Information Visualization Techniques in the Social Sciences and Humanities

Veslava Osinska
Nicolaus Copernicus University, Poland

Grzegorz Osinski
College of Social and Media Culture, Poland

A volume in the Advances in Human and Social
Aspects of Technology (AHSAT) Book Series

Published in the United States of America by
    IGI Global
    Information Science Reference (an imprint of IGI Global)
    701 E. Chocolate Avenue
    Hershey PA, USA 17033
    Tel: 717-533-8845
    Fax: 717-533-8661
    E-mail: cust@igi-global.com
    Web site: http://www.igi-global.com

Library of Congress Cataloging-in-Publication Data

Names: Osinska, Veslava, 1968- editor. | Osinski, Grzegorz, 1967- editor.
Title: Information visualization techniques in the social sciences and
  humanities / Veslava Osinska and Grzegorz Osinski, editors.
Description: Hershey, PA : Information Science Reference, [2018] | Includes
  bibliographical references.
Identifiers: LCCN 2017034014| ISBN 9781522549901 (h/c) | ISBN 9781522549918
  (eISBN)
Subjects: LCSH: Social sciences--Information resources. | Information
  visualization.
Classification: LCC H62 .I6417 2018 | DDC 300.72/8--dc23 LC record available at https://lccn.loc.gov/2017034014

This book is published in the IGI Global book series Advances in Human and Social Aspects of Technology (AHSAT) (ISSN: 2328-1316; eISSN: 2328-1324)

British Cataloguing in Publication Data
A Cataloguing in Publication record for this book is available from the British Library.

For electronic access to this publication, please contact: eresources@igi-global.com.

Advances in Human and Social Aspects of Technology (AHSAT) Book Series

Ashish Dwivedi
The University of Hull, UK

ISSN:2328-1316
EISSN:2328-1324

MISSION

In recent years, the societal impact of technology has been noted as we become increasingly more connected and are presented with more digital tools and devices. With the popularity of digital devices such as cell phones and tablets, it is crucial to consider the implications of our digital dependence and the presence of technology in our everyday lives.

The **Advances in Human and Social Aspects of Technology (AHSAT) Book Series** seeks to explore the ways in which society and human beings have been affected by technology and how the technological revolution has changed the way we conduct our lives as well as our behavior. The AHSAT book series aims to publish the most cutting-edge research on human behavior and interaction with technology and the ways in which the digital age is changing society.

COVERAGE

- Information ethics
- End-User Computing
- Technology adoption
- Computer-Mediated Communication
- Human Development and Technology
- Human Rights and Digitization
- Technology and Social Change
- ICTs and human empowerment
- ICTs and social change
- Human-Computer Interaction

IGI Global is currently accepting manuscripts for publication within this series. To submit a proposal for a volume in this series, please contact our Acquisition Editors at Acquisitions@igi-global.com or visit: http://www.igi-global.com/publish/.

Titles in this Series

For a list of additional titles in this series, please visit: www.igi-global.com/book-series

Psychological, Social, and Cultural Aspects of Internet Addiction
Bahadir Bozoglan (IF Weinheim Institute, Germany)
Information Science Reference • ©2018 • 390pp • H/C (ISBN: 9781522534778) • US $200.00 (our price)

Experience-Based Human-Computer Interactions Emerging Research and Opportunities
Petr Sosnin (Ulyanovsk State Technical University, Russia)
Information Science Reference • ©2018 • 294pp • H/C (ISBN: 9781522529873) • US $165.00 (our price)

Technology-Enhanced Human Interaction in Modern Society
Francisco Vicente Cipolla-Ficarra (Latin Association of Human-Computer Interaction, Spain & International Association of Interactive Communication, Italy) Maria Valeria Ficarra (Latin Association of Human-Computer Interaction, Spain & International Association of Interactive Communication, Italy) Miguel Cipolla-Ficarra (International Association of Interactive Communication, Italy) Alejandra Quiroga (Universidad Nacional de La Pampa, Argentina) Jacqueline Alma (Electronic Arts – Vancouver, Canada) and Jim Carré (University of The Netherlands Antilles, Curaçao)
Information Science Reference • ©2018 • 319pp • H/C (ISBN: 9781522534372) • US $205.00 (our price)

HCI Challenges and Privacy Preservation in Big Data Security
Daphne Lopez (VIT University, India) and M.A. Saleem Durai (VIT University, India)
Information Science Reference • ©2018 • 275pp • H/C (ISBN: 9781522528630) • US $215.00 (our price)

Handbook of Research on Human Development in the Digital Age
Valerie C. Bryan (Florida Atlantic University, USA) Ann T. Musgrove (Florida Atlantic University, USA) and Jillian R. Powers (Florida Atlantic University, USA)
Information Science Reference • ©2018 • 526pp • H/C (ISBN: 9781522528388) • US $275.00 (our price)

Optimizing Human-Computer Interaction With Emerging Technologies
Francisco Cipolla-Ficarra (Latin Association of Human-Computer Interaction, Spain & International Association of Interactive Communication, Italy)
Information Science Reference • ©2018 • 471pp • H/C (ISBN: 9781522526162) • US $345.00 (our price)

Designing for Human-Machine Symbiosis Using the URANOS Model Emerging Research and Opportunities
Benjamin Hadorn (University of Fribourg, Switzerland)
Information Science Reference • ©2017 • 170pp • H/C (ISBN: 9781522518884) • US $125.00 (our price)

701 East Chocolate Avenue, Hershey, PA 17033, USA
Tel: 717-533-8845 x100 • Fax: 717-533-8661
E-Mail: cust@igi-global.com • www.igi-global.com

To the memory of Eugene Garfield (1925 – 2017), one of the founders of the modern bibliometrics and scientometrics whose ideas made a great impact on the development of the large-scale data visualization methods.

Table of Contents

Foreword xvi

Preface xvii

Acknowledgment xxv

Section 1
The History of Human Knowledge From a Visual Perspective

Chapter 1
Shapes and Patterns in Visualizing Human Knowledge: Part 1: Origin From a Historical and
Cognitive Perspective 1
Grzegorz Osinski, College of Social and Media Culture, Poland
Veslava Osinska, Nicolas Copernicus University, Poland

Chapter 2
Shapes and Patterns in Visualizing Human Knowledge: Part 2 – Digital Visualisation Techniques ... 17
Veslava Osinska, Nicolaus Copernicus University, Poland
Grzegorz Osinski, College of Social and Media Culture, Poland

Chapter 3
Developing Visual Literacy Skills Through Library Instructions 32
Nevzat Özel, Ankara University, Turkey

Section 2
Visualization for Digital Humanity

Chapter 4
Infographics in Humanities: Communication of Information or Information Noise? Polish Case 50
Zbigniew Osiński, Maria Curie Sklodowska University, Poland

Chapter 5
The Vizualization of the Dynamics of the Relationship Between the Bridegrooms in the "Song of
Songs" 68
Monika Szetela, College of Social and Media Culture, Poland
Malgorzata Piotrkowska Dankowska, Cardinal Stefan Wyszynski University, Poland

Chapter 6

Text Preprocessing: A Tool of Information Visualization and Digital Humanities............................ 86
Piotr Malak, University of Wroclaw, Poland

Section 3
Visual Scientometrics

Chapter 7

Complex-Network Approach for Visualizing and Quantifying the Evolution of a Scientific
Topic 106
Olesya Mryglod, National Academy of Sciences of Ukraine, Ukraine
Bertrand Berche, Universite´ de Lorraine, France
Yurij Holovatch, National Academy of Sciences of Ukraine, Ukraine
Ralph Kenna, Coventry University, UK

Chapter 8

Bibliometric Maps of Science: The Visualization of Scientific Research......................... 121
Irina Marshakova-Shaikevich, Adam Mickiewicz University, Poland

Chapter 9

Visualizations of the GRUBA Bibliographic Database: From Printed Sources to the Maps of
Science 151
Anna Małgorzata Kamińska, University of Silesia in Katowice, Poland

Chapter 10

Visualization Methods for Exploring Transborder Indigenous Populations: The Case of Berber
Webosphere... 175
Abdelaziz Blilid, Charles de Gaulle University – Lille III, France

Section 4
Practical Application of Visualization Techniques

Chapter 11

Perspectives and Good Practices in Visualization of Knowledge About Public Entities 195
Jan Fazlagić, Poznan University of Economics and Business, Poland
Windham Loopesko, University of Colorado – Denver, USA
Leszek Matuszak, Poznan University of Economics and Business, Poland
Rigby Johnson, University of Colorado – Denver, USA

Chapter 12

Lighting Simulation Algorithms in Real-World Sacral Building Visualisation 214
Grzegorz Osinski, College of Social and Media Culture, Poland
Błażej Świętek, College of Social and Media Culture, Poland
Zbigniew Chaniecki, Lodz University of Technology, Poland

Chapter 13
From Visualization Framework on Teaching Process: New Methodical Approach to the Teaching
of Bookbinding in Graphic Technology 237
 Suzana Pasanec Preprotić, University of Zagreb, Croatia
 Gorana Petković, University of Zagreb, Croatia

Chapter 14
Generative Systems in Information Visualization 251
 Ilona Nowosad, College of Social and Media Culture, Poland

Chapter 15
Social Context: Visualisation of Cooperation – Evidence-Based Medicine in
Neurorehabilitation 274
 Emilia Mikołajewska, Nicolaus Copernicus University, Poland
 Tomasz Komendziński, Nicolaus Copernicus University, Poland
 Dariusz Mikołajewski, Kazimierz Wielki University, Poland & Nicolaus Copernicus
  University, Poland

Related References 294

Compilation of References 323

About the Contributors 348

Index 354

Detailed Table of Contents

Foreword xvi

Preface xvii

Acknowledgment xxv

Section 1
The History of Human Knowledge From a Visual Perspective

Chapter 1
Shapes and Patterns in Visualizing Human Knowledge: Part 1: Origin From a Historical and
Cognitive Perspective 1
    Grzegorz Osinski, College of Social and Media Culture, Poland
    Veslava Osinska, Nicolaus Copernicus University, Poland

The concepts of knowledge presentation have their origin in the early Middle Ages and establish contemporary trends in visualization activity. Using the latest scientific observations, it is possible to conclude that circles and spheres are the most common natural shapes in both micro- and macrospace. The next most often used metaphor in medieval literature is a tree: an instance of fractals that today determines the geometry of nature. The fractals are the strong attractors of human mind space. The problem is how these two forms interact with each other and how they coexist in the context of effective visualization of information. The chapter presents an intercultural historical outline of appropriate graphical forms for knowledge representation. The authors strive to prove the main hypothesis: fractals and spheres contribute to modern complex visualization. The reasons may be sought in human perception and cognition. This chapter discusses visualization problems in the form of tree-like fractal structures embedded in spherical shapes over time, different cultures, and inter-personal relationships.

Chapter 2
Shapes and Patterns in Visualizing Human Knowledge: Part 2 – Digital Visualisation Techniques ... 17
    Veslava Osinska, Nicolaus Copernicus University, Poland
    Grzegorz Osinski, College of Social and Media Culture, Poland

Excel or similar statistical software offers a lot of possibilities to generate different kinds of charts and diagrams. Throughout the variety of graphical representations, one can find common features among elementary patterns they consist of. Circles (spheres in 3D information space) and trees as effective and ergonomic shapes are the base of known historical and contemporary visualization techniques. The chapter introduces the most popular and ergonomic methods for visualizing large-scale data. The authors strive to find common visual properties in relation to their historical archetypes. The discussion about a series of both technical and aesthetical issues is also included.

Chapter 3

Developing Visual Literacy Skills Through Library Instructions 32
Nevzat Özel, Ankara University, Turkey

Visual literacy skills have become an inevitable part of life in today's world. Technological innovations leading to new literacy skills have changed traditional ways of communication and made it necessary to learn and understand symbols, pictures, photos, illustrations, diagrams, infographics, pictograms, simulations, graphical interfaces, digitized images, and other visual tools. Therefore, it is very significant to teach individuals about visual literacy skills: the ability to understand, interpret, evaluate, organize, and construct visual information. Infographics are essential tools for learners. One of the most prominent institution to teach visual literacy skills is libraries. Visual tools, strategies, and methods should be applied in library instructions for users to realize these skills. The aim of the chapter is to show the importance of visualization, visual literacy, and infographics and present suggestions regarding how to develop the visual literacy skills of learners by libraries.

Section 2
Visualization for Digital Humanity

Chapter 4

Infographics in Humanities: Communication of Information or Information Noise? Polish Case 50
Zbigniew Osiński, Maria Curie Sklodowska University, Poland

The purpose of the chapter is to join in the discussion of digital humanists on whether data and information visualizations can be an efficient way of communicating information and knowledge about the specificity of the humanities. The basis is to examine the problem of whether a visual communication containing far more graphical elements than text can be something more to the abovementioned group of recipients than a complement to the principal text (as is the case with school handbooks). Can it be a dominant form of communication? In order to obtain research data, a series of didactic tests were administered to a handpicked group of several dozen students. They were students with predominantly humanistic competencies but for whom modern technology poses no barriers in the cognitive process. The test results showed the usefulness of infographics as a form of organization and presentation but only of detailed data and information. The visualization of information did not turn out to be a good foundation for making generalizations and conclusions.

Chapter 5

The Vizualization of the Dynamics of the Relationship Between the Bridegrooms in the "Song of
Songs" 68
Monika Szetela, College of Social and Media Culture, Poland
Malgorzata Piotrkowska Dankowska, Cardinal Stefan Wyszynski University, Poland

The dominant theme in the "Song of Songs" is the relationship of love between Bridegrooms. The subject of interest is the dynamism of the relationship. The attitude and feelings expressed by love, depicted in this book of the Old Testament, don't express only a description of their beauty, but a description of expressing mutual delight of all your loved ones. Mutual learning is shaping a unique spousal bond, which as a result of the involvement of the beloved and the beloved of each event, not always easy, brings them together; and thus they can build their own language of communication. Narrative character of text is treated in its literal sense. Presented course of events highlights everything that deepens and develops relationships between characters and clearly shows what returns as the leitmotif of the story. Focusing attention on events, using visualization as a way to telling about the people and events, puts less emphasis on the lyrical parties – descriptions of the beauty of the Bride appear in the text of the "Song of Songs."

Chapter 6

Text Preprocessing: A Tool of Information Visualization and Digital Humanities..............................86
    Piotr Malak, University of Wroclaw, Poland

Digital humanities and information visualization rely on huge sets of digital data. Those data are mostly delivered in the text form. Although computational linguistics provides a lot of valuable tools for text processing, the initial phase (text preprocessing) is very involved and time-consuming. The problems arise due to a human factor – they are not always errors; there is also inconsistency in forms, affecting data quality. In this chapter, the author describes and discusses the main issues that arise during the preprocessing phase of textual data gathering for InfoVis. Chosen examples of InfoVis applications are presented. Except for problems with raw, original data, solutions are also referred. Canonical approaches used in text preprocessing and common issues affecting the process and ways to prevent them are also presented. The quality of data from different sources is also discussed. The content of this chapter is a result of a few years of practical experience in natural language processing gained during realization of different projects and evaluation campaigns.

Section 3
Visual Scientometrics

Chapter 7

Complex-Network Approach for Visualizing and Quantifying the Evolution of a Scientific
Topic 106
    Olesya Mryglod, National Academy of Sciences of Ukraine, Ukraine
    Bertrand Berche, Universite´ de Lorraine, France
    Yurij Holovatch, National Academy of Sciences of Ukraine, Ukraine
    Ralph Kenna, Coventry University, UK

Tracing the evolution of specific topics is a subject area that belongs to the general problem of mapping the structure of scientific knowledge. Often bibliometric databases are used to study the history of scientific topic evolution from its appearance to its extinction or merger with other topics. In this chapter, the authors present an analysis of the academic response to the disaster that occurred in 1986 in Chornobyl (Chernobyl), Ukraine, considered as one of the most devastating nuclear power plant accidents in history. Using a bibliographic database, the distributions of Chornobyl-related papers in different scientific fields are analysed, as are their growth rates and properties of co-authorship networks. Elements of descriptive statistics and tools of complex-network theory are used to highlight interdisciplinary as well as international effects. In particular, tools of complex-network science enable information visualization complemented by further quantitative analysis.

Chapter 8

Bibliometric Maps of Science: The Visualization of Scientific Research 121
Irina Marshakova-Shaikevich, Adam Mickiewicz University, Poland

This chapter is devoted to directions in algorithmic classificatory procedures: co-citation analysis as an example of citation network and lexical analysis of keywords in the titles. The chapter gives the results of bibliometric analysis of the international scientific collaboration of EU countries. The three approaches are based on the same general idea of normalization of deviations of the observed data from the mathematical expectation. The application of the same formula leads to discovery of statistically significant links between objects (publication, journals, keywords, etc.) reflected in the maps. Material for this analysis is drawn from DBs presented in ISI Thomson Reuters (at present Clarivate Analytics).

Chapter 9

Visualizations of the GRUBA Bibliographic Database: From Printed Sources to the Maps of
Science 151
Anna Małgorzata Kamińska, University of Silesia in Katowice, Poland

This chapter describes the author's experience of building the research environment for the implementation of bibliometric research on the science of mining, being developed in Poland in 1945-1989, on the basis of periodicals published by the major technical universities involved in teaching and research in that field at that time. The study was conducted on the volume of data entered (by typing), collected, and processed in a relational database. The data, covering information of more than 36,000 articles and more than 22,000 authors, formed bibliographic database named "GRUBA" (an acronym for polish phrase "Mining Register Enabling Bibliometric Analysis" and a word meaning mine in the Silesian dialect as well). The aim of this chapter is not to present a comprehensive and extensive bibliometric research results. Only a small part of it is a background for presenting the experience gained during the implementation of research, with the primary emphasis on the final stages – modeling and analyzing the visual maps created mainly using Gephi software and representing science development.

Chapter 10

Visualization Methods for Exploring Transborder Indigenous Populations: The Case of Berber
Webosphere 175
Abdelaziz Blilid, Charles de Gaulle University – Lille III, France

This chapter highlights the importance of information visualization using web mapping to shed light on the correlation between social actors. It shows how this method helps to understand if Berber identity beyond frontiers is a reality or just a motto in support of "cultural activism." The suggested web mapping presents the hyperlinks weaved between websites whose focus is Berber cultural identity. Berbers are the indigenous people of North Africa. They are scattered in Morocco, Tunisia, Algeria, and Libya; they have built a "resistance identity," including both cultural and political claims, long before the digital age. Since the 1960s they have been struggling for recognition against the state's cultural and political domination in which they live. The analysis of Berbers' relationships amongst each other on the internet is valuable for understanding the main features and issues of this digital connection, its shape, its contents, and actor typology.

Section 4
Practical Application of Visualization Techniques

Chapter 11

Perspectives and Good Practices in Visualization of Knowledge About Public Entities 195
Jan Fazlagić, Poznan University of Economics and Business, Poland
Windham Loopesko, University of Colorado – Denver, USA
Leszek Matuszak, Poznan University of Economics and Business, Poland
Rigby Johnson, University of Colorado – Denver, USA

Visualization of knowledge in public entities is becoming more and more popular due to the development of information technology tools, the demand for solutions allowing for reduction of information overload (IO), and new approaches to local government, including citizen participation. The chapter presents some case study examples of knowledge visualization in public entities with some conclusions and recommendations for policy makers. Additionally, it presents a complete map of certain Polish counties prepared by the authors. The authors applied, apart from the visualization in the form a map, the "Chernoff Faces" method (invented by Herman Chernoff in 1973). This method displays multivariate data on Polish counties in the shape of a human face. The individual parts, such as eyes, ears, mouth, and nose, represent values of the variables by their shape, size, placement, and orientation. The idea behind using faces is that humans easily recognize faces and notice small changes without difficulty. Chernoff Faces handle each variable differently.

Chapter 12

Lighting Simulation Algorithms in Real-World Sacral Building Visualisation 214
Grzegorz Osinski, College of Social and Media Culture, Poland
Błażej Świętek, College of Social and Media Culture, Poland
Zbigniew Chaniecki, Lodz University of Technology, Poland

The most commonly used rules of modeling are limited to determine the level and direction beam of the light. However, such an approach does not reflect the real impact of lighting on the object. More accurate selection of lighting parameters is important, especially in the case of design objects, when it is still possible to change the structure or any selection of location and type of lighting. The chapter presents the use of specialized numerical methods in the design of modern sacred buildings as well as visualization methods used in communication between professionals creating and managing such models.

Chapter 13

From Visualization Framework on Teaching Process: New Methodical Approach to the Teaching
of Bookbinding in Graphic Technology 237
Suzana Pasanec Preprotić, University of Zagreb, Croatia
Gorana Petković, University of Zagreb, Croatia

A framework for learning was developed with input from teachers, education experts, and business leaders to define and illustrate the skills and knowledge that students need to succeed in work, life, and citizenship, as well as the support system for learning outcomes. The critical system ensures student development and learning environment, including their personal skills, content knowledge, and important expertise, which they will need at Faculty, on the job, and generally in life. Students achieve better when they are actively engaged in solving meaningful problems. Today, among other academic courses, ICT-based learning provides an active learning process that enhances student-centered learning approaches, collaborative and participative forms of teaching and learning. Dialog, writing, and "high-order thinking" have significant importance, which directly improve communicative learning processes, including social network model of thinking. That process involves focusing on achieving a particular prior learning outcome (previous courses) and resolution comprehension of all aspects of the issue.

Chapter 14
Generative Systems in Information Visualization 251
Ilona Nowosad, College of Social and Media Culture, Poland

The author presents various approaches particularly in the field of visual arts and sound visualization based on hi-tech artificial agents and audiovisual systems. The number of digital artists and designers who tend to computational creativity has rapidly grown in recent years and their artworks and generative visuals that manifest the new cultural paradigm "Form Follows Data" meet with a wide interest. The author describes and presents a collection of tools and programming environments used for creating visual representations of sound as well as live coding visualizations which fall under so called generative art movement. Concepts of interactive audiovisual systems, sound-reactive programming software, and immersive environments refer to synergy of sound, visuals, and gestures. Another purpose is to point to applications of generative systems and agent-based frameworks in social and cognitive sciences to study environmental and social systems and their interactions.

Chapter 15
Social Context: Visualisation of Cooperation – Evidence-Based Medicine in
Neurorehabilitation 274
Emilia Mikołajewska, Nicolaus Copernicus University, Poland
Tomasz Komendziński, Nicolaus Copernicus University, Poland
Dariusz Mikołajewski, Kazimierz Wielki University, Poland & Nicolaus Copernicus
*   University, Poland*

Evidence-based medicine (EBM) and Evidence-based practice (EBP) are sets of standards and procedures created to search, verify, and select up-to-date findings implemented by medical staff as a basis for decision-making process in a daily clinical practice. Despite efforts of scientists and clinicians, neurorehabiltiation is regarded as a difficult area for EBM/EBP practices due to huge diversity of cases, clinical pictures, interventions, and scientific methodologies. More advanced tasks, including application of brain-computer interfaces and neuroprosteheses, show the need for a new approach from medical practitioners. This chapter presents challenges, barriers, and solutions in the aforementioned area based on the personal experiences of the authors. Visualisation tools provide cognitive support for social context, cooperation patterns, and data interpretation. Taking into consideration that social issues may extend the visibility of the results and allow for easier dissemination of the results, the aim was to show how visualisation helps identify cooperation networks and disseminate research results.

Related References 294

Compilation of References 323

About the Contributors 348

Index 354

Foreword

Visualization may refer to the process and the artifact of the process that transforms data into storytelling evidence or insightful and thought-provoking patterns. The process itself may differ considerably in terms of the extent to which the transformation can or should be repeatable and generalizable. The methodological tension between qualitative and quantitative approaches to scholarly inquiries often underlies some of the most fundamental differences between physical sciences and social sciences and humanities. In physical sciences, visualizations have been routinely applied in communicating the structure and dynamics of a wide variety of natural phenomena, ranging from microscopic to macroscopic worlds. Special-purpose instruments, such as astronomical telescopes and scanning tunneling microscopes, are built to investigate the unknown.

Traditionally, or at least until recently, research in social sciences and humanities largely remains to be an area that poses fundamental challenges to the development and application of visualization techniques. In physical sciences, researchers often need to study numerous instances of galaxies and storms. In contrast, researchers in social sciences and humanities often face the situation where a solo instance is all there is to study. There is only one William Shakespeare. There is only one Elbert Einstein.

The visualization as a transformation process is a process of abstraction. What is the gain for research in social sciences and humanities in the process of abstraction? What might be the loss? What does it take for researchers to find visualization techniques that can help them uncover insights that might be otherwise missed or overlooked? What are the ways information visualization can provide the clarify and effectiveness to the communication of research in social sciences and humanities?

Information Visualization Techniques in the Social Sciences and Humanities compiled by Veslava Osinka and Grzegorz Osinski presents a collection of 15 chapters. Contributors come from Croatia, France, Poland, Switzerland, Turkey, Ukraine, United Kingdom, and the United States. Collectively they represent disciplines such as cognitive science, condensed matter physics, physiotherapy, social and media culture, graphic arts, and economics and business. They address topics concerning visual literacy, knowledge visualization, infographics, digital storytelling, Bible visualization, tools for digital humanities, complex networks, bibliometric maps, and evidence-based medicine. Contributors also share several topics of common interest. For example, at least eight chapters address the role of visualization in communication and five chapters specifically discuss various applications of relevant tools. The 15 chapters provide an interesting window to reveal the current challenges and opportunities for a continued advance of digital humanities.

Chaomei Chen
Drexel University, USA

Preface

Information Visualization Techniques in the Social Sciences and Humanities constitutes a set of texts written by specialists in various visualization methods used in the broadly defined fields of humanity and social sciences. Despite the fact, that they often relate to highly specialised issues, both the language employed in the works and their substantive content are adapted for the recipients without professional background. Within the chapters, there are numerous references, a glossary and indices that enrich the texts with the specialist issues. Thus, the book can also constitute an important source of information for a reader who does not specialise in the given field (e.g., students, teachers, information management unit workers). Additionally, it can serve as a source of professional knowledge for the experts who, on a daily basis, employ the advanced visualisation techniques in their work.

The issues related to the application of the visualisation techniques currently constitute a very wide knowledge domain that covers all the areas of the scientific and technological activities. The interdisciplinarity of the discussed issues may, at first, somehow confuse the reader, as the subject area this book covers is extremely wide. Nowadays, within the scientific communities, the subject area of visualisation is most often associated with the big data analysis methods and their graphical representations. In fact, the majority of the scientific papers on the visualisation address the issues of the information visualisation in the form of various sets of data. Therefore, the visualisation techniques most often relate to the evaluation algorithms employed in the machine learning and data mining issues. The application of such methods requires the fundamental IT background, both in the use of the applied techniques and in the knowledge of the basics of mathematical methods employed in analyses. Thus, in the practical problems, it is necessary to establish a cross-disciplinary team of scientists representing various fields and cooperating to generate a proper final visualisation. However, at present, we are also dealing with the wide knowledge areas where we implement ready-made visualisation applications not requiring the employment of advanced mathematical and technological methods. In that case, the teams of the scientists working to create the visualisation representations do not require the direct support from the computer science specialists.

The editors' aim for the book, apart from its substantive content related to the newest visualisation technology, is to act as a particular memorial of remembrance of the eminent scientist Eugene Garfield, who passed away in February 2017. This American linguist and businessman was one of the founders of modern bibliometrics and scientometrics. He helped to create the most important database structures by introducing the analytical parametrisation of the scientific research such as: Current Contents, Science Citation Index (SCI) and Journal Citation Reports. In his works, he also used to employ some innovative visualisation analyses that remarkably contributed to the development of the visualisation processes as well as of the specialist algorithms used in testing and analysis of large and dynamic databases. Rapidly advancing modern science undoubtedly constitutes such a system; therefore, the methods he had proffered are presently developed and applied in various fields of research. Hence, in addition to the chapters discussing the results of the latest scientific researches, the book also comprises a special chapter written by Irina Marshakova-Shaikevich. The chapter features a compilation of historical achievements of Eugene Garfield, and constitutes an attempt of a holistic approach to the concept of knowledge and science visualisation. It is a specialist chapter relating directly to the major achievements of Garfield. In Chapter 8, "Bibliometric Maps of Science: The Visualisation of Scientific Research," in a historical chronology perspective, Irina Marshakova-Shaikevich discusses the directions of the algorithmic evaluation procedures for both the analysis of the quotations as an example of a quotation network, and for the lexical analysis of keywords in the titles of articles. It presents the results of the bibliometric analysis of an international scientific cooperation between the states of the European Union, by means of Garfield's methodology with whom she has been personally cooperating on many aspects of visualisation methods used in the scientometrics. Moreover, she describes various approaches based on the same general scientometric data normalisation concept: standard deviations observed in the data in relation to its mathematical simulation models. The application of this formula results in detecting statistically significant correlations between objects (publications, journals, keywords, etc.) visualised in the form of knowledge maps. The analytical material constitutes a content of currently the most popular database in the scientific world, the Web of Knowledge.

Besides, the visualisation is about more than simply processing the data obtained from various sources. The processes of creating graphical representations can also be primary ones, an image is being created in the simulation and modelling processes based on the vision of the author, the demand for a specific project or the required structure emerging within the Virtual Reality (VR). In that case, other methods and techniques are required, the ones that allow to create a visualisation not based on the available data, but directly in a creative process of the project's authors. Nowadays, for designing real-world physical objects: a building, an image or a knowledge structure, the architectural and industrial projects are developed by means of digital modelling techniques.

ORGANIZATION OF THE BOOK

The content of the book includes a wide range of topics related to the visualisation methods as well as to the use of specialist methods of graphical imaging within various fields of knowledge. The book structure consists of four parts. In the first section, "History of Human Knowledge From Visual Perspective," the matter discussed relates to the historical aspects of creating the visualisation images. The graphical contents have accompanied us for many centuries. Prior to the development of the symbolic alphabets that allowed for the creation of the original text-based communication forms, mankind had been leaving for successive generations cave paintings and characteristic graphic forms forged in durable structures of rock and stone. The illustrations in the medieval incunabula also constitute the first visualisations, they were not only the illustrations of the content, but also constituted an independent and isolated graphical message.

In the past, mankind has undergone similar revolutionary changes in the applied knowledge and information media. The historical aspects of these changes are discussed in Chapter 1, "Shapes and Patterns in Visualizing Human Knowledge: Part 1 – Origin From a Historical and Cognitive Perspective." Grzegorz Osinski and Veslava Osinskadescribe the origins of the modern concepts of the knowledge presentation that originated in the early Middle Ages. These historical concepts have affected the modern trends within the visualisation activity. While analysing the scientific activity over the recent years, it becomes clear that there occur universal shapes: circles and spheres. These are common, natural shapes occurring both in the micro- and macro-scales. Another universal shape that has lasted for centuries and at present is experiencing its renaissance, is a metaphor for a symbol of a branching tree. The trees have a fractal structure, just like the representations of the neural correlates we can observe while analysing the human brain activity by means of the neuroimaging techniques. Thus, the fractals are strong attractors, prevalent in the active representations of the human mind space. Accordingly, the main question of a well-prepared visualisation is how these two forms—the visualised fractal shape and the activity of the objects within the mind space—interact and how they create a universal visual communication. Within the content of the book, we shall also encounter a discussion on the cross-cultural and historical aspects of the graphic forms of the knowledge representation. The authors attempt to prove the main hypothesis that the fractals and spheres significantly contribute to the creation of the modern and universal forms of the complex visualisation. The causes for this should be sought within the mechanisms of the human perception effect and in the cognitive processes occurring in the human brain. This chapter discusses the issues of creating visualisations in the form of the tree-like fractal structures embedded within the spherical shapes in various eras and cultures.

Chapter 2, "Shapes and Patterns in Visualizing Human Knowledge: Part 2 – Digital Visualisation Techniques" by Grzegorz Osinski and Veslava Osinska, constitutes a compendium of practical knowledge about the employment of various tools in creating simple visualisations. The authors suggest that even the common Excel or other similar statistical software offer many opportunities to generate various graphs and diagrams. Within this set of pictorial representations, there occur numerous common features of basic shapes and visualisation standards. Among these, there are the fundamental and the oldest historical shapes, such as circles, spheres and trees, acting as effective and ergonomic elements of the modern visualisation techniques. This chapter features the most popular and ergonomic methods of the large-scale data visualisations. It also presents a discussion on the technical and aesthetic issues which constitute an immanent feature of a well-performed visualisation.

In Chapter 3, "Developing Visual Literacy Skills Through Library Instructions," Nevzat Ozel describes the reading and writing skills improvement methods that became an integral part of our lives. The modern communication is particularly abundant in terms of varied images. The technological innovations leading to new writing and reading skills have changed the traditional communication means. They have implemented, nowadays essential in the learning process, the skills to analyse: images, photographs, illustrations, schemes, infographics, pictograms, simulations, graphical interfaces, digital images and other visual tools. Therefore, the author puts a particular emphasis on teaching children reading and writing skills as an ability to understand, interpret, organise and construct the visual information. According to the author, modern infographics constitute the essential means for students requiring education in the field of accurate interpretation of the infographics. Despite the technological progress, the libraries are still the most important institutions teaching skills of a proper reading of modern texts. The visual tools, their strategies and procedures should be widely used in the library instruction manuals for users in order to shape their skills correctly.

The second section, "Visualisation for Digital Humanity," forms a set of studies on the practical implementation of the visualisation algorithms in the research in the field of humanistic sciences. Chapter 4, "Infographics in Humanities: Communication of Information or Information Noise? The Polish Case" by Zbigniew Osinski, is based on a particular example of the modern ICT methods application in the Polish higher education. The author describes his own study that constitutes an important element of an ongoing discussion on the broadly defined "digital humanities". He puts forward a question whether the data and information visualisations can form an effective measure for the transfer of information and knowledge under the particular circumstances of humanities. He attempts to answer the following question: whether the visual communication, featuring significantly more graphic constituents than a text, can form something more for a particular target group than just a graphic supplementation of the main text. Such circumstances are often encountered within various levels of education, from a primary school to an academic education. In order to answer the question, the author performed a series of didactic tests on a selected group of a several dozens of students. The test results showed a suitability of infographics as a form of organisation and presentation, but only in terms of detailed structures of data and information. The visualisation of information proved to be a good method in teaching techniques of synthesis, generalisations and drawing detailed conclusions. Thus, the improvement of the visualisation processes and the development of new methods of analysis becomes a crucial element of research and works in the field of the digital humanities. Presumably, both further studies and designing new, more functional visualisation algorithms allowing for the more effective synthesis of the presented content, will be necessary.

The analysis of the Biblical texts is probably the oldest issue related to the analysis of the literary texts. The Bible—the oldest and the most popular book in the world, has been an object of intensive analyses for thousands of years. The time frame as well as the spatial scope, vast number of characters and their interactions undoubtedly constitute a huge challenge even for the present scientists equipped with both the supercomputers and the latest analytical algorithms. This subject area is discussed by Monika Szetela and Małgorzata Piotrkowska-Dankowska in Chapter 5, "The Visualisation of the Dynamics of the Relationship Between the Bridegrooms in the 'Song of Songs.'" The authoresses analyse the relationships between the characters of the fragment of the Bible, Song of Songs. Since the dominant issue in the "Song of Songs" is a love relationship between the Bridegrooms, the dynamics of the relationship naturally becomes the object of algorithms implementation. The mutual learning of the characters creates an exceptional nuptial kinship which, in consequence of involving in every event, bonds them so they are able to create their own language of communication. In the process of visualisation, the narrative nature of the text has been handled literally. The authoresses employed the visualisations as measures of narration about people and events; they put a lesser emphasis on the lyrical elements and descriptions. The obtained results constitute an extremely interesting example of the visualisation techniques application in the analysis of the Biblical texts.

The second section of the book ends with a chapter written by Piotr Malak, "Text Preprocessing: A Tool of Information Visualisation and Digital Humanities," that relates to the application of the visualisation methods in studies on texts written in a natural language. The biggest problem in such analyses is a preliminary preparation of the texts for analysis. Even though the computational linguistics and natural language processing methods nowadays provide numerous tools for the word processing, the processing and analysis of the texts are very time-consuming. The author describes and discusses the main problems occurring during the preliminary phase of data collection for *InfoVis*. He propounds the implementation of the visualisation methods which would streamline and accelerate this critical stage of the analysis. The examples provided by the author result from his long-term practical experience in the natural language processing.

The third section of the book relates to the scientometrics issues. In Chapter 7, "Complex-Network Approach for Visualising and Quantifying the Evolution of a Scientific Topic," Olesya Mryglod, Bertrand Berche, Yurij Holovatch, and Ralph Kenna perform an analysis of the changes in the dynamics of the content of texts by means of the knowledge mapping methods. Based on the content of the bibliometric databases, they analyse the evolution of a particular scientific subject from its emerging in the public space up until its exhaustion or fusion with other topics. The authors perform an analysis based on the scientific works on the nuclear accident in the nuclear power plant in Chernobyl that happened in 1986. With the aid of the bibliographical database, the authors carried out an analysis of the distribution of the articles related to the Chernobyl disaster in different fields of science. They also determined appropriate indicators describing the dynamics of changes and the characteristics of the co-authors network. The employment of the analytic tool enabled the authors to create some innovative visualisations supplemented with a well performed quantitative analysis.

In Chapter 9, "Visualizations of the GRUBA Bibliographic Database: From Printed Sources to the Maps of Science," Anna Kaminska describes her own experience in the process of designing scientific environment in order to carry out the bibliometric studies in the field of mining science based on the analysis of the journals published by the major technical universities in Poland. The analysed data was collected from over 36,000 articles and it relates to approximately 22,000 authors; hence, it constitutes a typical issue of large data collection visualisation. The database that hosts all the data was named by the author the acronym GRUBA. The uttermost emphasis the author puts on the analysis' phases related to the modelling and analysis of the visual maps created by means of Gephi software.

An interesting issue associated with the cultural studies research of ethnic groups was presented in chapter "Visualization Methods for Exploring Transborder Indigenous Populations: The Case of Berber Webosphere," written by Abdelaziz Blilid. In his chapter, the author describes the problem of Berbers who, as a native population of North Africa, are dispersed in Morocco, Tunisia, Algeria and Libya, where they have created an "identity of resistance". It embraces cultural as well as political issues which Berbers had created long before the digital era. The author emphasises the importance of the information visualisation with the use of the Internet activity mapping. He explains how, with the aid of this method, to understand the Berber identity, as it constitutes the object of the analysis. Since the 1960s, the Berbers have fought for the recognition of their otherness in opposition to the political and cultural dominance of a country they live in. Whereas, the analysis of the internal relations amongst the Berber community scattered all over the world, is very valuable for the preservation of this ethnic group identity. The visualisation methods employed by the author require the application of the suitable algorithms used in the analysis of the scattered network data.

The fourth and last section of the book, "Practical Application of Visualisation Techniques," revolves around the use of practical issues of application in the matters related to creating visualisations from scratch. Not as a result of the analysis of the sets of data, but as an outcome of own visions and concepts of the authors who employ the visualisation algorithms for the creation of own objects, not just for the analysis of the existing theoretical concepts. In Chapter 11, "Perspectives and Good Practices in Visualisation of Knowledge About Public Entities," Jan Fazlagic, Windham Loopesko, Leszek Matuszak, and Rigby Johnson perform a visual analysis of public institutions based on public information. The issues discussed by them relate to both local authorities and active citizenship. The article presents exemplary visualisations related to the public bodies, and describes conclusions targeted directly at political dissidents. Apart from the visualisation in a form of a map, the authors employed "Chernoff Faces" method that displays multivariate data related to the Polish public bodies. The idea to employ the visualisation within a topological form of a human face allows for the unusual use of the final graphics that, during the analysis, use the elements of emotional graphics that engage the limbic system of the human brain.

Chapter 12, "Lighting Simulation Algorithms in Real-World Sacral Building Visualisation," written by Grzegorz Osinski, Blazej Swiatek, and Zbigniew Chaniecki, describes the use of visualisation techniques in the architectural design of a new object, The Shrine of Our Lady Star of the New Evangelisation and Saint John Paul II that has been built from the ground up over the period of 2012–2016, in Torun. The main subject of the chapter is a description of the meaning and an effect of the selection of the lighting parameters on the actual perception of the modelled sacral buildings. The visualisation of both the temple interior and its surroundings requires very thorough modelling of the lighting processes. In such works, the used modelling rules are most commonly limited to determining the level and direction of the light beams. Such an approach does not allow for the real-world simulations of the impact of illumination on the object. An adequate choice of the lighting parameters is more important, especially in the case of the facilities under design, when the changes of the structure or optional choice of material and a type of illumination are still possible. In such case, for the choice of the best lighting model, three-dimensional modelling should be chosen, with the preceding exact visualisation of the architectural object. The authors describe in detail the whole process of designing, construction and corrections implementation in close cooperation with the construction engineers and the investor for whom the aesthetic final effect is as important as the practical usability of the facility.

A new approach to the learning process with the use of visualisation methods is being propounded by Suzana Pasanec Preprotic and Gorana Petkovic in Chapter 13, "From Visualisation Framework on Teaching Process: New Methodical Approach to the Teaching of Bookbinding in Graphic Technology." Based on the example of the Croatian educational system, the authoresses discuss the issues of the identification of the students who can succeed at work and in the active citizenship. The critical evaluation system assures a development for the students and an appropriate learning environment. The students achieve higher scores when actively engaged in solving important problems. Nowadays, the best results are achieved in the active learning processes by focusing on the student. The teaching methods require participatory teaching methods. Therefore, a properly designed teaching process requires focusing on achieving the predefined effect, and visualisation methods are not just important in the process, but even necessary.

In Chapter 14, "Generative Systems in Information Visualization," Ilona Nowosad presents various approaches to the visual arts and, in particular, to the sound visualisation employing advanced technologies. Nowadays, a rapid increase in the activity of the "digital artists" is evident. Their works are mostly generative visualisations that present a new cultural paradigm "Form Follows Data". The authoress describes and presents a set of tools and software environments used for creating visual sound representations and live visualisations that fall under the scope of so-called generative art movement. The chapter describes various generative systems used in the visualisation processes.

The last chapter relates to the implementation of the visualisation methods in medicine, in particular in the process of neuro-rehabilitation. Chapter 15, "Social Context: Visualisation of Cooperation – Evidence-Based Medicine in Neurorehabilitation," written by Emilia Mikolajewska, Tomasz Komendzinski, and Dariusz Mikolajewski describes a methodology called Evidence-Based Medicine (EBM) and Evidence-Based Practice (EBP). These are sets of standards and procedures created in order to search, verify and select the newest findings implemented by medical staff as a basis for the decision-making processes in the clinical practice. By taking advantage of the newest technologies, such as BCI — Brain-

Computer Interface and neuroprostheses, we can now achieve rehabilitational effects far above the ones obtained in the standard medical procedures. Their implementation, however, requires a new approach to the analysis of the medical data used in the clinical practice. The contemporary visualisation tools provide appropriate support in the neuro-rehabilitation processes. Moreover, the consideration of the social factors can increase the results obtained and allow for faster mobilisation.

Figure 1. Visual representation of the publication's themes

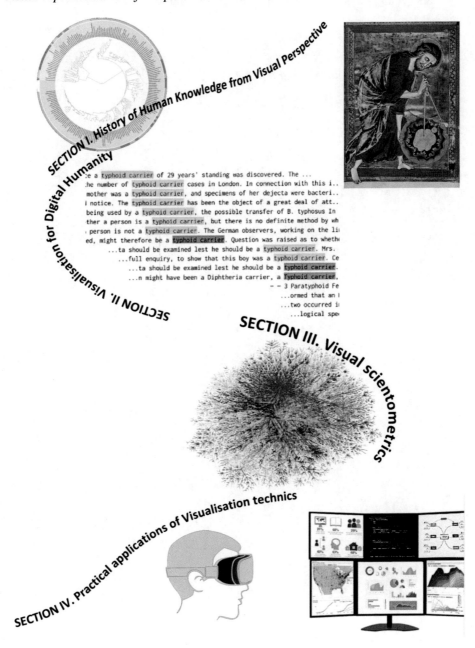

CONCLUSION

The above-presented description of the contents of the book clearly shows that the use of various techniques and methods of visualisation is, at present, an integral part of numerous applications employed not only in humanistic and social sciences, but also in numerous other fields of science. The authors hope that this short presentation of some practical examples will contribute to the further development of the applied visualisation methods and to the development of new scientific paradigm based on not only linear texts, but also on multi-dimensional, dynamic images.

Below the readers can perceive the map of content in visual form being able to provide overall view on the themes.

Grzegorz Osinski
College of Social and Media Culture, Poland

Veslava Osinska
Nicolaus Copernicus University, Poland

Acknowledgment

We wish to thank the members of the IGI Global Publishing team for giving us an opportunity to unite the visualization professionals in the space of the present book as well as share their knowledge with readers. Let us express our particular gratitude to Marianne Caesar for her assistance in developing this project.

We would like to thank Anna Ursyn for inspiring us with the texts in her widespreading monography *Maximazing Cognitive Learning Through Visualisation* published in IGI Global in 2015.

Thanks also to Włodzisław Duch, who keeps opening new perspectives on the human vision including visualization problems in the human mind.

Special thanks to Kevin Boyack for inspiring discussions and remarkable examples of science mapping.

Thanks also to Jan Kozłowski for his unforgettable lecture about the historical snapshots of knowledge visualization and valuable remarks.

Thanks to Casidy Suggimoto who made us meet the specialists in the field of visual scientometrcis and fruitfully start to collaborate with them.

Many thanks to the participants of the International Conference on *Information Visualization in Humanity* (which took place on Toruń, Poland in 2017) for contribution to the book as well as for the insightful reviews of text and improving them.

Section 1
The History of Human Knowledge From a Visual Perspective

Chapter 1
Shapes and Patterns in Visualizing Human Knowledge:
Part 1: Origin From a Historical and Cognitive Perspective

Grzegorz Osinski
College of Social and Media Culture, Poland

Veslava Osinska
Nicolas Copernicus University, Poland

ABSTRACT

The concepts of knowledge presentation have their origin in the early Middle Ages and establish contemporary trends in visualization activity. Using the latest scientific observations, it is possible to conclude that circles and spheres are the most common natural shapes in both micro- and macrospace. The next most often used metaphor in medieval literature is a tree: an instance of fractals that today determines the geometry of nature. The fractals are the strong attractors of human mind space. The problem is how these two forms interact with each other and how they coexist in the context of effective visualization of information. The chapter presents an intercultural historical outline of appropriate graphical forms for knowledge representation. The authors strive to prove the main hypothesis: fractals and spheres contribute to modern complex visualization. The reasons may be sought in human perception and cognition. This chapter discusses visualization problems in the form of tree-like fractal structures embedded in spherical shapes over time, different cultures, and inter-personal relationships.

Imagination is more important than knowledge. -Albert Einstein

DOI: 10.4018/978-1-5225-4990-1.ch001

BACKGROUND

Reading images is an extremely complicated process, it diverges from the classical reading of symbols-letters which are stacked in linear, successive strings. Images created by men are always meant to map the reality. But not always directly — the images of nature, objects from the world is just one of the ways of expressing the direct perceptive experiences. Much more important are the images that show the abstract results of the reasoning process that the information collected by man undergo. They are then not only the representation of the external world but above all they show what originated in the human mind in the process of observation and processing of information. They must therefore have both the component relating to the external world and the internal statuses of the human mind forming the image.

Can we find some universal patterns that make the visualized images not only comprehensible and acceptable for the others but also beautiful? When we analyze, from the historical point of view, the visual communications we can easily note that they are dominated by spherical shapes and representations in the form of branching boughs of trees. The geometric elements were not once too popular, only the use of automated computing devices disseminated the use of rectangular tables, bar charts or hierarchical diagrams. However, we rarely reckon such images as beautiful, we rather tend to associate them with an expert knowledge. We are going to try to explain this phenomenon and indicate that the evolution of the modern visualization techniques starts to drift toward the shapes of natural structures. In perception, they are closer to the complex tree-like structures, than simple geometrical shapes.

Do the modern visualization technologies tend to resume to the medieval concepts applied for illustrating the manuscripts? What is the reason? Perhaps the contemporary neuroscience will help us respond to such questions. Without going into details of biological nature, we are going to explain some concepts which will shed a new light on the issues of the development of visualization techniques. The computer technologies give us now a huge potential for processing and analyzing large data sets. Vast quantities of the available methods opens new cognitive horizons. Perhaps the combination of the conventional techniques of visualization structures used for hundreds of years and the modern technologies will allow us to create a universal visualization. Useful and beautiful, alike.

HISTORICAL DRAFT

The visual metaphors meant for the expression of the structures of the world that surrounds us have been humanity companions for thousands of years. Manuel Lima in the Book of Circles (2017) attempts to apply the methodology of historical sciences to explain why people are so much accustomed to the graphical representations in the form of circles. He proves that the first round inscriptions are dated at around 40,000 years ago, when the ancient people carved round characters called *Petroglyphs* in the rocks. These are important pre-literary forms of symbols used in the Neolith. The Petroglyphs from the African Twyfelfontein preserved 212 of stone plates covered with different shapes, where the circle or spiral were the predominant elements. If we want to treat the contemporary methods of visualization as visual patterns, then we should investigate the historical role of curvilinear shapes used in the visualization processes. Lima states in his book that he tries to prove that "the data visualization is much older discipline than it appears to us today". Although today we perceive it as a new and cutting-edge thing, trying to even assign this discipline the status of a new fourth scientific paradigm (Gray, 2007). However, a more detailed analysis will allow us to discover that the visualization of the structures of knowledge is closely linked with the form of language. Despite this, in the 21st century it must stand up to the new technological requirements, but it is rooted in the very distant past.

The popularity of the spherical shapes can be explained the simplest with referring to the anatomical construction of the human eye and the image creation process on the spherical retinal. After all, both eye, pupil and the spot light falling on the retina have spherical shapes. Therefore, the circles are perfect fits for our perceptive system. Any "angular" shapes or intersecting straight lines in the geometrical representations in such perceptive system suffer deformations, e.g. spherical aberrations. The spherical shapes are only mapped to the linear transformation ratio by creating elliptical structures. However, the geometric dependencies of image creation on the retinal do not yet form the perception process. Perception is a dynamic process which is closely coupled with the analysis of the seen object already at the eye level. Such an extension of perception we can illustratively describe as a process of "swallowing the image" by the eye with a simultaneous coming up to meet it. We cannot see something our brain is not able to recognize. Naming and simultaneous categorizing of the seen object seems to be of fundamental significance. It is the brain what determines what we see, i.e. we see what we want to see — and this is exactly what our brain wants to see. Therefore, the process of "vision" itself, the emergence of visual experience begins where the simple geometrical representation of the object on the retinal ends. In order to understand what processes occur in our brain in the course of viewing the reality that surrounds us, we need to use the latest research findings from the scope of neuroscience. Nevertheless, people living hundreds of years ago had no knowledge on such processes, and yet they knew how to create graphical representations that even today for us are not only useful but they also produce positive aesthetic experience.

In the beginning of the modern times, ca. 30 A.D., a Roman philosopher Lucretius in his work *Rerum natura* attempts a synthesis of the philosophical concept by Epicurus. His work is regarded as one of the canons of the Latin literature. Although over the centuries his views have prompted serious disputes of moral nature[1], we are only interested in his concept of the spherical structure of the world. Above all, he clearly indicates the curvilinear structure of the light propagation that lies at the heart of the perception process: "That sun, in winding onward, takes a year, through which illumining the sky and all the lands through which with curvilinear light." (Lucretius). Therefore the spherical, round shapes form the domain of heavens, phenomena which we can only observe on the inaccessible vault of heaven. In daily life, we do not observe perfect circles, only the Sun, Moon, and their movements in the sky feature universal, celestial shapes. The role of a link between the world of heavens and man plays the round eye which in our minds produces the representation of the world that we try to comprehend.

The spherical structures describing the world appear in the Middle Ages in many works, but the most extensive and of high aesthetic are the illustrations of works created by a mystic Hildegard of Bingen[2]. In her work *Scivias*[3], she describes and comments on her own mystical experiences, illustrated with numerous images that would become a graphic canon for multiple future medieval works. The concept of visualization using circles is particularly visible on the drawings illustrating the creation of the world and the Earth with a large number of links in the form of straight lines (Figure 1 A, B). They are supposed to show the relationships between the pictured objects. Especially ambiguous are the trees located in Figure 1 A. They simultaneously play roles of a metaphorical links between the heavenly structure and the earthly one and in shape they refer to the tree of life.

The circles and tree-like structures of the lines connecting the various graphical elements become the most important element of the image. The spherical structure of the graphic, despite the rectangular sheet of the book on which it was presented, attracts our vision to the center of the circle and seems to

Figure 1. Presentation of the Earth in the twelfth century treaty by Hildegard of Bingen Liber Divinorum Operum A); and The Universal Man, Liber Divinorum Operum of St. Hildegard of Bingen, 1165 Copy of the 13th century B) Public domain.

create a separate space. We can clearly see that the remaining space of the book sheet was not used as if someone had cut the place for the round visualization only in the rectangular structure of the painting.

Also during the Middle Ages, probably independently of Hildegard of Bingen, Joachim of Fiore[4] made a graphic connection of the heavenly circles with the earthly structure of a branched tree. His diagram of the Holy Trinity he presented in the relational form between the Divine Persons, combining the individual elements in the form of a graph (Figure 2). As he writes, he drew inspiration from the Biblical description of the Tree of Life from the Book of Genesis. The concept, initially very simple, was in later times expanded and became a canon of creating the theological visualizations where the circles are linked by means of relationship networks, often of complicated and extended structures. Such visual representations have become permanent elements of the sacred art, inspiring other creators, and have survived to the present times.

The shape of branched tree or one referring to this pattern for many years has been the primary form of illustrating the structured knowledge about the world. As we have already mentioned, according to Lima, the period of "of new knowledge flood" began in the historic times while the information visualization is not a new discipline that was only originated to "meet the needs of the era of *big data*". Even in the XII century Europe, to process the knowledge resulting from the compilation of backgrounds of the ancient Greeks and Romans, it took application of the new methods of visualization. On the cover of the XIII century encyclopaedia *Arbor Scientiae* (*Tree of Science*) by Spanish philosopher and polyhistor, Ramon Llulla, there is a tree (Figure 3) with branches symbolizing the sixteen basic areas of knowledge.

Figure 2. Trinity concept in an illustration to the Compendium Historiae in Genealogia Christi by Peter of Poitiers 1210. Public domain

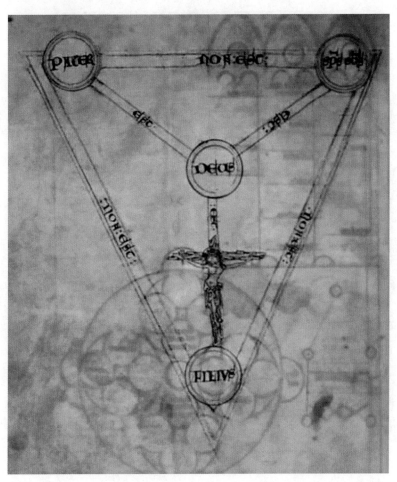

All grow out of a single trunk which shows the influence of the philosophy of Aristotle. The following sheets display further areas of science in the form of separate trees (Lima, 2011). Eighteen roots refer in turn to nine basic transcendental principles and nine techniques used in arts (difference, harmony, opposite, beginning, middle, end, majority, equality and minority).

Scott Weingard, one of the community members mindful of the development of Places&Spaces[5], is currently engaged in the analysis of the visual forms of knowledge representation in the history of humanity. He stresses that "in the beginning was the Tree" which we can find already in the Old Testament. He combined such objects as: the tree of life and the tree of knowledge, contradicting the good and evil. His blog entitled *Diagram of Knowledge* (Weingart, 2013) is a demonstration of unique examples of visualizations of structures for information and knowledge in medieval sources from VI century to XVIII century. In the Renaissance, the original schematic of illustrating the classified, accumulated philosophical and moral knowledge was replaced by picturesque images, necessarily presenting an abundant crown of leaves.

Figure 3. The Tree of Science on the cover of the XIII century encycloapedia Arbor Scientiae
Source: Wikipedia [on-line], public domain.

Lima notes that the models of trees from the XVIII–XIX centuries reveal clear abstract features (2013). Figure 4 shows "a graphics system of human knowledge" from *Encyclopaedia* by Diderot, however it is a diagram, rather than an image.

Charles Darwin in his famous work *On the Origin of Species by Means of Natural Selection* explains the theory of evolution and using the "Tree of Life" diagram he shows the complexity of the genealogical relationship in the time space (Figure 5). The tree schematism is justified by the necessity of representation of numerous links between the species. The hierarchical structure forming the basis for the trees: must include the primary element – root and secondary *elements*, nested levels — branches. This hierarchy is contemporary present in the organization of the corporations and universities, systems of folders and files on the hard drive, in the library classification systems of the genealogical data as well as in the definitions of classes of object-oriented programming languages. The tree-like visualization or ***dendrogram*** is currently used in the form of algorithms of the automatic clustering for the ongoing evaluations of the data grouping. Often this type of graphical presentation is attached to the other, for example to an array, in order to show a multi-faceted data spectra.

Figure 4. Figurative system of human knowledge from Encyclopaedia by Diderot, 1752 r. Public domain

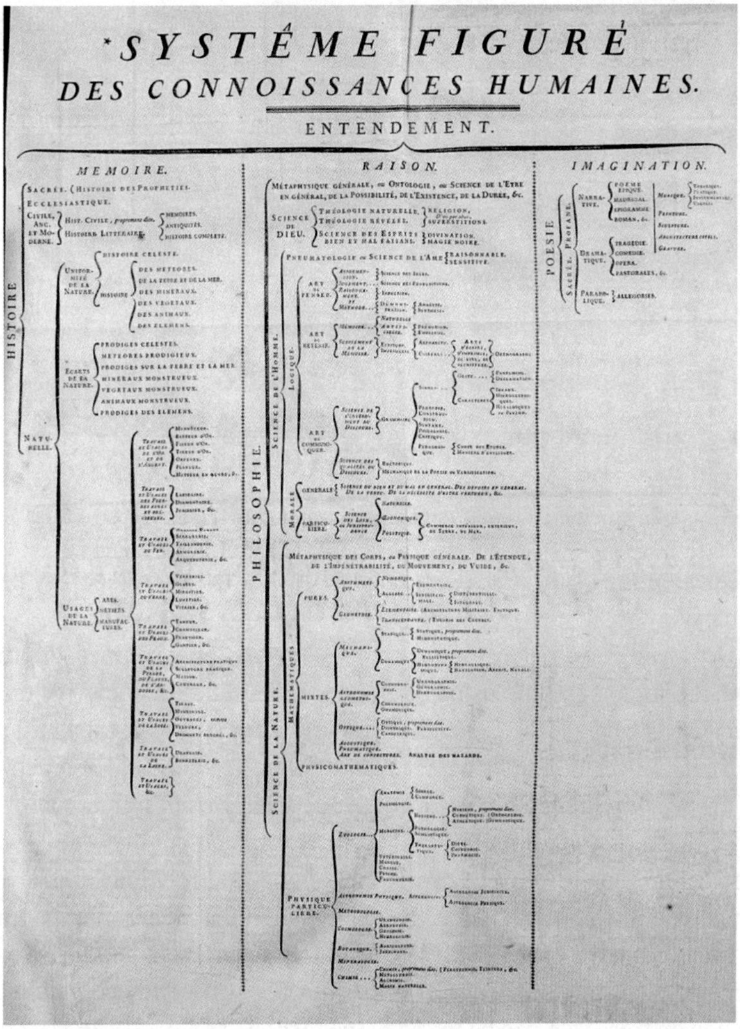

The major perceptive problem appears the provision of a good and effective representation of the spherical shape and the tree-like structure at the same time, on a two-dimensional flat surface. Probably today everyone has already seen a globe showing a model of the Earth and maps of the surface of our planet assembled in the form of the an atlas.

But not always everything was so simple, despite numerous attempts to construct good flat maps of the sphere surface. Some ideal spherical shapes people have seen only in heaven, the full Sun and Moon are shapes unobtainable in nature. Perhaps by analogy to the observed celestial objects people came to the conclusion that the Earth also must have been spherical? The problem of the Earth spherical shape have not always been so obvious. Today, for us it may be awkward that the ancient Romans and Greeks commonly accepted the fact of the Earth sphericity although the empirical confirmation of this concept appeared much later. So how this idea had become so universal before the proof came up? Today, the society would not be able to accept such a serious fact without a scientific confirmation. So were the societies of the Middle Ages so much different in terms of acceptance of the metaphysical concepts? If

Figure 5. The Tree of Life in the work by Ch. Darwin On the Origin of Species by Means of Natural Selection, 1859 r. Public domain.

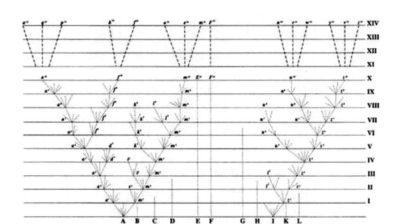

so, then maybe the perception of the visual experience was for the contemporary people other than the one that we imagine today?

In order to answer these questions, we must first understand how we measure the world around us. After all, before we produce a graphic or paint an image, we must first specify the dimensions of the objects that we want to display on the book sheets. Even if these are abstract structures, we still must specify the relationship between them using a sort of metric. The classical geometry allows us to solve these problems but as we have already mentioned, the geometry itself will not allow us to comprehend all the problems. So is it possible to precisely measure and calculate the reality which surrounds us? Yearning for understanding and discovery of the most important relationships in the world around us has accompanied people for a very long time. The initial attempts to measure the time we took as early as in the Neolith. Measurements of space were enabled by the ancient geometry but as early as in the Middle Ages it became clear that a ruler and caliper did not suffice to accurately measure the world. Important information on this issue can be found in the medieval edition of *Bible moralisee* dated 1250. The figure shows the structure of the Universe in the form of shape resembling a fractal, rather than an ideal Platonic solid, although fractal would become known for the humanity several hundred years later (Figure 6). Is this an effect of a stroke of an unknown author genius or just an intuitive attempt to present the complex structure of the world?

This we will probably never find out, but one fact is important — the figure does not display simple shapes of circles, lines and polygons, although such have been of interest for the geometry since the ancient times.

SHAPES: VISUAL PERCEPTION AND EMOTIONS

When we are looking at a complex image, our brain first analyses similar shapes and then recognizes the interconnections by trying to create a comprehensive object which is compared with already exist-ing ones in the long-term memory of the viewer. If the structure of the interconnections is recognized,

Figure 6. Anonymous 1220-1230. God as Architect, The Frontispiece of Bible Moralisee, public domain

a virtual representation appears in the space of mind (Osinska, Osinski, & Kwiatkowska, 2015). The natural capability of man of "viewing" makes our brain produce a projection showing an object from the real world that initially plays the role of reality imitation. Only then our brain compares, in a complex process that uses different modules, this imitation with the available known objects. Next, the space of our mind produces a new existence, recognized and manifested, as a seen object. Any theory concerning the visual perception will be incomplete without taking account of the problems arising from the origination of the language representation that semantically describes the viewed image (Jing Zhou, 2015).

This case triggers a natural question: how images can "talk" to our brains. Do they launch then natural mechanisms of the mathematics language or are they identical with the latter? Looking at the shapes of Figure 7 that show the representations of mandalas and angelic choirs — which are distant from each other in terms of time and space but above all in terms of the cultures — we feel, rather than analyze specific similarities. The mandala is here represented in a typical way as a fractal structure while the graphic from Hildegard work, which does not have such historical connotations, also features typical fractal characteristics. The self-similarity, the structure of the scaled elements and the large number of

Figure 7 Historical example: Hindu mandala[6] (A) and The structure of angelic choirs[7] (B)

the axes of symmetry arise from the spherical structure and make the graphics seem similar. And yet they represent completely different issues originated in the cultures that are very distant from each other.

The fractals are abstract objects created in the process of iteration of very simple mathematical expressions. First discovered and described by Benoit Mandelbrot[8], today they are regarded as important elements of the graphical representation of natural shapes found in nature (Mandelbrot, 1977). In the world around us, we do not find perfect squares, triangles and cubes, instead we see branched, complex, self-similar structures. Hence, if we want the images we create to "look naturally" we should use fractal algorithms in the visualization processes. The tree-like structures are the best examples.

We try to recognize the laws which govern the visual perception using imperfect empirical methods. They become more visible during the structural analysis of data originating from, as they may appear, totally different areas of knowledge. They can be viewed as visualized, spatial geometric forms. Obviously, the images created this way must feature structures comprehensible to our senses, fit on a two-dimensional sheet or a computer screen and ideally in a specially constructed three-dimensional virtual space. This does not mean, however, that these are images limited to a sheer copy of the world that surrounds us, sometimes they may greatly exceed it.

The projection of the multidimensional structures on the two-dimensional surface will always form a real shape, a reflection of reality on its own. Perhaps instead of looking for solutions to the difficult problems using only the observations and measurements, we should begin creating image atlases, based on analyses of large multidimensional data sets. They may prove helpful in a situation where the natural human perception cannot reach.

The resonance states in our brain can produce very complicated and individual feelings of beauty, reflection, etc. (Ramachandran, 2012). The search for a common definition of beauty is extremely complicated, the neurological-historical research show that it has evolved over time but it really is always very individual thing. The universal components of beauty must therefore pertain to those neuronal correlates that we have not only inherited in the genome, but which also have been shaped in the process of bringing up within a particular culture and in relations with other people. Why over the centuries we have been seeing the interpenetration of tree-like structures, which due to the fractal structure appear to be incidental, having only local symmetries and perfect shape circles, elements from the set of Platonic solids?

We can comment on this issue from the evolutionary perspective. Lima states that "We are returning to the original roots in nature, where the shapes are curvilinear in majority". He states further that the most enjoyed "are softer shapes as they provide some security, as opposed to angular shapes such as teeth of an animal or hard rock shapes. These are indications of danger" (Lima, 2017). This hypothesis is consistent with the neuroscience research. The human perception of images is always linked to the emotions, the visual routes run through the limbic system of the brain where the visual impression takes an individual, emotional coloring (Osinski, 2017). As early as in 1978, a psychologist, John N. Bassili, conducted an experiment in which he painted the faces of the participants in black and then he would add luminescent points. When the participants were asked to express happiness, the luminescent substance dots formed curvilinear shapes, open upwards. Whereas the expressions of wrath formed rectangular shapes facing downwards. Moreover, from everyday life we know that the expression of mouth with corners directed downwards reflects negative feelings, a smile is always "round". Hence the circles in our minds are represented in the positive context, while the acute-angled, triangular shapes represent fear and anger.

These experiments are complemented with newer concepts by Vilayanur S. Ramachandran (2012). According to his hypothesis, developed jointly with Edward M. Hubbardem, important factors responsible for the visual representations in our minds are phenomena of synesthesia (Osinski, 2017). They allow to explain not only the process of visual perception itself, but above all the secondary process of description of the resultant experience. This is of fundamental importance because our feelings must be described and interpreted in the form of a natural language. Therefore, if the visualization has a graphic form, ultimately it still must be converted into a syntactical representation. Then it becomes an element of language — visualization language.

Today, the theory of Noam Chomsky (1965) is very popular, concerning the hypothetical universal grammar that is to be a congenital grammar for a man. Ramachandran puts, however, a completely different hypothesis believing that the metaphors of language are closely related to the architecture of the human brain. The researchers repeated the Wolfgang Köhler[9] experiment, introducing the participants to two images: one composed of acute-angled triangular shapes and the second closed shape drawn with rounded contours. After the introduction of shapes the participants were asked to which shape fits word *bouba*, and to which *kiki*. The statistical majority of respondents (95%) stated that *bouba* was the name of a solid of rounded shapes, while *kiki* was the name of a solid with sharp edges. Hence, the visualization language has proved to be universal, not only inter-culturally, but also independently of the natural language. The universal shapes are responsible for the universal linguistic forms. After all, the experiment participants made their decision only based on the sound of the word and the shape of the solid. Word *bouba* comprises back and rounded vowels, whereas word *kiki* — front and flat ones. Therefore, we can conclude that people have a natural ability to associate certain sounds with certain shapes. Further, we can state that the visualization is a type of language because it uses properly aligned shapes and objects to forward a deeper sense and interconnections. The data is encoded in the symbolisms and semiology. Syntax and conventions of these schemes must be interpreted by human brains, they are not congenital.

VISUALIZATION PATTERNS IN CULTURES

Therefore, what we should do next, is to consider how the shapes are represented in different cultures. We already know that the visualization forms feature universal characteristics, independent of the times and places. So can we still today, in the age of globalization, note the specific characteristics of spherical shapes in different cultures? We clearly see that the degrees of compilation of individual shapes (Figure 8) tend to be various, Hindu culture is dominated by circles and spherical shapes. The Arabic circle consists of repetitive patterns, both round and consisting of straight lines, while the Chinese circle is filled with symbols. Therefore we can reckon the shape universal but its fillings, connections of the individual sections form structures specific for the cultural circles. Likewise the tree-like structures, the web-based and complex self-repeatable patterns in mandalas and schemas by Hildegard of Bingen feature fractal characteristics (Osinska, Osinski, Kwiatkowska, 2015). We can link them with shapes observed in nature, after all the fractals are representations of natural plants, features of the landscape of different geographical regions. They must have, therefore, affected the shapes and structures of the neuronal correlates that are responsible for the visual perception in people living for centuries in such places. Thus, the linkages of the fractal structures with the universal spherical shapes are natural, universal components of the visualization language.

We must realize that the visualization language has evolved, after all, the ongoing changes affect vegetation and landscapes viewed by people living in different locations. Furthermore, the wanderings and migrations of peoples create new qualities by mixing the original representations. If we therefore intent to historically analyze the issues of the visualization language universality, we must take account of the dynamics of time. Here, we may successfully apply the theory of Kuhn concerning the changes of the paradigm that uses the methodology enabling the analyses of important scientific events (the emergence of new theories), not from the point of view of a modern researcher, but from the perspective of the original creator living in another world "of the past". The full analysis of images originated hundreds of years ago is not possible from the point of view of the modern science alone. This is not only about the modern scientific paradigm, better and wider access to information, but above all about the images that prompt completely different feelings in the past and today in the minds of the analyzers.

Figure 8. The shapes corresponding to phrase "national circle" represented as the most frequently occurring in the graphical Google query[11] Public domain

China circle[10]　　　　Hindu circle　　　　Arabic circle

Similarly, we can investigate the issues related to the visual perception of the surrounding reality — already Władysław Strzemiński in "Theory of Vision" pondered on the evolution of visual awareness in man (2015). What we see directly affects who we are, but this has had different meanings and looked somewhat differently in different historical eras. Apart from that, the change in view of the world alters the way of its presentation by people in the act of the image creation. Both in the classical graphic form or increasingly today, in a digital form.

Thus, visualization means creating images for easier comprehension of the different forms of language. It is not supposed to substitute for the forms of language, but to creatively complement the latter. The natural languages using the semantic relations of words are extremely complex and difficult, for instance the translations between different languages produce enormous difficulties. The increasing specialization in research generates hermetic language styles origination. Encompassing the wording forms in such small groups means that they only develop within specific disciplines and not give insight in science as a whole. The original academic universality is displaced by scientific and financial corporations. In the search for the truth, we often have to cooperate, connect ideas and conceptions resulting in different environments. It appears then that the best, universal language will be an image, however constructed in the course of complex, often algorithmic processes. A visualization in a graphic form is to be the beginning of deeper studies, discussions that should be carried out using words. But the words somehow affixed in the universal graphical structure. The visualizations however must not be abstract, but they must constitute an attempt to genuinely reflect the reality, carried out based on the information available from different fields of research. Such a visualization will not only allow to broaden the horizons of knowledge, but above all it is capable of introducing us to a holistic seizure of description of the world from which a timeless order and truth emerge, truth which is unreachable with limited, closed horizons (Osinski, 2015).

CONCLUSION

To sum up, we see that the visualization processes for hundreds of years now have been engaged in the problem of connection of the ideal Platonic solids with the shapes that occur in nature. Today Colin Ware's in his book, *Information Visualization* (2012), wonders: Is visualization a science or a language? Shamir Zeki, a neuroscientist, indicates a close link between the activities of the neuronal correlates and our perception of beauty and harmony (2016). Even a new scientific discipline, called neuroesthetics, emerged, which deals with this issue. It will help us in the future to understand the aesthetic patterns, encoded in the space of mind. Only then we will be able to return to the questions concerning the cognitive experiences of the past generations. The neurodynamics language used by our brain still remains undiscovered, and probably it is what enables us to combine different complex structures originating from the perception system into a single consistent sensual feeling.

ACKNOWLEDGMENT

The work is sponsored by Polish National Science Center (NCN) under grant 2013/11/B/HS2/03048 "Digital knowledge structure and dynamics analyzing by means of information visualisation".

REFERENCES

Bassili, J. N. (1989). *On-line Cognition in Person Perception*. Psychology Press.

Chomsky, N. (1965). *Aspects of the Theory of Syntax*. MIT.

Hey, T., Tansley, S., & Tolle, K. (2009). *The Fourth Paradigm: Data-Intensive Scientific Discovery*. Microsoft Research.

Hildegard of Bingen. (1990). *Scivias - Classics of Western Spirituality*. Mahwah, NJ: Paulist Press.

Lima, M. (2011). *Visual Complexity: Mapping Patterns of Information*. New York: Princeton Architectural Press.

Lima, M. (2017). *The Book of Circles: Visualizing Spheres of Knowledge*. New York: Princeton Architectural Press.

Maldenbrot, B. (1982). *Fractal Geometry of Nature*. New York: W. H. Freeman and Company.

Osinska, V., Osinski, G., & Kwiatkowska, A. B. (2015). Visualization in Learning: Perception, Aesthetics, and Pragmatics. In A. Ursyn (Ed.), *Maximazing Cognitive Learning through Knowledge Visualization*. Hershey, PA: IGI Global. doi:10.4018/978-1-4666-8142-2.ch013

Osinski, G. (2015). Information Visualization. The research of information structures in the search for truth. *Fides Ratio et Patria, 3*. (in Polish).

Osinski, G. *Retarius contra Sekutor*. WSKSiM, Torun 2018. (in Polish)

Ramachandran, V. S. (2012). *The Tell-Tale Brain. A Neuroscientists' Quest for What Makes Us Human*. New York: W. H. Freeman and Company.

Strzeminski, W. (2015). Readability of Images. *Proceedings of the international conference devoted to the work of Władysław Strzemiński*.

Ware, C. (2012). *Information Visualization. Perception for Design*. Elsevier.

Weingart, S. (2013). *Diagrams of knowledge*. Retrieved July 20, 2017, from: http://www.scottbot.net/HIAL/

Weingart, S. (2013). From trees to webs: uprooting knowledge through visualization. In A. Slavic, A. Akdag Salah & S. Davies (Eds.). *Classification & visualization: Interfaces to knowledge. Proceedings of the International UDC Seminar*, (pp. 43-58). Würzburg: Ergon Verlag.

Zeki, S. (2012). *Splendor and Miseries of the Brain. Love, Creativity, and the Quest for Human Happiness*. Willey-Blackwell.

Zhou, J. (2015). Connecting the Dots: Art, Culture, Science and Technology. In A. Ursyn (Ed.), *Maximazing Cognitive Learning through Knowledge Visualisation. IGI Global 2015*. doi:10.4018/978-1-4666-8142-2.ch011

ADDITIONAL READING

Spence, I., & Wainer, H. (2001). William Playfair. In C. C. Heyde & E. Seneta (Eds.), *Statisticians of the Centuries* (pp. 105–110). New York: Springer. doi:10.1007/978-1-4613-0179-0_21

Yau, N. (2011). *Visualize This. The FlowingData Guide to Design Visualization and Statistics.* Indianopolis, USA: Wiley Publishing.

KEY TERMS AND DEFINITIONS

Fractal: Is a mathematically described object used to represent and simulate natural patterns. Fractals are very different from known geometric figures. Fractal structures are exceptionally intuitive in perception and reception because they originate from (or resemble) nature. This explains why fractal-like visualizations are perceived better.

Mind Space (MS): The concept, introduced and explained by authors. This abstract space will serve as a topological "place" in which we will describe the functions that connect our brain activity with the concepts referred to our mind states. At the beginning we will define MS metrics very generically, as a collection of all real observations and possible measurements of psychophysical activity. We do not ask about the size of MS; it should be as small as possible but universal enough for us to be able to carry out the necessary analysis. In such a space we will consider mental events that we can determine.

Neuroesthetics: A new cross-disciplinary research field related to art, history of art, cognitive and computer sciences, communication, and mathematics. Neuroaesthetics studies creative processes in art and tries to understand the mechanism of the human brain during such processes. This is not just the study of artistic experiences, but it also emphasizes the crucial influence of the brain study on the understanding of human nature.

Perception: Popular explanation of the term "percept," from which perception comes, defines the mental and conscious representation of the stimulus in the mind. However, such a definition does not explain anything; rather it generates another incomprehensible concept. The first problem relates to the notion of "consciousness": we do not yet have a strict and fully accepted theory of consciousness. Another problem is the location of a place "in the mind" where this representation occurs (see "mind space").

Synesthesia: A perceptual phenomenon in which one sense (for example, hearing) is simultaneously perceived as if by one or more additional senses such as sight. There are many forms synesthesia (for instance, where letters, shapes, numbers are joined with a sensory perception such as smell, color, or flavor). People who report a lifelong history of such experiences are called synesthetes.

Visualization: Generally can be defined as the representation of an object, situation, or set of data or information as chart, diagram, or other image. Regardless the technique, the main aim of visualization is to communicate a message that can be in abstract form or precise data.

ENDNOTES

1 Adam Mickiewicz, in his *Forefathers' Eve*, defines it clearly as the devil who wants to destroy the nature of man, quote: PETER: Who are you? GHOST: Lukrecy.

2 Hildegard of Bingen (1098-1179) — benedictine, reformer of religion, visionary, mystic, healer, recognized as a saint by the Roman Catholic Church, since 2012 a Doctor of the Church. A patron of the scientists and linguists.

3 *Scivias* is an illustrated work by Hildegard of Bingen, completed in 1151 or 1152. The title comes from the Latin phrase *"Sci vias Domini"* ("Know the Ways of the Lord"). The book is illustrated by 35 miniature illustrations, more than that are included in her two later books of visions.

4 Joachim of Flora and "Gioacchino da Fiore" [in Italian]) (c. 1135 – March 30, 1202)—was an Italian mystic, a theologian

5 Website is dedicated for collection of science maps created by researchers on the world: www.scimaps.org.

6 www.mandalas.com

7 Hildegard from Bingen, *Scivias* I.6: The Choirs of Angels. (from the Rupertsberg manuscript, fol. 38r.

8 Benoît B. Mandelbrot (1924-2010) — mathematician born in Warsaw. He solved problems of the topological representation of iterative mathematical expressions. He invented the word "fractal" itself and introduced the concept of fractal geometry. The most famous fractal, Mandelbrot set, is named after him.

9 Wolfgang Köhler (1887–1967), German psychologist who together with Max Wertheimer and Kurt Koffka, contributed to the creation of Gestalt psychology.

10 Tang Dynasty Mirror shows cycles in Chinese calendar. Innermost circle shows 4 cosmological animals depicting the 4 cardinal points N, S, E, W and the 4 seasons. Next ring shows 12 animals signifying the 12 year Jupiter cycle. Outer ring has 28 creatures representing the 28 Chinese 'hsiu' or stellar station.

11 The study was performed on 19.06.2017 with the use of Google search engine. A question was asked consisting of two "national-circle" members (china-circle, hindu-circle and arabic-circle). The figure shows the highest ranked shapes for the appropriate forms of the query.

Chapter 2
Shapes and Patterns in Visualizing Human Knowledge:
Part 2 – Digital Visualisation Techniques

Veslava Osinska
Nicolaus Copernicus University, Poland

Grzegorz Osinski
College of Social and Media Culture, Poland

ABSTRACT

Excel or similar statistical software offers a lot of possibilities to generate different kinds of charts and diagrams. Throughout the variety of graphical representations, one can find common features among elementary patterns they consist of. Circles (spheres in 3D information space) and trees as effective and ergonomic shapes are the base of known historical and contemporary visualization techniques. The chapter introduces the most popular and ergonomic methods for visualizing large-scale data. The authors strive to find common visual properties in relation to their historical archetypes. The discussion about a series of both technical and aesthetical issues is also included.

INTRODUCTION TO DIGITAL VISUALIZING

Today for the users familiar with a specialist software, visualization of data and information does not constitute a major challenge anymore. It may seem that the possibility of creating the computer diagrams offers unlimited possibilities in the design of original forms of graphical representation. For the interactive 3D visualizations such statement is reasonable. Creation of 3D scene, filling the three-dimensional space with data, high precision, modelling of information topology or interaction assurance is achieved using a computer program. A crucial fact is that this technology produces an instant, spectacular effect. However, the history of statistical infographics of the past centuries necessitates in this context a focus on 2D visualizations.

The era of digital plotting and graphing removes partly the creative thinking. It is particularly evident in the behavior of the majority of students attending the ICT classes. The audience brings some habits

DOI: 10.4018/978-1-5225-4990-1.ch002

to the spreadsheet handling course. They know that in order to generate a chart they need to select the columns of data and click "Create chart". Whilst the choice of the chart type is a real challenge for them. Were it not for the preview window, many of them could not even schematically draw what they intend to achieve visually. This dependence on the automation must not be attributed to a selected application, it has already become a common characteristic. The process of visualization is therefore reduced to specification of data column and selection of chart type that at any time can be reversed and transformed, which is already evident in all specialized applications.

The Graphic User Interface in the visualization software is designed to facilitate the work with data, while the cost of this is the loss of the user inventiveness. The instantly produced results do not allow us to comprehend the structure of the data and prevent its interpretation. So what have we lost deviating from the manual drawing of visualization? Before the digital era, were created the charts manually on the graph paper. At the beginning, we need to plot axes, specify the scales and measuring points. The insight at this stage would determine which method of visualization, matching and approximation should be used and in what sequence. This stepwise approach in the creation of the graphics provided a deeper, gradual recognition of the data and its nature. In the commonly used R programming environment, the "disable thinking" effect is minimized by cyclical forcing editing and processing of an appropriate code snippet until the effect is reached, by manually assigning the columns to the axes or by serial entering of the chart parameters.

The detailed analysis shows that the methods of numerical presentation, considered modern, in the great majority are only modifications of forms, used often in the past by an unknown author, forgotten, concealed in the old lexicons and atlases among charts and maps. Such search of historiographical evidence, leading to exploring innovative thinking tracks, deposits of inventiveness and imagination of XVIII and XIX century visualizers, became a popular subject among the information visualization researchers (Clegg & DeVarco, 2010; Lima, 2011; Lima, 2014; Moretti, 2005; Weingard, 2013). This shows how important the historical connotations are, especially today in the era of digital data processing.

CIRCLE- BASED CHARTS

Circles and spherical shapes were already described in detail in part one of the authors' chapter (*Shapes and Patterns in Visualizing the Human Knowledge. Origin from Historical and Cognitive Perspective*), both from the historical and neuroesthetic points of view. Now, let us go to the concept of repeatability resulting from application of the topology of circles.

The radial structures have a very long tradition in visualization. The cyclicality of the processes in nature and human life made the ancient illustrators frequently use the circle in the presentations of the knowledge on the world. The astronomers are used to describe phenomena using the current constellation of stars. Traditional astronomical calendar refers to the astrological knowledge; the outer ring which is made up of twelve zodiac signs. As we will see further, the evolution of various visualization forms has always comprised examples, most often proven and useful, of mapping the structures into a circle or sphere (Brath & MacMurchy, 2014).

The contemporary charts, based on a circle and symmetrical glyphs, are shown in Figure 1. The first one (Figure 1a) represents a circle chart, so called "pie chart", which illustrates the percentages of the component parts to the whole. Despite their popularity, in statistics such visualizations are regarded as too unprofessional and susceptible to tampering. A leading statistician, John Tukey, simply rejected them,

Figure 1. Pie chart A); Bubble chart B); Radar chart C) Scatter chart D)

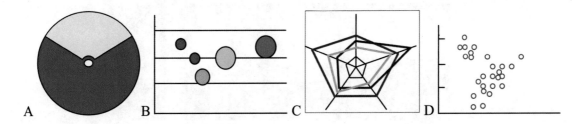

arguing that: "there is no such a pie chart which would not be replaceable by a better graphical presentation" (O'Connor & Robertson, 1999). With regard to the perception, a pie chart creates this difficulty that we tend to wrongly estimate the values of acute and widely obtuse angles, while the assessment of those depends on the vertical or horizontal positioning of a segment and the object projection. The pie chart was invented as early as in the XVIII century by William Playfair (Tufte, 1990; Friendly, 2008) who was the author of the most popular nowadays statistical charts, called *Playfair charts*.

Bubble chart (Figure 1b) became exceedingly popular in the last decade due to the aesthetic form (colorful, varied size circles) and to the possibility of manipulation of values. In the evaluation of the circle shape size, the diameter is preferred, while the surface area has a secondary significance. However, a simple calculation of the surface area ($\pi d^2/4$) produces as large as fourfold difference. Nevertheless, the *"bubbles"* have overwhelmed many services with the statistical infographics, such as a popular educational portal GapMinder[1] (Osinska, Osinski & Kwiatkowska, 2015). The automatic estimation of the analyzed size on the charts only pertains to two visual characteristics: length (bar charts, column charts) and the position in the coordinate system (line chart, scatter chart) (Few, 2009). This principle is used in the radar chart: the variable values are specified on centrifugal axes (Figure 1c). The series of data are presented as closed polygons and colored accordingly. In this way, the radar visualization is compact, though useless in the analysis of numerous series. The scatter charts (Figure 1d) facilitate searching the dependencies in the observed large-scale data; most often they are evident in the analysis of the empirical studies results. The data dispersion pattern in the Cartesian coordinate system, regardless of the complexity degree, is the most "sensitive" to decoding by human perception and cognition, as it enables an automatic capture of the homogeneity gaps, such as for example any clusters and holes in the layout of the points (Few, 2009). However, the images presented in the figures appear to be quite primitive; compared to the medieval visualizations they seem to contain no aesthetic elements. They are just simple representations of data.

TREE-BASED CHARTS

The visualizations will look entirely different when we use the previously described tree-like structures. In the natural environment, a mono-hierarchy is rather theoretical because predominantly the test objects fall simultaneously into several categories — facets. This fact however does not interfere with the tradition of research on the hierarchy visualization. The application meant to generate tree-like diagrams (treemaps) (Figure 2), quantitatively presenting the hierarchies was designed in 1991 by Ben Shneiderman (2009).

Figure 2. Treemap chart

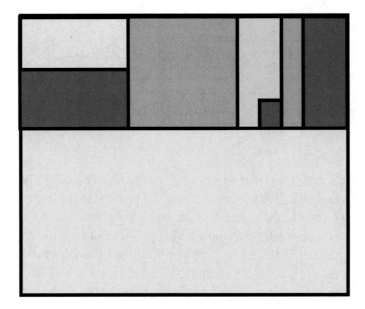

The concept of treemaps opted for the use of nested rectangles instead of the branches. Then, using the rectangle surface area, its color and grouping enables encoding of three variables in the data set. For example, in the demographic statistics of world, grouped by continents, where the figure size indicates the total population of a given country and the color within specified color scale— life expectancy for that area (Figure 3).

Through the research of the visual forms history, we are discovering analogies and similarities with the past. The treemaps were used as early as in 1870, when the idea of division of rectangles in proportion to the component values was used to visualize the demographic data in the United States in terms of race and origin ("Treemaps of Race," 2010). The palette specific for the era (*Vintage*, as the portal

Figure 3. Visualization of treemaps for demographic data Source: author's development based on the Treemap gnberated World Statistics eXplorer (2014)

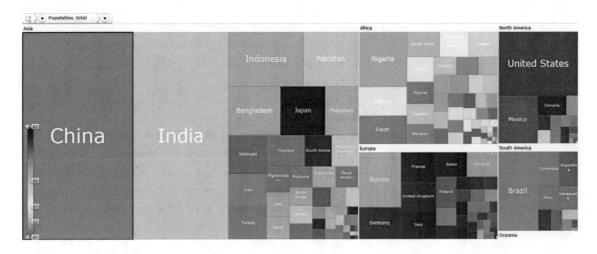

name) marked the following categories: white and colored Americans, born in the USA and abroad. The part of the white population, indigenous Americans, can be instantly estimated based on the area covered by the burgundy color, dominant in all the states. An added convenience is the order of the rectangles by size, which offers the ability to immediately conclude on the least (Nevada) and most (New York) populated states.

The treemaps have paved the way for experimentation with filling the data space with various figures. The history of this process was described in detail on the portal of the *treemapping* inventor, Schneiderman (2009). The rectangles were replaced with circles, and then the circular treemaps emerged — Figure 4a. In this concept, the root represents the outer circle, while the structure grows inwards with a partition of space by increasingly smaller circles. The idea of using the circles has been used in the John Stasko project, *Sunburst* (2001), which is shown on Figure 4B. The main level is situated in the center of the circle, the rings limited by segments represent the sub-levels with the specified sizes. The information structure is expanded on the outskirts of the configuration, thus the exploration space virtually features no limits.

The discussed examples concern the elementary geometric figures. The question arises therefore: how the previously described irregular fractal shapes can be implemented in the visualization algorithms? Let up go back to the beginning of the XX century. Then a Russian mathematician, Georgy Voronoy ("Georgy Fedoseevich Voronoy," 2007) invented the way of a plane division into irregular polygons. The visualization as well as the algorithm are called Voronoy tessellation and are commonly used by artists and designers because of the spectacular visual effect (Figure 4C). If there are *n* points in a set, then for each of them we can extract such an area on the plane that the distances between the points will be minimized[2]. Such fragmentation, clearly iterative including the coloring of the resulting areas, offers an express aesthetic effect. This method is particularly appreciated by artists. A portal with known Polish new-generation search engine Carrot2 offers an application for interactive Voronoy tessellation — FoamTree[3].

Open source software allows a large groups of users to create specific visualizations in the form of mutually self-similar fractal structures. According the FoamTree documentation, it enables visualization of over 100,000 objects on more than 100,000 hierarchy levels. This way generated graphical representation of numerous and interrelated data of phylogenetic tree[4] (in Figure 8) of organisms living on Earth is called the *tree of life* (*Foam Tree*, 20017).

Figure 4. Circular treemaps A) sunburst (B) and Voronoi diagram (C)

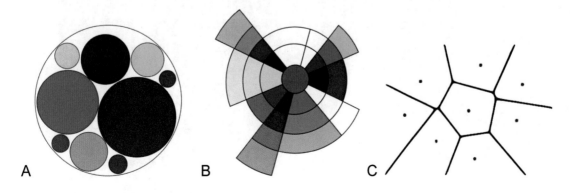

A   B   C

PATTERNS: NET VISUALIZATION

The concept of organized science structure has affected such thinkers as Francis Bacon or René Descartes. Descartes, in addition to the coordinate system is associated also with the concept of whirls aimed to explain the gravity and magnetism and which graphically, as Lima suggests (2013), is the prototype of the Voronoy diagram (Descartes, 1647). Figure 5 shows the specific polygons of solids outlines, filled with a hypothetical ether.

The most important part of a tree is the common root, superior for the whole. The branched structure without such a basis transforms to a network, i.e. it loses a hierarchy and order an takes a cluster of links of equivalent categories. From a formal perspective, the network structures are represented by graphs. The rapid increase of data, the development of ICT and the ubiquity of social network communication have determined the characterization of the contemporary phenomena and processes in each sphere of life in the form of graphs.

In the face of this new, visualization paradigm, the trees, instead of a decorative one, adopt a representative role (Osinska, 2016). A natural effect of this is the evolution of trees in the network configurations. The relationship between the investigated objects is best illustrated by graphs. They are used in the mathematical sciences, computing, communications, social studies and in the media space analysis. This form of graphical representation is already presented to the student of primary schools during the adding and subtraction operations. A graph, as a mathematical structure that consists of vertices imaging the investigated units and edges, symbolizes the interrelations. The edges can be defined using weights, i.e. the bond strengths, and shown graphically using distances. The greater the strength, the shorter the

Figure 5. The concept of whirls of René Descartes (1647) and scalable areas of Voronoy in a colorful outline

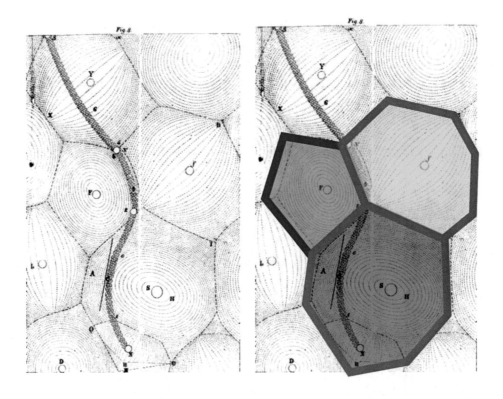

distance, i.e. the thickness of section and arrows symbolizing the direction of the information flow. The final visualization will depend on the interdependencies of three forces: gravity and repulsion between the vertices and summary, centripetal gravity of the entire system (Wilson, 2012). Therefore, the graph (network) representations by longer or shorter edges indicate the degree of similarity or mutual relations of objects. The degree of dissemination of the nodes shows the grouping as well as the entities irrelevant to the entire set. The resultant general configuration is very important from the perspective of the data structure analysis which is not visible on a traditional statistical chart.

In the studies on network structures the methodology basis relates to the *Social Network Analysis* — SNA that uses a graph theory, mathematics and statistics, data mining and *Network Science*. The inception of the graph theory is dated on XVIII century, when an outstanding mathematician, Leonhard Euler, solved the logistic problem of seven bridges of Koenigsberg using a graph (Barabási, 2010; Osinska, Osinski & Kwiatkowska, 2015). The Social Network Analysis enables analysis of diverse social relationships between individuals and organizations. The interpersonal interdependencies can be specified through various forms of communication, for example "who talks to whom?", "who paints/ calls to whom?". The SNA tests also include network transactional links: "Who sold whom a patent, technology or product?". In IT and telecommunications, the SNA is applied for testing the bandwidths of the Internet traffic channels, for the dynamics of the information dissemination in the networks and for testing the structures of the web portals communities, identification of regularities in the network of the recommended web pages. The nodes represent the websites, while the edges — URL links (Figure 6). It shows such Internet visualization from 1999, performed by Lucent Technologies, where the colors are used for indicating the country domains (*Internet Mapping Project*, 1998). In the period preceding the Web 2.0 era, such a map could have still featured legible traces of connections of a single domain or IP, which the authors of the project illustrate using many different color versions.

In the epidemiology, it enables prediction of the epidemic directions. What genes are responsible for human diseases? Here a visualization using the SNA shall be of assistance, showing the links between the disease characteristics with the pathogens (Goh et al., 2007).

The intelligence agencies and secret services treat SNA as an extremely useful tool for the detection of criminal groups and terrorist actions. After the attacks on WTC in 2011, thanks to the SNA the US intelligence identified the roles of the key members of Al-Qaida, their relationships and links. Furthermore, they recognized the structures of subgroups, including the prediction of the entire network developments. In the Internet, we can find the input data for these analyses and knowing the algorithmic methodology, we can carry out the simulations (Wu et al., 2015).

For large volumes of data, the resulting graphs are often illegible. Another problem is the distribution of the entire system on a limited plane of the screen. The unevenness featuring an excessive concentration of nodes in a single place and contrasting gaps in another is an undesirable effect of large data mapping (Chen, 2005). An improvement of the configuration can follow from changing the network topology with a circle. This type of example is a circular network visualization (Figure 8), implemented in Circos application, created mainly for the visualization of data of the human genome and their structural variation (*What is Circos*, 2009)). With live colors and compact layout, Circos has become a symbolic artistic measure in the art of presentation and visualization of large-scale data[5], while its author, Martin Krzywinski — a popular visualizer. In the circular graph, the nodes are deposited on a circle in the form of arcs of different lengths, while the bond strength between them is distinctive by the widths of the bands connecting the arcs' sections, rather than the distances. Therefore, the arcs and spherical structures once again appear today as a common form of visualization.

Figure 6. Map of the Internet of 1999 made by Bell Labs
Source: Flickr, n.d.

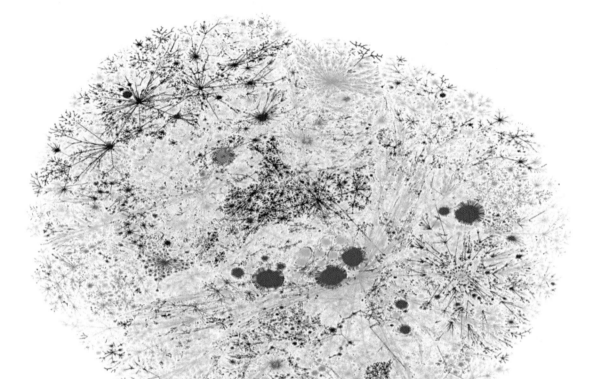

Another way to extend the scope of the exploration space is the 3D data presentation and hyperbolic distortion, consisting in that the selected portion is projected on the spherical vision area, thus stretching it locally. This method of visualization using both, spherical shapes and network fractal structures has been applied by Caida[6]. Its visualization application, Walrus allows to create comprehensive and beautiful visualization graphs in the 3D environment ("Walrus," 2005). Thanks to projects completed in this application, we can note that for the descriptions of visualizations we utilize the contemporary forms of mathematical language and clubby, specialized terms.

But if we visually compare the shapes of these visualizations with the previously presented historical counterparts, we will see completely different natural analogies. We can see the universal fractal forms and in Circos there are classical, positive spherical shapes. Does it not seem strange that despite the passage of almost a thousand years, the today's visualizations produced by the advanced computer technology, begin to resemble the graphical forms illustrating the works by Hildegard of Bingen? The transition from the classical, adversely associated by the limbic system, tables and line charts to the natural spherical and fractal structures is therefore an appropriate direction in the search for an universal measure of the visual communication. After all, it is clear that the invention of modern visualizers just pertains to the connections of the fundamental forms of visualization. The mapping of a network onto

Figure 7. An example of the circular network visualization of scientists' collaboration in Circos application

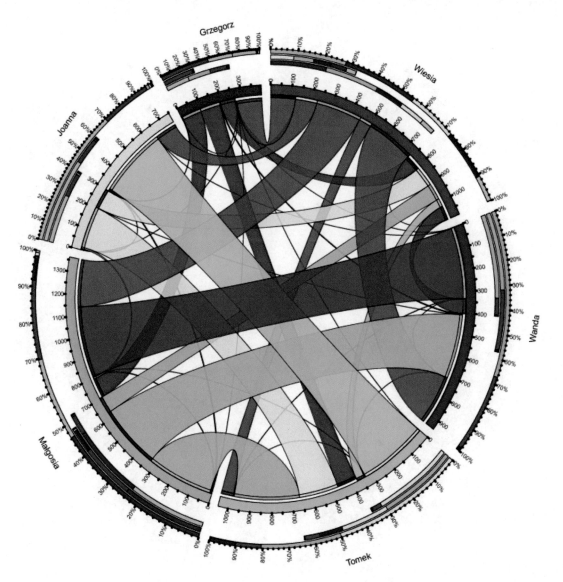

a circle or sphere has become a standard. A combination of a circle and a tree-like structure produces a radial tree which enables us to position hierarchical information on the circle, thus symmetrizing the structure – this structure is presented on Figure 8.

Therefore, the contemporary visualization methods to the full derive from the medieval concepts of deployment of the most important element in the center of the coaxial system, and the dependent components — on the outside. Since in the second half of the XX century, the development of processors and graphics cards allowed the powerful graphics rendering, the information trees started to resemble their counterparts in nature with abundant crowns without leaves, such as we see in winter, with clear contours, contrastive to the surroundings. This allegory shows the increasing importance of the fractals for understanding and imitating the geometries of nature and simulating the dynamic processes therein. The Euclidean geometry, enclosed in the elementary shapes known from school, does not describe the

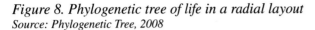

Figure 8. Phylogenetic tree of life in a radial layout
Source: *Phylogenetic Tree, 2008*

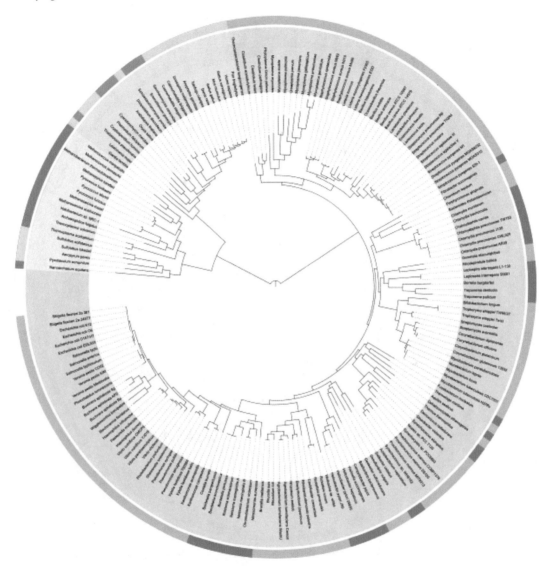

real world, for example jagged coastlines of the states, fancy shapes of clouds, life-giving blood vessels system or a dense tree crown.

As the iconographic sources show, over the centuries trees in different forms have made one of the primary forms of presentation of structures of knowledge on the world, God, on the human nature, role of man, place and transience in the continuum (Lima, 2014). In different cultures, over the centuries certain shapes have served as an inspiration and produced crisp emotions (Eco, 2013). For example, the pentagram, regarded as a symbol of freemasonry, can evoke curiosity mixed with fear (Brown, 2003). A prohibited Nazi symbol, swastika, for a long time in Asia has been associated with happiness and prosperity. Semiology investigates the symbol geometry effect on the human imagination, and combined with neurosciences it provides new observations. It has tried to understand how the human mind resonates with the shapes derived directly from nature. A tree turns out to be the most natural shape since the times of the medieval visualization tradition being the most popular metaphor in old books and manuscripts.

It has survived the great shocks in art and science which predominated in those times. It returns today, together with a new fractal algorithms and the use of spherical shapes, allowing for the creation of a new quality in the visualization techniques.

CONCLUSION

The overview of the numerous examples of visualizations from various periods of history leads to the conclusion that the new forms have emerged basically through experimenting with the classical geometry, through division of surfaces into components and subsequent combining them together, also through frequent use of timelines or bar charts in a variety of configurations and orientations, as in the case of initial dashboards that offered the possibility of data analysis from multiple perspectives (*Vintage visualization. Growth of the elements of the population: 1790 to 1890*, 2017; Osinska & Bala, 2015; Osinska, Jozwik & Osinski, 2015).

The modern trends in the information visualization are based on the representation traditions shaped over the ages. The medieval manuscripts show that the shape of a branched tree was then a basic form of presenting the structured knowledge on the world. Another often used ergonomic method was a round shape. The classical bar visualizations are too schematic. The bars and circles, the so-called "angular shapes" evoke negative feelings of fear. A prolonged exposure to angular shapes causes a natural habituation, i.e. neutralization. An excessive simplification and minimization following the principles of Gestalt make therefore the contemporary audience seek experience inspired by nature. Perhaps the nearest future will see new trends preferring the manual visualizations similar to those of the Middle Ages or Renaissance. Figure 9 shows an attempt to use both in the visualization process, manual drawing and subsequent artistic enhancement using digital techniques.

Figure 9. Authors conception of space-filling by irregular areas in hypothetical visualization

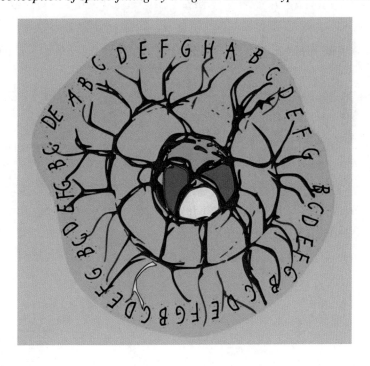

ACKNOWLEDGMENT

The work is sponsored by Polish National Science Center (NCN) under grant 2013/11/B/HS2/03048 *Digital knowledge structure and dynamics analyzing by means of information visualisation.*

REFERENCES

Barabási, A. L. (2016). *Network Science*. Cambridge, UK: University Printing House.

Brath, R., & MacMurchy, P. (2014). Information Visualization on Spheres. In E. Banissi, F. T. Marchese, & C. Forsell (Eds.), *Information Visualization: Techniques. Usability and Evaluation*. Cambridge Scholars Publishing.

Brown, D. (2003). *Angels and demons*. New York: Random House.

Clegg, E., & DeVarco, B. (2010). *What is the Shape of Thought?* Retrieved July 20, 2017, from: http://shapeofthought.typepad.com/shape_of_thought/what-is-the-shape-of-thought/

Descartes, R. (1647). *Prinzipien der Philosophie. Aether vortex around suns and planets*. Retrieved July 20, 2017, from: ttps://commons.wikimedia.org/wiki/File:Descartes_Aetherwirbel.jpg

Eco, U. (2010). *History of Beauty*. New York: Rizzoli.

Few, S. (2009). *Now You See It: Simple Visualization Techniques for Quantitative Analysis*. Oakland, CA: Analytics Press.

Flickr. (n.d.). *Networks of Abundance Lab*. Retrieved from https://www.flickr.com/photos/poptech/galleries/72157629723472161/

Foam Tree. (2017). *Web service by Carrot Search*. Retrieved July 20, 2017, from: http://carrotsearch.com/foamtree

Friendly, M. (2008). The Golden Age of Statistical Graphics. *Statistical Science*, *23*(4), 502–535. doi:10.1214/08-STS268

Friendly, M. (2010). *Re-Visions of Minard* Retrieved July 20, 2017, from: http://www.datavis.ca/gallery/re-minard.php

Georgy Fedoseevich Voronoy. (2007). Retrieved July 20, 2017, from: http://www-history.mcs.st-andrews.ac.uk/Biographies/Voronoy.html

Goh, K. I. (2007). The human disease network. *Proceedings of the National Academy of Sciences of the United States of America*, *104*(2). Retrieved from http://im.ft-static.com/content/images/b678abae-e6fa-11e3-88be-00144feabdc0.gif PMID:17502601

Howells, R., & Negreiros, J. (2013). *Visual Culture* (2nd ed.). Cambridge, UK: Polity Press.

Internet Mapping Project. (1998). *Map gallery*. Retrieved July 20, 2017, from: http://cheswick.com/ches/map/gallery/index.html

Lima, M. (2011). *Visual Complexity: Mapping Patterns of Information.* New York: Princeton Architectural Press.

Lima, M. (2014). *The Book of Trees. Visualizing Branches of Knowledge.* New York: Princeton Architectural Press.

Moretti, F. (2005). *Graphs, Maps, Trees. Abstract Models for Literary History.* Brooklyn, NY: Verso.

O'Connor, J. J., & Robertson, E. F. (1999). *John Wilder Tukey.* Retrieved July 20, 2017, from: http://www-history.mcs.st-and.ac.uk/Biographies/Tukey.html

Osinska, V. (2016). *Information Visualization. Information Science perspective.* Torun, Poland: Nicolaus Copernicus University Publishing. (in Polish)

Osinska, V., & Bala, P. (2015). Study of dynamics of structured knowledge: Qualitative analysis of different mapping approaches. *Journal of Information Science, 41*(2), 197–208. doi:10.1177/0165551514559897

Osinska, V., Jozwik, A., & Osinski, G. (2015). Mapping Evaluation for Semantic Browsing. In *Proceedings of the 2015 Federated Conference on Computer Science and Information Systems* (vol. 5, pp. 329-335). Los Alamitos, CA: IEEE. doi:10.15439/2015F50

Osinska, V., Osinski, G., & Kwiatkowska, A. B. (2015). Visualization in Learning: Perception, Aesthetics, and Pragmatics. In A. Ursyn (Ed.), *Maximazing Cognitive Learning through Knowledge Visualization.* Hershey, PA: IGI Global. doi:10.4018/978-1-4666-8142-2.ch013

Phylogenetic Tree. (2008). Retrieved on November 30, 2015 from https://en.wikipedia.org/wiki/Phylogenetic_tree#/media/File:Tree_of_life_SVG.svg

Shneiderman, B. (2009). *Treemaps for space-constrained visualization of hierarchies.* Retrieved July 20, 2017, from: http://www.cs.umd.edu/hcil/treemap-history/

Stasko, J. (2001). *Sunburst.* Retrieved July 20, 2017, from: http://www.cc.gatech.edu/gvu/ii/sunburst/

Treemaps of Race and Foreign-born by State. (n.d.). *Prints & posters of old maps, historic data viz and infographics from ages long past.* Retrieved July 20, 2017, from: http://vintagevisualizations.com/collections/charts-graphs/products/principal-constituent-elements-population-of-each-state

Tufte, E. (1990). *Envisioning Information.* Graphics Press LLC.

Vintage visualization. Growth of the elements of the population: 1790 to 1890. (2017). Retrieved July 20, 2017, from: http://vintagevisualizations.com/collections/charts-graphs/products/growth-of-the-elements-of-the-population-1790-to-1890

Walrus — Graph Visualization Tool. (2005, March 30). Retrieved July 20, 2017, from: http://www.caida.org/tools/visualization/walrus/

Weingart, S. (2013). From trees to webs: uprooting knowledge through visualization. In A. Slavic, A. Akdag Salah & S. Davies (Eds.), *Classification & visualization: Interfaces to knowledge. Proceedings of the International UDC Seminar,* (pp. 43-58). Würzburg: Ergon Verlag.

Weingart, S. (2013). *Diagrams of knowledge.* Retrieved July 20, 2017, from: http://www.scottbot.net/HIAL/

What is Circos? Circular visualization. (2009). Retrieved July 20, 2017, from: http://circos.ca/

Wilson, R. J. (2012). *Introduction to Graph Theory*. Cambridge, UK: Pearson Publishing.

World Statistics eXplorer. (2014). *Application developed by NComVA*. Retrieved July 20, 2017, from: https://mitweb.itn.liu.se/geovis/eXplorer

Wu, E., Carleton, R., & Davies, G. (2014). Discovering bin-Laden's Replacement in al-Qaeda, using Social Network Analysis: A Methodological Investigation. *Perspectives on Terrorism, 8*(1).

ADDITIONAL READING

Cairo, A. (2013). *The Functional Art. An Introducion to information graphics and visualization*. CA, USA: New Riders.

Maldenbrot, B. (1982). *Fractal Geometry of Nature*. New York: W. H. Freeman and Company.

Osinski, G. (2015). *Information Visualization. The research of information structures in the search for truth. Fides Ratio et Patria 3*.(in Polish).

Osinski, G. *Retarius Contra Secutor*. WSKSiM, Torun 2018 (in Polish).

Spence, I., & Wainer, H. (2001). William Playfair. In C. C. Heyde & E. Seneta (Eds.), *Statisticians of the Centuries* (pp. 105–110). New York: Springer. doi:10.1007/978-1-4613-0179-0_21

Yau, N. (2011). *Visualize This. The FlowingData Guide to Design Visualization and Statistics*. Indianopolis, USA: Wiley Publishing.

KEY TERMS AND DEFINITIONS

Circular Visualization: Circular layout of graph, where the vertices are placed on a circle, and edges may be depicted as hords or a types of curve. Popular application Circos to facilitate analysis of similarities and differences arising from comparisons of genomes implements this method using two visual variables: the length of arc (vertices attribute) and the width of the band (edge attribute).

Network Science: Is scientific field that studies complex networks in theoretical and technical contexts and their application in many areas of life. The field strongly relates to graph theory, mathematics, statistical mechanics, datamining, computer science, information visualization, and cognitive sciences.

Playfair Charts: Popular charts used today in data visualization, such as bar, circle, line, and bean charts; Gantt diagram derives from the original design of William Playfair (1759-1823), Scottish political economist.

Social Network Analysis (SNA): Is a method based on networks science for investigating social structures of both large and small communities. Network structure is represented in terms of nodes, which play the role of people or groups and the edges (i.e., relationships between them). SNA has emerged as a technique in modern social sciences and digital humanity that meets the challenges of big data in Web 2.0.

Sunburst: Is similar to treemaps technique, with space-dividing visualization that uses a radial rather than a rectangular layout.

Treemaps: Contemporary method for hierarchical information visualization that is used instead of traditional dendrogram. The main idea is recurrent division of rectangles proportionally to variable values. Each branch of the tree (dendrogram) is given a rectangle that is then tiled with smaller rectangles representing sub-branches.

ENDNOTES

[1]   Gapminder is an open source software for statistical data visualization and animation www.gapminder.org/.

[2]   An engine which demonstrates this method and can be tested at: http://alexbeutel.com/webgl/voronoi.html.

[3]   Foam Tree - a web service created and developed form 2005 by Carrot Search for efficient browsing of hierarchical data is accessible at: http://carrotsearch.com/foamtree.

[4]   Phylogenetics, a branch of biology devoted to investigating the developmental path of organisms and the phylogenetic tree shows the evolutionary interrelationships between species, just as a family tree for humans.

[5]   A video on the work of Martin Krzywinski can be view https://www.youtube.com/watch?v=mS8Q5_sZYH8.

[6]   CAIDA - Center for Applied Internet Data Analysis which investigates practical and theoretical aspects of the Internet offering many tools for mapping big data at: www.caida.org.

Chapter 3
Developing Visual Literacy Skills Through Library Instructions

Nevzat Özel
Ankara University, Turkey

ABSTRACT

Visual literacy skills have become an inevitable part of life in today's world. Technological innovations leading to new literacy skills have changed traditional ways of communication and made it necessary to learn and understand symbols, pictures, photos, illustrations, diagrams, infographics, pictograms, simulations, graphical interfaces, digitized images, and other visual tools. Therefore, it is very significant to teach individuals about visual literacy skills: the ability to understand, interpret, evaluate, organize, and construct visual information. Infographics are essential tools for learners. One of the most prominent institution to teach visual literacy skills is libraries. Visual tools, strategies, and methods should be applied in library instructions for users to realize these skills. The aim of the chapter is to show the importance of visualization, visual literacy, and infographics and present suggestions regarding how to develop the visual literacy skills of learners by libraries.

INTRODUCTION

The interests and attention in visuals have grown constantly because visuals or visualization can be observed everywhere in life and related with many disciplines. Moore and Dwyer (1994, p. ix) point out "scholars interested in the way visuals transmit information, emotion, and data are not limited to any one discipline because of the universal nature of images." Especially adoption of new information and communication technologies has enhanced its application. When we go back to its roots, its long history can be seen apparently.

Visuals are essential tools to understand the messages and meanings of words, concepts, ideas or expressions. Words, especially complex ones, are not enough alone to get the message. Thanks to the images, it becomes easier and faster to make interpretation and perception. Why visuals or visualization matters is explained by Card, Mackinlay and Shneiderman (1999, pp. 579-581) with numerous benefits. Visuals improve memory and make resources accessible, reduce the time to spend on research informa-

DOI: 10.4018/978-1-5225-4990-1.ch003

tion, make the patterns more comprehensible, allow perceptual inference, have perceptual attention and help to encode data in a suitable format.

Visual communication is an indispensable part of this digital age. From media to internet, it has a great role in sending and understanding messages. Visual learning which delivers educational content more effectively is also among the basic learning types. Both visual communication and learning are closely concerned with visual literacy.

Today it is suggested that a person should have different literacy types in the process of communication and learning such as *"information literacy"*, *"digital literacy"*, *"computer literacy"*, *"media literacy"*, *"technology literacy"*, *"political literacy"*, *"cultural literacy"*, *"multicultural literacy"* and *"visual literacy"*. All of them are equally important and necessary to be a competent and sophisticated person in this digital age. However, especially visual literacy may come into prominence since it is related to and part of every literacy type. When we critically read images or use them to increase comprehension, we realize the fundamentals of other literacy competencies. The statement by Velders, de Vries and Vaicaityte (2007) supported this idea. They announce "the development of visual competencies is fundamental to normal human learning and through the creative use of these competencies, he is able to communicate with others".

WHAT IS VISUAL LITERACY?

The integration of visuals into today's teaching and learning environment has been increasing with the help of technology such as computers, laptops, televisions, tablets, and smart phones. Visual literacy, one of the most important competence of the other literacy skills, can enrich and facilitate learning and understanding of information. It deals with the process of recognizing words and messages conveyed via images; for example, pictures, photos, charts, diagrams, graphics, tables, icons, websites, videos, symbols, maps, signs, pictograms, etc. Recently, infographics has come to the fore in this sense.

There is a more common point to be made here about the definition. Visual literacy is, in short, an ability to perceive, comprehend, construe and evaluate visual messages and images. There are numerous definitions as visuals are all around us and used in different disciplines. The first and the most comprehensive definition was made by Debes (as cited in Velders, de Vries and Vaicaityte, 2007, p. 1):

Visual Literacy refers to a group of vision-competencies a human being can develop by seeing and at the same time having and integrating other sensory experiences. The development of these competencies is fundamental to normal human learning. When developed, they enable a visually literate person to discriminate and interpret the visible actions, objects, symbols, natural or man-made, that he encounters in his environment. Through the creative use of these competencies, he is able to communicate with others. Through the appreciative use of these competencies, he is able to comprehend and enjoy the masterworks of visual communication.

According to Tillman (2012, p. 9) it is the capability of appreciating, utilizing, resolving, assessing and producing visual material as a fundamental part of a whole. Stokes (2002, p. 1) describes visual literacy "as the ability to interpret images as well as to generate images for communicating ideas and concepts". National Research Council (2000) characterizes visual literacy from a different point of view and clearly states that it is a sophisticated concept that has to do with the skills of monitoring; inquiring;

analyzing different sources in order to understand the proven issues; collecting, examining and evaluating information via tools; suggesting replies, justifications and estimations; and announcing the outcomes. In this definition, it especially emphasizes using mental questioning while trying to make the meaning of concepts clear and understandable. Avgerinou (2001), mostly interested in a history of visual literacy definitions expresses "visual literacy refers to a group of largely acquired abilities, i.e. the abilities to understand (read, and to use (write) images, as well as to think and learn in terms of images". Randhawa (1978) asserts visual literacy takes place in three stages; visual learning, visual thinking and visual communication. Visual learning is also the acquisition of information as a result of the interaction with the visual event; visual thinking is the skills that include shapes, lines, colors, texts and compositions; visual communication is the use of visual symbols in expressing thoughts and their meanings (as cited in Spitzer, Eisenberg and Lowe, 1998, pp. 26-27).

These definitions indicate that visual literacy helps learners read and grasp the information and messages conveyed by images which requires a mental performance and intellectual process. Careful and critical thinking is the key factor in this competency type.

VISUAL LITERACY STANDARDS

User-centered learning environments where one can question, solve problems, analyze and make decisions, think critically and creatively, convey ideas effectively and make sense of life meaningfully by using visual inputs require visual literacy competency. In accordance with lifelong learning, people who are adaptable, imaginative, enthusiastic, capable of taking his own responsibility, artistry, curious, innovative, self-disciplined and directed, collaborative and deliberate are required to cope with the demands of the 21st century. In this context, Association of College & Research Libraries (2011) determines the visual literacy standards, one of the most important ones to be competent in this century include seven skill areas for images: defining the need, finding and accessing, interpreting and analyzing, evaluating, using, creating, and understanding ethical and legal issues. All of these skills are analyzed in details as follows:

1. The visually literate person detects the characteristics and scope of the required visual material. He can recognize and express his need for an image and determines miscellaneous formats, kinds and supplies of visual materials.
2. The visually literate person acquires and reach the needed visuals and visual media effectively and efficiently. He can choose the most suitable visual sources and search strategy and access the needed visual material via proper technics and technologies.
3. The visually literate person comprehends the meanings of visual sources and materials. He can grasp the meanings of the messages conveyed by the images and identify the socio- cultural background of it; remarks the technologies and tools used in the creation of a visual.
4. The visually literate person assesses the visuals and their sources. He can reveal the effectiveness and reliability; aesthetic and technical characteristics of visuals and the reliability and accuracy of visual sources.
5. The visually literate person communicates with visuals and visual media effectively. He can apply images for different purposes, select the suitable visual tools and process to work with images, use creativity to solve problems, introduce the images efficiently and discuss them with others critically and communicate with others effectively via images.

6. The visually literate person produces expressive visuals and visual media. He can use his imagination and creativity to design a visual using various technologies and tools and evaluate his own production.
7. The visually literate person realizes ethical, legal, socio-economic points considering the creation and application of visuals and visual media. He can obey the laws and ethics while accessing, using and producing images and cite them in their studies.

These skills are all summarized in Figure 1.

Figure 1 shows the integration of visual literacy competency which covers various skills and mental process. Types/formats, exploration, sources, generating ideas and criteria in the definition section; researching, identifying, selecting, organizing and discovering in the section of finding; observation, related text, contexts, meanings and understanding in the interpreting/analyzing images part; source reliability, effectiveness, aesthetics, manipulation and accuracy in the evaluation section; project purpose, technol-

Figure 1. Visual Literacy Array based on ACRL's Visual Literacy Standards (Hattwig, Bussert, Medaille & Burgess, 2013, p. 75)

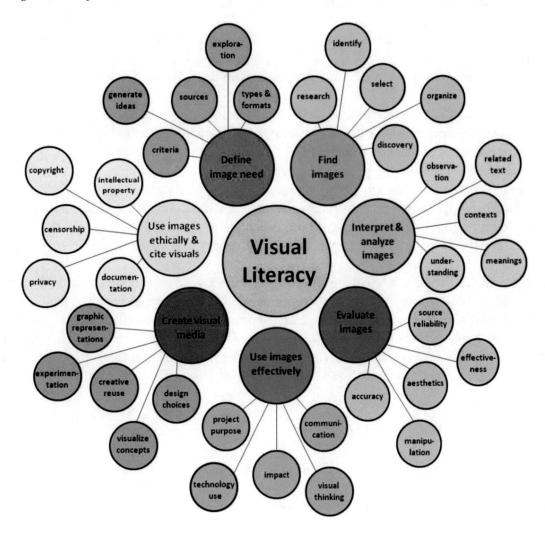

ogy use, impact, visual thinking and communication in the part of the application of images effectively; design choices, visualize concepts, creative reuse, experimentation and graphic representations in the production section; documentation, privacy, censorship, copyright and intellectual property in the section of ethics are taken into consideration. As seen in Figure 1, to be a visual literate person, one needs to have a set of abilities which are connected to each other. When one has these inseparable abilities, he can meet the needs of the rapidly changing world and deals with recent information and information systems and technological innovations.

Visual Resources Association (2009) takes the students of higher education into consideration and remarks that

students need assistance using visual information and developing digital literacies for their academic exercises. This includes identifying reliable image sources, judging the quality of images and associated descriptive data, accurate identification of historical content, and understanding intellectual property and how to cite images in their writing and assignments.

Brown (2004, p. 57) listed the skills or principles which should be the minimum requirement and included for all "*learners*" (elementary, secondary and tertiary):

- Learners need skills in understanding relationships between technological and meaning-creating practice.
- Learners need to develop a visual language/learnable grammar (including a technological language).
- Learners should be exposed to and have an understanding of visual design principles.
- Learners need experiences which allows them to understand, interpret and appreciate visual messages (including encoding and decoding).
- Learners should create and manipulate images.
- Learners need to conceptualize thoughts, knowledge and meaning visually.
- Learners need to see connections between aesthetics, visual communication and message design Learners need experiences using visual perception.
- Learners need experiences in viewing, thinking, reasoning in a critical manner.

To sum up, learners should be equipped with the abilities to identify their needs for the images, define the content of these images, understand the messages and meanings transmitted by these images or visuals by interpreting them, evaluate the visuals in terms of effectiveness, efficiency, originality, reliability, ethically and technically, organize the information for retrieval and reuse by the most appropriate systems and procedures, set up communication with the others, use and create their own visual materials by developing their interrogating skill and integrating ethics into their studies.

THE HISTORY OF VISUAL LITERACY

The origin of visual literacy is based on the ideas of Comenius in the 16th century or Plato two and a half millennium ago before the first definition was made by Debes as a concept. The first samples of communicating through images might even go back to about 32.000 years ago when primitive pictures was made by native tribes and 20,000 year-old wall paintings were drawn in the Lascaux cave in France (Linderman, 1997, p. 3).

As seen early communication is based on simple icons and symbols which would become more complex images in the future. From these visual representations, verbal communication has emerged. However, in relation to the new information and communication technologies and visual media, people have become more subject to images and visual messages. Therefore, while forming the meanings of concepts, visual sign systems have become a new type of language. When verbal and visual elements are unified, the concepts are easier to interpret.

Towards the late 18th century, Pestolozzi recognized the important effect of visual materials on learning and pioneered the use of manuals, a visual medium. In the second half of the 20th century, there has been an increased use in visual materials in schools (Andersen, Wagner & Warner, 2002). This was mostly due to the computer technology and internet used while searching, finding, understanding and reconstructing information. In this context, the acquisition of visual literacy skills during the learning process will make a significant contribution to the educational development of a person.

Visual literacy is not only concerned with education. As Bamford (2003) stresses that it has emerged from various disciplines such as visual arts, art history, aesthetics, linguistics, philosophy, psychology, perceptual physiology, sociology, cultural studies, media studies, instructional design, semiotics, communication studies and educational technology.

Since visuals are all around and related with all disciplines, its integration into the life is inevitable. Moreover, as known there have been a lot of literacy types and visual literacy is one of them but related to all of them.

PRESENTING INFORMATION VIA INFOGRAPHICS

A famous English idiom may be heard by everyone: *"A picture is worth a thousand words."* which shows the power of images. As Cleveland (1994) said, when the human brain transforms information into visual form, he can understand associations and patterns better. People can explain or present any information as quickly, meaningfully and clearly as possible using images. One of the best and latest ways to do that is infographics. By means of infographics, large amounts of data can be interpreted, presented or created in a shorter way.

"Information graphics, or infographics, combine elements of data visualization with design and have become an increasingly popular means for disseminating data" (Harrison, Reinecke and Chang, 2015, p.1). It is also defined as many varieties from simple graphics to complicated visual expressions of great amount of information and thoughts, occasionally on interactive web pages. It is able to deliver the complex messages from a data set fast and visually rather than textually (EDUCAUSE, 2013). Smiciklas (2012, p. 4) described it as "a visualization of data or ideas that tries to convey complex information to an audience in a manner that can be quickly consumed and easily understood".

Cairo (2013, p. xvi) differentiates infographics from information visualization and marks that information visualization utilize visual tools for the people to use for detection and analyzing of information sets. However, infographics use statistical charts, maps, and diagrams and tell stories created by communicators instead of allowing readers to grasp the stories on their own, which is aimed by information visualization. It can be concluded that all kinds of visuals are better than words to understand the message but infographics are more powerful and concrete.

Lee and Amirfar (2016) states that infographics has three parts:

- Stylized visuals to grab our attention and help us follow information in a fun and stimulating way,
- Content, including facts or statistics, we are expected to absorb,
- Knowledge representing the insight(s) we are meant to gain.

These parts produce an infographic and make sense of it together. As infographic is the ability to put simple or complicated information and data into visuals or images, it helps people perceive and interpret the meanings and messages in an easier and funnier way. In this framework, Schroeder (2004) mentions about many strengths of infographic including their flexible structures, opportunities for intelligent visualization and possibility to be prepared in alternative forms.

While creating a good infographic, some steps should be followed. Davis and Quinn (2013) list them as follows: purpose should be determined, which components can be used should be decided, infographic type to prepare should be chosen and information should be presented in a way that learners can understand. Shaltout adds more steps for a clear and distinguished infographic which include "choosing the main idea, preliminary drawing, choice of main headings and sub headings, being prudent to keep design parts as one unit, choice of colors, revising designs, representing the whole content, assuring drawings authenticity and final production" (as cited in Al-Mohammadi, 2017, pp. 30-31). When these circumstances are realized, infographics become more organized and planned to meet the needs of all related disciplines.

There are various sorts of infographics to introduce information. Some of them are given below (Model Systems Knowledge Translation Center, 2015):

- **Flowchart:** It can take people's attention and is used to solve problems. If the answer is easy, it tends to solve it in a humorous but an ideal way.
- **Timeline:** It makes people see the progresses and alterations in place of fixed data.
- **Versus Infographics:** It provides similar or new views different from each other so that people can make comparisons.
- **By the Numbers Infographics:** This gives numerical representations of large amount of information together with a great number of images and texts to make the message clear and comprehensible.
- **Data Visualization:** It turns information into charts and graphs with an attractive visual which allows to tell the story.

When appropriately used, these kinds of infographics can be useful and effective to present information. From the above, data visualization is seen to be the most common and classic way as infographics.

As to the infographic history, we should go back to 30.000 BC when the first examples of infographics were seen. In the late Stone Age, animal paintings on cave walls were found in France. In 3.000 BC, Egyptian hieroglyphics which used graphic symbols and icons were discovered. In 1350, French philosopher Nicole d'Orseme produced the first graphs which showed how to measure a moving thing. In 1510, Leonardo da Vinci presented human anatomy by combining the text with pictures. In 1786, Scottish engineer William Playfair was the initiator of data visualization. He explained numerical information through linear graphs, pie charts and bar graphs. In 1857, English nurse Florence Nightingale connected stacked bar with pie charts to show the number of casualties and reason for deaths during the Crimean War. Between 1850-1870, a civil engineer from France, Charles Joseph Minard connected maps with flow charts to make geographical statistics clearer. Between 1970-1990, infographics started to be widespread for news publications like The Sunday Times. They began to use them to make complex subjects and news easier to understand. Between 1930-1940, Otto Neurath developed a visual communication model in order to teach concepts through icons and illustrations (Smiciklas, 2012, pp. 8-9). These significant contributions created infographics and made concepts and ideas definite and perceptible. As seen, infographics is a phenomenon with a long history. It is not new but its value and importance are felt more today.

In today's modern world, infographics are very popular and have a widespread use. It can be used for educational purposes as well as various purposes such as art, business, advertisement, news, mass media, etc. Thanks to the implementation of technological innovations in education, integrating visualization and infographics into all processes of education has become possible. In this context, Krauss (2012) proposes that application of infographics in education allows learners to use more parts of their brain to look at a problem from different points of view; become active participant by giving response to the questions; take part in analysis and perception to infer the meaning; put the raw data into infographics with or without the help of computer programs to create or interpret the infographics; develop their critical skills to make them understand the charts, graphs, and infographics; realize that the way of representing data is as vital as the collection of data; narrate acceptable and correct representations in their infographics. In this way, it may be considered that using infographics in education develop students' skills for critical thinking, analysis and synthesis. It can also meet to the needs of students who learn by either linguistic or non-linguistic systems.

LIBRARIES AS A MEANS OF APPLYING AND TEACHING VISUAL LITERACY

Education is essential for all countries to compete with socio-economic and technological developments and changes. People can gain new skills, knowledge and habits and keep up with the changes and innovations by means of education. United Nations Educational, Scientific and Cultural Organization (UNESCO) adds that,

the goal of Education for All also involves the development of literate societies in the developing world, and cannot be attained solely by providing quality learning materials to schools. If people are to stay literate, the must have access to a wide variety of written materials and continue the habit of reading in their adult lives (Krolak, 2005, p. 3).

In this context, libraries come to the fore. In today's digital world schools are not enough alone to meet these skills and needs of learners, so they require the benefits of services of libraries.

It is clear that libraries highly have a significant role in education and literacy skills of learners. Libraries are one of the most effective education communities that provide learners with an environment in which they can develop a lot of skills and become life-long learners and literate. Adams, Krolak, Kupidura and Pahernik (2002, p. 28) specify that "libraries assist in finding, using and interpreting appropriate information that opens up opportunities for learning, literacy enhancement, entertainment, individual research, critical thinking and ultimately empowerment in an increasingly complex world". This idea is strongly supported by Krolak in her paper titled "*The Role of Libraries in the Creation of*

Literate Environments". She asserts that libraries introduce literate environments and enrich literacy by their free and reliable resources in printed, electronic or audiovisual form for every age and every literacy level and literacy classes for adults and families. They present chances to be life-long learners, sophisticated citizens, creative and imaginative researchers, critical thinkers and competent persons in the continually complicated word (Krolak, 2005, p. 3).

As mentioned, libraries take responsibility for the acquisition of all literacy skills, the role they play in empowering visual literacy is described within the scope of this study. Librarians or visual resources professionals effectively offer the visual literary standards including the abilities to "*find and access needed images and visual media effectively and efficiently*" and to "*understand many of the ethical, legal, social, and economic issues*" related to application or generation of visuals and visual media (Association of College & Research Libraries (2011).

To Marcum, for the interpretation of visual information, image manipulation is required as well as critical thinking. He adds that to deal with the age of information, librarians are supposed to become "*multi-literate*" and libraries must change the content of library instruction, and some of them help learners develop media production skills. In addition, librarians encourage students to produce their own visual materials in harmony with teaching faculty and other academic professionals (as cited in Hattwig, Bussert, Medaille and Burgess, 2013, p. 67).

Schellenberg (2015, pp. 37-38) discusses the visual and information literacy efforts of library instruction. Students' skills of finding and accessing visuals; assessing images in terms of accuracy, reliability and ethics; perception and analysis of texts are fostered by librarians via databases and search engines. Moreover, libraries help to increase the application of digital tools including editing software, web tools and cameras. Nelson (2004, p. 7), who studies on the concept of visual literacy and its implications for librarians teaching information, underlines the changing role of librarians in digital world and declares that:

Literacy components interfaces change, databases appear (and sometimes disappear), journals are discontinued or no longer available online, and new meta-search facilities are introduced which still do not cover all information sources. Students struggle to sift through this "stuff" trying to make sense of it all so that they can get the information needed for their paper, presentation or exercise. Serving as partners, supporters or collaborators with faculty, librarians respond to this situation by teaching technical skills and evaluative competencies in connection with course objectives and assignments.

As seen libraries support visual literacy instruction and increase learners' skills of visual literacy by providing a non-school setting. Therefore, Marcinek (2010) reminds the contributions of libraries to schools in this sense and states that schools are to have a tendency to cooperate with libraries in terms of visual literacy skills and create an organization to work with students, teachers, academicians, technologists, administration, and librarians to share ideas and discuss about this issue.

Zanin-Yost (2014) describes the following phases to develop and implement a visual literacy lesson by librarians to support a school in the context of ACRL Visual Literacy Standard:

- **Determine the Need of Students to Learn:** Librarians should cooperate with instructors, comprehend what is needed for the task and have information about the content of the course. To realize the task, librarians should teach students some abilities to know how they can use the library catalogue, how they can use the keywords effectively, and reach visuals using databases and the

Internet. At this point, they help students visualize their needs showing visuals at the beginning of the research section.

- **Detect what Standard, Performance Indicators and Outcomes to Apply:** After determining the needs of the students, librarians should decide about which standard, performance indicator and outcomes to apply.
- **Evaluation:** Here is the focus on level of understanding the students reach and an assessment is made to determine how well students are learning what the librarian has taught. This part can be integrated into the grade.

She explained these phases in Table 1:

On the other hand, she adds to the table one column to show the evaluation section if there is. In this section, "student will list where the resources used were found (book, magazine/ newspaper, etc.) and a brief explanation of which resources were selected over others."

Libraries provide best practices to teach visual literacy skills. For instance, for the ability to "find images", students can prepare poster presentations, create online image-based blogs, or find visual samples to support written assignments by using image databases like "Artstor" and many online, open-source image repositories available to all libraries such as "ALA Digital Images Collections Guide", "Digital Public Library of America" and "Open Content Program" and "Flickr's Creative Commons". For the ability to "manipulate images", some schools and libraries may present proprietary software like "Adobe Photoshop" or "Aperture". In addition, many open source, free image editing tools can also be found like "GIMP, Grokking the GIMP, Aviary, Pixlr and Pixlr Grabber feature". For the ability to "attribute images", library patrons and students have to control the license on every single image they use by applying "Creative Commons License". For the ability to "evaluate images", there is no CRAAP (Currency, Relevance, Authority, Accuracy and Purpose) test for images, but The University of California, Irvine and the University of Washington have very efficacious checklists for students and library patrons to evaluate images (Henrich, 2014).

Table 1. Phases of developing and implementing a visual literacy lesson

Task	Standard	Performance Indicator	Outcome
Learn how to use the catalog	2. Find and access needed images and visual media effectively and efficiently	1. Selects the most appropriate sources and retrieval systems for finding and accessing the needed images and visual media	a. Identifies interdisciplinary and discipline-specific images sources. e. Selects the most appropriate image source for the current project.
Learn how to use keywords		2. Conducts effective image searches	a. Develops a search strategy appropriate to the image need and aligned with with available resources. d. Identifies keywords, synonyms, and related terms forthe image needed, and maps those terms to the vocabulary used in the image source
Finds images with the databases			d. Identifies keywords, synonyms, and related terms forthe image needed, and maps those terms to the vocabulary used in the image source
Finds images online			e. Uses images to find other images through exploration, social linking, visual search engines, or browsing

Source: (Zanin-Yost, 2014)

Azmi (2014) suggested a good example of Media and Visual Literacy curriculum delivered by librarians at universities shown in Table 2.

This curriculum indicates the important role of libraries in equipping students with visual literacy skills. It should be kept in mind that librarians are supposed to have these skills before teaching students effectively and efficiently.

More detailed and concrete examples can also be given. Students can be canalized to do some activities while merging visual literacy with library teaching and programming. For example, in a science lesson for grade level 3, the students are asked to create recycling posters. A librarian can read a nonfiction book on recycling from which students can grasp the main ideas and how the pictures and images helped them understand how and why to recycle. Then they can apply a Web 2.0 tool like Glogster to prepare a poster with visuals and a short phrase about the reasons of recycling. Another example can be given from High School where the students are asked to create Mythology Picture Book for English lesson. To realize this, the elementary school librarian reads books about myths from other cultures to make students select images appropriate for the audience and the topic. He discusses with students how to find and ethically apply images besides how images are used to create a picture book and help provide meaning. Students then look for visuals and images to support the message of their myth. They can design these picture books using google docs and then upload them to the Web 2.0 tool Flipsnack (Literacy and School Libraries, 2013).

It is also observed that library exhibitions can teach visual literacy. A study "Rosenberg Library exhibition Project Survive 1995-2015" was evaluated with a written assignment given to four classes. Students are asked to locate, evaluate and interpret and ethically use visual and written information by

Table 2. Example of media and visual literacy curriculum

Modules to be Taught	Subject Areas
Module 1: Understanding the Role of Media in Society	"Citizenship", "Freedom of expression and information", "Access to information", "Democratic discourse and life-long learning", "Understanding the news, media and information ethics", "Communication, MIL and learning – Understanding the news", "Representation in media and information", "Languages in media and information" and "Audience"
Module 2: Accessing Media and Image Information Effectively and Efficiently	"Familiarization with information literacy and library skills", "Determining, defining and articulating the need for media and/or image", "Identifying the scope and purpose of a project for which media/image will be employed", "Identification of the variety of image sources, materials, and types", "Selection of the most appropriate sources and retrieval systems for finding and accessing needed images and visual media", "Investigating the scope, content, and potential usefulness of a range of image sources and formats" and "Organization of media/image and source information"
Module 3: Use and Assessment of Media and Image	"Identification, interpretation, and analyses of the meanings of images and visual media", "Situating images in their cultural, social, and historical contexts", "Identification of the physical, technical, and design components of an image", "Validation, interpretation and analysis of images through discourse with others", "Evaluation of the effectiveness and reliability of images as visual communications", "Evaluation of the aesthetic and technical characteristics of images", "Judging the reliability and accuracy of image sources", "Use of images effectively for different purposes" and "Use of problem solving, creativity, and experimentation to incorporate images into scholarly projects.
Module 4: Media/ Image Production and Social, Legal and Ethical Aspects	"The design and creation of meaningful images and visual media", "Use of design strategies and creativity in image and visual media production", "The employment of a variety of tools and technologies to produce images and visual media", "The evaluation of personally created visual products", "Understanding the ethical, legal, social, and economic issues surrounding images and visual media", "Adherence to legal best practices when accessing, using, and creating images" and "The citation of images and visual media in papers, presentations, and projects"

Source: (Azmi, 2014)

responding to information in a library exhibition, describing in a guided exhibition tour and accessing on the library's bookshelves. In all stages "teaching, leading tour and preparing the assessment rubric of the assignment", exhibition librarian took a main role (Connell, 2015). The study ended with students' high scores which expose that incorporating libraries in teaching, processing and evaluating visual literacy is very effective and efficient way to increase students' ability to express their visual literacy.

The changing role of libraries is well summarized "today's library is dynamic, multipurpose and flexible, supporting a broad range of community needs." (British Columbia, Ministry of Education, 2016). It should be kept in mind that in order to develop learners' visual skills, librarians should be equipped with this skill in advance and libraries become an institution that organizes visual instruction and foster learners' visual literacy skills. To realize this social responsibility, they should open their doors to the technological changes and digital developments and be aware of their vital role in developing learners' skills to cope with the world full of images and visual media. According to Beaudoin (2016, p. 377), like archives, libraries are supposed to organize programs so as to encourage users to perceive and apply visual content and define the images in their collections.

CONCLUSION

Visual literacy is one of the most important phenomenon in today's digital world. To increase the capacity of students to apply visual literacy skills is expected to realize for every nation. This competency empowers people with the critical and creative thinking skills as well as the skills of research, perception, organization, analysing and assessment. In this context, visual literate person is considered to be able to comprehend and perceive the meaning of visual images easily; discriminate, apply and produce conceptual visual representations effectively; and see, understand, think, and communicate graphically. Moreover, since text-based learning has been abandoned, new methodologies for teaching and learning are becoming more learner-centered and they are based on more visuals and multimedia environments. Thus, conveying one's ideas, needs and desires via visualization is of utmost importance and people are expected to create, produce, and share visual material to convey data, concepts, and emotions. Among visual tools, especially infographics are essential for learners to be equipped with visual literacy skills. They are quick and clear way to introduce information and thus they have come into prominence.

Libraries have many services which support education and learning. They provide facilities to find an accurate and confidential data; research, find and use the data efficiently; communicate their views effectively; become more aware of the world; adapt themselves to the changing technology and promote broader thinking and new ideas. Among their duties, one of the most important ones is to supply users with literacy skills which cause learners to gain knowledge via reading materials in addition to media and technology. As the numbers of visuals people are subject to increase, teaching learners to use and create them and communicate with them becomes more and more important. In this framework, providing people with visual literacy skills is accepted as a fairly striking issue to realize in libraries.

Visual literacy is regarded as an integral component in libraries and library instruction. They have a big role to help users to search, find, understand, interpret, use, evaluate, organize, construct and transmit information. When they do it, libraries should take the visual literacy standards, performance indicators and learning outcomes into consideration so that they can organize a standardized and fixed visual instruction to work in harmony with the other libraries and educational institutions. Most importantly, librarians are supposed to be familiar with visual literacy skills and they are expected to show these skills themselves. To do that, they should be educated about information literacy in their undergraduate program at university or an in-service education from time to time can be integrated into their workflows. In fact, teaching this kind of competencies from an early age should be enhanced.

This new and active role of libraries make them a remarkable and catchy places for learning and researching. Libraries are gradually regaining its strength by taking responsibilities to build literacy competencies. Libraries are not only places to find and read information materials, they change and reshape their services remarkably and become active participants of teaching 21st century skills to the learners.

As to further studies, the libraries should be ready for every change and adapt themselves accordingly today and in the future; therefore, libraries, library instruction and librarians should be flexible and keep in touch with technology and innovations. Within the concept of lifelong learning, librarians should be well-educated and qualified. Their lack of knowledge in visual literacy or the other literacy skills could be removed by ongoing education. They may take part in communication with teachers, instructors, and other related specialists about students' visual literacy learning. Moreover, it is clear that every technological change and development has a reflection in education and they have an effect on teaching methods, strategies and techniques. As a result, both instructors and librarians organize and plan their instructional content in accordance with recent visual literacy skills. Besides, some conferences, workshops, organizations could be held in which librarians, teachers and the other related participants will be invited in order to make discussion and share ideas about the visual literacy standards and the content of education and methods and techniques to teach learners these skills. This will help to create a standardized and up to date visual literacy instruction and curriculum. Lastly but the most importantly, user studies which will measure the level visual literacy skills of learners could be made and library instructions could be developed and organized in line with the results of these studies.

REFERENCES

Adams, S., Krolak, L., Kupidura, E., & Pahernik, Z. P. (2002). Libraries and resource centres: Celebrating adult learners every week of the year. *Convergence, 35*(2-3), 27–39.

Al-Mohammadi, N. (2017). Effectiveness of using infographics as an approach for teaching programming fundamentals on developing analytical thinking skills for high school students in the City of Makkah in Saudi Arabia. *Global Journal of Educational Studies, 3*(1), 22–42. doi:10.5296/gjes.v3i1.10854

Andersen, M., Wagner, J., & Warner, B. (2002). *Visual literacy, the Internet, and education.* Retrieved June 17, 2017, from http://www.cii.illinois.edu/InquiryPage/bin/docs/u12021_391finaldraft.doc

Association of College & Research Libraries. (2011). *ACRL visual literacy competency standards for higher education.* Retrieved June 15, 2017, from http://www.ala.org/acrl/standards/visualliteracy

Avgerinou, M. D. (2001). *Visual literacy: Anatomy and diagnosis* (Unpublished doctoral dissertation). University of Bath, UK.

Azmi, H. (2014). *Media and visual competencies for information professionals in the Arab world challenges of the digital environment.* Retrieved September 28, 2017, from http://library.ifla.org/888/1/139-azmi-en.pdf

Bamford, A. (2003). *The visual literacy white paper*. Retrieved June 17, 2017, from http://wwwimages. adobe.com/content/dam/Adobe/en/education/pdfs/visual-literacy-wp.pdf

Beaudoin, J. E. (2016). Describing images: A case study of visual literacy among library and information science students. *College & Research Libraries, 77*(3), 376–392. doi:10.5860/crl.77.3.376

British Columbia, Ministry of Education. (2016). *Inspiring libraries, connecting communities*. Retrieved June 20, 2017, from http://www2.gov.bc.ca/assets/gov/education/administration/community-partnerships/libraries/libraries-strategic-plan.pdf

Brown, I. (2004). Global trends in art education: New technologies and the paradigm shift to visual literacy. *The International Journal of Arts Education, 2*(3), 50–61.

Cairo, A. (2013). *The functional art: An introduction to information graphics and visualization*. Berkeley, CA: A New Riders. Retrieved June 17, 2017, from http://ptgmedia.pearsoncmg.com/images/9780321834737/samplepages/0321834739.pdf

Card, S. K., Mackinlay, J. D., & Shneiderman, B. (1999). *Readings in information visualization: Using vision to think*. San Francisco, CA: Morgan Kaufmann Publishers Inc.

Cleveland, W. S. (1994). *The elements of graphing data*. Hobart Press.

Connell, K. (2015). Library exhibitions teach visual literacy. *Assessment, 3*. Retrieved from https://www.ccsf.edu/dam/Organizational_Assets/Department/library/Assessment/Library%20Exhibition%20Assessment%203%20(1).pdf

Davis, M., & Quinn, D. (2014). Visualizing text: The new literacy of infographics. *Reading Today, 31*(3), 16–18.

Debes, J. (1969). The loom of visual literacy: An overview. *Audiovisual Instruction, 14*(8), 25–27.

EDUCAUSE. (2013). *7 things you should know about infographic creation tools*. Retrieved June 17, 2017, from https://net.educause.edu/ir/library/pdf/ELI7093.pdf

Harrison, L., Reinecke, K., & Chang, R. (2015). Infographic aesthetics: Designing for the first impression. In *Proceedings of the 33rd Annual ACM Conference on Human Factors in Computing Systems (CHI '15)*. New York: ACM. doi:10.1145/2702123.2702545

Hattwig, D., Bussert, K., Medaille, A., & Burgess, J. (2013). Visual literacy standards in higher education: New opportunities for libraries and student learning. *Libraries and the Academy, 13*(1), 61–89. doi:10.1353/pla.2013.0008

Henrich, K. J. (2014). *Visual literacy for librarians: Learning skills and promoting best practices*. Retrieved September 28, 2017, from https://theidaholibrarian.wordpress.com/2014/05/27/visual-literacy-for-librarians-learning-skills-and-promoting-best-practices/

Krauss, J. (2012). Infographics: More than words can say. *Learning and Leading with Technology, 39*(5), 10–14. Retrieved from http://files.eric.ed.gov/fulltext/EJ982831.pdf

Krolak, L. (2005). *The role of libraries in the creation of literate environments*. Retrieved June 18, 2017, from https://www.ifla.org/files/assets/literacy-and-reading/publications/role-of-libraries-in-creation-of-literate-environments.pdf

Lee, L., & Amirfar, V. A. (2016). Infographics: Presenting data, telling a story through visuals. *Pharmacy Today*, *22*(6), 46. doi:10.1016/j.ptdy.2016.05.021

Linderman, M. G. (1997). *Art in elementary school*. Boston: Mc Gnow-Hill.

Literacy and School Libraries. (2013). *Examples of visual literacy lessons & programming for school libraries*. Retrieved September 28, 2017, from https://literacyandschoollibraries.wikispaces.com

Marcinek, A. (2010). *Rethinking the library to improve information literacy*. Retrieved June 20, 2017, from https://www.edutopia.org/blog/rethinking-library-information-literacy

Model Systems Knowledge Translation Center. (2015). *Presenting data using infographics*. Retrieved June 18, 2017, from http://www.msktc.org/lib/docs/KT_Toolkit/MSKTC_KT_Tool_Infographics_508.pdf

Moore, D. M., & Dwyer, F. M. (Eds.). (1994). *Visual literacy: A spectrum of visual learning*. Englewood Cliffs, NJ: Educational Technology Publications.

National Research Council. (2000). *Inquiry and the National Science Education standards: A guide for teaching and learning*. Washington, DC: The National Academies Press.

Nelson, N. (2004). Visual literacy and library instruction: A critical analysis. *Education Libraries*, *27*(1), 5–10. doi:10.26443/el.v27i1.194

Schellenberg, J. (2015). *Visual literacy practices in higher education* (Unpublished master dissertation). Oslo and Akershus University College of Applied Sciences, Norway. Retrieved June 20, 2017, from https://oda.hioa.no/en/visual-literacy-practices-in-higher-education

Schroeder, R. (2004). Interactive info graphics in Europe--added value to online mass media: A preliminary survey. *Journalism Studies*, *5*(4), 563–570. doi:10.1080/14616700412331296473

Smiciklas, M. (2012). *The power of infographics: Using pictures to communicate and connect with your audiences*. Indianapolis, IN: Que Publishing. Retrieved June 17, 2017, from http://ptgmedia.pearsoncmg.com/images/9780789749499/samplepages/0789749491.pdf

Spitzer, K. L., Eisenberg, M. B., & Lowe, C. A. (1998). *Information literacy: Essential skills for the information age*. New York: ERIC Clearinghouse on Information & Technology.

Stokes, S. (2002). Visual literacy in teaching and learning: A literature perspective. *Electronic Journal for the Integration of Technology in Education, 1*(1), 10-19. Retrieved June 13, 2017, from https://wcpss.pbworks.com/f/Visual+Literacy.pdf

Tillmann, A. (2012). What we see and why it matters: How competency in visual literacy can enhance student learning. *Honors Projects*. Paper 9. Retrieved June 13, 2017, from http://digitalcommons.iwu.edu/education_honproj/9

Velders, T., de Vries, S., & Vaicaityte, L. (2007). Visual literacy and visual communication for global education: Innovations in teaching e-learning in art, design and communication. In *Designs on e-learning: the International Conference on Learning and Teaching in Art, Design and Communication, 12-14 September 2007, London, UK*. Retrieved June 13, 2017, from http://doc.utwente.nl/59769/1/Velders07visual.pdf

Visual Resources Association. (2009). *Advocating for visual resources management in educational and cultural institutions*. Retrieved June 16, 2017, from http://vraweb.org/wp-content/uploads/2016/09/vra_white_paper.pdf

Zanin-Yost, A. (2014). Visual literacy: Teaching and learning in the academic library of the 21st century and beyond. *AIB studi, 54*(2/3), 305-317. Retrieved June 20, 2017, from http://aibstudi.aib.it/article/download/9962/10179

ADDITIONAL READING

Abilock, D. (2008). Visual information literacy: Reading a documentary photograph. *Knowledge Quest, 36*(3), 7–13.

Brown, N. E., Bussert, K., Hattwig, D., & Medaille, A. (2016). *Visual literacy for libraries: A practical, standards-based guide*. Chicago: American Library Association.

Brumberger, E. (2011). Visual Literacy and the digital native: An examination of the millennial learner. *Journal of Visual Literacy, 30*(1), 19–47. doi:10.1080/23796529.2011.11674683

Carpenter, B. S. II, & Cifuentes, L. (2011). Visual culture and literacy online: Image galleries as sites of learning. *Art Education, 64*(4), 33–40.

ChanLin, L., & Chang, B. (2003). Web-based library instruction for promoting information skills. *Journal of Academic Librarianship, 30*(4), 265–276.

Felten, P. (2008). Visual literacy. *Change, 40*(6), 60–64. doi:10.3200/CHNG.40.6.60-64

Hsieh, M. L., & Holden, H. A. (2010). The effectiveness of a university's single-session information literacy instruction. *RSR. Reference Services Review, 38*(3), 458–473. doi:10.1108/00907321011070937

Little, D. (2015). Teaching visual literacy across the curriculum: Suggestions and strategies. *New Directions for Teaching and Learning, 141*(141), 87–90. doi:10.1002/tl.20125

Little, D., Felten, P., & Berry, C. (2015). *Looking and learning: Visual literacy across the disciplines: New directions for teaching and learning*. San Francisco: Jossey-Bass.

Mayer, J., & Goldenstein, C. (2009). Academic libraries supporting visual culture: A survey of image access and use. *Art Documentation, 28*(1), 16–28.

Metros, S. E. (2008). The educator's role in preparing visually literate learners. *Theory into Practice, 47*(2), 102–109. doi:10.1080/00405840801992264

Schoen, M. J. (2015). Teaching visual literacy skills in a one-shot session. *VRA Bulletin, 41*(1), Article 6.

KEY TERMS AND DEFINITIONS

Infographics: Information graphics – the combination of information and graphics that turn complex and big data into visuals to make the data more comprehensible.

Information Literacy: Skills helping learners become aware of their needs for information and search, access, analyze, use, evaluate, and transform this information.

Information Visualization: Visual representation of data to make it understandable.

Library Instruction: Library education, user education – educational programs for library users to learn how to search, access, analyze, use, evaluate, and transform information quickly and effectively.

Visual Literacy: Abilities to perceive, comprehend, construe, and evaluate visual messages and images.

Section 2
Visualization for Digital Humanity

Chapter 4

Infographics in Humanities:
Communication of Information or Information Noise? Polish Case

Zbigniew Osiński
Maria Curie Sklodowska University, Poland

ABSTRACT

The purpose of the chapter is to join in the discussion of digital humanists on whether data and information visualizations can be an efficient way of communicating information and knowledge about the specificity of the humanities. The basis is to examine the problem of whether a visual communication containing far more graphical elements than text can be something more to the abovementioned group of recipients than a complement to the principal text (as is the case with school handbooks). Can it be a dominant form of communication? In order to obtain research data, a series of didactic tests were administered to a handpicked group of several dozen students. They were students with predominantly humanistic competencies but for whom modern technology poses no barriers in the cognitive process. The test results showed the usefulness of infographics as a form of organization and presentation but only of detailed data and information. The visualization of information did not turn out to be a good foundation for making generalizations and conclusions.

INTRODUCTION

Since the mid-twentieth century there have been observable changes in the scientific and media communications, including those based on humanistic problems. Presentations of infographics, photos and films began to compete with the linear text. These tendencies intensified as the digital media developed, including the Internet, and in particular with the rise of the digital humanities, which undertook to study human digital products. The purpose of the study is to join in the discussion of digital humanists on whether the visualizations of data and information (the use of diverse graphical forms and techniques for presenting content) can be an efficient way of communicating information and knowledge about the specificity of the humanities. For the purpose of the research project, the author applies the last concept not only to refer to the knowledge about history and culture but also knowledge about education and

DOI: 10.4018/978-1-5225-4990-1.ch004

all other manifestations of human intellectual activity. In principle, the point is to stress that the studies are not concerned with the visualization of the functioning of devices, living organisms, physical and chemical processes, geological or climatic phenomena, etc. They are concerned with more or less abstract phenomena and processes. Efficacy will be examined, having in mind the receiver who is definitely less prepared for the visual form of communication than information visualization experts, i.e. the graduate of the Polish education system. The author is interested in the efficacy of visualization in the communication from the world of scientists and experts to the world of average users of the material with information and knowledge. To the world of persons to whom modern technologies are no obstacle in the cognitive process and who use elements of communication visualization, e.g. by using emoticons or creating and spreading graphical memes in social media. The article will be based on the investigation of the problem whether a visual communication containing far more graphical elements than a text can be something more to the recipient group (as is the case with school handbooks)? Can it be the dominant form of communication when we are speaking of abstract phenomena and processes, which are reflected not so much in the material reality as in the human mind? Are average graduates of the Polish education system able to understand the message contained in visualizations and find necessary information? Can such communication be useful in solving problems? This will be the way of verifying the thesis promoted by digital humanists, which says that in the days of the Internet, the writing and linear narrative can be superseded in describing the world for the visual forms of communication. It is also necessary to verify fears that visualizations only increase information noise or surplus information and their forms and sources, which make it difficult to distinguish true and essential information.

BACKGROUND

Graphical forms of the presentation of data and information (maps, charts, graphs, diagrams, drawings, photographs, etc.) have long been found in different forms of communicating humanistic knowledge. They usually accompany the primary text as the illustration of the content. The development of information technologies based on the capabilities of hardware and software as well as the Internet cause graphics to become an important form of information transmission in social and scientific communication. The emergence of the digital humanities definitely increased and even qualitatively changed the role and significance of the graphical forms of presentation of data, information, and knowledge. Robert Rosenstone (2008) and Hayden White (2008) proposed a thesis from which it follows that film can be a medium of knowledge equivalent to the written text. Using the example of the history of mankind they demonstrated that storytelling through picture and film is not encumbered with greater limitations and defects than storytelling through the printed text. We should also mention the thesis by David Staley (2003), who suggested that in the days of the dominance of visual content (the media, Internet), students should be taught to read and analyze multimedia and graphical media communications. I recognized these forms of communication as equivalent to the printed text but as having their separate grammar and genre characteristics. In Staley's conception the nontextual forms of communication are not a simple decoration or illustration to the text but a separate message. Polish humanist Andrzej Radomski (2016) advances the thesis that visualization entered the humanities not only as the way of illustrating the content but also as a research method. He argues that the visual communication of content begins to supersede the written word, and that the elites more often think in terms of figures and pictures rather than language. The scale of data and information production begins to impose visualization upon everyone, including humanists, both at the stage of analysis of research material and the presentation of results because the traditional linear narrative and written communication are unable to comprehend and describe the phenomena hidden in big data resources and various information bases. That author (Radomski, 2013) suggests that the future of scholarly works of the humanists is the so-called digital storytelling in the form of films, Web pages, multimedia presentations and narratives in computer games. Michał Paradowski (2011), in turn, says that in the communication process we are dealing with the shift from word to image. It has so far-reaching an impact on the acquisition and spread of knowledge as the transition from oral communication to the written word once did. The consequence is the change of not only the form of knowledge production and expression but also in the way of its reception and acquisition: from the linear and consecutive to simultaneous and holistic. Digital culture researcher, John Seely Brown (2002), recognized narrative visualization as the most adequate for the cognitive needs of people born and maturing in the realities of the digital world. Scholars specializing in visualization problems (Carswell & Wickens, 1987; Chen, 2006; Tufte, 1997, 2001; Ware 2004, 2008) argue that owing to the synthesis, integration and concentration of information, this form of communication serves the condensed knowledge communication, multiplying its interpretive potential as compared with the text communication. They assure that underlying the creation of effective visualizations are the results of scientific studies on visual perception and perception psychology, and they contend that visualizations use our brain more effectively than the text does, make complex data sets easier to understand, and enable their effective interpretation. By presenting information in an attractive and novel way, they attract attention, maintain the receiver's involvement, allow him/her to notice something that s/he might otherwise overlook, and facilitate remembering information. The authors of the concept of "macroscope" (a virtual tool in imitation of a microscope or telescope, but which makes it easier to see not so much the far-away or small but the large) in turn stress the growing importance of studying big data and visualization of the results of their analyses for the humanities (Graham & Milligan, Weingart, 2015). In this conception, by using glyphs (features of graphic signs), and by grouping, selecting, compressing and diminishing data complexity, the visualization should facilitate discovery of new connections, relationships, rules and regularities hidden in these big data sets.

However, even some digital humanists (Witek, 2014) admit that this kind of narrative requires the acquisition of different competencies to receive the content than the competencies developed during traditional school education and while reading written documents. This also requires mastering other vocabulary, grammar and syntax than those used in verbal discourse. It is believed (Schnettler, 2008) that in order to retrieve knowledge from a visual recording specific skills are needed, termed visual literacy. The skills are used to structure information, data and concepts based on the familiar cultural system of iconographic and esthetic visualization. The fact that education is based on the traditional text gives rise to fears that visualization recipients may become confused because of being accustomed to linear texts, spiced up with graphics at best. They may, because of the specificity of information competencies developed during the education process, be unable to translate the meaning contained in the material rich in diverse forms of visual communication into the knowledge they can understand. Consequently, visualizations may only intensify information noise. At present, despite the fact that they contain large stores of information and knowledge, they do not replace the written word on a larger scale, at least in the humanistic communication – both scientific and educational. What may be an obstacle is the uncertainty about the legibility and degree of understanding of the nontextual forms of communication. Although some educationists (Epstein Ojalvo & Doyne, 2010; Pulak & Tomaszewska 2011) speak enthusiastically of the usefulness of the visual and multimedia content in education, even they do not suggest departing from the written word and linear text as the basis of information and knowledge transfer. At best, they argue (Taraszkiewicz, 1999) that multimedia teaching materials facilitate concentration of attention and increase knowledge acquisition "because an image is three times as effective as the word itself, and the word combined with the image has a six times higher impact than the word itself "(p. 92). When analyzing scientific literature, we may get the impression that the foregoing digital humanists appear to be very optimistic about all visualizations as the forms of information communication, and they do so based more on the studies by educationists and psychologists than on their own research.

It should be mentioned that research on teaching methods that shapes competences in reading and creating infographics has been going on for more than a decade. The Collaborative Infographics for Science Literacy project is being implemented in the USA. It is based on the use of appropriate techniques for reading and interpreting infographics in science teaching, as well as on the science of creating infographics based on selected data (Lamb, Polman, Newman & Smith 2014). Also from the United States came information on how to conduct education based on the creation of an infographics by students, and the teachers of such classes are optimistic about the educational effectiveness of such a method (Davidson 2014). They claim that infographics allow students to understand that research and writing scientific works is a process of creation and design, and not just the extraction of data from various sources (Mendenhall & Summers 2015). Such reports confirm both the educational usefulness of the infographics and the necessity of including a infographics in the visual literacy education process.

THE MAIN FOCUS OF THE CHAPTER

When considering the problem posed in the title of the chapter, we have to take into account the fact that methods of producing and analyzing infographics and other visualizations derive from the disciplines that considerably differ from the humanities largely utilizing abstract knowledge. Consequently, when used in the realities of this domain, they (methods) make it difficult to unequivocally interpret the communication, whereas the human perception of humanistic abstract visual communication tends to reify, or treat the image, film and graphics as a concrete reflection of reality. We perceive the abstract as the concrete, which may distort the meaning of the communication. This problem is well rendered by the following quotations: "The persuasive and seductive rhetorical force of visualization performs such a powerful reification of information that graphics such as Google Maps are taken to be simply a presentation of "what is," as if all critical thought had been precipitously and completely jettisoned" (Drucker, 2012). Does the receiver without specialist competencies have a chance of interpreting the visual forms of the communication of humanistic knowledge in accordance with the author's intentions? Perhaps the problem comes down to the Paupers' Bible (Biblia Pauperum) dilemma? These are medieval illuminated codices consisting of graphics and their descriptions presenting biblical scenes. It is a common belief, expressed for example in "The Dictionary of Myths and Traditions of Culture" by Władysław Kopaliński and in the "Encyclopedia of Knowledge about the Book", that they were Bibles for the poor in spirit i.e. poorly educated. They were meant for preachers not very fluent in Latin and for the illiterate masses of the faithful, to whom the principles of faith would be presented in a picture form: they would be an equivalent of modern-day comic strips for the functionally illiterate. However, the scholar investigating these problems, Ryszard Knapiński (2011), challenged such opinions. He said that,

The complete perception of the [Bible] page required mastering the difficult technique of reading texts written in accordance with the rules adopted in scriptoria, where abbreviations (brachygraphy and elision) and special script and punctuation were used. It is therefore difficult to infer that so complicated a composition consisting of pictures and texts was intended for the illiterate. On the contrary, it presupposed thoroughgoing linguistic education (Latin, sometimes with the elements of Greek or national languages). The ability to read must have been accompanied by the ability of keen perception enabling recognition of iconographic components (p. 31).

Perhaps therefore it is the linear texts that are meant for the poorly educated while the picture and nonlinear communication is for those having non-standard competencies? Who is able to effectively read the visual forms of information and knowledge communication? And to whom visualization only increases information noise. This important research problem should be explicitly explained before the humanists begin to widely present the results of their research in a multimedia graphical form.

The previous studies on the perception of data and information visualization (Cleveland & McGill, 1984; Hollsanowa, Holmberg & Holmqvist, 2009; Francuz, 2007) focused mainly on marketing-advertizing, medical, statistical, and psychological applications. They provided answers to the questions of the type: How is visual material decoded? How is its form received? Which elements does the receiver pay attention to? How does information search proceed in this material? Researchers also conducted research on automatic recognition of the meaning of infographics, which led to the creation of a special application enriching automatic recognition of text in graphic files - OCR (Huang & Tan 2007). In contrast, only very few educationists deal with the educational application of visualization, their field of interest being mainly such problems as: visual teaching aids as an element of the teaching/learning set; methods of using visual teaching aids and the memorization of information taught using visualizations. However, in this case the results of investigations are without doubt connected with a specific model of education and typical school ways of using visualization. In the reality of Polish education, studies were conducted (Kierach & Ogonowski, 2012), which showed that the content enriched with graphics is better absorbed, but the role of graphics comes down only to drawing the learner's attention through an attractive form, the ratio between the amount of text and graphics not being essential. Thus the problem of the efficacy of infographics as the fundamental source of information needed by graduates of the Polish education system in order to understand a problem or execute a task should be regarded as open and worth investigating. What is essential is to what extent a specific system of education prepares a learner for the practical use of visualized data and information.

METHOD OF RESEARCH

The studies were conducted based on different types of material available on the Internet and meeting the criteria for infographics: they contain explanations and information in a visual form that integrates words and pictures; they function as self-contained sources of information and knowledge; they contain information given directly or hidden under symbols. In order to obtain research data enabling determination of the efficacy of searching for information in infographics and the degree of understanding the communication that they convey, a series of didactic tests with test materials were conducted. It was assumed that by using open-ended questions that require a short answer or writing a note (extended answer), the ability of students to perform specific intellectual tasks using visual forms of information communication would be investigated. Verification of the way and range of understanding of these forms of communication was also carried out through tasks requiring the creation of infographics on a set subject by students themselves. The tests were administered to a hand-picked group of forty students from the Faculty of Humanities of Maria Curie Skłodowska University in Lublin who took a degree course in Information Architecture. These are students who, on the one hand, chose education in the humanities, which, to some extent, shows their interests in and preferences for more humanistic knowledge and skills than others. On the other hand, they are not afraid of contact with new techniques and technologies because they chose the degree course whose curriculum offers many subjects associated with the use of computer hardware and software. In other words, these are students with predominantly humanistic competencies but to whom modern techniques and technologies are no obstacle to the cognitive process. It should be emphasized that the selected group can be identified with the typical graduate of the Polish education system in terms of his/her information competencies. The group performed test tasks containing diverse infographics which required: reading detailed information provided directly or guessable from the contexts and symbols, the ability to draw conclusions based on the analysis of a set of charts or materials making up a project in digital humanities; reading the general message of an infographic and specific issues contained in it, as well as creating a story based on infographics or materials making up a project in digital humanities. The next group of tasks required composing infographics by individual students according to specific criteria. All the questions and tasks required the students' own answers rather than selecting them from ready-made distractors. The point was to make the form of tests as close as possible to the practice of everyday use of information sources. The infographics were selected in such a way as to contain the main types of information: figures, text, location time and location in space. The information in those infographics was visualized as charts, graphs, diagrams, maps and pictures. What was significant in the selection of the infographics was also their internal diversity in accordance with Jacques Bertin's (1983) conception of glyphs (features of graphic signs), which include: shape, size, clarity, graininess, color shade, and spatial orientation. In the author's intention, diversity was meant to minimize the influence of single features on the efficacy of reading the test materials.

The following test tasks were used:

1. Using the following information -http://www.compareyourcountry.org/pisa/country/POL – compare the condition of education in Poland with: OECD, Finland, Japan and USA and answer the following questions:
   a. What issue/problem is illustrated by the charts?
   b. Itemize all the conclusions you have drawn from each individual chart/graph and from comparisons of Poland with other countries in each of the five thematic areas.
   c. List the difficulties that you encountered while reading the meaning of the charts/graphs.
   d. What decision about the place for educating your daughter would you take based on the knowledge you have now obtained? Why?
2. Use the data from infographic 1. *Psychologia konsumencka w e-commerce, nawyki, statystyki* [Consumer psychology in e-commerce, habits, statistics] – http://blog.bloomboard.co/2016/03/18/ zbior-22-najciekawszych-infographik-dla-branzy-e-commerce-cz-1/ - and write an essay (half-page long, font no. 12) on: *Zachowania klientów sklepów internetowych* [Behavior of Internet shop customers]
3. Study all the possibilities of data presentation and analysis in this project - http://republicofletters. stanford.edu/casestudies/voltaire.html. Then perform the tasks:

a. List all kinds of information on Voltaire's correspondence and contacts contained in the visualizations that make up the project.

b. Using the available visualizations, write a note that analyzes Voltaire's contacts by correspondence.

c. What difficulties do you experience while performing the above tasks?

4. Study all the functionalities offered by ORBIS - http://orbis.stanford.edu/. Then perform the tasks:

a. List all type of information that can be obtained from ORBIS on travelling around the ancient Roman Empire.

b. Using the ORBIS-based data and functionalities, create a description of the summer season journey from Rome to Constantinople by a person who is a civilian, has a horse and wishes to reach his/her destination as soon as possible.

c. What difficulties do you experience while performing the above tasks?

5. Using the infographic - http://scimaps.org/maps/map/napoleons_march_to_m_9/detail - describe those aspects of Napoleon's expedition to Moscow about which you will find information.

6. On the basis of the infographic - http://infographika.wp.pl/title,Marzec-najgorszy-miesiac-dla-alergikow,wid,18227287,wiadomosc.html – answer the question: In which regions of Poland do allergy sufferers feel worst in March and where does this come from?

7. On the basis of the infographic - http://infographika.wp.pl/title,Zly-sen-jest-typowy-dla-nowoczesnego-stylu-zycia,wid,18470320,wiadomosc.html – answer the question: Why do people have problems with falling asleep?

8. Using the available data in the infographic "10. *SMS marketing, a e-mail marketing, skuteczność, cechy* [SMS marketing and e-mail marketing – effectiveness, characteristics]" - http://blog.bloomboard.co/2016/03/18/zbior-22-najciekawszych-infographik-dla-branzy-e-commerce-cz-1/ - answer the question: What conclusions can a laundry owner draw from this data set for his/her activity?

9. Using the available data in the infographic "6. *Zakupy grupowe- trendy* [Group shopping – trends]" - http://blog.bloomboard.co/2016/03/18/zbior-22-najciekawszych-infographik-dla-branzy-e-commerce-cz-1/ - answer the question: Why in Denmark -unlike in Poland - is there a growing interest in group shopping?

10. Using the available data in the infographic "2. *Zakupy internetowe vs. zakupy tradycyjne, jak płacimy i co kupujemy* [Internet shopping vs. traditional shopping, how we pay and what we buy]" - http://blog.bloomboard.co/2016/03/18/zbior-22-najciekawszych-infographik-dla-branzy-e-commerce-cz-1/ - answer the questions:

a. Which product groups are not as a rule bought on the Internet?

b. Do we pay for Internet purchases with a debit card more often than for traditional purchases?

11. Using the available data in the infographic - http://najinfographiki.blogspot.com/2013/02/alkohol-spozycie-w-polsce-i-europie.html - answer the questions:

a. Drinking more than how many half-liter beers per day by a man is a risk behavior?

b. Is there an evident connection between permission to buy beer and wine already at the age of 16 and high alcohol consumption per capita in a given country?

c. Does the analyzed infographic contain information that the data present in it are reliable? Why do you think so?

12. On the basis of the following texts:

a. http://www.studiagdanskie.gwsh.gda.pl/tom10/129-141_Kedzierski.pdf;

b. http://www.ipsir.uw.edu.pl/UserFiles/File/Katedra_Socjologii_Norm/TEKSTY/ GasparskiStrzaleckaitpEtBiznesu.rtf;

c. http://yadda.icm.edu.pl/yadda/element/bwmeta1.element.desklight-4d0fb04b-f31f-4636-9212-a0ce6d415a74/c/22_R.Wojciechowska_Zachowania_etyczne....pdf;

design an infographic (using all the functionalities of the tool korzyshttps://venngage.com/) on: *Etyka w działalności informacyjnej traktowanej jako biznes* [Ethics in information activity treated as a business operation]

13. Using the knowledge acquired during classes and the functionalities of the tool https://venngage.com/ design an infographic on: *Cyfryzacja przestrzeni publicznej w Polsce* [Digitalization of public space in Poland]

14. Find two infographics on the Internet concerning the problem of personal information management. Then describe in your own words what content (facts and opinions, details and general knowledge) the infographics contain.

In order to avoid time pressure, the tasks were divided into several stages. Task no. 1 students performed in a computer lab within 45 minutes. Tasks no. 2 - 11 were performed outside classes at the university within 7 days. Each of the tasks no. 12,13 and 14 was connected with one university subject course. The preparation for its execution - acquiring the necessary knowledge - lasted for a whole semester, while the students had 14 days to complete the tasks.

TEST RESULTS

Test 1: Two-thirds of those tested were unable to name the problems presented in the graphs/charts; instead, some of them wrote in the names of graph groups (given in English) translated by the Google Translator. Half of the subjects correctly read the information contained in individual graphs and drew correct conclusions from them, while the others had problems noticing the variation over time of students' competencies and wrongly read the information from the charts. Each respondent was able to indicate in which country s/he would like to send his daughter to, but only two-thirds of them gave arguments based on the information from the graphs. As for the difficulties experienced with the execution of this task, for ca. 60% of the subjects it was a too small amount of data on the charts (despite the fact they contained all the information needed to perform the task), and for ca. 50% it was English used in the legends.

Task 2: Almost all the students wrote the essay on the set subject, correctly selected information for the subject and drew correct conclusions. It should however be stressed that the infographics used to perform the task operated mainly with the verbal and numerical format of information, the graphical elements being used mainly to organize the structure of information and for decoration.

Task 3: All the respondents correctly identified the information types but almost half of them did not notice the information shown on the margins of the infographics – the kinds of letters according to their subjects. Rather than make a note analyzing the correspondence, all the respondents made a list of detailed items of information about the contacts. No one took into consideration the infographics that compared the data on the range of Voltaire's correspondence with the appropriate data concerning J. Locke and B. Franklin. The principal difficulty for half of the students was to interpret the information presented in a graphical form.

Task 4: All the subjects correctly identified most of the information types. However, almost none of them named the types which appeared only after selecting the maximum accuracy of the map, this functionality being at the bottom side and of the interactive infographic. All the students created a comparatively correct description of the journey, but only half of them took into account the information that required magnifying the degree of map accuracy or discovering the data hidden under the point denoting a locality. Difficulties were mentioned by only one-third of students, this being English in the description of the functionalities of the infographic they used.

Task 5: All the subjects made a register of information contained in the infographic, mainly of the information items provided in the form of figures (dates, number of the troops) and words (place names). However, it was not a description of the expedition, taking into account such processes as the march on Moscow, retreat, the influence of frost, and the distance covered per time unit.

Task 6: Only one-third of the students performed the task correctly. The others were unable to correctly name the regions in Poland with the highest allergen concentration or indicate the plants causing most problems to the allergy sufferers.

Task 7: Almost two-thirds of the students did the task correctly. The others read only the information provided directly in the form of text. They did not take into consideration the information showing the relationship between good sleep and specific behaviors.

Task 8: Almost 85% of those tested gave the correct answer, taking information from the infographic into account. However, half of them did not take into account all the presented information that could be useful in the laundry business.

Task 9: only 25% of the students associated the problem with the fact that in Poland it is mainly young people who are interested in group shopping, while in Denmark – the elderly. The association could arise only on the basis of the infographic, which was not accompanied by the explanatory text.

Task 10: Both questions were correctly answered by over 90% of the respondents. Detailed information was given in the form of words and figures while the graphics served to organize and select information.

Task 11: in the first question, 15% of the answers were wrong, but what made things easier was that only one part of the infographic contained all the data necessary for calculations. In the second question it was necessary to compare the data from two parts and in this case already 25% of the answers were wrong. In the third question, the correct answer together with the arguments that required finding and assessing the reliability of the sources of the data presented in the verbal form, was given by 75% of the students.

Task 12: All students designed the infographic in accordance with the subject of the task, there was no reservation about the selection of substantive information. The graphics was used correctly to organize and systematize information. However, almost no one used the graphical and symbolic forms of communication exclusively. In the vast majority of infographics (80%) we can see a tendency for including in the graphics larger portions of verbal and numerical information, even in the form of a chart, diagram, photo or a drawing [Representative works is attached within the appendix].

Task 13: Exactly the same conclusions as in Task 12.

Task 14: One in three respondents had problems with correctly assigning the found infographics to the task subject. Almost all the students presented a simplified communication of the content as compared to the content of the graphical material they selected. They described what they saw instead of a creating a communication on the set subject. They did not emphasize factualinformation, descriptions, and opinions.

CONCLUSION

The infographics did not turn out to be a source of data, information and knowledge that would produce an insurmountable barrier. However, the following relationship was clearly seen: the more favorable the proportions between the text and graphics were, the fewer problems the students had with correct reading of the content. Another relationship was also observable: the more information the analyzed material contained, the more data, especially those on the edges, were disregarded when executing a task. The subjects did not have difficulties reading specific information, but making generalizations caused them problems. The students found the quantitative data easily, but found it difficult to notice the qualitative data. It was a serious challenge to correctly name the analyzed phenomenon unless the examined material presented it directly. There were also problems with reading the temporal and spatial variability of the phenomena presented as infographics, especially when this involved comparing several different graphical and textual elements. It was a great difficulty to interpret details read from an infographic and to translate their set into a consistent communication. This phenomenon was particularly intense with the subject matter that the students did not know well. The frequently observed behavior of the respondents was the attempts to find additional information although the items contained in the infographics were absolutely sufficient to perform the task. The infographics turned out to be most useful as the resource that organized and structured specific information.

To sum up, it should be emphasized that a typical graduate of the Polish education system is not adequately prepared to receive the visual content concerning abstract phenomena and processes. Hence, the expectations of digital humanists that writing and linear narrative can be superseded by visual forms of communication in describing the world are premature in the case of a large part of Polish society. It will be a long time before publications based on visualizations are a remedy for the observable decline in traditional reading in Poland. Admittedly, visualizations do not increase information noise but at present they are not becoming a significant form of communicating abstract knowledge from scientists and experts to society. An indisputable barrier is the model of education based on the verbal and textual, linear communication of knowledge. Information competencies of the graduate of this system do not allow him/her to efficiently use information visualizations. It is impossible, however, to indicate visualization types that cause the greatest problems because the observed relationship applies only to the proportions between the text and graphical elements – the more the latter, the more problems the students had.

SOLUTIONS AND RECOMMENDATIONS

The recommendations arising from the presented research results concern the system of education. It turned out that education, especially humanistic, based mainly on the verbal and textual transmission of knowledge (the handbook and the communication by the teacher), and requiring the work results above all in the verbal and textual form (oral utterances, compositions, essays, reviews) does not equip young people with a large portion of information competencies necessary in the reality dominated by the digital media and the Internet, thereby restricting the cognitive abilities of young people. This will change if two conditions are fulfilled. First of all, the authors of handbooks should, where possible, present information in visual forms or use references to the resources of such materials on the Internet. However, infographics, photographs or films should not be an addition to the verbal content or its illustration, but they should be primarily used as a legitimate source of new information and present not only quantitative but also qualitative data. This necessitates changes in the methods of teachers' work and the departure from providing knowledge to be remembered by the pupil/student, for setting tasks to be executed based on diverse, including visual, sources of information. It is important that tasks should require not only reading specific information but also comparing and generalizing it, as well as distinguishing essential features, and common and differentiating elements. Another group of tasks should come down to discussing problems, concrete and abstract ones, based on visual materials and on the use of these materials to create digital storytelling. What is also needed is exercises in associating the abstract humanistic content with graphical symbols that represent it. Good examples of educational activities based on the production of visualizations are provided by the increasingly numerous scientific studies, e.g. by Graham, Milligan & Weingart (2015), Tufte (2001) i Ware (2004, 2008), and by Internet guides, e.g. by Angela Zoss (2017) and Wiesława Osińska (2017).

REFERENCES

Bertin, J. (1983). *Semiology of graphics: diagrams, networks, maps*. Madison, WI: The University of Wisconsin Press.

Brown, J. S. (2002). Learning in the Digital Age. In *Forum Futures 2002* (pp. 20–23). New York: Educause.

Carswell, M., & Wickens, C. D. (1987). Information Integration and the Object Display: An Interaction of Task Demands and Display Superiority. *Ergonomics*, *30*(3), 511–527. doi:10.1080/00140138708969741

Chen, Ch. (2006). *Information Visualization: Beyond the Horizon*. London: Springer-Verlag.

Cleveland, W. S., & McGill, R. (1984). Graphical Perception: Experimentation and Application to the Development of Graphical Methods. *Journal of the American Statistical Association*, *79*(387), 531–554. doi:10.1080/01621459.1984.10478080

Davidson, R. (2014). Using Infographics in the Science Classroom: Three Investigations in Which Students Present Their Results in Infographics. *Science Teacher (Normal, Ill.)*, *3*(81), 34–39.

Drucker, J. (2012). Humanistic Theory and Digital Scholarship. In M. K. Gold (Ed.), *Debates in Digital Humanities*. Minneapolis, MN: University of Minnesota Press. Retrieved March 15, 2017, from http://dhdebates.gc.cuny.edu/debates/text/34

Epstein Ojalvo, H., & Doyne, S. (2010, August 24). Teaching with infographics. Social Studies, History, Economics. *The New York Times*.

Francuz, P. (2007). *Obrazy w umyśle. Studia nad percepcją i wyobraźnią [Images in the mind. Studies of perception and imagination]*. Warszawa: Wyd. Naukowe Scholar.

Graham, S., Milligan, I., & Weingart, S. (2015). *Exploring Big Historical Data. The Historian's Macroscope*. London: Imperial College Press. Retrieved March 15, 2017, from http://www.themacroscope.org/2.0/

Hollsanowa, J., Holmberg, N., & Holmqvist, K. (2009). Reading Information Graphics: The Role of Spatial Contiguity and Dual Attentional Guidance. *Applied Cognitive Psychology*, *23*(9), 1215–1226. doi:10.1002/acp.1525

Huang, W., & Tan, Ch. L. (2007). A system for understanding imaged infographics and its applications. In *Proceedings of the 2007 ACM symposium on Document engineering*, (pp. 9-18). New York: Association for Computing Machinery. doi:10.1145/1284420.1284427

Kierach, M., & Ogonowski, B. (2012). Wpływ ilości informacji i atrakcyjności wizualnej prezentacji na zapamiętywanie prezentowanych treści [The influence of the amount of information and visual attractiveness of the presentation on memorizing the presented content]. *e-Mentor*, 1. Retrieved March 15, 2017, from http://www.e-mentor.edu.pl/artykul/index/numer/43/id/905

Knapiński, R. (2011). Biblia Pauperum – rzecz o dialogu słowa i obrazu [The Bible of Pauperum: the dialogue of words and images]. In M. Kluza (Ed.), *Materiały konferencji „Wizualizacja wiedzy. Od Biblii Pauperum do hipertekstu"* [Conference proceedings "Visualization of knowledge. From the Bible Pauperum to hypertext"] (pp. 10-36). Lublin: Wiedza i Edukacja.

Lamb, G. R., Polman, J. L., Newman, A., & Smith, C. G. (2014). Science News Infographics: Teaching Students to Gather, Interpret, and Present Information Graphically. *Science Teacher (Normal, Ill.)*, *3*(81), 25–30.

Mendenhall, A. S., & Summers, S. (2015). Designing Research: Using Infographics to Teach Design Thinking in Composition. *Journal of Global Literacies, Technologies, and Emerging Pedagogies*, *1*(3), 359–371.

Osińska, W. (2017). *Wizualizacja informacji* [Visualization of information]. Retrieved March 15, 2017, from http://www.wizualizacjainformacji.pl/

Paradowski, M. (2011). Wizualizacja danych – dużo więcej niż prezentacja [Visualization of data - much more than presentation]. In M. Kluza (Ed.), *Materiały konferencji „Wizualizacja wiedzy. Od Biblii Pauperum do hipertekstu"* [Conference proceedings "Visualization of knowledge. From the Bible Pauperum to hypertext"] (pp. 37-60). Lublin: Wiedza i Edukacja.

Pulak, I., & Tomaszewska, M. (2011). Visual Literacy and Teaching with Infographics. In K. Denek (Ed.), Edukacja jutra. Edukacja w społeczeństwie wiedzy [Tomorrow's education. Education in the knowledge society]. Sosnowiec: Oficyna Wydawnicza "Humanitas".

Radomski, A. (2013). Digital storytelling. Kilka słów o wizualizacji wiedzy w humanistyce [Digital storytelling. A few words about the visualization of knowledge in humanities]. In R. Bomba & A. Radomski (Eds.), *Zwrot cyfrowy w humanistyce [Digital turnaround in humanities]*. Lublin: Wyd. E-Naukowiec.

Radomski, A. (2016). Wizualne analizy, wizualne narracje [Visual analyses, visual narrations]. In R. Bomba, A. Radomski, E. Solska (Ed.), Humanistyka cyfrowa. Badanie tekstów, obrazów i dźwięku [Digital humanities. Examination of texts, images and sound] (pp. 147-158). Lublin: Wyd. E-Naukowiec.

Rosenstone, R. (2008). Historia w obrazach/historia w słowach: rozważania nad możliwością przedstawienia historii na taśmie filmowej [History in images/history in words: reflections on the possibility of presenting a story on a film tape]. In I. Kurz (Ed.), *Film i historia. Antologia [Film and history. Anthology]* (pp. 93–116). Warszawa: Wyd. Uniwersytetu Warszawskiego.

Schnettler, B. (2008). W stronę socjologii wizualnej [Towards visual sociology]. *Przegląd Socjologii Jakościowej*, *3*, 116–142.

Staley, D. J. (2003). *Computers, visualization, and history: how new technology will transform our understanding of the past.* Armonk, NY: M. E. Sharpe.

Taraszkiewicz, M. (1999). *Jak uczyć lepiej? Czyli refleksyjny praktyk w działaniu [How to teach better? Reflective practitioners in action].* Warszawa: Wyd. CODN.

Tufte, E. R. (1997). *Visual Explanations: Images and Quantities, Evidence and Narrative.* Cheshire, CT: Graphics Press.

Tufte, E. R. (2001). *The Visual Display of Quantitative Information.* Cheshire, CT: Graphics Press.

Ware, C. (2004). *Information Visualization: Perception for Design.* San Francisco: Morgan Kaufman.

Ware, C. (2008). *Visual Thinking for Design.* San Francisco: Morgan Kaufman/Elsevier.

White, H. (2008). Historiografia i historiofotia (Historiography and historiophotics). In I. Kurz (Ed.), *Film i historia. Antologia [Film and history. Anthology]* (pp. 117–130). Warszawa: Wyd. Uniwersytetu Warszawskiego.

Witek, P. (2014). Metodologiczne problemy historii wizualnej [Methodological problems of visual history]. *Resena Historica (Mexico City, Mexico), 37*, 159–176.

Zoss, A. (2017). *Introduction to Data Visualization: About Data Visualization.* Retrieved March 15, 2017, from http://guides.library.duke.edu/datavis

KEY TERMS AND DEFINITIONS

Didactic Test With Test Materials: A properly constructed, objective method of measuring didactic achievements, whose results are presented in quantitative terms, whereas giving an answer to particular question or execution of a task is determined by the prior analysis of the appended materials (texts, photographs, maps, etc.).

Digital Humanities: The department of the humanities that studies man and his products in virtual, digital space; the kind of methodology of humanistic investigations that consists in the use of digital resources and tools for research work and for publishing its results; digital humanists study interdisciplinary subjects and combine qualitative and quantitative methods; they work in teams made up not only of professional scholars but also of experts and enthusiasts; they investigate big data, publish in the internet using free licenses, they undertake to investigate the manifestations of human activity available on the internet, presenting the results not only as text but also as graphics and film, and they participate in the digitalization of cultural assets.

Digital Storytelling: The presentation of scientific and educational content in the form of films, web pages, multimedia presentations, and computer games.

Infographics: The presentation of a condensed set of information, using mainly graphical elements containing information given directly or hidden under symbols.

Information Competencies: The ability to search, select, process, collect, and assess information, as well as to use it to solve problems and perform tasks.

Information Noise: An excess of information and its forms that makes it difficult to distinguish true and essential information; the imbalance between the amounts of provided information and man's capacity to process it.

Information Visualization: The use of diverse graphical forms and techniques (maps, charts/graphs, diagrams, schematics, photographs, animations, films) in order to present the content.

Open-Ended Test Questions: Questions in which the tested person formulates an answer on his/her own; the questions have three variants: with an extended answer, a short answer, or with a gap to be filled.

APPENDIX

Representative Works on Task Number 12

Figure 1. Infographic on "Ethics in information activity treated as a business operation"

Figure 2. Infographic on "Ethics in information activity treated as a business operation": Part 1

Figure 3. "Ethics in information activity treated as a business operation": Part 2

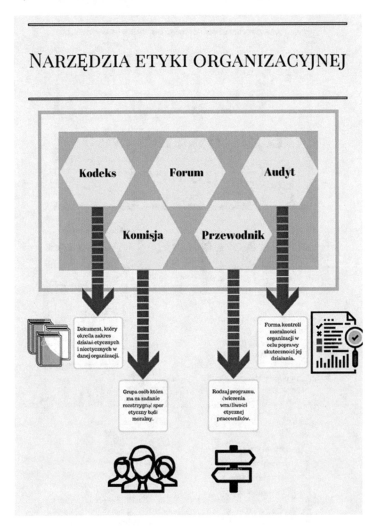

Figure 4. "Ethics in information activity treated as a business operation": Part 3

Chapter 5
The Vizualization of the Dynamics of the Relationship Between the Bridegrooms in the "Song of Songs"

Monika Szetela
College of Social and Media Culture, Poland

Malgorzata Piotrkowska Dankowska
Cardinal Stefan Wyszynski University, Poland

ABSTRACT

The dominant theme in the "Song of Songs" is the relationship of love between Bridegrooms. The subject of interest is the dynamism of the relationship. The attitude and feelings expressed by love, depicted in this book of the Old Testament, don't express only a description of their beauty, but a description of expressing mutual delight of all your loved ones. Mutual learning is shaping a unique spousal bond, which as a result of the involvement of the beloved and the beloved of each event, not always easy, brings them together; and thus they can build their own language of communication. Narrative character of text is treated in its literal sense. Presented course of events highlights everything that deepens and develops relationships between characters and clearly shows what returns as the leitmotif of the story. Focusing attention on events, using visualization as a way to telling about the people and events, puts less emphasis on the lyrical parties – descriptions of the beauty of the Bride appear in the text of the "Song of Songs."

INTRODUCTION

The text of the Song of Songs was studied and interpreted in many ways, not only by the biblical exegetes. Tradition of the readings of the book has its own history in patristic spirituality, especially in the Carmelite spirituality. The best solution seems to be the adoption of a polysemy interpretation of the text. None of the readings exclude the other (Murphy, 1986). This involves acceptance of the literal and allegorical meaning (the Bridegroom - God, the Bride - the Chosen People, the Church, the human soul)

DOI: 10.4018/978-1-5225-4990-1.ch005

and Targum reading, relating to the Exodus of the Chosen People from Egypt to the Promised Land. (Farmer, 2000, p. 802; Stachowiak, 1990, pp. 461-462).

The subject of our analysis is the development and formation of relationships between spouses (Bardski, 2010a, 2010b). Interesting is not only how the relationship between the characters, but under the influence of which events and experience the relationship dynamic is. Although the text for an object has a love – that assumes closeness, Song of Songs is often referred as a song of absence, of waiting, of seeking, more than the fulfillment (Bardski, 2010a, 2010b; Brzegowy, 2007, p. 151). It is important to analyze actions, activity of the woman and her beloved, and common space shaped by them (Falk, 1982).

The second subject of the research will be the answer to the question: how modern ways of presenting knowledge, the results of scientific research on the text of written words are a form of visualization, what has been verbalized as a result of scientific work and whether this visualization allows to expand the study itself in a selected aspect. It is important to recognize whether the new technologies actually allow not only to explain what has already been learned but also to intensify the cognitive process itself (Osińska, 2016, p. 14), and they are not only a decorative or aesthetic element, but as the creators of these tools think, they serve to analyze the presented phenomena (Osińska, 2016, p. 14, 60). Osińska argues that visualization "highlights the semantics of accompanying textual content, supports their analysis and memorization" (Osińska, 2016, p. 70).

Each song text will be analyzed in the chosen narrative aspect of the relationship between spouses. It was assumed that, despite the differences in the consistency of the text of the whole song, its final editor ordered the whole thing according to a certain concept. (Kręcidło, 2008, p. 39), (Balchin, 1970, pp. 579-580). Then, the visualization of the relationship will be made and the conclusions drawn from this statement will be presented. After this part of the research presented will be a visualization of the entire text in the perspective of dynamics of the observed relationship. The incomplete use of visualization techniques for text research, is due to the fact that the research methodology is treated with care in the work like this (Osińska, 2008, p. 176).

The aim is to use the methodology to such an extent that may be suitable for the selected topic. A separate issue is the study of the text of the Bible with using visualization techniques. Such works are carried out mainly at the level indicating the relationship between the characters, places, topics undertaken frequency occurring in the Old and New Testament (Bardski, 2011). The use of technology in Polish literary research concerns primarily stylometry and is conducted by J. Rybicki and M. Eder. It is difficult to point out the particular interests of Polish biblical scholars in this methodology.

BACKGROUND

Song I (1:2-2:7)

Description of the relationship between the Bridegroom and the Bride begins with the declaration of a woman who expresses a desire for love (Keel, 1997; Ravasi, 2005) when she says: „Let him kiss me with kisses of his mouth!" (Song of Songs 1:2a, New American Bible, [Revised Edition]). Compares love to wine but praises her superiority, even though the taste of wine was a symbol of pleasure, delight and joy (Keel, 1997, p. 62; Ravasi, 2005, p. 44). The highlighted scent values indicate a clear focus on the beloved:

better than the fragrance of your perfumes.
Your name is a flowing perfume (Song of Songs 1:3ab).

He himself becomes a spilled oil for her when he compiles his name with him (Keel, 1997, p. 62). He for her is „the most exciting oil, and its presence is fragrance" (Ravasi, 2005, p. 46). The desire to *let him kiss me* is strengthened with another: „Draw me after you! Let us run!" (Song of Songs 1: 4a). The Bride is not only open to love, she wants the Bridegroom's reaction. The threefold invitation is accepted, but the recipient of the text does not know how it happened. The song don't show how the first meeting took place. The Bridegroom don't speak about Her heart condition. From Her story we have learned that He responded generously to the invitation: *The king has brought me to his bed chambers.* (Song of Songs 1:4b).

The bridegroom in the Eastern tradition was called the king (Ravasi, 2005, p. 47). His reaction is instantaneous, as She describes with pride (Keel, 1997, p. 64). It looks like She's currently talking about a situation already known to Her. There are verbs in the plural: „Let us exult and rejoice in you;" (Song of Songs 1: 4c) highlight common experiences. „It's certainly a past history of the meeting, but it's also a surprisingly fresh presence, and it's also waiting for a new future that is tasted" (Ravasi, 2005, p. 44).

Ravasi writes about this part as perfect and fulfilled, on the other hand open to new ones (Ravasi, 2005, p.43). Living love does not reach its fullness, because the woman in the sequel tells about the search of „you whom my soul loves" (Song of Songs 1:7). The use of the Hebrew word *nefesz* indicates the importance of the presence of the beloved for the existence of the beloved, for all Her life (Ravasi, 2005, p. 53). The search process justifies the belief that „love isn't possessed but continuous acquisition" (Ravasi, 2005, p. 54). But don't want to wander and want directions on how to find him. Here we find out, that beloved is a shepherd. Also get to know the companions of the loving couple, it's the choir, that tells Her where to go, to find Him. „Whoever wants to find his beloved can't avoid the role of a love-seeker for the object of his love"(Keel, 1997, p. 72).

Again, without information about how the search was conducted, we have a return to the course of events. The first message is, that the beloved brought Her into His chambers. Now He speaks himself. He delights in Her beauty and declares to give Her precious jewelry. Then the narrative changes again and the experiences of the woman at the joint feast are described. She draws attention, not only on the scent values but also on the taste. His presence allows the Bride to realize Her own worth, Her own beauty:

While the king was upon his couch,
my spikenard gave forth its fragrance. (Song of Songs 1:12)

There's an intimate relationship between them, which is expressed poetically, He *fondly rests on the body of a woman* (Ravasi, 2005, p. 60):

My lover is to me a sachet of myrrh;
between my breasts he lies. (Song of Songs 1:13)

Not only myrrh is impersonated here (Walton, Matthews, & Chavalas, 2005, p. 665), but also the bunch of henna group (Pope, 2008, p. 347), because she calls Her Beloved. The feast takes place in the vineyards of Engaddi, in the oasis of greenery and vineyards (Keel, 1997, pp. 80-81). Verses 1:15-16 are alternate glimpses of the Bridegrooms, Ravasi calls it a *duet score* (Ravasi, 2005, p. 56). Vers 1:17

describes the construction of the house: the cedars (beams) and the cypresses (walls), indicate an oasis of tranquility and greenery (Ravasi, 2005, p. 61). After a series of mutual compliments, the Woman highlights the uniqueness of Her beloved with poetic comparison to the apple tree. She talks about realizing Her desire, to sit in His shade, which means that She gave herself under His care. The shadow symbolizes protection, a sense of security that „allows the woman to feel the taste of the apple fruit - delicacy and erotic devotion to the beloved as something sweet" (Keel, 1997, p. 97):

In his shadow I delight to sit,
and his fruit is sweet to my taste. (Song of Songs 2:3cd);
He brought me to the banquet hall
and his glance at me signaled love. (Song of Songs 2:4).

Not only She gave herself up into His care, but She also tasted His fruit. The Beloved introduced Her to the room, and this created a new situation among them. The banquet hall is also referred to as the home of wine, and the common drinking of wine has had in the world of the ancient East erotic connotations (Keel, 1997, p. 100).

Next, the woman narrate situation that He embraced Her and hugged Her (cf. 2:6). It's only here that he speaks himself, but his words are not addressed to the woman, but to the daughters of Jerusalem, so that she does not wake up, until it is ready. (Song of Songs 2: 7d). It is not so much a literal dream, but the recognition that in love there is particular time for everyting (Murphy, 2001, p. 549).

Timeline

The dynamics of the relation shown in the I song can be presented in the following diagram (Figure 1).

Figure 1. Dynamics of the relationship between the Bridegroom and the Bride in songs 1

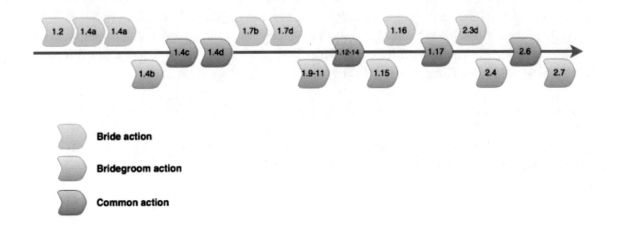

Commentary

Bride is talking about openness to love three times, clearly expecting the concrete actions of the Bridegroom. He introduced Her into Her room, but after a moment of joyful wedding or memories of them, Woman again is alone and looking for Him. She asks others about the way to Him. She doesn't want to get lost. These are not just declarations from Her, but specific actions to which He responds with delight and gifts. There is a time of feast and closeness and mutual compliment.

Woman seems to be more active in the event, maturing to deepen relationship. Bridegroom, on the other hand, had to express himself beforehand, and he is known because of his action. Part of them remains behind the veil. We get to know their effect from the bride's relationship. But the visualization of this relationship verifies this impression. In fact, in the first phase, Woman shows a lot of activity, but the trust She showed to Her beloved activates Him very concisely, and His expressions are an expression of delight over Her beauty and grace. Bridegrooms enjoy each other and this reciprocal relationship. It's a new situation in their lives. He invites to a feast, deepens the bond between them and cares for the beloved. One can therefore speak with reference to the whole song of the first equilibrium in the actions undertaken. These actions relate to the will (desire), expressing admiration, mutual exploration and deepening intimacy.

Song II (2:8-3:5)

The second song starts in a different place. Earlier sequences of events pointed to the closeness between the briedgrooms as they feasted. The Bride's story in Song of Songs 2: 8-14 and 2: 16-17 shows another space. There is no room, Woman is in a family home, She isn't with Her Beloved. She talks about what He does and says. In this song the Bridegroom shows a decent activity in His efforts. She urgently looks for it, and the growing excitement is expressed by exclamations:

The sound of my lover! here he comes
springing across the mountains,
leaping across the hills. (Song of Songs 2:8).

„Love gives Him supernatural strength" (Keel, 1997, p. 110). The stages of his activities are distinguished: „He speaks / calls (She hears His voice), comes, runs, jumps – this energetic behavior, full of youthful vigor, so natural comparisons are made to gazelles or young deer" (Song of Songs 2: 9ab). When He is under His beloved house: He is standing behind the wall, looking out the window, peering through the lattice. His determination to establish a closer contact is clear. And before, and now, totally devoted to what He does (Keel, 1997, p. 112). Repeats the invitation twice:

Arise, my friend, my beautiful one, and come! (Song of Songs 2:10cd).

Before repeating the request, He speaks of the joy of spring (2.11-13ab) (Ravasi, 2005, p. 71), and later expresses the desire to see Her gracefully and to hear Her voice:

My dove in the clefts of the rock,
in the secret recesses of the cliff,

Let me see your face,
let me hear your voice,
For your voice is sweet,
and your face is lovely (Song of Songs 2:14).

In this beautiful chiastical composition (Keel, 1997, p. 119), the Beloved compliments the chosen one. He emphasizes that the time for hiding in the rock clefts for the shy dove is over. He wants Her to appear in all Her wealth. Ravasi writes that this is „a proposal of intimacy that abolishes all divisions and secrets" (Ravasi, 2005, p. 75). The next two verses 16 and 17 are the response of a woman who expresses Her confession (Ravasi, 2005, p. 76) (Murphy, 2001, p. 550):

My lover belongs to me and to him (Song of Songs 2: 16a).

Then it turns out that He's not with Her, because She says: „roam, my lover, like a gazelle or a young stag, upon the rugged mountains" (Song of Songs 2:17). This part points to the following course of events: She expects – He is coming; He invites to go with Him, wants to see Her whole, hear Her voice – She has a sense of mutual belonging; He walks His herd – She calls him. He's still not with Her and She's very painfully experiencing this absence. She wakes up at night and looks for Him in bed. Exegeses think that this nightly search can be a dremy image (Keel, 1997, p. 131; Ravasi, 2005, p. 79). The desire to share with him every moment, is so great that without any regard for customs, the Bride gets up and walks at night through the city searching for Her Beloved (Keel, 1997, p.135; Ravasi, 2005, p. 80). The intensity of desire and search is expressed in four times of the verb "seek". The Hebrew word *seek* also means „to desire, to miss" (Keel, 1997, p. 133). She is looking for Him on a bed, looking and doesn't find, She will look for streets and squares. She met the night watchmen and asked if they had not seen Him. „The poet doesn't even notice the answer, which must have hit the vacuum. So empty and despair is the heart of a woman" (Ravasi, 2005, p. 81). Right after this situation She finds a Bridegroom and now She behaves very vigorously: She caught Him, doesn't let Him go; She wants to bring Him to Her mother's house. The term *mother's house* in the Bible is understood in the perspective of marriage (Farmer, 2000, p. 787). These actions clearly show that a Woman wants to be with Her beloved constantly: She wakes up at night and seeks Him, not paying attention to the inappropriateness of those searches in the city at this hour, and when She finds him, decides not to let go (Ravasi, 2005, p. 81).

The answer of the Bridegroom He gives in the next verse, is a refreshing rendition of 2:7, so as not to awaken the beloved. It isn't known whether what is shown above is a description of a real event plan or a dictated view.. Keel believes that this form „calls for not to interfere with passionate love that has achieved its purpose but to leave it to its own course" (Keel, 1997, p. 135). The desire of the Bride, to never separate from the Bridegroom, is deep.

As in the first song, descriptions of feasts appeared immediately, so here we come to know the expectations expressed by both sides of this love relationship. The diagram below shows that there is no common space. The song pervades the atmosphere of expectation (Ravasi, 2005, p. 77).

Timeline

The following diagram (Figure 2) illustrates the timeline.

Figure 2. Dynamics of the relationship between the Bridegroom and the Bride in songs 2

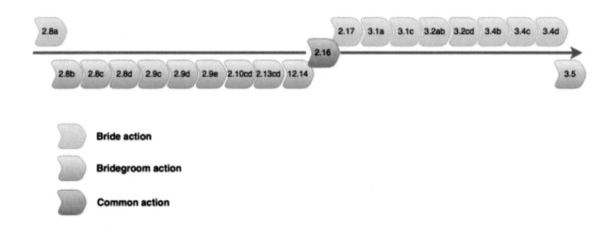

Commentary

The second song presents events from another perspective. This time, He is the one actively striving for the woman. She expresses a sense of reciprocal belonging, but there is nothing in this part about the intimate relationship that was the subject of the relationship building in the first song. First, His efforts and desires are presented, and then Woman begins to search for Him intensively. Both sides of this relationship are confirmed in their determination and decision not to leave anymore. Even assuming that the descriptions depicted in this song represent more dreamy than real events, the desires of the Bridegrooms are true and unequivocally defined. It's not only a result of the joy of intimate experiences, but of the importance of the presence of the beloved person as a result of Her lack of experience. Visualization presented on Figure 2 highlights the linearity of the action, first the entire sequence of actions of the Beloved, then Her. It is interesting that the amount of these activities is proportional.

Song III (3:6-5:1)

The third song begins with the choir's delight. Here she is „coming up from the desert" (Song of Songs 3:6). Her entrance to Jerusalem from the steppe or the desert (Keel, 1997, p. 136), surrounded by warriors, is full of dignity and wealth (Keel, 1997, p. 137). The Bridegroom is waiting for Her (Keel, 1997, p.139) and on a solemn wedding day She has a crown on Her head. „The crown in the East is a symbol of happiness" (Job 19: 9; Wisdom 2: 8), „and in Judaism the young spouses were crowned (Isaiah 61:10) at least until the seventh year after the Christ, the year of the destruction of Jerusalem (Ravasi, 2005, p. 86). This is the day of the joy of his heart (Song of Songs 3:11), and joy of the heart is the degree of supreme joy. This is the joy that comes from the center of man, embraces him all and makes him happy in every way" (cf. Ecclesiastes 5:19; Isaiah 30:29; Jeremiah 15:16; Keel, 1997, p. 147). It doesn't matter whether it is a description of Solomon's own marriage, or rather the custom of wedding ceremony (most exegetes tend to do so). It's essential that the Beloved is brought in solemnly in the litter, and He expects to meet Her with Her whole body. When they are in close proximity, the Bridegroom not only praises Her beauty (respecting the principles of the Arabian literary genre *wasf*) (Murphy, 2001, p. 550), but also the whole person (Ravasi, 2005, p. 90). She still seems unattainable and therefore he makes a decision (Farmer, 2000, p. 788):

Until the day grows cool
and the shadows flee,
I shall go to the mountain of myrrh,
to the hill of frankincense. (Song of Songs 4:6)

Expresses His desire to find himself as close to His Beloved as possible. He asks Her, and exclaims:

With me from Lebanon, my bride!
With me from Lebanon, come! (Song of Songs 4:8ab)

The justification for this request is She herself:

You have ravished my heart, my sister, my bride;
you have ravished my heart with one glance of your eyes,
with one bead of your necklace. (Song of Songs 4:9)

Bridegroom is delighted with Her love, loses His mind, and beautiful scents express His incredible felicity (Keel, 1997, pp. 172-175), but the woman is still His desire:

A garden enclosed, my sister, my bride,
a garden enclosed, a fountain sealed! (Song of Songs 4:12)

To this desire She responds. She blossoms with all Her beauty thanks to Her Beloved:

Let my lover come to his garden
and eat its fruits of choicest yield. (Song of Songs 4:16cd)

This is also the case in Song of Songs 5: 1a, and „*a Man responds to the invitation with joy. He's now in the garden of love*" (Ravasi, 2005, p. 99), He shares his joy with others. The joyful love of the Bridegroom, already flowing from their intimate relationship, radiates to those who are close to them. Metaphor of the *garden of love* is the term for the Bride in the Song of Songs, which describes the depth of the spousal relationship (Farmer, 2000, p. 789).

This time the scheme shows the way to a common space between spouses:

Timeline

The following diagram illustrates the timeline (Figure 3).

Figure 3. Dynamics of the relationship between the Bridegroom and the Bride in songs 3

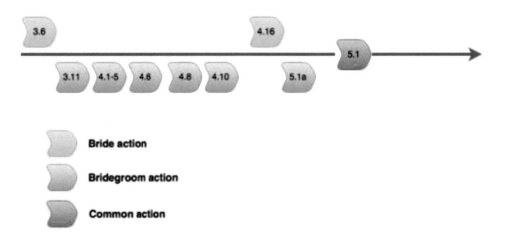

Commentary

In the first song the Bride talked about staying in His chambers, in the banquet hall. Now the Bridegroom radiates love and cheerfully proclaims it to His friends. In the second song the Bride said that He was Her and She was His. Now He says, that He is entering His garden. He Gives a full response to Her sense of mutual love and belonging. This is the answer to the level of being one. The survival of this love spreads, because love does not close people, but it opens and transforms others too, it can be called the radiation of love. „Love has in itself the power that spreads and tries to arouse love" (Ravasi, 2005, p. 99). The wedding song is the song of His action, and then full of love and joy.

Song IV (5:2-6:10)

In the fourth song we are dealing with the second nocturne. Exegesis wonder if this is a dream or not, and Keel is inclined to claim that it's a literary fiction that refers to real events and dreams and to sleep. „The Woman fell asleep, but Her heart is waiting, She is constantly watching" (Keel, 1997, p. 199). Thanks to this She hears every sound, hears the knock (the semantics of the word that indicates He is coming), Her beloved and asks Her to open the door (Farmer, 2000, p. 789). She, however, does not want to get up, explains Her activities before bed, expresses astonishment and indignation (Keel, 1997, p. 202):

I have taken off my robe,
am I then to put it on?
I have bathed my feet,
am I then to soil them? (Song of Songs 5:3)

The bridegroom tries to open the lock, but when He doesn't succeed, He leaves. Meanwhile, the Woman has just risen. Ravasi, interpreting the woman's reaction to the bride's attempt to open the door, writes that Her state was „deeply intimate excitement" (Ravasi, 2005, p. 104), but when She saw wat happend, She said: „at his leaving, my soul sank" (Song of Songs 5: 6c). She starts an intense search. She calls, looking for Him in the city until the wall guards mourned her (earlier nocturnal didn't carry this dramaturgy), She begs „the Daughters of Jerusalem" to seek Him. At their request, She describes His beauty. It is astonishing, that after asking the question, where the beloved departed, the Woman gives a very specific answer, although She had so desperately sought Him (Keel, 1997, p. 219). She says:

My lover has come down to his garden,
to the beds of spices,
To feed in the gardens
and to gather lilies. (Song of Songs 6:2)

Perhaps, according to Ravasi, in this brief concise way, we find out that She has found Beloved but physical remoteness allows a Woman to realize that love bonds can't be broken (Ravasi, 2005, p. 103). Then there's a repetition of the formula of mutual belonging. The Bridegroom once again describes the beauty of Her feminine beauty, which not only delights but terrifies (Keel, 1997, pp. 222-223). The song ends with a chorus of delight, distinguishing the Beloved among all women.

Scheme of emerging relationships:

Timeline

The following diagram illustrates the timeline (Figure 4).

Figure 4. Dynamics of the relationship between the Bridegroom and the Bride in songs 4

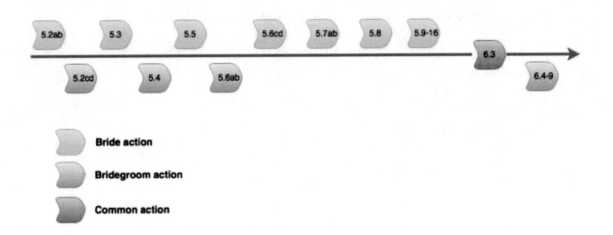

Commentary

The scheme Figure 4 emphasizes the dynamics of the first part of this song, which later focuses on the descriptions of Their beauty. This dynamism points to a great dramaturgy of events and the pace of their play. Certainly, however, the relationship between the Bridegrooms deepens, She is expecting His coming at night, but when He knocks, She turns His displeasure as if He came not in time. He tries to enter without Her consent, but quickly resolves. And when they meet after this event, none of them memorize that night. She had the opportunity to realize how important He was to Her and how captivating His charm was and bravely sought Him out at night in the city. When He speaks, He is focused only on Her charm, how much She admires Him with all Her person. The visualization in this case (Figure 4) illustrates what wasn't in the previous songs: the high tempo of events until the next night's search for the Bridegroom.

Song V (6:11-8:4)

The range of the fifth song (Song of Songs 6:11-8:4) not all scholars recognize. It's even more difficult to determine who, in some parts, is the speaker (Keel, 1997, p. 236) and who entered the walnut grove described in the song. Walnut is an unusual tree for Juda, imported, as suggested by the royal garden, but also „the garden of splendor, which is the body of his woman" (Ravasi, 2005, p. 115; Fox, 1985, p. 155). Similar doubts are expressed by the one who praises women's beauty in Song of Songs 7: 2-6 is is the Beloved or the choir marked the second, which didn't appear before in songs. It's evident that the choir in 7:1 calls the Shulammite (Walton, Matthews, & Chavalas, 2005, p. 658; Pope, 1977, p. 596; Barbiero, 2011, p. 364) so that She would dance or turn to tchem. Her reaction to this request is inspired by the delight expressed here in another descriptive song. Only, when words fall:

How beautiful you are, how fair,
my love, daughter of delights! (Song of Songs 7:7)

it is defined as the declaration of the bridegroom who speaks desires (Keel, 1997, p. 239):

Your very form resembles a date-palm,
and your breasts, clusters.

I thought, "Let me climb the date-palm!" (Song of Songs 7:8-9ab)

The Bride corresponds to the familiar formula of mutual belonging that She transforms, because She reacts to the expressing desires of Her Beloved:

I belong to my lover,
his yearning is for me. (Song of Songs 7:11)

Spouses speak the same language of desires. Next, the Woman proposes an interesting hike: to the fields, to the villages, to the vineyards, to enjoy intimacy there. She said that in their house already blooming mandrakes, fresh fruits(Keel, 1997, pp. 266-267). The next part of the song expresses Her dream of showing unconcerned feelings –e the customs of Eastern culture were strict (Keel, 1997, p. 269; Ravasi,

2005, p.124). She wants to bring Her beloved to Her mother's home, in which She will serve especially spicy wine and pomegranate juice. It may be a reward for teaching, although it is difficult to determine who is the teacher (Keel, 1997, p. 270; Murphy, 2001, p. 552). From the presentation of these desires, the Woman goes on to describe the situation in which She is:

His left hand is under my head,
and his right arm embraces me. (Song of Songs 8:3),

This situation is known from Song of Songs 2: 6. As it was then, the bridegroom now responds, repeating the request not to wake her until she wants to.

Timeline

The following diagram illustrates the timeline (Figure 5).

Commentary

There is relatively more description of the common space created by the bridegrooms in the fifth song, but it turns out that the delight of the Beloved is also intensified. This is another *wasf*. This time, the song describes the Woman from toe to head, highlighting Her high parentage, because sandals were worn only by rich people (Ravasi, 2005, p. 118). The Bridegroom is more boldly expressing His desire, but She speaks likewise. She changes the second part of the existing form of mutual affiliation:

My lover belongs to me and I to him (Song of Songs 2:16a)
I belong to my lover, and my lover belongs to me (Song of Songs 6:3a)
I belong to my lover, his yearning is for me (Song of Songs 7:11)

Figure 5. Dynamics of the relationship between the Bridegroom and the Bride in songs 5

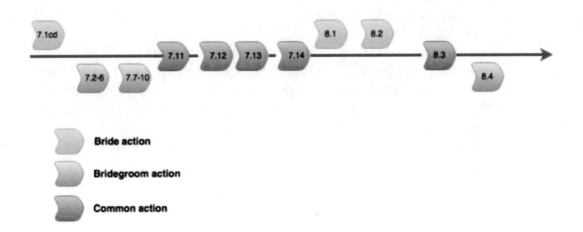

Subtle changes in this expression, point the barely perceptible but concrete dynamics of the relationship in their love (Farmer, 2000, p. 792):

- First attention is directed at Him: the Woman speaks of the affection of Her Beloved to Her, and then about Her,
- Then, affirmed in His reciprocity, as though She is realizes belonging to Him (Keel, 1997, p. 260),
- In the last formula She accepts His desire.

She proposes Him a *journey of love* in a world far from the riches of palaces and manors, the world of fields, villages, flowers and fruits. She speaks of Her desire to kiss Him unconcerned with moral attachments. We listen to love talks, expressing desires. He embraces Her and watches Her sleep again (Song of Songs 2:7 and 3:5 and 8:4). The common world of beloved, the common language of repetitive phrases, the calm of mutual belonging is formed.

Song VI (8:5-14)

The song begins with the phrase, that was already spoken by the choir, in Song of Songs 3:6:

Who is this coming up from the desert, (Song of Songs 8:5a),

But its second part is different:

leaning upon her lover? (Song of Songs 8:5b).

Keel highlights the transformation of a woman's attitude through love (Keel, 1997, p. 273), arrives with Her beloved, who says He woke Her up under the apple tree (where Her life began). In the original manuscript is described the opposite situation, the Woman speaks about the birth of the Beloved (Keel, 1997, p. 274; Murphy, 2001, p. 552). The power of love gives birth to a new life in the broad sense of this process (Farmer, 2000, p. 793). She deliver a hymn about the power of love, in which She expresses the desire for an inextricable connection with the Bridegroom:

Set me as a seal upon your heart,
as a seal upon your arm; (Song of Songs 8:6ab).

In this love hymn, once in the entire text of the Song of Songs, falls the name of the God of Israel. Described is a divine love (Kręcidło, 2008, p. 47). „Love in some way shares in the very power of God, being by nature his life as God, who in the full sense of the word is the living" (Ravasi, 2005, p. 129). The Woman feels mature and ready for love, clearly protesting when the brothers don't want to see it. It is important in our study to see Her pride and sense of dignity. „Love in a special way enriches the woman first, liberating her sense of dignity, responsibility for peace" (Stachowiak, 1990, p. 463), Her self-consciousness:

I am a wall,
and my breasts are like towers.
I became in his eyes
as one who brings peace. (Song of Songs 8:10-11).

He also becomes clearly connected with the Bride, He repeats with conviction:

My vineyard is at my own disposal (Song of Songs 8:12a).

Surrounded by friends, who had not previously appeared in songs, He asked His beloved, to let Him hear Her voice. It uses the phrase from 2:14, already known to His Beloved, but She was then hidden in the rock clefts. The Woman also responds to Him, using the familiar expression of the second song. She says:

Swiftly, my lover,
be like a gazelle or a young stag
upon the mountains of spices. (Song of Songs 8:14).

What the friends can consider as a request to leave, for the spouses is already the language of their own agreement, and in this case an invitation to further relationship (Ravasi, 2005, p. 136). Her dynamics is endless.

Timeline

The following diagram illustrates the timeline (Figure 6).

Figure 6. Dynamics of the relationship between the Bridegroom and the Bride in songs 6

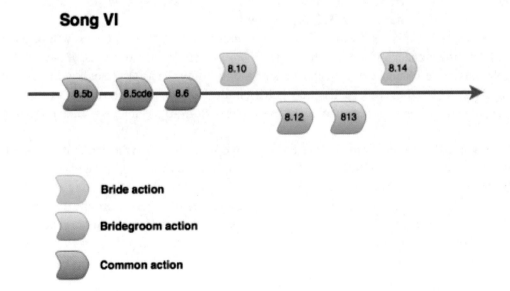

Commentary

In the last song the Bride and Bridegroom not only desire to be one but also become one. She appears supported and tucked into His arm, and in some way brings Him to life. The love hymn narrated by Her inscribes this relationship in the Divine economy of life. The Woman, by opening herself to love, has matured, and Her Beloved speaks of the inseparability of their relationship. The Spouses getting better understanding of eachother, they have their own language, and their relationship seems to have an infinite dimension, not only in the narrative field, though it's shrouded in the mystery of the continuation.

CONCLUSION

The visualization of subsequent songs, using a timeline, to determine the relationship between the Spouses makes it clear, that no words or actions of the character are unanswered. Their harmony and alternation makes an impression. It shows the bridegroom turned to each other, listening to the words and heart desires, and this gives the opportunity to deepen the relationship. As if in the rhythmic dance on Her steps were His steps. Although their dynamics in each song is unique. The relationship develops and the bridegrooms go beyond each other in order to build a more common space of both being and action.

The basic motive of common aspirations is the beauty of the people and the good that each represents. Love is therefore an important element of the personality of man, through which he can create an existential community of man and woman. (...). Human love not only comes from God, but also testifies of His love for man who participates in the creative plan of transmitting life. The description of love in the Song of Songs is open to the fullness of God's love (Potocki, 2007, p. 180).

Study doesn't address the issue of the literary genre Song of the Songs, because it's a genological problem. It doesn't appear from the study that the dramaturgical event shown would lead to a scenic interpretation of the form of the text, especially since the Judaic world did not know Hellenic theater. However, we see the narrative aspects of these songs (Stachowiak, 1990, pp. 457-459; Farmer, 2000, pp. 781-783; Hill, 1989; Landry, 1983; Murphy, 1990).

The overall view of this bond will be shown in Figures 6 and 7. As co-ordinates will be used on the horizontal axis the numbers of subsequent songs. In order to capture the progressive nature of changes in the relation on the vertical axis, the elements resulting from the narrative study will be introduced. For analysis are selected only those that are significant for the bride and bridegroom's actions.

Presented conclusions are specific observations that result from the analysis of the dendrogram:

- The nights of searching for the Beloved (song II and song IV) shape the depth of this relationship, allowing the Woman to self-aware of Her desire to be loved over everything else.
- During those nights that She experienced, the Beloved utters the delight songs (song III, IV) as if He added Her strength and determination, as they were together before the next experience of absence and search. These nights arouse in Women determination in expressing their love and allow the song of delight over the beauty and power of the Bridegroom (song IV), in response He confirms Her delight (song V).

Figure 7. The dynamics of the relationship on the Bridegroom side

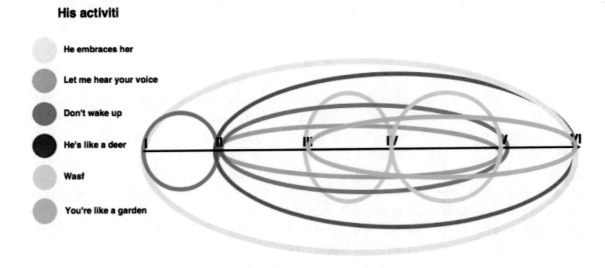

Figure 8. The dynamics of the relationship on the Bride side

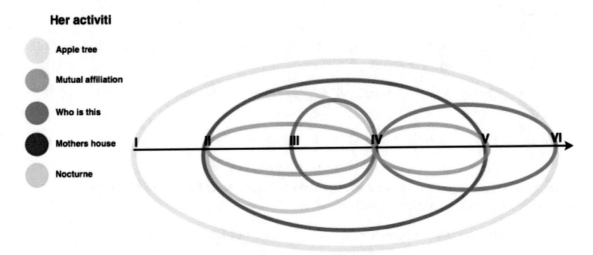

- In the same space of difficult searching, the Woman speaks of the formula of mutual belonging (song II, IV, V). This formula is pronounced in freedom, without the circumstances of cultural habits (I, II, V), then He also embraces Her (song I, V) as if this gesture strengthened the conviction of His love for the Bride.
- The deepening relationship between the Bridegrooms, also changes the look of the Bridegroom seen through the eyes of others. First, the attention is more focused on the litter in which She arrives, then She is admired by other women (song III, IV, VI).
- When a woman realizes the power of Her desire, She consistently strives to bring the Bridegroom to her mother's house (song II, V).

- When the night search begins (song II, IV), He wants to hear Her voice and see Her. Experienced difficulties build their common language – understandable only for them. (song II, VI).
- But above all, it is song about the bringing life through love (song I, VI). When She sits in His shade, under the apple tree, the whole dynamics of the event begins. She wakes up to Her full life, recognizes Her beauty, desires Her beloved. All this creates a new life.

The question arises: whether these observations don't emerge from linear analysis of the text? Part of it certainly yes, but the presentation of the dynamics of the relations between the Bridegrooms in the form of a graph, significantly facilitates their formulation in a designated aspect of the study. Therefore, the use of various technologies of visualization of knowledge doesn't contradict the analysis of the language text, it improves within the boundaries set by the research aspect.

A short theological commentary on the over-reading of the Song of Songs indicates how important it is for a man to crave God's care in life. The song of God shows how God accepts it, without restricting his freedom in any way, on the contrary, it gives birth to a new life. It seems that among the greatest darkness and search accompanies man and supports his presence, delight over his beauty. You also see how the person in this way is transformed and how this transformation is perceived by others.

REFERENCES

Balchin, J. A. (1970). The Song of Solomon. In The New Bible Commentary: Revised (3rd ed.; pp. 579-87). Grand Rapids, MI: Eerdmans.

Barbiero, G. (2011). *Song of Songs: A Close Reading*. Danvers, MA: Brill. doi:10.1163/ej.9789004203259.i-542

Bardski, K. (2010). Oblubienica. In *Encyklopedia Katolicka. t.14*. Lublin, Poland: Towarzystwo Naukowe KUL.

Bardski, K. (2011). *Lektyka Salomona. Biblia – Symbol – Interpretacja, Rozprawy Naukowe 6*. Warszawa, Poland: Wydawnictwo Archidiecezji Warszawskiej.

Brzegowy, T. (2007). *Pisma mądrościowe Starego Testamentu*. Tarnów, Poland: Biblos.

Falk, M. (1982). *Love Lyrics from the Bible: A Translation and Literary Study of the Song of Songs*. Sheffield, UK: The Almond Press.

Farmer, W. R. (Ed.). (2000). *Międzynarodowy komentarz do Pisma Świętego*. Warszawa, Poland: Vocatio.

Fox, M. V. (1985). *The Song of Songs and the Ancient Egyptian Love Songs*. Madison, WI: University of Wisconsin Press.

Hill, A. E. (1989). *The Song of Solomon. In The Evangelical Commentary on the Bible (pp. 452-66)*. Grand Rapids, MI: Baker Book House.

Keel, O. (1997). *Pieśń nad Pieśniami. Biblijna pieśń o miłości*. Poznań, Poland: Zyski i Spółka.

Kręcidło, J. (2008). Miłość – płomień Jahwe (Pnp 8,5-7): Potęga miłości jako klucz interpretacyjny do Pieśni nad pieśniami. *Collectanea Theologica, 78*(4), 39–62.

Landry, F. (1983). *Paradoxes of Paradise: Identity and Differences in the Song of Songs*. Sheffield, UK: The Almond Press.

Murphy, R. E. (1986). History of Exegesis as a Hermeneutical Tool, The Song of Songs. *Biblical Theology Bulletin, 16*(3), 87–91. doi:10.1177/014610798601600302

Murphy, R. E. (1990). *The Song of Songs. Hermeneia Commentary Series*. Philadelphia, PA: Fortress Press.

Murphy, R. E. (2001). Pieśń nad pieśniami. In R. E. Brown, J. A. Fitzmyer, & R. E. Murphy (Eds.), *Katolicki Komentarz Biblijny*. Warszawa, Poland: Vocatio.

Osińska, V. (2008). Wizualizacja i mapowanie przestrzeni danych w bibliotekach cyfrowych. *Toruńskie Studia Bibliologiczne, 1*, 167–176.

Osińska, V. (2016). *Wizualizacja informacji. Studium informatologiczne*. Toruń, Poland: Wydawnictwo Naukowe Uniwersytetu Mikołaja Kopernika.

Pope, M. H. (1977). *Song of Songs. In The Anchor Bible (vol. 7c)*. Garden City, NY: Doubleday & Sons, Inc.

Pope, M. H. (2008). *Song of Songs*. New Haven, CT: AYB.

Potocki, S. (2007). *Rady mądrości*. Lublin, Poland: Wydawnictwo KUL.

Ravasi, G. (2005). *Pieśń nad pieśniami…jak pieczęć na twoim sercu*. Kraków, Poland: Salwator.

Stachowiak, L. (Ed.). (1990). *Wstęp do Starego Testamentu*. Poznań, Poland: Pallotinum.

Walton, J. H., Matthews, V. H., & Chavalas, M. W. (2005). *Komentarz historyczno-kulturowy do Biblii Hebrajskiej*. Warszawa, Poland: Vocatio.

Chapter 6

Text Preprocessing:
A Tool of Information Visualization and Digital Humanities

Piotr Malak
University of Wroclaw, Poland

ABSTRACT

Digital humanities and information visualization rely on huge sets of digital data. Those data are mostly delivered in the text form. Although computational linguistics provides a lot of valuable tools for text processing, the initial phase (text preprocessing) is very involved and time-consuming. The problems arise due to a human factor – they are not always errors; there is also inconsistency in forms, affecting data quality. In this chapter, the author describes and discusses the main issues that arise during the preprocessing phase of textual data gathering for InfoVis. Chosen examples of InfoVis applications are presented. Except for problems with raw, original data, solutions are also referred. Canonical approaches used in text preprocessing and common issues affecting the process and ways to prevent them are also presented. The quality of data from different sources is also discussed. The content of this chapter is a result of a few years of practical experience in natural language processing gained during realization of different projects and evaluation campaigns.

INTRODUCTION

Big Data is a term used to describe a vast storage and source of data. Those data can be extremely valuable if properly gathered, compared and analyzed. Back, in the Machine Learning (ML) era, it was obvious to use charts in order to approximate to human analytical perspective and abilities any huge data set, presented originally in tables. Visualizing data allows us to easily detect and track changes and trends hidden in data sets, which are too extensive to analyze them only on the basis of raw data. Pie-, bar- and many other charts, are still useful tools for presenting and analyzing data. They are permanently used for analyzing huge amounts of structured data. Such data have clearly and strictly defined categories with clear, strong borders between types and distinct meaning. Typically, in the case of structured data, those categories are presented as columns or rows headers in data tables.

DOI: 10.4018/978-1-5225-4990-1.ch006

Information visualization (InfoVis), however, deals not only with data of clear, properly defined structure. This analytic and reasoning tool is also, if not mainly, used for data of latent structure or of a structure without strictly defined categories. One can find it useful in market analyzes, flow control or processes simulations. There is, of course, much more possibilities of applying InfoVis to analyzing real life processes. The ideas of use are limited by our imagination only.

One should be aware that Information visualization is so powerful tool, for it is a final step of automatic data analysis processes, called Machine Learning. InfoVis approximates, scales and presents in a comprehend manner results of ML data processing. Machine learning approach can help us to find and analyze any distinct and reliable relations, whether they are obvious or hidden, between data stored in different forms, not necessary in tables. As such, ML, can be and is successfully used also in Digital Humanities.

Any of those comprehend, very informative and nice looking graphical data or information presentation starts from raw data. Data which can, but not necessary are, cleared, unambiguous, and structured. The very preliminary step towards reliable graphical data, information, relations or trends presentation is text preprocessing. For properly prepared textual data we can apply ML approach and finally Information Visualization.

The goal of this chapter is to present preprocessing techniques and their role in modern and novel technique which is Information Visualization. We will discuss canonical approaches used in text preprocessing, common issues affecting the process and ways to prevent them. As substantial part of data can be, and already is, gathered from Web resources author presents chosen channels of gathering date for Digital Humanities (DH) purposes. The quality of data from different sources is also discussed. The content of this chapter is a result of few years of practical experience in Natural Language Processing (NLP) gained during realization of different projects and evaluation campaigns.

BACKGROUND

Big Data components and sources, such as data bases, Web- and Web2.0 sites, social media etc. are ever-growing sources of digital data. Despite of improving data transferring speed over the Internet, which make it possible to present in real time sounds, pictures and video, textual data are still the most popular in scale of document types. And text documents themselves are still the richest source of data to analyze and visualize.

From the human comprehension perspective the reception of text is a complex system, that employs not only reading abilities but also other cognitive predispositions. We, the humans, do always comprehend text in the context, which is defined by our education, knowledge and experience. Thus we can clearly detect and understand metaphors, and social-, political- and any other context and relations included non-explicitly in the text. Thanks to the ability of reading the latent information, so called "reading between the lines", a raw text itself can be very informative for us, while, in contrast, not for computer systems.

There are, of course, similarities in perception of texts by humans and by computers, but in the very core of the process there are substantial differences. Computational text analysis are surface processes, this is recognizing of graphical representations of sounds and words. In order to adjust any meaning to recognized signs and their sequences computer needs a background guidance information. In order to make computational text processes useful and reliable we, humans, need to provide for computers additional data, relations descriptions, meaning linkage, disambiguation rules, computational routines, etc.

Such support, in the form of multiple relations between words of natural language, delivers e.g. WordNet[1] and its national clones, like one of the best developed - Polish WordNet - Słowosieć[2], developed and maintained by (CLARIN-PL). There are also tools composed of text corpora which annotate syntactic or semantic sentence structure, called treebanks, e.g. Penn (Treebank) allowing, among the others, to adjust meaning to words or at least to determine polarization of opinions given by specific sequence of words. There are many, many other tools available for processing and analyzing data from texts. But the clue is the knowledge of language we gain, poses and use in a natural manner, computers need to have delivered directly and strictly together with set of rules how to apply and use that knowledge. From this point of view Machine Learning and further Information Visualization are not cognitive processes, these are rather reasoning and presenting on the basis of frequency and distribution of recognizable patterns instead of meaning.

Only with background support of NLP, as described in preceding lines, computer systems are able to detect and visualize for example a scientific communication between XVII/XVIII centuries philosophers and scientists, called *The Republic of Letters*. Stanford University project *Mapping The Republic of Letters* (Mapping) is one of the greatest examples of applying Digital Humanities and Information Visualization techniques in order to present global, at its times, scientific cooperation and ideas dissemination. An example of the project output is geographical visualization of Voltaire's correspondence presented in Figure 1. On current political map of Europe we can track sending and destination places of individual letters as. Thickness of connecting lines represents the intensity of mutual correspondence. However, different settings of start and end years of such communication shows there is in average only 10% of available correspondence processed and plotted. This observation is confirmed by time-chart displayed below the mapping as well as information site (Voltaire). On Figure 1 there is time-chart visualizing numbers of letters for each year from a given period, with additional division into plottable and not plottable ones.

Another worth mentioning DH project, which also applies Information Visualization, is *The Venice Time Machine*, launched by EPFL and the University Ca'Foscari of Venice. The project is an attempt to digitize over a thousand years of historical Venetian records and make them searchable. It aims to create a multidimensional model of Venice - Republic and city - and its evolution covering a period of ten centuries (Venice). Visualizations cover spatial development of Venice, political and economic relations between influential families, etc. There are also other mapping projects, like *Nobel journeys in chemistry: Mapping the lives of laureates* provided by Chemical & Engineering News (Nobel). Here we can see geographical locators and display biographical notes of Nobel Prize winners in the field of chemistry. The categorization of visualized data can be done by born place, place of affiliation in time of winning the Nobel Prize and place of passing away. Data for this visualization are relatively not challenging, as they are facts of constant categories, like: year, birth date, living place, main scientific journey, etc. The main challenge here is gathering the data. An example of the visualization, with focus on Europe is presented in Figure 3.

A little bit more challenged is project of mapping metaphor (Mapping Metaphor). Project visualizes *all of knowledge in English: every word in every sense in the English language for over a millennium.* Such representation of meaning requires high level of human supervision, exampling InfoVIs is not a fully automated process but it requires human supervision. Example visualization of metaphorical relations between terms categories is presented in Figure 4.

Mentioned above projects are referred to only as the prominent examples of possibilities of using Information Visualization. There are thousands of other information or data visualization projects running each year. Either scientific or media and business related, like data journalism. Selected projects are

Figure 1. Mapping the Republic of Letters and Voltaire correspondence
Source: (ink.designhumanities, n.d.)

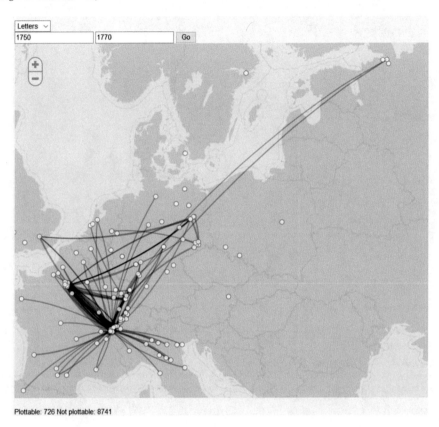

Figure 2. Timechart with indication of the fraction of plotable letters for each year from a given period
Source: (ink.designhumanities, n.d.)

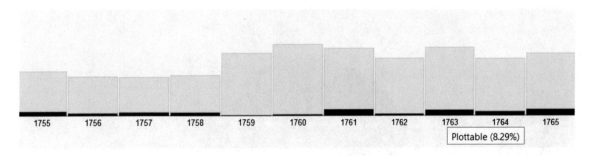

available for example at (Flowingdata). Information on different Digital Humanities projects, including Information Visualization, with public voting on the project is available at *Digital Humanities Awards* (DH Awards). InfoVis approach caused also developing of appropriate tools, either open and proprietary ones. There are, for example, data manipulation and presentation (including visualizations) libraries available, like two almost the most famous D3.js[3] – a set of a JavaScript library for manipulating documents based on data (D3.js) or vis.js[4] - a dynamic, browser based visualization library (vis.js). There

Figure 3. An example of visualizing of Nobel journeys in chemistry, according to Born places
Source: (Davenport, 2016)

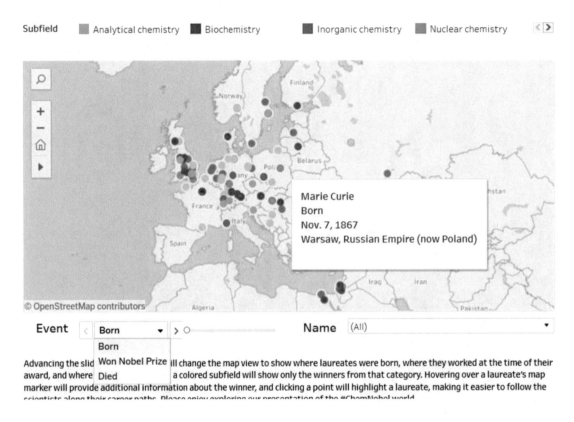

Advancing the slid[...]ill change the map view to show where laureates were born, where they worked at the time of their award, and where [...] a colored subfield will show only the winners from that category. Hovering over a laureate's map marker will provide additional information about the winner, and clicking a point will highlight a laureate, making it easier to follow the scientists along their career paths. Please enjoy exploring our presentation of the #ChemNobel world.

Figure 4. Visualization of metaphorical relations for group of concepts concerning people
Source: (Mapping Mataphor, n.d.)

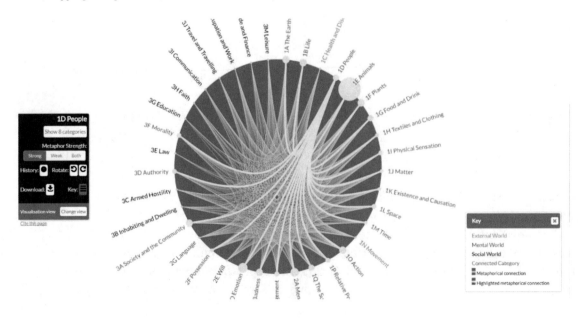

are also Information Visualization platforms, like Gephi – the Open Graph Viz Platform (Gephi). And again – all the tools process, compare, classify and visualize text data which are expected to be properly preprocessed in order to make any reasonable and reliable visualizations on them.[5]

Very comprehensive view into text processing and analysis process one may get using voyant-tools service - a web-based reading and analysis environment for digital texts. (Voyant-tools). Figure 5 presents results of an analysis of an example text, here part of current chapter, from *Grammatical normalization* subsection, a paragraph starting with *Each of the two approaches...* The analysis of a text provides information on frequencies of terms (in original form), distribution of term as line chart, statistical details of the text, like vocabulary density, average number of words per sentence and most frequent words. It is worth to underline the flexibility of the tool. Each separate window, displaying chosen analyses, can be detached from the main window as well as replaced by other tool. Available tools operate on corpus and document levels. For educational value Voyant-tool is a very good choice for introduction tool to digital humanities.

As mentioned earlier in this chapter, most of visualizations rely on textual data, which are originally unstructured and unclassified. In order to extract valuable information from texts we need to process text documents, recognize distinct units on different levels of language structure, compare data and finally present them. Here we describe phases of text preprocessing.

Phases of Computational Text Processing

1. Text preprocessing,
2. Disambiguation,
3. Tagging, including part-of-speech tagging (pos tagging),

Figure 5. An example of initial analyses of text
Source: (Voyant-tools, 2017)

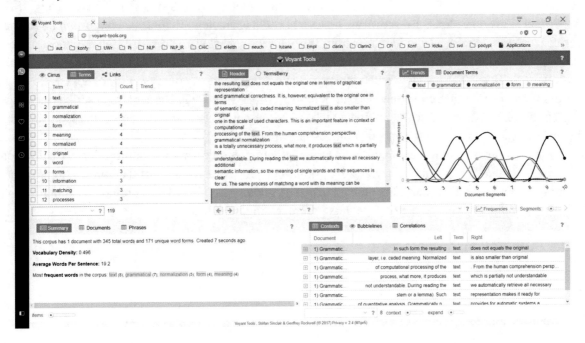

4.   Classification or categorization.

Preparing text in order to make proper visualizations is a task for text preprocessing assignment. Author's experience shows that the stage of preprocessing takes 60% up to even 90% of the whole Information Visualization process. Such work overload is due to the human factor – each set of analyzed data consists of units prepared by different humans. Despite of using similar standards, the output data sources are mostly quite different from others in terms of inner data sets organization, thus they require typically individual, personalized preprocessing stage.

Any of the other listed here phases of computational text processing does also need many work and is very challenging. They need constant development, but their results are universal. One set of disambiguation we can use for many different text sources. POS tagging works well for any proper texts in a given language as well as automatic text classification. TC is similarly efficient and effective for texts in given language, under condition we provide enough data. As such, Text Classification (TC) bases, in general, on words frequencies, words order and/or words types in documents. Thus, to a great extent, one can say the TC is language independent. One of widely used open text classification systems WEKA developed by The University of Waikato (Hall at all, 2009; Frank, Hall & Witten, 2016) is able to classify texts in different languages with similar efficiency and accuracy. Concluding one may say, any of further phases of computational texts processing is of multiple use and of multiple applications. Only text preprocessing phase is individual each time we work with a new data set. However, such substantial phase of any text processing related project, is disproportionally unrepresented in the literature. There are, of course, some exceptions.

David Palmer (2010) provides extended and comprehensive introduction to text preprocessing. Author defines text preprocessing as a task of converting raw text file(s) into a well-defined sequence of units which have linguistic meaning. Those units are e.g.: characters representing individual graphemes of a language written system, distinct words or sentences. Palmer describes also character encoding issues, discussing in detail the character-set dependencies. He presents evolution of the encoding standards starting from 7-bit ASCII, which covered 128 (2^7) characters, through 8-bit, 256 (2^8) characters, ISO-8859 (and Win-…) up to UTF-8, covering up to 1,111,998 characters. He notes an important issue, that influences automatic encoding identification. It is caused by backward compatibility, i.e. most of new introduced encoding standards preserved capability of mapping of the first 128 characters compatible with the ASCII set. The problem noted by Palmer appears when text consists only of those 128 ASCII covered characters, which can be encoded either as ASCII, ISO- or UTF. Palmer also describes language detection, tokenization and segmentation which are important in Natural Language Processing as such, but are of limited influence for Information Visualization.

Except of raw text preprocessing one may apply data preprocessing for Information Visualization purposes. García, Luengo and Herrera (2015) describes process and stages of data processing for data mining purposes. Authors state data preparation as mandatory step in order to provide meaningful data for data mining. They provide phases of data preprocessing, which are as follow:

Data Preparation Phases

1.   Cleaning,
2.   Transformation,
3.   Integration,

4. Normalization,
5. Missing Data Imputation,
6. Noise Identification.

It is worth to mention that authors of presented book exclude data preparation phase from overall data preprocessing, as substantial part of providing meaningful data for ML processes. Data cleaning consists of correcting bad data, filtering incorrect data and reducing details of data to reasonable level. During transformation data are consolidated, discretized and generalized. Integration, further, deals with merging data from multiple sources, while data normalization is attaching appropriate attributes (features) to data and scaling the weights of the attributes, which is especially useful in statistical ML methods. Missing data cause ambiguity of research data. Data imputation stands, in general, for methods of providing substitute values for missing data on the basis of statistics, for example. The last phase, noise identification allows researcher to detect any noise among data in order to omit them in analysis.

MAIN FOCUS OF THE CHAPTER

In present chapter author will describe chosen techniques of text data preprocessing in order to provide useful sets of data for TC and for Information Visualization. Discussed subjects will be delivered with sample codes of Python scripts.

Python ("Python Programming Language," 2017) is an interpreted, scripting language very popular in many web applications, including Natural Language Processing, Text Classification and Information Visualization. A Python application itself consists of one or a few scripts which source code needs to be executed by appropriate interpreting environment. Though scripting languages are more resource-consuming than compiled languages, the scripts are more universal than compiled executables. They can run in different operating systems mostly without any additional adjustments. A lot of Pythons libraries are precompiled in C, a very efficient compiled language, which guaranties they are very fast in execution. As a fork called Django, Python serves among others Google, YouTube and many different web services. In Bird et al. (2009) authors claim Python characterize clear syntax and using chain-type variables. One of pointed advantages of Python is it's object programming orientation.

Decoding

Palmer raised an importance of automatic charset detection. In practice charset of the text in a file is often given in a file heading. Theoretically trivial operation of matching the coding description is not so easy to perform. One must keep in mind many different file types and ways of providing the charset identification. Even using XML a few possibilities of providing coding information are expected, thus automatic detection of encoding used in a file appears not a trivial operation.

However very useful and with great support of libraries, Python 2.7+ offers a handicap – decoding. By default all texts are expected to be ASCII encoded and any other decoding needs proper encoding, as well as proper decoding of output text files. Python3 works by default with UTF-8 encoding, while still is outperformed by 2.7 in terms of available libraries and forks.

Gathering data from the Internet one may encounter almost all text encoding standards. In author's experience with digital libraries and scientific repositories three encoding standards were available:

ISO-8859, UTF-8 and UTF-16. In order to make Python2.7 script flexible in terms of recognized encoding, the *try-except* statement were used, as shown in listing below this paragraph. Due to the archiving function of the Internet there are still available files coded using standards that are still valid ones, but not the most current. Thus during automatic corpus building one can meet some files using ASCII coding, quite a lot of ISO-88.. (or Win-..) and similar number or more files with UTF-8 or even UTF-16.

with open(afile) as data:
try:
doc = data.read().decode('utf-16')
except:
doc = data.read().decode('utf-8')

In the code above a file is open with *open()* function, then the content of the file is confronted with UTF-16 decoding, in case it fails another attempt of decoding, this time with UTF-8 standard is done. Using *try.. except...* allows to avoid application exit in case of inappropriate encoding used in a file. The statement is of wider usage, of course.[6] Once properly recognized, thus reed, content of text files can be further preprocessed, i.e. confronted with other kinds of issues.

Meta Descriptions

Another frequent issue in web files preprocessing is a difference in XML tags names and comments tags in the role of section limiters. Here are examples of different content start tags from stylometric analyze of about 300 web blogs:

- * *
- *<!-- .entry-header -->*
- *<!-- more -->*
- * *
- * *
- * *
- * *
- * *
- * *

Such differentiation requires additional procedures for detecting chosen parts of blog content, which is additional work for application developers.

Grammatical Normalization

A grammatical normalization term stands for transforming inflected words into canonical forms. This can be either a basic grammatical form or a stem (or a root) representing the whole set of possible, correct grammatical forms of the word. Those forms of one word, being subject of inflection or conjugation, are called *a synset*. Grammatical normalization stands for matching and replacing any item from one synset by its representative. In case of replacing for grammatically correct word, a basic form, we use lemmatization, in case of replacing with stem or root we use stemming.

Each of the two approaches reduces original texts into normalized form. In such form the resulting text does not equals the original one in terms of graphical representation and grammatical correctness. It is, however, equivalent to the original one in terms of semantic layer, i.e. ceded meaning. Normalized text is also smaller than original one in the scale of used characters. This is an important feature in context of computational processing of the text. From the human comprehension perspective grammatical normalization is a totally unnecessary process, what more, it produces text which is partially not understandable. During reading the text we automatically retrieve all necessary additional semantic information, so the meaning of single words and their sequences is clear for us. The same process of matching a word with its meaning can be performed by computer systems, but is an order of magnitude slower than human cognitive processes. The execution time is the reason we perform stemming or lemmatization as one of the initial phases of NLP processes. After such normalization computers work on reduced texts, where each different meaning is represented by an universal unit (whether a stem or a lemma). Such text representation makes it ready for Information Retrieval seeking and matching processes or classifying on the basis of quantitative analysis. Grammatically normalized text provides for automatic systems a valuable information on the meanings, not only on the graphical representations of concepts. Normalized representation of text is also suitable for features selection, which will be discussed later in the chapter.

Lemmatization

The approach of replacing inflected words with their base forms is called lemmatization. During lemmatization we seek to extract a morphological base form of a word, which represents the whole synset. The basic grammatical form of the word is called a lemma, thus the name of the process. For English verb *to be* the basic form covers all possible forms: *am, are, is, was, were, been, being.*

English, as a language of relatively simple and easy grammar is not very challenging for grammatical normalization. The problem rises for flexional languages of complex grammar, like, for example Polish. In called example of the verb *to be,* there exist following, grammatical correct, forms (here given in an alphabetical order).

a lemma: *być*
forms:

być, bądź, bądźcie, bądźcież, bądźmy, bądźmyż, bądźże, będą, będąc, będąca, będącą, będące, będącego, będącej, będącemu, będący, będących, będącym, będącymi, będę, będzie, będziecie, będziemy, będziesz, bycia, byciach, byciami, bycie, byciem, byciom, byciu, byli, byliby, bylibyście, bylibyśmy, byliście, byliśmy, był, była, byłaby, byłabym, byłabyś, byłam, byłaś, byłby, byłbym, byłbyś, byłem, byłeś, było, byłoby, byłobym, byłobyś, byłom, byłoś, były, byłyby, byłybyście, byłybyśmy, byłyście, byłyśmy, byto, jest, jestem, jesteś, jesteście, jesteśmy, niebędąca, niebędącą, niebędące, niebędącego, niebędącej, niebędącemu, niebędący, niebędących, niebędącym, niebędącymi, niebycia, niebyciach, niebyciami, niebycie, niebyciem, niebyciom, niebyciu, niebyć, są (Słownik SJP – a digital dictionary of Polish).

One can also call the example of a noun, like, *a man* (*człowiek* in Polish) (Słownik SJP, n.d.):

człowiek, człowiecze, człowieka, człowiekiem, człowiekowi, człowieku, ludzi, ludziach, ludzie, ludziom, ludźmi

The above examples approximate the complexity and challenge level of grammatical normalization for words in flexional languages. One can distinguish two main approaches of lemmatization: algorithmic and dictionary based. There is, of course, a hybrid approach too, which connects the preceding two approaches. In general dictionary based approach relays on provided full synsets dictionary in order to match the basic form of a word. The advantage of such solution is high level of control over the process, thus high quality of basic forms extraction. It is also easy to provide a dictionary, as there are a lot of linguistic resources for different languages available online. Disadvantage of dictionary based approach is a gap for words not included into a dictionary. Dictionaries require constant updates, but still do not secure a 100% coverage of a language vocabulary. It is also a time consuming process. Coding appropriate matching and replacing procedures may also appear to be a challenging task for flexional languages, due to many similar or equal forms of different words. Algorithmic approaches are more flexible. Using set of rules of pattern matching, words and sysnets recognition they attempt to extract a proper lemma for a given word. The transformation rules base also on a kind of dictionary. The dictionary, however, is not an explicit list of the vocabulary but rather the set of rules that transform a word into its basic form or can expand a basic form into grammatically correct inflected forms. Algorithmic approach is more efficient in case of unknown words, i.e. words that are not included in the dictionary.

Stemming

A process of extracting a stem (or a root) out of the word is called *stemming*. In reverse to lemmatization, stemming does not provide grammatically correct words, however it may happen the stem equals the lemma. In general stemming deals with suffixes, which are reduced. Stems serve the same function as lemmas – represent the whole set of all possible, and grammatically correct, forms of the word. An example of output, stemmed text provides (Manning, Raghavan & Schütze, 2008) in Stemming and lemmatization subsection.

Stemmers are much faster in performing normalization tasks than lemmatizers, thus are one of the basic tools used in Information Retrieval. IR needs are specific, in comparison to other NLP activities. The main goal is to immediately match all documents that are relevant to a user query. Hence stemming, due to its working speed and reasonably good accuracy of normalization is appropriate technique for IR. In Kühni (2013) author describes comparison of efficiency between an algorithmic stemmer and a dictionary-based lemmatizer for German. Normalization over a test corpus took 9 milliseconds for stemming and about 23 seconds for lemmatizing. (Kühni, 2013) observed about 90% of stemming time for one word is consumed by seeking the word index, which means applying reduction rules is almost immediate process. In general similar disproportion of execution time between stemming and lemmatization may be observed for most languages. Additional speed advantage for stem extraction may be achieved by use of the *light stemming,* i.e. deriving stems only for nouns or for nouns and adjectives. (Savoy, 2006) proves the efficiency and accuracy of light stemming for French, Portuguese, German and Hungarian languages. This approach was also tested and validated for Polish (Malak, 2013). Despite of substantial outperformance of stemming it is not commonly used in other NLP fields, especially in Text Classification, and further in Information Visualization.

Similarities

For TC purposes the execution time of normalization is not the most important factor while the accuracy of meaning representation is more important. TC and InfoVis operate on classes of data or information in order to make general conclusions on the basis of available data. And, again, any reasoning and similar data, concepts or information gathering in order to provide graphic visualization, needs prior classification or clustering of analyzed units. These two terms stand for automatic grouping of chosen units on the basis of sharing similar feature or features. The features can be various and of different message levels. Classification attempts to adjust units to one of predefined class, where conditions of class membership are already given. Clustering, in reverse, attempts to detect distinct differences in features set and group units according to detected conditions of differentiation. In case of text data sources the features taken under consideration may be pure frequencies or semantic features. The latter are recognized and defined during process called Part-of-Speech tagging.

Figure 6 presents visualization of clustering of XIX century Polish novels according to Ward's hierarchical cluster analysis algorithm (Murtagh & Legendre, 2011). On current example the similarity of documents was established for grammatical features, like: grammatical 3-grams and bigrams (e.g. adv_adj_interp = adverbs + adjectives + punctuation signs). The whole process was conducted using NLP services developed by CLARIN-PL (CLARIN, 2015). After individual preprocessing phase all the texts were send to WCRFT2 service for POS tagging (Przepiórkowski, 2011), then Fextor and Featfil services were used in order to prepare features – document matrix. Once having comparison matrix one can make similarity measuring according to chosen method. Ward's hierarchical clustering is claimed as one of very effective. In order to allow evaluation of similarity measurement there are caption for each meeting point, indicating evaluated similarity of objects. For the last level documents are compared objects, while for any other higher level of hierarchy there are documents groups compared.

Part-of-Speech Tagging

POS tagging is a process of enriching a textual layer of a document with semantic information. All words are adjusted to appropriate grammatical class. In advanced systems POS is executed in connection to lemmatizing – once recognized semantic feature is used to derivate a correct lemma (or all possible lemmas in case of ambiguous entry). Properly tagged part of the speech is suitable base for further processing. There is a lot of POS taggers available either open or proprietary. Figure 7 gives an example output with graphical visualization of detected parts of speech. Each grammatical entity is represented by different colour.

One example can be WCRFT2 (Radziszewski & Warzocha, 2014; WCRFT2) available as service of CLARIN-PL. It is a morphosyntactic tagger for Polish, which joins Conditional Random Fields (CRF) and tiered tagging of plain text. The service itself is available at (Tager), the webpage provides also English version available at (TagerEn). The examples of work of both tagger versions are presented in following lines.

For the original Polish texts (CLARIN-PL):

Programy udostępniane w ramach sieci CLARIN pozwalają wykorzystać opracowane już zbiory archiwów cyfrowych i korpusów. W obrębie CLARIN tworzymy także, przechowujemy i udostępniamy nowe

Figure 6. Example of clustering XIX century novels
Source: (CLARIN-PL, n.d.)

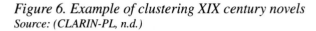
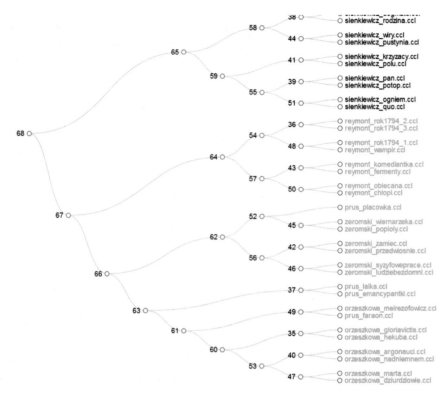

Figure 7. An example of POS for English text
Source: (Parts-of-speech.info, n.d.)

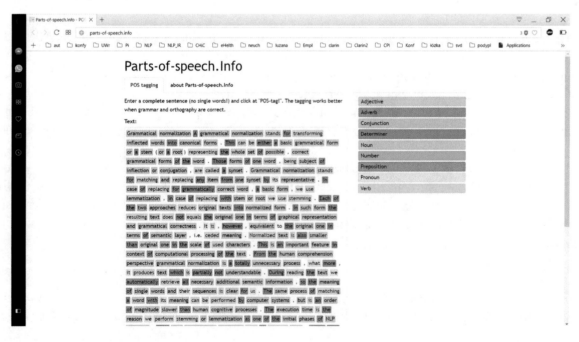

zasoby. Możliwa jest również praca na „surowych" tekstach publikowanych w Internecie, w postaci informacji prasowych, artykułów, blogów, dokumentów itp. W przyszłości powstaną narzędzia do analizy zarejestrowanej mowy (wideoblogów, transmisji czy audycji).

in English:

The CLARIN network provides software which enables the use of the previously developed digital archives and corpora, and new resources are created, stored and shared. It is also possible to work on raw text published on the Internet in such forms as press releases, articles, blogs and other documents. Future plans include the construction of tools for the analysis of recorded speech in broadcasts, video blogs and so on.

we receive following tagged XML output:

```xml
<?xml version="1.0" encoding="UTF-8"?>
<!DOCTYPE chunkList SYSTEM "ccl.dtd">
<chunkList>
 <chunk id="ch1" type="p">
  <sentence id="s1">
   <tok>
    <orth>Programy</orth>
    <lex disamb="1"><base>program</base><ctag>subst:pl:nom:m3</ctag></lex>
   </tok>
   <tok>
    <orth>udostępniane</orth>
    <lex disamb="1"><base>udostępniać</base><ctag>ppas:sg:nom:n:imperf:aff</ctag></lex>
   </tok>
   <tok>
    <orth>w</orth>
    <lex disamb="1"><base>w</base><ctag>prep:acc:nwok</ctag></lex>
   </tok>
   <tok>
    <orth>ramach</orth>
    <lex disamb="1"><base>rama</base><ctag>subst:pl:loc:f</ctag></lex>
   </tok>
   <tok>
    <orth>sieci</orth>
    <lex disamb="1"><base>sieć</base><ctag>subst:sg:gen:f</ctag></lex>
   </tok>
   <tok>
    <orth>CLARIN</orth>
    <lex disamb="1"><base>CLARIN</base><ctag>ign</ctag></lex>
```

```
     </tok>
....
```

Equivalent English text POS tagged gives following output, which is noticeably easier than for Polish, as English is a language of relatively simple grammar:

```
<?xml version="1.0" encoding="UTF-8"?>
<!DOCTYPE chunkList SYSTEM "ccl.dtd">
<chunkList>
 <chunk>
  <sentence>
   <tok>
    <orth>The</orth>
    <lex disamb="1"><base>the</base><ctag>DET</ctag></lex>
   </tok>
   <tok>
    <orth>CLARIN</orth>
    <lex disamb="1"><base>clarin</base><ctag>PROPN</ctag></lex>
   </tok>
   <tok>
    <orth>network</orth>
    <lex disamb="1"><base>network</base><ctag>NOUN</ctag></lex>
   </tok>

...
```

As we can see in the above example, WCRFT2 provides not only POS tagging, there are other preliminary text preprocessing operations, which are performed in the background of tagging process. These operations are segmentation and delivering lemmas, base grammatical forms of words. Each individual token is tagged by <tok> </tok> marks and include a word in original form bracketed by <orth> </orth> tags. The orthographic form is then followed by lexical characteristic, consisting of a base form in <base> </base> marks and grammatical indicators marks in <ctag> </ctag> tags. The output file is information rich source of further preprocessing steps, like lemmatizing or feature extraction. Extensive introduction into CLARIN-PL services, infrastructure, work-flow and algorithms is described by Walkowiak (2016).

Feature Extraction

Extracting features which are not explicitly available in text files e.g. grammatical signatures of words (membership of certain grammatical class) can be performed on the basis of grammatical information provided in POS tagging process. Different features, describing texts on different levels of abstraction, are the base for further classification operations. Distinction between classes of vocabulary may be performed on the base of frequential characteristics of a raw text, i.e. number of occurrences of individual words. This, easy and straightforward, approach can be used for example for detecting of characteristic vocabulary, i.e. words which quite frequently appear in texts of one subject, while are rare of absent in other texts. However pure frequencies may be not distinctive enough for classification purposes. Then features and their distribution are analyzed. Example features of grammatical layer of text can be nouns or any other grammatical class and their combinations (called bigrams for pairs, trigrams for triplets and generally n-grams for n-classes). Staying within described already NLP web services of CLARIN-PL one can call Fextor as a service for feature extraction. As Piasecki (2017) writes:

Fextor is a tool for extracting features from the collections of texts. It is characterized by high flexibility, while maintaining the performance and simplicity.

Features are extracted from text snippets, defined according to the type of pointer (token, annotation or pair annotations). This allows the simultaneous generation of multiple features for a single document. Fextor creates a vector representing a document, on the basis of chosen features (FextorEn, 2017). As an input file the services accepts a CCL format file, derived from XCES (CCL, 2017), and output is a vector of chosen features, describing individual text. Example result presents following listing:

3-gram_count:inf_adv_interp;3-gram_count:praet_adv_ppas;3-gram_count:adv_adj_interp;3-gram_count:ppas_fin_subst; ....

3;2;13;2; ....

where the first line are features or their combinations and second line are values derived from features frequencies. Features vectors can be used for further classification or clustering of documents.

CONCLUSION

Preparing text documents in order to make them valuable source for information classification and visualization is not a trivial task. First of all, especially when dealing with languages other than English, one should consider detecting used encoding standards. Writing own application for preprocessing a developer should provide solutions to decode if not all possible, then at least all the most popular encoding standards. We do also need to carefully detect the internal structure of processed files, like for example XML tags used for distinguish different parts of the files. During tags identification it is wise to pay attention they may be not appropriate XML tags but user tags (as in case of blogs contents starting part, described in this chapter). Each tag, important for traversing file structure, should be explicitly defined in processing application. One may not assume all the files from one data source are delivered with preserving the same internal structure and tags. If we collect data from long period of time, we need to be aware there could occur few format changes and try to detect them. The differences can be small, but of vital influence on preprocessing quality.

During the whole preprocessing phase, we need to analyze a lot of latent information and provide algorithms for normalizing all gathered texts to common write form. For languages of relatively easy flexion, like English, stemming is good choice, while for those of complex flexion, like e.g. Polish, lemmatization give better results of normalization. However, due to higher grammatical correctness of lemmatization it is also advised to lemmatize texts in English-like languages too. Stemming is much faster than lemmatization, thus is perfect for Information Retrieval applications, and everywhere where response time is a vital factor. Information Visualization typically is not a real-time process. We accept the price of time for data processing, classification and comparison, thus the use of lemmatization is wise choice here.

All the tasks described in current chapter are preprocessing tasks. The better preprocessed text is, the better, more reliable and less affordable results we get.

ACKNOWLEDGMENT

This research was supported by Polish National Science Center (NCN) under grant 2013/11/B/HS2/03048 "Digital knowledge structure and dynamics analyzing by means of information visualisation".

REFERENCES

D3.js: Data-Driven Documents. (2017). Retrieved October 20, 2017 from https://d3js.org

Bird, S., Klein, E., & Loper, E. (2009). *Natural language processing with Python. Analyzing text with the Natural Language Toolkit.* Pekin.

Cambridge University Press. (2008). *Stemming and Lemmatization.* Retrieved from https://nlp.stanford.edu/IR-book/html/htmledition/stemming-and-lemmatization-1.html

CCL. (2013). Retrieved August 25, 2017, from http://nlp.pwr.wroc.pl/redmine/projects/corpus2/wiki/CCL_format

CLARIN-PL. (2015). Retrieved August 25, 2017, from http://clarin-pl.eu/pl/strona-glowna/

CLARIN-PL. (n.d.) Retrieved from http://ws.clarin-pl.eu/websty.shtml

Davenport, M. (2016, September). Nobel journeys in chemistry: Mapping the lives of laureates. *Chemical and Engineering News, 94*(37), 24–25. Retrieved from https://cen.acs.org/articles/94/i37/Nobel-journeys-chemistry-Mapping-lives.html

DH Awards: Digital Humanities Awards. (n.d.). Retrieved October 19, 2017 from http://dhawards.org

Digital Humanities Awards. (n.d.). Retrieved August 25, 2017, from http://dhawards.org

FextorEn. (2013). Retrieved August 25, 2017, from http://nlp.pwr.wroc.pl/redmine/projects/nlprest2/wiki/Fextor2_en

Flowingdata. (2017). Retrieved October 19, 2017 from http://flowingdata.com

Frank, E., Hall, M. A., & Witten, I. H. (2016). *The WEKA Workbench. Online Appendix for "Data Mining: Practical Machine Learning Tools and Techniques"*. Morgan Kaufmann. Retrieved October 19, 2017, from https://www.cs.waikato.ac.nz/ml/weka/Witten_et_al_2016_appendix.pdf

García, S., Luengo, J., & Herrera, F. (2015). *Data preprocessing in data mining*. New York: Springer. doi:10.1007/978-3-319-10247-4

Gephi. The Open Graph Viz Platform. (2017). Retrieved October 21, 2017 from https://gephi.org

Hall. (2009). The WEKA Data Mining Software: An Update. *SIGKDD Explorations, 11*(1). Retrieved October 19, 2017, from http://www.kdd.org/exploration_files/p2V11n1.pdf

Ink.designhumanities. (n.d.). Retrieved from http://ink.designhumanities.org/voltaire/

Junho, S. (in press). Roadmap for e-commerce standardization in Korea. *International Journal of IT Standards and Standardization Research*.

Kühni, J. A. (2013). *Stemming and Lemmatizing for Natural Language Processing* (Unpublished master report). University of Neuchatel.

Malak, P. (2013) *The Polish Task within Cultural Heritage in CLEF (CHiC) 2013. In CLEF 2013 Evaluation Labs and Workshop Working Notes*. Retrieved August 25, 2017, from http://www.clef-initiative.eu/documents/71612/b00f7561-fadb-47a8-ab67-74f116ce062a

Manning, C. D., Raghavan, P., & Schütze, H. (2008). *Introduction to information retrieval*. Cambridge University Press. Retrieved October 21, 2017 from: https://nlp.stanford.edu/IR-book/html/htmledition/irbook.html

Mapping Metaphor. (n.d.). Retrieved August 25, 2017, from http://mappingmetaphor.arts.gla.ac.uk

Mapping the Republic of Letters. (2013). Retrieved June 15, 2017, from http://republicofletters.stanford.edu/index.html

Murtagh, F., & Legendre, P. (2011). *Ward's hierarchical clustering method: clustering criterion and agglomerative algorithm*. Retrieved October 21, 2017 from https://arxiv.org/pdf/1111.6285v2

Palmer, D. D. (2010). Text Preprocessing. In N. Indurkhya & F. J. Damerau (Eds.), Handbook of Natural Language Processing (pp. 9-30). Chapman & Hall/CRC.

Parts-of-speech.info. (n.d.). Retrieved from http://parts-of-speech.info/

Piasecki, M. (n.d.). *Fextor*. Retrieved August 25, 2017, from https://clarin-pl.eu/dspace/handle/11321/12

Przepiórkowski, A. (2011). *NKJP Tagset*. Retrieved October 23, 2017 from http://nkjp.pl/poliqarp/help/ense2.html

Python Programming Language – Official Website. (2017). Retrieved August 25, 2017, from http://www.python.org/

Radziszewski, A., & Warzocha, R. (2014). *WCRFT2, CLARIN-PL digital repository*. Retrieved August 25, 2017, from http://hdl.handle.net/11321/36

Savoy, J. (2006). Light Stemming Approaches for the French, Portuguese, German and Hungarian Languages. *Proceedings ACM-SAC*, 1031-1035. doi:10.1145/1141277.1141523

Słownik, S. J. P. (n.d.). Retrieved October 21, 2017 from https://sjp.pl/

Tager. (n.d.). Retrieved August 25, 2017, from http://ws.clarin-pl.eu/tager.shtml

TagerEn. (n.d.). Retrieved August 25, 2017, from http://ws.clarin-pl.eu/tagerEn.shtml

Treebenk. (2017). Retrieved October 20,2017 from https://en.wikipedia.org/wiki/Treebank

Venice Time Machine. (2016). Retrieved June 15, 2017, from https://vtm.epfl.ch/

Vis.js. (n.d.). Retrieved October 20, 2017 from https://visjs.org/

Voltaire and the Enlightenment. (2013). Retrieved October 19, 2017, from http://republicofletters.stanford.edu/casestudies/voltaire.html

Voyant-tools. (2017). Retrieved October 21, 2017 from https://voyant-tools.org

Walkowiak, T. (2016). Asynchronous System for Clustering and Classifications of Texts in Polish. In W. Zamojski, J. Mazurkiewicz, J. Sugier, T. Walkowiak, & J. Kacprzyk (Eds.), *Dependability Engineering and Complex Systems. Advances in Intelligent Systems and Computing* (Vol. 470). Cham: Springer. doi:10.1007/978-3-319-39639-2_46

WCRFT2. (2017). Retrieved August 25, 2017, from http://nlp.pwr.wroc.pl/redmine/projects/wcrft/wiki

ENDNOTES

[1] WordNet – a lexical database for English: https://wordnet.princeton.edu/

[2] PlWordNet. Słowosieć – wielka sieć wyrazów: http://plwordnet.pwr.wroc.pl/wordnet/

[3] https://d3js.org/

[4] http://visjs.org/

[5] e.g. D3.js operates on JSON input files.

[6] Other *try- except* usage scenarios, please review at: https://docs.python.org/2/tutorial/errors.html or at: https://stackoverflow.com/

Section 3
Visual Scientometrics

Chapter 7

Complex–Network Approach for Visualizing and Quantifying the Evolution of a Scientific Topic

Olesya Mryglod
National Academy of Sciences of Ukraine, Ukraine

Bertrand Berche
Universite´ de Lorraine, France

Yurij Holovatch
National Academy of Sciences of Ukraine, Ukraine

Ralph Kenna
Coventry University, UK

ABSTRACT

Tracing the evolution of specific topics is a subject area that belongs to the general problem of mapping the structure of scientific knowledge. Often bibliometric databases are used to study the history of scientific topic evolution from its appearance to its extinction or merger with other topics. In this chapter, the authors present an analysis of the academic response to the disaster that occurred in 1986 in Chornobyl (Chernobyl), Ukraine, considered as one of the most devastating nuclear power plant accidents in history. Using a bibliographic database, the distributions of Chornobyl-related papers in different scientific fields are analysed, as are their growth rates and properties of co-authorship networks. Elements of descriptive statistics and tools of complex-network theory are used to highlight interdisciplinary as well as international effects. In particular, tools of complex-network science enable information visualization complemented by further quantitative analysis.

INTRODUCTION

The subject of this chapter unites two major topics: complex-network science and scientometrics. Both topics reflect new trends in the evolution of science and, on a more general scale, in the evolution of human culture as a whole. Both are tightly related to the notion of complex systems which is gradually appearing as one of central concepts of our times. Usually by "complex system" one means a system that

DOI: 10.4018/978-1-5225-4990-1.ch007

is composed of many interacting parts, often called agents, which display collective behavior that does not follow trivially from the behaviors of the individual parts (for recent discussions see e.g. Thurner 2017, Holovatch et al. 2017). Inherent features of complex systems include self-organization, emergence of new functionalities, extreme sensitivity to small variations in initial conditions, and governing power laws (fat-tail behaviour). In this sense science itself, both as an enterprise that produces and systematizes knowledge as well as the body of this knowledge, is an example of a complex system. The above inherent features are ubiquitously present in different forms of scientific activity. Some of them will be a subject of analysis in this chapter.

Science is an integral part of general human culture. In this sense scientometric research is related to humanities. It is meaningless to talk about any metrics isolated from the context, which is caused by the history and philosophy of science. In the field of scientometrics, science itself is the subject of analysis: What is the structure of science? How do interactions between different scientific fields occur? What is the impact of a certain field, certain scientific article or of certain academic institutions? These and many more questions lie within the parameters of scientometric studies. Numerous indicators have been invented in order to quantify answers to these questions. Currently almost everyone in the academic world is familiar with metrics such as the impact factor, citation index, Hirsch factor and similar 'magic' numbers frequently used in science-policy and management contexts. These metrics are usually based on citation and bibliographic data. To acquire interpretable information from such large amounts of interconnected data, special tools must be used. The results are highly applicable in this case; new knowledge about how the system of science is organized can be used to improve it on different scales. Therefore, visual representation of data and of the results of its analysis becomes vital.

An analysis of the evolution of a scientific topic is considered in this chapter. Such a case study is used here to describe some of the tools and methods useful for bibliographic data analysis. The questions discussed previously in the work (Mryglod et al. 2016) concern a very subtle effect one can experience in the evolution of scientific studies: How does a new topic in science emerge? When does it appear? How does it evolve? What are the principal factors involved in its development? Amongst different ways to approach these questions, and to quantify the answers, an obvious idea is to analyze the dynamics of scientific publications paying attention to content analysis, disciplinary targeting, institutional involvement, etc. In the case study presented below, authors map out the academic response to the disaster that occurred in 1986 in Chornobyl (Chernobyl), Ukraine, considered as one of the most devastating nuclear power plant accidents in history (Alexievich & Gessen 2006). The results from (Mryglod et al. 2016) are used in this chapter to create an appropriate canvas to illustrate the application of visualization techniques.

The science of complex networks gives an essential methodological framework enabling one to describe complex-systems behaviour in a quantitative and predictive way (Albert & Barabási 2002, Dorogovtsev & Mendes 2003, Newman, Barabási, & Watts 2006). Moreover, another goal of a complex-network approach is that very often it allows one to visualize the system under consideration. In turn, both quantitative descriptions and visualizations enable understanding of complex-system behaviour. One of the goals of this chapter is to show how such an approach works when combined with other ways of scientometric analysis using the above case study as an example.

The rest of this chapter is organized as follows: first, authors make a very short introduction to the field of complex networks, giving main definitions and introducing principal observables used to quantify them. Then they pass to the above question of interest, displaying some of our results that concern quantification of the evolution of a scientific topic. There, the complex-network representations are used to visualize certain processes involved and complement their analysis by elements of descriptive statistics. The conclusion summarizes the results obtained and proposes an outlook.

COMPLEX NETWORKS: BACKGROUND

Here, the authors provide a brief introduction of what network science is about and define some of the main observables used to quantify complex networks. Complex network is a central notion of our time. An explosion of interest in networks in social and cultural phenomena has been observed at the end of last century. Currently, there is a vast amount of literature on networks. Entire journals or journal sections are devoted to networks too. Therefore, in this chapter the authors introduce only some basic notions which are necessary for the further account, referring interested readers to the available sources for a more detailed introduction (see e.g. Albert & Barabási, 2002; Dorogovtsev & Mendes, 2003; Newman, Barabási, & Watts, 2006 and references therein).

A *network* is an assemblage of *nodes* connected by *links* (also called edges), see Figure 1. In the case discussed below the nodes will be countries and links between pairs of them are formed if authors from each have jointly published a paper on the Chornobyl topic, which is recorded in the *Scopus* database. The degree of a node is the number of links emanating from it. In principle, if there are N nodes in the network, they could be interconnected by $N(N-1)/2$ links. If the actual number of links in a network is M instead, the density of the network is $2M/[N(N-1)]$.

Some parts of a network may be denser than others and there are various ways to capture such features. Indeed, the network itself may be fragmented into a number of *components* which are not connected to each other through links. The largest possible component, in principle, is the entire network itself (if each node can be reached from every other node by a sequence of links). The smallest possible component is a single isolated node, disconnected from all other nodes of the network. Usually the largest component is smaller than the entire network and in this case it is called the giant component. This is usually the focus of interest in such fragmented networks.

The statistics involving lengths of paths in the network is a frequent matter of interest. Paths between nodes are formed by sequences of links. The shortest path between any two nodes is called a *geodesic*. If the network is fragmented, only geodesics within a given fragment is considered because there are no paths interconnecting two separate fragments (in a sense the distance between them is infinite). The longest finite geodesic in the entire network is called the network *diameter*. This is the longest shortest path in the network. One can be also interested in the *mean path length* formed by averaging over the distances between all pairs of nodes which are connected by a path. This notion became famous by American psychologist Stanley Milgram's experiment in the 1960s to investigate the "small world problem" (Milgram 1967). This was related to a suggestion that, despite the world's population of over 7 billion people, everyone is connected to everyone else by six or fewer steps or "a friend of a friend" statements.

In Figure 1, authors present a simple network for demonstration purposes. The network has $N = 8$ nodes interconnected by $M = 11$ links. Since 8 nodes could, in theory, be connected together by $N(N-1)/2 = 28$ links, the density of the network is $11/28 = 0.39$. The degree of each node varies, e.g., Node A has degree 3 while B has four links. The average number of links per node is $11/8 = 1.375$. There is no fragmentation in this network – every node belongs to the giant component. The network diameter is 4 because the longest shortest paths (longest geodesics) have this length. These are paths joining F to G (namely FCBAG or FCBEG) or F to H (FCBEH).

The *clustering coefficient* provides one measure of how dense a local part of a network is. In a social network, for example, if an individual has two friends, it is fairly likely that these two are also acquainted. In Figure 1 node A has 3 neighbours (namely B, G and H). There are therefore three potential relationship triads involving node A, (namely ABG, ABH and AGH). Of these, only one is realised (namely

Figure 1. A small network comprising N = 8 nodes interconnected by M = 11 links. The nodes may represent people in real life, characters in a text, stations in a transport system or countries producing scientific publications. Links represent some sort of interactions or relationships between them. In network science one seeks to capture the statistics relating to how these links are distributed. In social networks links may have different features, e.g., here, the solid light-blue links and the dashed purple ones may represent positive (friendly) and negative (hostile) relations.

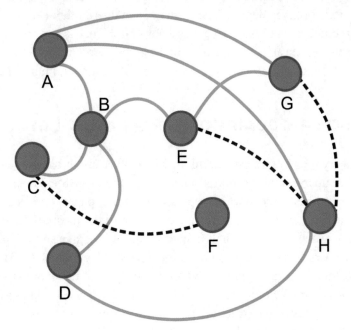

AGH). One can say that the clustering coefficient for node A is one out of three or 1/3. It is possible then to proceed and to calculate the clustering coefficients for each node on the entire network. Taking an average of all of the resulting numbers is gives the clustering of the entire network.

If a network has a small path length and a high clustering coefficient, it is called a *small world*. To decide how small the path length has to be and how high the clustering has to be for a network to be small world, it should be compared to a random graph of the same size and average degree. If the path lengths are comparable in magnitude but the clustering of the network at hand is far greater than that of the random network, the network is deemed small world. In small worlds, every node is close to every other node, in a sense.

Sometimes a subset of nodes can be very highly clustered – very tightly connected. If a subset of nodes is complete, i.e., if every distance pair of nodes is connected by a link, it is called a *clique*.

It is often desirable to decide if some nodes are particularly important or influential. One way to do this is to consider that those with highest degree are most important. Another is to consider nodes with the highest *betweenness* centralities as most important. Betweenness counts the number of shortest paths (geodesics) which pass through the given node. To define it for a specific node, all geodesics that go through it should be counted and then divided by the total number of paths on the network. The result then should be divided again by $(N-1)(N-2)/2$ in order to normalise it in such a way that it is one if all geodesics pass through node.

Another measure of the importance of a node is its *closeness* centrality. This is defined by first taking the sum of the distances from the given node to all other nodes in a connected component of the network. This is termed its farness. The reciprocal of farness is a simple measure of how central a node is and is termed its closeness.

Many other statistics have been invented to capture and compare various characteristics of networks. In particular, defining the mean degree one naturally arrives to the notion of node *degree distribution*: a probability to find a node of given degree. The form of such distribution is crucial in defining network properties. For many complex networks it decays as a power law. Such networks are called scale-free. But here authors have given the measures that are used in the remainder of this chapter. The reader is referred to the literature (e.g., Newman 2010) for more extensive discussions of multitudes of such measures.

VISUALIZING THEMATIC COAUTHORSHIP: A CASE STUDY

Complex-network theory provides a set of useful tools to analyze also bibliographic data. For this reason modern scientometrics operates with different kinds of networks such as citation and co-citation networks, coauthorship networks or those which represent scientific papers connected by common authors or key words. In particular, coauthorship data constitute one of the most useful sources of information for detection of links between papers, journals or even countries. To give an example of such an analysis, authors refer to a recent work where a case study is considered (Mryglod 2016). These results contribute to a direction of scientometrics research focused on the analysis of the evolution of separate scientific topics. The knowledge about how new topics emerge and evolve is useful, in particular, to describe the forefront of research and to reveal the structure of scientific disciplines as well as their interconnections.

The main aim of the work was to study the reaction of academic community to a particular important event. Similar to how society's response can be tracked through the analysis of news, discussions in mass media or activity in social networks, the interest of academics is reflected in scientific publications. Since periodicals provide the most common way to present and interchange new results, it is natural to consider the set of publications in scientific journals. To give an example, the bibliographic data about papers relevant to the problem of poverty were analyzed in (Zuccala, & van Eck, 2011). General publication activity on a given topic, interdisciplinary landscape, as well as international collaboration patters, was studied in this work. The suggested set of methods were applied, not to analyze the core of papers relevant to a permanently important problem, but rather to highlight the dynamics of new trends in response to single event.

The Chornobyl catastrophe was chosen as the trigger event for our study. Several reasons (besides the fact that two of us are Ukrainians) led to such a choice:

- The consequences of this disaster can be felt in different spheres of humanity and, therefore, attract the attention of researchers of various disciplines.
- The worldwide scale of the Chornobyl accident implies international interest in the problem. At the same time the reaction of the academic community on a national level is strong enough to make comparisons and to reveal the role of Ukraine in the international scene within the topic.
- The exact time of "birth" can be defined for Chornobyl-related research topics: 26 April 1986 (of course, papers using name Chornobyl and published before 1986 can also be found but the number

of post-accident paper is obviously larger: 1.8 publication per year on average between 1966 and 1985 comparing to above 200 publications already in 1986).

Over 9500 records about research papers containing words "Chornobyl" (and its variations: "Chornobyl'", "Chernobyl" or "Chernobyl'") in their titles, abstracts or authors' key words were collected from Scopus[1]. Almost 75% of records contain the "affiliation" field, which is useful to find countries related to authors. Using these data international collaborations on the Chornobyl topic are studied. The coauthorship network at the level of countries is built; nodes represent separate countries while each link connects two nodes if two different countries were mentioned in the affiliation list of the same publication. The aggregated network incorporating all the data starting from 1986 and until the beginning of 2015 is considered below. Therefore, it also includes a number of countries that do not exist anymore as political entities, such as Czechoslovakia or the USSR.

The network consists of 97 nodes connected by 761 links (see Table 1 for these and some other numerical characteristics of the network). On one hand, such a ratio indicates quite a sparse network; only approximately 16% of possible links are actualized. On the other hand, most nodes are mutually reachable since over 82% of them belong to the largest connected (giant) component. This means that the majority of countries are interconnected through Chornobyl-related research collaboration. Moreover, starting from a randomly chosen country, one can reach another one in just 2 steps on average. The longest geodesic (network diameter) connects Yugoslavia and the Faroe Islands and still takes only 4 steps. It is interesting to note that the large connected component is in fact the only connected fragment in the network. The remaining 17 nodes are isolated: the authors from countries such as Lebanon, Iran, Pakistan and others were not involved in the international collaboration on Chornobyl topic.

The remaining network statistics are given in Table 1 can be easily interpreted as well. The average value of the node degree indicates that each country collaborates with more than 15 other countries on average. The highest level of collaboration activity, represented by the maximal node degree, corresponds to the USA: 1082 papers (the second largest number after Russia which produced 1180 publications) were coauthored with 51 other countries. Being the largest hub, the USA also occupies an influential place in the network. This is confirmed by special quantitative node properties – betweenness centrality and closeness centrality. The maximal value of the former means that the largest number of shortest paths between any other two countries passes through the USA. Taking into account that such shortest paths on average consists of 2 steps, the USA appears to be a direct bridge between the majority of the other countries. The latter centrality value gives the closeness of a particular node to any other node in the network – and it is maximal for USA as well.

The Watts-Strogatz clustering coefficient is another numerical value which describes the network connectedness. It reflects the average probability of nodes to be a part of the fully connected clusters – *cliques*. Clustering coefficients can be calculated for connected fragments that imply that the majority of nodes are taken into account in our case. The neighbours of a node are interconnected in their own turn with probability 0.78.

A visual representation of the network (Figure 2) provides a more intuitive way to understand the structure discussed above. One can instantly distinguish the connected component surrounded by a comparatively small set of isolated nodes. Textual labels with short names of countries can also contain the exact values of node attributes: total numbers of papers, population, degree values or any others. However, it is often hard to visualize large network consisting of a lot of nodes and numerous links in a simple and intuitively clear way. Therefore, it is convenient to use different possible "dimensions" of

Table 1. Some of numerical values which characterize coauthorship network on the level of countries for Chornobyl-related publications (1986 – January 2015) visible in Scopus.

Number of Nodes	Number of Links (Network Density)	Average Node Degree	Max Degree	The Longest Geodesic	Watts-Strogatz Clustering Coefficient	Number of Isolated Nodes (%)	Number of Nodes Within the Largest Connected Component (%)
97	761 (0.16)	15.7	51	4	0.78	17 (17.5%)	80 (82.5%)

visual attributing of network representation depending on the purpose. The layout, size and color can be used to highlight particular fragments of the network or to distinguish nodes or links by an attribute.

The same coauthorship network as in Figure 2 is presented in Figure 3 using a different kind of representation:

- TOP10 nodes characterized by highest degree value are positioned in the center;
- The links connecting central nodes are highlighted in yellow;
- Node size is proportional to the total number of papers, where a particular country is mentioned in affiliation list.

Such a visualization approach allows one instantly to see the most active countries – collaborators within the Chornobyl-related topic – and to compare the absolute contributions in terms of numbers of publications. One can wonder about the factors which play a role to manifest these hubs: geographical closeness to the epicenter of the tragedy (Ukraine, Russia and Belarus) and the active position of developed countries (USA, United Kingdom, France, Germany, Austria, Japan, Denmark). Eight of these countries are also in the TOP10 list of the most productive countries in terms of numbers of publications (Austria and Denmark were in 12th and 21th positions, respectively, in the most recent rating).

One could expect the role of Ukraine to be the most significant, since it is the geographical center of the accident. Indeed, Ukraine is one of the main centers of collaborators. However, it is not the leader due to several natural reasons. First of all, Ukraine became an independent country only in 1991 – before that year USSR, Ukraine or even Russia could be found in affiliations of Ukrainian authors. Secondly, our visualization shows that Ukraine still plays a noticeable role. If we compare the collaboration maps for Chornobyl and any other randomly chosen topic (not related geographically to Ukraine) – we will probably see the clear difference.

The highly connected fragment highlighted in yellow in Figure 3 demonstrates the high level of connectedness amongst the TOP10 most actively collaborating countries which is rather natural. In fact, these countries form a clique.

Another way of representing of the same coauthorship network is used in Figure 4:

- The nodes colors and the layout depend on the part of the world each country belongs to;
- Node size is proportional to the node degree.

In this case one can explore the geographical aspect of international collaboration. The differentiation of the nodes by their degree allows one to speculate about the typical collaboration patters. E.g., it

Figure 2. Collaboration network of countries for Chornobyl-related research based on Scopus data (publication period: 1986–2015). Visualization of this and further networks is performed using Pajek network visualization software (Vlado 2015).

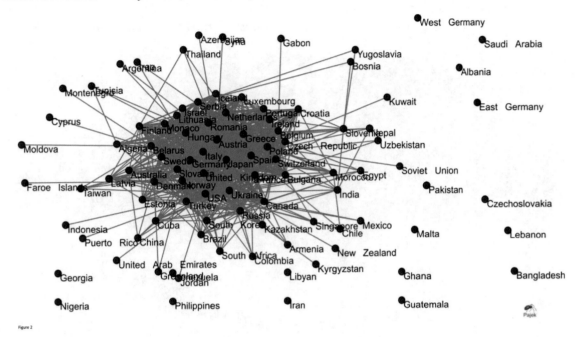

is easy to distinguish the most connected countries for the Asia region: Russia and Japan each have 42 coauthorship links to other countries while a majority of the rest countries has one or no links. A more balanced situation is observed for European countries: e.g., 8 of them have at least 40 collaborators and 9 of them have no more than 1 collaborator.

Finally information about the year when each country introduced the first Chornobyl-related publications is used in Figure 5. Again, the same network is presented, but this time visualized in such a way to see how countries from different parts of the world entered "into the game". Obviously, the largest number of countries reacted immediately after the accident in 1986 or one year later. A sort of anniversary effect can be seen here: new countries joined 5 (6) and 10 years later. It is natural that geographical position is important: the first reaction wave came mostly from Eurasian countries. Supposedly, the more distant countries started to discuss the Chornobyl problem (i) when remote consequences became worldwide and (ii) after Fukushima catastrophe in 2011.

Besides the variety of ways to represent the same data, network theory allows us to consider "slices" of network. Any node attributes can be used to group them and to extract subnetworks for further consideration. In Figure 6 the evolution of the network described above can be seen: the first subfigure represent the picture of collaboration during the first several years after the accident (1986–1990), the second subfigure shows the network built on the data about publications during the several later years (2011–2015). The so-called sliding window technique is preferable due to a change of historical circumstances. This means that different periods of time are considered and separate coauthorship networks are built for each of them taking into account only data "visible" within the particular time window. Such an approach is also useful in order to see the non-aggregative nature of collaboration patterns dynam-

Figure 3. Collaboration network of countries for Chornobyl-related research based on Scopus data (publication period: 1986–2015). TOP10 of nodes with the highest degrees are centered and the links connecting these nodes are highlighted in lighter color. Node size is nonlinearly proportional to the total number of papers, published by authors from the corresponding country. Link widths are nonlinearly proportional to the numbers of common publications by authors from two given countries.

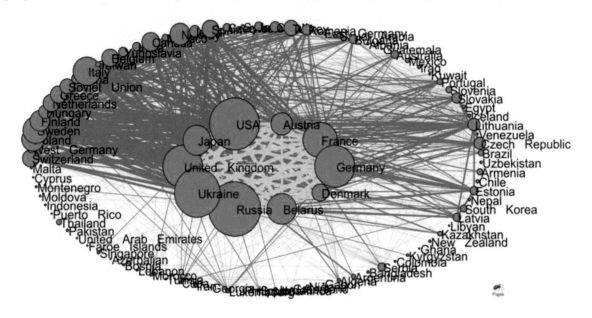

Figure 4. Collaboration network of countries for Chornobyl-related research based on Scopus data (publication period: 1986–2015). The nodes of different kinds (different colors online) represent different part of the world – for the sake of visual simplicity the same attribute is used to include a node to corresponding circle. A node size is proportional to its degree.

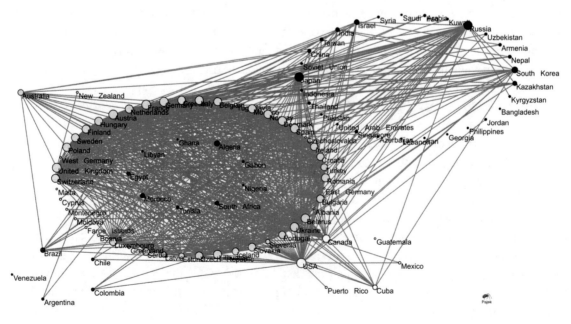

Figure 5. Collaboration network of countries for Chornobyl-related research based on Scopus data (publication period: 1986–2015). The nodes of different kinds (different colors online) represent different part of the world. Nodes are grouped by the year of the first Chornobyl-related publication of a country.

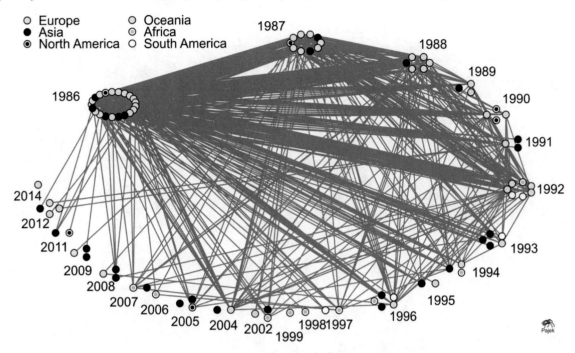

ics: new links can appear while some old relations become broken. Thus, the visual densification of the network can be clearly seen in Figure 6. Such an effect when the network becomes denser accumulating more nodes and links was described for different real networks (Leskovec et al. 2007). Network evolution is considered as an integral process to check this numerically, i.e. all the links and nodes are taken into account starting from 1986. Similarly as in (Leskovec et al. 2007) the increase of the average node degree is observed: it grows starting from 1.4 for the first snapshot made for interval 1986-1990 and ending with 15.7 for 1986-2015 data. The network diameter decrease is not observed supposedly due to the small statistics, but this value is obviously not increasing – it fluctuates around 4. The number of links increases much faster than the number of nodes: it is also hard to make a reliable quantitative conclusion about the shape of this dependence, but it is not far from being power-law (see Figure 7) which characterizes the network densification process. Such a densification can be interpreted as the intensification of international collaboration about the topic: along with new countries joining new links between the former members of collaboration network appears.

The visualization of the data can be completed by other kinds of graphics. The variation of numerical values with time is often better presented using traditional methods: e.g., the number of Chornobyl-related papers within different disciplines for different years is presented in Figure 8. The change of publication activity within TOP10 disciplines can be seen here. Two conclusions can be made instantly from the figure: there is no distinct decreasing tendency and the local maxima correspond to the "anniversary years" passed after the disaster.

Figure 6. Collaboration network of countries for Chornobyl-related research based on Scopus data. Publication period: (a) 1986–1990, (b) 2011–2015. The size of each node is proportional to the number of papers for the corresponding country.

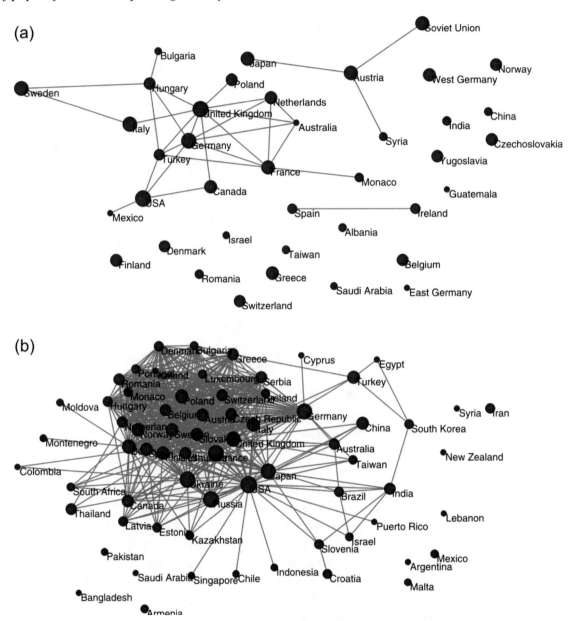

Network representation can be frustrating when the network contains a lot of links. For example, some aspects visualized in Figure 5 are also represented in Figure 9: share of countries which belong to different parts of the world and the time of their entering into the ``game'' (the increment in cumulative data corresponds to the year when new countries appear on a map). Additionally the collaboration links are shown in Figure 5, but the more connected nodes are, the less informative such visualization.

Figure 7. Number of links L versus number of nodes N for integral network built for every 5 years starting from 1986 (symbols). The linear fit is schematically shown by broken line.

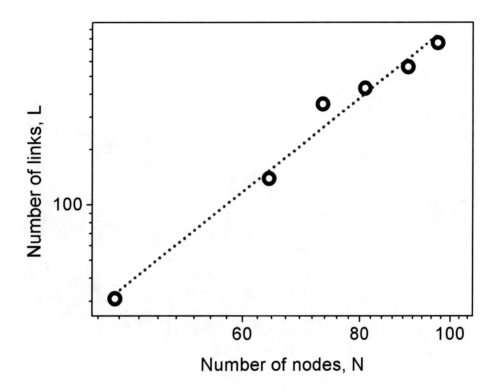

Figure 8. Number of Chornobyl-related papers within different disciplines changing with time in the Scopus database, see also (Mryglod et al. 2016).

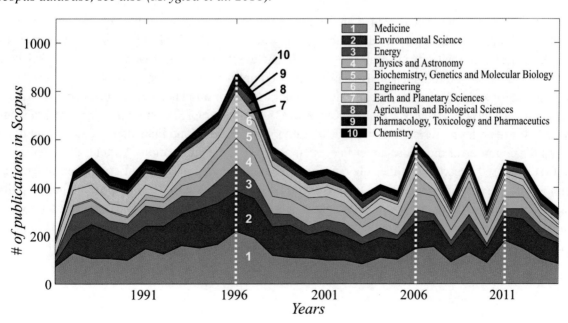

Figure 9. Cumulative number of countries from different parts of the world, involved in Chornobyl-related research, see also (Mryglod et al. 2016).

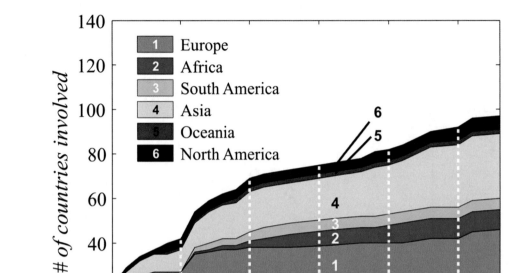

CONCLUSION

In this chapter, authors have provided an example of how visualization of information can be used in order to deduce more insights into the problem analyzed. The example chosen is that of scientific publications related to the Chornobyl disaster of 1986. Relevant publications were selected via keywords queries and we went through an analysis inspired by complex-network theory which has proven to be a very powerful tool in various other contexts, e.g. public transportation networks (Von Ferber et al 2012), mythological networks (Mac Carron and Kenna 2012). Various graphical representations were then proposed, where nodes represent the countries of authors' affiliations, and links between nodes are drawn when the countries of the nodes under interest appear in a same publication. A "neutral" visualization is first proposed according to the rules indicated above, which shows a giant component containing almost all nodes and a periphery of a few isolated nodes. Authors have then proposed other graphical representations, with e.g. the nodes with highest degrees in central positions, node sizes proportional to the number of papers, or to the node degrees, geographical characteristics of nodes of the chronology of their appearance in the set emphasized via color codes, etc. Each of these visualizations facilitates a focus on specific features of the set analyzed.

ACKNOWLEDGMENT

The research was supported by 7th FP, IRSES projects No. 612707 "Dynamics of and in Complex Systems" and No. 612669 "Structure and Evolution of Complex Systems with Applications in Physics and Life Sciences" and by the COST Action TD1210 "Analyzing the dynamics of information and knowledge landscapes" (OM and YuH). YuH acknowledges kind hospitality of Veslava and Grzegorz Osiński at the Conference on Information visualization in humanities (Toruń, 23-24 March 2017) where a part of this work was reported.

REFERENCES

Albert, R., & Barabási, A.-L. (2002). Statistical mechanics of complex networks. *Reviews of Modern Physics*, *74*(1), 47–97. doi:10.1103/RevModPhys.74.47

Alexievich, S., & Gessen, K. (2006). *Voices from Chernobyl: The oral history of a nuclear disaster*. London: Macmillan.

Dorogovtsev, S. N., & Mendes, J. F. F. (2003). *Evolution of Networks*. Oxford, UK: Oxford University Press. doi:10.1093/acprof:oso/9780198515906.001.0001

Holovatch, Yu., Kenna, R., & Thurner, S. (2017). Complex systems: Physics beyond physics. *European Journal of Physics*, *38*(2), 023002. doi:10.1088/1361-6404/aa5a87

Leskovec, J., Kleinberg, J., & Faloutsos, C. (2007). Graph evolution: Densification and shrinking diameters. *ACM Transactions on Knowledge Discovery from Data*, *1*(1), 2, es. doi:10.1145/1217299.1217301

Mac Carron, P., & Kenna, R. (2012). Universal properties of mythological networks. *EPL*, *99*(2), 28002. doi:10.1209/0295-5075/99/28002

Milgram, S. (1967). The small world problem. *Psychology Today*, *1*(May), 61–67.

Mryglod, O., Holovatch, Yu., Kenna, R., & Berche, B. (2016). Quantifying the evolution of a scientific topic: Reaction of the academic community to the Chornobyl disaster. *Scientometrics*, *106*(3), 1151–1166. doi:10.1007/s11192-015-1820-2

Newman, M. (2010). *Networks: An Introduction*. Oxford, UK: Oxford University Press. doi:10.1093/acprof:oso/9780199206650.001.0001

Newman, M., Barabási, A.-L., & Watts, D. J. (2006). *The Structure and Dynamics of Networks*. Princeton University Press.

Pazienza, M. T., Pennacchiotti, M., & Zanzotto, F. M. (2005). Terminology extraction: An analysis of linguistic and statistical approaches. In S. Sirmakessis (Ed.), *Knowledge mining* (pp. 255–279). Berlin: Springer. doi:10.1007/3-540-32394-5_20

Thurner, S. (Ed.). (2017). *43 Visions for Complexity*. Singapore: World Scientific. doi:10.1142/10360

Vlado, A. (2015). *Pajek: Program for large network analysis.* Retrieved April 1, 2015, from http://vlado. fmf.unilj.si/pub/networks/pajek/

Von Ferber, C., Berche, B., Holovatch, T., & Holovatch, Yu. (2012). A tale of two cities. *Journal of Transportation Security, 5*(3), 199–216. doi:10.1007/s12198-012-0092-9

Zuccala, A., & van Eck, N. J. (2011). Poverty research in a development policy context. *Development Policy Review, 29*(3), 311–330. doi:10.1111/j.1467-7679.2011.00535.x

KEY TERMS AND DEFINITIONS

Chornobyl (Chernobyl) Disaster: A catastrophic nuclear accident that occurred on 26 April 1986 in the reactor at the Chernobyl Nuclear Power Plant (Ukraine, then USSR).

Complex Network: A graph with non-trivial topological features that do not occur in such networks as lattices or uncorrelated random graphs. Usually it is said that any network that is more complex than classical Erdös-Rényi random graph is a complex network. Many real-world networks manifest features of complex networks, in particular they are scale-free small worlds. Examples are given by the internet, www, technological, communication, social networks.

Complex Systems: Systems composed of many interacting parts, often called agents, which display collective behavior that does not follow trivially from the behaviors of the individual parts. Inherent features of complex systems incorporate self-organization, emergence of new functionalities, extreme sensitiveness to small variations in the initial conditions, governing power laws (fat-tail behaviour).

Scale-Free Network: A network where the probability $P(k)$ to find a node of degree k (i.e., with k attached links) decays at large k as a power law: $P(k) \sim k^\lambda$. The decay exponent plays an important role in governing different network properties.

Scientometrics: The field of knowledge about measuring and analysing science, technology, and innovation.

Small World Network: A network with small shortest path length (number of steps from one node to another) and high clustering coefficient (i.e., when neighbors of any node are likely to be neighbours of each other). Usually it is said that a network is a small world if its typical size l grows with number of nodes N slower than a power law (e.g., logarithmically: $l \sim \ln N$).

ENDNOTE

[1]   The data collected during January–February 2015 are used.

Chapter 8
Bibliometric Maps of Science:
The Visualization of Scientific Research

Irina Marshakova-Shaikevich
Adam Mickiewicz University, Poland

ABSTRACT

This chapter is devoted to directions in algorithmic classificatory procedures: co-citation analysis as an example of citation network and lexical analysis of keywords in the titles. The chapter gives the results of bibliometric analysis of the international scientific collaboration of EU countries. The three approaches are based on the same general idea of normalization of deviations of the observed data from the mathematical expectation. The application of the same formula leads to discovery of statistically significant links between objects (publication, journals, keywords, etc.) reflected in the maps. Material for this analysis is drawn from DBs presented in ISI Thomson Reuters (at present Clarivate Analytics).

INTRODUCTION

The present chapter is devoted to direction in algorithmic classificatory procedures: co-citation analysis as an example of citation network and lexical analysis of keywords in the titles. The chapter will give the results of bibliometric analysis of the international scientific collaboration of EU countries. The five approaches are based on the same general idea of normalization of deviations of the observed data from the mathematical expectation. The application of the same formula leads to discovery of statistically significant links between objects (publication, journals, keywords, etc.) reflected in the maps.

This chapter includes five parts: (1) Co-citation maps of publications and authors, (2) Journal co-citation analysis , (3) bibliometric maps of the international scientific collaboration of EU countries, (4) the map of scientific organizations based on their thematic specters, (5) MEMORY and MEMORIES in lexical environment.

Material for this analysis is drawn from DBs presented in ISI Thomson Reuters (at present Clarivate Analytics)..

Since the beginning of the 1960-s a new direction in the study of science has been gaining ground – quantitative analysis of information flows. As is well known bibliometrics is one of the approaches to

DOI: 10.4018/978-1-5225-4990-1.ch008

the study of science. Items of bibliometric analysis are publications grouped according to a multitude of aspects: journals, authors, countries, thematic fields, etc. The specific feature of bibliometrics is the use of secondary information: all kinds of bibliographic indexes: abstracts, and so on presented in various DBs The corresponding statistics may be of great interest for the analysts of science development, it may help in planning and management of science.

It is very important to underline two important sides of these directions of analysis should be mentioned at once.

1. Bibliometrics is based on the huge amount of easily accessible secondary information well represented in various databases, particularly in the databases of the ISI (Thomson Reuters). It was exactly those databases that served as a starting point for the development of bibliometrics.
2. Bibliometrics is primarily a quantitative study of the flow of documents. It is not aimed at finding a particular bit of information, it concentrates on discovering middle- and long-range trends, on strategic monitoring the development of science. The results are visualized in maps of science.

CO-CITATION ANALYSIS OF PUBLICATIONS AND AUTHORS

The research in field of the science of science in the 1960-1970 was concentrated mainly in elaborating of synchronic classifications. The inclusion of time factor was one of the aims of present author in elaborating methods of prospective coupling. Two methods of automatic clustering were worked out, which could be applied to dynamic corpora of documents. The author's further work in this direction was divided between 1) co-citation analysis of publications and authors and 2) journal co-citation analysis (see part 2).

The present part of the chapter is based to the idea of co-citation as a tool of automatic classification of a set of items (a citation network). The method was worked out by the author from 1970 and was called 'prospective coupling' (Marshakova,1973) as contrasted to Kessler's 'bibliographic coupling'(Kessler, 1963).

From the mathematical point of view Citation network is a set of documents with the relation of citing imposed on it. In other words it is a union of a set of citing papers and a set of cited papers. A citation network is a potential base for various classifications of member-papers. Search for practical algorithmic (automatic) classification is a characteristic feature of present-day bibliometric analysis of citation networks. It was M. Kessler who in 1963 formulated the concept of 'bibliographic coupling' as a measure of similarity of two documents based on the number of common references. The method relies on past literature and may be called *retrospective.*

The logical opposite of bibliographic coupling is the concept of co-citation proposed in 1973 independently by H. Small in the USA and by the present author in the USSR. The similarity of two documents depends on the number of papers citing both documents. When a new paper appears it is not linked to any other paper until it starts to be cited in scientific literature. This connection was called *prospective* by the author for it is based on citations in future literature. Henry Small's term 'co-citation' proved a happier coinage and the author accepted it into Russian as *kocitacia* or *kocitirovanie* (Marshakova, 1973; Small, 1973).

The proposed method is the logical opposite of the method of bibliographic coupling. From the mathematical point of view citation network is a set of documents with the relation of citing imposed on it. In other words it is a union of a set of citing papers and a set of cited papers. A citation network is a potential base for various classification of member-papers.

Both methods establish a measure of similarity of two papers, but they differ in the in the principles, underlying this measure. In bibliographic coupling the connection of two papers, once measured, does not change with the further growth of the corpus of scientific papers.

Co-citation or prospective coupling entirely depends on the future development of science. At the beginning a paper (no matter, how many references it contains) shows no links to other documents, until it starts to be cited by future papers. This bias for the future makes co-citation especially interesting for scholars, engaged in the study of cognitive and social structure of science.

Below some results are given of co-citation classifications. They are based on two kinds of items: 1) publications figures 1-2, and 2) authors figure 3. The choice of various tools gives many-sided information interesting to philosophers and sociologists of science, social sciences and humanities.

The results of visualization are presented on figures 1-3:

Figure 1. Map of publications 1966–67
Figure 2. Map of publications 1968–69
Figure 3. Map of authors for 1968–69

The co-citation map was carried out in two separate stages 1) for 1966-1967 and 2) for 1968-1969. On the basis of the formal mathematical model and resulting procedure 7 autonomous groups were

Figure 1. Map 1966–67 Research Fronts in Laser's field
Source: Marshakova-Shaikevich, 2010a

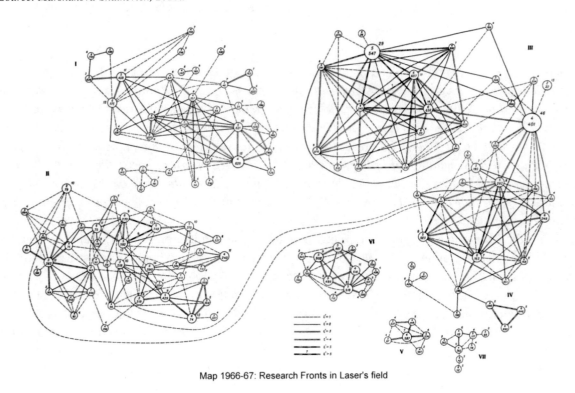

Map 1966-67: Research Fronts in Laser's field

Figure 2. Map 1968–69 of Research Fronts in Laser's field
Source: Marshakova-Shaikevich, 2010a

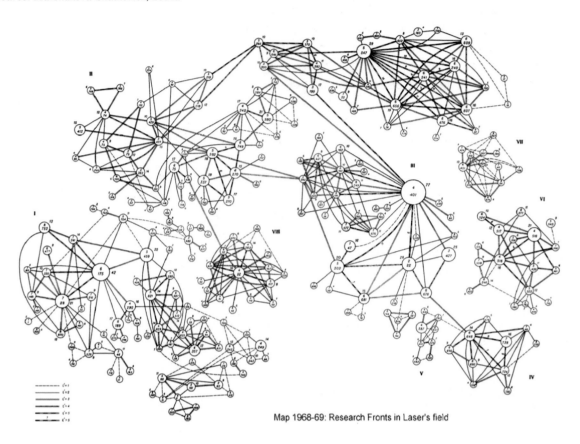

Map 1968-69: Research Fronts in Laser's field

found for 1966-1967 (Figure 1) and more than 20 groups for 1968-1969 (Figure 2: those groups are easily interpreted and labeled e.g. *Problems of linear optics, Theoretical problems of optical quantum generators, Stimulation of laser radiation, Selection of oscillation types, Research on distribution of laser radiation, Lamb's theory of laser, Semiconductor lasers, Laser on water vapors, Gas lasers, Liquid lasers, Zeeman effect in lasers, Theoretical problems of He-Ne laser, Quantum theory of OKG; Laser in magnetic field; Stimulation of laser radiation; Self- focusing of laser beams; Brillouin scattering; Interaction of oscillations; Zeeman effect in lasers; Giantpulse laser; Research on distribution of laser radiation; Generation of optical harmonics; Solidstate laser; Organic dyer laser; Molecular gas lasers; Liquid lasers; Ion lasers* etc.)

Using the same terminology one can speak of co-citation communities of authors (groups of researches linked by co-citation coupling). The 1968-69 map, which included 442 publications, served as a source for establishing links between authors. The productivity (number of publications) of each author in 1968-69 was taken into consideration, when the sum of mutual prospective links was calculated. On the basis of those normalized links between authors a measured symmetrical matrix was built (see details Marshakova, 1988, p.188). Graphic representation of that matrix was published as a map of author-to-author links (see Figure 3. Co-citation map of authors). This map reflects professional communication between authors in the Laser's field 1968- 69. There is a difference between maps of co-citation publications and

Figure 3. Co- citation map of authors
Source: Marshakova-Shaikevich, 2010a

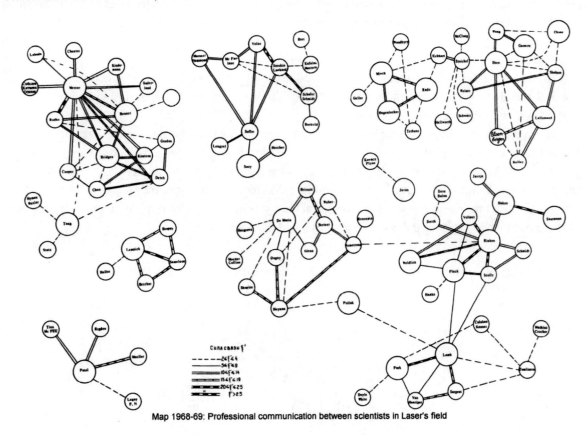

Map 1968-69: Professional communication between scientists in Laser's field

maps of co-citation authors, which means that cognitive and social structures of a field of knowledge differ as well. For a more extensive treatment of the subject (see Marshakova, 2010a).

The changes in configuration are due to: a) stabilization of groups, b) division of a group into related groups, c) appearance of new groups. Stable groups are characterized by strong co-citation links. Documents with weak prospective links are unstable and can be easily regrouped. Changes in classification usually show landmarks in the development of the given field of science. Group 'Laser on water vapors', which appears on 1968–69 map, is the result of research, done in 1964–1965. W.E. Lamb's paper of 1964 (number 4 401 on the maps, a 'classical' work in Price's terms) is the core of the 'Theory of gas lasers' group (Lamb, 1964).

The proposed method of co-citation coupling may prove useful for monitoring development of a direction of research. It helps to identify thematic groups, leaders of particular directions and 'classical' works, e.g. the paper by De Maria, Stetse, & Heyhau (1966), (see number 6.175 at Figure 2).

In 1990 Prof. Robert Merton and myself discussed co-citation maps of science. The difference between the map of publications and map of their authors was the central point of our discussion. We agreed that the map of co-citation publications representing the cognitive structure of a scientific field does not coincide with the map of co- cited authors where some social factors are reflected. The method of co- citation analysis (method of structural bibliometrics) serves to identify cognitive and social structures of science and the nature of their correlations (congruence, non- congruence), as well as forms of professional communication. This method should be used in scientific knowledge and identification of social institutes of science. Maps of science produced by the method of co-citation reflected one more way of knowledge existence — prospective connections between publications determined by relationships within the scientific community (on the whole).

Prof. Merton acknowledged that such maps should be regarded as an objective picture of the cognitive and social structures of science; they could lead to discovery of important individual papers, true leaders in new fields and directions of science.

The idea of co-citation coupling was extended by the author to constructing networks of scientists. The authors co-citation in the field of USSR's Information Science is presented on the map –Figure 4 (see details in Marshakova, 1981). Material for this investigation was 13 volumes of journal "Nauchno-tekhnicheskaya Informatsiya (NTI) and Cumulative Subject and Authors Index, Volumes 1-13, Moscow,1975". The limited scope of this investigation (analysis of a single journal) might be overcome with the help of Science Citation Index and Social Science Citation Index.

Figure 4. Map of authors co-citation in the field of Information Science in USSR in 1975.
Source: Marshakova, 1981

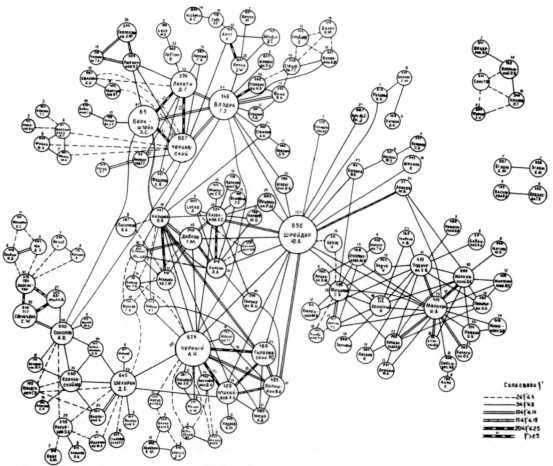

Map: authors co-citation in the field of USSR's Information Science (1975)

JOURNAL CO-CITATION ANALYSIS

Classification of journals, based on their citation behavior, may correspond to heuristically established fields of science, or, conversely, it might be quite different from the latter. The citation behavior of a scholarly journal is determined by a host of factors. Of course, the thematic similarity of papers is the main reason for citing previous work, but other motives, both scientific and social, also come into play. Due to this fact 'citation' classification may seem suspicious to adherents of 'logical' classification schemes in science and humanities. Those traditional schemes have proved their utility, efficiently organizing researchers' behavior in their search of information.

However, new approaches to classification of fields of science might be useful, paving the way to revisions of existing framework, and discovering subtler links transcending the boundaries of hierarchical classifications.

The idea to compare the categories of ISI Journal Citation Reports with the results of some algorithmic approach, based on citation, is not new. L. Nordstrom found a significant overlap of cited literature between ecology and biogeography (Nordstrom, 1990). Pudovkin and Fuseler (1995) mapped the field of marine and freshwater biology journals, with the core group of journals at the center of a two-dimensional diagram and narrow topic journals at its periphery. Huge area of environment research was studied by Sigogneau (1995). An impressive attempt to build a multilevel classification of scientific journals was made by Bassecoulard and Zitt (1999). They found that algorithmic procedures were quite efficient in differentiating some disciplines (medicine, agriculture, and engineering), but failed in chemistry or physics.

Methodology of Journal Co-Citation Analysis

It is known the idea of co-citation was first put forward in 1973 Marshakova (1973) and by Small (1973), it may be concisely expressed by the following maxim: two papers are similar when they are simultaneously cited by other papers. Here, the maxim should be read as: two journals are similar when both of them are often cited in the same third journals. Thus the present part will exclude the direct transactions within pairs of journals (Marshakova-Shaikevich, 2003, 2004a, 2004b).

Algorithm includes the next steps (Marshakova-Shaikevich, 2005)

1. To facilitate the calculation, the bottom part of the list of citing journals was excluded from the analysis. The cut-off point was determined as:

0,01× (number of total cites – number of self-cites).

For example, the journal *JASIST* has 1916 cites, of which 434 are cites of itself, thus the cut-off point is $0,01 \times (1916\text{-}434) = 14.82$

the journal 'PSYCHOL WOMEN QUART' has 1046 cites, of which 128 are cites of itself, thus the cut-off point is $0,01 \times (1046 - 128) = 9.18$

The minimal cut-off point is arbitrarily set at 2.

2. For each citing journal its citing capacity (CC) is calculated. Citing capacity of the given citing journal (CC) is defined as the sum of its frequencies in all the core lists of cited journals of the category.

3. Assuming (for time being) the null hypothesis of uniform distribution of cites in journals within the category, let us calculate the mathematical expectation of a journal (*a*) being cited by a citing journal (*i*). This mathematical expectation (*m*) will be defined as the product of a portion of total number of cites (*p*) of the cited journal by the citing capacity (CC) of the citing journal:

$$m_{ai} = p_a \times CC_i \tag{1}$$

$$p = \frac{\sum C_a}{\sum \sum C} \tag{2}$$

where $\sum C_a$ – total cites for a journal (*a*)

4. The real number of journal (*i*) citing journal (*a*) may deviate from *m*. The magnitude of this deviation will be calculated as

$$S = \frac{x - m - 1}{\sqrt{m}} \tag{3}$$

where *x* is the actual number of times that journal *a* was cited by journal *i*. The (-1) in the numerator is introduced to cut off unique experimental events which should not be used as evidence no matter how small is ***m*** .

5. The resulting value of co-citation relatedness of two journals (a and b) will be calculated according to

$$R_{ab} = n \times \sum \lg(S_{ai} \times S_{bi}) \tag{4}$$

where *n* is the number of common non-zero positive deviations (with $S \geq 2$) from mathematical expectation.

The journal co-citation analysis was first tested on the ISI Journal Citation Reports: 2001 Social Sciences Edition category '*Information Science and Library Science*'. This category in 2001 edition included 55 journals, differing widely in the number of articles (36 articles on average, but '*The Scientist*' claiming 249, in the number of cites (with an average figure of 252 and the record of 1916 of *Journal of the American Society for Information Science and Technology*), in impact factor (with an average 0.5 and the record 2.02 of *Journal of Documentation*). The total number of cites is 13850, each journal making a small portion (*p*) of this sum (Marshakova-Shaikevich 2004b, 2005)

Maps for fields "Information Science and Library Science" are given in this part (Figure 5, 6, 7).

The maps presented on Figures 5 and 6 clearly demonstrate the existence of a separate cluster of 8 journals (figure 7), in no way connected with the rest of our category. Among the citing journals of this cluster many more journals can be found which are not part of JCR: Social Science Edition *Information Science and Library Science* category, but which appear on the list of JCR: Science Edition *Computer*

Science, Information Systems category. These are: *Decis Support Sys, Eur J Inform Syst, Inform, Software Tech, Internet Res, J Comput Inform Syst, Wirschaftsing*. This list may be extended by many journals in Social Science outside our category (Information and Library Science): *Comput Educ, Comput Hum Behav, Int J Electr Co, Int J Hum-Comput, Int J Oper Prod M, IEEE T Eng Manage, J Comput Assist L, Leadership Quart, J Bus Res, Omega- Int J Manag, Organ Sci*.

Analysis of bibliometric maps gives an opportunity to discuss some general problems. Researchers in scientometrics (or bibliometrics) usually see a map of discrete set with subsets in them as the final result of their study. Failure to attain such a picture seems a disappointment. However, another alternative to thinking in customary cluster terms may be suggested. Maps 5 and 6 evoke a metaphor of space: the two tentative clusters, represented here, are not separated by any barrier – they are bridged by *Libr Quart, Libr Trends, LIBRI* (and to a certain degree – *Coll Res Libr* and *ASLIB Proc*).

However, the opposite poles: e.g. *Libr J, Online, Electr Libr* on the one hand, and *JASIST, J Inform Sci, Annu Rev Inform Sci* on the other are not connected anywhere. The journals in the upper part of the combined picture (Figure 5 and Figure 6) are mostly preoccupied with theoretical problems, while the journals at the bottom part (Figure 6) more often try to solve practical problems. Nevertheless, the composite character of this large combined cluster is evident. This conclusion is supported by journals with low *R* values, which can be seen at the periphery of Figure 5 and Figure 6. *Scientometrics, Proc ASIS Annu Meet* (to a lesser extent *Can J Inform Libr Sci*) are in the upper part of the picture. *Database,*

Figure 5. Co-citation relatedness in some journals in LIS field
Source: Marshakova-Shaikevich, 2005

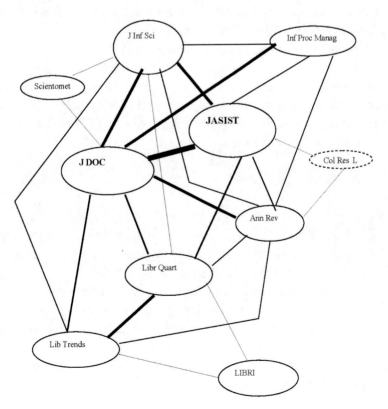

Figure 6. Co-citation relatedness in some journals in LIS field
Source: Marshakova-Shaikevich, 2005

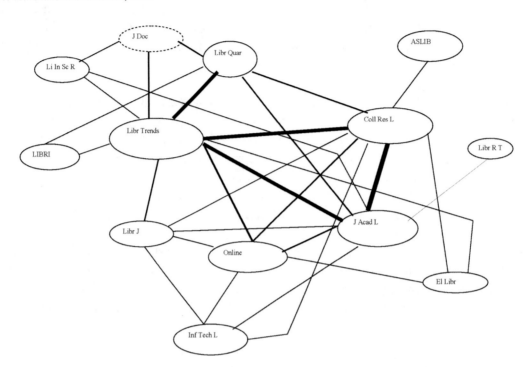

Interlend Doc, Supply, Libr Collect Acquis, Online Inform Rev, J Scholarly Publ, Knowl Organ evidently belong to Library Science he bottom part of the picture).

In conclusion the visualization on research results presented on journal co-citation maps discovered two clusters of journals within the JCR:SSE category of Information and Library Science. The lesser of the clusters Information Systems and Management (Figure 7) has consistent inner links, the greater cluster show some characteristics of a space (figures 5-6). The well-cited journals, which did not show links to those clusters, turned out to be outright mistakes and should be excluded from the category of Information and Library Science (Marshakova-Shaikevich, 2003).

Maps for Field "Women's Studies"

The same method was applied to the journals of the field *"Women's Studies"*. The results are reflected on maps for this field (Figures 8 and 9). Some examples of the results of this study are given in tabular form. The binary links between words discovered in this way may form triplets or other groups with more than two member words (see Marshakova-Shaikevich, 2004a)

Seventeen journals of the field under study of the 25 journals belonging to Women's Studies field showed positive values of R. The corresponding links are presented in Figures 8, 9.

Three clusters are clearly seen in this map. This result is quite meaningful which is demonstrated by the analysis of keywords (supplied by the authors or editor). For each journal a frequency list of keywords was formed. Common keywords of a pair of journals (or of all journals of the cluster) show their thematic similarity. Let us turn to the three clusters in Figure 8

Figure 7. Co-citation relatedness in some journals in Information Systems and Information Management fields
Source: Marshakova-Shaikevich, 2009

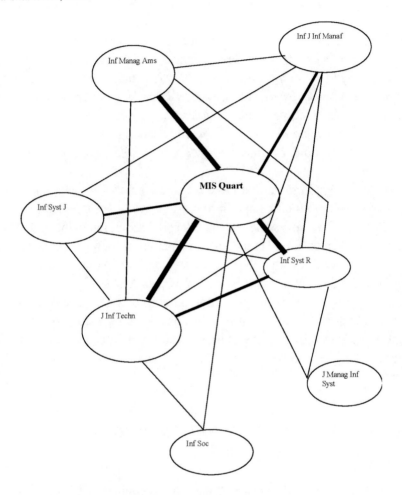

Cluster 1 includes 3 journals (*Sex Roles, Psychology of Women Quarterly* and *Feminism and Psychology*) with all R values exceeding 6. For the first two journals R is 26. The thematic coherence of this cluster is reflected in the list of keywords: *gender, girls, identify, knowledge, men, mental health, personality, psychology, rape, sex, students, women.*

The first pair of journals have many additional keywords: *dissatisfaction, psychology, stress, stereotypes, aggression, experiences, self-esteem, weight.* All these keywords belong to the central thematic component of the cluster, i.e. PSYCHOLOGY. The same conclusion is supported by keywords denoting methodological concept of psychological research: *college students, inventory, model, objectification, reliability, responses, scale, students, validation, validity.*

There are six journals in cluster 2: *Gender and Society, Signs, Women Studies International Forum, Feminist Review, Journal of Gender Studies, Feminist Studies*, but R values are low. Common keywords are few, nevertheless we find here: *gender, labor, movement, population, power, war, women, work.* All those words show the thematic center of the cluster: SOCIOLOGY and POLITICS concerning women. A few more journals may be added to the cluster (with R values < 2): *European Journal of Women's*

Study, Social Politics, Women & Therapy (see Fig 8a). Those additional journals support the same thematic conclusion.

Cluster 3 includes 5 journals: *Women & Health, Journal of Women Health & Gender-Based, Women Health Issues, Journal of Women Aging, Journal of Women Health*; all devoted to the theme WOMEN's HEALTH. There are 145 keywords, common at least to one of pair of journals. They are often medical terms: *Alzheimer's disease, blood pressure, breast cancer, cancer, coronary heart diseases, disorders, epidemiology, estrogen replace therapy, hip fracture, HIV infection, hormone replace therapy, intervention, mammography, menopause, osteoporosis, risk, risk factor(s)*. Demographic terms are reflection of standard experimental research procedure: *adolescent, African-American, age, black, education, employment, older women, population, race*. Keywords denoting behavior traits are also conspicuous here, e.g.: *abuse, assault, cocaine, contraception, domestic violence, exercise, homeless, pregnancy, smokers, smoking, victims*.

However, it should be kept in mind that there are a few keywords common to all 3 clusters (*gender, women, United States*) or to the first and third clusters (*attitudes, behavior, depression, inventory, knowledge, men, risk factor, sex, stress*). The keyword *work* is common to the second and third clusters.

In conclusion we could emphasize that the journal co-citation analysis, carried out in this study, discovered three clusters of journals within the JCR:SSE category of Women's Studies: *PSYCHOLOGY; SOCIOLOGY and POLITICS concerning women; WOMEN's HEALTH*.

Co-citation procedure provides its greater differentiating power as compared to use of keywords. To be sure the keywords *gender* and *women* may be considered characteristic of the field as a whole. On the other hand most keywords of singe clusters would unite them with psychology, sociology or medicine. Perhaps a better solution for a thematic cluster would be to use a group of keywords, rather than single terms.

BIBLIOMETRIC MAPS OF THE INTERNATIONAL SCIENTIFIC COLLABORATION OF EU COUNTRIES

Scientific collaboration of EU countries is becoming a significant issue in bibliometric and webometric studies of science. Only some of them should be mentioned in the context of this study: Lamirel et al. presented a new approach for evaluation of collaboration between European universities (Lamirel, 2005). Science collaboration of in the field of social sciences was discussed by the present author at Collnet 2006 in Nancy (Marshakova-Shaikevich, 2006), bibliometric perspectives of an integrated EU research was presented by Robert J.W. Tijssen at Collnet 2008 in Berlin (Tijssen, 2008). An attempt at visualization of international collaboration of 27 EU countries in science and social sciences is made here. The resulting maps could serve for better understanding of structure of scientific cooperation in Europe.

The main object of the present study is international scientific collaboration within the EU countries. However, lest essential information should be lost, the data for some countries outside European Union were also included into material of this study. Those countries are – USA, Japan, People's Republic of China, Canada, Australia, India, Russia, Switzerland, Israel, Norway, Iran, Croatia and Iceland. The statistics of academic publications of 40 states under study are given in Table 1.

The EU countries contribute some 40% to the world output in science proper and 33% in social sciences. Bibliographic data were drawn from DBs Web of Science: SCIex 2006 and SSCI 2006.

Figure 8. Map of journal co-citations in the Women's Study field
Source: Marshakova-Shaikevich, 2004a

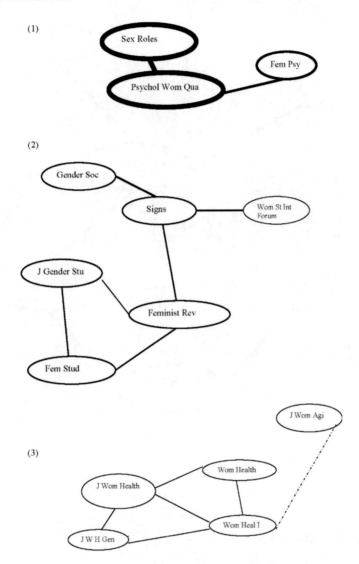

The source data call for some modifications for our purpose. The tradition of British authors to indicate parts of UK (England, Scotland, Wales, Northern Ireland) rather than the kingdom as a whole gives those parts undue prominence. The figures of that 'internal collaboration' should be subtracted from the sum of four parts to give the true result for UK.

Methodology for Construction Maps of Collaboration of Countries

To calculate specific collaboration relatedness of two countries the following formula was used:

Figure 9. Map of journal co-citations in the fields Sociology and Politics concerning Women
Source: Marshakova-Shaikevich, 2004a

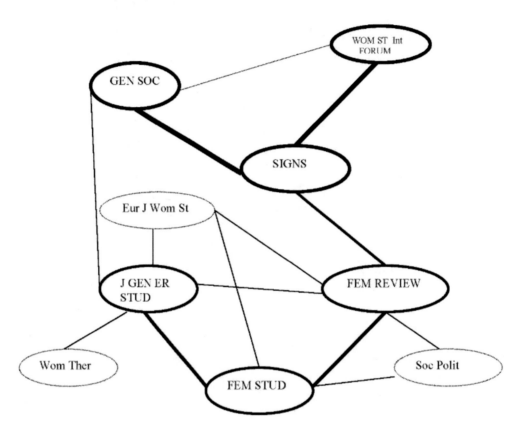

$$S_{ij} = \frac{\left(C_{ij} - m\right)}{\sqrt{m}} \qquad (5)$$

C_{ij} – real number of joint publications of countries i and j.

m - mathematical expectation of number of joint publications of countries i and j.

The mathematical expectation of the number of joint publications, entirely due to chance, was calculated as:

$$m = N_i \times P_j \qquad (6)$$

with N_i – total collaboration publications of country i,

$P_j = N_j/\sum N$ – the weight of country j in the total number of publications of the world.

Table 1. Research activity in science and social sciences: 2006

Country	Social Sciences: Total N = 150 th		Science: World Total N= 1218 th	
	SSCI 2006 Number publications	Weight in world total %	SCIex 2006 Number of publications	Weight in world total %
Austria	722	0.48	10750	0.88
Belgium	1465	0.98	15471	1.27
Denmark	998	0.66	11047	0.91
Finland	1111	0.74	9556	0.78
France	2934	1.96	61899	5.08
Germany	**6928**	**4.62**	**89306**	**7.33**
Greece	593	0.39	10463	0.86
Ireland	654	0.44	7067	0.56
Italy	2441	1.63	50886	4.18
Luxembourg	0		265	0.02
Netherlands	4725	3.15	28315	2.32
Portugal	405	0.27	7488	0.61
Spain	2855	1.90	37808	3.10
Sweden	2290	1.53	19466	1.60
United Kingdom	19691*	13.13	100575*	8.52
Czech Republic	270	0.18	7203	0.59
Poland	403	0.27	17021	1.40
Hungary	317	0.21	5974	0.49
Slovakia	151	0.10	2305	0.19
Slovenia	124	0.08	2225	0.18
Estonia	88	0.06	874	0.07
Cyprus	57	0.04	364	0.03
Lithuania	107	0.07	1213	0.10
Malta	14	0.01	72	0.01
Latvia	20	0.01	343	0.03
Romania	70	0.05	3219	0.26
Bulgaria	51	0.03	1863	0.15
USA	**74567**	**49.7**	**376833**	**30.94**
Australia	6676	4.45	32718	2.69
Canada	8951	5.97	51725	4.25
Russia	530	0.35	23188	1.90
Croatia	334	0.22	2118	0.17
Israel	1669	1.11	14310	1.17
Japan	1828	1.21	88851	7.29
Norway	1148	0.76	7712	0.63
Switzerland	1808	1.20	21055	1.73
Iceland	82	0.05	574	0.05
Peoples-R-China	1965	1.3	86025	7.06

*The sum of UK publications adjusted for 'internal collaboration'.

135

One can see that the of French and German joint publications corresponds exactly to what might be expected as a null-hypothesis, i.e. those countries are statistically independent as far as international collaboration is concerned. $S = 0$ here. The number of German and Italian joint publications is even less than expected ($S = -4$), which might be interpreted as the effect of a very weak factor hindering the collaboration between the two countries. On the other hand, all other cells are positive deviations from mathematical expectation. In the pair 'France-Austria' this association is negligible, in all other pairs it is significant or highly significant (Marshakova-Shaikevich, 2007a).

A matrix of 27 x 27 would be too cumbersome. A graphic representation on the maps 10 and 11 is easily visualized and gives better ground for interpretation (Figure 10, 11).

Analysis of Bibliometric Maps in Science and Social Science

In Figure 10 a map of international collaboration of countries in science is given. The four degrees of thickness of the lines reflect values of S as follows:

1. $S = 50$ and more (e.g. UK – Ir, CzR – Sk, Au – Ge),
2. $S = 25$-49 (e.g. Fr – Swt, De – Ic, Fi – Es, Sl - Cr),
3. $S = 15$-24 (e.g. Fr – It, Ge – Ru, CzR – Pl, Hu – Ro),
4. $S = 10$-11 (e.g. UK – M, Sp – It, Bu – Gr, Sw – Li).

A very compact cluster of countries is seen in the upper part of the map: it comprises five Scandinavian countries with three small Baltic states. One bridge to the rest of Europe is formed by United Kingdom with three states: Australia, Ireland and Malta. Another bridge (of weaker S) connects Scandinavia with Germany, Netherlands and Belgium. Specific links of the countries of Romance languages are manifest in the left part of the map. Switzerland with its languages and its scientific tradition is a virtual hub of the map. It has strongest ties with Germany and Austria, who show various specific links with the states of Central and Eastern Europe (Russia included). Some of those countries (especially Hungary and Bulgaria) are apt to participate in international collaboration to an uncommon degree. In addition to the links of the map we can mention Hungary's links with Finland, Sweden and Poland, or Bulgaria's ties with France, Italy, Austria and Romania. On the contrary, Poland's involvement in this cluster is not so great, although its weak ties ($S = 6$-8) with Austria, Germany, Russia and Lithuania might be mentioned. No specific links were observed outside Europe (with the single exception of 'UK-Australia' pair).

In Figure 11 a map of the international collaboration in social science is given specific links in social sciences to some extent resemble the outlines of Figure 10 on a lesser scale. The output of publications in social sciences is eight times less than that in science proper. Accordingly the values of S are much lower. The four degrees of thickness of the lines reflect values of S as follows:

1. $S = 20$ and more (e.g. Be – Ne, CzR – Sk, Es – La),
2. $S = 15$-19 (e.g. Ge – Swt, Li – Es, Sl - Cr),
3. $S = 9$-14 (e.g. Sw – No, Ge – Au, CzR – Pl, Hu – Bu),
4. $S = 4$-8 (e.g. De – Fi, Sp – It, Fr – Swt Sw – Li).

United Kingdom disappears from the map altogether. Scando-Baltic cluster remains intact. The linguistic preponderances are evident in Western Europe (with German and Romance languages very

Figure 10. Map of collaboration in science
Source: Marshakova-Shaikevich, 2010b

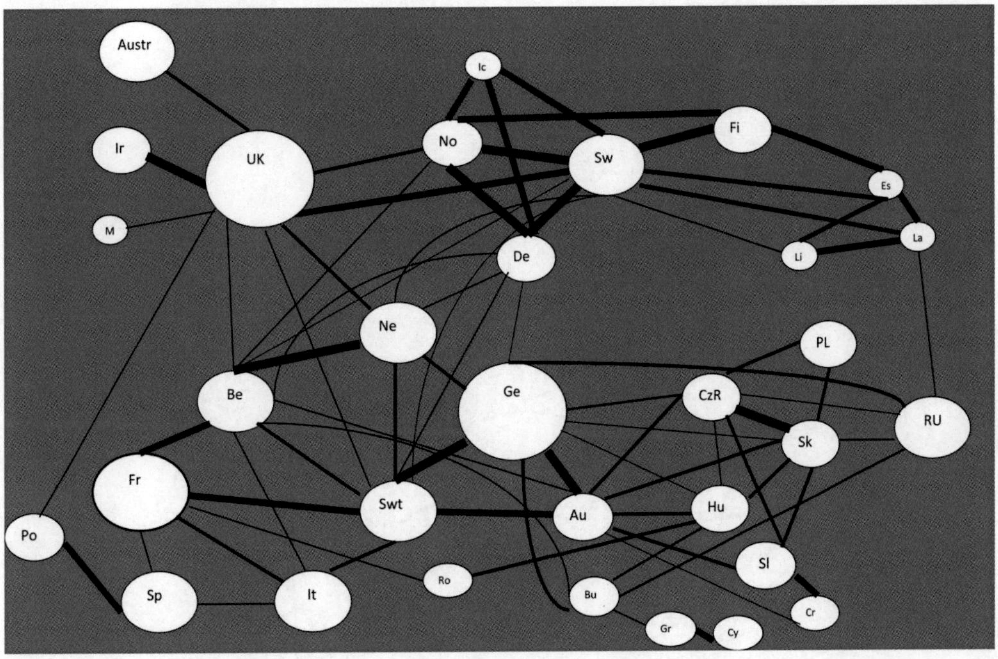

active as cultural factor). But East European cluster with its Soviet and more ancient Austro-Hungarian traditions is alive. It is interesting to note that there is no connection between USA and EU countries, USA only have a weak links with Norway (S=6) and Israel (S=3). China appears quite isolated. It does not show any links to the countries under study.

Atlas of Science issued at ISI may serve as a basis for further bibliometric studies.

Bibliometric study of ISI Atlas of Science: Biotechnology and Molecular Genetics was aimed at analysis of the contribution of various countries and scientific organizations to the progress of world science. An attempt was made to construct a space of scientific organizations based on their thematic spectra. A map of science built on "ISI Atlas of science: Biotechnology and Molecular Genetics 1981/82" served as a visualization of space of science organizations sharing common thematic specters. Links between two organizations were determined by the number of common Specialties presented in the Atlas of Science for these organizations (ISI Atlas of Science: Biotechnology and Molecular Genetics, 1984; Garfield, 1984)

So the link between a pair of organizations was calculated according the expression:

$$p = \frac{F_{xy} - m}{\sqrt{(m+1)}} \qquad (7)$$

where Fxy – is the sum of minimal number of common documents of organization x and y;

Figure 11. Map of collaboration in social science
Source: Marshahova Shaikovich, 2010bThe map of scientific organizations based on their thematic spectres

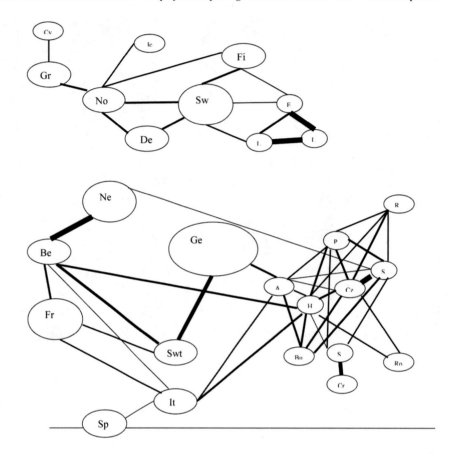

m - the mathematical expectation of the number common papers for specialty "x" and specialty "y" (see details Marshakova, 1988, p.277).

Figure 12 is a resulting map of research institutions, it may be considered a grand world social institution of biotechnology and molecular genetics (as distinct from 127 Research Fronts registered in the Atlas of Science). Such map may facilitate general orientation in scientific professional communication of a given field of science. This map of organizations (universities, research institutions, important hospitals) working on problems of biotechnology and molecular genetics.

Values of *p:*

- 2: Berkeley Univ (CA), USA
- 5: Scripps Found (la Jolla), USA
- 6: Univ of California, San Diego, USA
- 7: Univ of California, Los-Angeles, USA
- 8: Univ of South-Ca, Los-Angeles, USA
- 9: California Inst of Tech, Passada, USA
- 10: Salk Inst.of Biol Stud (San Diego,CA), USA

Figure 12. Map: A space of scientific organizations on based ISI Atlas of Science:Biotechnology and Molecular Genetics 1981/82
Source: Marshakova, 1988

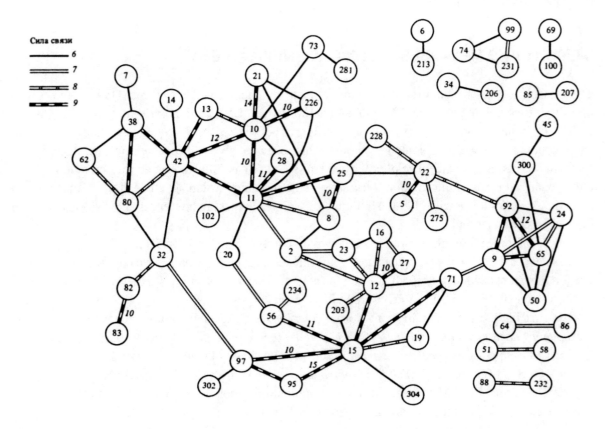

- 11: Univ.of California (San Francisco), USA
- 12: Stanford Univ. (CA), USA
- 13: Univ of Colorado, Denver, USA
- 15: Yale Univ., USA
- 14: Univ of CT, Famington, USA
- 16: Univ. of Chicago, USA
- 19: Dept of Embrion, Carnegie Inst, MA, USA
- 20: J-H Univ, USA
- 21: NCI, Bethesda, USA
- 22 - NIAD, Bethesda, USA
- 25: Harvard Univ., USA
- 28: MTI, USA
- 42: Rockefeller Univ (N-Y), USA
- 65: Royal Melbourn Hospital, Australia
- 71: MRC (Medical Research Centre), Cambridge, UK
- 80: Univ. of Uppsala, Sweden
- 92: Basel Inst of Immunology, Switzerland95: Univ of Zurich, Switzerland

- 97: CNRS, Strasburg, France
- 102: Inst of Mol Biology, Moscow, USSR
- 300: Osako Univ, Japan

MEMORY AND MEMORIES IN LEXICAL ENVIRONMENT

The present study is an exercise in application of distributional statistical analysis (DSA) to the corpus of abstracts, containing words MEMORY and MEMORIES. DSA is an algorithmic procedure, based entirely on graphic word (chain of letters and/or figures between spaces) frequencies in the text without any recourse to the semantic content of words. This formal analysis 'discovers' multiword sequences (potential terms of a science discipline). The results of DSA is followed by an interpretation, taking into account all kinds of information, accessible to the researcher (Shaikevich A, 2001). This two-step procedure belongs to the wider field of bibliometrics, aimed at making inferences about science through the analysis of quantified data.

The data for the present bibliometric study was drawn from SSCI DB 2005, including many fields of social sciences (Economics, I & L sciences, Neurosciences, Psychology etc.). Two corpora were formed: one for documents with word MEMORY and the other for documents with word MEMORIES (Table 2):

Two frequency dictionaries (FDs) were built for each corpus.

The first FD (33 thousand different words) contains single graphic words with their frequencies, e.g. *counter-memory* 1, *countermemory* 2, *eyewitness-memory* 4, *human-memory* 10, *long-memory* 26, *long-term-memory* 75, *mci-memory* 2, *memorability* 6, *memories* 448, *memorization* 12, *memorized* 17, *memory* 8521, *1st-episode* 38, *episode* 43, *episode-specific* 4, *episodes* 42, *episodic* 589, *episodic-like* 18, etc. The second FD (285 thousand different combinations) includes binary combinations of graphic words in two versions: alphabetically arranged according to left and right word (Table 3):

FD of binary combinations is an extensive source of potential multiword terms. The most frequent sequence '*working memory*' (f = 963) is evidently a terminological collocation, on the other hand the inverse sequence '*memory working*' occurring 19 times is not terminological. The sequence '*delayed memory*' (f=17) is a good candidate for being a term (the sequence '*memory delayed*' never occurred in the text).

The analysis of word pairs with MEMORY as left member is instructive, when the frequency of the pair is compared to the mathematical expectation (*m*), calculated on the assumption of mutual independence (Table 4):

The grammatical words after MEMORY (5 first examples in the left column) are good syntactic signals, which exclude terminological interpretation. Other examples may be interpreted as terms or rather

Table 2. Statistics of two corpora under study

	MEMORY Corpus	MEMORIES Corpus
Number of abstracts	3 297	156
The corpus size (total number of words in the text)	680 556	31 436

Table 3. Frequencies of binary combinations of graphic words

FD Arranged According to Left Word		FD Arranged According to Right Word	
F	Binary combination	F	Binary combination
31	1st-episode schizophrenia	5	1 st episode
20	cingulated gyrus	2	an episode
13	depressive episode	1	caching episode
5	episode schizophrenia	1	drinking episode
41	episodic and	1	eating episode
11	episodic memories	7	first episode
398	episodic memory	26	and episodic
11	episodic recall	11	between episodic
6	episodic recognition	46	in episodic

Table 4. Term frequency (F) and mathematical expectation (m) with MEMORY as left member

F	M	Word Pairs	F	m	Word Pairs
458	251	memory and	22	2	memory load
30	18	memory but	43	12	memory model
302	70	memory for	16	4	memory paradigm
93	47	memory is	229	29	memory performance
85	50	memory was	74	5	memory processes
27	3	memory bias	129	11	memory retrieval
68	5	memory capacity	139	28	memory task
49	1.3	memory complaints	134	15	memory tasks
72	2.5	memory consolidation	50	8	memory tests
66	12	memory deficits	25	5	memory traces
122	11	memory impairment			

term-like collocations that may be easily grouped on a semantic *basis - capacity, load, span; complaints, deficits, impairment; task(s), tests, performance, retrieval; model, paradigm.* The only true term in table 2 is *'memory bias'* (along with *'attentional bias'* (f=25), *'response bias'*(f=27).

Even more significant are word pairs with MEMORY as right member (Table 5):

These terms do not form large semantic groups, but are sometimes linked into antonymic pairs (delayed vs. immediate, explicit vs. implicit, long-term vs. short-term, verbal vs. nonverbal).

For further analysis four multiword terms were chosen *WORKING MEMORY, EPISODIC MEMORY, SEMANTIC MEMORY* and *AUTOBIOGRAFICAL MEMORY.* Accordingly four subcorpora of documents were built (WM, EM, SM, AM) and corresponding FDs were generated. The share of those subcorpora in the general corpus is as follows: WM - 27%, EM - 8.5%, SM - 2.7%, AM - 2.5%. From the largest WORKING MEMORY subcorpus a subcorpus of 2-order was formed, which included 3-line fragments of text around 'working memory' (the share of that subcorpus was 2.7% of the general corpus).

Table 5. Term frequency (F) and mathematical expectation (m) with MEMORY as right member

F	M	Word Pairs	F	m	Word Pairs
149	3	autobiographical memory	29	5	phonological memory
31	7	collective memory	25	1.1	procedural memory
125	2	declarative memory	78	1.8	prospective memory
17	2.3	delayed memory	420	18	recognition memory
398	7	episodic memory	21	1.3	reference memory
16	0.2	episodic-like memory	13	0.5	remote memory
135	4.5	explicit memory	161	10	semantic memory
43	1.4	eyewitness memory	35	2.2	sensory memory
50	3.5	false memory	206	3.7	short-term memory
20	2.3	immediate memory	150	12	special memory
165	6	implicit memory	27	2	subjective memory
21	3.4	location memory	31	5	transactive memory
51	2.8	long memory	111	11	verbal memory
116	5	long-term memory	95	15	visual memory
20	12	nonverbal memory	19	2.4	visuospatial memory
34	1.5	organizational memory	963	12	working memory

Specific features of a subcorpus within the framework of DSA were elicited by means of lexical markers. A lexical marker is a word or word combination, whose frequency in the subcorpus deviates significantly from the mathematical expectation, calculated on the null hypothesis of a uniform general corpus .

This deviation was measured with the help of the formula:

$$S = \frac{(x - m - 1)}{\sqrt{m}} \qquad (8)$$

where

x is observed frequency of the word in the subcorpus,

$m = Np$ - mathematical expectation,

N - frequency of the word in the general corpus,

p - share of the subcorpus in the general corpus.

All former experience proves that values of S=3 and more are statistically significant.

The transition to specific subcorpora brought forth two important results. It helped to formally extend the central term of the subcorpus, e.*g. n-back working memory* (f=5), *nonspatial working memory* (f=5), *spatial working memory* (f=114), *verbal working memory* (f=99), *visual working memory* (f=37), *visuospatial working memory* (f=31). But the main finding was the discovery of lists of lexical markers (a few hundred terms) for each subcorpus.

This final result of the formal procedure was done by the author) was followed by a semantic interpretation. It turned out that lexical markers of a subcorpus as a rule can be brought together into semantic groups. For example, *'working memory'* was associated with such groups as

1. **Brain:** *Prefrontal cortex (PFC), cingulated cortex,* etc.;
2. **Disease:** *Alzheimer's disease, schizofrenia, autism,* etc.;
3. **Experiments:** *Task, test, functional magnetic resonance imaging (FMRI),* etc.,
4. **Characteristics:** *Age, children, IQ, extremely low birthweight ELBW,* etc.
5. **Substances:** *Dopamine, protein, protein TGCRND8*

'Episodic memory' was associated with such groups as

1. **Brain:** *Prefrontal cortex (PFC), anterior prefrontal cortex (aPFC), anterior temporal lobe, frontal lobe, frontal gyres, parahippocampal gyrus, medial prefrontal cortex, medial temporal lobe (MTL), ventral medial prefrontal cortex (vmpc)*
2. **Disease:** AD, epilepsy, amnesia, *retrograde amnesia, transient global amnesia (TGA), autobiographical amnesia, semantic dementia,*
3. **Methods:** *Functional magnetic resonance imagin (fmri), electroconvulsive therapy (ECT), positron -emission-tomography*
4. **Memories:** Picture recognition, recollection process, episodic recollection, autobiographical memories.

'Semantic memory' was associated with such groups as

1. **Brain:** *Hippocampus, hippocampal, lobe, gyrus, fronral lobe gyrus, medial temporal lobe (MTL), rhinal cortex,* cortex, prefrontal, PFC, frontal, dlpfc, anterior cingulated cortex,
2. **Disease:** *Epilepsy, dementia, semantic, PNFA, dementia, TLE, left TLE, mesial TLE,*
3. **Linguistics:** *Grammatically, verb, modality-specific, property, syntagmatic, paradigmatic, wr,*
   a. (semantics): *thematic, naming, category, property, object(s), structures, couterexamples, semantic processing, knowledge, artifactual, associative, lexico-semantic*
4. **General Words:** *Animals, patients, nonliving things, pictures, stimulations*

The first two groups are common to first three subcourpora, but some details would be different, e.g. EM and SM would stress hippocampus, gyrus and temporal lobes in Brain group, epilepsy and dementia in Disease group (with EM stressing amnesia). SM has many linguistic terms (Figures 13, 14, 15).

'Autobiographical memory' was associated with such groups as

Figure 13. Semantic field of working memory
Source: Marshakova-Shaikevich, 2007b

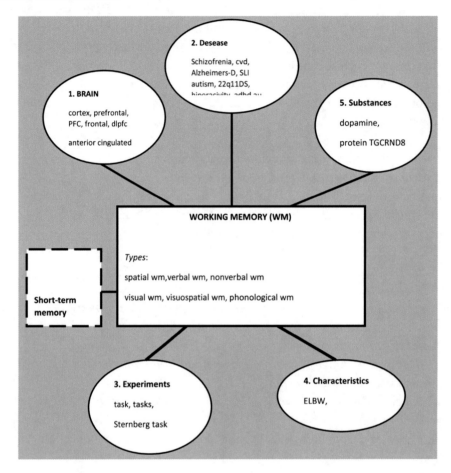

1. **Personality:** *ego*, *self-focus*, *self-defining*, *self-recognition*, *self-awareness*, *self-devaluative*, *self-focused*, *self-information*, *self-perception*, *self-reported*, *self-continuity*,
2. Self-related, self-verification;
3. **Emotions:** angry, depressed, expressiveness, *memory bump, inner speech*
4. **Memories:** episodic memories, false memories, autobiographical memories, episodic autobiographical memories, episodic memory retrieval
5. **Past:** *ago, past, earliest, retrograde, remote time period, life, early-life, life, early-life, childhood, mother-child, mothers, reminiscence bump, autobiographical reminiscence bump, episodic*
6. **Events:** *events, town, kibbutz, earthquake, Toronto*

The picture of the terminological field is absolutely different in AM (with some weak links to EM), which seems closer to psychology in contrast to first three subcourpora, which belong to neurosciences (Figure 16). Total semantic picture of MEMORY is presented at Figure 17.

Figure 14. Semantic field of episodic memory
Source: Marshakova-Shaikevich, 2007b

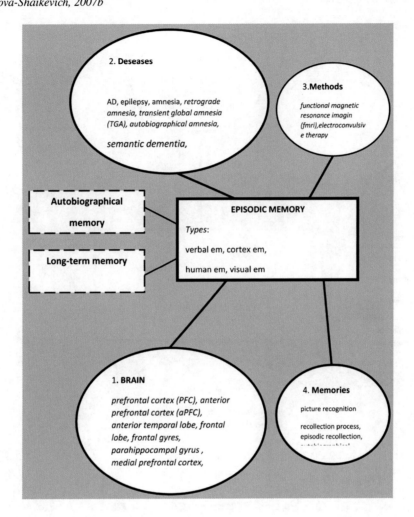

CONCLUSION

The bibliometric maps of science presented here were manually constructed by the author in the course of four past decades. The first co-citation maps were made possible by the appearance in 1963 of the Science Citation Index created by Dr. Garfield at the Institute for Science Information (ISI). Soon followed electronic versions of those book indices (ISI: SCI, SSCI, A&HCI, JCR,) on CDs and later in Internet (Web of Science, Web of Knowledge). Those databases gave much material for numerous bibliometric studies with their new quantitative methods of the analysis of science.

The five approaches to construction of maps presented in this Chapter are based on the same general idea of normalization of deviations of the observed data from the mathematical expectation. The application of the same formula leads to discovery of statistically significant links between objects (publications, authors, journals, countries, scientific organizations and keywords) reflected in the maps. The map of co-citation publications representing the cognitive structure of a scientific field does not coincide

Figure 15. Semantic field of SEMANTIC MEMORY
Source: Marshakova-Shaikevich, 2007b

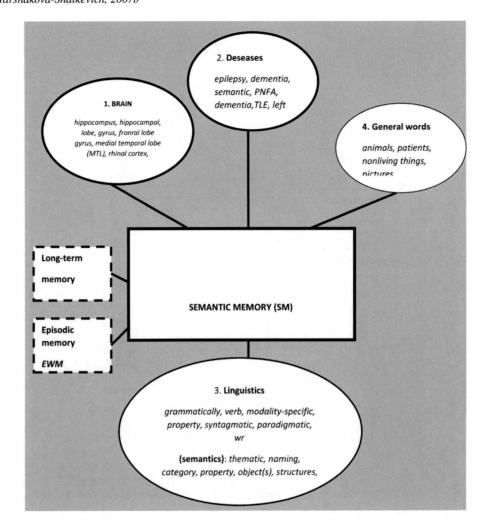

with the map of co-citation authors where some social factors are reflected. The method of co-citation analysis (method of structural bibliometrics) serves to identify cognitive and social structures of science and the nature of their correlations (congruence, non-congruence), as well as forms of professional communication. Maps of science produced by the method of co-citation or journal co-citation reflected one more way of knowledge existence – prospective connections between publications or authors or journals determined by relationships within the scientific community (on the whole). The maps of international scientific collaboration of EU countries discover that specific links in social sciences to some extent resemble the outlines of science on a lesser scale. The output of publications in social sciences is eight times less than that in science proper. The map of scientific organizations reflects connections between thematic specters of these organizations working on problems of biotechnology and molecular genetics. MEMORY maps reflect semantic fields both of the general term MEMORY and specific terms *working memory, episodic memory, semantic memory, autobiographical memory.*

Figure 16. Semantic field of autobiographical memory
Source: Marshakova-Shaikevich, 2007b

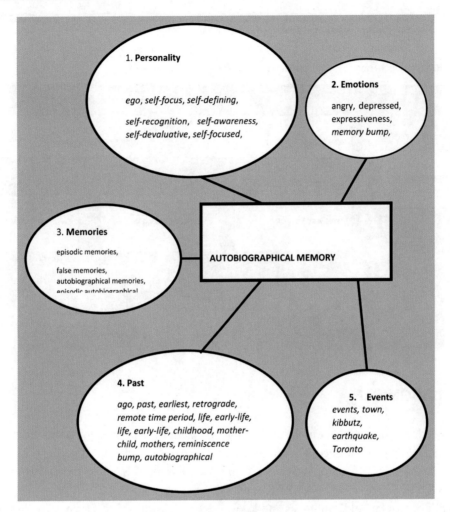

Visualization of scientific research results acknowledged the fact that such maps may be regarded as an objective picture of the cognitive and social structures of science ; they could lead to discovery of important individual papers and journals, true leaders in new fields and directions of science. Bibliometric maps may facilitate general orientation in scientific professional communication of a given field of science. The maps of science given in the Chapter are valid for the time of their creation. At present they are interesting from the point of view of history and development of science.

Figure 17. Memory
Source: Marshakova-Shaikevich, 2007b

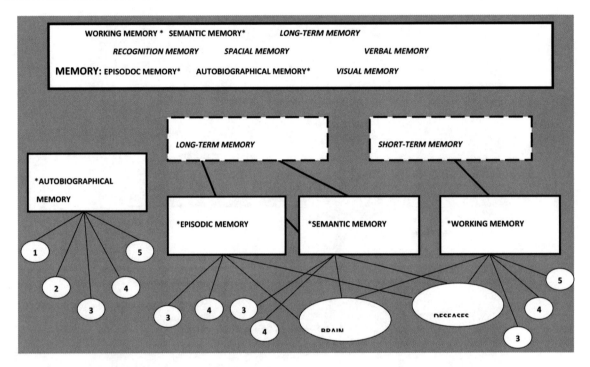

ACKNOWLEDGMENT

This Chapter is dedicated to the memory of Dr Eugene Garfield . The present author enjoyed the generosity of Dr Garfield who gave access to the data (such as Atlas of science: Biotechnology and molecular genetics; databases JCR, National Science Indicators, Essential Science Indicators on) and to such networks as Web of Science, later Web of Knowledge.

The breadth of Dr Garfield's interests and knowledge was astonishing. His personality was a unique amalgam of thoroughness of a scientist, of managerial talents, of almost poetic insights of a humanitarian. At the beginning of the 1960s he created the Science Citation Index, which immediately gained popularity among researchers as a source of information. Soon the system was extended to social sciences, and later to arts and humanities. Besides serving practical purposes those citation indices became testing grounds for experiments in bibliometric research. Exclusive bibliometric information was supplied by Journal Citation Reports – Garfield's favorite of the 1970s. In the 1980s appeared Atlases of science, showing nascent research fronts (an experiment never repeated since then). That was a materialization of an idea (he had long cherished) to combine bibliographic and encyclopedic information.

Dr Garfield was a generous man: thanks to that side of his nature many large libraries of Eastern Europe were enriched with the products of ISI.

REFERENCES

Anscombe, G. E. M. (1981). Memory, "Experience", and Causation. In G.E.M. Anscombe (Ed.), Collected Philosophical Papers (vol. 2, pp. 120-130). Oxford, UK: Blackwell.

Bassecoulard, E., & Zitt, M. (1999). Indicators in a research institute: A multi-level classification of scientific journals. *Scientometrics*, *44*(3), 323–345. doi:10.1007/BF02458483

Carruthers, M. (1990). *The Book of Memory*. Cambridge, UK: Cambridge University Press.

Garfield, E. (1984). Introducing The ISI Atlas of science: Biotechnology and molecular genetics, 1981/82 and bibliographic update for 1983/84. Essays of an Information Scientist, 7, 313-325.

ISI Atlas of science: Biotechnology and molecular genetics, 1981/82 covering 127 Research Fronts Specialities. (1984). Philadelphia: Academic Press.

Kessler, M. (1963). Bibliografic coupling between scientific papers. *American Documentation*, *14*(1), 10–25. doi:10.1002/asi.5090140103

Lamb, W. E. Jr. (1964). Theory of an Optical Maser. *Physical Review*, *134*(6A), A1429–A1450. doi:10.1103/PhysRev.134.A1429

Lamirel, J. C., Al Shehabi, S., & Francois, C. (2005). Evaluation of collaboration between European universities using dynamic interaction between multiple sources. In P. Ingwersen, & B. Larsen (Eds.), *Proceedings of ISSI 2005: 10th international conference of the International Society for Scientometrics and Informetrics, Stockholm, Sweden, July 24-28* (pp. 740-749). Stockholm: Karolinska University Press.

Marshakova, I. (1973). System of document connections based on references [in Russian]. *Nauchno-Tekhnicheskaja Informacya. Ser. 2, N6*, 3–8.

Marshakova, I. (1981). Citation Networks in Information Science. *Scientometrics*, *3*(1), 13–26. doi:10.1007/BF02021861

Marshakova, I. (1988). *The SCI system as a mean of monitoring of science development*. Moscow: Nauka. (in Russian)

Marshakova-Shaikevich, I. (2003). Journal Co-Citation Analysis in the Fields of Information Science and Library Science. In W. Krzemińska & P. Nowak (Eds.), *Language, Information and Communication Studies* (pp. 87–96). Poznań: Sorus.

Marshakova-Shaikevich, I. (2004a). Journal co-citation analysis in the field of Women's Studies. In H. Kretschmer, Y. Singh, & R. Kudra (Eds.), *WIS-2004, International Workshop on Webometrics, Informetrics and Scientometrics, 2-5 March 2004* (pp. 247-259). Roorkee: Central Library, Indian Institute of Technology.

Marshakova-Shaikevich, I. (2004b). Journal co-citaton analysis. *Journal of Information Management and Scientometrics*, *1*(2), 27–36.

Marshakova-Shaikevich, I. (2005). Bibliometric maps of Field of Science. *Information Processing & Management*, *41*(6), 1534–1547. doi:10.1016/j.ipm.2005.03.027

Marshakova-Shaikevich, I. (2006). Science collaboration of new 10 EU countries in the field of social sciences. *Information Processing & Management, 42*(6), 1592–1598. doi:10.1016/j.ipm.2006.03.023

Marshakova-Shaikevich, I. (2007a). The visualization of scientific collaboration of 15 'old ' and 10 'new' EU countries in the field of social sciences. *Collnet Journal of Scientometrics and Information Management, 1*(1), 9–16. doi:10.1080/09720502.2007.10700948

Marshakova-Shaikevich, I. (2007b). Memory and Memoriesa in lexical environment: Bibliometric analysis of SSCI DB. *Collnet Journal of Scientometrics and Information Management, 1*(2), 41–52. do i:10.1080/09737766.2007.10700830

Marshakova-Shaikevich, I. (2009). Information management as the part of Information and library science: bibliometric study. In B. F. Kubiak & A. Korowicki (Eds.), *Information Management* (pp. 498–506). Gdańsk: Gdansk University Press.

Marshakova-Shaikevich, I. (2010a). Meeting Robert Merton: Discussion of co-citation maps of science and evaluation of scientific journals. *Sotsologija Nauki i Tekhnologij, 1*(4), 118-123.

Marshakova-Shaikevich, I. (2010b). Bibliometric maps of scientific Collaboration of UE countries in science and social science. *Sotsologija Nauki i Tekhnologij, 1*(2), 57-63.

Nordstrom, L. O. (1990). 'Bradford's Law' and the relationship between Ecology and Biogeography. *Scientometrics, 18*(3-4), 193–203. doi:10.1007/BF02017761

Pudovkin, A. I., & Fuseler, E. A. (1995). Indices of journal citation relatedness and citation relationships among aquatic biology journals. *Scientometrics, 32*(3), 227–236. doi:10.1007/BF02017642

Pudovkin, A. I., & Garfield, E. (2002). Algorithmic Procedure for finding semantically related journals. *Journal of the Association for Information Science and Technology, 53*(13), 1113–1110. doi:10.1002/asi.10153

Shaikevich, A. (2001). Contrastive and comparable corpora: Quantitative aspects. *International Journal of Corpus Linguistics, 6*(2), 229–255. doi:10.1075/ijcl.6.2.03sha

Sigogneau, A. (1995). *The delimitation of the 'environment' research field by using reviews and journal citations.* In *Fourth International Conference on Science and Technology Indicators*, Antwerp, Belgium.

Small, H. (1973). Co-citation in the scientific literature: A new measure of the relationship between two documents. *Journal of the Association for Information Science and Technology, 24*(July/August), 256–269.

Tijssen, R. J. W. (2008). Are we moving towards an integrated European Research Area? Some macro-level bibliometric perspectives. In H. Kretschmer & F. Havemann (Eds.), *Proceedings of WIS 2008, Berlin. Fourth International Conference on Webometrics, Informetrics and Scientometrics & Ninth COLLNET Meeting* (pp. 19-25). Berlin: Humboldt-Universität zu Berlin.

Tulving, E. (1972). Episodic and semantic memory. In E. Tulving & W. Donaldson (Eds.), *Organization of memory* (pp. 381–403). New York: Academic Press.

Chapter 9

Visualizations of the GRUBA Bibliographic Database:
From Printed Sources to the Maps of Science

Anna Małgorzata Kamińska
University of Silesia in Katowice, Poland

ABSTRACT

This chapter describes the author's experience of building the research environment for the implementation of bibliometric research on the science of mining, being developed in Poland in 1945-1989, on the basis of periodicals published by the major technical universities involved in teaching and research in that field at that time. The study was conducted on the volume of data entered (by typing), collected, and processed in a relational database. The data, covering information of more than 36,000 articles and more than 22,000 authors, formed bibliographic database named "GRUBA" (an acronym for polish phrase "Mining Register Enabling Bibliometric Analysis" and a word meaning mine in the Silesian dialect as well). The aim of this chapter is not to present a comprehensive and extensive bibliometric research results. Only a small part of it is a background for presenting the experience gained during the implementation of research, with the primary emphasis on the final stages – modeling and analyzing the visual maps created mainly using Gephi software and representing science development.

INTRODUCTION

Research to discover rules hidden in the collection of related documents becomes necessary as a result of the growing number of scientific publications in the second half of the twentieth century. This has resulted from the rapid increase in scientific research, which resulted in a doubling in the production of books and a fourfold increase in the number of scientific journals. In part to keep track of this increase, Eugene Garfield, in an article published in *Science* (Garfield, 1955), proposed to build a citation index for science, as a tool for the evaluation of scientific journals. The first Science Citation Index (SCI) was published in 1963 and included 102,000 articles published in 1961 by 613 selected journals.

DOI: 10.4018/978-1-5225-4990-1.ch009

Since then, quantitative methods have been applied ever more purposefully to identify rules hidden in communication artifacts, resulted in establishing the discipline of bibliometrics, a term first proposed in 1969 by Alan Pritchard.

Initially, bibliographic data were collected in tabular form, and to this day they are most often managed by relational database management systems that store them in data tables. The use of such mechanisms naturally suggests presentation of the results of bibliometric analyzes in tabular form. But such tabular analyses are not conducive to recognizing certain phenomena, for which graphical displays of networks may be more convincing.

It is worth noting that bibliographic data naturally have a network (or graph) structure rather than a tabular structure. Whether these graphs represent citations between articles or co-operation between the authors, the nodes of the graph represent the analyzed units, and the edges of the graph represent the relationships between these entities.

The above observation has led to the hypothesis of this chapter – using visualization techniques implemented in proposed analytical environment, allow for gaining better both general and specific knowledge about co-authoring data. The second, minor aim of this chapter is to present some research results on state of mining science, as it developed in the post-war years from 1945 to 1989 in Poland. Since the source data used for these analyses have not previously been collected in any national bibliographic database, these results are novel. In order to achieve the above, the chapter presents the realization of the following partial objectives:

- Description of the structure and scope of the source data,
- Presentation the experience of performing research using an analytical visualization environment,
- Description of obtained visualizations as a result of research,
- Verification of the initial hypothesis underpinning this study.

This chapter may primarily be of interest to researchers studying the development of science and scholarly publication, who can adapt these visualization methods to their own ends. But is will also prove of relevance to those interested in the development of mining science in Poland after World War II, as this country was then a major player in European coal mining. Lastly, researchers in other fields, who are looking for an effective visualization tool for large volumes of network data, may find the author's experience with the proposed visualization tool to be useful.

The purpose of this chapter, however, is not to present the results of author's bibliometric research (which will be presented in separate publications), but specifically to show the application of selected visualization methods to the results obtained by applying social network analysis (SNA) metrics to bibliographic data. The author wishes to point out that it is possible to conduct such research on bibliometric data collected independently from commercial sources such as Web of Science Core Collection (WoS), and encourages other researchers to follow this path.

BACKGROUND

Equitable stimulation of the development of science centers and individual researchers, by providing better conditions for more efficient entities, requires the ability to correctly quantify their contributions. One way to measure this contribution is to aggregate bibliographic data to the level of institutions or authors, the latter is the subject of this chapter. It should not be surprising that such analyzes have been carried out for quite some time.

Already in 1979, Beaver and Rosen (1979) demonstrated that scientific collaboration leads to increased productivity. This caused increased interest in this research area. Recognizing the facts that the data structures describing co-authoring are networked and the rapid development of methods of examining network structures have led to the application of these methods in the scientific collaboration field. One of the most significant contributions to the analysis of co-authoring networks is the research on collaboration databases by Mark E.J. Newman (Newman, 2004, 2001). He used social network analysis to co-authoring data and the results he got indicate that co-authoring networks have high clustering coefficient and small average distance between pairs of nodes, thus being "small-world" networks. Since then, research on these network structures and their visualizations has been undertaken by many researchers.

Some of them use visualization techniques to describe relatively few data to illustrate the values of certain measures attributed to individual authors. For example, Wolfgang Glänzel (2014) has shown a simple visualization of an ego network with different sizes of nodes resulting from author's publication output. In similar applications, it seems that the Pajek (Mrvar & Batagelj, 2016) program is often chosen. It was used for example by Loet Leydesdorff to visualize a fairly small amount of data (Leydesdorff, 2010a) and to present multimodal collaboration graphs (Leydesdorff, 2010b). It is worth noting that in the above mentioned papers the size of labels is not correlated with the size of nodes, which may affect the overall readability of the graph. A similar case is in an article written by Katy Börner, Luca Dall'Asta, Weimao Ke and Alessandro Vespignani (2005), but here we can also see a quite strange feature resulting from the application of the Kamada-Kawai layout algorithm (Kamada & Kawai, 1989) which edge weights interpret as the distances between vertices. This results in considerable distance from the authors working closely together, what seems not intuitive. Visualization of co-authoring networks, applying the same layout algorithm, is also used in the analysis of data limited by date range and specific departments (Perianes-Rodríguez, Olmeda-Gómez, & Moya-Anegón, 2010) where the authors show methods for detecting collaborating communities.

Visualization of collaboration networks is also used in the analysis of large data structures to illustrate the general characteristics and shapes of analyzed networks, rather than focusing on its individual components, and a good example here is work of Theresa Velden, Asif-ul Haque and Carl Lagoze (2010). An interesting way of presenting data aggregated to countries visualized as heliocentric networks was presented by Zaida Chinchilla-Rodríguez, Benjamin Vargas-Quesada, Yusef Hassan-Montero, Antonio González-Molina and Félix Moya-Anegóna (2010). While the article dedicated to the application of the Pajek program in visualization of large networks was written by Andrej Mrvar and Vladimir Batagelj (2016), also Gephi platform is often used for visualization of large networks as shows for example Zinaida Apanowicz and Pavel Vinokurov (2010a,2010b), applying Fruchterman-Reingold layout algorithm. Presenting large networks is not always necessary, as it is often enough to focus only on the most important nodes. The methods of reducing large networks on example of co-authoring networks describe Milos Kudelka, Zdenek Horak, Vaclav Snasel and Ajith Abraham (2010).

More about other visualization techniques in collaboration networks analysis can be found in article written by Carson Kai-Sang Leung, Christopher L. Carmichael, and Eu Wern Teh (2011), while a more comprehensive review of literature was published by Sameer Kumar (Kumar, 2015).

It also should be noted that even contemporary analyzes whether performed at author level (Arnaboldi, Dunbar, Passarella, & Conti, 2016) or at journal level (Santos & Santos, 2016) not always require the use of visualization of network structures, as this depends on the purpose of the analyzes performed.

This chapter tries to go beyond the visualization techniques, which are intended only to make more attractive data already readable in raw forms and beyond visualizations showing difficult-to-analyze, without further research, clouds of nodes, which are hard to read about outstanding individual participants. Trying to fill this gap it shows the visualizations of quite large data sets realized in a way that recognizes the most important actors.

DATA SOURCE

The subject of wider research then the one presented in this article was to evaluate the state of mining science, developing in the years from 1945 to 1989 in Poland, based on selected periodicals, using a variety of bibliometric methods – from the classic and the already known approaches used exclusively in bibliometrics (e.g. co-citation and bibliographic coupling methods) through methods currently used in the analysis of social networks and adapted already for analysis of bibliographic data (e.g. the method based on the PageRank algorithm) to the metrics defined for the purpose of social network analysis which were not yet commonly being used in the analysis of bibliographic records. All the periodicals published by all major scientific centers in Poland at this time were being analyzed (called later generally as the subject bibliography):

- For „Akademia Górniczo-Hutnicza":
  ◦ „Zeszyty Naukowe Akademii Górniczo-Hutniczej im. Stanisława Staszica. Elektryfikacja i Mechanizacja Górnictwa i Hutnictwa",
  ◦ „Zeszyty Naukowe Akademii Górniczo-Hutniczej im. Stanisława Staszica. Górnictwo",
  ◦ „Zeszyty Naukowe Akademii Górniczo-Hutniczej im. Stanisława Staszica. Wiertnictwo Nafta Gaz",
  ◦ „Zeszyty Naukowe Akademii Górniczo-Hutniczej w Krakowie. Elektryfikacja i Mechanizacja Górnictwa i Hutnictwa",
  ◦ „Zeszyty Naukowe Akademii Górniczo-Hutniczej w Krakowie. Górnictwo",
- For „Politechnika Śląska w Gliwicach":
  ◦ „Zeszyty Naukowe Politechniki Śląskiej. Górnictwo",
- For „Politechnika Wrocławska":
  ◦ „Prace Naukowe Instytutu Górnictwa Politechniki Wrocławskiej. Konferencje",
  ◦ „Prace Naukowe Instytutu Górnictwa Politechniki Wrocławskiej. Monografie",
  ◦ „Prace Naukowe Instytutu Górnictwa Politechniki Wrocławskiej. Studia i Materiały",
- For „Politechnika Lubelska":
  ◦ „Prace Naukowe Politechniki Lubelskiej. Górnictwo".

The author, using only standard personal computer system and mostly free and open source software, walked most of the way the development history of bibliometrics did. At the beginning it was necessary to build the database by use bibliographic data of the aforementioned periodicals. This information contained structured descriptions of the notebooks and included articles with the authors of articles and individual items of bibliographic record for each article. The scale of the project turned out to be quite similar (in terms of order of magnitude) to the world's first index of scientific citations. To be able to start any research, the author must first enter (by typing) information about more than 36 thousand articles. All the preparatory work to enable only the start of the research lasted almost two and a half years. All data have been collected in a relational database using a simple application with a graphical user interface.

However, how can one compare to the examples of other national bibliographic databases, the period of two and a half years for collecting such a large volume of data proved to be surprisingly short, which was achieved thanks to the author's method of creating bibliographic databases described in another article (Kamińska, 2017a). The so built bibliographic database, named "GRUBA" (acronym for polish phrase "Mining Register Enabling Bibliometric Analysis" and a word meaning a mine in the Silesian dialect as well), provided research material of excellent quality for further analysis. The data were collected according to the conceptual data model presented in Figure 1.

The diagram, expressed in the UML, shows classes, their attributes and relations that are a subset of the data used in this study. The central point of the diagram is the "Article" class with attributes such as title, pages, etc. This is an abstract class what means that concrete articles must be either "NativeArticle" or "ForeignArticle" classes. "Native" articles are those whose content is published in the analyzed journals, while "foreign" ones are those only listed in the references of articles. It is important that the above terms not be used interchangeably with cited article and citing article because a "native" article can be both citing and cited, while a "foreign" article can only be cited. As is evident from the diagram, the way of assigning authors to both "native" and "foreign" articles is the same – through the association class "Authorship" with an attribute that allows to specify the order of authors in a concrete article. The second association class "Reference" implements a link between citing and cited articles. "Native" articles are assigned to the aforementioned journals within specific journal issues. Thanks to

Figure 1. Class diagram of the conceptual data model
Source: own work

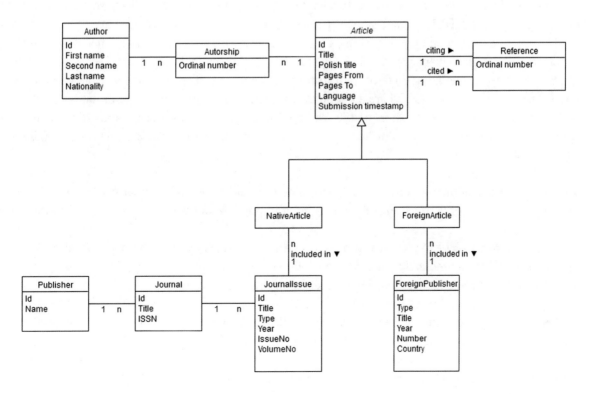

such a tree structure it is possible to conduct research with aggregation of results both at the journal and publisher level. In the case of foreign articles, a simplified way of registering the publisher was adopted.

Finally, according to the data model presented above, 36056 articles (4375 "native" articles), 22685 authors and 42185 references were collected. The average number of citations for a "native" article is 9.64, and the average number of its authors is 1.74.

TOOLS AND TECHNIQUES

As previously mentioned all of analyzed data were gathered in a relational database management system. The database platform was the primary source of data from which it was exported to other dedicated analytical tools. In some cases, to carry out basic quantitative research, calculations and aggregations were performed directly inside database platform using SQL (structured query language).

Research described in this chapter, using SNA methods and visualization of the achieved results, was conducted using Gephi (Bastian, Heymann, & Jacomy, 2009) software. It is obvious that the data model must meet a number of conditions to enable for building graph structures with "traversable edges". More on the method enabling data collection for building such citation graphs can be found e.g. in another author's article (Kamińska, 2017a).

This choice of Gephi has been influenced by desire to explore new tool as the author was already familiar only with Pajek and Cytoscape. At the start of the research the current version of Gephi was 0.8.2 beta. As it turned out later, it was the last version before a total refactoring of the core of system. The subsequent versions discontinued support for hierarchical graphs and redesigned dynamic graphs mechanisms (Heymann, 2013).

Gephi application was provisioned with data directly from the database thanks to implementation of exporting to files of GEXF format. Using the extensive documentation (Heymann et al., 2009) the author tried to generate one general file describing all of the collected data and relations so that it could suffice to perform all assumed analysis in Gephi by using such graphs manipulating operations as aggregating, splitting, cutting, normalizing (in terms of transforming graphs to unimodal form – i.e. all nodes are the same class, e.g. all are articles, all are authors, etc.) and filtering data to the range of dates.

Unfortunately, the idea of exporting the whole bibliographic data as a one complete structure that could be processed later in Gephi turned out to be a dead end, at least because of the following limitations of that tool:

- The plug-in Multimode Networks Transformations could not handle correctly networks with such a large number of vertices and edges, making it impossible to convert the general graph into unimodal forms,
- The mechanisms of hierarchical graphs (in particular edges aggregation and virtual edges creation) worked unpredictable making the results of SNA not credible,
- There were problems with filtering graphs according to time periods.

Above factors resulted in decision of building multiple GEXF files dedicated to specific profiles of analysis (i.e. several unimodal graphs representing citations, authorship, co-authorship, etc.) at concrete levels of aggregation and for concrete periods of time. The sample content of the GEXF file defining the graph of cooperation between authors is presented below.

Sample of GEXF File for Cooperation Between Authors

```
<?xml version = "1.0" ?>
<gexf xmlns = "http://www.gexf.net/1.2draft" version = "1.2" >
<meta lastmodifieddate = "2016-06-26" >
 <creator> Gruba </creator>
 <descritpion> Coauthorings in Gruba </descritpion>
</meta>
<graph mode = "static" defaultedgetype = "undirected" >
 <attributes class = "node" mode = "static" >
 <attribute id = "0" title = "nazwa" type = "string" />
 <attribute id = "2" title = "jestobce" type = "boolean" />
 <attribute id = "20" title = "nazwisko" type = "string" />
 <attribute id = "21" title = "imie" type = "string" />
 <attribute id = "22" title = "imie2" type = "string" />
 <attribute id = "23" title = "narodowosc" type = "string" />
 <attribute id = "24" title = "zeszytowy" type = "boolean" />
 <attribute id = "25" title = "instytucje" type = "string" />
 <attribute id = "26" title = "inst_part" type = "integer" />
 </attributes>
 <attributes class = "edge" mode = "static" >
 <attribute id = "weight" type = "float" />
 </attributes>
 <nodes>
 <node id = "AUT001494" label = "Wan Da Lin NN" >
 <attvalues>
 <attvalue for = "0" value = "Wan Da Lin NN" />
 <attvalue for = "2" value = "true" />
 <attvalue for = "20" value = "Wan Da Lin" />
 <attvalue for = "21" value = "NN" />
 <attvalue for = "22" />
 <attvalue for = "23" value = "NN" />
 <attvalue for = "24" value = "false" />
 <attvalue for = "25" />
 <attvalue for = "26" value = "5" />
 </attvalues>
 </node>
 <node id = "AUT001495" label = "Paraybiek G.">
 <attvalues>
 <attvalue for = "0" value = "Paraybiek G." />
 <attvalue for = "2" value = "true" />
 <attvalue for = "20" value = "Paraybiek" />
 <attvalue for = "21" value = "G." />
```

```
<attvalue for = "22" value = "E." />
<attvalue for = "23" value = "NN" />
<attvalue for = "24" value = "false" />
<attvalue for = "25" />
<attvalue for = "26" value="5" />
</attvalues>
</node>
. . . . . . . . . . . .
</nodes>
<edges>
<edge id = "S000100T002600" source = "AUT000100" target = "AUT002600">
<attvalue for = "weight" value = ".166667" />
</edge>
<edge id = "S000100T001102" source = "AUT000100" target = "AUT001102">
<attvalue for = "weight" value = "1.000000" />
</edge>
. . . . . . . . . . . .
</edges>
</graph>
</gexf>
```

As we can see above defined graph is static and undirected (as the co-author is a reflexive relationship). For nodes there are several attributes defined:

- nazwa (the visual label of the node),
- jestobce (boolean value indicating the fact of being the author of at least one cited unit that is not a subject bibliography),
- nazwisko (the last name of a given author),
- imie (the first name of a given author),
- imie2 (the second name of a given author),
- narodowosc (the nationality of a given author),
- zeszytowy (boolean value indicating the fact of being the author of at least one unit that is a subject bibliography – i.e. a "native" author),
- instytucje (a comma-separated list of all affiliations of a given author),
- inst_part (the identifier of the main affiliation of a given author).

For edges only float value has been defined indicating the strength of cooperation relation (the greater value the strongest cooperation).

The possibilities of calculating SNA metrics (either using of built-in algorithms and those provided by several plug-ins), networks visualizations mechanism (defining the colors or sizes of nodes and edges derived from previously calculated metrics in terms of both ranking and partitioning) and layout algorithms have proven to be powerful tools, and affected the final positive assessment of Gephi software. It is worth mentioning that the layout algorithms based on simulation of gravity forces even when using multi-threaded calculation (what is possible for ForceAtlas2 plug-in) must perform many hours for graphs of similar size. Given that it is an n-body problem that is very demanding computationally (Diacu, 1996), we have no choice but to accept this fact or use other, less accurate, heuristic layout methods (i.e. OpenOrd layout plug-in).

It seems that some of the above-mentioned problems which encountered the author during own research have been recognized by the developers of Gephi software which resulted in the release with version 0.9 a kind of manifesto in which it is stated about improving of certain functions or ending of the support for those that caused the most trouble (e.g. hierarchical graphs).

RESULTS

Gathered data volume was so large that just by reviewing the raw data, it would be difficult to support further analysis. In such cases, it works through implementing the rough sketch (just vertices and edges, without names, identifiers or any metrics values), where can be observed some symptoms or phenomena, and later drill down the data for further analysis in more detail. An example of such a rough sketch showing the citation between the registered citing articles is illustrated in Figure 2.

Figure 2. The rough sketch of citation between the registered citing articles
Source: own work

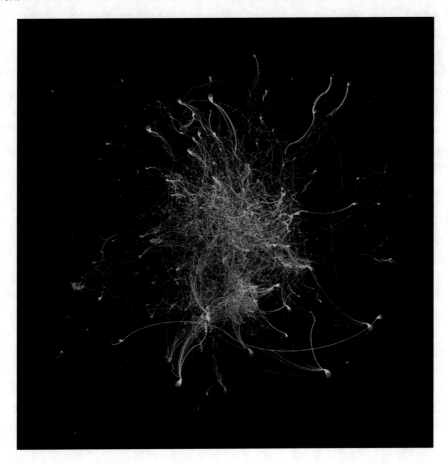

The red color identifies the articles published by "Politechnika Śląska", the green one published by "Akademia Górniczo-Hutnicza", while the blue one published by "Politechnika Wrocławska".

In the Figure 3 the cooperation (co-authoring) between "native" authors was shown. "Native" means here authors of articles published in analyzed printed sources (contrary to "foreign" what means authors of articles registered only in references of the aforementioned articles). In other words, a "native" author is the author of at least one "native" article. To facilitate the analysis of the map and make it more transparent the least significant edges have been removed.

It should be mentioned that the deployment of nodes results from the use of layout algorithm based on simulation of gravity forces (provided by ForceAtlas2 plug-in), but the force impact between two nodes is not derived from their masses but from the edge weights resulting directly from cooperation intensity. This approach allows drawing a map where distribution of nodes is not random or driven by aesthetic considerations but carries directly interpretable information about the "collaboration distance" between authors.

The size of the node, which represents an author, indicates one's PageRank value. The larger the point, the more important person in the context of cooperation between authors. Edges connecting nodes indicates a fact of cooperation between given authors. The thicker is the arc, the closer is the cooperation between individuals. The red color identifies the authors from "Politechnika Śląska", the green one from "Akademia Górniczo-Hutnicza", while the blue one from "Politechnika Wrocławska".

Already the first look at the map allows one to notice the most important and largest groups of cooperating authors. Strong, sharp curves indicate more frequent cooperation. The dominant colors are red and green. The red color, very intense in several places of the graph, indicates a strong collaboration between the authors from "Politechnika Śląska". One will notice that the authors from the "Politechnika Śląska" work together intensively, the strong arches and proximity to each other on a graph testifies this fact. The undisputed leader here is Mirosław Chudek from "Politechnika Śląska". Many authors, as well as the connections between them, forming a dense network of cooperation, indicate the popularity of this author. The most significant authors that cooperate with him are Marcin Borecki, Kazimierz Rułka and Kazimierz Podgórski. Other important authors from "Politechnika Śląska", forming strong cloud of points on the map of cooperation are: Jerzy Antoniak, Włodzimierz Sikora, Walery Szuścik, Florian Krasucki, Stefan Ziemba, Jerzy Nawrocki and Wiesław Gabzdyl. In contrast to the authors from "Politechnika Śląska", the authors from "Akademia Górniczo-Hutnicza", are not focused in one place, but rather spread out in smaller groups, but nearer the other authors affiliated with "Akademia Górniczo-Hutnicza". Green color and bold arches of cooperation most often focused around Stanisław Jucha, Ludger Szklarski and Henryk Filcek. It is noteworthy that Mieczysław Lasoń from "Akademia Górniczo-Hutnicza" and a group of authors localized near Henryk Filcek - Stanisław Takuski, Mieczysław Hobler and Jan Walaszczyk, as well as Roman Bromowicz and Mieczysław Jawień whose position on the graph and arches of cooperation between authors, indicate very close cooperation with the authors from "Politechnika Śląska".

On the cooperation map one can see a single group of collaborating authors from "Politechnika Wrocławska", marked in blue color. The most powerful group of authors from the university, whose main author is Jan Sajkiewicz, is located between the authors from the "Akademia Górniczo-Hutnicza" and connected with them by edges, that indicates the strong links and cooperation between them.

The practical value of using such a layout, discussed in the above example, lies in the possibility of literal interpretation – size of given node and author's name indicates the tendency to cooperate with others, while the nearest surroundings indicates the scientists with whom this cooperation is enhanced.

Figure 3. Co-authoring map
Source: own work

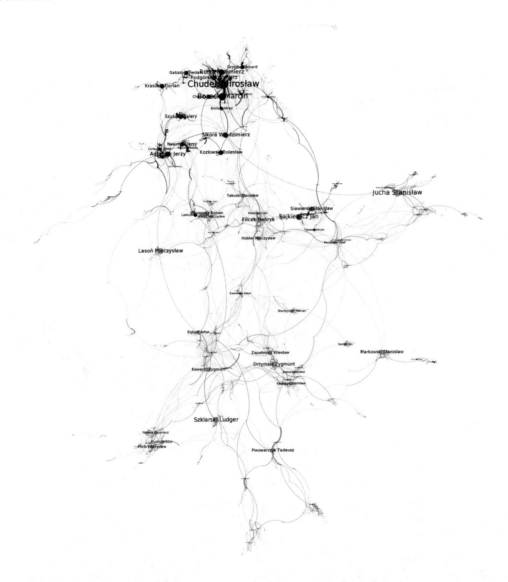

To draw the next graph (Figure 4) a different layout algorithm has been used. The measured characteristic remains the same – the strength of cooperation between authors. But layout used for this graph (provided by Radial Axis Layout plug-in) makes it possibly to sort and partition nodes. Already one glance is enough to observe collaboration ranking for authors divided into universities where they worked.

An undirected graph (see Figure 4) presents individuals with the highest PageRank collaboration between authors. The size of the point, which indicates the concrete labeled person, indicates its PageRank cooperation. The larger the node, the more important person in the context of cooperation between authors. The red color indicates the authors from "Politechnika Śląska", the green color the authors from "Akademia Górniczo-Hutnicza", and the blue one the authors from "Politechnika Wrocławska". The color pink has been marked individuals with other affiliations. The authors were ordered along the

Figure 4. Co-authoring ranking
Source: own work

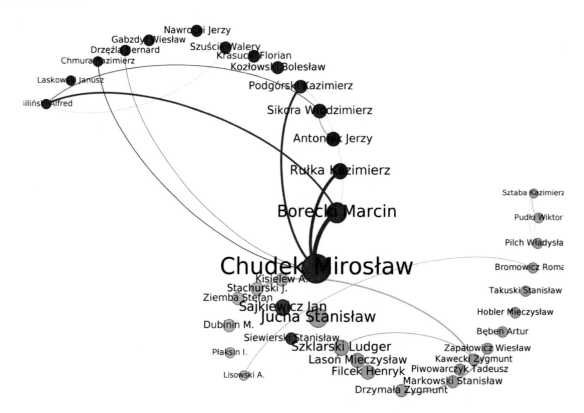

four axes of the graph. In the center of the graph the authors of the highest PageRank collaboration are placed. The farther from the center, the smaller is PageRank of cooperation. On the graph, one can also notice marked edges between individuals, which indicate the direct co-operation between them. The thicker is the line, the closer is the cooperation between authors.

Authors of the highest PageRank cooperation are Mirosław Chudek and Marcin Borecki from "Politechnika Śląska", Stanisław Jucha from "Akademia Górniczo-Hutnicza" and Jan Sajkiewicz from "Politechnika Wrocławska".

The practical value of using above described layout results from several of its properties. It is partitioned what means the scientists are grouped according to their affiliation. Thanks to the spiral arm of each partition, the picture is very compact and in the middle of it there are scientists with the biggest tendency to cooperate with others. The scientists are sorted – the less tendency to cooperate, the more they are placed outside the image. In addition, the thicknesses of the edges linking them show the intensity of collaboration between them.

The next figures present graphs using Erdős number for authors with the highest PageRank cooperation between authors from various universities. The first one (Figure 5) shows Erdős numbers calculated for Mirosław Chudek from "Politechnika Śląska".

To find out how scientists worked closely with relation to one selected author, one can use very popular and trendy in science environments measure, as Erdős number. It describes the "distance cooperation" and to be able to get it, one need to be co-author of the article with someone who already has assigned the value of this measure. The selected author has the value k = 0. Each co-author gets number k + 1, where k is the lowest value of all the co-authors of given article.

Visualization of Erdős number for Mirosław Chudek was shown in the Figure 4. This time yet another deployment algorithm is used (provided by Layered layout plug-in). For each author the Erdős number (related to Mirosław Chudek) was evaluated. The values obtained were the basis for assigning a particular author to one of the layer (orbit). The graph was limited to two orbits.

In the center of the graph Mirosław Chudek was placed, and in two rings around him people cooperating with him (directly or indirectly). In the first, the inner, there are those working directly (Erdős

Figure 5. Erdős graph for Mirosław Chudek
Source: own work

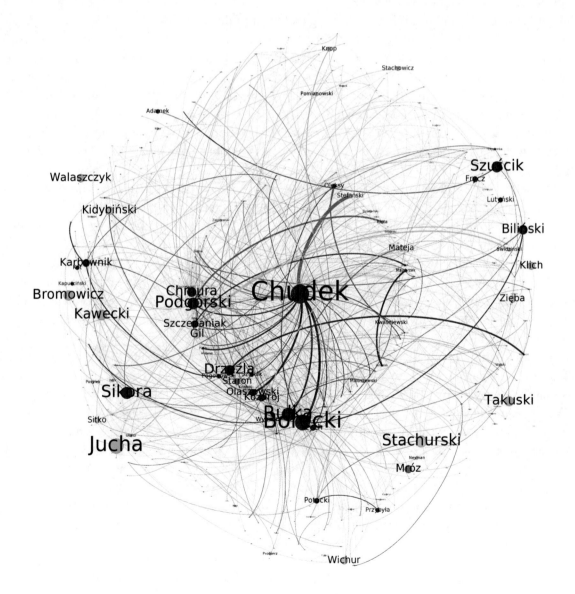

number 1) with Mirosław Chudek. In the second orbit, outside, there are the authors cooperating with those placed in the inner one (Erdős number 2).

The size of the node, which represents the person, indicates its PageRank. The larger the node, the more important person in the context of cooperation between authors. Edges connecting individuals indicates a direct cooperation between them. The thicker is the line, the closer is the cooperation between authors.

The red color indicates the authors from "Politechnika Śląska", the green color the authors from "Akademia Górniczo-Hutnicza", and the blue one the authors from "Politechnika Wrocławska". The color pink has been marked individuals with other affiliations.

Mirosław Chudek from "Politechnika Śląska" wins the PageRank cooperation ranking between the authors. Many authors, as well as the connections between them, form a dense network of cooperation, showing the great popularity of this author.

To make the graph more readable in the Figure 6 a similar to the previous graph is shown, but with removed nodes with the lowest PageRank.

After "cleaning the graph", it is worth noting that most of the authors placed in the inner ring, are form "Politechnika Śląska". Authors of the highest PageRank cooperation from "Politechnika Śląska" are: Marcin Borecki, Kazimierz Rułka and Kazimierz Podgórski. In the outer circle, most authors come from the "Politechnika Śląska", but several from "Akademia Górniczo-Hutnicza". The authors of the highest cooperation PageRank in this circle are: Stanisław Jucha from "Akademia Górniczo-Hutnicza" and Włodzimierz Sikora from "Politechnika Śląska".

The author with the greatest value of PageRank measure from "Akademia Górniczo-Hutnicza" is Stanisław Jucha. His collaboration network limited to Erdős number value less or equal 2 and a significant PageRank value is shown in Figure 7.

A densely populated outer orbit indicates that the authors who collaborated with Stanisław Jucha were active and also worked intensively with other prominent scientists (e.g. with Mirosław Chudek). It is worth noting that in Figure 7 Mirosław Chudek is located in an outer orbit (having Erdős number of Stanisław Jucha equal to 2) and in the Figure 6 Stanisław Jucha is located in an outer orbit (having Erdős number of Stanisław Chudek equal to 2). This is because the relation of Erdős number is reflexive.

As we can see Stanisław Jucha was a type of rather independent researcher preferring to cooperate with lesser known scientists. This fact seems to confirm both the sparsely populated inner orbit and nodes in that orbit are connected by very thin edged with the central apex. The position of Stanisław Jucha on the border of the map shown in the Figure 3 also confirms this observation.

The author with the greatest value of PageRank measure from "Politechnika Wrocławska" is Jan Sajkiewicz. His collaboration network limited to Erdős number value less or equal 2 and a significant PageRank value is shown in Figure 8.

We can immediately see that Jan Sajkiewicz preferred cooperation with scientists from his home institution. The only scientist with a significant PageRank measure not coming from the home institution is Andrzej Dunikowski from "Akademia Górniczo-Hutnicza". It is worth noting that Jan Sajkiewicz did not cooperate directly with the second highest PageRank researcher from "Politechnika Wrocławska" – Stanisław Siewierski. The biggest bridge of cooperation was in this case Adam Fiszer.

The practical value of the layout presented above on four examples can be surprisingly large. Inner orbit shows the ego network (also known as personal network) of a scientist (so-called ego) placed in the middle. This scientist probably knows all of his co-workers (so-called alters) and the intensity of collaboration that connects him to each of them. But graph of inner and outer orbit (i.e., for Erdős number $\leq$ 2) is the assembly of ego networks for every alter of a given scientists. Thus, in the outer orbit lie

Figure 6. More readable Erdős number graph for Mirosław Chudek
Source: own work

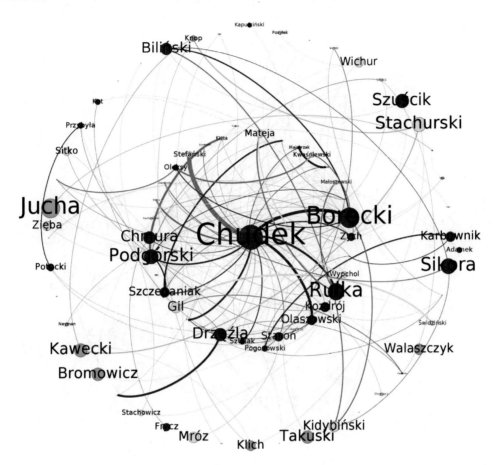

scientists working directly with alters of a given ego, but not with him directly. A scientist looking for new development opportunities may, based on such layout, identify potential new contributors. The help in this can additionally be the size of the nodes indicating the tendency to cooperate, calculated for the entire graph of cooperation and not only for the subgraph for Erdős number $\leq$ 2. Such layouts could be particularly very useful in a social networking sites for scientists and researchers such as ResearchGate or Academia.

All previously described layout algorithms are taking into account such properties as node size, weight of edges and geometric trajectories. But beyond the size and color, which in the pictures illustrated before present background and additional information, the nodes have their labels that present principal information – the names of the authors. It's obvious that the desirable feature of legible drawings is not overlapping labels. As we can see e.g. in pictures of the Erdős number metric where the layered layout plug-in has been used, the nodes are not perfectly positioned on concentric circles. This is because there was a need to adjust their layout so that their labels would not overlap roughly. Such functionality offers the Label Adjust layout plug-in. Unfortunately, it is impossible to overlook a flaw that does not arise even from the implementation of the application but from the general concept of the whole system. The Gephi application lets us to manipulate graphs from three different perspectives:

Figure 7. Erdős number graph for Stanisław Jucha
Source: own work

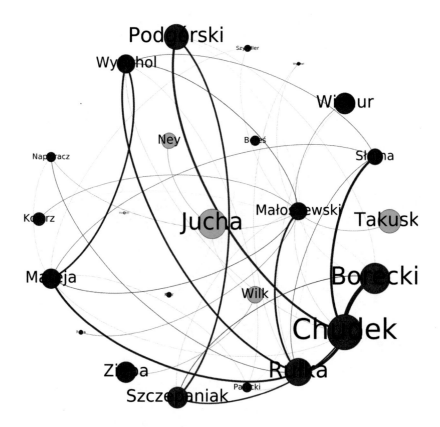

- **Overview:** The main perspective for analysis and visual development of graphic design using rough sketches of graphs – here one can use the layout and analytical plug-ins,
- **Data Laboratory:** The tabular perspective of graph details information,
- **Preview:** The final "post-processing" perspective for rendering beautiful and ready to use image files.

The problem results from the fact of use two completely different mechanisms for defining labels (i.e. fonts, styles, sizes, scales) and once one gets a satisfactory result of labels deployment in the overview perspective, then during the picture processing in the preview perspective (where there is no ability to correct layout of nodes with labels) the final result can be severely disturbed.

FUTURE RESEARCH DIRECTIONS

Bibliometric studies (or even more generally – scientometrics) require extensive research between the various artifacts, scientists and their relationships. Although this chapter is limited to analyzing co-authoring relationships only, there are many other directions of research on bibliographic data:

Figure 8. Erdős number graph for Jan Sajkiewicz
Source: own work

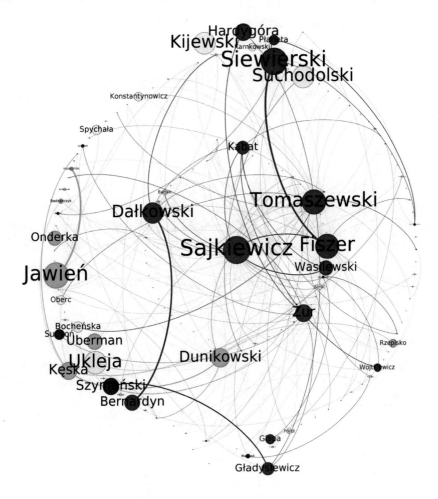

- Citation relationships between individual authors,
- Citation relationships between articles,
- Bibliographic coupling relationships,
- Co-citation relationships,
- Aggregation of the citation relationships between the articles to the level of periodicals or publishers,
- Aggregation of the citation (and co-authoring) relationships to the level of universities or countries.

All the above-mentioned data perspectives may require the use of other measures and different ways of visualization. Besides the use of layout algorithms based on gravity emulation, many platforms provide ready to use implementations of clustering algorithms. Thanks to them and taking into account the dynamics of the process (the variability of the strength of relationships of given type changing over time) it is possible to observe the development, the emergence of new ones, the merging or the disappearance of existing domains of science. Some of the concepts given above were already fulfilled but on the basis of the other national bibliographic database CYTBIN (Kamińska, 2017b), that gathers data about both the library science and the scientific information.

The second interesting issue is the development of an environment to enable "cross-domain" research and visualization. This would lead to the ability to easily copy some information calculated for nodes of one type of graph to another type of graph (assuming that both graphs have corresponding nodes). This would facilitate, for example, the analysis of the cooperation (what require analysis of co-authoring graph) of researchers with a Hirsch index value (what require analysis of citation graph) greater than the one given.

CONCLUSION

This chapter presents a subset of the visualized results of bibliometric research conducted on data collected during the development of bibliographic database GRUBA. The main goal was to present a visualization techniques of the results of bibliographic research on the relationships of collaboration between scientists. The author presents her experience with the final stages of bibliometric analyzes, which includes analysis involving SNA methods and visualization of the results in Gephi application.

Table 1. The tabular form of nodes from Figure 6

Id	Label	Partition	PageRank	Erdös Number
AUT000410	Chudek Mirosław	3	0.0022592101108925115	0
AUT000411	Podgórski Kazimierz	3	5.506852732432206E-4	1
AUT003083	Drzęźla Bernard	3	4.6053554071340513E-4	1
AUT002347	Rułka Kazimierz	3	6.742005373062928E-4	1
AUT004171	Borecki Marcin	3	9.508663434401075E-4	1
AUT000368	Szuścik Walery	3	5.072585447909566E-4	2
AUT000533	Stachurski J.	5	5.3211372229303335E-4	2
AUT001401	Jucha Stanisław	2	8.36240773938287E-4	2
AUT002523	Kawecki Zygmunt	2	4.6661909143542226E-4	2
AUT013516	Sikora Włodzimierz	3	5.923480146530545E-4	2

Table 2. The tabular form of edges from Figure 6

Source	Target	Weight
AUT000410	AUT000411	7.514286
AUT000410	AUT003083	1.1
AUT000410	AUT002347	10.166667
AUT000410	AUT004171	14.466667
AUT000411	AUT004171	0.3
AUT000533	AUT002523	4.909524

This platform used for these analysis and visualizations, despite many previously described "beta version problems", proved to be both an effective and user-friendly tool for SNA research on bibliographic data.

The author, focusing in this research on the relationships of scientific collaboration, presented only a few techniques and possibilities of graphical representation of bibliographic data but hopes that they can provide inspiration also for other researchers. The author also hopes that she has demonstrated the practical relevance of applying the SNA approach and its visualization to bibliometric studies, and that her visualizations allow understanding phenomena taking place in scientific communities more easily than analyzing data presented in traditional tabular layouts.

Looking at the data in Tables 1 and 2 that correspond only to small subset of the nodes and edges visualized in Figure 6, it seems that the hypothesis formulated at the beginning of the chapter, that proposed visualization techniques of co-authoring allow for gaining better both general and specific knowledge about analyzed data, can be accepted. In addition, as the volume of collected and processed bibliographic data continues to grow, it seems that visual presentations of bibliometric analysis results will continue to gain in importance. Obviously, the degree of usefulness of the proposed techniques may vary from one recipient to another, as the perception phenomenon of particular individuals of the human species is not identical.

It should finally be noted that the use of different methods of visualization entails the risk of over-interpretation of certain facts, and even manipulate of them (the same risk carries any use of statistical methods). For example, neighboring scientists in Figure 4 – Chudek, Jucha, Sajkiewicz, are very remote from one another in the Figure 3. Although both figures visualize co-authoring relationships, without further clarification to the recipients, it is possible to suggest either closeness or distance separating the mentioned scientists by presenting only one of these figures.

REFERENCES

Apanovich, Z. V., & Vinokurov, P. S. (2010a). An extension of a visualization component of ontology based portals with visual analytics facilities. *Bulletin of the Novosibirsk Computing Center*, *31*, 17–28.

Apanovich, Z. V., & Vinokurov, P. S. (2010b). *Ontology based portals and visual analysis of scientific communities*. Paper presented at the First Russia and Pacific Conference on Computer Technology and Applications (RussiaPacificComputer 2010), Vladivostok.

Arnaboldi, V., Dunbar, R. I. M., Passarella, A., & Conti, M. (2016). Analysis of Co-authorship Ego Networks. In A. Wierzbicki, U. Brandes, F. Schweitzer, & D. Pedreschi (Eds.), *Advances in Network Science* (pp. 82–96). Springer International Publishing. doi:10.1007/978-3-319-28361-6_7

Bastian, M., Heymann, S., & Jacomy, M. (2009). Gephi: an open source software for exploring and manipulating networks. In *Proceedings of the Third International Conference on Weblogs and Social Media* (pp. 361–362). AAAI Press.

Beaver, D. D., & Rosen, R. (1979). Studies in scientific collaboration: Part II: Scientific co-authorship, research productivity and visibility in the French elite. *Scientometrics*, *1*(2), 133–149. doi:10.1007/BF02016966

Börner, K., Dall'Asta, L., Ke, W., & Vespignani, A. (2005). Studying the emerging global brain: Analyzing and visualizing the impact of co-authorship teams. *Complexity, 10*(4), 57–67. doi:10.1002/cplx.20078

Chinchilla-Rodríguez, Z., Vargas-Quesada, B., Hassan-Montero, Y., González-Molina, A., & Moya-Anegóna, F. (2010). New approach to the visualization of international scientific collaboration. *Information Visualization, 9*(4), 277–287. doi:10.1057/ivs.2009.31

Diacu, F. (1996). The Solution of the n-body Problem. *The Mathematical Intelligencer, 3*(3), 66–70. doi:10.1007/BF03024313

Garfield, E. (1955). Citation index for science: A new dimension in documentation through association of ideas. *Science, 122*(3159), 108–111. doi:10.1126/science.122.3159.108 PMID:14385826

Glänzel, W. (2014). Analysis of co-authorship patterns at the individual level. *Transinformação, 26*(3), 229–238. doi:10.1590/0103-3786201400030001

Heymann, S. (2013). *Rebuilding Gephi's core for the 0.9 version.* Retrieved May 1, 2017, from https://gephi.wordpress.com/2013/03/05/rebuilding-gephis-core-for-the-0-9-version/

Heymann, S., Bastian, M., Jacomy, M., Maussang, C., Rohmer, A., Bilcke, J., & Jacomy, A. (2009). *GEXF File Format.* Retrieved March 13, 2017, from https://gephi.org/gexf/format/

Kamada, T., & Kawai, S. (1989). An algorithm for drawing general undirected graphs. *Information Processing Letters, 31*(1), 7–15. doi:10.1016/0020-0190(89)90102-6

Kamińska, A. M. (2017a). ProBIT – Prospektywna metoda tworzenia indeksów cytowań a problemy organizacji przestrzeni informacji w tradycyjnych bibliograficznych bazach danych [ProBIT - the prospective method of creating the traversable citation indices and the contemporary problems of the information space organization in traditional bibliographic databases]. *Zagadnienia Informacji Naukowej, 1*(109).

Kamińska, A. M. (2017b). (in press). Wizualizacje wybranych wskaźników bibliometrycznych na przykładzie bibliograficznej bazy danych CYTBIN [Visualizations of selected bibliometric indicators on the example of the bibliographic database CYTBIN]. *Toruńskie Studia Bibliologiczne, 2*(19).

Kudelka, M., Horak, Z., Snasel, V., & Abraham, A. (2010). Social Network Reduction Based on Stability. *2010 International Conference on Computational Aspects of Social Networks.* Retrieved from IEEE Xplore Digital Library. doi:10.1109/CASoN.2010.120

Kumar, S. (2015). Co-authorship networks: A review of the literature. *Aslib Journal of Information Management, 67*(1), 55–73. doi:10.1108/AJIM-09-2014-0116

Leung, C. K. S., Carmichael, C. L., & Teh, E. W. (2011). Visual analytics of social networks: mining and visualizing co-authorship networks. In D. D. Schmorrow & C. M. Fidopiastis (Eds.), *Foundations of Augmented Cognition. Directing the Future of Adaptive Systems* (pp. 335–345). Berlin: Springer. doi:10.1007/978-3-642-21852-1_40

Leydesdorff, L. (2010a). Eugene Garfield and algorithmic historiography: Co-words, co-authors, and journal names. *Annals of Library and Information Studies, 57*(3), 248–260.

Leydesdorff, L. (2010b). What Can Heterogeneity Add to the Scientometric Map? Steps towards algorithmic historiography. In M. Akrich, Y. Barthe, F. Muniesa, & P. Mustar (Eds.), *Débordements: Mélanges offerts à Michel Callon* (pp. 283–289). Paris: Presses des Mines. doi:10.4000/books.pressesmines.756

Mrvar, A., & Batagelj, V. (2016). Analysis and visualization of large networks with program package Pajek. *Complex Adaptive Systems Modeling, 4*(1), 6. doi:10.1186/s40294-016-0017-8

Newman, M. E. J. (2001). The structure of scientific collaboration networks. *Proceedings of the National Academy of Sciences of the United States of America, 98*(2), 404–409. doi:10.1073/pnas.98.2.404 PMID:11149952

Newman, M. E. J. (2004). Coauthorship networks and patterns of scientific collaboration networks. *Proceedings of the National Academy of Sciences of the United States of America, 101*(Suppl. 1), 5200–5205. doi:10.1073/pnas.0307545100 PMID:14745042

Newman, M. E. J. (2010). *Network: An introduction.* Oxford, UK: Oxford University Press. doi:10.1093/acprof:oso/9780199206650.001.0001

Perianes-Rodríguez, A., Olmeda-Gómez, C., & Moya-Anegón, F. (2010). Detecting, identifying and visualizing research groups in co-authorship networks. *Scientometrics, 82*(2), 307–319. doi:10.1007/s11192-009-0040-z

Santos, J. A. C., & Santos, M. C. (2016). Co-authorship networks: Collaborative research structures at the journal level. *Tourism & Management Studies, 12*(1), 5–13. doi:10.18089/tms.2016.12101

Velden, T., Haque, A., & Lagoze, C. (2010). A new approach to analyzing patterns of collaboration in co-authorship networks: Mesoscopic analysis and interpretation. *Scientometrics, 85*(1), 219–242. doi:10.1007/s11192-010-0224-6

ADDITIONAL READING

Abbasi, A., Altmann, J., & Hossain, L. (2011). Identifying the effects of co-authorship networks on the performance of scholars: A correlation and regression analysis of performance measures and social network analysis measures. *Journal of Informetrics, 5*(4), 594–607. doi:10.1016/j.joi.2011.05.007

Abbasi, A., Chung, K. S. K., & Hossain, L. (2012). Egocentric analysis of co-authorship network structure, position and performance. *Information Processing & Management, 48*(4), 671–679. doi:10.1016/j.ipm.2011.09.001

Abbott, A., Cyranoski, D., Jones, N., Maher, B., Schiermeier, Q., & Van Noorden, R. (2010). Do metrics matter? *Nature, 465*(7300), 860–862. doi:10.1038/465860a PMID:20559361

Abramo, G., D'Angelo, C., & Rosati, F. (2013). Measuring institutional research productivity for the life sciences: The importance of accounting for the order of authors in the byline. *Scientometrics, 97*(3), 779–795. doi:10.1007/s11192-013-1013-9

Abramo, G., D'Angelo, C. A., & Di Costa, F. (2011). National research assessment exercises: A comparison of peer review and bibliometrics rankings. *Scientometrics*, *89*(3), 929–941. doi:10.1007/s11192-011-0459-x

Abramo, G., D'Angelo, C. A., & Viel, F. (2013). The suitability of h and g indexes for measuring the research performance of institutions. *Scientometrics*, *97*(3), 555–570. doi:10.1007/s11192-013-1026-4

Aggrawal, N., & Arora, A. (2016). Visualization, analysis and structural pattern infusion of DBLP co-authorship network using Gephi. In *2016 2nd International Conference on Next Generation Computing Technologies (NGCT)*, Dehradun, India: IEEE. doi:10.1109/NGCT.2016.7877466

Biscaro, C., & Giupponi, C. (2014). Co-authorship and bibliographic coupling network effects on citations. *PLoS One*, *9*(6), e99502. doi:10.1371/journal.pone.0099502 PMID:24911416

Blakeslee, J. E., & Keller, T. E. (2012). Building the youth mentoring knowledge base: Publishing trends and coauthorship networks. *Journal of Community Psychology*, *40*(7), 845–859. doi:10.1002/jcop.21494

Borgatti, S. P., Everett, M. G., & Johnson, J. C. (2013). *Analyzing social networks*. London: SAGE Publications Ltd.

Börner, K., & Polley, D. E. (2014). *Visual Insights: A Practical Guide to Making Sense of Data*. Cambridge, MA: The MIT Press.

Bornmann, L., & Marx, W. (2014). How should the societal impact of research be generated and measured? A proposal for a simple and practicable approach to allow interdisciplinary comparisons. *Scientometrics*, *98*(1), 211–219. doi:10.1007/s11192-013-1020-x

De Freitas, A. R. R., Fleming, P. J., & Guimarães, F. G. (2015). Aggregation Trees for visualization and dimension reduction in many-objective optimization. *Information Sciences*, *298*, 288–314. doi:10.1016/j.ins.2014.11.044

Emmert-Streib, F., Dehmer, M., & Shi, Y. (2016). Fifty years of graph matching, network alignment and network comparison. *Information Science*, *346–347*, 180–197. doi:10.1016/j.ins.2016.01.074

Frankel, F. C., & DePace, A. H. (2012). *Visual Strategies: A Practical Guide to Graphics for Scientists & Engineers*. Yale University Press.

Gazni, A., & Didegah, F. (2016). The relationship between author's bibliographic coupling and citation exchange: Analyzing disciplinary differences. *Scientometrics*, *107*(2), 609–626. doi:10.1007/s11192-016-1856-y

Hsin-Ning, S. (2012). Visualization of Global Science and Technology Policy Research Structure. *Journal of the American Society for Information Science and Technology*, *63*(2), 242–255. doi:10.1002/asi.21520

Li, E. Y., Liao, C. H., & Yen, H. R. (2013). Co-authorship networks and research impact: A social capital perspective. *Research Policy*, *42*(9), 1515–1530. doi:10.1016/j.respol.2013.06.012

Michels, C., & Schmoch, U. (2014). Impact of bibliometric studies on the publication behaviour of authors. *Scientometrics*, *98*(1), 369–385. doi:10.1007/s11192-013-1015-7

Park, H. W., Yoon, J., & Leydesdorff, L. (2016). The normalization of co-authorship networks in the bibliometric evaluation: The government stimulation programs of China and Korea. *Scientometrics, 109*(2), 1017–1036. doi:10.1007/s11192-016-1978-2

Uddin, S., Hossain, L., Abbasi, A., & Rasmussen, K. (2012). Trend and efficiency analysis of co-authorship network. *Scientometrics, 90*(2), 687–699. doi:10.1007/s11192-011-0511-x

Uddin, S., Hossain, L., & Rasmussen, K. (2013). Network effects on scientific collaborations. *PLoS One, 8*(2), e57546. doi:10.1371/journal.pone.0057546 PMID:23469021

Wallace, M. L., Lariviere, V., & Gingras, Y. (2012). A small world of citations? The influence of collaboration networks on citation practices. *PLoS One, 7*(3), e33339. doi:10.1371/journal.pone.0033339 PMID:22413016

Xiang, L., Tingting, J., & Feicheng, M. (2013). Collective dynamics in knowledge networks: Emerging trends analysis. *Journal of Informetrics, 7*(2), 425–438. doi:10.1016/j.joi.2013.01.003

Yau, N. (2011). *Visualize This: The FlowingData Guide to Design, Visualization, and Statistics*. Indianapolis, IN: Wiley Publishing, Inc.

KEY TERMS AND DEFINITIONS

Bibliographic Database: A database of bibliographic records including sometimes additional information such as citations, abstracts, keywords, full text, and other descriptive content. These digital collections of published literature, including journal and newspaper articles, conference proceedings, reports, patents, books, etc. are often focused on a specific academic discipline. A well-structured bibliographic database could be an indispensable tool for researchers to find descriptive records of relevant information sources. There is a significant number of bibliographic databases that are proprietary, available by licensing agreement from vendors.

Bibliographic Record: A structured unit of information describing a specific resource. As this resource can be a book, a chapter, an article, and many other types, the structure must vary to meet their specificity. Bibliographic records that form the enumerative bibliography should be consistently written using one of many standards (formats, styles) of which the most popular are APA, Chicago, MLA, and Harvard.

Bibliography: A scientific discipline of study of books as physical and cultural objects (in this sense, it is also known as bibliology), but also the organized listing of publications (enumerative bibliography) and systematic description of publications (descriptive bibliography). This chapter is focused on the enumerative bibliography (called also references), that consisting of the bibliographic records placed at the end of scientific articles traces sources and inspirations for author of given article.

Bibliometrics: Statistical analysis of written publications used in the field of library and information science to analyze the development of given domain and measure the author's influence or impact. Currently, as scientific activities move toward word wide web and scientific social portals, it is evolving into disciplines called webometrics and altmetrics, but the basis remain still the same and rely on analyzing the various types of relationships (authoring, citing, downloading, etc.) that have occurred between the authors or products of their work. Studies can be conducted at different levels of aggregation (article-level metrics, author-level metrics, journal-level metrics, etc.) and are more often used for so-called evaluation of science.

Citation Index: A data structure of bibliographic records containing citation references, allowing the user to easily establish which later documents cite which earlier documents. Citation indexes can be built on the bases of well-designed bibliographic databases and are used as the source of data for bibliometric analysis. Examples of popular citation indexes are Web of Science, Scopus, Google Scholar, CiteSeer, and others.

Gephi: A general purpose visualization and exploration software written in Java on the NetBeans platform for all kinds of graphs and networks. This open-source and free tool is cross platform (available on Windows, Mac OS X, and Linux) and customizable by plugins (layouts, metrics, data sources, manipulation tools, rendering, and more). The latest version 0.9.1 was released on 14.02.2016 and introduced several new features and many bugfixes.

Graph: A structure amounting to a set of objects in which some pairs of the objects are "related." The objects are called vertices (and also nodes or points) and each of the related pair of vertices is called an edge (and also an arc or line). Depending on the relation type, the edges may be directed or undirected (for example, co-authoring relation is reflexive so it forms undirected graph). A weighted graph is a graph in which a number (the weight) is assigned to each edge. Such weights might represent intensity of the relationship for example number of coauthored articles written by two authors.

Multimodal Graph: A graph containing vertices representing objects of different classes (e.g., authors and articles). Applying SNA metrics to multimodal graphs could lead to results that are difficult to interpret, so most often these graphs are reduced to unimodal form before analysis.

Periodicals: Magazines, scholarly journals, newspapers, and newsletters that are published at regular intervals. This chapter focuses on journals as collections of articles written by scholars in an academic field. Usually an editorial board reviews these articles to decide whether they should be accepted.

SNA: The abbreviation of social network analysis – discipline of quantitative and qualitative analysis of a social networks/graphs. SNA provides both a visual and a mathematical method of discovering facto and rules hidden behind an often large volume of networked data.

Unimodal Graph: A graph containing vertices representing objects of one class. Unimodal graphs can be directly analyzed with SNA metrics, and the results can be easily interpreted.

Chapter 10
Visualization Methods for Exploring Transborder Indigenous Populations:
The Case of Berber Webosphere

Abdelaziz Blilid
Charles de Gaulle University – Lille III, France

ABSTRACT

This chapter highlights the importance of information visualization using web mapping to shed light on the correlation between social actors. It shows how this method helps to understand if Berber identity beyond frontiers is a reality or just a motto in support of "cultural activism." The suggested web mapping presents the hyperlinks weaved between websites whose focus is Berber cultural identity. Berbers are the indigenous people of North Africa. They are scattered in Morocco, Tunisia, Algeria, and Libya; they have built a "resistance identity," including both cultural and political claims, long before the digital age. Since the 1960s they have been struggling for recognition against the state's cultural and political domination in which they live. The analysis of Berbers' relationships amongst each other on the internet is valuable for understanding the main features and issues of this digital connection, its shape, its contents, and actor typology.

INTRODUCTION

The Amazighs[1] (or the Berbers) are the indigenous populations of North Africa. In the past, the Amazighs occupied a large territory extending from the Nile valley, in Egypt, to the Atlantic Ocean, and from the Mediterranean to the south of the Niger. These people are today unequally distributed in countries such as Morocco, Algeria, Tunisia, Libya, Egypt, and the Tuareg in the south. The Amazighs share similar languages and customs. They are, separated from each other, according to the state's political frontiers that don't match the Amazigh nation according to them.

DOI: 10.4018/978-1-5225-4990-1.ch010

The Amazighs began using the Internet in the 1990s in order to attain a visible presence, after many years of activism in associations.

The author uses visualization techniques to identify how Amazigh people shape their digital presence on the Web and represent themselves as a unique and unified identity, despite their geographic fragmentation which generated variations of their language and culture. This chapter will show how Amazighs interact on the Internet to remain united despite their linguistic and cultural diversity. Similarly, the author will analyze how this people uses the Internet to protect their oppressed culture. First, the author will present the methodology used and data collection. Then he will expose our results about the Berber webosphere. Finally, he will analyse these results related to the issues of Amazigh activism.

Visualizing Amazigh Webosphere Identification With Using Hypertext Web Mapping

Web Mapping: A Method of Data Visualization

The visualization of the data is a graphical and visual representation of a raw data with the objective of analyzing them for a good understanding of their contents. It has been present in the world of research since the first civilizations (Vaisman, 2015) in various forms and disciplines. By visualizing it, data transform into information and knowledge.

The visualization of data has several relevant roles in the social sciences. First, it seeks to understand, explain and predict human behavior by observing, reflecting, and measuring social phenomena. Second, it helps formulate new hypotheses based on these data and to confirm or refute existing assumptions. In this sense, the visualization method makes it possible to create informative illustrations of data by summarizing on the same diagram a large amount of information.

The importance of the data visualization method (*Mayer-Schnonberger and Cukier, 2014*) lies in its ability to reveal, among other things, connections that we have never suspected. For Tufte (*1983*), graphic visualization is a well-designed representation of a set of data of interest for the analysis of a study. It communicates ideas with clarity and effectiveness that were complex beforehand.

A broad disciplinary and interdisciplinary literature is interested in the analysis of visualizations of social phenomena has emerged in recent decades in the social sciences. Geographers, sociologists, political scientists and economists have used various datasets and methodologies to analyze different phenomena of societies (Erickson, 1996 ; Haythornthwaite & Laat, 2010 ; Boullier, 2015 ; Healy & Moody, 2014 ; Ollion & Boelaert, 2015 ; Zinovyev, 2012 ; Firebaugh, 2008). Some of them were interested in the analysis of transborder populations (Praham, 2004 ; Diminescu, 2008 ; Oiarzabal, 2012 ; Severo & Zuolo, 2012 ; Hiller & Franz, 2004 ; Nedelcu, 2009), others to the relationship between the geographic territory and the digital territory (Ghitalla, 2008 ; Helland, 2007 ; Adams & Ghose, 2003 ; Musso, 2010 ; Perriault, 2012), and still others in the identity struggle of indigenous peoples (Virtanen, 2015 ; Ginsburg, 2001 ; Schleser, 2012 ; Budka & al., 2013 ; Srinivasan, 2006; Nakata, 2008). These studies are valuable in that they set a precedent for the study of the links and volumes of interaction between different social actors in the digital world.

The foundations of our research on the spatial structures of the Internet and web content come from this research. These studies provide a descriptive analysis of data sets from web pages of different communities. Their purpose is to analyze the content and structure of the web, usually from the point of view of computer and communication techniques in order to understand the structure and composition of cultural identity interactions on the Internet.

The social sciences are transformed with the digital world in general, but especially with the visualization of data (*Diminescu & Wieviorka, 2015*) which deal with social phenomena by the use of algorithms. Some researchers, such as Anderson (*2008*), speak of a revolution insofar as this method could put an end to the preliminary elaboration of theories. The advent of ICT has given rise to new forms of visualization through the analysis of massive data gathered in a single graph. These new methods improve understanding, facilitate data analysis, and ensure certainty of results.

One of these new methods of data visualization is the Web Mapping or digital mapping (*Fry, 2007*) which is composed of a number of websites represented by nodes, linked by hypertext represented by arcs (links). According to Lima (*2014*), the objective of the data collected must first be known and the question to be answered by analyzing the data; This question will allow to collect relevant data that increase the chances of understanding the phenomenon studied. The Web Mapping makes it possible to visualize the web synoptically and to deduce hypotheses on the positioning, and the role of the actors. Boechat and Venturini (*2016*) state that the analysis of visual data follows a process of discovery which begins with the discovery of the results and ends with the justification of this discovery. Web mapping is based on the hypertext links created between websites, which can be the equivalent of social links in the real world (*Kondratov, 2016*).

Data Collection

Severo and Zuolo (*2012*) distinguished between two types of tools in the graphical visualization of data; the tools of exploration of the web, and the tools of its representation. The first are crawlers which navigate a list of websites and explore the hyperlinks between them. The latter visualize these hypertext links in the form of a graph; several tools of representation such as Gephi, Adobe R, Pajek can be cited.

Digital methods (*Rogers, 2013*) combine a very heterogeneous set of visualization methods based on digital traces as a source of information for the study of social phenomena. The representation of the data in the form of graphs comes after the collection of all the traces using a certain number of numerical tools.

Cyber Metering (*Rogers, 2005*) applies a number of web analytics methods by collecting hyperlinks using software such as Issuecrawler and Navicrawler which crawl websites, identify links, and represent these relationships in the form of network graphs.

For the analysis of the Berber webosphere, we formed, as a starting point, a list of 20 Amazigh websites which we provided to the similar sites application. A tool available on the web in the form of a website called www.similarsites.com. We have collected 121 websites identified by the application as sites dealing with the Berber identity. Afterwards, we tried to detect the links between these sites thanks to a semi-automatic crawl tool, Navicrawler. The latter is a tool for extracting hyperlinks from a list of websites that we propose to analyze. It comes in the form of a sidebar of the Mozilla Firefox browser which includes a set of indexing features. We used a set of parameters to collect relevant data for the creation of a graph of the hypertext links of Amazigh websites. In the parameters of this tool, we chose the distance '2' to collect links with a doubled depth, with an interval of 32 milliseconds between downloading two hyperlinks. Navicrawler automatically navigates to all websites. This tool was able to collect a raw corpus that contains 382 nodes and 430 links. For the elaboration of the graph, we have imported this corpus into Gephi.

Gephi is a tool developed in Java and which focuses on the visualization of networks and interactivities (*Heymann, 2014; Le Béchec, 2016*). Visualizing the Berber webosphere, we have chosen a number of criteria provided by Gephi (*Jacomy, et al. 2014*). This makes it possible to visualize which are the most central elements of the network, the most remote, and the best connected. We checked the "Dissuade Hubs" box to push back nodes with a considerable number of links. We also checked the box "Mode LinLog" which allows us to increase the repulsion force. And to prevent overlapping of the nodes, we checked the box "Preventing overlap". We have created this graph by choosing a 10.0 scale as a measure of the intensity of the forces of repulsion and attraction between the nodes.

The size of the nodes extends from 50 to 900. It is proportional to the number of hypertext links created by each website (Degree). The more links there are, the larger the size of the node. To choose the color of each node, we considered the modularity class. Nodes with the same number of links have the same color (*Figure 1*).

Figure 1. Hyperlinks of Berbers' web sites

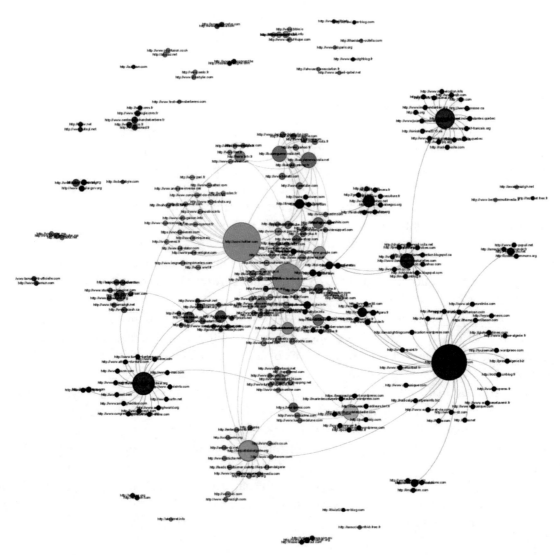

Amazighs Web Mapping: Observation and Analysis

Unity Within Diversity

The graph represents the set of websites created by the Amazighs on the Internet, and the hyperlinks they form between themselves and with other non-Amazigh websites.

This cartography illustrates all the territories occupied by this people, whether in North Africa or the West. These territories are identified by the name of the site: www.kabyleuniversel.com, www.amazigh-montreal.org, or by its domain www.fadma.be, www.amazigh.nl. Nevertheless, it is sometimes difficult to identify the geographical territory to which the website belongs without a consultation of its contents. These sites use general names and domains with no territorial reference such as www.mondeberbere. com, and www.amazighnews.org.

Figure 2 illustrates the links between several websites belonging to different geographical boundaries. Www.kabyle.com, a site for the Amazigh identity in Kabylia, is linked to www.mondeberbere.com, which is generally interested in the identity of the Amazigh people in southern Morocco. The latter establishes links with several other sites in geographical territories beyond its own, such as www.tamazgha.fr created by the Amazigh diaspora of France, and also that of the Movement for the Self-Determination of Kabylie (MAK) www.makabylie.info, as well as other non-Amazigh Algerian sites such as www.1dependance. com, and www.lequotidien-oran.com.

We found that all the sites that have hypertext links between them often share the same thematic. Although the central theme is the Amazigh identity, websites usually connect when they share the same subtheme. Moreover, the reason for the presence of non-Amazigh websites in the graph is the sharing of the same theme with these Amazigh sites.

For example, the website www.amazigh-montreal.org, which presents itself as a site that works for the well-being of the Amazigh community and the revival of its civilization, is linked to several sites including www.tunisie-berbere.com, www.algerie.info, www.souss.com, www.tamazgha.fr, www.tawalt. com. (*Figure 3*).

Language is also a criterion for forming hypertext links between sites. The Amazigh web generally uses French and Arabic or the Amazigh and English languages. Other diaspora languages are present on some sites, but they have no influence on hypertext links between websites.

Unconnected Web Sites

A number of nodes remain isolated in the graph, without linking to any other web site (*Figure 4*). These are usually internal or private sites. We can mention two web associatives: that of the Franco-Berber Association in Paris www.associationfbkb.fr, and the blog of the Association Tiwizi59 in Lille www. tiwizi59.over-blog.com. These two associations are not in contact with any other organizations on the Internet. By observing the content of their sites, we note that they are mainly interested in internal communication by focusing on the publication of information about the events organized by the association. Www.atmazret.info does not share any link because it remains the only website that gives courses of Amazigh language in Tunisian language. This site does not open to other Amazigh-speaking users and does not share any links with them. As for the site of the Thaddarth Oufella village in Algeria, www. thaddarth-oufella.com, it is isolated in the graph because of the focus of its publications on the history and current affairs of the village. The other two unrelated websites are www.awalamazigh.net which is

Figure 2. Links between websites belonging to different geographical boundaries

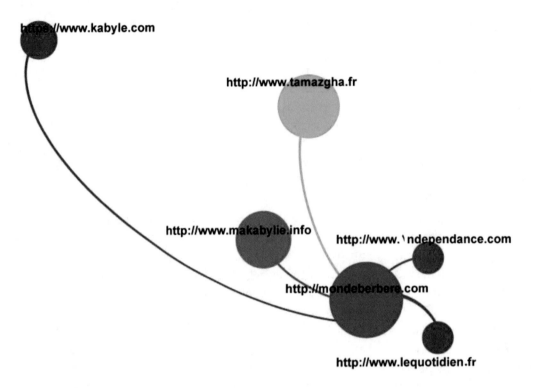

Figure 3. Berber Web sites sharing the same theme

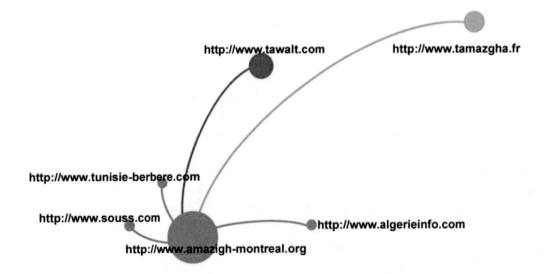

Figure 4. Unconnected web sites

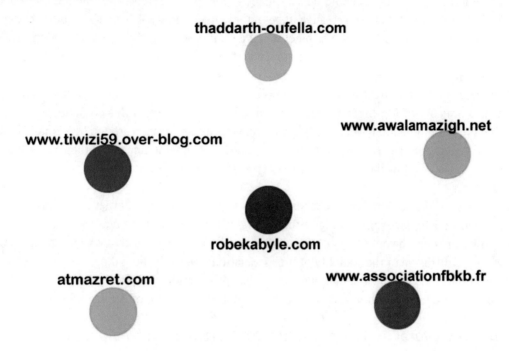

a simple discussion forum, as well as www.robekabyle.com which is a private website for the exhibition of Kabyle addresses.

The Amazigh community has gathered since the 1960s in associations and non-governmental organizations throughout North Africa, notably in Morocco and Algeria. Other associations were created by the Amazighs in the West, primarily, in France, to form "an identity-resistance" (*Castells, 1997*), considerably devalued and stigmatized by the dominant identity. These organizations, which demand recognition of the Amazigh identity by their states, resist and come before a "legitimating identity" introduced by the leading institutions of society in order to extend their domination over the social actors. These associations form a social movement called the "Amazigh movement", with the aim of preserving their culture, threatened with disappearance, in order to transmit it to future generations. A creator of an Amazigh site claims that "the internet is the only media accessible to the Amazigh at a time when television and newspapers are monitored by the North African authorities" (*Oulhadj, 2005*). Apart from the "Berber TV" channel, based in Paris, and created by Kabyles of France, all channels are either state-controlled or. Similarly, although Amazighs have the right to publish their own newspapers, the content and ideas developed are not immune to state control.

The Amazighs led a cyber-activism for cultural revitalization by inviting members of this community to learn more about their ancestral cultures. Traditional knowledge crosses the boundaries of nation-states to bring together on the digital web a people that has long shared a common ethnic and cultural origin before being arbitrarily divided by modern geopolitics.

The Amazighs have shown by their adaptation to different technologies, especially the internet, that their culture is not locked in the past. They have found ways to integrate their culture in a contemporary context. Digital tools therefore bring a new dimension to the survival of the Amazigh cultural identity.

The development of digital technologies has made it possible to democratize and facilitate access to information. The Amazighs have taken advantage of these means to get to know each other better and to make themselves known to other peoples by creating a multitude of websites. They used the internet to disclose a cultural knowledge, a historical memory and identity in order to establish links between the generations. This work ensures the continuity and transmission of their intangible cultural heritage. The network of networks is thus used for its two functions: communication and information: Communication insofar as it is a means of forging links between the different members of this community; information by ensuring the dissemination of ideas on websites and discussion forums around the Amazigh identity. The younger generations use the Web to discover this identity communicated by their ancestors. These means of transmission allow them to build up a deep knowledge and strengthen the construction of their cultural identity.

The isolation of the associations websites testifies to the use of the Internet as a portal that makes the association known, far from linking with other social actors, in particular the other associations. This non-link illustrates the continuity of the work realized in the real world to which is added a website whose use is the diffusion of the actuality of the association. Similarly, the village websites, which have the same utility as those of the associations, were created in the form of portals that make the village's heritage and culture known, while keeping their isolation from the rest of the digital world.

Internet and Cultural Activism: Culture as a Weapon of Resistance

Hyperlinks are a relevant means for analyzing the connections between the Amazighs in the digital world and the correlation between their presence in both the real sphere and the digital arena.

The analysis of the presence of the Amazighs on the Internet forces us to distinguish two levels: on the one hand, we analyze the hypertext links established between Amazigh websites. This must be corroborated, on the other hand, by analyzing the content of each web site, studying the reasons for the hypertext links established with the other sites.

A Berber Webosphere Designed for Cultural Activism

After their independence, the North African states adopted an identity centralism based on the "Arab-Muslim" identity by excluding all other components of their identities, including the Amazigh identity. The marginalization of the Amazigh cultural heritage by these states during the post-colonial period led to the loss of an important part of this legacy, which is highly oral. Many poems, tales, customs of traditional marriages and so various other Amazigh celebrations have disappeared due to a policy of oppression led by state governors.

The cultural heritage of indigenous peoples, such as Amazighs, has been marginalized by those responsible for their states (*Watson, 2012*). They take specific measures to eradicate, suppress or discredit indigenous culture. In creating their media, indigenous peoples engage in "cultural activism" (*Buser & Arthurs, 2013*) as a set of practices and activities that challenge the interpretations and constructions of the dominant world while presenting socio-political alternatives. It is a type of organization in which culture, activism and politics meet, mingle and interact (*Verson, 2007*). This includes engaging with a variety of creative practices such as theater, music, art, poetry, literature, and other cultural forms that challenge dominant practices and envision an alternative world.

The Amazighs use culture as a weapon of resistance which opposes the centralism of identity imposed by their states. The political concerns that characterize this activism are closely linked to issues of cultural affirmation. Amazigh cultural activism is not only a tool of cultural revitalization that reinforces knowledge and identity rootedness, but also a means of conducting a political struggle that expresses a set of ethnic claims. The visual and written documents on the Amazigh oral culture have an important place in the identity claim of this people. In an article published on the amazigh website www.monde-berbere.com, under the title "The Amazigh cause between culture and politics", Benyounès affirms that it is culture that gives birth to politics for the Amazigh people. Culture as a vehicle of identity and history must resist the oppression of the dominant identity established by States. Through the mediation of culture, Amazighs try to transform the status of their identity in the state sphere, and to end a dominant discourse that marginalizes and oppresses the Amazigh identity.

Amazighs are creating their media both to demonstrate against the marginalization of their states and to preserve and transmit their cultural identities. They have successfully used technological tools for their socio-cultural needs. They have allowed them to make their voices heard, to connect with each other, to pass on information, to revitalize their cultures and languages, and to commit themselves to their political rights.

Cultural activism has allowed the Amazighs to forge ties with other peoples who are more or less oppressed, notably indigenous peoples, but also with several international human rights organizations. They were the guests of the Bretons in France for a film festival in 1993. They later became members of the International Working Group for Indigenous Peoples (GITPA), headquartered in Vienna before becoming, in 2001, "the Permanent Forum" by changing the seat in New York. At the same time, the Amazighs joined the Office of the High Commissioner for Human Rights and established links with other organizations such as the European Union, UNESCO and the United Nations.

The cultural activism of the Amazighs has taken a new lease of life with the advent of the Internet. This digital tool has offered these people and their organizations plenty of opportunities to spread and strengthen their demands through the digitization of their culture. The Internet has created free trade spaces between the different components of the Amazighs people, and has been a revolution for the so-called traditional media. Amazigh websites address topics related to the cultural and political development of their countries.

Amazigh Cultural Activism on the Social Media

Activism culture is very present in the Amazigh web. The audio-visual and written documents on the Amazigh identity have a crucial place in all Amazigh websites. Texts and documents on Amazigh culture and tradition are constantly being published. Many articles and videos are often broadcasted by websites to celebrate certain festivals such as *Id Yennayer*, the Amazigh New Year, or to recall certain periods of Amazigh history, or to honor historical Amazigh personalities such as Yuba, Massinissa, and Yugerten in addition to the Amazigh heroes like Moha Ou Hemmou Azayyi, and Abdelkarim El Khattabi. Also, there are personalities adopted by the Amazigh movement as symbols for their contribution to the activism for the Amazigh identity like the singer Lounès Matoub or the historian Ali Sidqi Azaykou.

Social networks, especially YouTube and Facebook, have become a meeting place for many identities and the development of several cultures around the world. Pages and Facebook accounts are vectors of identity promotion of all by putting in relation the social identity and the digital identity of the users of these digital social networks. These networks are thus a widely used tool for Amazigh cultural activism.

Many videos have been published on YouTube for the diffusion of culture and Amazigh political demands. Collado (*2012*) distinguishes between four types of videos on YouTube: the first are those that exalt the past and history; The second show the artistic production of the Amazighs, the third are composed of speeches by Amazigh activists, and finally the different cultural and political manifestations of the movement.

Similarly, Facebook has been a place where the Amazighs exercise their cultural activism *par excellence*. Far from their private identities (name, first name, age ...), many young Amazighs who create their accounts on this social network choose a digital identity of a cultural nature. The use of pseudonyms with Amazigh cultural meanings by a very large number of Facebook users remains the first remark that can be made by looking at the Facebook accounts of Amazighs or by looking for a concept that reflects Belonging to the Amazigh identity on Facebook.

Proud of the ancient history of Tamazgha and her heroes, Amazigh youth choose for their pseudonyms on Facebook the names of the ancient Amazigh kings who have marked the history of North Africa.

One of the names of the most widespread kings on the canvas is that of *Massinissa*. In Amazighe, *Massinissa* or *Massnssen* as his name was found in his tomb in Cirta means "Their Lord". To justify this choice, an Amazigh youth who chose "Massinissa Boutfounast" as pseudonym asserts that he was fascinated by the courage and bravery of this king who marked the ancient history, "Massinissa is one of the most intelligent kings in history. I find in Him a model to follow. "Said the young" Massinissa Amazigh." Like *Massinissa*, *Yuba* is the name of the Amazigh kings most used as pseudonyms on Facebook. Among other things, *Yuba Wissin* (Yuba II), *Yuba Amazigh*, *Yuba ihihi*, Amazigh king Yuba I and his son Yuba II were two kings who marked the history of the Amazighs. The youth of the Amazigh movement are proud of today.

Likewise, the names of Amazigh queens are widely used as pseudonyms of the Amazigh girls on Facebook, *Tihya Tamghnast* (Tihya the activist), *Tihya Tamazight*, *Tihya Tanirte* (Tihya angel) or *Tinhinan Tameqrant, Tin-hinan Tamazight* are pseudonyms that illustrate the presence of the names of the Amazigh queens on Facebook. This reflects the pride of the young Amazighs *vis-à-vis* the place of women in their society, Having queens which reign over the whole of North Africa thousands of centuries ago, reflects the important place of women in the Amazigh society for a long time, it is also a sign of respect and valorization, but above all of the equality between men and women. Having the pseudonym of an Amazigh queen on Facebook is "a pride for me", says a young Amazigh activist.

The speech and claims of the Amazigh movement are very clear on the pseudonyms of the Facebook accounts of militants and sympathizers of the movement. In this regard, claims in the public arena have transposed to the digital and virtual sphere.

Since the creation of the first amazigh association, AMREC in 1967, the Amazighs claim their identity and their Amazighity. Currently, on the pseudonyms of the Facebook, the most common concept is that of "Amazigh" or "Tamazight". The choice of this denomination refers to its cultural and historical value in as much as the name "Amazigh" is that of a whole people with a long history and a specific culture to which the users of these accounts on Facebook belong. To express pride in their identity, Amazigh youths have chosen pseudonyms such as *Igidr Amazigh, Massinissa Amazigh, Tamazight Tudertinu* (Tamazight my life), *Tafokt Tamazight* (Amazigh Sun) to illustrate Their attachment to that identity and culture.

Freedom is one of the claims of the Amazigh movement whether in Morocco or elsewhere. Far from street protests, and press releases, the concept of freedom in the Amazigh culture is the subject of several pseudonyms on the Facebook. *Tiderfit, Tilelli or Tililli* are symbols of freedom claim on Facebook. *Tilelli*

Tamazight (Tilelli Tunaruz), Tiderfit Souss (Tilelli Tamazight), illustrate the presence of the demand for this freedom, which remains today one of the objectives of member activism of the Amazigh movement.

Another concept that refers to this "e-militancy", and to the claim of the Amazigh identity through the Facebook pseudonyms is that of *Ameghnas* (militant) / *Tameghnast* (female militant), which is used by a multitude of Amazigh militants such as *"Adrar Ameghnas"* (militant mountain), *Ameghnas Anzruf* (activist from Anzruf) *Tihya Tamghnast* (Tihya Militant), *Tamghnast Tamazgha* (Activist from Tamazgha), to discuss this activism within the Movement of Amazigh identity, and also to express this pride of being Amazighs.

The expression of the Amazigh identity on the Web also manifests itself in several forms. Examples include the use of recognition symbols in Facebook profiles, such as the so-called Amazigh flag, the *"Aza"* letter of the Tifinagh alphabet, which represents the Amazighs as "free men", or the fibula very present In Amazigh culture through tapestry, jewelry or costumes. Sometimes, in social network profiles, pseudonyms are used, such as "Imazighen" or "Amazigh" associated with the real names of cybernauts. In other cases, *Yougurtha*, *Massinisa*, *Kahina* or *Youba*, it is used as a sign Recognition, and even commitment to the Amazigh cause *(Suarez-Collado, 2013)*.

The pseudonyms of Facebook accounts play a very important role in the promotion of the Amazigh language and the preservation of its lexicon especially in the cultural field insofar as most of these terms have a linguistic value and a cultural charge.

This very important role of the pseudonyms used on the Facebook profiles applies to the published photos that these young people use as profile images. Visuals of identity, culture, history, politics, and Facebook's profiles play an essential role in promoting the Amazigh as the identity and culture of these young Internet users.

Similarly, the images of the profiles of young Amazighs symbolize their deep attachment to this identity, and their work for its promotion through this social network. These images published by young Amazighs on Facebook always have a link with the cultural life and the identity claims of the Amazighs.

The ancestral culture of the Amazighs has found its place on ICT in general, and on social networks in particular.

Facebook, frequented by a very large number of young Amazighs, remains a place of promotion of this Amazigh culture. An amazighe cultural identity is very clear on Facebook thanks to these beautiful images that deeply illustrate the culture and the Amazigh cultural heritage.

Highly aware of the role that images play on Facebook in promoting their culture, Amazigh youth publish daily on their accounts many images having a cultural and identity aspect as well as a vital value in their everyday life .

The Amazigh marriage, as an example, is clearly illustrated with images on Facebook. Images of the Amazigh bride are numerous. These images usually illustrate the bride's clothing at Imazighen such as the jewelry, *Lqdib* (traditional scarf), *Addal* (tradition cover), as well as also the traditions and customs of the Amazigh marriage ceremony.

The clothes of the Amazighs are also the object of the promotion of the Amazigh culture by images of the profile. Many images depict women who wear these traditional Amazigh dresses, fibula, jewelry, and slippers with amazigh colors.

The fibula is also the symbol of Amazigh culture on Facebook images. Several kinds of fibula from different regions have been posted on the Facebook profiles to illustrate the richness of their culture and the attachment of these young people to their roots and their identity.

Figure 5. Customs of the Amazigh mariage ceremony

The Amazigh cultural festivities are also portrayed in these images. Among others, we can mention the carnaval *Bilmawn* that the Amazigh youth organize each year on the occasion of the sacrifice festival throughout North Africa, but especially in the southern Moroccan region; or the masquerade of *Imaâchar* that the young people celebrate in the city neighborhoods of Tiznit located in the south of Morocco during the *Ashoura* ceremoney. Far from the demonstrations and releases of the Amazigh associations and organizations, Amazigh youths use profile images to demonstrate their claims on Facebook. One can say that the word Amazigh is very linked on Facebook in the image of the Amazigh flag. The image of this flag which represents the Amazigh people in the world is the image most shared by the young people who claim this identity and who work for its promotion. According to them, this tricolor flag with a letter "Z" in Tifinagh, character Amazigh, does not mean the autonomy of the Amazighs of their states, for them this flag represents and unites all the amazighs of the world.

Other young people choose images of historical personalities, Amazigh intellectuals and singers to promote and valorize the works of these personalities and to pay tribute to those who have created a glorious history of these people. One of the most widely shared images of Facebook profiles are those of Rif Mohamed Ben Abdelkarim El-Khattabi, the leader of the resistance movement against Spain and France during the Rif Represented on Facebook via his photos shared by the majority of Amazigh young people very active on this social network. In addition, the singer Kabyle Lounès Matoub, who thanks to his committed discourse and his work to promote the Amazigh identity, is today an emblematic figure on digital social networks. Similarly, the photos of the Moroccan French-speaking writer Mohamed Khair Eddine are widely shared by Facebook youth given his literary and cultural heritage and his promotion of Amazigh culture and identity through his literary writings.

Figure 6. Amazigh fibula

Social networks represent a space open to the promotion of all the identities of the world since they gather people from all over the world far from these geographical borders. In this sense, the Amazigh youth is very present on the social network Facebook for the promotion of its identity and its culture via this means of communication.

The pseudonyms that draw their originality from the Amazigh culture have contributed to the promotion of identity and to making it known to other people who do not belong to this Northern African community.

Like pseudonyms, the images of the profiles aim to promote the culture and literary heritage of the Amazighs. This presence of the Amazighs in the public arena and in the virtual sphere creates a sort of feedback relationship (*Suarez-Collado 2013*).

Figure 7. Amazigh carnaval (Bilmawen)

FUTURE RESEARCH DIRECTIONS

Future research may focus on the study of how transnational peoples organize themselves on the Internet. Being scattered across geographical territories, the Internet allows transnational peoples to create other boundaries by sharing hypertext links between their websites, or their accounts and Facebook pages. Among these transnational peoples, future research can focus on indigenous peoples. The latter, oppressed by their states, find in the Internet an alternation to meet and, particularly, to carry out "cultural activism", this study can be carried out by analyzing the hypertext links established between their separate websites.

CONCLUSION

The visualisation is a crucial means for the representations and the data analysis. This method utilized in this research has two main advantages. First, the visualization of the hypertext links of the Amazigh websites. The latter allows the visibility of the both the commonalities and the differences between all the components of these communities. Also, this method shows the visual representations that the Amazighs chose for themselves; a visual unreal representation attempting to represent the Amazigh people under one homogeneous identity.

REFERENCES

Kondratov, A. (2016). Analyser les matérialités de l'espace public contemporain avec la méthode quantitative de visualisation. In *Les cahiers numériques: La visualization de données* (Vol. 12). Paris: Lavoisier. doi:10.3166/lcn.12.4.93-129

Zinovyev, A. (2010) Data Visualization in Political and Social Sciences. International Encyclopedia of Political Science, 8.

Collado, A. S. (2012). Cyberactivisme et liens transnationaux au Rif. In Diaspora, Community and Communication: Internet Use in Transnational Haiti, Global Networks (Vol. 4). Academic Press.

Najar, S. (Ed.). (2012). *Les nouvelles sociabilités du Net en Méditerranée*. Paris: IRMC/Karthala.

Collado, A. S. (2013). Mouvement sociaux sur la Toile: les effets des TIC sur le militantisme Amazigh au Maroc. In *Le cyberactivisme au Maghreb et dans le monde arabe*. Paris: IRMC/Karthala.

Fry, B. (2007). *Visualizing Data*. Sebastopol, CA: O'Reilly Media.

Haythornthwaite, C. (2010). Social Networks and Learning Networks: Using Social Network Perspectives to Understand Social Learning. *7th International Conference on Networked Learning*.

Anderson, C. (2008). *The End of Theory: The Data Deluge Makes the Scientific Method Obsolete*. Retrieved April 13, 2017, from https://www.wired.com/2008/06/pb-theory/

Helland, C. (2007). Diaspora on the Electronic Frontier: Developing Virual Connections with Sacred Homeland. *Journal of Computer-Mediated Communication, 12*.

Vaisman, C. (2015). La visualisation, un langage sans parole. *NETCOM, 29*(3/4), 2015.

Diminescu, D. (2008). The Connected Migrant: An Epistemological Manifesto. *Social Sciences Information. Information Sur les Sciences Sociales, 47*(4), 565–579. doi:10.1177/0539018408096447

Boullier, D. (2015). Les Sciences Sociales Face aux Traces du Big Data? Société, Opinion et Répliques. *Fondation Maison des Sciences de l'Homme, 88*.

Edouard Tufte, E. (1983). *The Visual Display of Quantitative Information*. Cheshire, CT: Graphics Press.

Ollion, E., & Boelaert, J. (2015). Au Delà des Big Data: Les Sciences Sociales et la Multuplication des Données Numériques. Sociologie, 6(3).

Ginsburg, F. (2002). *Mediating Culture: Indigenous Madia, Ethnographic film, and the Production of Identity. In The Anthropology of Media*. Oxford, UK: Backwell.

Ghitalla, F. (2008). La "Toile Européenne" Parcours Autour d'une Cartographie Thématique de Documents Web Consacrés au Thème de l'Europe et à ses Acteurs sur le Web Francophone. Communication & langages, 1(158).

Hiller, H., & Franz, T. (2004). New Ties, Old Ties and Lost Ties: The Use of the Internet in Diaspora. *New Media & Society, 6*(731).

Watson, I. (2012). The Future Is Our Past: We once were sovereign and we still are. *Indigenous Law Bulletin, 8*(3).

Perriault, J. (2012). Réseaux Socionumériques et Frontières. Hermès, La revue, 2(63).

Schleser, J. (2013). Unprotected Memory: User-Generated and the Unintentional Archive. In *Proceedings of the Memory of the World in the Digital Age: Digitization and Preservation*. UNESCO.

Verson, J. (2007). Why We Need Cultural Activism? In *Do it Your Self: A Handbook for Changing our World*. London: Pluto Press. Retrieved April 05, 2017, from http://trapese.clearerchannel.org/chapters/HandbookForChangingOurWorld_chap11.pdf

Wheeldon, J., & Ahlberg, M. (2011). *Visualizing Social Sciences Research*. New York: SAGE Publications.

Healy, K., & Moody, J. (2016). Data Visualisation in Sociology. *Annual Review of Sociology, 40*(105).

Oulhadj, L. (2005). *La ruée vers Internet*. Retrieved March 15, 2017, from http://tawiza.x10.mx/Tawiza92/oulhadj.htm

Lima, M. (2014). *The Book of Trees: Visualizing Branches of Knowledge*. New York: Princeton Architectural Press.

Castells, M. (1997). *The Power of Identity, The Information Age: Economy, Society and Culture* (Vol. 2). Cambridge, MA: Blackwell.

Le Béchec, M. (2016). Le territoire comme un graphe: Pratiques, formes, éthique. In *Les cahiers numériques: La visualization de données* (Vol. 12). Paris: Lavoisier. doi:10.3166/lcn.12.4.131-156

Boechat, M., & Venturini, T. (2016). From analysis to presentation: Information visualization for reifying issues and reenacting insights in visual data analysis. In *Les cahiers numériques: La visualization de données* (Vol. 12). Paris: Lavoisier.

Severo, M., & Zuolo, E. (2012) Egyptian e-diaspora: migrant websites without a network? In Social Science information, (n° 51, pp. 521-533). Paris: SAGE Publications. doi:10.1177/0539018412456772

Nakata, M., Nakata, V., Gardiner, G., McKeough, J., Byrne, A., & Gisbon, J. (2008). Indigenous Digital Collections: An Early Look at the Organisation and Culture Interface. *Australian Academic and Research Libraries, 49*(4).

Jacomy, M., Venturini, T., Heymann, S., & Bastian, M. (2014). ForceAtlas2, a Continuous Graph Layout Algorithm for Handy Network Visualization Designed for the Gephi Software. *PLoS One, 9*(6), 2014. doi:10.1371/journal.pone.0098679 PMID:24914678

Buser, M., & Arthurs, J. (2013). *Connected Communities: Cultrual Activism in the Community*. Retrieved May 01, 2017, from http://www.culturalactivism.org.uk/wp-content/uploads/2013/03/CULTURAL-ACTIVISM-BUSER-Update.3.pdf

Wieviorka, M., & Diminescu, D. (Eds.). (2015). Le tournant numérique...et après ? *Socio, 4.*

Nedelcu, M. (2009). Du Brain Drain à l'E-diaspora: Vers une Nouvelle Culture du Lien à l'ère du Numérique. TIC & Diaspora, 3(1-2).

Musso, P. (2010). Le Web: Nouveau Territoire et Vieux Concept. *Annales des Mines – Réalités Industrielles, 4.*

Virtanen, P.K. (2015). Indigenous Social Media Pratices in Southwestern Amazonia. *AlterNative: An International Journal of Indigenous Peoples, 11*(4).

Budka, P., Brandi, B., & Fiser, A. (2009). MyKnet.org: How Northen Ontario's First Nations Communities Made Themeselves at Home on the World Wide Web. Community Informatics, 5(2).

Adams, P., & Ghose, R. (2003). India.Com: The Construction of a Space Between. *Progress in Human Geography, 27*(4), 414–437. doi:10.1191/0309132503ph437oa

Oiarzabal, P. (2012). Diaspora Basques and Online Social Networks: An Analysis of Users of Basque Institutional Diaspora Groups on Facebook. *Journal of Ethnic and Migration Studies, 38*(9), 1469–1485. doi:10.1080/1369183X.2012.698216

Srinivasan, R. (2006). *Indigenous, Ethnic and Cultural Articulations of New Media, International Journal of Cultural Studies.* London: Sage Publications.

Rogers, R. (2005). *Digital Methods.* Boston, MA: The MIT Press.

Heymann, S. (2014). *Exploratory link stream analysis for event detection. Social and Information Networks.* Paris: Université Pierre et Curie.

Erickson, T. (1996). The World Wide Web as Social Hypertext. *Communications of the ACM, 39*(1), 15–17. doi:10.1145/234173.234174

Mayer-Schnonberger, V., & Cukier, K. (2014). *Big Data: A Revolution That Will Transform How We Live, Work, and Think.* Boston: Houghton Mifflin Harcourt.

KEY TERMS AND DEFINITIONS

Amazigh: An indigenous ethnic group in North Africa. Known in antiquity under the names of Libyans, Moors, Gétules, Garamantes, or Numides. Their land stretched from the Canary Islands to Egypt. Today they are found in Morocco, Algeria, Libya, Tunisia, and Egypt.

Cultural Activism: Set of practices and activities that challenge the interpretations and constructions of the dominant world while presenting socio-political alternatives.

Data Visualization: A general term that describes any effort to help staff understand the meaning of the data by placing it in a visual context. Thus, data visualization software will help highlight and identify patterns, trends, and correlations that may go unnoticed in textual data.

Gephi: A free software for analysis and visualization of networks, developed in Java and based on the NetBeans platform. Originally developed by students at the Compiègne University of Technology (UTC) in France, Gephi was selected for the Google Summer of Code five consecutive years between 2009 and 2013. In 2010, he won the Duke's Choiced'Oracle The Innovative Technical Data Visualization category.

Indigenous People: A population settled in a given territory before all the others, and who has established special, ancient, and ever-present relations with this territory and its environment, and which has its own customs and culture.

Web-Mapping: It is the process that brings together all the technologies for displaying a map via the internet. It makes it possible to transform invisible data beforehand into a visual mapping.

ENDNOTE

[1] Amazigh translates as the "free man". Berber is widely used to refer to the Berber people in Academia, however, it is a derogatory term that the Romans used to name the Amazigh when they conquered North Africa. *Amazigh* means "free man". "Berber" is widely used in the academic world: it refers to the name given by the Romans when they conquered North Africa.

APPENDIX

This map illustrates the origin of the websites visualized in Figure 1. It represents North Africa, region of origin of the Amazighs, and the diaspora in the Western.

Figure 8. Distribution of websites by country of origin

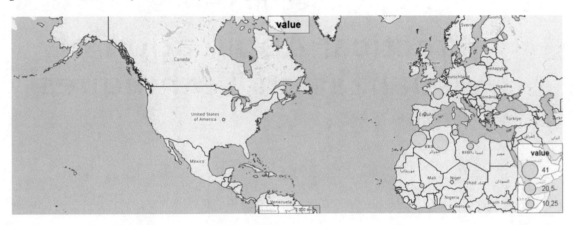

Section 4
Practical Application of Visualization Techniques

Chapter 11
Perspectives and Good Practices in Visualization of Knowledge About Public Entities

Jan Fazlagić
Poznan University of Economics and Business, Poland

Windham Loopesko
University of Colorado – Denver, USA

Leszek Matuszak
Poznan University of Economics and Business, Poland

Rigby Johnson
University of Colorado – Denver, USA

ABSTRACT

Visualization of knowledge in public entities is becoming more and more popular due to the development of information technology tools, the demand for solutions allowing for reduction of information overload (IO), and new approaches to local government, including citizen participation. The chapter presents some case study examples of knowledge visualization in public entities with some conclusions and recommendations for policy makers. Additionally, it presents a complete map of certain Polish counties prepared by the authors. The authors applied, apart from the visualization in the form a map, the "Chernoff Faces" method (invented by Herman Chernoff in 1973). This method displays multivariate data on Polish counties in the shape of a human face. The individual parts, such as eyes, ears, mouth, and nose, represent values of the variables by their shape, size, placement, and orientation. The idea behind using faces is that humans easily recognize faces and notice small changes without difficulty. Chernoff Faces handle each variable differently.

DOI: 10.4018/978-1-5225-4990-1.ch011

INTRODUCTION

The inventor of the "Chernoffs Faces" method of visualization of knowledge is Hermann Chernoff (now Professor Emeritus of Applied Mathematics, Department of Statistics at Harvard University). He created the method in 1973 for the graphic representation of statistical data, to represent specific multivariate data using only one symbol (a human face) changing its features. In the late 1970's Chernoff faces began to be popular outside of the USA. Today, the processing of data using Chernoff faces is a common feature of statistical software (e.g. Statistica, S-PLUS or Systat). The underlying motive for using Chernoff faces is that humans possess an innate ability easily recognize distinct faces and notice small, even subtle changes in facial features.

Creating visualizations of data is becoming more and popular as a method of communicating and sharing knowledge. In a world where complexity is growing at an accelerating rate and where time is increasingly the scarce resource, traditional ways of exchanging knowledge are perceived as insufficiently efficient. Text and numbers are yielding to visualization as a tool for exchanging knowledge. But a wide variety of visualization techniques have been developed; choosing the technique that is best suited for the nature and details of the knowledge the researcher desires to convey is thus a critical research task (Meyer, n.d.)

The visualization technique used should also take into consideration the audience for which the information is intended. Remo Aslak Burkhard noted in his doctoral thesis that architects presenting information about the same object (a skyscraper) used different complementary visualization techniques in addressing various target groups (e.g., lawyers, engineers, clients and workers) with diverse knowledge backgrounds and a need to understand different levels of detail (Burkhard, 2005).

Visual descriptions of data provide meaning to information which may be especially useful in intercultural communication, as well as an answer to the IO challenge. Through knowledge visualization, complex sets of data are displayed in a graphical interface – for example, in a chart or on a map – which allows the viewer to gain deeper insight into patterns and trends. Visualized knowledge is highly sharable on social media channels and social networks. Visualization of knowledge is very useful to communicate science to lay audiences. Thus, knowledge visualization serves educational purposes.

Knowledge visualization is a relatively new field of research that focuses on the creation and transfer of knowledge by visualizations with and without the help of computers. It has the possibility to be a mediator between many different disciplines. Knowledge visualization (and modeling) is a term used to describe the use of visual representations to transfer knowledge between a minimum of two people. Its purpose is to improve the transfer of knowledge by using a mix of computer and non-computer-based visualization methods.

During the process of learning and problem solving, visualization can help the learner overcome problems. Combining computer-based information systems with human cognitive capabilities, while using visualization as the link between the two, is seen to be far more powerful than just using human cognitive processes. In an educational context, learner visualizations may foster constructive cognitive processing and visual/spatial strategies (Burkhard, 2005).

KNOWLEDGE VISUALIZATION VS. INFORMATION VISUALIZATION

Knowledge visualization and information visualization are related techniques, as they both assist in visualizing different abstraction levels of data (Burkhard, 2005). Robert Meyer distinguishes among:

- *Data*, which are symbols or facts that are isolated and have not yet been interpreted;
- *Information*

. . . is more sophisticated. It is data that has been interpreted or processed and therefore contains some meaning and can give answers to questions like 'who?', 'what?', 'where?', 'why?' or 'when?' For those who do not comprehend the meaning it still stays data.

- *Knowledge* is a step further, being information that has been processed and integrated into someone's existing knowledge structure. While information is outside the brain, knowledge is inside.

Thus, the content and process of information- and knowledge visualization differ. While both are based upon the abilities of the human perception system, information visualization is much more linked to computer-based visualizations; it cannot process non-computer-based visualizations and knowledge types (Meyer, 2008-2009). Burkhard argues, however, that as a new field, knowledge visualization lacks a theoretical basis and an interdisciplinary mediating framework; while information visualization researchers have succeeded in creating new insights based upon abstract data, they have not been able to develop a means of transmitting this information to the recipients, which Burkhard hopes will result from the recognition and pursuit of knowledge visualization as a new field of research (Meyer, 2008-2009).

To this end, Burkhard proposes a knowledge visualization model, developed around the principle that knowledge cannot be transferred directly from one person to another; the recipients must integrate the transferred knowledge (which to them is initially information) into their own knowledge base developed from their individual background and experience. The vehicle for this transfer is the use of complementary visualizations for the successive steps in the knowledge transfer process from sender to receiver. Burkhard's proposed model seeks to answer five questions:

- What is the aim and the effect of externalizing knowledge into visual representations?
- What is relevant and should be visualized?
- Which audience should be addressed?
- What is the interest of the recipient?
- What is the most efficient way to visualize the knowledge?" (Meyer, n.d.).

Burkhard proposes a staged substructure that does not rely upon a single knowledge visualization technique for the knowledge transfer process but rather complementary visualizations for different purposes. Burkhard suggests the following stages:

- The first stage involves catching the *attention* of the recipient – for example, by a provoking image;
- In the second stage, the sender must:

- ◦ Illustrate the *context* of the knowledge to make the recipient aware of the importance of the knowledge to him;
- ◦ Provide an *overview* of the information, showing the "big picture" of the topic;
- ◦ Offer some *options to act*, enabling the recipient to focus his interest;
- In the third stage, the sender presents the *details* of the knowledge to be transferred.

Burkhard notes as a caveat, however, the limitations of the model due to different abilities of all humans to interpret visual stimuli, while suggesting that the model can provide general guidelines for using knowledge visualization.

ADVANTAGES OF KNOWLEDGE VISUALIZATION

Knowledge visualization offers many benefits. Burkhard (2005) identified the following functions of knowledge visualization:

- Coordination: Visual representations (VRs) help to coordinate individuals in the communication process.
- Attention: VRs help to get and keep the viewer's attention by addressing emotions.
- Understanding: VRs help to identify patterns, outliers, and trends.
- Recall: VRs improve memorability, remembrance, and recall.
- Motivation: VRs inspire, motivate, energize, and activate viewers.
- Elaboration: VRs foster the elaboration of knowledge in teams.
- New insights: VRs support the creation of new insights by embedding details in context, showing relationships between objects, and leading to "ah-ha" effects.

The attention function overlaps with that used in the AIDA model — "Attention, Interest, Desire, and Action," developed by E. St. Elmo Lewis in 1898 (Vakratis, 1999) — where drawing the attention of the recipient of information is a prerequisite for successful communication.

These functions are part of an overall Knowledge Visualization Framework that includes the following additional elements:

- Knowledge type:
  - ◦ Know-what;
  - ◦ Know-how;
  - ◦ Know-why;
  - ◦ Know-where; and
  - ◦ Know-who.
- Recipient type
  - ◦ Individual;
  - ◦ Group;
  - ◦ Organization; and
  - ◦ Network.
- Visualization type (see discussion in the next section, "Tools of knowledge visualization").

Other functions of knowledge visualization can be achieved through:

- **Stress Reduction:** Uncertainty is one of the main causes of stress and the subsequent decrease in the ability to process information (Rock, 2009). A simplified version of the reality presented in a visual representation of knowledge is conducive for stress reduction and, as a consequence, may improve learning outcomes.
- **Metaphor:** A metaphor consists in giving a thing a name that belongs to something else (Sontag, 1988). In visualizing knowledge, different commonly known objects such as a tree, an iceberg, a mountain, a pyramid, a ladder, and dice, are frequently used to describe a process or a phenomenon. Morgan (1998) used metaphors to describe the complexity of organizations. Metaphors enable understanding reality through sense making (Weick, 1995).

Visualization of knowledge is often used in strategic management. Strategy visualization is defined as the systematic use of complementary visual representations to improve the analysis, development, formulation, communication, and implementation of strategies in organizations (Burkhard 2005). Barrett (1994) distinguishes between *business visions* (the organization's values, philosophy, or beliefs) and the *process visualization* (which tells how to do those things right and focus, motivate, and engage individuals). La Rooy (2000) emphasizes the importance of visualization as a *visual motivation*, which involves employees in the implementation of many small improvements by using photographs of "before and after" situations tagged with ideas and findings of the improvement ideas.

TOOLS OF KNOWLEDGE VISUALIZATION

Burkhard (2005) has developed a taxonomy of seven tools that can be used in knowledge visualization that researchers can use to achieve "knowledge communication", which Martin Eppler defines as an "...activity of interactively conveying and co-constructing insights, assessments, experiences or skills through verbal and non-verbal means" (Eppler, 2004). The seven are:

- *Sketches* (simple designs helping to visualize key features and the main idea quickly);
- *Diagrams* (abstract, schematic representations used to display, explore and explain relationships);
- *Maps* (plans that present entities on a different scale and allow two-dimensional representations of three-dimensional objects);
- *Images* (renderings, photographs or paintings);
- *Objects* (physical models to show projects from different perspectives);
- *Interactive visualization* (visualizations allowing the recipient to access, combine, control, explore, and manipulate different types of complex data); and
- *Visions/stories* (non-physical, imaginary visualizations that transfer knowledge across time and space).

Some complex formats of knowledge visualization are theory-drive conceptual maps, concept maps, interactive visual metaphors, or knowledge maps (Meyer, 2016).

Another tool for visualization of knowledge is difficult to classify. It is based on humans' innate ability to process visual information related to face recognition. Inspired by this unique feature of the human brain, Hermann Chernoff developed a unique type of knowledge visualization tool now commonly called "Chernoff Faces". Chernoff created Chernoff Faces as a method for multiple variables data presentation method in 1973 (Chernoff, 1973). Its underlying principle is the use of the human face (especially its features) to show the intensity or level of different variables.

THE BACKGROUND OF THE CHERNOFF FACE METHOD

Chernoff used the human face because the face is the easiest way for humans to determine differences; people recognize others thanks to differences in, for example, the shape of the head, the nose and the mouth. Chernoff wasn't the first person using shapes to represent k-dimensional variables. Anderson in 1957 was using glyphs, a "graphical object whose properties represent data values" (e.g., Anderson in 1957 was using glyphs, a "graphical object whose properties represent data values" (Anderson, 1957) (e.g., circles with fixed diameters and rays that have different angles and lengths), but the glyph method was not as intuitive as Chernoff's idea of faces. Some researchers were using triangles (up to 4 variables - three lengths of sides and position). Chernoff wrote that he was using profiles with series of n bars (n = number of variable), but the use of such bars was not intuitive — a bar graph with more than 3 - 4 variables is difficult to examine, especially when searching for similarities. Standardization of data puts numbers into a range between -3 and 3 (with the mean = 0) and helps to compare relations between objects. For example, without standardization the importance of variables counted in billions would be higher than others counted in tens - because differences are counted in billions, not in tens. The data must be standardized (to range from 0 to 1, with standardization using a z-score) to have identical/nearing range. In 1970, he concluded that using bars was a very promising method of representation multivariate data, but it is highly vulnerable to noise in one group of variables overspreading differences between others.[1] Among other methods used nowadays, the most common still are polygons (stars, stars presentations, star coordinate systems and similar representations), classic bar-charts, and lines (Chambers, 1983). Chernoff claims that it is possible to show up to 18 different variables. Statistical packages offer over 40 different face features.

Chernoff Faces are used in many field of science – for example, in mechanics (Zhang, 2017), chemistry (Kim, 2012), geographical information systems, and cartography. Using Chernoff Faces and other specific diagrams in showing differences and similarities between areas is the most popular use of Chernoff Faces. The method was first used publicly by Eugene Turner in the map "Life in Los Angeles, 1970". In the 90's, Chernoff Faces were used to show differences in spatial structures of British electors (Dorling, 1991), feature salience and the election results in the United States of America - one of the most popular and most often-cited diagrams (Fabrikant, 2000) - in its most popular form, it uses the face, but in a simplified carto-diagram.

In 1997, a team of researchers from San Diego State University tested which features are the easiest and most efficient to detect within Chernoff Faces in a cartographic setting (Nelson, 1997). They concluded that subjects were the fastest and most accurate in determining changes in head size, with the greatest difficulty in detecting changes in mouth orientation; in between were eye size and nose size. While they did not use color in their study, they suggested that using color could be very effective in emphasizing one of many variables.

According to Hungarian and Argentine researchers, Chernoff Faces are a perfect base and concept for creating multivariable diagrams - instead of faces, researchers can use pictures of factory, mine, car, tank/artillery units and many other objects (Nuñez, 2011). Reyes and others (including Turner) proposed using additional features (filling in the head) and changing some parameters to make the diagrams more understandable (Reyes, 2009).

CRITICSM OF THE CHERNOFF FACES METHOD

Most of the criticism of the Chernoff Face method comes from the very different way that humans react to faces compared with other glyphs or symbols. Martin Elmer notes,

...human beings have ridiculously strong hard wiring for identifying faces. We sport an entire part of our brain dedicated to process images of faces, which snaps on faster than you can blink when a face comes into view. Our ability to recognize faces is famously overzealous. Chernoff was curious if he could co-opt our powerful face-spotting abilities to help humanity deal with something our brains are notoriously bad at comprehending: numbers. Thus, the Chernoff face: a face-like symbol where the various proportions of the facial features each correspond to some sort of data item (Elmer, 2013).

This innate human face-recognition capability raises a number of issues. One such issue is *pareidolia*, or the phenomenon of seeing faces in inanimate objects (e.g., the "man in the moon"). The Merriam-Webster defines pareidolia as:

The tendency to perceive a specific, often meaningful, image in a random or ambiguous visual pattern. The human brain is optimized to recognize faces, which could also explain why we are so good at picking out meaningful shapes in random patterns (Pareidolia, 2017).

A perhaps even clearer example is the use of aligned punctuation symbols to convey emotions. Examples include the following (Kosara, 2007):

;) : (>: P : ^ D

This tendency of humans to ascribe emotions to inanimate objects or sets of typographical characters suggests how faces as an analytical tool can confuse or mislead an audience. As Elmer notes, the academic term for this problem is *"correspondence"*, which he defines as "simply how intuitive the relationship is between any given symbol and the thing it is symbolizing" (Elmer, 2013). Elmer criticizes Chernoff's use of human faces in his original 1973 article to represent the characteristics of various minerals. He provides examples of faces that Chernoff used to represent such characteristics (Figure 1).

As Elmer notes,

... we don't associate human faces with anything other than, well, human faces, so using them for numerical data seems silly. . . It makes a lot more sense to see a human face stand in for actual humans (Elmer, 2013).

Since Chernoff's 1973 articles, most authors have used Chernoff Faces for socio-economic data – i.e., data that involves human beings (and not, as in the original Chernoff article, inanimate items such as

Figure 1. Examples of Chernoff faces.
Source: Meyer, op. cit., citing Chernoff, op. cit., footnote 9

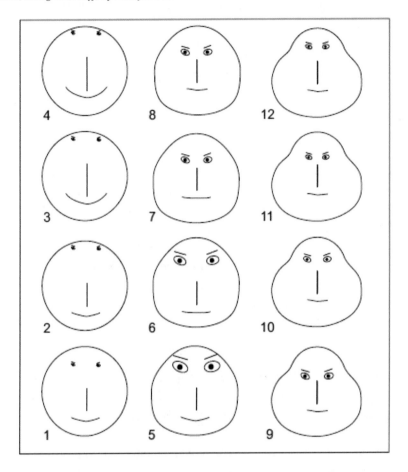

minerals). Thus, the most effective uses of Chernoff Faces have been where the data represented in the faces corresponds to the emotions that the faces derived from the data evoke in the intended audience.

Elmer cites as a famous example of an appropriate use of Chernoff Faces (i.e., "good correspondence") Eugene Turner's map showing socio-economic conditions in various parts of the City of Los Angeles. In this study, Turner mapped four variables over sixteen different regions of the City:

- "Affluence" (based upon various income, education and housing factors);
- Unemployment rate;
- "Urban stresses" (bsed upon various health, crime and transportation factors); and
- Racial composition (defined as the percentage of whites in the total population).

Here Turner used

- Rounder faces (compared with gaunt, emaciated faces) to show greater affluence;
- Smiles/frowns to show lower/higher levels of unemployment, respectively;
- Relaxed/tense eyes to show lower/higher levels of urban stress), and

●   Different shades of beige/brown to show racial composition.

The correspondence works, because the more fortunate data results in happier-looking, more relaxed faces, while the less fortunate data produces unhappier, angrier-looking expressions. As a result, readers have a relatively intuitive understanding of the differences in socio-economic conditions within the City.

The problem with using Chernoff Faces is that good correspondence is hard to achieve. Elmer cites another example, using the data described in Figure 3.

In the example presented in Figure 3, lower unemployment rates generate a smile, while higher rates create a frown – all well and good. But higher divorce rates are represented by longer noses. While higher divorce rates are generally considered socio-economically less desirable, it's not intuitive that a face with a longer nose is less desirable than one with a shorter nose. Similarly, higher crime rates are represented by longer ears. While higher crime rates are clearly socio-economically negative, longer ears do not, at least for the authors of this study, generate either a positive or negative response. Perhaps the most glaring example of bad correspondence, however, (particularly in the politically correct environment of 2017; the example used dates from 2004) is the use of angry eyes to denote a higher percentage of women

Figure 2. Life in Los Angeles.
Source: Eugene Turner - Life in Los Angeles (1977)

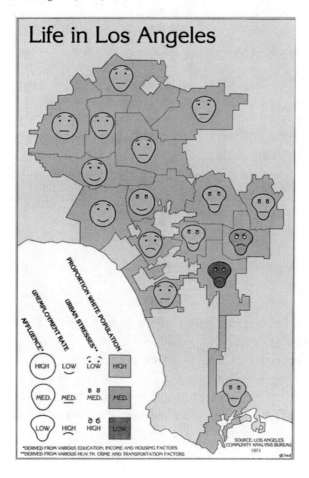

Figure 3. Examples of unintuitive correspondence.
Source: From Joseph Spinelli and Yu Zhou (2004)

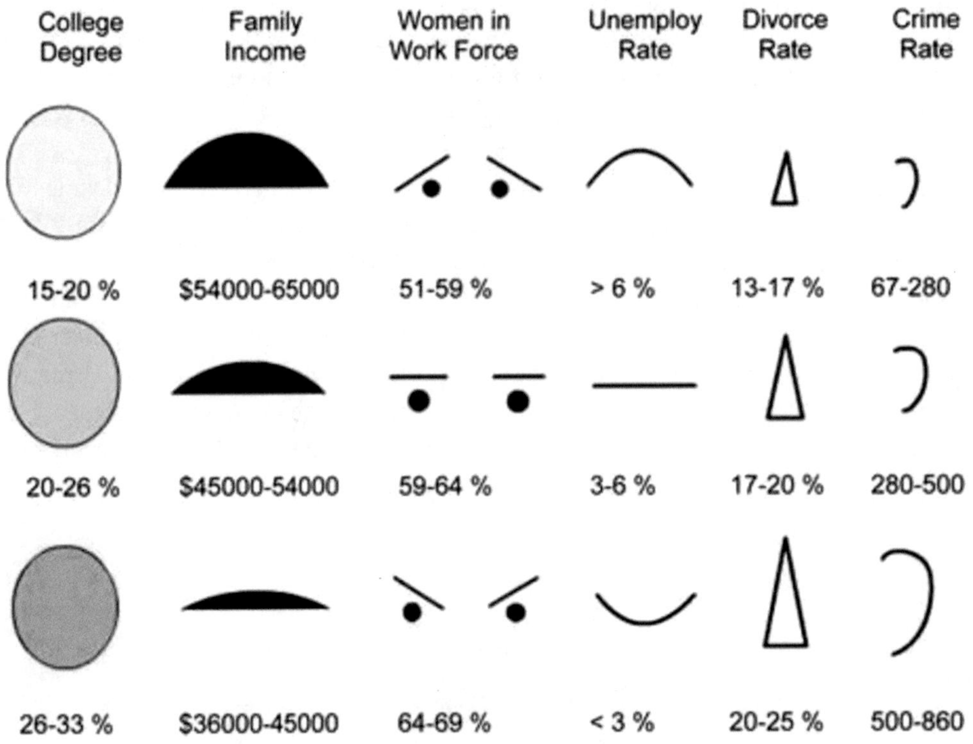

College Degree	Family Income	Women in Work Force	Unemploy Rate	Divorce Rate	Crime Rate
15-20 %	$54000-65000	51-59 %	> 6 %	13-17 %	67-280
20-26 %	$45000-54000	59-64 %	3-6 %	17-20 %	280-500
26-33 %	$36000-45000	64-69 %	< 3 %	20-25 %	500-860

in the workforce. This choice of symbolism seems clearly counter-intuitive, as a higher percentage of women in the workforce (again, for the authors of this article) seems as if it should generate a positive emotion rather than the increasing anger that the symbol for the eyes evokes.

Elmer suggests two fundamental difficulties with using faces to depict multivariate data symbolization:

1. *Facial features are not generally ordinal.*
2. *Humans treat faces as more than the sum of their parts.*

Re. 1: In data theory, data is ordinal if it can be arranged in groups with a meaningful order. Elmer contrasts two different types of data:

*   Crime figures (which can be meaningfully order, as high crime rates are more than medium and low crime rates); and
*   Nationality (American, British, German, etc. cannot be meaningfully ordered).

While some types of data can be meaningfully ordered, many facial features (e.g., eyes and eyebrows) cannot. Maps using Chernoff Faces often use the position of eyebrows as a data representation, with the angle of the eyebrows varying depending on a data value (see Figure 4).

Figure 4. Examples of faces showing non-ordinal emotions.
Source: Eugene Turner - Life in Los Angeles (1977)

Elmer describes (accurately in the authors' view) the emotions generated by these faces as angry, bored/indifferent and sad. He notes:

These emotions aren't orderable: an angry person is not "more bored" than a sad person. A sad person is not "less angry" then a person with a blank expression. These emotions don't fit along a sliding scale, so pairing them with data that does (e.g., the high/medium/low urban stresses in Turner's map) is inappropriate at best and misleading at worst (Elmer, 2013).

Re. 2: Elmer provides an example of the following face (which could have, but did not, occur in the Turner study, as it would imply high urban stress but low unemployment) (Figure 5).
Using the Chernoff criteria, this face would be happy but angry. Elmer asserts:

Figure 5. A mixed-attribute face. Source: Eugene Turner - Life in Los Angeles (1977), cited in Elmer, op. cit.

... facial expressions are, visually, more than the sum of their parts. Place a happy grin and angry eyebrows onto a face, and the result is not "both happy and angry", but rather an entirely new emotion (impishness) that is not relatable to the components that created it. This creates problems in the context of the map, because mixed-up facial expressions like these A) just plain look silly and B) obscures the actual goings-on of the data (Elmer, 2013).

Elmer notes a fundamental distinction between facial features that convey emotion and those that do not. He cites a cartoonist asserting that the facial features that convey emotion are:

- Eyes;
- Eyebrows;
- Mouth shape; and
- Cheeks.

He adds that the text-based emoticons (see, e.g., the examples above) always display the eyes and mouth; they do not include noses, ears or hairlines, which generally do not provide information about how a person is feeling. When a facial feature does not convey emotion, it's hard to convey any meaningful information by differences in that features. While such differences may be perceptible, responses to those differences will not be intuitive.

Elmer offers the following criteria for effective use of Chernoff Faces, the data should be:

- Socio-economic in nature;
- Devoid of mixed attributes (as in the smiling/angry face above); and
- "Plottable" to emotion-linked facial features (he adds head-silhouette – as the use by Turner in the City of Los Angeles data suggests – as a possible emotion-linked feature).

He concludes:

That's a lot of barriers to be overcome, and even if they are, the product is still going to have to tangle with all the emotional and cultural and biological baggage that humans have when it comes to looking at faces. I honestly don't know if truly good Chernoff faces can ever be pulled off (Elmer, 2013).

THE RELIABILITY OF THE CHERNOFF FACES METHOD

Data used in creating Chernoff Faces must be standardized and assigned to different features of the face. Researchers should avoid using data with low variation coefficients. The process of assignment is the most difficult part of creating the diagram. While popular statistical software (i.e. STATISTICA, R, STATGRAPHICS) assigns data and standardizes it automatically, we do not recommend this practice.

The most popular features used in analysis are length of the nose and mouth, curvature of the mouth, slant of the eyebrows, size of the eyes and ears, eccentricity of the upper- and lower-face, visibility of the eyeballs and many other features (filling the eyes and face with gradients). Study designers should assign features in a logical way, correlating stimulant variables with positive images, while using negative images for depressants (i.e., higher incomes should relate to a more curved/bigger smile; a higher unemployment rate shouldn't). Connecting face features with variables is the most important and most difficult issue.

Researchers can encounter many problems, raised both by critics and followers of Chernoff Faces, including:

- Hiding interesting patterns by using the wrong feature connected with a variable (for example, the face shape or nose length can change the perception of the mouth);
- Using the wrong feature for more important variables;
- Encountering pareidolia;
- Finding different perceptions of the human face (there are more and less important features) – which can result in over-emphasizing or understating some variable (intentionally or by accident); and
- Recognizing the human face not by analyzing every feature and connecting it; people just recognize a person, or judge her/his character, personality, mood, etc.

Followers would say that Chernoff Faces, despite these disadvantages, are the best way to find patterns and similarities in multivariate objects, because careful researchers can avoid most of the disadvantages. Additionally, intuitive analysis of the same sets of faces by different analyst would give similar (but not identical) results.

THE APPLICATION OF THE CHERNOFF METHOD TO VISUALIZE KNOWLEDGE ABOUT POLISH COUNTIES

The applications of the methods are multifarious. Gifford (1997) conducted an interesting research study using the Chernoff method to test its reliability. He used Chernoff Faces to depict certain financial indicators (e.g., working capital, profitability) in periodic reports. Gifford asked two groups of professionals to provide their financial forecasts of the analyzed companies. One group was using traditional numerical data; the other was using Chernoff Faces to analyze the financial standing of the same companies' historical data. Those analysts who based their forecasts on visual information were more accurate in predicting the financial future.

In this study, we endeavored to use the Chernoff Faces method to visualize certain socio-economic indicators, establishing a set of variables describing some selected statistical information about Polish counties. We chose the features of a face listed below and matched with the variables indicated Table 1).

An extended list of 15 variables the differentiation among faces/counties is higher:

1. Width of the face: cultural accessibility
2. Level of ears: employment rate
3. Mid-face: long-term unemployment
4. Shape of the upper part of face: migration balance
5. Shape of the lower part of face: number of divorces
6. Length of nose: average salary
7. Mid-mouth: number of areas covered by local development plans (MPZ[2])
8. Curvature of mouth: value of completed projects

Table 1. Features of a face matched with the variables.

Feature	Variable
Face width	Accessibility of cultural goods (the wider the face, the more accessible cultural goods)
Ear positioning	Unemployment rate (low ears = low unemployment rate)
Length of nose	Number of square meters of living space per inhabitant
Mouth position	Foreign capital invested per employment age inhabitant
Mouth gesture	Number of businesses (high number = smiling mouth)
Length of mouth	Accessibility through transportation network (rail, plane, road)
Upper face shape	Divorces per 1000 inhabitants (higher divorce rate = more rounded face)
Lower face shape	Average gross salary in divorces (higher salary = more rounded face)
Mid-face shape	Migration balance among communes in the county

Source: own elaboration

9. Length of mouth: number of square meters of living area per inhabitant
10. Height of ears: amount of foreign capital
11. Distance between eyes: number of businesses
12. Slant of eyes: businesses per 1,000 inhabitants in production age
13. Eyes' slant: number of entrepreneurs.
14. Eyes' length: NGOs per 1,000 inhabitants
15. Level of pupils in eyes: communication accessibility

As we look at such counties as Sopot, Łódź and Kraków and compare them with Leżajsk county, one can see that in urban counties, the number of divorces is higher (the face is more rounded). The size of the eyes indicates that Sopot and Krakow have the highest number of registered businesses and NGO's. A comparison of Legionowo (in the northwestern Warsaw suburbs) and Debica (in rural southeastern Poland) demonstrates how quickly and dramatically viewers can perceive differences in variables such as average salary (length of nose), value of completed projects (mouth curvature) and foreign (height of ears). Similarly, comparing two counties from the same Polish region (Upper Silesia) quickly shows the vast differences between an industrial (Katowice) and a rural county (Rybnik) in terms of various business statistics (eye-related features) and unemployment (mouth-related features).

First, we created three sets of faces by using a large number of variables – a list of variables from 2014 was mentioned above; in 2012 it was the same (except one additional variable: the number of square meters of an average flat. The differences between the three faces are easy to notice: "Perfect county" face has big, round eyes; a long nose; a smile; horizontal eyebrows, etc. There are only a few problems in recognizing the differences – the perfect county has a smaller size and a different shape for the lower part of the face; one can believe that the bigger face is better, so it should have been changed. The next issue is the shape of the mouth; it is one of the most popular and visible features of the face, so there is a risk that the weight of mouth shape would be too high. But generally it is easy to recognize similarity; almost everybody says, that "Powiat poznański" is closer to being perfect than to being the worst; there are some issues with the smile and nose length, but similarities are easy to recognize.

In the last case, where we applied only five variables -- the dynamic of changes in migration balance (level of ears), the dynamic of divorces ratio (mid-face shape), the dynamic of communication accessi-

Figure 6. "Faces" of selected Polish counties.

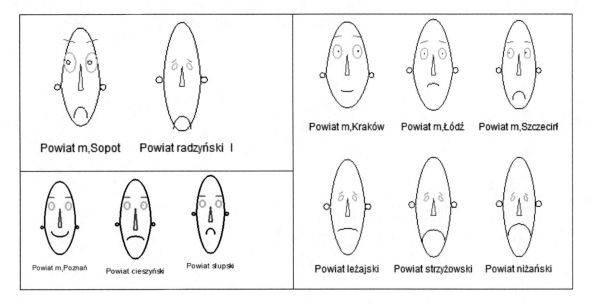

bility (lower part of face), average salary (upper part of face) -- the differences are harder to discern. All the faces are happy and have similar noses, eyes and mouth. The only differences apply to face shape, but it is not the perfect solution. That is why Chernoff Faces can be used both to finding similarities and showing multiple variables on one picture, but also to manipulate, showing the lack of differences or emphasizing less important things.

CONCLUSION

We have used the Chernoff Face knowledge visualization technique to analyze a complex set of 15 socio-economic variables shedding light on the lives and living conditions of citizens of various Polish counties (*powiats*). Our primary purpose is to demonstrate the utility of Chernoff Faces for researchers seeking to analyze these types of political/economic data. Secondarily, we wish to show how these results can be a tool for policy makers and their advisers in making decisions based upon this research.

Before providing the data analysis, we discuss why, in an increasingly data-rich (or data-cluttered) 21st-century context, knowledge visualization is becoming an increasingly attractive and significant research tool, particularly across cultures. We seek to distinguish knowledge information from information visualization and discuss the advantages that knowledge visualization offers and the variety of its uses in strategic management. We then consider the traditional tools used in knowledge visualization and suggest the unique features of Chernoff Faces that differentiate this technique from older knowledge visualization techniques.

We believe that the comparisons show that Chernoff Faces are a useful tool for comparing data between counties, and, using a finer measurement scale, for areas within counties. Among the subjects that we feel merit further research are:

Table 2.

Absolute values	Description	
2014, 14 variables	From left: Powiat poznański, perfect county, worst county	
2012, 16 variables	From left: Powiat poznański, perfect county, worst county	
2010, 13 variables	From left: Powiat poznański, perfect county, worst county	
Dynamics 2004 - 2014, 5 variables	From left: Powiat poznański, perfect county, worst county	

Source: Original creation.

- Whether the emotions conveyed by the face (happy, indifferent, sad) create a bias or distortion in the viewer's perception;
- How switching the assignment of specific data to certain features changes the perception of the face; and
- Whether recipients can glean useful information for analysis or policy making from the Chernoff Face depictions.

Finally, we believe that Chernoff faces will become an increasingly frequently used tool for 21st century socio-economic research.

REFERENCES

Anderson, E. (1957). A Semi-Graphical Method for the Analysis of Complex Problems. *Proceedings of the National Academy of Sciences*, *13*(3), 923-927.

Barrett, J. L. (1994). Process Visualization: Getting the Vision Right Is the Key. *Information Systems Management*, *11*(2), 14–23. doi:10.1080/10580539408964631

Burkhard, R. A. (2005). Strategy Visualization: A New Research Focus in Knowledge Visualization and a Case Study. *Proceedings of I-KNOW*.

Cañas, A. J., Carff, R., Hill, G., Carvalho, M., Arguedas, M., . . . Carvajal, R. (2005). Concept Maps: Integrating Knowledge and Information Visualization. In Lecture Notes in Computer Science: Vol. 3426. Knowledge and Information Visualization. Springer.

Chambers, J.M., Cleveland W.S., & Kleiner, B. (1983). *Graphical Methods for Data Analysis*. Wadsworth International Group.

Chernoff, H. (1973). The Use of Faces to Represent Points in k-Dimensional Space Graphically. *Journal of the American Statistical Association*, *68*(342), 361–368. doi:10.1080/01621459.1973.10482434

Dorling, D. (1991). *The Visualization of Spatial Structure* (PhD dissertation). Department of Geography, University of Newcastle upon Tyne, UK.

Elmer, M. (2013). *The Trouble with Chernoff*. Retrieved October 29, 2017, from http://maphugger.com/post/44499755749/the-trouble-with-chernoff

Eppler, M. J. (2004). *Knowledge Communication Problems between Experts and Managers - an Analysis of Knowledge Transfer in Decision Processes*. University of Lugano. Retrieved October 29, 2017, from http://doc.rero.ch/record/5197

Fabrikant, S. I. (2000). *Cartographic Variations on the Presidential Election 2000 theme*. Retrieved October 29, 2017, from https://web.archive.org/web/20100818112308/

Keller, T., & Tergan, S. (2005). *Knowledge and Information Visualization Searching for Synergies*. Berlin: Springer.

Kim, J. H., Iyer, V., Joshi, S. B., Volkin, D. B., & Middaugh, C. R. (2012). Improved Data Visualization Techniques for Analyzing Macromolecule Structural Changes. *Protein Science*, *21*(10), 1540–1553. doi:10.1002/pro.2144 PMID:22898970

Kosara, R. (2007). *A Critique of Chernoff Faces*. Retrieved October 29, 2017, from https://eagereyes.org/criticism/chernoff-faces

La Rooy, G. (2000). Charting Performance. *NZ Business*, 14.

Marchese, F. T., & Banissi, E. (2013). *Knowledge visualization currents: from text to art to culture*. London: Springer. doi:10.1007/978-1-4471-4303-1

Meyer, R. (2009). *Knowledge Visualization*. Retrieved October 29, 2017, from http://citeseerx.ist.psu.edu/viewdoc/download?doi=10.1.1.164.3759&rep=rep1&type=pdf

Morgan, G. (1998). *Images of Organization*. Thousand Oaks, CA: Sage Publications.

Nelson, E., Dow, D., Lukinbeal, C., & Farley, R. (1997). Visual Search Processes and the Multivariate Point Symbol. *Cartographica*, *34*(4), 19–33. doi:10.3138/15T3-3222-X25H-35JU

Nuñez, J. J. R., Rohonczi, A., Juliarena de Moretti, C. E., Garra, A. M., Rey, C. A., . . . Campos, M. A. (2011). Updating Research on Chernoff Faces for School Cartography. In A. Ruas (Eds.), Advances in Cartography and GI Science (vol. 2). Springer.

Pareidolia. In (2017). In *Merriam-Webster's dictionary* (11th ed.). Springfield, MA: Merriam-Webster.

Reyes, J. J. (2009). Ideas for the Use of Chernoff Faces in School Cartography. The World's Geospatial Solutions. *CD Proceedings of ICA 24th ICC*.

Rock, D. (2009). *Your Brain at Work: Strategies for Overcoming Distraction, Regaining Focus, and Working Smarter All Day Long*. New York, NY: HarperBusiness.

Sontag, S. (1998). *AIDS and Its Metaphors. New York: Farrar, Straus and Giroux* .

Ursyn, A. (Ed.). (2014). *Perceptions of knowledge visualization: explaining concepts through meaningful images*. Hershey, PA: Information Science Reference. doi:10.4018/978-1-4666-4703-9

Ursyn, A. (Ed.). (2015). Handbook of research on maximizing cognitive learning through knowledge visualization. Hershey, PA. Information Science Reference/an imprint of IGI Global. doi:10.4018/978-1-4666-8142-2

Vakratsas, D., & Ambler, T. (1999). How Advertising Really Works: What Do We Really Know? *Journal of Marketing*, *63*(1), 26–43. doi:10.2307/1251999

Ware, C. (2000). *Information Visualization: Perception for Design*. London: Springer.

Weick, K. E. (2009). *Sensemaking in Organizations*. Sage.

Zhang, H., Hou, Y., Zhao, J., Wang, L., Xi, T., & Li, Y. (2016). Automatic Welding Quality Classification for the Spot Welding Based on the Hopfield Associative Memory Neural Network and Chernoff Face Description of the Electrode Displacement Signal Features. *Mechanical Systems and Signal Processing*, *85*. doi:10.1016/j.ymssp.2016.06.036

KEY TERMS AND DEFINITIONS

AIDA Model: Attention, interest, desire, and action. This model works under the assumption that drawing the attention of the recipient of information is a prerequisite for successful communication.

Business Visions: A for-profit organization's values, philosophy, and/or beliefs.

Chernoff Faces: A method of visualization of knowledge developed by Herman Chernoff using a graphical representation of statistical data to represent specific multivariate data using only one symbol—a human face—to represent e data in question.

Emoticons: A visual representation of a facial expression using only typed symbols, such as colons and parentheses.

Herman Chernoff: Professor Emeritus of Applied Mathematics from Harvard University's Department of Statistics, creator of Chernoff Faces.

Information Technology: Telecommunication technology used for storing, retrieving, and sending information data.

Information Visualization: Using visual mediums and methods to convey information and/or data to an audience.

Knowledge Base: An individual's lifelong collection of knowledge and wisdom.

Pareidolia: The phenomenon of seeing faces in inanimate objects.

Process Visualization: A visualization given to members of a team so that they may better understand the methods that are expected to be utilized to achieve a collective goal.

Socio-Economic: Pertaining to an individual or group's combination of social and economic factors which determine their social standing.

Unintuitive Correspondence: A situation in which the intuitive or presumed correspondence of a visual representation of knowledge and its underlying data and truth is skewed by poor design.

ENDNOTES

In the case of small differences between objects (in areas of one variable), it is not appropriate to use standardization, because differences would be strengthened (and thus would appear bigger than they are).

2   *Miejscowy Plan Zagospodarowania* (Local Development Plan): a strategy for local spatial development which defines what can be constructed and where in the area covered by the plan. These plans in Poland can be very controversial, as they often cause chaotic development and/or stall development and investment.

Chapter 12
Lighting Simulation Algorithms in Real–World Sacral Building Visualisation

Grzegorz Osinski
College of Social and Media Culture, Poland

Błażej Świętek
College of Social and Media Culture, Poland

Zbigniew Chaniecki
Lodz University of Technology, Poland

ABSTRACT

The most commonly used rules of modeling are limited to determine the level and direction beam of the light. However, such an approach does not reflect the real impact of lighting on the object. More accurate selection of lighting parameters is important, especially in the case of design objects, when it is still possible to change the structure or any selection of location and type of lighting. The chapter presents the use of specialized numerical methods in the design of modern sacred buildings as well as visualization methods used in communication between professionals creating and managing such models.

INTRODUCTION

The works on the information visualization usually focus on the measures and methods of graphical presentation of large sets of data (BIGDATA). However, it is not the only current within a wide spectrum of issues that is currently embraced by the visualization paradigm. The visualization methods are well-known and widely applied in engineering disciplines that deal with designing technological equipment as well as industrial processes. Since it is a domain strictly associated with technical sciences, it is usually being ignored in discussions on issues concerning humanities. This is a reasonable approach, for the literature on the subject covering issues on technological visualizations is quite extensive and constitutes a completely remote current within the visualization domain.

DOI: 10.4018/978-1-5225-4990-1.ch012

However, it is quite uncommon to encounter works on the visualizations employed in the reconstructions and developments of new buildings that constitute a cultural heritage of nations, religions or objects relevant for the entire modern civilization. An attempt to support designing sacral buildings featuring large cubic capacity and numerous architectural elements, aiming to ensure appropriate lighting of the interiors of the facility, constitutes an innovative use of the visualization methods. The visualizations works are then being carried out as early as at the stage of building design, in order to ensure a particular atmosphere of the visual effects that is specific for the facilities of this type. In this case, the scope of modelling and computer simulation works that in effect will create the final interior visualizations require the application of particular methods involving issues of visual perception, aesthetic sensations and inclusion of historical and ethnological aspects. These issues go beyond the domain of technical sciences that need to be complemented with a creative in-depth analysis supported by a methodology and by the results of the works of humanistic sciences. In this chapter, we shall discuss the use of specific tools in the process of designing the interiors of The Shrine of Our Lady Star of the New Evangelization and Saint John Paul II[1] that has been built from the ground up over the period of 2012–2016, in Torun. The visualizations works commenced as early as at the stage when the dome has been put over the building, but the interior works have not yet begun (Figure 1). Thus, the carried out visualizations could have been employed as early as at the stage of the constructional changes inside the Shrine (Figure 2).

The detailed works included an assessment of the methodology and the algorithms employed in the visualization process and also the comprehensive visualization design based on designs created by visual artists, such as paintings, frescoes, mosaics, stained glass windows, sculptures and ornaments. The choice of an artificial lighting and its blending with natural lighting aimed to adjust the location of the stainedglass windows in order to obtain the anticipated effect of *shading*.

Figure 1. The Shrine: Outside view (© 2017, WSKSiM, Used with permission)

Figure 2. The shrine: Inside view (© 2017, WSKSiM, Used with permission)

With the aim of achieving the correct results, a surface texturing has been adopted along with considering and adjusting its function in the context of the artists' requirements driven by the sacral nature of the individual objects, such as aisles, sections and respective rooms. A proprietary software designed for application of computing server and various software for design and rendering of individual scenes served as tools.

The designated aim of the final effect has been achieved in the process of visualization of obtaining the end results of the rendering process in 4k and converting thus created graphics into target resolution enabling an accurate view of the effects on a standard computer or smartphone. In addition to the traditional design technique, there has also been a *Virtual Reality* (VR) visualization performed. The 3D visualization allowed for the validation of employing the right algorithms, in terms of the aesthetic visual sensations expressed by the artists and architects, hence they were able to test particular architectural ideas within the virtual environment.

The monumental nature of the building resulted in the necessity that the authors employ specialized visualization methods. The merging, but also intersecting, architectural forms, the symbolism of the message of the form and shading became a quite difficult challenge. The form of the temple represents two eras. Its exterior neoclassicistic structure symbolizes the tradition of the architecture and detail of the churches, practiced during the past architectonic periods. The cubic interior part constitutes a modern symbol of our time. The combination of these two forms creates a sensation of power and eternalness of Christian fate. The top level of the church covers approximately 50 percent of the total surface area, whereas the space in the centre of the church accounts for 30 percent of the total. Additionally, this level houses traffic routes: footpaths, staircases and passenger lifts. Also on this level, there are support rooms, such as vestries, liturgical and broadcast rooms, washing facilities and technical support rooms for radio and TV recordings (Figure 3).

Figure 3. The visualization of the cross-section of the temple picturing themodelled interiors. (© 2017, B.Świętek, Used with permission)

VISUALISATION ALGORITHMS

The process of creating a visualization of the architectural structures constitutes a multi-stage and complex process. Apart from the structural complexity of the building, the reason for this is mainly the number of the operations required and the necessity to seek acceptance for each step of the computation process from the investor and the architect. To ensure the proper implementation of the design, a proprietary algorithm has been designed in compliance with a character of the works carried out in a particular order related to the execution of the construction of the whole structure. The entire procedure is divided into six main stages:

Stage 1: The Organization of Architectural Instructions, Sketches and Photographs

A close cooperation between an IT specialist and an architect, based on so-called architectural instructions, that is, particular task orders according to the architect's intentions, has been crucial in the works. These instructions can be handed over in varied forms. The first phase, after receiving the set of the instructions, is organizing them in a sequence they will be entered in a digital form into the design. This process is called the organization of the instructions. A manual instruction usually takes the form of a sketch with the designer's descriptions. It provides a graphic representation of the architect's concept along with measurements and all the mathematical calculations associated with the project's measurements.

A digital engineering drawing saved in DWG file format is created in an advanced engineering software. It is employed in construction, engineering, subjects of materials resistance, and constructional modelling. Such images have vectorial records. The unrestricted vector scalability enables creating drawings with an accuracy expressed in the smallest units of the given measurement. There are symbols and blocks, as well as detailed measurements along with their referents, located in the drawing (Figure 5). The direct transfer of the design into the *Computerised Numerical Control*, CNC machines and 3D

Figure 4. Classic type of a manual architectural instruction, created during the design works. (© 2017, B.Świętek, Used with permission)

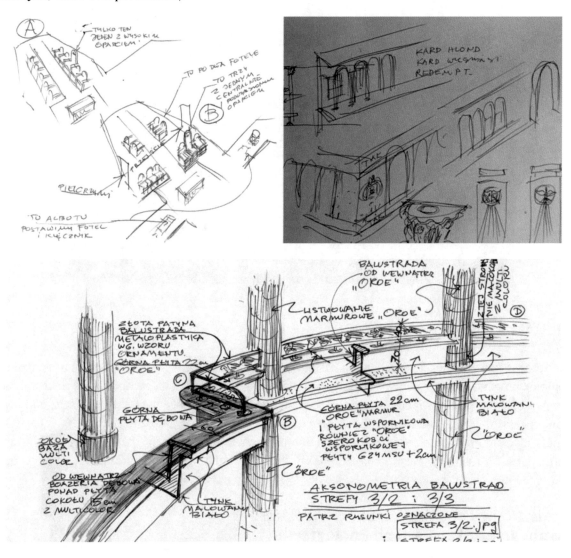

printers allows e.g. to print full-size building components from a special concrete. Additionally, it facilitates cutting ornaments in granite or marble by means of *WaterJet* machines with a collimated jet of water under very high pressure (Murdock, 2013). These technologies were employed in the production process of the ornaments in the featured temple.

Stage 2: Visualization Software Environment Interface Personalisation and Selection of the Modifiers

V-Ray, a visualization system, has been employed in the visualization works for the standardization of the add-ons and the preparation of the measurements within the proprietary algorithm. All the measurements were performed on the real-world object and they required the implementation of the appropriate

Figure 5. Typical architectural instruction in a digital format with manual amendments added to the initial visualisation. .(© 2017, B.Świętek, Used with permission).

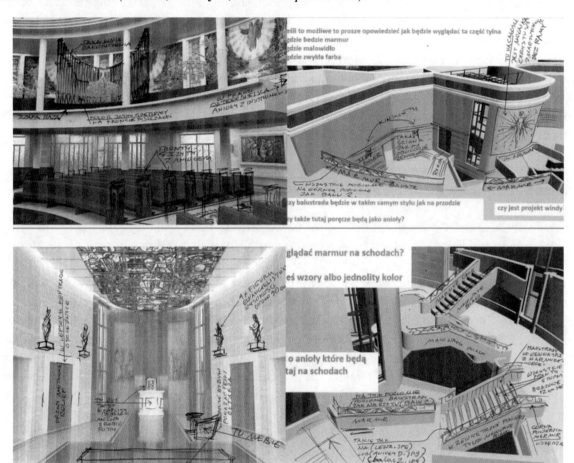

measurement tools. The initial *coarse modelling* of the building, combined with *grid errors* detection, has been performed at the beginning, followed by the appropriate amendments in compliance with the architectural instructions.

The works have been carried out in a visualization software equipped with a toolkit supporting import and conversion of the external files. However, when we do not create the files, but only receive them within other external software, their standardization for custom requirements is needed. The ability to use various commercial software, such as AutoCAD, SketchUp, Illustrator or Photoshop[2], is thus very important. Therefore, initially, within the main visualization application, it is necessary to standardize the measurement units that the imported files, as well as the constructed designs, will be relating to. An important tool, employed within this process, is a *Box Modeling* procedure that involves creating base objects, representing basic shape of the object, e.g. *box*, within a *ViewPort* window, and then, developing geometry and shaping through the operations available from the menus of numerous elements. Whereas, *sculpting*, another modelling method, is based on adjusting the polygon components of the created sphere, by shifting, scarifying, densification, deletion, addition and merging. All these operations are performed by means of a virtual brush that consists of various tips. The tips are bitmaps with a specific pattern that characterise the particular brush shapes. Since this is a tedious and laborious procedure, it can be shared among various computer graphic designers working on different elements of the designed details.

Due to the extent of the graphical material, the modelling procedures have been demonstrated on the example of designing the pipe organs situated in the temple. The organs form a permanent and important architectural element of the sacral buildings. Their shape and proper location within the object depend not only on aesthetics but also on the individual acoustic properties of the building (Štěpánek, 2015). The sophisticated shape of the pipe organs required an application of specific symmetry and proportions to its form, therefore their visualization involved employing numerous modifiers. Figure 6 illustrates the process of generating the final visualization.

Stage 3: The Processes of Specifying the Lighting, Selection of Data Resources and Camera Settings

Even the best completed graphical design, set in sceneries of other buildings, traffic infrastructure, vehicles and pedestrians, could not be perceived realistically without taking account of the specific play of lights. The light, both natural and artificial, either set up intentionally or entirely incidentally or even whilst illuminating another object, gives life to the least attractive building. Thus, completely dull wall, sculpture or painting can influence the perception of the observer. It is equally easy to spoil the best performed architectural visualisation by means of poorly chosen lighting. Traders see the lighting advantages, they use the appropriate colour of light in illuminating fruits and vegetables making them look fresh and full of life. The purpose of every graphic designer is not a desire to manipulate the viewer, but to present their work in "the right light". The proper aim of the work of a computer graphic designer is, thus, to show the purpose of "illumination in the right light" in order to get the best final effect. The variety of the objects in the light and shadow blends shapes with the background at certain places or sets off against it, in others (Strzeminski, 2016).

From the artistic point of view, the most important notion associated with lighting is *chiaroscuro* (from Italian *chiaro* — "light" and *scuro* — "dark"). It has been introduced by Leonardo da Vinci who applied this technique in 1483 in his painting 'The Virgin of The Rock'. This notion became one of the most important techniques imparting three dimensional effects to the flat paintings, whereas in the case of the three-dimensional objects, the right play of light and shadow emphasizes sensations and the depth, thus, in Polish language a concept of 'światłocień' (light and shadow) has been adopted, although it is quite inaccurate (Cremante, 2014). The choice of lighting strongly influences the viewer's perception of the image. By means of appropriate operation of the lighting, many different tasks concerning the final visualisation effect can be accomplished: to arrange the scene, to indicate primary and secondary objects, to control perspective, to create depth sensation or enhance three-dimensionality (Constant, 2015).

Regarding the materials used in the objects, it is possible to differentiate the texture of the materials (plaster, wood grain, convexities and concavities), operate with the structure of the shadows, create and observe the caustic surface (Ball, 2013). The individual character of a setting can be achieved with a colour modulation, proper planning of an illumination of the entire design, choice of appropriate kind of source of light including its colour, temperature, light beam current, and an angle of the light and shadows (Figure 7). In the process of modelling the scattering of light, the detailed composition of atmospheric air should be taken into account. It is worth to mention that after a storm, when the ozone concentration in the air is higher, the yellow glow appears and blue shades recede. Around the setting,

Figure 6. The procedure of creating the pipe organs by means of the modifiers. (© 2017, B. Świętek, Used with permission)

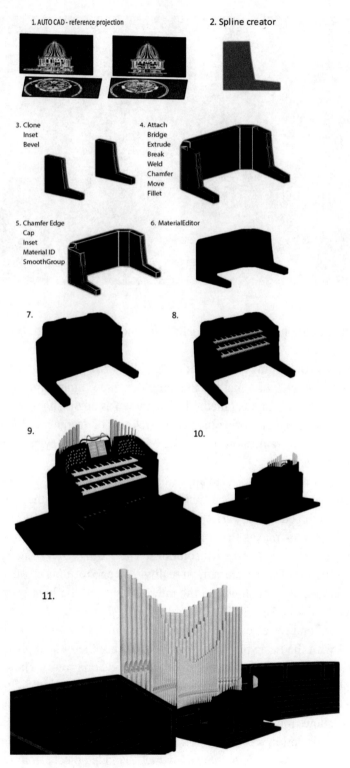

Figure 7. Visualization of types of light sources employed in computing algorithms, in the main view inside the temple. .(© 2017, B.Świętek, Used with permission)

also the changes in illumination should be modelled depending on other atmospheric conditions such as cloudiness and downfall.

In general, two methods of lighting design are applied: *classical*, created on the basis of the actual site measurements, and a *computer-based* method that employs three-dimensional design techniques. The most important advantage of the classical method, also known as an on-site method, is the possibility to view the design simulation on a real-world object. The architect or designer can perform experiments in chosen atmospheric conditions (rain, snow, fog), time of year and day; they also can run tests of various settings of real light sources.

The photorealistic light rendering takes to apply a proper light beam structure and also to determine preferences calculated according to physical phenomena. In the case of the employed V-Ray render engine, the operator is equipped with a variety of types of light (Sannino, 2012). The increasing speed of V-Ray rendering algorithms makes the use of these methods by professionals indisputable. Also, the preferences of the employers suggest such solutions. The settings of V-Ray lights, by means of the parameters, allow creating the effects occurring in reality. The end result is an outcome of such intuitive scene design that the emission of photons and the interaction of all the light sources give a physically correct realistic image (Kuhlo & Eggert, 2010; Kuhlo, 2013) (Figure 8).

The emitted, scattered and reflected light inside the visualized facility is determined by numerous parameters associated with the basic physical theory describing the optical phenomena. In particular, for proper practical implementation, they can be divided into several groups. The general parameters are common for all the light sources, but often have different names within individual visualization tools. These are: *target* as a value of a proper orientation of a camera aiming at the particular point of a setting, *shadow* — activates shadows rendering, *use global settings* — corresponds to the uniform settings of a light shading parameter this option was chosen for. There is also an entire group of parameters available, relating to the visualized objects: *exclude / include* which exclude objects from receiving light or casting shadows, *intensity/colour/attenuation* determine the intensity and colour, and, in the case of V-Ray,

Figure 8. Visualisation of the employed sources of lighting for the main view of the upper level of the temple. (© 2017, B.Świętek, Used with permission)

enable selection of the temperature and the units of energy and illumination. A similar role is fulfilled by an advanced parameter, *attenuation* inducing light extinguishing, that is, determining the manner of light fading with increasing distance from the source. The best example that explains the use of this parameter in practice is a candle set in the middle of a room observed from different distances. When determining the distance parameter, we can then simulate various levels of light intensity in different radial distances from the object. For this purpose, additional parameters are available: *Inverse* determining intensity that is inversely proportional to distance *Inverse Square* setting the fading inversely proportional to the square of the distance. The proper application of these parameters not only allows for achieving realistic end results but also enables the ergonomics of the planned numerical simulations. Not all the areas within the visualised graphics are equally important. The appropriate manipulation of these parameters enables reducing the calculation time and obtaining equally realistic end effect. The additional parameters facilitate subtle changes in the lighting systems: *spotlight / directional* feature — softens shadow edges, *shape* sets a shape of the exterior spotlight light affects shadow colour blends the colour of the shadow with the colour of the light.

The implementation of the light algorithms in the view of the paradigm of computer design can be divided into two basic types: *Local Illumination* (*direct illumination*) employs realization models of the building illumination originating directly from the following sources: natural — sun, artificial — electricity-powered bulb, spotlight etc. While the second model, *Global Illumination* (*indirect illumination*) realizes the calculations of the light intensity through the indirect effects resulting from direct light reflections from the objects located on the scene. Figs 9 and 10 illustrate the results of the implementation of these models in the realization of the temple visualization. Particular attention should be paid to the difference in brightness of the light reflection from heterogeneous surfaces when employing dispersion algorithms.

The appropriate parameters setting of the camera realizing the end result of the simulation is a crucial element of the visualization process. In this chapter, we shall discuss only one of the many parameters that is essential in the processes of lighting simulation of spacious objects with numerous interior archi-

Figure 9. Direct illumination visualization Local Illumination within the design scene of the temple interior. .(© 2017, B.Świętek, Used with permission)

Figure 10. Visualisation of direct illumination model Local Illumination within the design scene of the temple interior. (© 2017, B.Świętek, Used with permission)

tectural elements. It is the f-number parameter that sets the diameter of the hole in the lens of the camera. The mechanism of this function is modelled on the iris and pupil of a human eye. It sets the amount of light present in the visualized scene as well as the trajectory of the light rays in the design software required for capturing by camera matrices. Depending on the size of the opening, the focus depth is determined, and also the light exposure changes. Thus, by means of the aperture, it is possible to manage the primary and secondary scenes and adjust frames. The core values of the f-number parameter are determined for two basic values: f / 1.4 — extended aperture, smaller depth of focus, lighter exposure, sharp foreground and blurred background. It is employed in portrait photography. The second value is f / 22 — narrower aperture, greater depth of focus, darker exposure and the entire frame is sharp. It is appropriate for landscape photography and shooting large architectural objects. Figs 11 and 12 illustrate the net results of the above parameters' implementation in the realization of the temple visualization.

In addition to the parameters defining the aperture, a parameter determining *ISO,* that represents the CCD matrix sensitivity to light in the camera, play an important role in the process. Since the visualization process occurs within the natural environment, then this parameter, in fact, simulates an actual situation familiar to photographers from the classic methods of photography. The value of *ISO* is determined, ranging from 50 to 25600. Of great importance is the fact that the lower the value of *ISO*, the lower sensor *sensitivity*. Thus, the end results of the visualization process can also be obtained for different values of the matrix speed parameter (Figures 13-15).

Stage 4: Final Rendering

Rendering is a process of analyzing three-dimensional scenes and depicting it as a two-dimensional static graphics or animation. The main factors under consideration are the processes occurring within the setting, such as simulation and light propagation, and the interpretation of the calculated shapes and textures of the facilities (Ursyn & Mostowfi, 2015). Thereby, in terms of the end product, the rendering and camera setting are concurrent processes. In real cameras, the image is generated based on the record of light rays falling on the photosensitive material. Whereas during rendering, it is generated by means of sampling and light rays analysis at the points of its incidence, reflection and refringence.

The rendering process is usually carried out in Renderer, an external and usually plug-in type software. By means of a light ray tracing algorithm, the Renderer converts the setting, described with vectors *XYZ* in three-dimensional space, into a two-dimensional image. Renderer V-Ray[3] has been employed in the

Figure 11. The result of employing f/22 aperture on the focus depth in the final effect of visualization. .(© 2017, B.Świętek, Used with permission)

Figure 12. The result of employing f/1.4 aperture on the focus depth in the final effect of visualisation. (© 2017, B.Świętek, Used with permission).

Figure 13. Visualisation of the closing scene for the value of ISO 200 (© 2017, B.Świętek, Used with permission)

visualization works. It features hybrid approach to the structure of such algorithms as *Global Illumination* (Berner, 2015). It enables effective application of CPU processor for calculating final effect by means of adaptive techniques, *bucket rendering* and *path trace.*

Apart from tracking methods, the techniques differ in computing algorithms. *Bucket Rendering* module allows further optimization of RAM memory and the processor, for the calculations are carried out in relatively smaller sections. The 3D scene is projected parallel to the camera lens. It creates an array of

Figure 14. Visualisation of the closing scene for the value of ISO 700. (© 2017, B.Świętek, Used with permission)

Figure15. Visualisation of the closing scene for the value of ISO 3200. (© 2017, B.Świętek, Used with permission)

pixels of a density equal to the resolution of the final image. Depending on the purpose of the algorithm, triangulation and models prioritization are performed. The *Bucket Rendering* algorithm consists of the fixed area expressed in pixels, e.g. (16x16, 32x32) where ray tracing is performed. The targets of this technique stem from *Raytracing*, a tracking method. The collection of samples commences on the *sub-pixel* level, determined in a few processes (Legrenzi, 2010). Firstly, the minimum values are applied in order to determine the base, whereas the decision about a necessity of further algorithmization is reached

Figure 16. The bucket rendering technique realization in the visualized scene of the temple interior. (© 2017, B.Świętek, Used with permission)

with respect to the value of noise threshold set by the user. The processes run in the individual selections are hidden and the end result is visible as a pixel colour. A number of rendering sections often depends on a number of cores in the processor.

The progressive targets are quick in completing the rendered scene. The calculations are performed simultaneously in the entire setting, thereby significantly increasing the computing resources usage. Information about light characteristic is gathered, and the resulting image is presented in a very low resolution in the first processing. It is a standard procedure in the test renderings which do not always require high-quality imaging. Scene specialization is performed at the same time as the consecutive procedures. The emerging of the details is associated with sending and reading the increasing amount of objects. The time limitation, as well as a parameter of sent light rays, can be adjusted individually to the computed scene.

The limitation of the above method can be observed when the application of one light ray disables the creation of the intermediate, so-called "blurred", values, that is, the reading of a light beam scattered on the reflecting and refracting surfaces, caustics, diffraction, depth of focus and motion blur. Further examination of the individual rendered images allows noticing the unsatisfactory result of edge *anti-aliasing*. The only solution in such situation is the computation of the higher amount of points within the visual field. However, it increases the amount of time needed for rendering the objects and of the computing power. The above defects have been modified within a new method based on an analysis and sampling of a higher amount of *primary* and *secondary* rays. This method is called *path tracing*. It is an advanced method of rendering calculations based on a Monte Carlo probabilistic method. It builds on multiplying the analyzed paths of light. The development of the method resulted in numerous conclusions, of which the most fundamental turned out to be the optimization of computing power, expressed in a necessity to schedule the amount of distributed light rays, depending on the requirements. Codes of many algorithms contain the implementation of the standard version of the Monte Carlo method which pseudo randomly designates numbers, thus, each following iteration of the same frame slightly differs

Figure 17. Final visualisation of the final scene by means of the progressive rendering. (© 2017, B.Świętek, Used with permission)

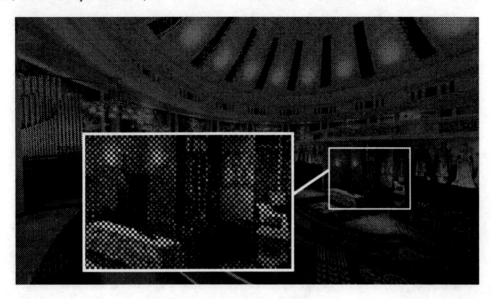

from the previous one. In graphics, such phenomenon is defined as a lack of repeatable solutions. It is, therefore, possible to say that the employment of the advanced rendering methods by probabilistic algorithms allows obtaining unique visualization results that would not reoccur in the same process. Since the works on improving the rendering algorithms continue, the further analysis of this issue goes far beyond the framework of this study.

VIRTUAL REALITY

On the basis of the obtained visualization of the temple interior, a system of a direct insight into the three-dimensional structure of the visualized facility by means of VR technology has been developed. A proper transformation of the created models of the temple was implemented in a VR environment allowing for direct insight into the three-dimensional interior of the object. This is a very useful tool that allows both the architects and interested viewers to see the interior of a building that is still under construction before the completion of the building finish.

Figures 18–20 illustrate the results of the works using VR technique. Thus, it should be noted that the translation of the visual modelling results allows for the creation of the visual experience of being inside the temple.

EXAMPLES OF ARCHITECTURAL CHANGES BASED ON VISUALIZATION

As a result of the virtual modelling and visualization by means of 3D technology, several significant changes in the architectural project of the constructed temple has been made. Originally open from the top stained glass plafond above the main altar, has been illuminated by covering it with an unplanned

Figure 18. Visualization presentation in a VirtualReality technology. .(© 2017, B.Świętek, Used with permission)

Figure 19. Rendering performed during the works in the three-dimensional project of the temple interior. (© 2017, B.Świętek, Used with permission)

special reflector. Moreover, additional single stained glass panels were added on its entire circumference. Its prototype present in the *Capella Pontificia* chapel is narrower and consists of 3 panels, whereas the presbytery in the Shrine is wider. In order for the plafond to fill the entire space above the presbytery, it has been enlarged to 5 panels. The original draft proposed white flares in these planes, but this idea resulted in some kind of perceptional discomfort (Figure 21). Therefore, the new planes were styled matching the message from the prototype.

Figure 20. Rendering performed during the works in the three-dimensional project of the temple interior. (© 2017, B.Świętek, Used with permission)

Changes were also made within the structure of the central stairs which originally were to be illuminated by wall lamps. During a "virtual tour" of such illuminated stairs, the designers noticed a necessity to introduce some lighting corrections. The illumination of the frescoes was also changed, in terms of both the homogeneity of lighting and the angle of the light incidence. Lighting system correction was also performed, considering the spectral layout of sources of LED light in order to achieve a global effect. Figure 22 illustrates the changes in the impact of the overall lighting on the colour and texture of the wood panelling and main floor.

FUTURE VISION

Due to the computer modelling, not only the models of the temple were created, but also of its surroundings including characteristic features of the landscape and the natural objects in the vicinity. Such virtual model allows not only for constructing and altering the appearance of the building, but it also enables creating entirely new designs of the surroundings and building new additional objects. Thus, employing the same visualisation technologies, completely new objects, not taken previously into account, can be created.

The most important facility scheduled for prospective construction is a roofed amphitheatre located close to the temple. Since the construction works are currently being performed, the visualisations of the amphitheatre and its view, both in a full light and at night, can be viewed only on the final images of a graphical visualisation. Virtual concepts of the amphitheatre illustrated by Figures 23–25, will be implemented on the basis of such representations. The above results prove that the use of visualisation techniques in sacral objects designs is a very good method supporting the classic architectural design process and construction.

Figure 21. Central plafond replacement carried out during construction works on the basis of the lighting visualisation results. (A — a prototype of the plafond from Capella Pontificia chapel, B — architectural instruction including the reflecting side panels, C — plafond with the side panels visualisation, D — visualisation of a final, modified version of the plafond. .(© 2017, B.Świętek, Used with permission)

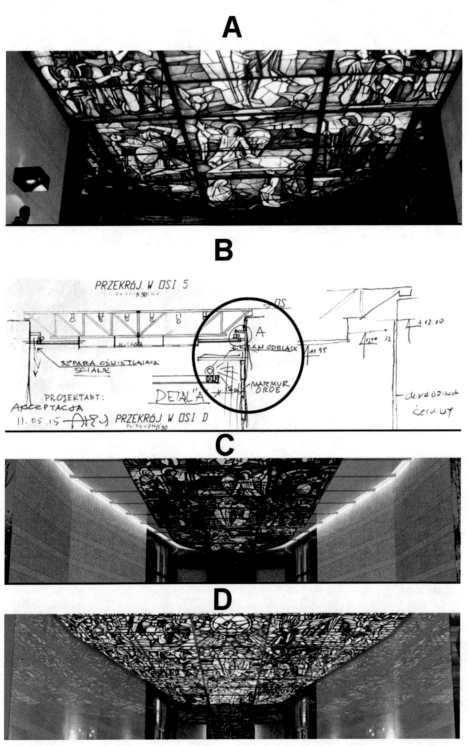

Figure 22. Visualisation of the wood panelling colour and imaging of two types of wood textures (top) and the impact of the illumination on the floor (bottom). (© 2017, B.Świętek, Used with permission)

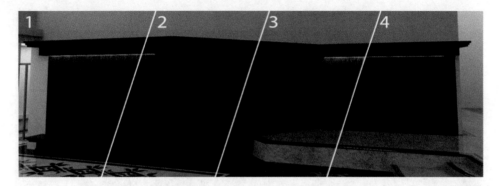

Figure 23. Visualisation concept of an amphitheatre in the vicinity of the site of the temple. Night view in a simulated moonlight and artificial illumination. (© 2017, B.Świętek, Used with permission)

CONCLUSION

Visualization design works for real sacral objects involve a comprehensive approach to building designing and finishing. The selected sacral building allowed for presenting the artistic character of the tools available to a present-day graphics engineer as well as all scientists working on humanistic field interesting in visualization algorithm used in real life. The entire designing phase includes the cooperation between a computer graphic designer employing visualization techniques with an investor and architect. As a result of such approach, the works could have produced results of character analogous to the completed structure. A particular attention should be paid to the lighting process that allows impacting a quality and nature of the building. On the one hand, the visualizations aid in the implementation process and serve the investor and architect in implementing consecutive corrections, but also after completion they

Figure 24. Amphitheatre visualisation based on lighting simulation at sunset. (© 2017, B.Świętek, Used with permission)

Figure 25. Amphitheatre visualisation, view from the water reservoir, allowing for light reflections from the water surface. (© 2017, B.Świętek, Used with permission)

constitute significant advertising materials. A visualization can also act as a historical document. In addition, a presentation in a *VirtualReality* technology can constitute the only means of a close encounter with the Shrine for people who, due to an illness or large distance — e.g. from other continents, are not able to travel to the temple.

REFERENCES

Berner, A. (2015). AiryLight: Ambient Enviromental Data. In A. Ursyn (Ed.), *Maximazing Cognitive Learning through Knowledge Visualization*. IGI Global. doi:10.4018/978-1-4666-8142-2.ch017

Constant, J. (2015). Random Processes and Visual Perception. In A. Ursyn (Ed.), *Maximazing Cognitive Learning through Knowledge Visualization*. IGI Global. doi:10.4018/978-1-4666-8142-2.ch006

Cremante, S. (2014). *Leonardo da Vinci. The Complete Works*. A David and Charles Book.

Kuhlo, M. (2013). *Architectural Rendering with 3ds Max and V-Ray*. Taylor & Francis.

Kuhlo, M., & Eggert, E. (2010). *Architectural Rendering with 3ds Max and V-Ray: Photorealistic Visualization*. Focal Press.

Legrenzi, F. (2010). *VRay The Complete Guide* (2nd ed.). Industrie Grafiche Stilgraf.

Long, B. (2014). *Complete Digital Photography* (8th ed.). Boston: Cengage Learning PTR.

Murdock, K. L. (2013). *3ds Max 2012 Bible*. Indiana: Willey.

Sannino, C. (2012). *Photography and Rendering with V-Ray*. GC Edizioni.

Štěpánek, J., Syrový, V., Otčenášek, Z., Taesch, Ch., & Angster, J. (2005). Spectral features influencing perception of pipe organ sounds. *Proceeding of Forum Acusticum*.

Strzemiński, W. (2016). Theory of Vison-the first edition with the critical commentary. Łódź Art Museum.

Ursyn, A., & Mostowfi, M. (2015). Visualization by Coging: Drawing Simple Shapes and Forms in Various Programing Language. In A. Ursyn (Ed.), *Maximazing Cognitive Learning through Knowledge Visualization*. IGI Global. doi:10.4018/978-1-4666-8142-2.ch008

ADDITIONAL READING

Boeykens, S. (2013). *Unity for Architectural Visualization*. Birnigham.

Chen, C. H. (Ed.). (2012). *Emerging Topics in Computer Vision and its Applications*. Word Scientific.

Osinski, G. (Ed.). (2012). *The Chaos in the mind: the brain and life. Inowrocław*. Aspekt Press. (in Polish)

Pasek, J. (2013). *Wizualizacje architektoniczne. 3ds Max 2013 i 3ds Max Design*. Gliwice, Poland: Szkoła efektu (in Polish).

Turlo, J., Karbowski, A., Służewski, K., & Osinski, G. (2008). *Examples of Information Technology in Science Education*. Torun, Poland: UMK. (in Polish)

ENDNOTES

1   http://sanktuarium.radiomaryja.pl/

2   http://www.sketchup.com/; http://www.adobe.com/pl/products/illustrator.html; https://www.adobe.com/pl/products/photoshop.html

3   https://docs.chaosgroup.com/display/VRAY3MAX/V-Ray+for+3ds+Max+Help.

Chapter 13

From Visualization Framework on Teaching Process:
New Methodical Approach to the Teaching of Bookbinding in Graphic Technology

Suzana Pasanec Preprotić
University of Zagreb, Croatia

Gorana Petković
University of Zagreb, Croatia

ABSTRACT

A framework for learning was developed with input from teachers, education experts, and business leaders to define and illustrate the skills and knowledge that students need to succeed in work, life, and citizenship, as well as the support system for learning outcomes. The critical system ensures student development and learning environment, including their personal skills, content knowledge, and important expertise, which they will need at Faculty, on the job, and generally in life. Students achieve better when they are actively engaged in solving meaningful problems. Today, among other academic courses, ICT-based learning provides an active learning process that enhances student-centered learning approaches, collaborative and participative forms of teaching and learning. Dialog, writing, and "high-order thinking" have significant importance, which directly improve communicative learning processes, including social network model of thinking. That process involves focusing on achieving a particular prior learning outcome (previous courses) and resolution comprehension of all aspects of the issue.

INTRODUCTION

Graphic technologies represent one of the largest professions in the world. The profession embraces change, requiring those pursuing graphic technology careers to learn new and diverse skills. The graphic technologies program appeals to a variety of individuals including students with interest in creativity, technology and management. The graphic technologies include traditional printing and electronic,

DOI: 10.4018/978-1-5225-4990-1.ch013

publishing, packaging, digital imaging, computer graphics, website development, digital photography, printable electronics and related areas. The discipline includes media and mass communication involving creation, production, management and distribution of advertising, marketing, web sites, books, magazines, newspapers, catalogues, packages and other media in printed and digital form. Graphic engineering is the part of technology field that requires the application of scientific and engineering knowledge and methods combined with technical skills in support of engineering activities; it lies in the occupational spectrum between crafting and engineering but more close to the engineering. Engineering is the profession in which knowledge of the mathematical and natural sciences gained by study, experience, and practice is applied with judgment to develop ways to utilize economically the materials and forces of nature for the benefit of humankind.

The market for traditional print products offers more variety. Usually, printed products are categorized into commercial printing and periodicals. This classification differentiates printed matter with regard to its frequency of publication. Since the production process also depends largely on these basic conditions, print shops usually specialize in one or the other market segment. Commercial printing refers to print products that are produced occasionally (e.g. catalogues, brochures, leaflets, business cards). Periodicals are printed matter that appears periodically (e.g. newspapers, journals, magazines). Publishing houses and companies are the typical clients for periodicals printing (Kipphan, 2001, p. 4)

Gutenberg's work and his invention, printing with movable lead type, in the middle of the fifteenth century triggered a revolution in book production. A much greater proportion of the population had a chance to acquire education, culture, and information than had ever been possible with hand-written books. Consequently, illiteracy decreased in the following centuries. Books continued to be colored by hand even after Gutenberg's invention and a lot more colorful volumes has been produced in high quality comparable to earlier ones. For over 500 years, letterpress was the dominant printing technology for books. Only when phototypesetting and lithographic printing became widespread, in 1970s, printed books have turned into a low cost mass medium. It was because more efficient production processes and availability of inexpensive paper who were the main reasons why books have become a mass medium. The printed book has developed its independent look and form over the years, which is still used today, and the number of produced new book titles has been growing continuously since Gutenberg's invention. Even today, in the age of electronic media, annual growth rates in book production are still recorded in Germany, Great Britain and China (Kipphan, 2001, p. 5).

The extensive range of books is classified on the one hand in terms of content; on the other, it extends from high quality, thread-stitched leather volumes with a gilt edge to simple perfect-bound pocket books or paperbacks. Books are offered both in one color as well as in top-quality multicolor art publications. Along with advertising inserts, which we find daily in newspapers and magazines, there is a large market for leaflets and product descriptions. Such printed matter is referred to as brochures. Unlike magazines and newspapers, brochures are not published periodically. Brochures are commercial print work. Another significant difference from newspapers or magazines is the usually low print volume. Today, brochures are generally printed in color and are available as either folded individual sheets or bound copies. Also, brochures are in better quality than newspapers and magazines because are mainly used to advertise, describe and sell some company products (Kipphan, 2001, p. 6).

Every book product is usually made of book block as a carrier of printed information and cover as protection unit, produced independently and then assembled into a single unique product. To analyze the organization of the processing procedure it is useful to structure the bookbinding finishing processes into individual process sections. Each section characterizes the transformation of the materials with regard to the desired processing outcome. The designations of these processing sections use unique terminology including classification in bookbinding (Kipphan, 2001, p. 776). The frame of bookbinding engineering contributes to student engagement and comprehension of a complex network of binding technology as well as a one-man craft bookbinding (Pasanec, 2014). The course follows finishing processes throughout publishing and craft bookbinding. It studies the bookbinding process and binding block system types. It focuses on establishing the characteristics of bookbinding with regard to book shelfs system, binding unit, adhesive and paper types. The paper grade bindability is the most relevant factor in bookbinding engineering process. Paper properties (thickness, bulk, grain direction, roughness, smoothness, mechanical strength, adhesive wetting) directly determine papers suitability in the act of choosing between different binding block systems (perfect, thread-stitching, thread-sealing, side wire-stitching, wire saddle-stitching, spiral). Today offset and bulky printing paper, matte and satin coated paper, recycled and office paper, newsprint, art, magazine and Bible paper are being put into printing process without exchanging knowledge and skills with bookbinding experts. Project manager often overlook some of the rules and interrelations of graphic engineering, which are then not in accordance with defined print production range - mass, serial or craft-made book production.

The aim of the Bookbinding course is finding the best solutions within the bookbinding engineering frameworks. Practical work is focusing on specific details, including individual handmade books. It allows students to understand a complex binding technology network. Course topics support student engineering activities with integrated education environment and interdisciplinary approach to learning that provides hands-on a relevant learning experience for students. Teaching and learning goes beyond the mere transfer of knowledge. It engages students and equips them with critical thinking, problem solving, creative and collaborative skills, and ultimately establishes connections between the Faculty and labor market (Pasanec, 2017). Also knowledge from previous courses dramatically enable development of student`s work portfolios in Bachelor degree according to the Croatian Qualifications Framework (CROQF) of Ministry of Science, Education and Sports establishes by CROQF (2013) based on learning outcomes. Learning outcomes are defined in terms of knowledge, skills, responsibility and independency. It is a single, comprehensive eight-level framework, which incorporates credit systems (ECTS). It includes qualifications from all levels and subsystems of formal education, training and informal learning. Apart from offering transparency, the CROQF is seen as an important tool for reforming national education and training; this includes setting up a system for validating and recognizing non-formal an informal learning, and creating a well-founded quality assurance system (National Qualifications Framework-Anniversary edition, 2015, p. 26).

LEARNING METHODS AND PROCESSES IN HIGHER - EDUCATION QUALIFICATIONS FRAMEWORK

Professional development influence teacher's classroom practice significantly and lead to improvement of student achievement throughout particular courses according to instruction of the Project about Teaching Tolerance (2017). Pervious research on professional development is scattered throughout course areas, with its focus ranking from classroom processes and structures to teachers' professional attribute. Researches showed that professional development leads to better instruction processes and improve students learning when is connected to the curriculum materials that teacher use, the district and state academic standard that guide their work, and by measuring assessment and accountability that evaluate their success (Cohen & Hill, 2001).

Further, Garet et al. (2001) presented in their research that teachers were more likely to change their instructional practices and gain greater course knowledge and improved teaching skills when their professional development are linked directly to their daily experiences and aligned with standards and assessments. The P21 Framework for 21st Century Learning was developed with input from educator, education experts and business leaders to define and illustrate the skills, knowledge, expertise, and support system that students need to succeed in work, life and citizenship in the USA. Framework provides the students skills at the centre of learning, all elements of the Frameworks are critical to ensure 21st century readiness for every student, learning environments improve students' engagement in learning process and graduate better prepared to progress in nowadays digitally and globally interconnected world. Divjak (2005) claim that nowadays, extremely rapid accumulation and development of new knowledge is not enough for a teacher to teach ex-cathedra -"from the seat of authority", while the student is listening, writing, and more or less reproduces on exam what is written or read in the class book. In fact, the student has to overcome basic knowledge in the scope, but also learn how to use literature, so that way student could continue to learn independently. On the other hand, the student should be involved in real situation that will enable him or her to develop the strategies how to solve problems, but also think critically about the problems. This approach encourage teacher to use contemporary teaching methods, which the student will recognize as a learning subjects, just not as a teaching objects. It means that the Bologna Process also forces teachers to continue their lifelong learning and training. Teachers have to be focused on students' load, not the teacher. The learning outcomes are important, the teaching content is not. Teaching methods put student at the centre of teaching process. Now, the students are preparing for lifelong learning, employment and self-employment. The Bologna Process is agreement between European countries to ensure comparability in the standards and quality of higher-education qualifications framework. The Bologna Process has created the European Higher Education Area. According to CROQF (2013), "Active Learning and Critical Thinking in Higher Education" is a program developed under the International Reading and Writing for Critical Thinking (RWCT) project and it was originally Croatian product (Figure 1).

The program is designed to help teachers and all those attending university classes in Croatia. The program, apart from its philosophy, also contains a system of steps and concrete teaching techniques based on the cognitivist learning theory. The special quality of the project represents the direct applicability of the lessons learned as well as the flexibility of application in different academic disciplines. Through 80 hours of instructions, teachers learn how to apply more than 80 different teaching methods and techniques, they learn how to stimulate the development of new skills for open and responsible interaction in the classroom, enrich the existing curriculum and devise an innovative teaching process and classes based on ERR (Early Reading Research) system. The evaluation of the entire program since its beginning in 2005 has shown that the active application of the learned content in daily teaching process makes different in three levels:

1. **In Teaching Process:** Organizing class based on ERR system contributes diversity, dynamism, enthusiasm in content preparation, thinking about teaching method according the students experience.
2. **For Students:** More satisfaction for them, "students are cheerful!" They are active in teaching process (motivated, regularly attend classes).

Figure 1. A plan view of training program for Croatian teachers

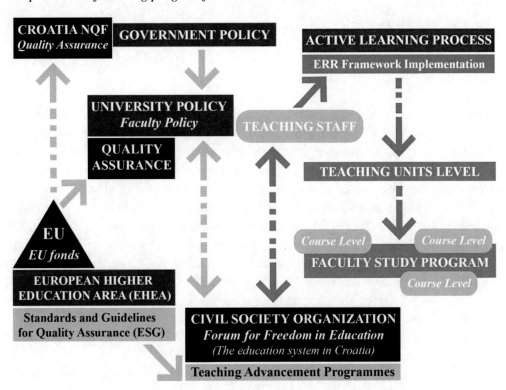

3. **Personal Level:** Student satisfaction, a growing sense of competence, students become aware of the importance of teaching process quality and improvement possibilities.

Generally, teachers emphasize that they have completely changed their approach and focus from teacher to student. Program participant statements are excellent on social networks, and that is why the ALCT (Active Learning and Critical Thinking) Program improves quick analysis of teacher quality in teaching process. ERR Framework system and cooperative learning use a specially designed assessment scale for student, which contribute cognitive, conative and affective students' development and strength their competence for 21st century. The certain taxonomy has to match the learning outcomes hierarchy. Bloom taxonomy directly pronounce the "deepness" of learning process, while teaching content gives information about covered learning themes.

Further, students' way of thinking and presenting graphic technology-oriented knowledge is based on practical visual communication and visual data organization, with a focus on the meaning, not exclusively on data and facts. Data visualization provides clearer way to see and understand data analyses than just through a narrative explanation. Design of visualizations is relevant and selective method for gathering the data. Lima (2011) claimed that approaching and creating network visualization involves roughly eight principles:

1. Start with a question.
2. Look for a relevance.
3. Enable multivariances.

4.   Embrace time.
5.   Enrich your vocabulary.
6.   Expose grouping.
7.   Maximize scaling.
8.   Manage intricacy (Lima, 2011, pp. 82-92).

Visual Mental Imagery or paper-based concept map visualizations created by students is one of excellent teaching technique that has been proven to be successful in producing learning outcomes. Data visualization functions as a way of visually represent data set; the idea is to representing data in illustrative ways. Students are making connections among specific keywords, ideas, research and sketches. It is very important for students because human being has a strong need to see and understand data visually. Mapping Patterns of information is a process of producing graphic and bookbinding technology-oriented knowledge and critical representation of the processes, ideas and concepts of making data comprehensibly, logically and visually beautiful. Further, students are able to analyze knowledge and new information through more connective, comparative and critically thoughtful way. Now, teaching and learning are highly complex, individual and subjective. Teaching process becomes inspirational and exciting. This kind of interactive visualizations offers the multiple level of information, which represent the numerous layers of teaching and learning process. The main point is to work out a way to capture the various patterns and meanings that teacher and student notice when they directly watch, view, read and interpret actual teaching and learning.

Knowledge visualization have four typical knowledge tasks throughout idea generation, knowledge sharing, evaluating option and planning. All of these provide support for the selection of adequate visualizations for individual and collaborate cognitive tasks. Key lessons of such an approach include:

1.   Design in way that is self-sustaining and conductive to growth.
2.   Develop community relationship patterns.
3.   Keep learning.
4.   Keep creating and inventing (Taylor, 2015).

Manovich (2011) wrote: "Visualizations can also function as art in a different sense: an activity aimed at making statements and asking questions about the world by selecting parts of it and representing these parts in particular way. Some of the most well-known artistic visualizations projects do exactly that: they make strong assertions about our world not only through the choice of visualization techniques, but also through the choice of data sets" (Manovich, 2011, p. 13). Generally, learning and making about bookbinding requires an understanding of consequences and constrains of media and ground. Education process requires that students and teachers think deeply about how their work may provoke action, understanding, awareness and simple appreciation through bookbinding process and curriculum. Teaching implementation of Information and Communication Technologies (ICT) based learning environment gives new scenarios face-to-face and virtual learning. Different learning effects contribute changing study habits and long-term teaching effects. E-learning is recognized that the roles assumed by teachers are related to the information transmission to leading students' actions. The teachers' acts more as learning guides because when the teachers have used internet and multimedia, they have to change style, who has wanted to keep traditional teaching style, they just quit. Teacher-student and student-student interactions in e-learning environment generate communicative learning processes and the adoption social mode of thinking. In general, learning innovations challenge the teaching function, teaching roles and education culture. The changes in the teacher and student roles as result of using ICT affect classroom organization and teaching approach has applied of placing emphasis on the learning process rather than the learning outcomes and on social learning rather than individual learning process (Barajas, 2001).

This paper presents implementation of ERR framework system process and virtual learning for the Undergraduate Study Course of Graphic Technology. The study program for Bachelor of Science in Graphic technology contributes earning of basic and for graphic engineering specific knowledge and skills in core course Bookbinding on Department for Bookbinding and Packaging at Faculty of Graphic Arts in Zagreb, Croatia. Framework promotes students active learning and critical thinking through the training program ALCT. Students engage with the materials, participate in the class and collaborate with teachers. The teacher becomes a facilitator, coordinator and seeks to enable students to become active teaching process participants.

ABOUT ERR FRAMEWORK SYSTEM AS TEACHING METHOD WITHIN THE BOOKBINDING COURSE

Through the training program "Active Learning and Critical Thinking in Higher Education" attended by teachers, students become people who think and learn critically. Independent learning enables them to acquire a set of new and important skills. The aim study of this methodical approach is problem solving suited to the surrounding of bookbinding publishing environment. Instrumental learning, dialogic learning and self-reflective learning are included through effective framework system: evocation (E), realization of meaning (R) and reflection (R). In the first phase (E), students are stimulated to use their knowledge and experience on a particular topic and determine the purpose of teaching and learning. In this phase student connects the previous knowledge or prior learning outcomes with new knowledge given to them (course outcomes). In the second phase (R), students make a new text analysis of thematic presentations and contents. Students are expected to integrate new contents into their own knowledge. In the final, reflection phase (R), students think about what they have learned in the context of their existing knowledge. Thus, students repeat, build and create a link between existing and new knowledge and create a new quality (Bjelanović, 2012; Terzić, 2012; Urbanc & Kleteči, 2007).

In order to develop a practical understanding of the ERR framework system for teaching and learning, Terzić (2012) presented how the system must be tested in the context of teaching as part of guided and each teaching unit passes through the aforementioned phases of system framework. Estimated system for teaching and learning allows teacher to:

1. Organize instructions.
2. Identify purpose and objective of teaching.
3. Plan additional activities.
4. Involve students in purposeful learning.
5. Establish a correlation between the subjects.
6. Watch the needs and interests of students.

Duron (2006) presented technique that encourages critical thinking where teaching process is allowing students to discover information and make decisions to solve problems according to 5-Step Model to move students toward critical thinking. The first step includes learning objectives determination, the second step each through questioning, the third step includes practice before assessing, the forth step is review, refine and improvement and the final fifth step includes provide feedback and assessment of learning process. Duron concluded that 5-step Framework helps students to learn critical thinking skills and pushed out traditional lecture-based (ex-cathedra) format of teaching process in 21st century. Lloyd & Bahr (2010) consider that students have to learn in small work groups about 3-5 students, having fun by learning from each other in a trusting environment.

Students of first BSc year have written an anonymous online opinion in academic survey that critical thinking as an outcome included student ability to think a topic; "Its benefits, how I can use this items, products,…". Students can look at all possibilities and analyze the situation, look beyond literal information available and make inferences, draw conclusion, predict, reflect, be able to think independently and critique what they hear, think about problems and issues in a way that doesn't necessarily conform the main discourse but confronts and challenges it as well (Lloyd & Bahr, 2010, p. 7). With this approach to teaching and learning students motivation is encouraged, the bookbinding teachers directly promotes critical thinking by questions and students are encouraged to think and ask questions. Students are working on real bookbinding current problems in learning environment (Figure 2), which helps them to develop

Figure 2. Collaborative teaching process that includes community, collaboration, interaction, brainstorming, discussion and ideas sharing

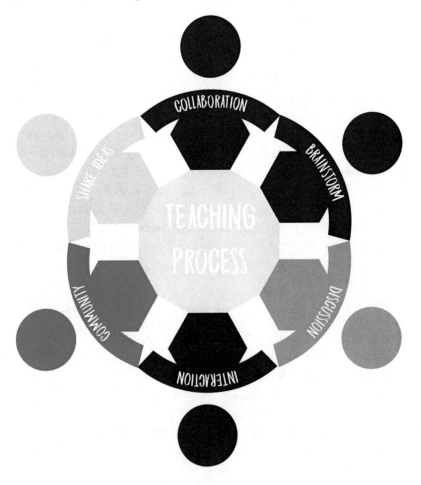

critical thinking, student's habits, need to learn and grow individually. In this phase, prior knowledge and prior learning assessment is simple process for educator/teacher, because student's practical skills of critical thinking, reasoning and conclusions become measurable with course tasks for achieving new outcomes in bookbinding.

It can involve focusing on achieving a particular prior learning outcome in graphic materials, graphic design and graphic management resolution or simply to better understanding all aspects of a binding technology issue. In this way, the teaching process is focused on learning outcomes and it can provoke further questions or areas to research. The fact is that students must be able to think deeply and logically as result of studying fundamental disciplines where critical thinking can be integrated into student activities (Vizek, 2009). Vizek (2009) claimed that Bloom classification of cognitive domain active verbs directly provide active learning process in ERR framework system in which one can build upon prior learning to develop more complex levels of understanding (Figure 3).

Budimir, Pasanec and Lukić (2013) presented active learning process in ERR framework system in core course Packaging on same Department at Faculty of Graphic Arts. Trusting learning environment lies in flexible active teaching through Croatian e-learning "Merlin" system. Actually, teacher has become tutor and directly supports the self-learning process through bookbinding problems solving and updating the contents of courses for learning via electronic media, internet. As a result, students have

Figure 3. Teaching method based on Bloom classification

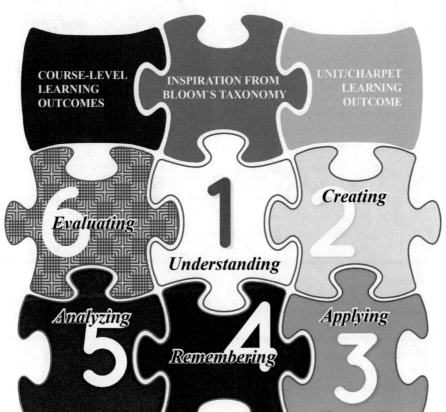

greater responsibility in learning activities by the use of ICT-based learning environment incorporate to training program ALCT (Figure 4).

Active/cooperative learning is very effectively used in conjunction with bookbinding lectures. The simple active learning techniques (about 10 different styles) have replaced traditional lecture-based format (Figure 5).

Figure 4. Concept map of active learning process

Figure 5. Example of teaching framework technique in 5 steps, course Bookbinding 1

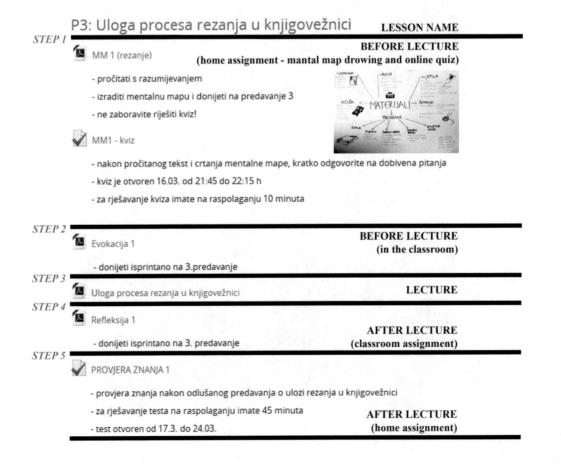

Dialog, writing and "high-order thinking" include main course outcomes such as analysis, synthesis and evaluation. Teacher-student interaction and vice versa has significant importance because ICT bookbinding learning environment improve communicative learning processes and social network model of thinking (individual/group learning). This methodical approach has improved learning and teaching progress. Active learning can be achieved without great effort, but teacher has to assure organized, understandable and interesting course lecture with different learning materials like tests, quises, tables, funny stories, articles and similar. Divjak (2005) noticed that all course materials and interaction during the lecture has to be held by teacher who has to maintain interest in the subject of lecture, stimulate students to ask interesting questions and develop habits of critical thinking in bookbinding subject (Figure 6). Through this way of learning, exceptional achievement progress of the learning outcomes are presented by Divjak (2008). For that reason, the unique bookbinding social game was designed to follow the "deep" learning process.

Generally, assessment technique for effective learning and grading criteria are achieved by multiple-choice tests like paper and pencil, e-learning tests and mental-drawing maps. A scoring guide tool is opportunity for mark systematization throughout student learning activities (Kennedy, 2006; Lončar & Dolaček, 2009), so final grade directly presents students learning outcomes in bookbinding (Figure 7).

At the end of course, the evaluation questions recommended for teaching and learning is part of the review process in which students individually give critique and evaluate quality of teaching and learning process. The ultimate aim of this evaluation review is improvement of student learning outcomes. Anonymous students' surveys for bookbinding course "pencil and paper" showed more interest for course topics because teacher prepares lectures according the students experience. Students concluded and have written: "We are cheerful!"; "Finally, we are involved in teaching process!"; "We can give our opinion about bookbinding problems on different ways!", "We have bookbinding knowledge for real life in labor market!"; "We are able to discuss and resolve different bookbinding case studies!"; "We are having experience in bookbinding engineering!"

Figure 6. Personalized unique social game that includes Bloom classification, designed for practical lessons in Bookbinding course

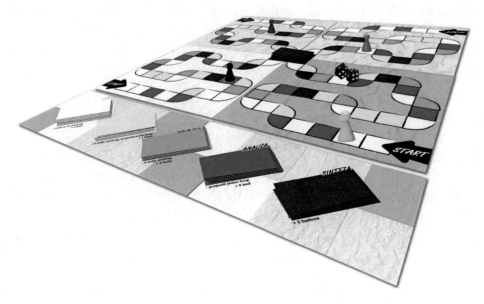

Figure 7. Score/mark table for systematization and evaluation of students learning activities, course Bookbinding 1

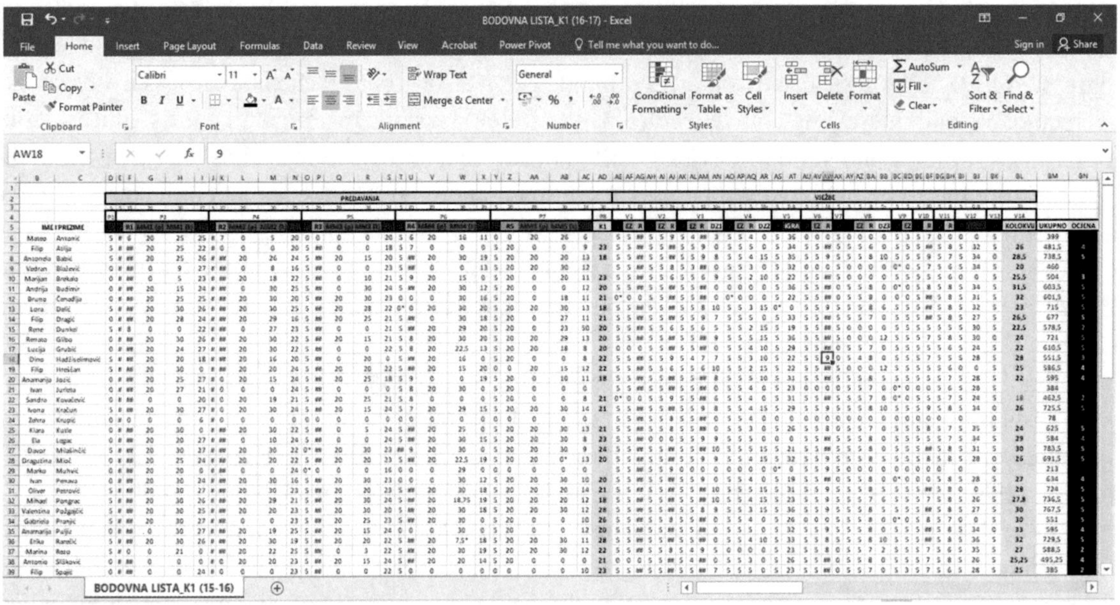

CONCLUSION

Learning outcomes play a key role in ensuring students professional development in solving meaningful problems. Communicative learning process directly provides social network model of critical thinking in various environments (traditional classroom, electronic media). Reaching a basic learning outcome must be provided with minor levels of students' engagement. Teacher professional development, developed skills and high knowledge of the presented topics are the most important parameters for improvement of student critical thinking on the subject. Teacher has to continuously make activities focused on high-quality topic-matter content. ERR framework system directly provides teachers creativity throughout collaborative learning and visual data organization which are applicable in everyday situations and useful for resolving problem situations and tasks. From experience, it can be concluded that students prefer lectures that are based on a cooperative learning process.

REFERENCES

Barajas, M. (2001). *Monitoring and evaluation of research in learning innovations (Merlin) - Final Report of project HPHA-CT2000-00042 funded under the Improving Human Research Potential & the Socio-economic Knowledge Base Directorate General Science, Research and Development European commission.* Retrieved December 15, 2016, from http://www.ub.edu/euelearning/merlin/docs/finalreprt.pdf

Bjelanović Dijanić, Ž. (2012). Some Methods for the Development of Students' Critical Thinking by ERR System. *Methodical Review. Journal of Philosophy of Education*, *19*(1), 163–179.

Budimir, I., Pasanec Preprotić, S., & Lukić, D. (2013). Cross-curricular linkage of mathematics and technology with applications in graphic technology. *The Holistic Approach to Environment*, *3*(4), 223–230.

Cohen, D. K., & Hill, H. C. (2001). *Learning Policy: When State Education Reform Works*. New Haven, CT: Yale University Press. doi:10.12987/yale/9780300089479.001.0001

Divjak, B. (2005). *First Steps in the Bologna Process), Tempus project, Croatia Bologna promoters team Cro4 Bologna*. Retrieved February 15, 2015, from http://www.kif.unizg.hr/_download/repository/Bologna.pdf

Divjak, B. (2008). *O ishodima učenja u visokom obrazovanju*. Retrieved July 19, 2017, from http://iu.foi.hr/upload_data/knjiga/Ishodi_ucenja_u_visokom_obrazovanju_12122008_F.pdf

Duron, R. (2006). Critical Thinking Framework for any discipline. *International Journal on Teaching and Learning in Higher Education*, *17*(2), 160–166.

Garet, M. S., Porter, A. C., Desimone, L., Birman, B. F., & Yoon, K. S. (2001). What makes Professional Development Effective? Results from a National Sample of Teachers. *American Educational Research Journal*, *38*(4), 915–945. doi:10.3102/00028312038004915

Kennedy, D. (2006). *Writing and Using Learning Outcomes*. Retrieved December 9, 2016, from https://www.cmepius.si/wp-content/uploads/2015/06/A-Learning-Outcomes-Book-D-Kennedy.pdf

Kipphan, H. (Ed.). (2001). *Handbook of Print Media*. Berlin: Springer. doi:10.1007/978-3-540-29900-4

Lima, M. (2011). *Visual complexity: Mapping patterns of information*. New York: Princeton Architectural Press.

Lloyd, M., & Bahr, N. (2010). Thinking Critically about Critical Thinking in Higher Education. *International Journal for the Scholarship of Teaching and Learning*, *4*(2), 1–16.

Lončar Vicković, S., & Dolaček Alduk, Z. (2009). *Ishodi učenja, priručnik za sveučilišne nastavnike*. Retrieved March 5, 2017, from http://www.azoo.hr/images/Natjecanja_2014./ishodi_ucenja.pdf

Manovich, L. (2011). *Visual complexity: Mapping patterns of information* (M. Lima, Ed.). New York: Princeton Architectural Press.

National Qualifications Framework-Anniversary edition. (2015). *CROQF-Developments in Europe*. Retrieved March 12, 2016, from https://www.cedefop.europa.eu/files/4137_en.pdf

Partnership for 21st Century Learning. (2015). *P21's Framework for 21st Century Learning*. Retrieved July 05, 2017, from http://www.p21.org/about-us/p21-framework

Pasanec, P. S. (2017, March). *From Visualization framework in teaching bookbinding at the Faculty of Graphic Arts*. Paper presented at the meeting International Conference Information Visualization in Humanities, Torun, Poland.

Pasanec Preprotić, S. (2017). *Informacijski paket - Preddiplomski sveučilišni studij grafičke tehnologije*. Retrieved July 15, 2017, from http://www.grf.unizg.hr/informacijski-paket/

Taylor, P. G. (2015). *Handbook of Research on Maximizing Cognitive Learning through Knowledge Visualization* (A. Ursyn, Ed.). Hershey, PA: IGI Global.

Teaching Tolerance. (2017). *Teaching Teachers: PD To Improve Student Achievement*. Retrieved August 8, 2017, from https://www.tolerance.org/professional-development/teaching-teachers-pd-to-improve-student-achievement

Terzić, F. (2012). ERR Framework system and cooperative learning. *Metodički obzori, 7*(3), 47-50.

Urbanc, K., & Kletečki Radović, M. (2007). Active learning and critical thinking in the context of supervisory, educational and helping relationship. *Annual of Social Work, 14*(2), 355-366.

Vizek Vidović, V. (Ed.). (2009). *Planiranje kurikuluma usmjerenoga na kompetencije u obrazovanju učitelja i nastavnika - Priručnik za visokoškolske nastavnike*. Zagreb, Croatia: University of Zagreb, Faculty of Humanities and Social Sciences & Faculty of Teacher Education.

KEY TERMS AND DEFINITIONS

Assessment of Prior Knowledge: In the context of this chapter assessment of prior learning (APL) and assessment of prior knowledge are synonymous; they both refer to the assessment of students' knowledge, skills, and competences prior to engagement with a course of study.

Assessment of Prior Learning (APL): The assessment of students' knowledge, skills, and competences prior to engagement with a course of study.

Bookbinding Engineering: It combines different skills from other trades: paper and fabric crafts, leatherwork, model making, and graphic arts. It requires knowledge about numerous book structure varieties according to assembly point details, forms, and types. This is an artistic craft including antiquity and highly mechanized industry (mass production) on the other hand.

E-Learning: The use of information communications technology (ICT), hardware, and software to facilitate online learning.

Educator: One who engages with the theory, practice, and skill/art of teaching.

Graphic Technology: Graphic technologies encompasses the world of print, everything from creating the design to producing it in various forms on numerous types of materials. The industry includes electronic and traditional printing, publishing, packaging, digital imaging, computer graphics, website development, digital photography, printable electronics, and other related areas.

Learning Motivation: Main factor for internal (intrinsic) or external (extrinsic) forces that give students power to learn effectively. Teachers are the best source of motivation in the teaching-learning interaction.

Portfolio: It refers to a purposeful and selective collection of work that tells the story with reflection and self-assessment, and provides authentic evidence of the individual's efforts, skills, abilities, achievement, and contributions over time.

Teacher Motivation: Main factor for internal (intrinsic) or external (extrinsic) forces that give teachers power to run their daily routine.

Teachers' Beliefs: A set of strong feelings and attitudes of teachers about things that can affect the teaching-learning interaction. What teachers believe has a direct implication on the teaching-learning transaction.

Chapter 14
Generative Systems in Information Visualization

Ilona Nowosad
College of Social and Media Culture, Poland

ABSTRACT

The author presents various approaches particularly in the field of visual arts and sound visualization based on hi-tech artificial agents and audiovisual systems. The number of digital artists and designers who tend to computational creativity has rapidly grown in recent years and their artworks and generative visuals that manifest the new cultural paradigm "Form Follows Data" meet with a wide interest. The author describes and presents a collection of tools and programming environments used for creating visual representations of sound as well as live coding visualizations which fall under so called generative art movement. Concepts of interactive audiovisual systems, sound-reactive programming software, and immersive environments refer to synergy of sound, visuals, and gestures. Another purpose is to point to applications of generative systems and agent-based frameworks in social and cognitive sciences to study environmental and social systems and their interactions.

Things which are made, such as houses, furniture, and machines, are an assemblage of parts put together, or shaped, like sculpture, from the outside inwards. But things which grow shape themselves from within outwards—they are not assemblages of originally distinct parts; they partition themselves, elaborating their own structure from the whole to the parts, from the simple to the complex. (Watts, 1958)

GENERATIVE SYSTEM

To start off the story about generative systems in information visualization the author defines and familiarizes a notion of generative systems as systems which consist of a pre-determined set of rules that give rise to a range of unpredictable results. By this definition, it is obvious that for each generative system it is necessary to determine the set of rules and the rules determine the results.

DOI: 10.4018/978-1-5225-4990-1.ch014

When one prepares a series of written instructions, which describe several emotional states with corresponding exact manners of facial expression to be performed, then each person's interpretation of the instructions will certainly be different, but all of them shall be remarkably similar. This simple example shows the concept of a generative system, because it uses a couple of basic rules to yield patterns which can be unpredictable and extremely varied. Obviously, one can classify it as a generative system.

To better understand a notion of a generative system one can also consider a dice having its squares colored in six different colors. A simple rule is to roll the dice six times and emerging property is determined by a sequence of six horizontal colored squares as a result. Following this concept *8vo* - the design group of typographic designers with experience in visual identity and brand communications - developed such a system in which pre-designed typographic rules could determine the final outcome. The objective of the system was to bring *a freedom from the tyranny of aesthetics* (8vo, 2005). The system was used for generating a series of posters for the Flux Festival.

The above examples show the set of rules can be described in an everyday language. In fact, sets of rules and instructions can be written in every language, like everyday language. The explicitness and straightforwardness are strongly required properties of the pre-defined instructions and rules. For this reason, programming languages are the most useful and frequently used, as they best satisfy the mentioned properties. Programming codes are the most precise way of determining a set of instructions, particularly when these instructions are to be executed by computerized machines.

More often than not, programming codes of generative systems appear quite complex, however, a simple generative system can be described in a couple of code lines, as Listing 1 below shows:

```
void setup(){
size(800,600);
}
void draw(){
if (mousePressed){
   fill(250,115,180);
} else {
   fill(90, 230, 245);
}
ellipse(mouseX, mouseY, 50, 50);
}
```

Listing 1: The Code of the Simple Generative System

The generative system showed in Listing 1 consists of two functions: setup and draw, which are responsible for setting the size of the frame (canvas) and drawing visual objects, respectively. An important feature of this generative system is its interactivity and reactiveness to the user's actions. The system continuously draws circles in the present mouse location, changing their colors in response to pressing the mouse button, as shown in Figure 1. Obviously, every time when the system runs on demand of the user, a different output is generated with regard to the user's mouse control, although all outputs will be remarkably similar and fit in a range of possible patterns.

Generative systems can be considered with respect to the level of their autonomy. The author shall recall after Hyacinth S. Nwana that

Figure 1. The visual output of the generative system presented in Listing 1
Source: own elaboration

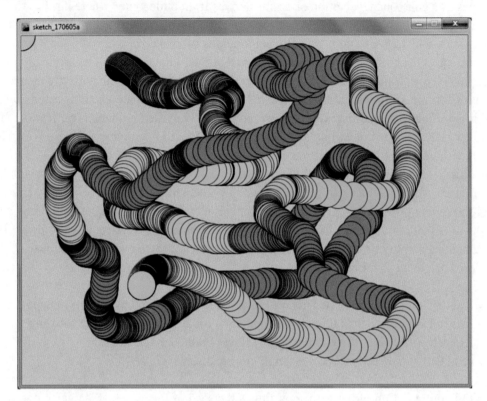

Autonomy refers to the principle that agents (systems) can operate on their own without the need for human guidance, even though this would sometimes be invaluable. Hence agents have individual internal states and goals, and they act in such a manner as to meet its goals on behalf of its user. (Nwana, 1996)

From this point of view, they can be purely reactive systems on one end and fully autonomous systems on the other. Between these two extremes all intermediate guises are possible, which can automate tasks partially, for instance, a computer assisted creativity system. Purely reactive systems have no autonomy, like Windows Paint or MS Excel. "They act using a stimulus/response type of behavior by responding to the present state of the environment in which they are embedded" (Ferber, 1994). Completely autonomous systems do not require any further input when they start their task on demand, so they complete it without any interference. Some generative systems can also interact with humans, such as what was shown in the above example. The interaction can also be a sort of dialogue between the system and its user or an even wider environment. Most software is interactive in a classical meaning, i.e., such systems interact with humans via interfaces and every input is mapped to a particular reaction. The level of the mapping complexity in such a case can also vary. Hence, what exactly one should understand by interactive systems? The system is interactive if it takes input in real time in order to perform its tasks. Again, there is a range of interactivity levels for generative systems. Some of them are low interactivity level systems, they can only react to the input, for this reason they are often named reactive systems. Some generative systems represent a high level of interactivity. In such a case, agents that can be natural or artificial, influence actions of one another, moreover, it is rather difficult to predict their actions and the outcomes as a consequence. Notion of agents derives from philosophy, where it refers to a capability to act, in contrast to objects, which are not proactive. By an artificial agent the author understands a computer system which is capable to perform autonomous actions.

Also, one can consider generative systems in terms of their knowledge and its origin. Some systems have static knowledge, while some can change it over time. Thus, some of them will have their knowledge inserted once forever along with a pre-determined set of rules, some can take it or extend by learning from the input. Finally, generative systems can represent diversified architectures, from archetypally simple, threw reflexive one containing an inner feedback loop, to interactive and adaptive architecture which includes a feedback loop with its outer environment.

John Conway's Game of Life is a well-known example illustrating a generative system and the power of a tiny little set of rules, which can generate various visual patterns. The game, shortly called Life, is set in an infinite two-dimensional grid of square cells. Every cell has its own neighborhood consisting of all eight cells that are adjacent. Each cell can represent one of two states: alive or dead. There are four fundamental, simple rules that interpose transitions into the game evolution (Gardner, 1970). John Conway described them as follows:

- Any live cell with fewer than two live neighbors dies, as if caused by underpopulation.
- Any live cell with more than three live neighbors dies, as if caused by overcrowding.
- Any live cell with two or three live neighbors lives on the next generation.
- Any dead cell with exactly three live neighbors becomes a live cell.

The initial configuration of the game constitutes the seed of the system. The game doesn't require any further input and operates within an infinite iteration process, in which each such iteration is called a tick. In every tick the above four rules are applied simultaneously to every single cell of the game universe. The rules are applied repeatedly so that consecutive generations emerge. Patterns can evolve in surprising ways so that observers have no idea what they are going to look like. They grow and extend in their life cycles to very complex ones. The patterns are examples of emerging and self-organizing structures, which are specific to generative systems. Brian Eno, the British musician and visual artist, who has introduced the concept of generative systems into his compositions and artistic work in general, made an important note about generative systems that *one makes seeds rather than forests*, and these seeds produce a great richness. This feature makes generative systems so powerful.

On the other hand, patterns are very dependent on their initial conditions and this causes them to also be very fragile in terms of sensitivity to changes. When one changes though a single cell in the game life cycle, the pattern will occur to lose some primal property. For instance, if it was symmetric, it would become skew. John Conway's Game of Life sparked off research in a new field of cellular automata, which can simulate a variety of real-world systems. There is a strong analogy between Conway's Game of Life and alterations of a society of living organisms, including its rise and fall. For this reason, it belongs to a growing class of games resembling real life processes, involving generative systems.

Therefor generative systems are frequently used for doing simulations of very complex phenomenon. As an example, the author can indicate one of a well-known series of computer games called SimCity, which is built on generative systems with very simple rules for traffic, crime, energy, health and education systems, even environment pollution etc. Underneath the graphical layer, which illustrates the virtual city with streets, buildings and factories, as shown on Figure 2, there is the simple grid-based generative

Figure 2. Screenshots of the SimCity game based on a generative system
Source: Hopkins, 2006

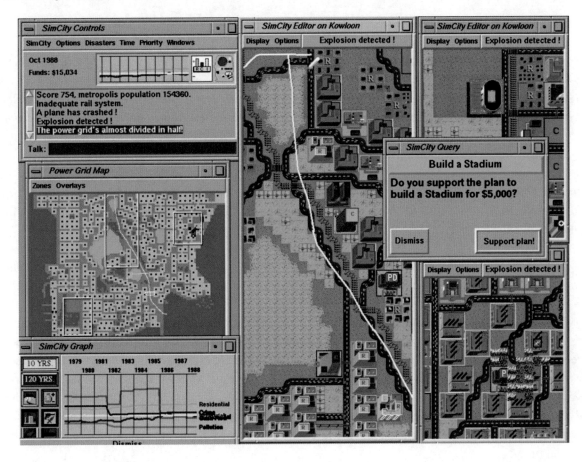

system, which is responsible for all the simulation of the urban advancement. SimCity is an agent-based model simulating and visualizing a complex, dynamic nature of urban problems.

Wishart et al. (2004) described how generative systems approaches are capable to capture the stochastic properties of many biological processes. To perform simulations described in their paper, the educational biology game, called SimCell, was developed. The game is a simulator of cellular and biochemical processes in plants and humans, which allows users to understand scientific information about the cell and the mechanics of cell biology. The SimCell is meant to teach high school students about the human cell in particular. The game allows users to create objects like protein or DNA molecules, membranes and genes, and next observe the way those cellular elements interact among themselves. At any time, the user can also interact with the system and change its visual content in real time. The SimCell moreover includes music compositions obtained as a procedural sound design based on generative systems defined within a generative music synthesizer. The aim was to generate live music which well corresponds to every single user's actions and experience of drowning into what life is. Some samples of the SimCell project, in particular the generative music and procedural sound design of Sim Cell, one can see in this youtube video: https://www.youtube.com/watch?v=0xr4aL1C24E

GENERATIVE ART

Lev Manovich (2008) in his Info-Aesthetics Manifesto wrote:

Since we are physical beings, we have always required and continue to require various physical forms in order to house and transport our bodies, our information-processing machine, and information itself. (…) Therefore, although the word "information" contains the world "form" inside it, in reality it is the other way around: in order to be useful to us, information always has to be wrapped up in some external form.

Further Manovich explained that

Info-aesthetics refers to those contemporary cultural practices that can be best understood as responses to the new priorities of information society: making sense of information, working with information, producing knowledge from information and put questions: what is the shape of information? and

If the shift from industrial to information society has been accompanied by a shift from form to information flows, can we still map these information flows into forms meaningful to a human? (Manovich, 2008)

In other words, how can this be reduced and translated to the scale of human perception and cognition? As an information-processing species people need to design forms for information that they create, record and manipulate. Thus, Manovich declared a new info-aesthetics paradigm that can be expressed as "Form Follows Data", that is the form is generated by the data. Data structures encode the form of systems through computational logic and generative processes fed by data sets. Hence data sets generate dynamic forms, patterns and evolutionary behavior of the system, and in addition through the deployment of various detecting or sensing technologies, this can generate dynamic data structures that evolve in real time.

Generative systems have given rise to generative art in a contemporary approach. The introductory quotation of Alan Watts emphasizes a sharp distinctiveness between the world of nature and the man-made one, the organic realm, full of generative forces and natural agents, and the mechanical systems being results of human creativity. The subject of generative art is quite well described as "things which grow", however it is difficult to qualify them as organic ones, since they are products of creative tasks, in particular computational creativity. They derive from the mechanical world as the outcome of logical decisions, mathematics and frequently computer programming.

So that the author defines generative art as art being a creation for part or entirely produced by an autonomous system (process, machine or other procedural invention) theretofore described or developed by an artist or designer. Often generative art involves computational processes for creative tasks. These include various algorithms adopted from artificial intelligence, machine learning or artificial life. In such a case, as Marius Watz (Pearson, 2011) described, generative art is "perfectly placed at the intersection of code and creative thinking."

However, generative art does not require any use of a computer. The generative system used to produce an artwork can be fully conceptual. An important note is generative art does not refer to a content of the outcome, nor to a reason it is made, but to the method it is produced.

It is crucial to clearly make one more important note to the above definition, which also proves that generative art is different from a classical art approach. Usually people imagine an artist working directly on his or her piece of artwork, for instance a sculptor sculpting a marble or a musician writing notes of his or her new composition. Generative art does not consist of building the artwork with materials and tools using designs or blueprints. In generative art, an artist first conceptualizes a process and then this process is used to perform and generate the artwork. The work of art is grown similarly to an organic plant, although it is not self-structuring, since the process is based on a set of rules or series of instructions that are executed by others. In this process, many artifacts can be machine-generated. The British artists Harold Cohen (1995) described evolution of the system and development process on the computer program and robotic machine called AARON. In 1973 Cohen began with the simple question: "what is the minimum condition under which a set of marks functions as an image?" The artist's intention was to develop a program that *would need to exhibit cognitive capabilities* quite like humans use for making and understanding images. From its beginning, AARON makes paintings autonomously, but as a result of continuous development, extending set of rules of the generative system that AARON is, the outcomes of AARON's processes became original and have been exhibited in many galleries such as the Tate Gallery in London. Due to Raymond Kurzweil, one of the world's leading inventors and futurists, presently AARON is the fine art screensaver that continuously creates original paintings on PCs and in this process utilizes artificial intelligence. AARON is now recognized as the Cybernetic Artists.

At this moment it is worth mentioning that generative art is nothing new. Philip Galanter (2006) said that generative art is as old as art itself. Moreover it is not specific to any medium, say electronic or digital technologies, and has been practiced in various forms for centuries. Indeed in ancient cultures, for instance, there were known patterns and techniques which were used to generate visual ornaments. Ancient generative art obviously was non-computerized. Nevertheless, in the present topic the author shall focus mainly on electronic medium, computational and digital systems, hence generative fruits of emerging cyberculture, which include particularly algorithmic composition, computer graphics and animation, demo scene, VJ culture, even industrial design and architecture that was presented by Nassery, F. and Sikorski, P. (2015).

Generative art cannot be simplified by describing it as either programming or art itself. Generative art is a strict combination of them both and is placed in their intersection area. Equally important are subjective emotional content which is expressive, illogical, unpredictable and on the other hand logical, with clean processes, and strictly defined algorithms. Thus both disciplines are combined into one entity called generative art.

When one investigates a creative process questions always arise, whether it is possible to model it and to build a simulator. Why should one ask these questions when there are many artificial intelligence algorithms which simulate and solve problems, for instance, they play games, perform automated discussions, regulate city traffic? A common property of the mentioned tasks is a precise, rational goal, which obviously cannot be associated with creative tasks for the clear reason, that an optimal or best result for them does not exist. Creative processes are not rational-based problems, at least not entirely, they do not have to manifest utilitarian functions, also it is often difficult to optimize them, etc. These questions have opened a new domain of research called computational creativity, which covers studies on processes that make art, models of human creativity, computational systems supporting creativity and artificially creative systems, among others. Computational creativity derives from generative art but is not its subdomain. It concerns various human or machine creative tasks, not only purely artistic but also those including functional elements. So that, tasks considered and researched in computational creativity are not identical with artistic ones. On the other hand, as it was mentioned above, generative art does not have to involve computational processes at all, in contrast to computational creativity.

Modern generative systems, based on computational processes, are the response to the needs of a creative and entertainment market nowadays. They are widely present in many creative disciplines including generative music composition, generative levels of video games, generative animations and video, generative comics and literature etc. Some research on visual computing and models for design based on generative algorithms are presented by Calvano (2016). Generative systems allow users to move from linear to non-linear media. They decrease costs of non-linear media prediction. For example they allow users to personalize music for every single video game player playing the same game simultaneously with many others. Moreover the music and sounds will react and adapt to scenes and events in the player's game instance. By analogy, the same concerns apply to the visuals, the animations and other elements of the game universe. Generative systems play a great role in those creative processes, helping artists and designers to obtain results automatically, making their work more efficient and strengthening visual and audiovisual perception and cognition of art processes.

AGENT-BASED SYSTEMS

The fundamental notion of the present research, according to the author, is an agent, which was already mentioned before. One can distinguish natural and artificial agents. The agents are considered as intentional systems from the philosophy of mind point of view. Daniel Dennet (2009) in his essay on intentional systems wrote:

The robot poker player that bluffs its makers seems to be guided by internal states that function just as a human poker player's intentions do, and if that is not the original intentionality, it is hard to say why not.

The robot poker player belongs to the class of artificial agents. It is the example of the artificial intentional system, while the human poker player is obviously the natural agent.

All artificial agents can be formally viewed as mappings from a set of percepts into a set of actions, which are called agents' programs. The term percept refers to the agent's perceptional inputs. Therefore, a simple agent program is an abstract concept of an agent function, which can invoke various principles of decision making. However, being pro-active and autonomous systems, they cannot be reduced to objects. As systems, they are embedded in some space, so they can interact with it and take inputs via certain sensors and affect the environment in return. In particular, they are able to interact with other agents and humans (natural agents), and accordingly respond in time. Thus, most cybernetic systems can be seen as agents. Multi-agents or multi-agent systems or shortly MAS, are systems that consist of a number of agents, which interact with their environment and if possible also with one another to achieve a goal that could not be accomplished by a single agent acting alone. In addition to the agents' architectural design, they require the societal design, which is implied by an ability to interact with other agents and humans. In order to cooperate, agents need to possess a social ability, i.e. the ability to interact with other agents and possibly humans via some communication language (Wooldridge & Jennings, 1995a). The agents in multi-agents have certain important characteristics. They are at least partially autonomous, none of these agents has a full global view of the system and none of them is designated as a controlling agent.

So far agents have been classified as software, virtual and physical agents. Software agents are situated as digital. For all above reasons they have become the dominant paradigm of modern software engineering as well as artificial intelligence. Along with the concept of agents we have a raising number of programming languages with increasing level of abstraction (from machine code to agent-oriented programming languages and numerous frameworks). It is enough to list just a few high-level abstraction languages and frameworks like object-oriented Java, Python, Ruby or agent-oriented Jason, Jade, Goal.

LIVE-CODING

There exist many specific programming languages and runtime environments designed for particular purposes. Extempore, which supports cyber-physical programming, is a good example of this sort of tool. The notion of cyber-physical programming encompasses a human programmer who acts as an active agent in a real-time distributed network of environmentally oriented systems. Procedural interaction between the programmer and the distributed real-time system is held on-the-fly by modifying the code. The idea of programming as an activity that takes place along with a real-time computational process and its interactions with the physical world gave rise to live coding, which in practice most often emerges as a live audiovisual performance. Sorensen and Gardner (2010) wrote "live-coding is a computational arts practice that involves the real-time creation of generative audiovisual software for interactive multimedia performance." Commonly, the programmer and his actions are exposed to the audience by displaying the editing environment with a code and its real-time modifications. Screens are projected for to display the entire process to the audience, which makes computer-based performance more inclusive. Live-coding most often is understood as the improvisations of video or/and music using computer systems and programming language. There are several closely related terms that are used interchangeably which describe the live coding processes, like on-the-fly, just-in-time, conversational, and interactive programming.

Live-coding has developed in recent years into an active field of research and arts practice. There arise numerous projects and groups of researchers which study live coding, for instance the Temporary Organization for the Promotion of Live Algorithm Programming (TOPLAP), Live Coding Research Network, which aim at integration of people and researchers dealing with live programming. Also the International Conference on Live Coding (ICLC) has taken place every year since 2015. The term live programming is used to denote all systems which support the direct programmer's intervention in a runtime execution of a program. It is made possible due to dynamic language interpreters, which allow codes to run while they are being modified, so that changes are loaded without making breaks in the audiovisual output generated by the code. Visualization is central to live-coding. Typical live-coding performance begins with no code and no audiovisual output. When the code grows, the output becomes more complex. In last decades many artist-oriented programming languages have arised. There are various live programming languages and interfaces, like text -based systems in which a programmer inserts characters that are immediately interpreted and acted, for instance processing or actionscript, or visual environments using visual paradigms, e.g. Fluxus, Max/MSP and Pure Data, where a signal processing graph is updated immediately in response to changes and data input. The visual presentation of code has shaped its own aesthetic, for example by making use of colors to highlight syntax, fonts specially designed for codes or visual tools for navigation around code blocks. Live coding is the unique opportunity to visualize processes which are being formed just in time the code runs. This technique makes a bridge between a particular process and its abstract description in the form of a code. This helps the audience to figure out the underlying processes and appreciate live programming and live coding performance, however, from the viewpoint of the psychology of programming the visualization of live code is still under-investigated.

Yet in 70's appeared systems, which have been classified as livecoding examples. In 1974, Thomas DeFanti designed GRASS ("The Graphic Symbiosis System") denoted as interactive and interpreted programming language to help artists interactively deal with and explore computer art without a constant presence and support of programmers. The main concept of GRASS was to define and manipulate vector graphic so that its users have no need to be expert programmers. Its later expanded version called "The Circle Graphics Habitat" was widely used for preparing animated educational materials, DeFanti (1976). Although a capability of music visualization was a leading feature of the system. Graphics in GRASS were programmed on-the-fly in a synchro with music and directly displayed along with codes in a resulted video. This approach gave rise to various real-time interactive computer graphics systems.

Visual forms of generative art accomplished by generative systems started to appear in the 1960's as an obvious implication of technology evolution, dissemination of computers and their useful convenience. Initially they were outputted to plotters, later with visual display units or various forms of print or video. One of the pioneers was Manfred Mohr, the author of *Artificiata I*, the collection of computer-generated artworks from 1969. The algorist, which means a generative artist using algorithms in their work, designed his own software for the purpose of presenting technique and the beauty of algorithmic art.

TurTan is another example of a live coding language. It was introduced by Gallardo et al. in 2008, based on technology of the formerly designed ReacTable by Jordà et al. in 2007, that exploits a tangible user interface (TUI) in which a user interacts with digital data through the physical environment. It is a novel and alternative paradigm to Graphical User Interface (GUI), which is broadly in use as the conventional computer interface. To bring it closer the author presents a nice example of TUI which is designed in the SandScape device exhibited at "Get in Touch" exhibition at the Ars Electronica Center in Linz (2002) and presently installed in the Children's Creativity Museum in San Francisco. The SandScape interface uses sand along with computational simulations, which together allow users to design, manipulate and understand variety of landscape models. The users can quickly construct physical models of the terrain and manipulate physical forms, then choose a real-time computational analysis on 3D viewing window and observe a projection on the surface of sand. The implementation of the SandScape uses infrared light to capture a landscape geometry. The amount of light passing through the model is being registered by a camera mounted above the model. More light passes through where the sand has less depth and less light passes through where sand forms the hills. In this way users can better and with greater ease understand spatial relationships and make GIS analysis. The illustration of the SandScape TUI one can see on vimeo: https://vimeo.com/44538789 Another research on alternative interfaces for GIS landscape analysis algorithms and simulations is described by Piper, Ratti and Ishii (2002).

TurTun is a geometric visual live coding language which was prepared for programming entertainment and creative purposes, particularly for non-programmers and children. It may help to explore basic programming concepts in a creative and playful manner. TurTan is a tangible programming language which takes the advantage of tabletop interfaces. It consists of named task blocks called tangibles, which are real-time-generated physical representations of the virtual programming instructions. One variable parameter is attached to every instruction. The user determines the parameters by the rotations applied to the corresponding tangibles. The instructions are performed while the user modifies them and the results of any instruction are presented in real time. This allows users to understand quickly their operations. The main technical concept of TurTan is the use of a projector and a camera under the tabletop surface. The system makes use of the open source tracking software designed for the ReacTable. The camera captures the user's activity, identifies and positions the objects and the fingers, and the projector is responsible for the visual output of the system, which is drawn continuously on the table surface. The output vector graphics is plotted on a virtual canvas which also can be manipulated due to some gesture recognition. Examples of some TurTun videos can be seen on vimeo: https://vimeo.com/13178171

The TurTun-like projects have inspired other novel visual/geometric live-coding systems like Scheme Bricks, Daisy Chain or Al-Jazari by Dave Griffiths. All of them are derived from Fluxus. Scheme Bricks generates visual output that shows a correspondence between sound events and the code. The visualization process makes the relationship between the code structure and sound in a way that the instruction which triggered a sound event lightens up when the sound is played. It appears very useful for performers as it allows them to locate immediately the code that generates a particular sound event.

Daisy Chain system is a visual gamepad programming language that uses a petri net model of computation and force-directed graph drawing algorithms, which are another powerful information visualization method frequently used in social sciences and humanities. To give one example of its applications, the author shall mention an open-source network analysis and visualization software called Gephi, used in a number of academic projects, journalism, social network analysis, digital humanities and elsewhere. For instance Gephi was used for network traffic visualizations of Twitter under particular social conditions or global connectivity of New York Times content.

In Daisy Chain, all instructions and activator tokens form dynamic graphs which grow. The system is designed for live coding performances to visualize interactive soundscapes. An example of a Daisy Chain visualization can be seen on youtube: https://www.youtube.com/watch?v=I2PpBdr1BV0

Al Jazari, named after a scholar and engineer who lived in XIII century and worked on plans of automatons and humanoid robots, is a live coding system based on a simple graphical language, which allows an interaction between robot characters and their movements over a virtual terrain, where cartoon depictions of robots are placed on a grid and programmed live, given a short programs for navigating them. The code that is run is being displayed, visibly floating and modified in bubbles over the robots using a game pad. Al Jazari is an installation derived from musical live coding performances dedicated for art students in south London. One of Al Jazari installations was exhibited in 2008 during Seville Biennal in the Alhambra, Granada. This version of Al Jazari was very accessible for the audience. It was designed for four users playing at once, with simplified instructions of the original performance software which enhanced users to experience live coding themselves. In order to introduce live coding to schools and familiarize people with concepts of higher level programming in recent versions Al Jazari has become an exploration of virtual worlds inspired by Minecraft. To see a sample of Al Jazari performance one can go to: https://www.youtube.com/watch?v=Uve4qStSJq4

A visual or data-flow programming is a new direction of research that has emerged from live-coding practice. To not misunderstand the notion, the author shall note that visual programming languages are not those using environments based on GUI forms, but those which make intense use of visual elements in the code. A simple example of visual programming can be a program that is notated as a graphical diagram. According to the theory of Paivio (1990) of dual coding in humans a visuospatial cognition runs parallel to linguistic cognition, where a mental imagery is a crucial support of visuospatial thought separate from language. This can be related to programming languages, in which abstract codes can be expressed simultaneously within linguistic grammar and visuospatial structures. Following this idea, live coding performance can be understood as dual activity of language and spatial perception. McLean and Wiggins (2011) also wrote about cognitive dimensions of notation, which is a framework designed to aid discussion on programming languages features, a syntactic value of colors and the role of geometry as syntax. This approach represented by Fluxus, Max/MSP and Pure Data is particularly present in the field of media arts. The name Fluxus comes from the idea of constant change in time, an act of flowing, a continuous succession of changes. It is an environment that allows users to quickly code 3D live animations and make audiovisual performances as well as change them flexibly in reaction to external input in real time. The Fluxus interface presents code and its visual output together on one screen as it is shown on Figure 3:

Using one window to build scripts and play live is a characteristic feature for most live-coding software. Fluxus can be used in an immediate mode in which there is one state stack with the current context on its top and everything is drawn once per frame. Code does not have to be called by (every-frame) function, though. Another method is a use of the build functions that create primitive objects and copy the current render state into the scene graph in a container named a scene node. Fluxus is capable to take external data in order to control the visual output. Its original purpose was a mapping sound to light VJ application. At present Fluxus can take an input from various sources, among others from a sound card or some application providing sound, keyboard, mouse, time or OSC (Open Sound Control) which is a standard protocol for networking computers, sound synthesizers and other multimedia devices. OSC has become an inherent element of programming environments and has achieved a wide use in fields including computer-based new interfaces for musical expression. It provides real-time control of sound, data exchange between computers, instruments, synthesizers, MIDI controllers. There are many implementations of OSC, like real-time sound and media processing environments, web interactivity tools or devices for sensor measurement. Due to WAN, LAN and internet communication, which is supported by OSC, it is possible to set multimedia system of a complex architecture, like wide-area and local-area networked distributed music systems. Data taken from linked system components are transformed into

Figure 3. The code and its visualization in the Fluxus
Source: own elaboration

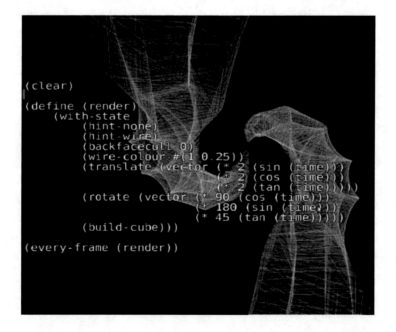

parameters used for graphical object manipulation, animations and changes in visualizations, for instance setting a new position, translation or rotation in 3D scene.

MAX/MSP and Pure Data (Pd) belong to a class of visual programming languages which are used for interactive computer music and multimedia performances. They enable visual artists, performers and researchers to create their original software graphically instead of writing lines of codes. MAX/MSP is found in dozens of educational institutions, particularly schools of arts, connects objects with virtual patches in order to generate and process interactive sound, 2D and 3D graphics, video and other visual effects. It makes technology a medium of creative expression, can work over local and remote networks integrating various kind of equipment including also wearable technology, lighting rigs or complex systems for large-scale projects. Max and Pd allow musicians and visual artists to connect via LAN as well as in dispersed parts of the world to create music and visual shows together in real time. Visual boxes called simply objects represent algorithmic functions in Pd. They are placed within a patcher or a visual canvas which is a patching window for projects. Data flow between objects is obtained through visual connections named patch cords. Each object may receive input via one or more visual inlets, generate output through visual outlet, or both, and is responsible for a particular task, which can be for example a low-level mathematical operation, audio or video function, FFT transformations or coding/decoding of video. Pd and MAX/MSP are very similar in scope and design. With the addition of the set of externals like Graphics Environment for Multimedia (GEM) which provide graphics functionality to Pd, giving support for many objects such as polygon graphics, lighting, texture mapping, camera motion and image processing, it is possible to generate and manipulate audiovisual performances in real-time including interactivity with audio, external sensors etc.

CUSTOM GENERATIVE SYSTEMS

The artist Helen Alexandra uses custom generative software to code generative algorithms in order to create real-time generative animations. She is the author of the generative system consisting of, as she describes, "moving agents that make colorful digital marks" and each time the system runs, it creates a unique animation (Pangburn, 2017). The outputs of the system are digital paintings which can be compared to still frames from a video. The artist also combines generative outcomes with traditional painting with acrylic or ink.

Another interesting generative system is Wild Growth by Chang Liu. It is an interactive processing application that generates outcomes from data gathered from registered live videos. The Wild Growth employs a live camera which records colors of natural environments when positioned toward them. The creative process of the system reminds a growth process of a wild plant situated in a digital world, which explains the name of the system.

Jonathan McCabe is a generative artist who is interested in theories of natural pattern formation and their applications to computer art and design. Completely different generative approaches can be found in his artworks, which result in a visual richness of the outcomes. In the Nervous States project each image is a map of complex dynamics, states of a system being a small neural network. The coordinates of the image pixels correspond to two variables in the connections of the network and the pixels colors are determined by the network behavior for relevant parameters. Areas of consistent colors in the resulting image represent relative stable states or gradual changes, edges present sharp jumps in states, other patterns can be complex oscillations. McCabe rendered his images using the parallel pixel processor on a graphics card supported by Brook language for modern graphics hardware. One can see an example of the outcome on Figure 4 and the collection of the artworks on flickr: https://www.flickr.com/photos/jonathanmccabe/albums/72157614673650974

The Butterfly Origami is a generative system involving four cellular automata depending on one another, so one can think of them as four layers. All four cellular automata form a sort of neural network of sixteen connections. At each time step a cell state determines its own future state looking at its neighborhood in the same layer, as well as checking the states of equivalent cells in remaining three layers. Next it changes its own state based on a table of transition rules. Moreover the rules that each cell uses can also be transformed by the past states of its recent history. The output image pixels take their red, green and blue channels from three of four layers of the system. An example of the outcome is shown on Figure 5. The system illustrates quite a philosophical issue that the way things are at present controls the rules that determine what they will become next. To see visuals of the Butterfly Origami project one can go to flickr: https://www.flickr.com/photos/jonathanmccabe/albums/72157619224237107

There exist a number of custom programming environments designed by programming artists or artists in cooperation with programmers, which aim is to generate visual representations of change over time, in particular visual forms in response to sound signals changing with time. However, all of them

Figure 4. Nervous States by Jonathan McCabe
Source: McCabe, n.d.

Figure 5.

use some standardized methods of creating sound visualization. They can be classified as symbolic representation, spectral analysis and average level indication. Symbolic representation uses graphic notation based on set of symbols. Spectral analysis employs various devices (spectrograph etc.) and mathematical tools in form of FFT to decompose sound into a number of sinusoids and then plot them on a graph. Among average level indicators one can find decibel meters (dB), peak program meter (PPM) and volume unit (VU). In 1985, Stephen Malinowski, inspired by works of Oscar Fischinger - a visual musician, designed a software which allowed communication about music through visual means. The Music Animation Machine (MAM) that he implemented was able to take information from a MIDI file and generate animated graphical scores. Malinowski said "music moves, and can be understood just by listening. But a conventional musical score stands still, and can be understood only after years of training. The Music Animation Machine bridges this gap, with a score that moves — and can be understood just by watching." (Popova, n.d.) The MAM generates various types of graphical shapes in response to data input from an MIDI file while it plays. It displays those shapes in sync with the MIDI data as well as in response to live MIDI input. The music visualization is shown horizontally, the time line is oriented left-to-right and pitch is shown bottom-to-top. Colorful displays appear on the right side of the window and move left along the time line accordingly to a pace of music piece. With usage of a special technique based on chromostereoscopy, it is possible to obtain spatial sound visualization with a depth sensation.

The music visualization allows the audience not acquainted with common music notation to understand music scores intuitively. Thus the MAM is considered a useful educational tool in the field of music and is broadly exploited during concerts, presented on conferences and exhibitions worldwide. The fragment of the concert played on the festival Sounds of Childhood in Holon, Israel 2013, is available on youtube: https://www.youtube.com/watch?v=KwcfzORcZmA (Back To The Future, Music Animation Machine Children's Concert, Holon, Israel, 2013).

Though the MAM is limited to the Windows platform and was last upgraded in 2006, it is still used for various audiovisual projects. The mobile application *Biophilia* released in 2011 by a singer and composer Björk along with interactive artist, Scott Snibb, is an interactive and extraordinary visualization to the music album of the musician inspired by the work of Malinowski. Biophilia is an innovative multimedia exploration of music, technology and nature. Each music piece of the album resembles a 3D galactic computer game. At present, Biophilia is a large-scale educational project aimed mainly at children aged 10 – 12 years and involves many scientists, artists, teachers and students. It serves as an example of dynamic collaboration between different areas in society.

Systems of real-time sound visualization arise on a base of various programming languages and graphics environments. They also cooperate with a number of peripherals and signal or data converters. The custom system, Partitura, designed by the artistic group Abstract Birds and Quayola generates on-the-fly 3D graphics which visualizes sound. The software was developed mainly with use of VVVV software and Max4Live, a customized plug-in for audio analysis. The VVVV is a hybrid textual-visual environment designed for live programming and rapid prototyping media applications which allow real-time audio, video, motion graphics and interactivity with many users simultaneously. The main property of Partitura is a capability to translate sound into visual forms, which appear along horizontal linear structure of the output window, as it is in the MAM. The visual sound representation is obtained by generating images based on a certain system of relationships between various types of geometries. Abstract elements are created just-in-time according to the sound and evolving over time while Partitura receives inputs in the form of musical structure, audio analysis or manual gestures being sent via OSC. The abstract landscapes that Partitura creates, can expand from a single dot to very complex structures. The concept of Partitura has been developed by Quayola and Sinigaglia into another generative system called Dedalo, which can be seen as an instrument "to see" the sound. This generative system is a collection of engines and tools for generating, mapping and exchange of data between a number of graphics modules and renderer. The system consists of two main submodules (graphics and system) working on two separate computers, which constantly communicate over a network and cooperate with a couple of iPads for parameters control. The system submodule is called a manager which is a repository of all parameters and their temporary states, thus controls sound analysis and provides data output. The rendered is a graphics submodule which is responsible for mapping states of parameters into specific values of graphics objects, lighting, materials and shaders. The artistic duo Abstract Birds focuses their research and work on the simultaneous generation of abstract compositions both musical and graphical based on synesthetic relationships between sound and images. They make use of modern digital technology to analyze and process sound sourcing from electronic and acoustic musical instruments, digital synthesizers etc. The whole process is based on a real-time technique, which results in rendering virtual visual forms responding to sound respectively to particular frequencies. Those dynamic graphical forms make it possible to see the sound. This becomes particularly obvious when silence seems the present aural impression. The human hearing perception is relatively limited and moreover varies among human population. Interactive audiovisual systems are experimental approaches that aim at translating sound to an image and back again as an aid for the deaf and hard of hearing in particular but not exclusively. They become instruments which smooth away such hearing imperfections, reinforce perception of soundscapes through the human body in an unusual, visual manner and also make the sound exposure and reception more objective. The instruments of this kind are employed in a field of audio-phonology, where they serve for speech signal visualizations, support early oral development diagnosis and appear particularly helpful for people with serious dysfunction of hearing apparatus as they allow their communication with the environment. Many research projects work on special interactive audiovisual systems supporting the deaf and hard of hearing to help them respond to sounds from their environment through translating the sound signals into useful visual information easy to interpret in real-time and also turn it back into sound. The project of M. Griegson (2008) from Goldsmiths College in London focused on the sound conversion into a real-time spectrogram which further was processed and modified into an image depicting a set of two-dimensional concentric rings. The visuospatial sound representation was calculated with use of the computer video hardware supported by FFT and OpenGL packages. The obtained visual pattern illustrating non-linearly spaced rings meets with neurological patterns of human visual cortex structures and mirrors human perception of audible frequencies. The system Lumisonic released by Griegson allows users two-way communication, which means the sound translation into an image, editing the image, which results in perceptually relevant changes in the sound, and re-translation back into sound signals. All is processed in real-time without significant time delay and since Lumisonic is available on iPhones, the software gives possibility to visualize sounds in any location.

Spectrographic three-dimensional sound visualizations are based on spectral analysis of audio signal. The main task of spectrographs is to convert sound frequencies into a sound spectrogram. Paul Prudence, an artist, researcher and programmer presents in his artworks the way sound, space and geometric forms emerge and unite into visual-musical experience. On the basis of information about sound frequencies transmitted from the input devices there are generated colorful graphical segments moving in the space in response to the musical pace. The generative system of sound visualization called Fast Fourier Radials (FFR) was developed in VVVV for the purpose of the live audiovisual performance on the Hactronic conference in Boston in 2007 and further upgraded. The photo-relation of the event can be seen on: https://www.flickr.com/photos/transphormetic/sets/72157606705986957/ FFR – Paul Prudence;

In 2012, during the festival of media arts, Ars Electronica in Linz the audience had a unique opportunity to not only hear but also see the music of human brain frequencies. Monitoring and reception of physiological parameters of human body is nowadays possible thanks to medical technologies such as EEG, MR, MMG. Non-visible internal human body activity becomes an interesting source of data input that control software systems generating sound and visual forms on-the-fly. Bio-interfaces which enable registering bio-signals more and more frequent are used as submodules for data input of complex generative systems exploited on dynamic interactive audiovisual spectacles. The representative of hybrid arts Joao Martinho Moura, a Portuguese artist and programmer, designed his custom generative system SuperColliderShape on the base of two visual programming environments, SuperCollider and Processing, linked together via OSC. The system was integrated with EEG bio-interface, which registered and analyzed the artist's brain signals in real-time. Next it converted inputted data into sound files and transferred them through the radio network to the main system module responsible for visualization processes. The minimalistic audiovisual translation of the sound in SuperColliderShape arose on the ground of generative algorithms, which exploit rules of self-organization in order to search for optimal spatial arrangement, see Figure 6. This is due to the SuperCollider environment, which is designed for algorithmic composition, real-time audio synthesis and interactive programming.

Figure 6. Still frame from SuperColliderShape visualization
Source: *Moura, 2011*

Generative artworks inspired by models of memory and self-organizing processes were also developed by Bogart and Pasquier (2013). Their Context Machines is a series of autonomous, conceptual image-makers with creative behavior, which manifest some cognitive processes. In fact, the output consisting of media artifacts presented to the audience is a creation of the system built by the artists, not the artists themselves, and due to complex and nondeterministic processes the visual results appear surprising. The installation involves a computer controlled camera for capturing and collecting images of the visual environment and uses computational methods in order to generate novel, creative composition.

There are plenty of generative systems examples being used in digital and media arts, which emerge and evolve on the ground of visualization techniques. Some of them has already been described by the author in *Sound and Datasets Graphical Visualizations* (2015). Every year yields new ideas, new projects and new implementations of generative systems which represent some information visualization methods not only in the area of media and visual arts but many others too. Agent-based computational modelling is broadly used in social sciences. Yet in 1996 Epstein and Axtell wrote the book "Growing artificial societies", in which they presented one of the most paradigmatic examples of the generative approach to social science. The computational model presented in the book shows a finite, heterogeneous population of autonomous agents, which compete for unequally distributed renewable resources in the plane environment represented by a two-dimensional grid. The agents are given the ability to realize various activities which characterize the human population, described precisely in a set of rules. The model is named Sugarscape as the agents' role is to collect the greatest amount of sugar, which is placed in some cells of the environment. All cells are colored accordingly to their sugar capacity. Over time one can observe among others the emergence in communication and cooperation within artificial societies. The standard Sugarscape vision system to obtain information about the world gave rise to new software systems for empirical investigations of evolving agent societies, in which agents are equipped with certain special features to meet challenges of their world. The generative systems allow researchers to study the development of the agents' behavior under varying conditions appearing in real-life situations, examples of such modelling are presented by Axtell, Epstein and Young (2001), by Epstein in his publications (2002) and (2007), and by Millington, O'Sullivan and Perry (2012). The research of evolution of agent societies and their growing communication is described by Buzing, Eiben and Schut (2005). Epstein (2014) developed his research and introduced in generative social science a new theoretical entity called agent-zero. His fourteen generative agent-based modeling animations and computational simulations with the agent-zero individual behavior that can generate various group behaviors, e.g financial panic, violence, rebellions and other complex social phenomena, are presented on internet: https://vimeopro. com/princetonuniversitypress/epstein-animations

CONCLUSION

The generative agent-based modeling allows researchers to explore and understand the dynamics of many cultural processes, past ecosystems and the operation of coupled human and natural systems. There are many challenges focused on human-environment interactions, for instance what factors drive emergence of agricultural economies, their spreading and intensification, what factors drive or constrain population growth in history etc. Generative modeling using palaeoecological data relies on process-based models in which the agents seek to fulfill some goal interacting with their environment. The agents may be individual organisms and then they may represent family groups, settlements or tribes. For example Brewer, Jackson, and Williams (2012) applied geohistorical data to ecological questions, and Wainwright (2016) used CybErosion system, which is an agent-based model representing interactions between Neolithic agriculturalists and Mesolithic hunter-gatherers and their environment. In result of the research he explored a couple of scenarios of human pressure on the landscape, which respectively can result in periods of stability or instability. Generative modeling provides tools for experiments on theory, to explore the past human-environment interactions and for testing hypothesis of the sort "what if ...?". However, the agent-based approach in this field appears useful under several conditions, among others the environment is heterogeneous in time and space and the agents interact in the decision-making process, which may be true although are not universal. Generative simulation modeling provides a useful framework to study the dynamics of multi-agent organizations, to investigate the interactions of individual heterogeneous agents through time and across space and how they produce system-level patterns. The study of a model of social coherence in multi-agent organizations is presented in Martinez, Kwiatkowski and Pasquier (2011). This approach is increasingly being applied to study social and environmental systems along with their two-way interactions.

There are radically new representational techniques unique to own time - in the era of information overload. Frequently non-deterministic algorithms play a significant role in generative systems. Such systems enable dynamic visualizations having a non-deterministic component. Generating artifacts using stochastic process can produce endless interesting and meaningful outputs. Stochastic processes refer to those where the system looks at the average and then codifies the average and the best approach. Such systems, unlike static models, are focused on computational logic and they constitute an open system, which Marius Watz described as "a group of interacting, interrelated, or interdependent elements forming a complex whole" (Pearson, 2011). They are composed of interconnected agents, as a whole generating a complex behavior that is not obvious regarding the properties of the individual agents. In this model certain emergent properties are exhibited as a result. It allows users to establish relations between patterns, forms, structures, processes and to model evolutionary behaviors. This technique enables not only to simulate real-world phenomena, particularly fed by large amounts of dynamically generated semantically-rich data and providing high-quality, realistic examples. There arise various projects like frameworks modeling the real-time energy system behavior (Open Energy or Internet of Energy), the complexity of cities (Internet of Cities) which help to understand dynamic cities, and other data driven responsive environments of urban data visualization category. The model usually consists of multiple interconnected layers and its computation is distributed in urban infrastructure. It includes sensing technology that allows the monitoring of different urban, energy, environmental parameters. Large amount of data generated, explored and analyzed via this technology forms visual representation which allow users to reveal new dynamics of behavior in the city. The confluence between the city and the data leads to a new concept of *real-time city* in which the citizens can influence their patterns of behavior in relation to the dynamic information systems with an evolutionary and auto adaptive dimension. *Real-time city* can influence evolution of cities and generate new forms of participation, analysis, governance and information management. LIVE Singapore! is an interdisciplinary *real-time city* project that presents five different urban views of Singapore dynamic which is graphically visualized based on selected digital data generated by people in Singapore and their actions. The project involves vast system of communication devices, sensors and microcontrollers commonly present in urban environment. The data recorded and captured in real-time is then analyzed and the obtained information is mapped onto multi-dimensional maps of Singapore showing interesting mobility, economic and social patterns. The mentioned example of generative systems including non-deterministic components demonstrates the potential of the technology of visualizing so called processuality (the notion introduced by Bruce Sterling) and a new form of visual language.

REFERENCES

Axtell, R., Epstein, J. M., & Young, H. P. (2001). The Emergence of Economic Classes in an Agent-Based Bargaining Model. In S. In Durlauf & H. P. Young (Eds.), *Social Dynamics*. Cambridge, MA: MIT Press.

Bogart, B. D. R., & Pasquier, P. (2013). Context Machines: A Series of Situated and Self-Organizing Artworks. *Leonardo*, *46*(2), 114–122. doi:10.1162/LEON_a_00525

Brewer, S., Jackson, S. T., & Williams, J. W. (2012). Paleoecoinformatics: applying geohistorical data to ecological questions. In *Trends in ecology and evolution* (vol. 27, Issue 2, pp. 104–112). Retrieved February 24, 2017 from http://www.cell.com/trends/ecology-evolution/fulltext/S0169-5347(11)00269-2

Buzing, P., Eiben, A., & Schut, M. (2005). Emerging communication and cooperation in evolving agent societies. *Journal of Artificial Societies and Social Simulation*, *8*(1), 2. Retrieved from http://jasss.soc.surrey.ac.uk/8/1/2.html

Calvano, M. (2016). Models for Design: From Geometries to Generative Algorithms. In Handbook of Research on Visual Computing and Emerging Geometrical Design Tools (pp. 825-855). IGI Global.

Cohen, H. (1995). The further exploits of Aaron, painter. *Stanford Humanities Review*, *4*(2), 141–158.

DeFanti, T. A. (1976). The digital component of the circle graphics habitat. In *National Computer Conference* (pp. 195-203). Retrieved August 10, 2015 from http://excelsior.biosci.ohio-state.edu/~carlson/history/PDFs/cgh-defanti.pdf

Dennett, D. (2009). *Intentional Systems Theory*. Retrieved July 24, 2017 from https://ase.tufts.edu/cogstud/dennett/papers/intentionalsystems.pdf

Epstein, J.M., (1996). *Growing artificial societies: Social Science From the Bottom Up (Complex Adaptive Systems)*. Brookings Institution Press and MIT Press.

Epstein, J. M. (2002). Modeling civil violence: An agent-based computational approach. In *PNAS* (vol. 99, suppl. 3, 7242). Retrieved February 25, 2017 from http://www.pnas.org/content/99/suppl_3/7243.full.pdf

Epstein, J. M. (2007). *Generative Social Science: Studies in Agent-Based Computational Modeling*. Princeton University.

Epstein, J. M. (2014). *Agent_Zero: Toward Neurocognitive Foundations for Generative Social Science*. Princeton University.

Ferber, J. (1994). Simulating with Reactive Agents. In E. Hillebrand & J. Stender (Eds.), *Many Agent Simulation and Artificial Life* (pp. 8–28). Amsterdam: IOS Press.

Galanter, P. (2006). *Generative art and rules-based art*. Retrieved July 24, 2017 from http://vagueterrain.net/

Gallardo, D., Julià, C. F., & Jordà, S. (2008). *TurTan: a Tangible Programming Language for Creative Exploration*. Third annual IEEE international workshop on horizontal human-computer systems (TABLETOP). doi:10.1109/TABLETOP.2008.4660189

Gardner, M. (1970). Mathematical Games. *Scientific American, 223*, 120-123.

Grierson, M. (2008). Making music with images: Interactive audiovisual performance systems for the deaf. In *Proceedings of 7th ICDVRAT with ArtAbilitation*. Retrieved August 10, 2015 from http://doc.gold.ac.uk/~mus02mg/wp-content/uploads/m-grierson-icdvrat_artabilitation_2008_submissiondoc.pdf

Hopkins, D. (2006). *Multi Player SimCity for X11 TCL/Tk running on SGI Indigo workstation*. Retrieved from https://commons.wikimedia.org/w/index.php?search=simcity&title=Special:Search&go=Go&searchToken=69rsbzp0coqdrn4b8qst7y6po#/media/File:SimCity-Indigo.gif

Manovich, L. (2008). *Introduction to Info-Aesthetics*. Retrieved September 22, 2017 from http://manovich.net/content/04-projects/060-introduction-to-info-aesthetics/57-article-2008.pdf

Martinez, E., Kwiatkowski, I., & Pasquier, P. (2011). *Towards a Model of Social Coherence in Multi-Agent Organizations*. Springer.

McCabe, J. (n.d.). *Nervous States*. Retrieved from https://www.flickr.com/photos/jonathanmccabe/albums/72157614673650974

McCabe, J. (n.d.). *Origami butterfly_0076*. Retrieved from https://www.flickr.com/photos/jonathanmccabe/albums/72157619224237107

McLean, A., & Wiggins, G. (2011). *Texture: Visual Notation for Live Coding of Pattern*. Centre for Cognition, Computation and Culture Department of Computing Goldsmiths, University of London.

Millington, J. D. A., O'Sullivan, D., & Perry, G. L. W. (2012). Model histories: Narrative explanation in generative simulation modelling. *Geoforum, 43*(6), 1025–1034. doi:10.1016/j.geoforum.2012.06.017

Moura, J. M. (2011). *Joao Martinho Moura*. Retrieved from http://jmartinho.net/

Nassery, F., Sikorski, P. (2015). New possibilities of using processing and modern methods of the "generative art" graphics in architecture. *Technical Transactions Architecture, 4-A/2015.*

Nowosad, I. (2015). *Sound and Datasets graphical visualizations.* Fides, Ratio et Patria. In *Studia Toruńskie* (no. 3, pp. 82-98). Academic Press.

Nwana, H. S. (1996). Software Agents: An Overview. *The Knowledge Engineering Review, 11*(3), 1–40. doi:10.1017/S026988890000789X

Paivio, A. (1990). *Mental Representations: A Dual Coding Approach.* Oxford University Press. doi:10.1093/acprof:oso/9780195066661.001.0001

Pangburn, D. D. (2017). *Generative Algorithms and Acrylic Paint Create Profound Digital Paintings.* Retrieved from https://creators.vice.com/en_us/article/78e5qb/generative-paintings-acrylic-algorithms-helen-alexandra

Pearson, M. (2011). *Generative Art: A practical guide using Processing.* Manning Publications.

Perry, G. L. W., Wainwright, J., Etherington, T. R., & Wilmshurst, J. M. (2016, October). Experimental Simulation: Using Generative Modeling and Palaeoecological Data to Understand Human-Environment Interactions. *Frontiers in Ecology and Evolution, 13.* Retrieved from http://journal.frontiersin.org/article/10.3389/fevo.2016.00109/full

Piper, B., Ratti, C., & Ishii, H. (2002). Illuminating Clay: A Tangible Interface with potential GRASS applications. *Proceedings of the Open source GIS - GRASS users.* doi:10.1145/503376.503439

Popova, M. (n.d.). *The Music Animation Machine.* Retrieved from https://www.brainpickings.org/2010/11/09/stephen-malinowski-music-animation-machine/

Sorensen, A., & Gardner, H. (2010). Programming With Time. Cyber-physical programming with Impromptu. *ACM SIGPLAN Notices, 45*(10), 822–834. doi:10.1145/1932682.1869526

8. vo. (2005). *On the outside.* Lars Müller Publishers.

Watts, A. (1958). *Nature, Man and Woman.* New York: Vintage Books.

Wishart, D. S., Yang, R., Arndt, D., Tang, P., & Cruz, J. (2004). Dynamic cellular automata: an alternative approach to cellular simulation. In Silico Biology 4, 0015. Bioinformation Systems e.V.

ADDITIONAL READING

Grierson, M. (2005). *Audiovisual Composition*. Retrieved July 25, 2017 from http://www.strangeloop.co.uk/Dr.%20M.Grierson%20-%20Audiovisual%20Composition%20Thesis.pdf

Wolfram, S. (1984). Computational Theory of Cellular Automata. *Communications in Mathematical Physics*, *96*(1), 15–57. doi:10.1007/BF01217347

Chapter 15
Social Context:
Visualisation of Cooperation – Evidence–Based Medicine in Neurorehabilitation

Emilia Mikołajewska
Nicolaus Copernicus University, Poland

Tomasz Komendziński
Nicolaus Copernicus University, Poland

Dariusz Mikołajewski
Kazimierz Wielki University, Poland & Nicolaus Copernicus University, Poland

ABSTRACT

Evidence-based medicine (EBM) and Evidence-based practice (EBP) are sets of standards and procedures created to search, verify, and select up-to-date findings implemented by medical staff as a basis for decision-making process in a daily clinical practice. Despite efforts of scientists and clinicians, neurorehabiltiation is regarded as a difficult area for EBM/EBP practices due to huge diversity of cases, clinical pictures, interventions, and scientific methodologies. More advanced tasks, including application of brain-computer interfaces and neuroprosteheses, show the need for a new approach from medical practitioners. This chapter presents challenges, barriers, and solutions in the aforementioned area based on the personal experiences of the authors. Visualisation tools provide cognitive support for social context, cooperation patterns, and data interpretation. Taking into consideration that social issues may extend the visibility of the results and allow for easier dissemination of the results, the aim was to show how visualisation helps identify cooperation networks and disseminate research results.

INTRODUCTION

Evidence Based Medicine (EBM) and Evidence Based Practice (EBP) are sets of standards and procedures created to search, verify and select up-to-date findings implemented by medical staff as a basis for decision-making process in a daily clinical practice. Cause of emergence of EBM has been significant increasing of data flow (e.g. easier access to electronic databases of medical articles). There become

DOI: 10.4018/978-1-5225-4990-1.ch015

hard to distinguish reliable and unreliable medical evidences. As a result - there was hard to develop medical knowledge of the staff. The priority become selection and elimination unreliable findings at the beginning. It was noticed, that rehabilitation methods should be as reliable as other methods in clinical use. Concept Evidence Based Medicine licked into shape Evidence Based Practice (Bridges et al. 2007; Dean-Baar & Pakieser-Reed 2004).

The following chapter presents challenges, barriers, and solutions in the aforementioned area based on the personal experiences of the authors. Chapter begins from familiarizing of fundamentals of EBM/EBP, including also debate with opponents. Paper contains also outcomes of the own research, their useful visualizations, and results of practical implementation of EBM/EBP based on experience and findings in Poland and abroad. Vizualization tools provide cognitive support for pattern recognition and data interpretation toward usable information and knowledge (Osińska & Bala 2015, Osińska 2011). Our aim was to show how visualisation helps identify co-operation networks and disseminate research results.

BACKROUND: EVIDENCE BASED MEDICINE IN NEUROREHABILITATION – STATE OF THE ART

Neurological diseases are popular in main population and constitute one of the main cause of disability in adult people. Interdisciplinary rehabilitation teams deal with neurologically disabled patients applying the newest methods, drugs, and approaches to rehabilitation process (Członkowska & Sarzyńska-Długosz 2002). Rehabilitation should start as early as possible (Hömberg 2010). Integrative neurorehabilitation science based on dedicated rehabilitation research focused on neurorehabilitation is necessary (Kwakkel 2009; Gillen 2010). Therapeutic procedures should be evidence-based and modified to find patient-tailored solutions. General rules derived from neuroscience confirm their usefulness in designing new therapeutic techniques in neurorehabilitation. (Hömberg 2010).

Searching and reading the research literature seem be essential activities for enhancing the use of research and optimizing the quality of current clinical practice in neurorehabiltiation (figure 1). From the other hand neurorehabilitation is regarded very hard area for EBM/EBP practices, especially due to huge diversity of cases, their clinical pictures, interventions, and scientific methodologies. Thus neurorehabilitation may be perceived clinical area with lacking evidences (Grimmer-Somers et al. 2007; Iles & Davidson 2006).

Enormous growth of knowledge in the neurosciences may cause significant progress in neurorehabilitation. EBM/EBP is a complex process that can be facilitated by the use of the Knowledge to Action Process model. It provides a sequence of phases for researchers and clinicians to follow in order to optimize knowledge translation (KT) across various fields of practice. Thus our ultimate aim is creating effective KT interventions to increase clinicians' knowledge and use of EBM/EBP among for clinicians, health care managers, and researchers (figure 2). Clinical application of the new tool/method, approach requires research on its:

- Reliability (interrater reliability, intrarater-reliability, test-retest reliability, etc.), i.e. measurement error associated with an instrument,
- Validity, i.e. extent to which an instrument measures itself in the absence of the "gold standard" (including compartmental studies with other existing clinical scores and scales),

- Responsiveness, i.e. minimal degree of change that is clinically significant (including *floor effect* and *ceiling effect*),
- Acceptability to patients and assessors (Prokopowicz et al. 2017; Jette et al. 2003; Stevenson et al. 2004; Palfreyman et al. 2003).

Despite many challenges in the implementation of evidence in neurorehabilitation the increasing use of EBM/EBP concepts and an early KT from the neurosciences into everyday clinical neurorehabilitation practice contribute to therapeutic advances, providing further occupations for enhancing results of neurorehabilitation (Ramírez-Vélez et al. 2015; Teasell 2012; Pereira et al. 2012; Hömberg 2010; Petzold et al. 2010; Sackett et al. 1996; Rosenberg & Donald 1995).

Scientists and clinicians should be aware general situation concerning publications in rehabilitation and physical therapy. Widely discussed review by Shadgan et al. showed 100 top-cited English language articles from 30 rehabilitation dedicated journals published between 1959 and 2002. Average citations per article was 200, ranging from 131 to 1109. The most common fields of the study were neurorehabilitation (41%), disability (19%), and biomechanics (18%). The most common article type was original article (84%), prospective (76%) case series studies (67%) on humans, what more 67% articles was published in the USA (Shadgan et al. 2010). Partial key may be also characteristics of bibliometric indicators and analysis of associated information. Review by Franchignoni et al. showed scientific productivity of 24 randomly selected leading European authors of publications in the area of physical medicine and reahabilitation (PM&R). Median values of their bibliometric parameters were not high: number of publication: 31 (Web od Science - WoS), 46 (Publish or Perish - PoP), number of citations: respectively 171 and 317, Hirsch index: respectively 6.5 and 8.5 (Franchignoni et al. 2011). Deeper assessment may show causes of such situation. Gender gap within peer-reviewed publication productivity in physical therapy were reported by Kaufman & Chewan: 0.51-0.58 fewer articles per year for women than for men was observed (Kaufman & Chewan 2011). Study by Ahmed et al. assessed top cited ((≥50, WoS) articles concerning disability published between 1980 and 2015. Collaborative studies enjoy wider citation, what

Figure 1. Hierarchy of evidences according to EBM/EBP paradigm

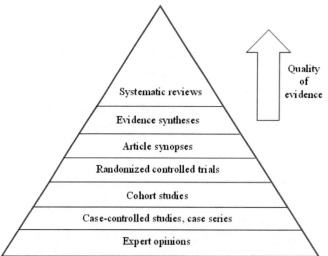

Figure 2. Sources of evidence for patient-centred evidence-based practice (Rycroft-Molone et al. 2003)

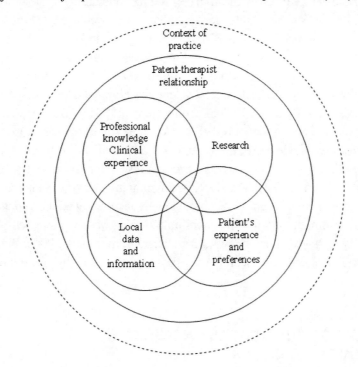

more articles with 11 to 20 pages were the most often cited (Ahmed 2016). True may be an assumption that collaboration increases influence of publication, thus co-author network may be important factor.

EVIDENCE BASED MEDICINE IN NEUROREHABILITATION - BARRIERS

Scientists and clinicians can try subjectively, not always directly, assess the effectiveness of EBM/EBP implementation in neurorehabiltiation .There may be defined three primary areas of limitations to physical therapists' implementation of EBM/EBP

- **Organizational Barriers:** Support and resources,
- **Practitioner Barriers:** Education, attitudes and beliefs, interest and perceived role, and self-efficacy,
- **Technical Barriers:** Quick development of innovative solutions requiring randomized controlled trials covering their efficacy, long-term effects observations, and clinical guidelines (Brandt & Bertram 2016; Sidiakina et al. 2015).

The most valuable clinical trials face problems of recruitment, retention, treatment fidelity, outcome measure selection, and control intervention selection. A problem may constitute even such basic factor as within-group homogeneity which contributes to successful conduct of a clinical trial.

Lack of education, negative perceptions about research and physical therapists' role in EBM/EBP, and low self-efficacy to perform EBM/EBP activities represent barriers to implementing them into neurorehabilitation that can be addressed through continuing education. Organizational provision of access to Web-based resources is likely insufficient to enhance research use by clinicians: despite Internet access at work for 80% of respondents, only 8% were given protected work time to search and appraise the literature (Salbach et al. 2010; Salbach et al. 2009; Salbach et al. 2007).

The evidence base on neurorehabilitation is often limited and clear definitions are lacking. The observed spread in opinion may reflect the absence of clear guidelines and knowledge in the particular area and need for further research (Lynch et al. 2017; Sjöholm et al. 2011). But EBM/EBP paradigm is not obvious: despite lack of clear agreement only 19% stroke care professionals required a large randomized controlled trial or a systematic review to be convinced of early mobilization after stroke benefits (Sjöholm et al. 2011). From the other hand awareness of an ongoing research trials among professionals may lead to changes in opinions before the efficacy of the experimental intervention is known (Lynch et al. 2017).

General tendency may be unfavorable. Recent review by Jesus showed discrepancy between number of clinical trials and systematic reviews in rehabilitation. Number of published yearly clinical trials increased, while number of systematic reviews did not change since early 1990s. What important neurologic conditions (particularly cerebrovascular) were the most addressed by aforementioned publications (Jesus 2016).

SOCIAL CONTEXT OF PUBLICATION IN MEDICAL AND ALLIED HEALTH SCIENCES

The social context must respond to the transformation in society due to global changes: environmental, cultural, technological, etc. Digital change may shorten distance between research and publication, but easier way may result in thousands of scientific publications a day. Current research should be more effectively disseminated and showed impact on state-of the-art to play a significant role in the global scientific discussion and development. Long lifespan and chances of survival have only the best of them. Aforementioned approach is linked with the model of science development chosen to follow. Popular scientists want to maintain their position, but more and more younger scientists want share similar achievements and lifestyle. The social analysis cannot remain marginal to global change concerning research. Despite pitfalls and mistakes, we need to find a path toward a more secure and sustainable development of science in the future. Some phenomenon within current system cannot be understood only by measuring traditional bibliometric parameters. Purely technical details may diminish the main issue, uneven and inadequate elsewhere. Qualitative and quantitative studies need for novel methods and tools. Pressure on science to be relevant may fall heavily. Priorities and mainstreams may differ across the region. Traditional scientific paradigms and approaches may be increasingly distrusted and questioned. Interdisciplinary approaches with the capacity to investigate changes may help solve them. Thus current social analysis should be interconnected with a multitude of other point of view to the same question. No doubt interdisciplinary programmes and policymaking should be related to sound, independent research.

In the past the single-author paper was the common habit, but over the past decades, the average number of authors on scientific articles has drastically increased (Borry et al. 2006). Contemporary scientific success may be significantly influenced by cooperation and competition thus research collaboration occurs more frequently now than in the past. Levsky et al showed that number of authors per medical article increased from 4.66 to 5.73 between 1995 and 2005 (Levsky et al. 2007). But multiauthored publications have also disadvantages, e.g. in some disciplines authors publishing more often as first authors have fewer publications in the short period of time than authors publishing more often as last authors (Wardil & Hauert 2015). This may show variety of possible strategies applied by scientists/ authors and evolution of cooperation in multi-authored publications. From the other hand rule that number of publications and citations is a principal factor for scientific career advancement may lead to natural selection of poorer science. Poor research design and data analysis is probably quicker and simpler. Rewarding full understanding instead of rewarding knowledge is hard but possible, e.g thanks to computational analysis of data sets showing potential correlations and gaps within current theories (Smaldino & McElreath 2016). Study by Slone (Slone 2016) showed that despite over half of the papers published in the American Journal of Roentgenology (AJR) have five or more coauthors, the first two authors made almost all of work in almost all researched papers. Honorary authorship is still discussed (Bonekamp et al. 2012, Eisenberg et al. 2014). Aforementioned trends are still challenges for the editors of journals. Moreover there is expected gender revolution: during the last 3 decades, the proportion of women authoring manuscripts in the 3 major general dermatology journals increased from 12% to 48% (Feramisco et al. 2009). There are proposed alternative indicators for progress in the field of publication: e.g. number of publications listed in the particular classification of the top publication in the particular medical discipline during recent years/decades (Bas et al. 2011). From the other hand study by Abu-Dawas et al. showed that despite an increase in quantitative research productivity of Gulf countries over the last 3 years, no increase in quality of research publications was noted based on the mean reports of mean journal IF (Abu-Dawas et al. 2015).

EVIDENCE BASED MEDICINE IN NEUROREHABILITATION:SOLUTIONS

We need to begin from identification of characteristics that are associated with writing, searching or reading the research literature among physical therapists involved in neurorehabilitation. Results may point modifiable practitioner characteristics, including self-efficacy for implementing EBM/EBP and participation in research, appear to be key determinants of EBM/EBP. Own studies will focus on afore-mentioned factors.

Own Studies

Publication analysis may help find collaborators, identify main trends and find your own scientific way/ field. Our own study will show if previous studies concerning scarce evidence in neurorehabilitation were right. It is worth noting and comprehend current status in this field. First of all 45% top cited rehabilitation journals strictly covers field of neurorehabilitation or any subfield (e.g. stroke rehabilitation)[1], all of them publish articles in English only. Six main bibliographic databases was searched. The most of articles concern orthopedic rehabilitation, next neurorehabilitation and pulmonary rehabilitation (figure 3).

Article type influences the strength of evidence. The most common are reviews, then clinical trials and comparative studies (figure 4).

Demands for evidences may miss needs. Where are there needs located? Figure 5 shows the most common searches within neurorehabilitation publication versus number of publications. The most frequent topic is stroke neurorehabilitation.

The most common are articles concerning adult patients. The most popular age of patients are:

Figure 3. The percentage proportion of covered topics by publications analyzed within six main bibliographic databases

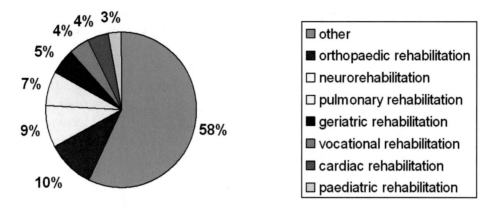

Figure 4. The percentage proportion of types of articles concerning neurorehabilitation analyzed within six main bibliographic databases

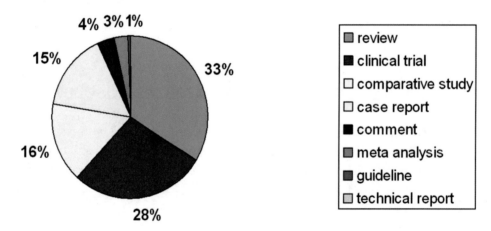

- **Adults Aged 65+ Years:** 8132 publications,
- **Adults Aged 19-44 Years:** 7509 publications,
- **Children (Birth-18 Years):** 2696 publications (while infants: birth-23 months: only 446 publications).

Compartmental study of co-author networks of four European specialists in neuroscience or neurorehabilitation show figures 6-9. Used data sets were gathered by Harzing's Publish or Perish ver. 5.28 (bibtex files) (Harzing, 2016) analyzed using Science of Science (Sci2) Tool (Sci2 Team, 2009; Börner & Polley 2014). Information on the similarity/distance/co-author weights is used to calculate node positions and distances. Similar nodes are proximal. More publications and more citations were associated with number of nodes and structure and density of connections with co-authors. Four GUESS layouts were selected: a) traditional, b) circular, c) GEM (Generalized Expectation Maximalization, Gupta & Chen 2010, Einicke 2012), d) MDS (Multidimensional Scaling, Cox & Cox 2001). Layout menu and

Figure 5. The most common searches within neurorehabilitation publication versus number of publications

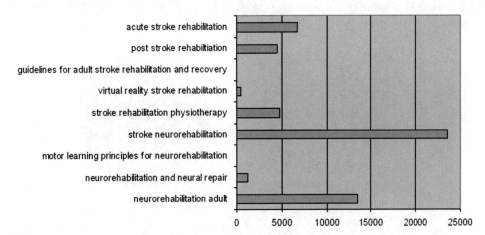

BinPack use allows to "pack" the nodes more closely in space. Node degree shows the number of each individual's co-authors. MDS layout shows graph where node-node distances are defined by the connecting edge weight (co-occurrence frequencies). GEM shows projects more frequently acknowledged together in publications.

Reader should obtain from the graphs orientation concerning number of co-authors and frequency of co-operation. It seems even top level of publications is achievable for specialists in neurorehabilitation. But no doubt such achievements are rare and remarkable. Figures 6-9 provide increased information about the structure and direction of co-operation within research being done. Further enhanced analysis may increase aforementioned information to past successes (the most cited researchers, affiliations, collaborations, and topics/areas of research) and future chances (frequently cited but rarely studied issues, occupations for future collaboration, etc.). Enormous number, diversity and complexity of diseases and injuries in neurorehabilitation makes particularly important that specialists in neurorehabilitation and neuroscience research, and scientists in the biomedical field in general (including biocybernetics and biomedical engineers) should pay particular attention to collaborate through resource sharing, exchange of ideas and knowledge dissemination, as far as information acquisition and analysis. No doubt scientists belonging to different institutions (countries, research areas) should be encouraged to collaborate. Focusing studies on diverse key issues accompanied by reasonable interdisciplinary suggestions, polices, and evidences may help to effectively diagnose, prevent, treat, rehabilitate and care (Huang & Huang 2006, Strotmann et al. 2009, Wu & Duan 2015, Morris &Yen 2004, Leydesdorff 2007).

DISCUSSION

Wider dissemination and increased visibility of evidences in neurorehabilitation need for interdisciplinary studies and denser network of co-authors. Despite unquestionable quality of studies social issues remain very important. It may provide strengthening position of the EBM-based neurorehabilitation.

Individualization of therapy in neurorehabilitation creates severe limitations of scientific and clinical research. Even such relatively basic factors as hard to assess similar knowledge and experience of the

Figure 6. Neuroscience publications co-author network of worldwide recognized expert in neuroscience, 980 papers, h=90, 30021 citations. Layouts: a) traditional, b) circular, c) GEM, d) MDS.

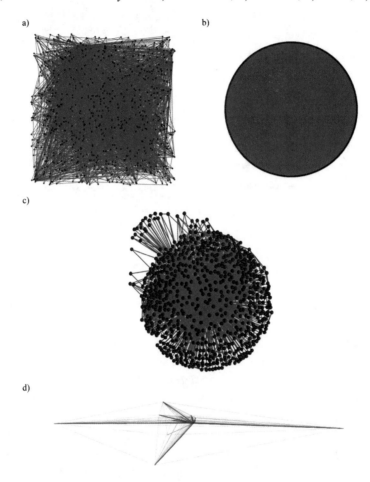

therapists or environment and of exercises may influence results of the study. Various societal and cultural needs of the patients may create diverse context of the treatment (Doucet 2013). Increasing number of RCTs may lead to misunderstanding: review by McIntyre et al. showed that number of RCTs in stroke rehabilitation have increased over the past forty years with an associated increase in methodological quality, but not sample size (McIntyre et al. 2014). Moreover careful analysis of publications may cause confusion or malfunction: recommendations may be separated for target variables and time after accident thus huge specific knowledge and experience is needed to incorporate them into the particular neurorehabilitation programme. E.g. Dohle et al. showed that in the area of functional restoration of gait in post-stroke survivors:

- Many factors, including pathophysiological insights into functional restoration of stance and gait after stroke should be taken into consideration,
- Gait velocity may be improved by intensive gait training, including incorporation of rehabilitation robots,

Figure 7. Neuroscience publications co-author network of worldwide recognized expert in neuroscience, 352 papers, h=71, 26928 citations. Layouts: a) traditional, b) circular, c) GEM, d) MDS.

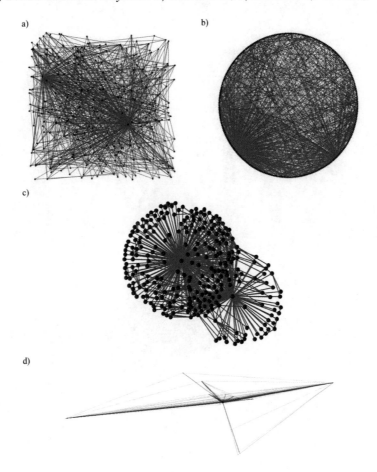

- Gait distance can be improved by aerobic endurance exercises (with a cardiovascular effect) in a functional context,
- Balance may be improved by intensive functional gait training.
- Functionally relevant training program may incorporate additional stimulation techniques (Dohle et al. 2016).

EBM/EBP did not answer all our questions (Tilson et al. 2008; Timio & Antiseri 2000; Turner & Whitfield 1997). Action observation treatment (AOT), derived from neurophysiology, constitutes novel but not explored approach in neurorehabilitation where patients observe an action and then execute it in context (Buccino 2014). Such reducing the evidence-practice gaps requires active management strategies (Walker et al. 2013).

DIRECTIONS FOR FUTURE RESEARCH

Professor Henry Markram established following challenges for neuroscience:

Figure 8. Neurorehabilitation publications co-author network of European scientists, authority in neuro-rehabilitation, 391 papers, h=69, 20130 citations. Layouts: a) traditional, b) circular, c) GEM, d) MDS.

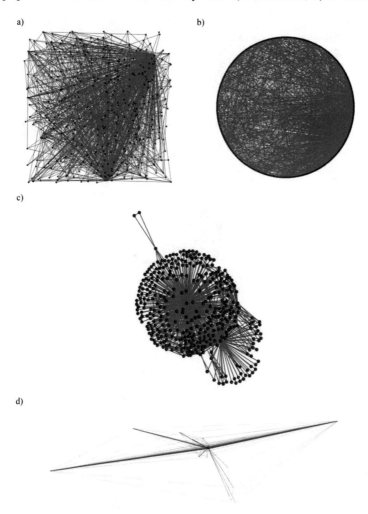

- Big teams alble to solve the big problems,
- Interlinked sets of data providing a complete picture of single areas of the brain at their different levels of organization,
- Efficient predictive tools,
- Hardware and software powerful to simulate the brain,
- New ways of classifying and simulating brain disease, leading to better diagnosis and more effective drug discovery,
- Brain-inspired technologies, with potentially huge benefits for industry and for society,
- Public awareness and support for neuroscience, associated research and possible benefits (Markram 2013).

Figure 9. Neurorehabilitation publications co-author network of Polish scientists, specialist in neuro-rehabilitation, 216 papers, h=10, 564 citations. Layouts: a) traditional, b) circular, c) GEM, d) MDS.

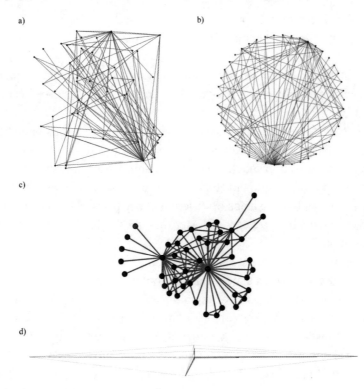

Similar challenges for neurorehabilitation were established by Harris and Winstein:

- Primary and secondary prevention, including secondary prevention of lifestyle-related diseases and participation,
- Simple, environmentally relevant predictive measures,
- Cooperation of clinicians and researchers to provide deeper understanding processes such as exercise-induced brain plasticity effects via neuroimaging,
- Interdisciplinary cooperation on advances in mindful health and patient-centered clinical practice (Harris & Winstein 2017).

Neurorehabilitation focus on decreasing impairment and improving function toward higher health-related quality of life. Clinical evidence for most neurorehabilitative treatments is still sparse. Interventions (both conventional and modern)) are usually optimized toward needs of specific target groups of patients. The best direction of further research seems be better understanding of the neuroscience of self-healing and stimulated recovery coupled with outcomes from small-scale and well-focused clinical trials (Luft 2012).

Low number of the clinical trials to testing efficacy and effectiveness of therapeutic interventions within neurorehabiltiation constitutes huge problem. Our ultimate goal is to increase effectiveness of neurorehabilitation. There is need for three-fold development of existing approaches:

- Development and validation of instruments quantitatively and qualitatively measuring functional outcomes,
- Dissemination of research that supports particular methods,
- Disseminate negative outcomes confirming lack of efficacy.

Academic-clinical alliances, objective assessment of evaluation and intervention methods, education of practitioners, and evidence-driven everyday clinical practice would be the best solution for current problems (Doucet 2013).

Visualization technology should be used to track scientists from various branches in neurorehabilitation research, and look for possible associations and occupations to co-operate with the most fruitful scientists. Topic-related visualization should be used to acquire more valuable information, identify the most popular issues, and promote rapid development of rare research areas. Exploring the knowledge domain of publications thanks to crossmaps of different entity pairs, should be complemented by identification of front timelines and base reference cluster timelines (Khosrow-Pour et al. 2016, Byrne et al. 2015, Rosiek & Leksowski 2016).

Unification of tools and methods in not always possible. Scientists and clinicians should be aware of differences between studies. It is worth a mention, that tool or method without evidence-based efficacy (or which did not show superiority) is not always non-effective (due to e.g. methodological problems) – scientists need to find them and provide doubtless evidences (Liepert 2012; Pereira et al. 2012).

Neurorehabilitation constitutes unique challenge due to the complexity of human nervous system (associated physiological and pathological motor and cognitive processes/responses), variability of interventions and wealth of clinical/research staff interaction. Variety of kinds and levels of impairment is remarkable as far as their causes: usually most patients have had a stroke, but other traumatic brain injuries, spinal cord injuries, severe poisonings, metabolic diseases, damaged nerves, etc. Thus translation of evidence to clinical practice and the improvement of patient outcomes and qualify of life requires close partnerships of scientists, clinicians, and administrators (Behrman et al. 2013). Three international solutions were described so far by Walker et al.:

- Development of an evidence-based consensus document combined with qualitative and quantitative methods (England),
- Research program covering synthesis of evidence, creation of user friendly information, and development of multimodal knowledge transfer strategies (Canada),
- Multistep process covering audit, feedback, identification of barriers, and tailored education (Australia) (Walker et al. 2013).

Proposed approach to vizualization of social co-author networks in neurorehabilitation is still at the beginning of its development. There is need for development of the most efficient tools, simple and practical in everyday use. Thus compartmental studies will be useful in the future. There is lack of one predominant approach to vizualization of the aforementioned data sets, thus careful tests and dedicated software modernization may be necessary, even as third party visualization tools supported by existing software, e.g. PoP 5.

CONCLUSION

There is a discrepancy between scientific research, current knowledge, and need of clinical practitioners. Positive attitude to EBM/EBP in neurorehabiltiation and interest of medical staff in learning about or improving the skills are necessary to adopt EBM/EBP in their clinical practice. More guidelines, RCTs, and research concerning long-term results of the particular neurorehabilitation programmes (approaches, tools, etc.) would be very valuable. New goals associated with patient-tailored therapy need new and more precise diagnostic tools, which can be the main challenge for scientists and clinicians from the aforementioned areas. Taking into consideration social issues thanks to application of visualization tools may extend visibility of results and allow for easier dissemination of results.

ACKNOWLEDGMENT

This work was conducted as a part of work within the InteRDoCTor project.

REFERENCES

Abu-Dawas, R. B., Mallick, M. A., Hamadah, R. E., Kharraz, R. H., Chamseddin, R. A., Khan, T. A., & Rohra, D. K. et al. (2015). Comparative analysis of quantity and quality of biomedical publications in Gulf Cooperation Council countries from 2011-2013. *Saudi Medical Journal*, *36*(9), 1103–1109. doi:10.15537/smj.2015.9.12369 PMID:26318469

Ahmed, A., Adam, M., Ghafar, N. A., Muhammad, M., & Ebrahim, N. A. (2016). Impact of article page count and number of authors on citations in disability related fields: A systematic review article. *Iranian Journal of Public Health*, *45*(9), 1118–1125. PMID:27957456

Bas, K., Dayangac, M., Yaprak, O., Yuzer, Y., & Tokat, Y. (2011). International collaboration of Turkey in liver transplantation research: A bibliometric analysis. *Transplantation Proceedings*, *43*(10), 3796–3801. doi:10.1016/j.transproceed.2011.09.081 PMID:22172849

Behrman, A. L., Bowden, M. G., & Rose, D. K. (2013). Clinical trials in neurorehabilitation. *Handbook of Clinical Neurology*, *110*, 61–66. doi:10.1016/B978-0-444-52901-5.00005-8 PMID:23312630

Bonekamp, S., Halappa, V. G., Corona-Villalobos, C. P., Mensa, M., Eng, J., Lewin, J. S., & Kamel, I. R. (2012). Prevalence of honorary coauthorship in the American Journal of Roentgenology. *AJR. American Journal of Roentgenology*, *198*(6), 1247–1255. doi:10.2214/AJR.11.8253 PMID:22623536

Börner, K., & Polley, D. E. (2014). *Visual Insights: a practical guide to making sense of data*. Cambridge, MA: Massachusetts Institute of Technology.

Borry, P., Schotsmans, P., & Dierickx, K. (2006). Author, contributor or just a signer? A quantitative analysis of authorship trends in the field of bioethics. *Bioethics*, *20*(4), 213–220. doi:10.1111/j.1467-8519.2006.00496.x PMID:17044155

Brandt, T., & Bertram, M. (2016). Evidence-based neurorehabilitation. *Der Nervenarzt*, *87*(10), 1041–1042. doi:10.1007/s00115-016-0202-1 PMID:27613178

Bridges, P. H., Bierema, L. L., & Valentine, T. (2007). The propensity to adopt evidence-based practice among physical therapists. *BMC Health Services Research*, *7*(1), 103. doi:10.1186/1472-6963-7-103 PMID:17615076

Buccino, G. (2014). Action observation treatment: A novel tool in neurorehabilitation. *Philosophical Transactions of the Royal Society of London. Series B, Biological Sciences*, *369*(1644), 20130185. doi:10.1098/rstb.2013.0185 PMID:24778380

Byrne, P et al. (Eds.). (2015). *Maximizing cognitive learning through knowledge visualization*. IGI Global.

Cox, T. F., & Cox, M. A. A. (2001). *Multidimensional scaling* (2nd ed.). London: Chapman & Hall.

Członkowska, A., & Sarzyńska-Długosz, I. (2002). Aims of neurorehabilitation. *Neurologia i Neurochirurgia Polska*, *36*(Suppl 1), 23–31. PMID:12189684

Dean-Baar, S., & Pakieser-Reed, K. (2004). Closing the gap between research and clinical practice. *Topics in Stroke Rehabilitation*, *11*(2), 60–68. doi:10.1310/GVP2-8CTV-QNGM-NG3U PMID:15118968

Dohle, C., Tholen, R., Wittenberg, H., Quintern, J., Saal, S., & Stephan, K. M. (2016). Evidence-based rehabilitation of mobility after stroke. *Der Nervenarzt*, *87*(10), 1062–1067. doi:10.1007/s00115-016-0188-8 PMID:27531212

Doucet, B. M. (2013). Five years later: Achieving professional effectiveness to move neurorehabilitation forward. *The American Journal of Occupational Therapy*, *67*(5), e106–e119. doi:10.5014/ajot.2013.008417 PMID:23968801

Einicke, G. A. (2012). *Smoothing, filtering and prediction: estimating the past, present and future*. Rijeka, Croatia: Intech.

Eisenberg, R. L., Ngo, L. H., & Bankier, A. A. (2014). Honorary authorship in radiologic research articles: Do geographic factors influence the frequency? *Radiology*, *271*(2), 472–478. doi:10.1148/radiol.13131710 PMID:24475845

Feramisco, J. D., Leitenberger, J. J., Redfern, S. I., Bian, A., Xie, X. J., & Resneck, J. S. Jr. (2009). A gender gap in the dermatology literature? Cross-sectional analysis of manuscript authorship trends in dermatology journals during 3 decades. *Journal of the American Academy of Dermatology*, *60*(1), 63–69. doi:10.1016/j.jaad.2008.06.044 PMID:19103359

Franchignoni, F., Muñoz Lasa, S., Ozçakar, L., & Ottonello, M. (2011). Bibliometric indicators: A snapshot of the scientific productivity of leading European PRM researchers. *European Journal of Physical and Rehabilitation Medicine*, *47*(3), 455–462. PMID:21946402

Gillen, G. (2010). Rehabilitation research focused on neurorehabilitation. *The American Journal of Occupational Therapy*, *64*(2), 341–356. doi:10.5014/ajot.64.2.341 PMID:20437922

Grimmer-Somers, K., Lekkas, P., Nyland, L., Young, A., & Kumar, S. (2007). Perspectives on research evidence and clinical practice: A survey of Australian physiotherapists. *Physiotherapy Research International, 12*(3), 147–161. doi:10.1002/pri.363 PMID:17624895

Gupta, M. R., & Chen, Y. (2010). Theory and Use of the EM Algorithm. *Foundations and Trends in Signal Processing, 4*(3), 223–296. doi:10.1561/2000000034

Harris S.R., Winstein C.J. (2017) The Past, Present, and Future of Neurorehabilitation: From NUSTEP Through IV STEP and Beyond. *Journal of Neurologic Physical Therapy, 41*(Suppl 3), S3-S9.

Harzing, A. W. (2016). *Publish or Perish*. Retrieved on May 15, 2017, from https://harzing.com/resources/publish-or-perish

Hömberg, V. (2010). Neurological rehabilitation. *Internist, 51*(10), 1246–1253, 1248–1253. doi:10.1007/s00108-010-2624-3 PMID:20848072

Huang, T. H., & Huang, M. L. (2006). *Analysis and visualization of co-authorship networks for understanding academic collaboration and knowledge domain of individual researchers.* IEEE Xplore. doi:10.1109/CGIV.2006.20

Iles, R., & Davidson, M. (2006). Evidence based practice: A survey of physiotherapists' current practice. *Physiotherapy Research International, 11*(2), 93–103. doi:10.1002/pri.328 PMID:16808090

Jesus, T. S. (2016). Systematic Reviews and Clinical Trials in Rehabilitation: Comprehensive Analyses of Publication Trends. *Archives of Physical Medicine and Rehabilitation, 97*(11), 1853–1862.e2. doi:10.1016/j.apmr.2016.06.017 PMID:27424809

Jette, D. U., Bacon, K., & Batty, C. (2003). Evidence-based practice: Beliefs, attitudes, knowledge, and behaviors of physical therapists. *Physical Therapy, 83*(9), 786–805. PMID:12940766

Kaufman, R. R., & Chevan, J. (2011). The gender gap in peer-reviewed publications by physical therapy faculty members: A productivity puzzle. *Physical Therapy, 91*(1), 122–131. doi:10.2522/ptj.20100106 PMID:21127164

Khosrow-Pour, M et al. (Ed.). (2016). *Big data: Concepts, methodologies, tools, and applications*. IGI Global.

Kwakkel, G. (2009). Towards integrative neurorehabilitation science. *Physiotherapy Research International, 14*(3), 137–146. doi:10.1002/pri.446 PMID:19634129

Levsky, M. E., Rosin, A., Coon, T. P., Enslow, W. L., & Miller, M. A. (2007). A descriptive analysis of authorship within medical journals, 1995-2005. *Southern Medical Journal, 100*(4), 371–375. doi:10.1097/01.smj.0000257537.51929.4b PMID:17458396

Leydesdorff, L. (2007). On the normalization and visualization of author co-citation data: Salton's Cosine versus the Jaccard index. *Journal of the Association for Information Science and Technology*. doi:10.1002/asi.20732

Liepert, J. (2012). Evidence-based methods in motor rehabilitation after stroke. *Fortschritte der Neurologie-Psychiatrie, 80*(7), 388–393. PMID:22760510

Luft, A. R. (2012). How to gain evidence in neurorehabilitation: A personal view. *Biomedical Engineering*, *57*(6), 427–433. PMID:23023795

Lynch, E. A., Cumming, T., Janssen, H., & Bernhardt, J. (2017). Early mobilization after stroke: Changes in clinical opinion despite an unchanging evidence base. *Journal of Stroke & Cardiovascular Diseases*, *26*(1), 1–6. doi:10.1016/j.jstrokecerebrovasdis.2016.08.021 PMID:27612626

Markram, H. (2013). Seven challenges for neuroscience. *Functional Neurology*, *28*(3), 145–151. PMID:24139651

McIntyre, A., Richardson, M., Janzen, S., Hussein, N., & Teasell, R. (2014). The evolution of stroke rehabilitation randomized controlled trials. *International Journal of Stroke*, *9*(6), 789–792. doi:10.1111/ijs.12272 PMID:24621406

Morris, S. A., & Yen, G. C. (2004). Crossmaps: Visualization of overlapping relationships in collections of journal papers. *Proceedings of the National Academy of Sciences of the United States of America*, *101*(Supplement 1), 5291–5296. doi:10.1073/pnas.0307604100 PMID:14762168

Osińska V. (2011) Fractal Analysis of Knowledge Organization in Digital Library. *New Trends in Qualitative and Quantitative Methods in Libraries,* 17–23.

Osińska, V., & Bala, P. (2015). Study of dynamics of structured knowledge: Qualitative analysis of different mapping approaches. *Journal of Information Science*, *41*(2), 197–208. doi:10.1177/0165551514559897

Palfreyman, S., Tod, A., & Doyle, J. (2003). Comparing evidence-based practice of nurses and physiotherapists. *British Journal of Nursing (Mark Allen Publishing)*, *12*(4), 246–253. doi:10.12968/bjon.2003.12.4.11165 PMID:12671571

Pereira, S., Graham, J. R., Shahabaz, A., Salter, K., Foley, N., Meyer, M., & Teasell, R. (2012). Rehabilitation of individuals with severe stroke: Synthesis of best evidence and challenges in implementation. *Topics in Stroke Rehabilitation*, *19*(2), 122–131. doi:10.1310/tsr1902-122 PMID:22436360

Petzold, A., Korner-Bitensky, N., & Menon, A. (2010). Using the knowledge to action process model to incite clinical change. *The Journal of Continuing Education in the Health Professions*, *30*(3), 167–171. doi:10.1002/chp.20077 PMID:20872771

Prokopowicz, P., Mikołajewski, D., Mikołajewska, E., & Kotlarz, P. (2017) Fuzzy system as an assessment tool for analysis of the health-related quality of life for the people after stroke. In *Artificial Intelligence and Soft Computing: 16th International Conference, ICAISC 2017, Proceedings, Part I*. Springer. doi:10.1007/978-3-319-59063-9_64

Ramírez-Vélez, R., Correa-Bautista, J. E., & Muñoz-Rodríguez, D. I. (2015). Evidence-based practice: Beliefs, attitudes, knowledge, and skills among Colombian physical therapists. *Colombia Médica (Cali, Colombia)*, *46*(1), 33–40. PMID:26019383

Rosenberg, W. M., & Donald, A. (1995). Evidence-based medicine: An approach to clinical problem solving. *BMJ (Clinical Research Ed.)*, *310*(6987), 1122–1126. doi:10.1136/bmj.310.6987.1122 PMID:7742682

Rosiek, A., & Leksowski, K. (Eds.). (2016). *Organizational culture and ethics in modern medicine*. IGI Global. doi:10.4018/978-1-4666-9658-7

Rycroft-Malone, J., Seers, K., Titchen, A., Harvey, G., Kitson, A., & McCormack, B. (2004). What counts as evidence-based practice? *Journal of Advanced Nursing*, *47*(1), 81–90. doi:10.1111/j.1365-2648.2004.03068.x PMID:15186471

Sackett, D. L., Rosenberg, W. M., Gray, J. A., Haynes, R. B., & Richardson, W. S. (1996). Evidence-based medicine: What it is and what it isn't. *BMJ (Clinical Research Ed.)*, *312*(7023), 71–72. doi:10.1136/bmj.312.7023.71 PMID:8555924

Salbach, N. M., Guilcher, S. J., Jaglal, S. B., & Davis, D. A. (2009). Factors influencing information seeking by physical therapists providing stroke management. *Physical Therapy*, *89*(10), 1039–1050. doi:10.2522/ptj.20090081 PMID:19661160

Salbach, N.M., Guilcher, S.J., Jaglal, S.B., & Davis, D.A. (2010). Determinants of research use in clinical decision making among physical therapists providing services post-stroke: A cross-sectional study. *Implementation Science*, *14*(5), 77.

Salbach, N. M., Jaglal, S. B., Korner-Bitensky, N., Rappolt, S., & Davis, D. (2007). Practitioner and organizational barriers to evidence-based practice of physical therapists for people with stroke. *Physical Therapy*, *87*(10), 1284–1303. doi:10.2522/ptj.20070040 PMID:17684088

Sci2 Team. (2009). *Science of Science (Sci2) Tool*. Indiana University and SciTech Strategies. Retrieved on May 15, 2017 from http://sci2.cns.iu.edu

Shadgan, B., Roig, M., Hajghanbari, B., & Reid, W. D. (2010). Top-cited articles in rehabilitation. *Archives of Physical Medicine and Rehabilitation*, *91*(5), 806–815. doi:10.1016/j.apmr.2010.01.011 PMID:20434622

Sidiakina, I. V., Dobrushina, O. R., Liadov, K. V., Shapovalenko, T. V., & Romashin, O. V. (2015). The role of evidence-based medicine in the neurorehabilitation: The innovative technologies (a review). *Voprosy Kurortologii, Fizioterapii, i Lechebnoi Fizicheskoi Kultury*, *92*(3), 53–56. doi:10.17116/kurort2015353-56 PMID:26285335

Sjöholm, A., Skarin, M., Linden, T., & Bernhardt, J. (2011). Does evidence really matter? Professionals' opinions on the practice of early mobilization after stroke. *Journal of Multidisciplinary Healthcare*, *4*, 367–376. PMID:22096341

Slone, R. M. (1996). Coauthors' contributions to major papers published in the AJR: Frequency of undeserved coauthorship. *AJR. American Journal of Roentgenology*, *167*(3), 571–579. doi:10.2214/ajr.167.3.8751654 PMID:8751654

Smaldino, P. E., & McElreath, R. (2016). The natural selection of bad science. *Royal Society Open Science*, *3*(9), 160384. doi:10.1098/rsos.160384 PMID:27703703

Stevenson, K., Lewis, M., & Hay, E. (2004). Do physiotherapists' attitudes towards evidence-based practice change as a result of an evidence-based educational programme? *Journal of Evaluation in Clinical Practice*, *10*(2), 207–217. doi:10.1111/j.1365-2753.2003.00479.x PMID:15189387

Strotmann, A., Zhao, D., & Bubela, T. (2009) Author name disambiguation for collaboration network analysis and visualization. *Proceedings of the Association for Information Science and Technology.* doi:10.1002/meet.2009.1450460218

Teasell, R. (2012). Challenges in the implementation of evidence in stroke rehabilitation. *Topics in Stroke Rehabilitation*, *19*(2), 93–95. doi:10.1310/tsr1902-93 PMID:22436356

Tilson, J. K., Settle, S. M., & Sullivan, K. J. (2008). Application of evidence-based practice strategies: Current trends in walking recovery interventions poststroke. *Topics in Stroke Rehabilitation*, *15*(3), 227–246. doi:10.1310/tsr1503-227 PMID:18647727

Timio, M., & Antiseri, D. (2000) Evidence-based medicine: reality and illusions. *Extension of epistemological reflexions, 1*(3), 411-414.

Turner, P., & Whitfield, T. W. (1997). Physiotherapists' use of evidence based practice: A cross-national study. *Physiotherapy Research International*, *2*(1), 17–29. doi:10.1002/pri.76 PMID:9238748

Walker, M. F., Fisher, R. J., Korner-Bitensky, N., McCluskey, A., & Carey, L. M. (2013). From what we know to what we do: Translating stroke rehabilitation research into practice. *International Journal of Stroke*, *8*(1), 11–17. doi:10.1111/j.1747-4949.2012.00974.x PMID:23280264

Wardil, L., & Hauert, C. (2015). Cooperation and coauthorship in scientific publishing. *Physical Review E: Statistical, Nonlinear, and Soft Matter Physics*, *91*(1), 012825. doi:10.1103/PhysRevE.91.012825 PMID:25679674

Wu, Y., & Duan, Z. (2015). Visualization analysis of author collaborations in schizophrenia research. *BMC Psychiatry*, *15*(1), 27. doi:10.1186/s12888-015-0407-z PMID:25884451

KEY TERMS AND DEFINITIONS

Evidence-Based Medicine (EBM): Approach of practicing medicine with the goal to improve and evaluate patient care. Requires the judicious integration of best research evidence with the patient's values to make decisions about medical care (i.e., make proper diagnosis, devise best testing plan, choose best treatment and methods of disease prevention, and develop guidelines for large groups of patients with the same disease).

Evidence-Based Practice (EBP): Way of providing healthcare guided by a thoughtful integration of the best available scientific knowledge with clinical expertise. It allows the practitioner to critically assess research data, clinical guidelines, and other information resources in order to correctly identify the clinical problem, apply the most high-quality intervention, and re-evaluate the outcome for future improvement.

Neurological Rehabilitation: Physician-supervised programs designed to rehabilitate people with diseases, trauma, or disorders of the nervous system.

ENDNOTE

[1]   https://scholar.google.com/citations?view_op=top_venues&hl=en&vq=med_rehabilitationtherapy

Related References

To continue our tradition of advancing academic research, we have compiled a list of recommended IGI Global readings. These references will provide additional information and guidance to further enrich your knowledge and assist you with your own research and future publications.

Abdelaziz, H. A. (2013). From content engagement to cognitive engagement: Toward an immersive web-based learning model to develop self-questioning and self-study skills. *International Journal of Technology Diffusion, 4*(1), 16–32. doi:10.4018/jtd.2013010102

Acha, V., Hargiss, K. M., & Howard, C. (2013). The relationship between emotional intelligence of a leader and employee motivation to job performance. *International Journal of Strategic Information Technology and Applications, 4*(4), 80–103. doi:10.4018/ijsita.2013100105

Agrawal, P. R. (2014). Digital information management: preserving tomorrow's memory. In S. Dhamdhere (Ed.), *Cloud computing and virtualization technologies in libraries* (pp. 22–35). Hershey, PA: IGI Global. doi:10.4018/978-1-4666-4631-5.ch002

Akram, H. A., & Mahmood, A. (2014). Predicting personality traits, gender and psychopath behavior of Twitter users. *International Journal of Technology Diffusion, 5*(2), 1–14. doi:10.4018/ijtd.2014040101

Akyol, Z. (2013). Metacognitive development within the community of inquiry. In Z. Akyol & D. Garrison (Eds.), *Educational communities of inquiry: Theoretical framework, research and practice* (pp. 30–44). Hershey, PA: IGI Global. doi:10.4018/978-1-4666-2110-7.ch003

Albers, M. J. (2012). How people read. In *Human-information interaction and technical communication: Concepts and frameworks* (pp. 367–397). Hershey, PA: IGI Global. doi:10.4018/978-1-4666-0152-9.ch011

Albers, M. J. (2012). What people bring with them. In *Human-information interaction and technical communication: Concepts and frameworks* (pp. 61–113). Hershey, PA: IGI Global. doi:10.4018/978-1-4666-0152-9.ch003

Ally, M. (2012). Designing mobile learning for the user. In B. Khan (Ed.), *User interface design for virtual environments: Challenges and advances* (pp. 226–235). Hershey, PA: IGI Global. doi:10.4018/978-1-61350-516-8.ch014

Almeida, L., Menezes, P., & Dias, J. (2013). Augmented reality framework for the socialization between elderly people. In M. Cruz-Cunha, I. Miranda, & P. Gonçalves (Eds.), *Handbook of research on ICTs for human-centered healthcare and social care services* (pp. 430–448). Hershey, PA: IGI Global. doi:10.4018/978-1-4666-3986-7.ch023

Alonso, E., & Mondragón, E. (2011). Computational models of learning and beyond: Symmetries of associative learning. In E. Alonso & E. Mondragón (Eds.), *Computational neuroscience for advancing artificial intelligence: Models, methods and applications* (pp. 316–332). Hershey, PA: IGI Global. doi:10.4018/978-1-60960-021-1.ch013

Ancarani, A., & Di Mauro, C. (2013). The human side of supply chains: A behavioural perspective of supply chain risk management. In *Supply chain management: Concepts, methodologies, tools, and applications* (pp. 1453–1476). Hershey, PA: IGI Global. doi:10.4018/978-1-4666-2625-6.ch086

Andres, H. P. (2013). Collaborative technology and dimensions of team cognition: Test of a second-order factor model. *International Journal of Information Technology Project Management, 4*(3), 22–37. doi:10.4018/jitpm.2013070102

Arora, A. S., Raisinghani, M. S., Leseane, R., & Thompson, L. (2013). Personality scales and learning styles: Pedagogy for creating an adaptive web-based learning system. In M. Raisinghani (Ed.), *Curriculum, learning, and teaching advancements in online education* (pp. 161–182). Hershey, PA: IGI Global. doi:10.4018/978-1-4666-2949-3.ch012

Ashcraft, D., & Treadwell, T. (2010). The social psychology of online collaborative learning: The good, the bad, and the awkward. In web-based education: concepts, methodologies, tools and applications (pp. 1146-1161). Hershey, PA: IGI Global. doi:10.4018/978-1-61520-963-7.ch078

Aston, J. (2013). Database narrative, spatial montage, and the cultural transmission of memory: An anthropological perspective. In D. Harrison (Ed.), *Digital media and technologies for virtual artistic spaces* (pp. 150–158). Hershey, PA: IGI Global. doi:10.4018/978-1-4666-2961-5.ch011

Asunka, S. (2013). Collaborative online learning in non-formal education settings in the developing world: A best practice framework. In V. Wang (Ed.), *Technological applications in adult and vocational education advancement* (pp. 186–201). Hershey, PA: IGI Global. doi:10.4018/978-1-4666-2062-9.ch015

Attia, M. (2014). The role of early learning experience in shaping teacher cognition and technology use. In P. Breen (Ed.), *Cases on teacher identity, diversity, and cognition in higher education* (pp. 1–21). Hershey, PA: IGI Global. doi:10.4018/978-1-4666-5990-2.ch001

Ávila, I., Menezes, E., & Braga, A. M. (2014). Strategy to support the memorization of iconic passwords. In K. Blashki & P. Isaias (Eds.), *Emerging research and trends in interactivity and the human-computer interface* (pp. 239–259). Hershey, PA: IGI Global. doi:10.4018/978-1-4666-4623-0.ch012

Bachvarova, Y., & Bocconi, S. (2014). Games and social networks. In T. Connolly, T. Hainey, E. Boyle, G. Baxter, & P. Moreno-Ger (Eds.), *Psychology, pedagogy, and assessment in serious games* (pp. 204–219). Hershey, PA: IGI Global. doi:10.4018/978-1-4666-4773-2.ch010

Bagley, C. A., & Creswell, W. H. (2013). The role of social media as a tool for learning. In E. McKay (Ed.), *ePedagogy in online learning: New developments in web mediated human computer interaction* (pp. 18–38). Hershey, PA: IGI Global. doi:10.4018/978-1-4666-3649-1.ch002

Balogh, Š. (2014). Forensic analysis, cryptosystem implementation, and cryptology: Methods and techniques for extracting encryption keys from volatile memory. In S. Sadkhan Al Maliky & N. Abbas (Eds.), *Multidisciplinary perspectives in cryptology and information security* (pp. 381–396). Hershey, PA: IGI Global. doi:10.4018/978-1-4666-5808-0.ch016

Banas, J. R., & Brown, C. A. (2012). Web 2.0 visualization tools to stimulate generative learning. In D. Polly, C. Mims, & K. Persichitte (Eds.), *Developing technology-rich teacher education programs: Key issues* (pp. 77–90). Hershey, PA: IGI Global. doi:10.4018/978-1-4666-0014-0.ch006

Bancroft, J., & Wang, Y. (2013). A computational simulation of the cognitive process of children knowledge acquisition and memory development. In Y. Wang (Ed.), *Cognitive informatics for revealing human cognition: Knowledge manipulations in natural intelligence* (pp. 111–127). Hershey, PA: IGI Global. doi:10.4018/978-1-4666-2476-4.ch008

Bartsch, R. A. (2011). Social psychology and instructional technology. In *Instructional design: Concepts, methodologies, tools and applications* (pp. 1237–1244). Hershey, PA: IGI Global. doi:10.4018/978-1-60960-503-2.ch508

Bertolotti, T. (2013). Facebook has it: The irresistible violence of social cognition in the age of social networking. In R. Luppicini (Ed.), *Moral, ethical, and social dilemmas in the age of technology: Theories and practice* (pp. 234–247). Hershey, PA: IGI Global. doi:10.4018/978-1-4666-2931-8.ch016

Berwick, R. C. (2013). Songs to syntax: Cognition, combinatorial computation, and the origin of language. In Y. Wang (Ed.), *Cognitive informatics for revealing human cognition: Knowledge manipulations in natural intelligence* (pp. 70–80). Hershey, PA: IGI Global. doi:10.4018/978-1-4666-2476-4.ch005

Best, C., O'Neill, B., & Gillespie, A. (2014). Assistive technology for cognition: An updated review. In G. Naik & Y. Guo (Eds.), *Emerging theory and practice in neuroprosthetics* (pp. 215–236). Hershey, PA: IGI Global. doi:10.4018/978-1-4666-6094-6.ch011

Bhattacharya, A. (2014). Organisational justice perception: A work attitude modifier. In N. Ray & K. Chakraborty (Eds.), *Handbook of research on strategic business infrastructure development and contemporary issues in finance* (pp. 296–322). Hershey, PA: IGI Global. doi:10.4018/978-1-4666-5154-8.ch021

Biggiero, L. (2012). Practice vs. possession: Epistemological implications on the nature of organizational knowledge and cognition. In M. Mora, O. Gelman, A. Steenkamp, & M. Raisinghani (Eds.), *Research methodologies, innovations and philosophies in software systems engineering and information systems* (pp. 82–105). Hershey, PA: IGI Global. doi:10.4018/978-1-4666-0179-6.ch005

Bishop, J. (2014). The psychology of trolling and lurking: The role of defriending and gamification for increasing participation in online communities using seductive narratives. In J. Bishop (Ed.), *Gamification for human factors integration: Social, education, and psychological issues* (pp. 162–179). Hershey, PA: IGI Global. doi:10.4018/978-1-4666-5071-8.ch010

Blasko, D. G., Lum, H. C., White, M. M., & Drabik, H. B. (2014). Individual differences in the enjoyment and effectiveness of serious games. In T. Connolly, T. Hainey, E. Boyle, G. Baxter, & P. Moreno-Ger (Eds.), *Psychology, pedagogy, and assessment in serious games* (pp. 153–174). Hershey, PA: IGI Global. doi:10.4018/978-1-4666-4773-2.ch008

Borah, P. (2014). Interaction of incivility and news frames in the political blogosphere: Consequences and psychological mechanisms. In A. Solo (Ed.), *Handbook of research on political activism in the information age* (pp. 407–424). Hershey, PA: IGI Global. doi:10.4018/978-1-4666-6066-3.ch024

Borri, D., & Camarda, D. (2011). Spatial ontologies in multi-agent environmental planning. In J. Yearwood & A. Stranieri (Eds.), *Technologies for supporting reasoning communities and collaborative decision making: Cooperative approaches* (pp. 272–295). Hershey, PA: IGI Global. doi:10.4018/978-1-60960-091-4.ch015

Boukhobza, J. (2013). Flashing in the cloud: Shedding some light on NAND flash memory storage systems. In D. Kyriazis, A. Voulodimos, S. Gogouvitis, & T. Varvarigou (Eds.), *Data intensive storage services for cloud environments* (pp. 241–266). Hershey, PA: IGI Global. doi:10.4018/978-1-4666-3934-8.ch015

Boyle, E. (2014). Psychological aspects of serious games. In T. Connolly, T. Hainey, E. Boyle, G. Baxter, & P. Moreno-Ger (Eds.), *Psychology, pedagogy, and assessment in serious games* (pp. 1–18). Hershey, PA: IGI Global. doi:10.4018/978-1-4666-4773-2.ch001

Boyle, E., Terras, M. M., Ramsay, J., & Boyle, J. M. (2014). Executive functions in digital games. In T. Connolly, T. Hainey, E. Boyle, G. Baxter, & P. Moreno-Ger (Eds.), *Psychology, pedagogy, and assessment in serious games* (pp. 19–46). Hershey, PA: IGI Global. doi:10.4018/978-1-4666-4773-2.ch002

Breen, P. (2014). Philosophies, traditional pedagogy, and new technologies: A report on a case study of EAP teachers' integration of technology into traditional practice. In P. Breen (Ed.), *Cases on teacher identity, diversity, and cognition in higher education* (pp. 317–341). Hershey, PA: IGI Global. doi:10.4018/978-1-4666-5990-2.ch013

Buchanan, A. (2014). Protective factors in family relationships. In M. Merviö (Ed.), *Contemporary social issues in east Asian societies: Examining the spectrum of public and private spheres* (pp. 76–85). Hershey, PA: IGI Global. doi:10.4018/978-1-4666-5031-2.ch004

Burke, M. E., & Speed, C. (2014). Knowledge recovery: Applications of technology and memory. In M. Michael & K. Michael (Eds.), *Uberveillance and the social implications of microchip implants: Emerging technologies* (pp. 133–142). Hershey, PA: IGI Global. doi:10.4018/978-1-4666-4582-0.ch005

Burusic, J., & Karabegovic, M. (2014). The role of students' personality traits in the effective use of social networking sites in the educational context. In G. Mallia (Ed.), *The social classroom: Integrating social network use in education* (pp. 224–243). Hershey, PA: IGI Global. doi:10.4018/978-1-4666-4904-0.ch012

Caixinha, A., Magalhães, V., & Alexandre, I. M. (2013). Do you remember, or have you forgotten? In R. Martinho, R. Rijo, M. Cruz-Cunha, & J. Varajão (Eds.), *Information systems and technologies for enhancing health and social care* (pp. 136–146). Hershey, PA: IGI Global. doi:10.4018/978-1-4666-3667-5.ch009

Carbonaro, N., Cipresso, P., Tognetti, A., Anania, G., De Rossi, D., Pallavicini, F., & Riva, G. et al. (2014). Psychometric assessment of cardio-respiratory activity using a mobile platform. *International Journal of Handheld Computing Research, 5*(1), 13–29. doi:10.4018/ijhcr.2014010102

Castellani, M. (2011). Cognitive tools for group decision making: The repertory grid approach revisited. In J. Yearwood & A. Stranieri (Eds.), *Technologies for supporting reasoning communities and collaborative decision making: Cooperative approaches* (pp. 172–192). Hershey, PA: IGI Global. doi:10.4018/978-1-60960-091-4.ch010

Cawthon, S. W., Harris, A., & Jones, R. (2010). Cognitive apprenticeship in an online research lab for graduate students in psychology. *International Journal of Web-Based Learning and Teaching Technologies, 5*(1), 1–15. doi:10.4018/jwltt.2010010101

Cederborg, T., & Oudeyer, P. (2014). Learning words by imitating. In *Computational linguistics: Concepts, methodologies, tools, and applications* (pp. 1674–1704). Hershey, PA: IGI Global. doi:10.4018/978-1-4666-6042-7.ch084

Cervantes, J., Rodríguez, L., López, S., Ramos, F., & Robles, F. (2013). Cognitive process of moral decision-making for autonomous agents. *International Journal of Software Science and Computational Intelligence, 5*(4), 61–76. doi:10.4018/ijssci.2013100105

Chadwick, D. D., Fullwood, C., & Wesson, C. J. (2014). Intellectual disability, identity, and the internet. In *Assistive technologies: Concepts, methodologies, tools, and applications* (pp. 198–223). Hershey, PA: IGI Global. doi:10.4018/978-1-4666-4422-9.ch011

Chan, E. C., Baciu, G., & Mak, S. C. (2010). Cognitive location-aware information retrieval by agent-based semantic matching. *International Journal of Software Science and Computational Intelligence, 2*(3), 21–31. doi:10.4018/jssci.2010070102

Chen, C. (2014). Differences between visual style and verbal style learners in learning English. *International Journal of Distance Education Technologies, 12*(1), 91–104. doi:10.4018/ijdet.2014010106

Chen, K., & Barthès, J. A. (2012). Giving personal assistant agents a case-based memory. In Y. Wang (Ed.), *Developments in natural intelligence research and knowledge engineering: Advancing applications* (pp. 287–304). Hershey, PA: IGI Global. doi:10.4018/978-1-4666-1743-8.ch021

Chen, S., Tai, C., Wang, T., & Wang, S. G. (2011). Social simulation with both human agents and software agents: An investigation into the impact of cognitive capacity on their learning behavior. In S. Chen, Y. Kambayashi, & H. Sato (Eds.), *Multi-agent applications with evolutionary computation and biologically inspired technologies: Intelligent techniques for ubiquity and optimization* (pp. 95–117). Hershey, PA: IGI Global. doi:10.4018/978-1-60566-898-7.ch006

Chiriacescu, V., Soh, L., & Shell, D. F. (2013). Understanding human learning using a multi-agent simulation of the unified learning model. *International Journal of Cognitive Informatics and Natural Intelligence, 7*(4), 1–25. doi:10.4018/ijcini.2013100101

Christen, M., Alfano, M., Bangerter, E., & Lapsley, D. (2013). Ethical issues of 'morality mining': Moral identity as a focus of data mining. In H. Rahman & I. Ramos (Eds.), *Ethical data mining applications for socio-economic development* (pp. 1–21). Hershey, PA: IGI Global. doi:10.4018/978-1-4666-4078-8.ch001

Cipresso, P., Serino, S., Gaggioli, A., & Riva, G. (2014). Modeling the diffusion of psychological stress. In J. Rodrigues (Ed.), *Advancing medical practice through technology: Applications for healthcare delivery, management, and quality* (pp. 178–204). Hershey, PA: IGI Global. doi:10.4018/978-1-4666-4619-3.ch010

Code, J. (2013). Agency and identity in social media. In S. Warburton & S. Hatzipanagos (Eds.), *Digital identity and social media* (pp. 37–57). Hershey, PA: IGI Global. doi:10.4018/978-1-4666-1915-9.ch004

Combs, R. M., & Mazur, J. (2014). 3D modeling in a high school computer visualization class: Enacting a productive, distributed social learning environment. In *K-12 education: Concepts, methodologies, tools, and applications* (pp. 1020–1040). Hershey, PA: IGI Global. doi:10.4018/978-1-4666-4502-8.ch061

Cook, R. G., & Sutton, R. (2014). Administrators' assessments of online courses and student retention in higher education: Lessons learned. In S. Mukerji & P. Tripathi (Eds.), *Handbook of research on transnational higher education* (pp. 138–150). Hershey, PA: IGI Global. doi:10.4018/978-1-4666-4458-8.ch008

Correa, T., Bachmann, I., Hinsley, A. W., & Gil de Zúñiga, H. (2013). Personality and social media use. In E. Li, S. Loh, C. Evans, & F. Lorenzi (Eds.), *Organizations and social networking: Utilizing social media to engage consumers* (pp. 41–61). Hershey, PA: IGI Global. doi:10.4018/978-1-4666-4026-9.ch003

Cowell, R. A., Bussey, T. J., & Saksida, L. M. (2011). Using computational modelling to understand cognition in the ventral visual-perirhinal pathway. In E. Alonso & E. Mondragón (Eds.), *Computational neuroscience for advancing artificial intelligence: Models, methods and applications* (pp. 15–45). Hershey, PA: IGI Global. doi:10.4018/978-1-60960-021-1.ch002

Crespo, R. G., Martíne, O. S., Lovelle, J. M., García-Bustelo, B. C., Díaz, V. G., & Ordoñez de Pablos, P. (2014). Improving cognitive load on students with disabilities through software aids. In *Assistive technologies: Concepts, methodologies, tools, and applications* (pp. 1255–1268). Hershey, PA: IGI Global. doi:10.4018/978-1-4666-4422-9.ch066

Cró, M. D., Andreucci, L., Pinho, A. M., & Pereira, A. (2013). Resilience and psychomotricity in preschool education: A study with children that are socially, culturally, and economically disadvantaged. In M. Cruz-Cunha, I. Miranda, & P. Gonçalves (Eds.), *Handbook of research on ICTs for human-centered healthcare and social care services* (pp. 366–378). Hershey, PA: IGI Global. doi:10.4018/978-1-4666-3986-7.ch019

Cummings, J. J., & Ross, T. L. (2013). Optimizing the psychological benefits of choice: information transparency and heuristic use in game environments. In R. Ferdig (Ed.), *Design, utilization, and analysis of simulations and game-based educational worlds* (pp. 142–157). Hershey, PA: IGI Global. doi:10.4018/978-1-4666-4018-4.ch009

Curumsing, M. K., Pedell, S., & Vasa, R. (2014). Designing an evaluation tool to measure emotional goals. *International Journal of People-Oriented Programming, 3*(1), 22–43. doi:10.4018/ijpop.2014010102

Cuzzocrea, F., Murdaca, A. M., & Oliva, P. (2013). Using precision teaching method to improve foreign language and cognitive skills in university students. In A. Cartelli (Ed.), *Fostering 21st century digital literacy and technical competency* (pp. 201–211). Hershey, PA: IGI Global. doi:10.4018/978-1-4666-2943-1.ch014

DaCosta, B., & Seok, S. (2010). Human cognition in the design of assistive technology for those with learning disabilities. In S. Seok, E. Meyen, & B. DaCosta (Eds.), *Handbook of research on human cognition and assistive technology: Design, accessibility and transdisciplinary perspectives* (pp. 1–20). Hershey, PA: IGI Global. doi:10.4018/978-1-61520-817-3.ch001

DaCosta, B., & Seok, S. (2010). Multimedia design of assistive technology for those with learning disabilities. In S. Seok, E. Meyen, & B. DaCosta (Eds.), *Handbook of research on human cognition and assistive technology: Design, accessibility and transdisciplinary perspectives* (pp. 43–60). Hershey, PA: IGI Global. doi:10.4018/978-1-61520-817-3.ch003

Danielsson, U., & Öberg, K. D. (2011). Psychosocial life environment and life roles in interaction with daily use of information communication technology boundaries between work and leisure. In D. Haftor & A. Mirijamdotter (Eds.), *Information and communication technologies, society and human beings: Theory and framework (Festschrift in honor of Gunilla Bradley)* (pp. 266–282). Hershey, PA: IGI Global. doi:10.4018/978-1-60960-057-0.ch020

Daradoumis, T., & Lafuente, M. M. (2014). Studying the suitability of discourse analysis methods for emotion detection and interpretation in computer-mediated educational discourse. In H. Lim & F. Sudweeks (Eds.), *Innovative methods and technologies for electronic discourse analysis* (pp. 119–143). Hershey, PA: IGI Global. doi:10.4018/978-1-4666-4426-7.ch006

De Simone, C., Marquis, T., & Groen, J. (2013). Optimizing conditions for learning and teaching in K-20 education. In V. Wang (Ed.), *Handbook of research on teaching and learning in K-20 education* (pp. 535–552). Hershey, PA: IGI Global. doi:10.4018/978-1-4666-4249-2.ch031

Deka, G. C. (2014). Significance of in-memory computing for real-time big data analytics. In P. Raj & G. Deka (Eds.), *Handbook of research on cloud infrastructures for big data analytics* (pp. 352–369). Hershey, PA: IGI Global. doi:10.4018/978-1-4666-5864-6.ch014

Demirbilek, M. (2010). Cognitive load and disorientation issues in hypermedia as assistive technology. In S. Seok, E. Meyen, & B. DaCosta (Eds.), *Handbook of research on human cognition and assistive technology: Design, accessibility and transdisciplinary perspectives* (pp. 109–120). Hershey, PA: IGI Global. doi:10.4018/978-1-61520-817-3.ch007

Derrick, M. G. (2013). The inventory of learner persistence. In M. Bocarnea, R. Reynolds, & J. Baker (Eds.), *Online instruments, data collection, and electronic measurements: Organizational advancements* (pp. 271–290). Hershey, PA: IGI Global. doi:10.4018/978-1-4666-2172-5.ch016

Doolittle, P. E., McNeill, A. L., Terry, K. P., & Scheer, S. B. (2011). Multimedia, cognitive load, and pedagogy. In *Instructional design: Concepts, methodologies, tools and applications* (pp. 1564–1585). Hershey, PA: IGI Global. doi:10.4018/978-1-60960-503-2.ch706

Dourlens, S., & Ramdane-Cherif, A. (2013). Cognitive memory for semantic agents architecture in robotic interaction. In Y. Wang (Ed.), *Cognitive informatics for revealing human cognition: Knowledge manipulations in natural intelligence* (pp. 82–97). Hershey, PA: IGI Global. doi:10.4018/978-1-4666-2476-4.ch006

Dubbels, B. (2011). Cognitive ethnography: A methodology for measure and analysis of learning for game studies. *International Journal of Gaming and Computer-Mediated Simulations*, *3*(1), 68–78. doi:10.4018/jgcms.2011010105

Dunbar, N. E., Wilson, S. N., Adame, B. J., Elizondo, J., Jensen, M. L., Miller, C. H., & Burgoon, J. K. et al. (2013). MACBETH: Development of a training game for the mitigation of cognitive bias. *International Journal of Game-Based Learning*, *3*(4), 7–26. doi:10.4018/ijgbl.2013100102

Dunham, A. H., & Burt, C. D. (2012). Mentoring and the transfer of organizational memory within the context of an aging workforce: Cultural implications for competitive advantage. In *Organizational learning and knowledge: Concepts, methodologies, tools and applications* (pp. 3076–3099). Hershey, PA: IGI Global. doi:10.4018/978-1-60960-783-8.ch817

Durrington, V. A., & Du, J. (2013). Learning tasks, peer interaction, and cognition process an online collaborative design model. *International Journal of Information and Communication Technology Education*, *9*(1), 38–50. doi:10.4018/jicte.2013010104

Duțu, A. (2014). Understanding consumers' behaviour change in uncertainty conditions: A psychological perspective. In F. Musso & E. Druica (Eds.), *Handbook of research on retailer-consumer relationship development* (pp. 45–69). Hershey, PA: IGI Global. doi:10.4018/978-1-4666-6074-8.ch004

Dwyer, P. (2013). Measuring collective cognition in online collaboration venues. In N. Kock (Ed.), *Interdisciplinary applications of electronic collaboration approaches and technologies* (pp. 46–61). Hershey, PA: IGI Global. doi:10.4018/978-1-4666-2020-9.ch004

Egan, R. G., & Zhou, M. (2011). Re-conceptualizing calibration using trace methodology. In G. Dettori & D. Persico (Eds.), *Fostering self-regulated learning through ICT* (pp. 71–88). Hershey, PA: IGI Global. doi:10.4018/978-1-61692-901-5.ch005

El-Farargy, N. (2013). Refresher training in clinical psychology supervision: A blended learning approach. In A. Benson, J. Moore, & S. Williams van Rooij (Eds.), *Cases on educational technology planning, design, and implementation: A project management perspective* (pp. 295–317). Hershey, PA: IGI Global. doi:10.4018/978-1-4666-4237-9.ch016

El Louadi, M., & Tounsi, I. (2010). Do organizational memory and information technology interact to affect organizational information needs and provision? In M. Jennex (Ed.), *Ubiquitous developments in knowledge management: Integrations and trends* (pp. 1–20). Hershey, PA: IGI Global. doi:10.4018/978-1-60566-954-0.ch001

Estrada-Hernández, N., & Stachowiak, J. R. (2010). Evaluating systemic assistive technology needs. In S. Seok, E. Meyen, & B. DaCosta (Eds.), *Handbook of research on human cognition and assistive technology: Design, accessibility and transdisciplinary perspectives* (pp. 239–250). Hershey, PA: IGI Global. doi:10.4018/978-1-61520-817-3.ch016

Fitzpatrick, M., & Theoharis, R. (2010). Assistive technology for deaf and hard of hearing students. In S. Seok, E. Meyen, & B. DaCosta (Eds.), *Handbook of research on human cognition and assistive technology: Design, accessibility and transdisciplinary perspectives* (pp. 179–191). Hershey, PA: IGI Global. doi:10.4018/978-1-61520-817-3.ch012

Francis, A. G. Jr, Mehta, M., & Ram, A. (2012). Emotional memory and adaptive personalities. In *Machine learning: Concepts, methodologies, tools and applications* (pp. 1292–1313). Hershey, PA: IGI Global. doi:10.4018/978-1-60960-818-7.ch507

Gagliardi, F. (2014). A cognitive machine-learning system to discover syndromes in erythemato-squamous diseases. In J. Rodrigues (Ed.), *Advancing medical practice through technology: Applications for healthcare delivery, management, and quality* (pp. 66–101). Hershey, PA: IGI Global. doi:10.4018/978-1-4666-4619-3.ch005

Gaines, B. R., & Shaw, M. L. (2013). Sociocognitive inquiry. In *Data mining: Concepts, methodologies, tools, and applications* (pp. 1688–1708). Hershey, PA: IGI Global. doi:10.4018/978-1-4666-2455-9.ch088

Gardner, M. K., & Hill, R. D. (2013). Training older adults to improve their episodic memory: Three different approaches to enhancing numeric memory. In R. Zheng, R. Hill, & M. Gardner (Eds.), *Engaging older adults with modern technology: Internet use and information access needs* (pp. 191–211). Hershey, PA: IGI Global. doi:10.4018/978-1-4666-1966-1.ch010

Ghili, S., Nazarian, S., Tavana, M., Keyvanshokouhi, S., & Isaai, M. T. (2013). A complex systems paradox of organizational learning and knowledge management. *International Journal of Knowledge-Based Organizations*, 3(3), 53–72. doi:10.4018/ijkbo.2013070104

Gibson, D. (2012). Designing a computational model of learning. In *Machine learning: Concepts, methodologies, tools and applications* (pp. 147–174). Hershey, PA: IGI Global. doi:10.4018/978-1-60960-818-7.ch203

Gibson, M., Renaud, K., Conrad, M., & Maple, C. (2013). Music is the key: Using our enduring memory for songs to help users log on. In *IT policy and ethics: Concepts, methodologies, tools, and applications* (pp. 1018–1037). Hershey, PA: IGI Global. doi:10.4018/978-1-4666-2919-6.ch046

Godine, N., & Barnett, J. E. (2013). The use of telepsychology in clinical practice: Benefits, effectiveness, and issues to consider. *International Journal of Cyber Behavior, Psychology and Learning*, 3(4), 70–83. doi:10.4018/ijcbpl.2013100105

Gökçay, D. (2011). Emotional axes: Psychology, psychophysiology and neuroanatomical correlates. In D. Gökçay & G. Yildirim (Eds.), *Affective computing and interaction: Psychological, cognitive and neuroscientific perspectives* (pp. 56–73). Hershey, PA: IGI Global. doi:10.4018/978-1-61692-892-6.ch003

Goswami, R., Jena, R. K., & Mahapatro, B. B. (2013). Psycho-social impact of shift work: A study of ferro-alloy industries in Orissa. In P. Ordóñez de Pablos (Ed.), *Business, technology, and knowledge management in Asia: Trends and innovations* (pp. 166–174). Hershey, PA: IGI Global. doi:10.4018/978-1-4666-2652-2.ch013

Graff, M. (2011). Can cognitive style predict how individuals use web-based learning environments? In *Instructional design: Concepts, methodologies, tools and applications* (pp. 1553–1563). Hershey, PA: IGI Global. doi:10.4018/978-1-60960-503-2.ch705

Griffiths, M., Kuss, D. J., & Ortiz de Gortari, A. B. (2013). Videogames as therapy: A review of the medical and psychological literature. In M. Cruz-Cunha, I. Miranda, & P. Gonçalves (Eds.), *Handbook of research on ICTs and management systems for improving efficiency in healthcare and social care* (pp. 43–68). Hershey, PA: IGI Global. doi:10.4018/978-1-4666-3990-4.ch003

Guger, C., Sorger, B., Noirhomme, Q., Naci, L., Monti, M. M., & Real, R. ... Cincotti, F. (2014). Brain-computer interfaces for assessment and communication in disorders of consciousness. In G. Naik & Y. Guo (Eds.), Emerging theory and practice in neuroprosthetics (pp. 181-214). Hershey, PA: IGI Global. doi:10.4018/978-1-4666-6094-6.ch010

Güngör, H. (2014). Adolescent suicides as a chaotic phenomenon. In Ş. Erçetin & S. Banerjee (Eds.), *Chaos and complexity theory in world politics* (pp. 306–324). Hershey, PA: IGI Global. doi:10.4018/978-1-4666-6070-0.ch022

Hai-Jew, S. (2013). Interpreting "you" and "me": Personal voices, PII, biometrics, and imperfect/perfect electronic memory in a democracy. In C. Akrivopoulou & N. Garipidis (Eds.), *Digital democracy and the impact of technology on governance and politics: New globalized practices* (pp. 20–37). Hershey, PA: IGI Global. doi:10.4018/978-1-4666-3637-8.ch003

Hainey, T., Connolly, T. M., Chaudy, Y., Boyle, E., Beeby, R., & Soflano, M. (2014). Assessment integration in serious games. In T. Connolly, T. Hainey, E. Boyle, G. Baxter, & P. Moreno-Ger (Eds.), *Psychology, pedagogy, and assessment in serious games* (pp. 317–341). Hershey, PA: IGI Global. doi:10.4018/978-1-4666-4773-2.ch015

Hainey, T., Soflano, M., & Connolly, T. M. (2014). A randomised controlled trial to evaluate learning effectiveness using an adaptive serious game to teach SQL at higher education level. In T. Connolly, T. Hainey, E. Boyle, G. Baxter, & P. Moreno-Ger (Eds.), *Psychology, pedagogy, and assessment in serious games* (pp. 270–291). Hershey, PA: IGI Global. doi:10.4018/978-1-4666-4773-2.ch013

Haque, J., Erturk, M., Arslan, H., & Moreno, W. (2011). Cognitive aeronautical communication system. *International Journal of Interdisciplinary Telecommunications and Networking, 3*(1), 20–35. doi:10.4018/jitn.2011010102

Hauge, J. B., Boyle, E., Mayer, I., Nadolski, R., Riedel, J. C., Moreno-Ger, P., & Ritchie, J. et al. (2014). Study design and data gathering guide for serious games' evaluation. In T. Connolly, T. Hainey, E. Boyle, G. Baxter, & P. Moreno-Ger (Eds.), *Psychology, pedagogy, and assessment in serious games* (pp. 394–419). Hershey, PA: IGI Global. doi:10.4018/978-1-4666-4773-2.ch018

Haykin, S. (2013). Cognitive dynamic systems. In Y. Wang (Ed.), *Cognitive informatics for revealing human cognition: Knowledge manipulations in natural intelligence* (pp. 250–260). Hershey, PA: IGI Global. doi:10.4018/978-1-4666-2476-4.ch016

Henderson, A. M., & Sabbagh, M. A. (2014). Learning words from experience: An integrated framework. In *Computational linguistics: Concepts, methodologies, tools, and applications* (pp. 1705–1727). Hershey, PA: IGI Global. doi:10.4018/978-1-4666-6042-7.ch085

Hendrick, H. W. (2011). Cognitive and organizational complexity and behavior: Implications for organizational design and leadership. In D. Haftor & A. Mirijamdotter (Eds.), *Information and communication technologies, society and human beings: Theory and framework (Festschrift in honor of Gunilla Bradley)* (pp. 147–159). Hershey, PA: IGI Global. doi:10.4018/978-1-60960-057-0.ch013

Henrie, K. M., & Miller, D. W. (2013). An examination of mediation: Insights into the role of psychological mediators in the use of persuasion knowledge. In R. Eid (Ed.), *Managing customer trust, satisfaction, and loyalty through information communication technologies* (pp. 106–117). Hershey, PA: IGI Global. doi:10.4018/978-1-4666-3631-6.ch007

Ho, W. C., Dautenhahn, K., Lim, M., Enz, S., Zoll, C., & Watson, S. (2012). Towards learning 'self' and emotional knowledge in social and cultural human-agent interactions. In *Virtual learning environments: Concepts, methodologies, tools and applications* (pp. 1426–1445). Hershey, PA: IGI Global. doi:10.4018/978-1-4666-0011-9.ch705

Holt, L., & Ziegler, M. F. (2013). Promoting team learning in the classroom. In V. Wang (Ed.), *Technological applications in adult and vocational education advancement* (pp. 94–105). Hershey, PA: IGI Global. doi:10.4018/978-1-4666-2062-9.ch008

Honey, R. C., & Grand, C. S. (2011). Application of connectionist models to animal learning: Interactions between perceptual organization and associative processes. In E. Alonso & E. Mondragón (Eds.), *Computational neuroscience for advancing artificial intelligence: Models, methods and applications* (pp. 1–14). Hershey, PA: IGI Global. doi:10.4018/978-1-60960-021-1.ch001

Hoppenbrouwers, S., Schotten, B., & Lucas, P. (2012). Towards games for knowledge acquisition and modeling. In R. Ferdig & S. de Freitas (Eds.), *Interdisciplinary advancements in gaming, simulations and virtual environments: Emerging trends* (pp. 281–299). Hershey, PA: IGI Global. doi:10.4018/978-1-4666-0029-4.ch018

Huang, C., Liang, C., & Lin, E. (2014). A study on emotion releasing effect with music and color. In F. Cipolla-Ficarra (Ed.), *Advanced research and trends in new technologies, software, human-computer interaction, and communicability* (pp. 23–31). Hershey, PA: IGI Global. doi:10.4018/978-1-4666-4490-8.ch003

Huang, W. D., & Tettegah, S. Y. (2014). Cognitive load and empathy in serious games: A conceptual framework. In J. Bishop (Ed.), *Gamification for human factors integration: Social, education, and psychological issues* (pp. 17–30). Hershey, PA: IGI Global. doi:10.4018/978-1-4666-5071-8.ch002

Huijnen, C. (2011). The use of assistive technology to support the wellbeing and independence of people with memory impairments. In J. Soar, R. Swindell, & P. Tsang (Eds.), *Intelligent technologies for bridging the grey digital divide* (pp. 65–79). Hershey, PA: IGI Global. doi:10.4018/978-1-61520-825-8.ch005

Huseyinov, I. N. (2014). Fuzzy linguistic modelling in multi modal human computer interaction: Adaptation to cognitive styles using multi level fuzzy granulation method. In *Assistive technologies: Concepts, methodologies, tools, and applications* (pp. 1481–1496). Hershey, PA: IGI Global. doi:10.4018/978-1-4666-4422-9.ch077

Hussey, H. D., Fleck, B. K., & Richmond, A. S. (2014). Promoting active learning through a flipped course design. In J. Keengwe, G. Onchwari, & J. Oigara (Eds.), *Promoting active learning through the flipped classroom model* (pp. 23–46). Hershey, PA: IGI Global. doi:10.4018/978-1-4666-4987-3.ch002

Ilin, R., & Perlovsky, L. (2010). Cognitively inspired neural network for recognition of situations. *International Journal of Natural Computing Research, 1*(1), 36–55. doi:10.4018/jncr.2010010102

Ilin, R., & Perlovsky, L. (2011). Cognitive based distributed sensing, processing, and communication. In B. Igelnik (Ed.), *Computational modeling and simulation of intellect: Current state and future perspectives* (pp. 131–161). Hershey, PA: IGI Global. doi:10.4018/978-1-60960-551-3.ch006

Jenkins, J. L., Durcikova, A., & Burns, M. B. (2013). Simplicity is bliss: Controlling extraneous cognitive load in online security training to promote secure behavior. *Journal of Organizational and End User Computing, 25*(3), 52–66. doi:10.4018/joeuc.2013070104

Jennings, D. J., Alonso, E., Mondragón, E., & Bonardi, C. (2011). Temporal uncertainty during overshadowing: A temporal difference account. In E. Alonso & E. Mondragón (Eds.), *Computational neuroscience for advancing artificial intelligence: Models, methods and applications* (pp. 46–55). Hershey, PA: IGI Global. doi:10.4018/978-1-60960-021-1.ch003

Jin, S., DaCosta, B., & Seok, S. (2014). Social skills development for children with autism spectrum disorders through the use of interactive storytelling games. In B. DaCosta & S. Seok (Eds.), *Assistive technology research, practice, and theory* (pp. 144–159). Hershey, PA: IGI Global. doi:10.4018/978-1-4666-5015-2.ch010

Johnson, R. D., De Ridder, D., & Gillett, G. (2014). Neurosurgery to enhance brain function: Ethical dilemmas for the neuroscientist and society. In S. Thompson (Ed.), *Global issues and ethical considerations in human enhancement technologies* (pp. 96–118). Hershey, PA: IGI Global. doi:10.4018/978-1-4666-6010-6.ch006

Johnson, V., & Price, C. (2010). A longitudinal case study on the use of assistive technology to support cognitive processes across formal and informal educational settings. In S. Seok, E. Meyen, & B. DaCosta (Eds.), *Handbook of research on human cognition and assistive technology: Design, accessibility and transdisciplinary perspectives* (pp. 192–198). Hershey, PA: IGI Global. doi:10.4018/978-1-61520-817-3.ch013

Kalyuga, S. (2012). Cognitive load aspects of text processing. In C. Boonthum-Denecke, P. McCarthy, & T. Lamkin (Eds.), *Cross-disciplinary advances in applied natural language processing: Issues and approaches* (pp. 114–132). Hershey, PA: IGI Global. doi:10.4018/978-1-61350-447-5.ch009

Kammler, D., Witte, E. M., Chattopadhyay, A., Bauwens, B., Ascheid, G., Leupers, R., & Meyr, H. (2012). Automatic generation of memory interfaces for ASIPs. In S. Virtanen (Ed.), *Innovations in embedded and real-time systems engineering for communication* (pp. 79–100). Hershey, PA: IGI Global. doi:10.4018/978-1-4666-0912-9.ch005

Khan, T. M. (2011). Theory of mind in autistic children: multimedia based support. In P. Ordóñez de Pablos, J. Zhao, & R. Tennyson (Eds.), *Technology enhanced learning for people with disabilities: Approaches and applications* (pp. 167–179). Hershey, PA: IGI Global. doi:10.4018/978-1-61520-923-1.ch012

Khetrapal, N. (2010). Cognition meets assistive technology: Insights from load theory of selective attention. In S. Seok, E. Meyen, & B. DaCosta (Eds.), *Handbook of research on human cognition and assistive technology: Design, accessibility and transdisciplinary perspectives* (pp. 96–108). Hershey, PA: IGI Global. doi:10.4018/978-1-61520-817-3.ch006

Khetrapal, N. (2010). Cognitive science helps formulate games for moral education. In K. Schrier & D. Gibson (Eds.), *Ethics and game design: Teaching values through play* (pp. 181–196). Hershey, PA: IGI Global. doi:10.4018/978-1-61520-845-6.ch012

Kickmeier-Rust, M. D., Mattheiss, E., Steiner, C., & Albert, D. (2011). A psycho-pedagogical framework for multi-adaptive educational games. *International Journal of Game-Based Learning*, *1*(1), 45–58. doi:10.4018/ijgbl.2011010104

Kiel, L. D., & McCaskill, J. (2013). Cognition and complexity: An agent-based model of cognitive capital under stress. In S. Banerjee (Ed.), *Chaos and complexity theory for management: Nonlinear dynamics* (pp. 254–268). Hershey, PA: IGI Global. doi:10.4018/978-1-4666-2509-9.ch012

Kiili, K., & Perttula, A. (2013). A design framework for educational exergames. In S. de Freitas, M. Ott, M. Popescu, & I. Stanescu (Eds.), *New pedagogical approaches in game enhanced learning: Curriculum integration* (pp. 136–158). Hershey, PA: IGI Global. doi:10.4018/978-1-4666-3950-8.ch008

Kiliç, F. (2011). Structuring of knowledge and cognitive load. In G. Kurubacak & T. Yuzer (Eds.), *Handbook of research on transformative online education and liberation: Models for social equality* (pp. 370–382). Hershey, PA: IGI Global. doi:10.4018/978-1-60960-046-4.ch020

Kim, E. B. (2011). Student personality and learning outcomes in e-learning: An introduction to empirical research. In S. Eom & J. Arbaugh (Eds.), *Student satisfaction and learning outcomes in e-learning: An introduction to empirical research* (pp. 294–315). Hershey, PA: IGI Global. doi:10.4018/978-1-60960-615-2.ch013

Kinsell, C. (2010). Investigating assistive technologies using computers to simulate basic curriculum for individuals with cognitive impairments. In S. Seok, E. Meyen, & B. DaCosta (Eds.), *Handbook of research on human cognition and assistive technology: Design, accessibility and transdisciplinary perspectives* (pp. 61–75). Hershey, PA: IGI Global. doi:10.4018/978-1-61520-817-3.ch004

Kirwan, G., & Power, A. (2012). Can forensic psychology contribute to solving the problem of cybercrime? In G. Kirwan & A. Power (Eds.), *The psychology of cyber crime: Concepts and principles* (pp. 18–36). Hershey, PA: IGI Global. doi:10.4018/978-1-61350-350-8.ch002

Klippel, A., Richter, K., & Hansen, S. (2013). Cognitively ergonomic route directions. In *Geographic information systems: Concepts, methodologies, tools, and applications* (pp. 250–257). Hershey, PA: IGI Global. doi:10.4018/978-1-4666-2038-4.ch017

Knafla, B., & Champandard, A. J. (2012). Behavior trees: Introduction and memory-compact implementation. In A. Kumar, J. Etheredge, & A. Boudreaux (Eds.), *Algorithmic and architectural gaming design: Implementation and development* (pp. 40–66). Hershey, PA: IGI Global. doi:10.4018/978-1-4666-1634-9.ch003

Kokkinos, C. M., Antoniadou, N., Dalara, E., Koufogazou, A., & Papatziki, A. (2013). Cyber-bullying, personality and coping among pre-adolescents. *International Journal of Cyber Behavior, Psychology and Learning, 3*(4), 55–69. doi:10.4018/ijcbpl.2013100104

Konrath, S. (2013). The empathy paradox: Increasing disconnection in the age of increasing connection. In R. Luppicini (Ed.), *Handbook of research on technoself: Identity in a technological society* (pp. 204–228). Hershey, PA: IGI Global. doi:10.4018/978-1-4666-2211-1.ch012

Kopp, B., & Mandl, H. (2012). Supporting virtual collaborative learning using collaboration scripts and content schemes. In *Virtual learning environments: Concepts, methodologies, tools and applications* (pp. 470–487). Hershey, PA: IGI Global. doi:10.4018/978-1-4666-0011-9.ch303

Kumar, S., Singhal, D., & Murthy, G. R. (2013). Doubly cognitive architecture based cognitive wireless sensor networks. In N. Chilamkurti (Ed.), *Security, design, and architecture for broadband and wireless network technologies* (pp. 121–126). Hershey, PA: IGI Global. doi:10.4018/978-1-4666-3902-7.ch009

Kutaula, S., & Talwar, V. (2014). Integrating psychological contract and service-related outcomes in emerging economies: A proposed conceptual framework. In A. Goyal (Ed.), *Innovations in services marketing and management: Strategies for emerging economies* (pp. 291–306). Hershey, PA: IGI Global. doi:10.4018/978-1-4666-4671-1.ch016

Kyriakaki, G., & Matsatsinis, N. (2014). Pedagogical evaluation of e-learning websites with cognitive objectives. In D. Yannacopoulos, P. Manolitzas, N. Matsatsinis, & E. Grigoroudis (Eds.), *Evaluating websites and web services: Interdisciplinary perspectives on user satisfaction* (pp. 224–240). Hershey, PA: IGI Global. doi:10.4018/978-1-4666-5129-6.ch013

Kyritsis, M., Gulliver, S. R., & Morar, S. (2014). Cognitive and environmental factors influencing the process of spatial knowledge acquisition within virtual reality environments. *International Journal of Artificial Life Research, 4*(1), 43–58. doi:10.4018/ijalr.2014010104

Laffey, J., Stichter, J., & Schmidt, M. (2010). Social orthotics for youth with ASD to learn in a collaborative 3D VLE. In S. Seok, E. Meyen, & B. DaCosta (Eds.), *Handbook of research on human cognition and assistive technology: Design, accessibility and transdisciplinary perspectives* (pp. 76–95). Hershey, PA: IGI Global. doi:10.4018/978-1-61520-817-3.ch005

Lai, S., & Han, H. (2014). Behavioral planning theory. In J. Wang (Ed.), *Encyclopedia of business analytics and optimization* (pp. 265–272). Hershey, PA: IGI Global. doi:10.4018/978-1-4666-5202-6.ch025

Lawson, D. (2013). Analysis and use of the life styles inventory 1 and 2 by human synergistics international. In M. Bocarnea, R. Reynolds, & J. Baker (Eds.), *Online instruments, data collection, and electronic measurements: Organizational advancements* (pp. 76–96). Hershey, PA: IGI Global. doi:10.4018/978-1-4666-2172-5.ch005

Lee, L., & Hung, J. C. (2011). Effect of teaching using whole brain instruction on accounting learning. In Q. Jin (Ed.), *Distance education environments and emerging software systems: New technologies* (pp. 261–282). Hershey, PA: IGI Global. doi:10.4018/978-1-60960-539-1.ch016

Levin, I., & Kojukhov, A. (2013). Personalization of learning environments in a post-industrial class. In M. Pătruţ & B. Pătruţ (Eds.), *Social media in higher education: Teaching in web 2.0* (pp. 105–123). Hershey, PA: IGI Global. doi:10.4018/978-1-4666-2970-7.ch006

Li, A., Li, H., Guo, R., & Zhu, T. (2013). MobileSens: A ubiquitous psychological laboratory based on mobile device. *International Journal of Cyber Behavior, Psychology and Learning*, 3(2), 47–55. doi:10.4018/ijcbpl.2013040104

Li, R. (2013). Traditional to hybrid: Social media's role in reshaping instruction in higher education. In A. Sigal (Ed.), *Advancing library education: Technological innovation and instructional design* (pp. 65–90). Hershey, PA: IGI Global. doi:10.4018/978-1-4666-3688-0.ch005

Li, X., Lin, Z., & Wu, J. (2014). Language processing in the human brain of literate and illiterate subjects. In *Computational linguistics: Concepts, methodologies, tools, and applications* (pp. 1391–1400). Hershey, PA: IGI Global. doi:10.4018/978-1-4666-6042-7.ch068

Li, X., Ouyang, Z., & Luo, Y. (2013). The cognitive load affects the interaction pattern of emotion and working memory. *International Journal of Cognitive Informatics and Natural Intelligence*, 6(2), 68–81. doi:10.4018/jcini.2012040104

Lin, T., Li, X., Wu, Z., & Tang, N. (2013). Automatic cognitive load classification using high-frequency interaction events: An exploratory study. *International Journal of Technology and Human Interaction*, 9(3), 73–88. doi:10.4018/jthi.2013070106

Linek, S. B. (2011). As you like it: What media psychology can tell us about educational game design. In P. Felicia (Ed.), *Handbook of research on improving learning and motivation through educational games: Multidisciplinary approaches* (pp. 606–632). Hershey, PA: IGI Global. doi:10.4018/978-1-60960-495-0.ch029

Linek, S. B., Marte, B., & Albert, D. (2014). Background music in educational games: Motivational appeal and cognitive impact. In J. Bishop (Ed.), *Gamification for human factors integration: Social, education, and psychological issues* (pp. 259–271). Hershey, PA: IGI Global. doi:10.4018/978-1-4666-5071-8.ch016

Logeswaran, R. (2011). Neural networks in medicine. In *Clinical technologies: Concepts, methodologies, tools and applications* (pp. 744–765). Hershey, PA: IGI Global. doi:10.4018/978-1-60960-561-2.ch308

Low, R. (2011). Cognitive architecture and instructional design in a multimedia context. In *Instructional design: Concepts, methodologies, tools and applications* (pp. 496–510). Hershey, PA: IGI Global. doi:10.4018/978-1-60960-503-2.ch301

Low, R., Jin, P., & Sweller, J. (2014). Instructional design in digital environments and availability of mental resources for the aged subpopulation. In *Assistive technologies: Concepts, methodologies, tools, and applications* (pp. 1131–1154). Hershey, PA: IGI Global. doi:10.4018/978-1-4666-4422-9.ch059

Lu, J., & Peng, Y. (2014). Brain-computer interface for cyberpsychology: Components, methods, and applications. *International Journal of Cyber Behavior, Psychology and Learning*, 4(1), 1–14. doi:10.4018/ijcbpl.2014010101

Ludvig, E. A., Bellemare, M. G., & Pearson, K. G. (2011). A primer on reinforcement learning in the brain: Psychological, computational, and neural perspectives. In E. Alonso & E. Mondragón (Eds.), *Computational neuroscience for advancing artificial intelligence: Models, methods and applications* (pp. 111–144). Hershey, PA: IGI Global. doi:10.4018/978-1-60960-021-1.ch006

Lützenberger, M. (2014). A driver's mind: Psychology runs simulation. In D. Janssens, A. Yasar, & L. Knapen (Eds.), *Data science and simulation in transportation research* (pp. 182–205). Hershey, PA: IGI Global. doi:10.4018/978-1-4666-4920-0.ch010

Mancha, R., Yoder, C. Y., & Clark, J. G. (2013). Dynamics of affect and cognition in simulated agents: Bridging the gap between experimental and simulation research. *International Journal of Agent Technologies and Systems*, 5(2), 78–96. doi:10.4018/jats.2013040104

Manchiraju, S. (2014). Predicting behavioral intentions toward sustainable fashion consumption: A comparison of attitude-behavior and value-behavior consistency models. In H. Kaufmann & M. Panni (Eds.), *Handbook of research on consumerism in business and marketing: Concepts and practices* (pp. 225–243). Hershey, PA: IGI Global. doi:10.4018/978-1-4666-5880-6.ch011

Mancilla, R. L. (2013). Getting smart about split attention. In B. Zou, M. Xing, Y. Wang, M. Sun, & C. Xiang (Eds.), *Computer-assisted foreign language teaching and learning: Technological advances* (pp. 210–229). Hershey, PA: IGI Global. doi:10.4018/978-1-4666-2821-2.ch012

Manrique-de-Lara, P. Z. (2013). Does discretionary internet-based behavior of instructors contribute to student satisfaction? An empirical study on 'cybercivism'. *International Journal of Cyber Behavior, Psychology and Learning*, 3(1), 50–66. doi:10.4018/ijcbpl.2013010105

Markov, K., Vanhoof, K., Mitov, I., Depaire, B., Ivanova, K., Velychko, V., & Gladun, V. (2013). Intelligent data processing based on multi-dimensional numbered memory structures. In X. Naidenova & D. Ignatov (Eds.), *Diagnostic test approaches to machine learning and commonsense reasoning systems* (pp. 156–184). Hershey, PA: IGI Global. doi:10.4018/978-1-4666-1900-5.ch007

Martin, J. N. (2014). How can we incorporate relevant findings from psychology into systems methods? *International Journal of Systems and Society*, 1(1), 1–11. doi:10.4018/ijss.2014010101

Mayer, I., Bekebrede, G., Warmelink, H., & Zhou, Q. (2014). A brief methodology for researching and evaluating serious games and game-based learning. In T. Connolly, T. Hainey, E. Boyle, G. Baxter, & P. Moreno-Ger (Eds.), *Psychology, pedagogy, and assessment in serious games* (pp. 357–393). Hershey, PA: IGI Global. doi:10.4018/978-1-4666-4773-2.ch017

Mazumdar, B. D., & Mishra, R. B. (2011). Cognitive parameter based agent selection and negotiation process for B2C e-commerce. In V. Sugumaran (Ed.), *Intelligent, adaptive and reasoning technologies: New developments and applications* (pp. 181–203). Hershey, PA: IGI Global. doi:10.4018/978-1-60960-595-7.ch010

McLaren, I. (2011). APECS: An adaptively parameterised model of associative learning and memory. In E. Alonso & E. Mondragón (Eds.), *Computational neuroscience for advancing artificial intelligence: Models, methods and applications* (pp. 145–164). Hershey, PA: IGI Global. doi:10.4018/978-1-60960-021-1.ch007

McMurray, B., Zhao, L., Kucker, S. C., & Samuelson, L. K. (2013). Pushing the envelope of associative learning: Internal representations and dynamic competition transform association into development. In L. Gogate & G. Hollich (Eds.), *Theoretical and computational models of word learning: Trends in psychology and artificial intelligence* (pp. 49–80). Hershey, PA: IGI Global. doi:10.4018/978-1-4666-2973-8.ch003

Mena, R. J. (2014). The quest for a massively multiplayer online game that teaches physics. In T. Connolly, T. Hainey, E. Boyle, G. Baxter, & P. Moreno-Ger (Eds.), *Psychology, pedagogy, and assessment in serious games* (pp. 292–316). Hershey, PA: IGI Global. doi:10.4018/978-1-4666-4773-2.ch014

Misra, S. (2011). Cognitive complexity measures: An analysis. In A. Dogru & V. Biçer (Eds.), *Modern software engineering concepts and practices: Advanced approaches* (pp. 263–279). Hershey, PA: IGI Global. doi:10.4018/978-1-60960-215-4.ch011

Mok, J. (2010). Social and distributed cognition in collaborative learning contexts. In S. Dasgupta (Ed.), *Social computing: Concepts, methodologies, tools, and applications* (pp. 1838–1854). Hershey, PA: IGI Global. doi:10.4018/978-1-60566-984-7.ch121

Moore, J. E., & Love, M. S. (2013). An examination of prestigious stigma: The case of the technology geek. In B. Medlin (Ed.), *Integrations of technology utilization and social dynamics in organizations* (pp. 48–73). Hershey, PA: IGI Global. doi:10.4018/978-1-4666-1948-7.ch004

Moore, M. J., Nakano, T., Suda, T., & Enomoto, A. (2013). Social interactions and automated detection tools in cyberbullying. In L. Caviglione, M. Coccoli, & A. Merlo (Eds.), *Social network engineering for secure web data and services* (pp. 67–87). Hershey, PA: IGI Global. doi:10.4018/978-1-4666-3926-3.ch004

Moseley, A. (2014). A case for integration: Assessment and games. In T. Connolly, T. Hainey, E. Boyle, G. Baxter, & P. Moreno-Ger (Eds.), *Psychology, pedagogy, and assessment in serious games* (pp. 342–356). Hershey, PA: IGI Global. doi:10.4018/978-1-4666-4773-2.ch016

Mpofu, S. (2014). Memory, national identity, and freedom of expression in the information age: Discussing the taboo in the Zimbabwean public sphere. In A. Solo (Ed.), *Handbook of research on political activism in the information age* (pp. 114–128). Hershey, PA: IGI Global. doi:10.4018/978-1-4666-6066-3.ch007

Mulvey, F., & Heubner, M. (2014). Eye movements and attention. In *Assistive technologies: Concepts, methodologies, tools, and applications* (pp. 1030–1054). Hershey, PA: IGI Global. doi:10.4018/978-1-4666-4422-9.ch053

Munipov, V. (2011). Psychological and social problems of automation and computerization. In D. Haftor & A. Mirijamdotter (Eds.), *Information and communication technologies, society and human beings: Theory and framework (Festschrift in honor of Gunilla Bradley)* (pp. 136–146). Hershey, PA: IGI Global. doi:10.4018/978-1-60960-057-0.ch012

Najjar, M., & Mayers, A. (2012). A cognitive computational knowledge representation theory. In *Machine learning: Concepts, methodologies, tools and applications* (pp. 1819–1838). Hershey, PA: IGI Global. doi:10.4018/978-1-60960-818-7.ch708

Nakamura, H. (2011). Cognitive decline in patients with Alzheimer's disease: A six-year longitudinal study of mini-mental state examination scores. In J. Wu (Ed.), *Early detection and rehabilitation technologies for dementia: Neuroscience and biomedical applications* (pp. 107–111). Hershey, PA: IGI Global. doi:10.4018/978-1-60960-559-9.ch013

Nankee, C. (2010). Switch technologies. In S. Seok, E. Meyen, & B. DaCosta (Eds.), *Handbook of research on human cognition and assistive technology: Design, accessibility and transdisciplinary perspectives* (pp. 157–168). Hershey, PA: IGI Global. doi:10.4018/978-1-61520-817-3.ch010

Nap, H. H., & Diaz-Orueta, U. (2014). Rehabilitation gaming. In J. Bishop (Ed.), *Gamification for human factors integration: Social, education, and psychological issues* (pp. 122–147). Hershey, PA: IGI Global. doi:10.4018/978-1-4666-5071-8.ch008

Naranjo-Saucedo, A. B., Suárez-Mejías, C., Parra-Calderón, C. L., González-Aguado, E., Böckel-Martínez, F., Yuste-Marco, A., … Marco, A. (2014). Interactive games with robotic and augmented reality technology in cognitive and motor rehabilitation. In Robotics: Concepts, methodologies, tools, and applications (pp. 1233-1254). Hershey, PA: IGI Global. doi:10.4018/978-1-4666-4607-0.ch059

Ndinguri, E., Machtmes, K., Hatala, J. P., & Coco, M. L. (2014). Learning through immersive virtual environments: An organizational context. In J. Keengwe, G. Schnellert, & K. Kungu (Eds.), *Cross-cultural online learning in higher education and corporate training* (pp. 185–199). Hershey, PA: IGI Global. doi:10.4018/978-1-4666-5023-7.ch010

Ninaus, M., Witte, M., Kober, S. E., Friedrich, E. V., Kurzmann, J., Hartsuiker, E., … Wood, G. (2014). Neurofeedback and serious games. In T. Connolly, T. Hainey, E. Boyle, G. Baxter, & P. Moreno-Ger (Eds.), Psychology, pedagogy, and assessment in serious games (pp. 82-110). Hershey, PA: IGI Global. doi:10.4018/978-1-4666-4773-2.ch005

Nobre, F. S. (2012). The roles of cognitive machines in customer-centric organizations: Towards innovations in computational organizational management networks. In F. Nobre, D. Walker, & R. Harris (Eds.), *Technological, managerial and organizational core competencies: Dynamic innovation and sustainable development* (pp. 653–674). Hershey, PA: IGI Global. doi:10.4018/978-1-61350-165-8.ch035

Norris, S. E. (2014). Transformative curriculum design and program development: Creating effective adult learning by leveraging psychological capital and self-directedness through the exercise of human agency. In V. Wang & V. Bryan (Eds.), *Andragogical and pedagogical methods for curriculum and program development* (pp. 118–141). Hershey, PA: IGI Global. doi:10.4018/978-1-4666-5872-1.ch007

Norris, S. E., & Porter, T. H. (2013). Self-monitoring scale. In M. Bocarnea, R. Reynolds, & J. Baker (Eds.), *Online instruments, data collection, and electronic measurements: Organizational advancements* (pp. 118–133). Hershey, PA: IGI Global. doi:10.4018/978-1-4666-2172-5.ch007

O'Connell, R. M. (2014). Mind mapping for critical thinking. In L. Shedletsky & J. Beaudry (Eds.), *Cases on teaching critical thinking through visual representation strategies* (pp. 354–386). Hershey, PA: IGI Global. doi:10.4018/978-1-4666-5816-5.ch014

Okrigwe, B. N. (2010). Cognition and learning. In S. Seok, E. Meyen, & B. DaCosta (Eds.), *Handbook of research on human cognition and assistive technology: Design, accessibility and transdisciplinary perspectives* (pp. 388–400). Hershey, PA: IGI Global. doi:10.4018/978-1-61520-817-3.ch027

Ong, E. H., & Khan, J. Y. (2013). Cognitive cooperation in wireless networks. In M. Ku & J. Lin (Eds.), *Cognitive radio and interference management: Technology and strategy* (pp. 179–204). Hershey, PA: IGI Global. doi:10.4018/978-1-4666-2005-6.ch010

Orlova, M. (2014). Social psychology of health as a social-psychological situation. In Ş. Erçetin & S. Banerjee (Eds.), *Chaos and complexity theory in world politics* (pp. 331–335). Hershey, PA: IGI Global. doi:10.4018/978-1-4666-6070-0.ch024

Orr, K., & McGuinness, C. (2014). What is the "learning" in games-based learning? In T. Connolly, T. Hainey, E. Boyle, G. Baxter, & P. Moreno-Ger (Eds.), Psychology, pedagogy, and assessment in serious games (pp. 221-242). Hershey, PA: IGI Global. doi:10.4018/978-1-4666-4773-2.ch011

Ortiz Zezzatti, C. A., Martínez, J., Castillo, N., González, S., & Hernández, P. (2012). Improve card collection from memory alpha using sociolinguistics and Japanese puzzles. In C. Ortiz Zezzatti, C. Chira, A. Hernandez, & M. Basurto (Eds.), *Logistics management and optimization through hybrid artificial intelligence systems* (pp. 310–326). Hershey, PA: IGI Global. doi:10.4018/978-1-4666-0297-7.ch012

Ota, N., Maeshima, S., Osawa, A., Kawarada, M., & Tanemura, J. (2011). Prospective memory impairment in remembering to remember in mild cognitive impairment and healthy subjects. In J. Wu (Ed.), *Early detection and rehabilitation technologies for dementia: Neuroscience and biomedical applications* (pp. 98–106). Hershey, PA: IGI Global. doi:10.4018/978-1-60960-559-9.ch012

Ouwehand, K., van Gog, T., & Paas, F. (2013). The use of gesturing to facilitate older adults' learning from computer-based dynamic visualizations. In R. Zheng, R. Hill, & M. Gardner (Eds.), *Engaging older adults with modern technology: Internet use and information access needs* (pp. 33–58). Hershey, PA: IGI Global. doi:10.4018/978-1-4666-1966-1.ch003

Özel, S. (2012). Utilizing cognitive resources in user interface designs. In B. Khan (Ed.), *User interface design for virtual environments: Challenges and advances* (pp. 115–123). Hershey, PA: IGI Global. doi:10.4018/978-1-61350-516-8.ch007

Parsons, T. D., & Courtney, C. G. (2011). Neurocognitive and psychophysiological interfaces for adaptive virtual environments. In M. Ziefle & C. Röcker (Eds.), *Human-centered design of e-health technologies: Concepts, methods and applications* (pp. 208–233). Hershey, PA: IGI Global. doi:10.4018/978-1-60960-177-5.ch009

Peden, B. F., & Tiry, A. M. (2013). Using web surveys for psychology experiments: A case study in new media technology for research. In N. Sappleton (Ed.), *Advancing research methods with new technologies* (pp. 70–99). Hershey, PA: IGI Global. doi:10.4018/978-1-4666-3918-8.ch005

Perakslis, C. (2014). Willingness to adopt RFID implants: Do personality factors play a role in the acceptance of uberveillance? In M. Michael & K. Michael (Eds.), *Uberveillance and the social implications of microchip implants: Emerging technologies* (pp. 144–168). Hershey, PA: IGI Global. doi:10.4018/978-1-4666-4582-0.ch006

Pereira, G., Brisson, A., Dias, J., Carvalho, A., Dimas, J., Mascarenhas, S., ... Paiva, A. (2014). Non-player characters and artificial intelligence. In T. Connolly, T. Hainey, E. Boyle, G. Baxter, & P. Moreno-Ger (Eds.), *Psychology, pedagogy, and assessment in serious games* (pp. 127-152). Hershey, PA: IGI Global. doi:10.4018/978-1-4666-4773-2.ch007

Pereira, R., Hornung, H., & Baranauskas, M. C. (2014). Cognitive authority revisited in web social interaction. In M. Pańkowska (Ed.), *Frameworks of IT prosumption for business development* (pp. 142–157). Hershey, PA: IGI Global. doi:10.4018/978-1-4666-4313-0.ch010

Phebus, A. M., Gitlin, B., Shuffler, M. L., & Wildman, J. L. (2014). Leading global virtual teams: The supporting role of trust and team cognition. In E. Nikoi & K. Boateng (Eds.), *Collaborative communication processes and decision making in organizations* (pp. 177–200). Hershey, PA: IGI Global. doi:10.4018/978-1-4666-4478-6.ch010

Plunkett, D., Banerjee, R., & Horn, E. (2010). Supporting early childhood outcomes through assistive technology. In S. Seok, E. Meyen, & B. DaCosta (Eds.), *Handbook of research on human cognition and assistive technology: Design, accessibility and transdisciplinary perspectives* (pp. 339–359). Hershey, PA: IGI Global. doi:10.4018/978-1-61520-817-3.ch024

Prakash, S., Vaish, A., Coul, N., Saravana, G. K., Srinidhi, T. N., & Botsa, J. (2014). Child security in cyberspace through moral cognition. In *Cyber behavior: Concepts, methodologies, tools, and applications* (pp. 1946–1958). Hershey, PA: IGI Global. doi:10.4018/978-1-4666-5942-1.ch102

Prescott, J., & Bogg, J. (2013). Self, career, and gender issues: A complex interplay of internal/external factors. In *Gendered occupational differences in science, engineering, and technology careers* (pp. 79–111). Hershey, PA: IGI Global. doi:10.4018/978-1-4666-2107-7.ch004

Prescott, J., & Bogg, J. (2013). Stereotype, attitudes, and identity: Gendered expectations and behaviors. In *Gendered occupational differences in science, engineering, and technology careers* (pp. 112–135). Hershey, PA: IGI Global. doi:10.4018/978-1-4666-2107-7.ch005

Pressey, A., Salciuviene, L., & Barnes, S. (2013). Uncovering relationships between emotional states and higher-order needs: Enhancing consumer emotional experiences in computer-mediated environment. *International Journal of Online Marketing, 3*(1), 31–46. doi:10.4018/ijom.2013010103

Qin, X., Li, C., Chen, H., Qin, B., Du, X., & Wang, S. (2014). In memory data processing systems. In J. Wang (Ed.), *Encyclopedia of business analytics and optimization* (pp. 1182–1191). Hershey, PA: IGI Global. doi:10.4018/978-1-4666-5202-6.ch109

Ramos, I., & Oliveira e Sá, J. (2014). Organizational memory: The role of business intelligence to leverage the application of collective knowledge. In H. Rahman & R. de Sousa (Eds.), *Information systems and technology for organizational agility, intelligence, and resilience* (pp. 206–223). Hershey, PA: IGI Global. doi:10.4018/978-1-4666-5970-4.ch010

Ratten, V. (2013). The development of social e-enterprises, mobile communication and social networks: A social cognitive perspective of technological innovation. *Journal of Electronic Commerce in Organizations, 11*(3), 68–77. doi:10.4018/jeco.2013070104

Reddy, Y. B. (2013). Nanocomputing in cognitive radio networks to improve the performance. In N. Meghanathan & Y. Reddy (Eds.), *Cognitive radio technology applications for wireless and mobile ad hoc networks* (pp. 173–193). Hershey, PA: IGI Global. doi:10.4018/978-1-4666-4221-8.ch010

Redien-Collot, R., & Lefebvre, M. R. (2014). SMEs' leaders: Building collective cognition and competences to trigger positive strategic outcomes. In K. Todorov & D. Smallbone (Eds.), *Handbook of research on strategic management in small and medium enterprises* (pp. 143–158). Hershey, PA: IGI Global. doi:10.4018/978-1-4666-5962-9.ch008

Remmele, B., & Whitton, N. (2014). Disrupting the magic circle: The impact of negative social gaming behaviours. In T. Connolly, T. Hainey, E. Boyle, G. Baxter, & P. Moreno-Ger (Eds.), *Psychology, pedagogy, and assessment in serious games* (pp. 111–126). Hershey, PA: IGI Global. doi:10.4018/978-1-4666-4773-2.ch006

Renaud, P., Chartier, S., Fedoroff, P., Bradford, J., & Rouleau, J. L. (2011). The use of virtual reality in clinical psychology research. In *Clinical technologies: Concepts, methodologies, tools and applications* (pp. 2073–2093). Hershey, PA: IGI Global. doi:10.4018/978-1-60960-561-2.ch805

Revett, K. (2012). Cognitive biometrics: A novel approach to continuous person authentication. In I. Traore & A. Ahmed (Eds.), *Continuous authentication using biometrics: Data, models, and metrics* (pp. 105–136). Hershey, PA: IGI Global. doi:10.4018/978-1-61350-129-0.ch006

Rødseth, I. (2011). A motive analysis as a first step in designing technology for the use of intuition in criminal investigation. In A. Mesquita (Ed.), *Sociological and philosophical aspects of human interaction with technology: Advancing concepts* (pp. 276–298). Hershey, PA: IGI Global. doi:10.4018/978-1-60960-575-9.ch015

Rothblatt, M. (2014). Mindclone technoselves: Multi-substrate legal identities, cyber-psychology, and biocyberethics. In *Cyber behavior: Concepts, methodologies, tools, and applications* (pp. 1199–1216). Hershey, PA: IGI Global. doi:10.4018/978-1-4666-5942-1.ch062

Rückemann, C. (2013). Integrated information and computing systems for advanced cognition with natural sciences. In C. Rückemann (Ed.), *Integrated information and computing systems for natural, spatial, and social sciences* (pp. 1–26). Hershey, PA: IGI Global. doi:10.4018/978-1-4666-2190-9.ch001

Rudnianski, M., & Kravcik, M. (2014). The road to critical thinking and intelligence analysis. In T. Connolly, T. Hainey, E. Boyle, G. Baxter, & P. Moreno-Ger (Eds.), *Psychology, pedagogy, and assessment in serious games* (pp. 47–61). Hershey, PA: IGI Global. doi:10.4018/978-1-4666-4773-2.ch003

Rufer, R., & Adams, R. H. (2012). Adapting three-dimensional-virtual world to reach diverse learners in an MBA program. In H. Yang & S. Yuen (Eds.), *Handbook of research on practices and outcomes in virtual worlds and environments* (pp. 606–619). Hershey, PA: IGI Global. doi:10.4018/978-1-60960-762-3.ch033

Saadé, R. G. (2010). Cognitive mapping decision support for the design of web-based learning environments. *International Journal of Web-Based Learning and Teaching Technologies*, 5(3), 36–53. doi:10.4018/jwltt.2010070103

Saeed, N., & Sinnappan, S. (2014). Comparing learning styles and technology acceptance of two culturally different groups of students. In T. Issa, P. Isaias, & P. Kommers (Eds.), *Multicultural awareness and technology in higher education: Global perspectives* (pp. 244–264). Hershey, PA: IGI Global. doi:10.4018/978-1-4666-5876-9.ch012

Samuelson, L. K., Spencer, J. P., & Jenkins, G. W. (2013). A dynamic neural field model of word learning. In L. Gogate & G. Hollich (Eds.), *Theoretical and computational models of word learning: Trends in psychology and artificial intelligence* (pp. 1–27). Hershey, PA: IGI Global. doi:10.4018/978-1-4666-2973-8.ch001

Sanjram, P. K., & Gupta, M. (2013). Task difficulty and time constraint in programmer multitasking: An analysis of prospective memory performance and cognitive workload. *International Journal of Green Computing*, 4(1), 35–57. doi:10.4018/jgc.2013010103

Sato, Y., Ji, Z., & van Dijk, S. (2013). I think I have heard that one before: Recurrence-based word learning with a robot. In L. Gogate & G. Hollich (Eds.), *Theoretical and computational models of word learning: Trends in psychology and artificial intelligence* (pp. 327–349). Hershey, PA: IGI Global. doi:10.4018/978-1-4666-2973-8.ch014

Scalzone, F., & Zontini, G. (2013). Thinking animals and thinking machines in psychoanalysis and beyond. In F. Orsucci & N. Sala (Eds.), *Complexity science, living systems, and reflexing interfaces: New models and perspectives* (pp. 44–68). Hershey, PA: IGI Global. doi:10.4018/978-1-4666-2077-3.ch003

Schafer, S. B. (2013). Fostering psychological coherence: With ICTs. In M. Cruz-Cunha, I. Miranda, & P. Gonçalves (Eds.), *Handbook of research on ICTs for human-centered healthcare and social care services* (pp. 29–47). Hershey, PA: IGI Global. doi:10.4018/978-1-4666-3986-7.ch002

Scheiter, K., Wiebe, E., & Holsanova, J. (2011). Theoretical and instructional aspects of learning with visualizations. In *Instructional design: Concepts, methodologies, tools and applications* (pp. 1667–1688). Hershey, PA: IGI Global. doi:10.4018/978-1-60960-503-2.ch710

Seo, K. K., Byk, A., & Collins, C. (2011). Cognitive apprenticeship inspired simulations. In *Gaming and simulations: Concepts, methodologies, tools and applications* (pp. 346–358). Hershey, PA: IGI Global. doi:10.4018/978-1-60960-195-9.ch202

Serenko, N. (2014). Informational, physical, and psychological privacy as determinants of patient behaviour in health care. In V. Michell, D. Rosenorn-Lanng, S. Gulliver, & W. Currie (Eds.), *Handbook of research on patient safety and quality care through health informatics* (pp. 1–20). Hershey, PA: IGI Global. doi:10.4018/978-1-4666-4546-2.ch001

Shibata, T. (2013). A human-like cognitive computer based on a psychologically inspired VLSI brain model. In J. Wu (Ed.), *Technological advancements in biomedicine for healthcare applications* (pp. 247–266). Hershey, PA: IGI Global. doi:10.4018/978-1-4666-2196-1.ch027

Shirkhodaee, M., & Rezaee, S. (2013). Evaluating the persuasive and memory effects of viral advertising. *International Journal of Online Marketing*, 3(3), 51–61. doi:10.4018/ijom.2013070104

Simzar, R., & Domina, T. (2014). Attending to student motivation through critical practice: A recommendation for improving accelerated mathematical learning. In S. Lawrence (Ed.), *Critical practice in P-12 education: Transformative teaching and learning* (pp. 66–116). Hershey, PA: IGI Global. doi:10.4018/978-1-4666-5059-6.ch004

Smart, P. R., Engelbrecht, P. C., Braines, D., Strub, M., & Giammanco, C. (2010). The network-extended mind. In D. Verma (Ed.), *Network science for military coalition operations: Information exchange and interaction* (pp. 191–236). Hershey, PA: IGI Global. doi:10.4018/978-1-61520-855-5.ch010

Smith, M. A. (2011). Functions of unconscious and conscious emotion in the regulation of implicit and explicit motivated behavior. In D. Gökçay & G. Yildirim (Eds.), *Affective computing and interaction: Psychological, cognitive and neuroscientific perspectives* (pp. 25–55). Hershey, PA: IGI Global. doi:10.4018/978-1-61692-892-6.ch002

Soliman, F. (2014). Could knowledge, learning, and innovation gaps be spiralling? In F. Soliman (Ed.), *Learning models for innovation in organizations: Examining roles of knowledge transfer and human resources management* (pp. 1–29). Hershey, PA: IGI Global. doi:10.4018/978-1-4666-4884-5.ch001

Somyürek, S. (2012). Interactive learning in workplace training. In J. Jia (Ed.), *Educational stages and interactive learning: From kindergarten to workplace training* (pp. 498–514). Hershey, PA: IGI Global. doi:10.4018/978-1-4666-0137-6.ch027

Spadaro, L., Timpano, F., Marino, S., & Bramanti, P. (2013). Telemedicine and Alzheimer disease: ICT-based services for people with Alzheimer disease and their caregivers. In V. Gulla, A. Mori, F. Gabbrielli, & P. Lanzafame (Eds.), *Telehealth networks for hospital services: New methodologies* (pp. 191–206). Hershey, PA: IGI Global. doi:10.4018/978-1-4666-2979-0.ch013

Spiegel, T. (2014). An overview of cognition roles in decision-making. In J. Wang (Ed.), *Encyclopedia of business analytics and optimization* (pp. 74–84). Hershey, PA: IGI Global. doi:10.4018/978-1-4666-5202-6.ch008

Stachon, Z., & Šašinka, C. (2012). Human cognition: People in the world and world in their minds. In T. Podobnikar & M. Čeh (Eds.), *Universal ontology of geographic space: Semantic enrichment for spatial data* (pp. 97–122). Hershey, PA: IGI Global. doi:10.4018/978-1-4666-0327-1.ch005

Stefurak, J. R., Surry, D. W., & Hayes, R. L. (2011). Technology in the supervision of mental health professionals: Ethical, interpersonal, and epistemological implications. In D. Surry, R. Gray Jr, & J. Stefurak (Eds.), *Technology integration in higher education: Social and organizational aspects* (pp. 114–131). Hershey, PA: IGI Global. doi:10.4018/978-1-60960-147-8.ch009

Stieglitz, S. (2014). The American memory project. In J. Krueger (Ed.), *Cases on electronic records and resource management implementation in diverse environments* (pp. 106–116). Hershey, PA: IGI Global. doi:10.4018/978-1-4666-4466-3.ch006

Suárez, M. G., & Gumiel, C. G. (2014). The use of sensorial marketing in stores: Attracting clients through their senses. In F. Musso & E. Druica (Eds.), *Handbook of research on retailer-consumer relationship development* (pp. 258–274). Hershey, PA: IGI Global. doi:10.4018/978-1-4666-6074-8.ch014

Sugiura, M. (2013). A cognitive neuroscience approach to self and mental health. In J. Wu (Ed.), *Biomedical engineering and cognitive neuroscience for healthcare: Interdisciplinary applications* (pp. 1–10). Hershey, PA: IGI Global. doi:10.4018/978-1-4666-2113-8.ch001

Sujo-Montes, L. E., Armfield, S. W., Yen, C., & Tu, C. (2014). The use of ubiquitous learning for children with Down Syndrome. In F. Neto (Ed.), *Technology platform innovations and forthcoming trends in ubiquitous learning* (pp. 160–176). Hershey, PA: IGI Global. doi:10.4018/978-1-4666-4542-4.ch009

Tamba, H. (2013). Workers' mental health problems and future perspectives in Japan: Psychological job stress research. In J. Wu (Ed.), *Biomedical engineering and cognitive neuroscience for healthcare: Interdisciplinary applications* (pp. 370–379). Hershey, PA: IGI Global. doi:10.4018/978-1-4666-2113-8.ch038

Tatachari, S., Manikandan, K. S., & Gunta, S. (2014). A synthesis of organizational learning and knowledge management literatures. In M. Chilton & J. Bloodgood (Eds.), *Knowledge management and competitive advantage: Issues and potential solutions* (pp. 122–147). Hershey, PA: IGI Global. doi:10.4018/978-1-4666-4679-7.ch008

Taxén, L. (2010). Cognitive grounding. In L. Taxen (Ed.), *Using activity domain theory for managing complex systems* (pp. 108–124). Hershey, PA: IGI Global. doi:10.4018/978-1-60566-192-6.ch006

Te'eni, D. (2012). Knowledge for communicating knowledge. In *Organizational learning and knowledge: Concepts, methodologies, tools and applications* (pp. 1656–1665). Hershey, PA: IGI Global. doi:10.4018/978-1-60960-783-8.ch501

Terras, M. M., & Ramsay, J. (2014). E-learning, mobility, and time: A psychological framework. In E. Barbera & P. Reimann (Eds.), *Assessment and evaluation of time factors in online teaching and learning* (pp. 63–90). Hershey, PA: IGI Global. doi:10.4018/978-1-4666-4651-3.ch003

Thapa, A. (2013). A study on worker's perceptions of psychological capital on their earnings. *International Journal of Applied Behavioral Economics*, 2(3), 27–42. doi:10.4018/ijabe.2013070103

Thatcher, A., & Ndabeni, M. (2013). A psychological model to understand e-adoption in the context of the digital divide. In *Digital literacy: Concepts, methodologies, tools, and applications* (pp. 1402–1424). Hershey, PA: IGI Global. doi:10.4018/978-1-4666-1852-7.ch074

Thompson, K., & Markauskaite, L. (2014). Identifying group processes and affect in learners: A holistic approach to assessment in virtual worlds in higher education. In S. Kennedy-Clark, K. Everett, & P. Wheeler (Eds.), *Cases on the assessment of scenario and game-based virtual worlds in higher education* (pp. 175–210). Hershey, PA: IGI Global. doi:10.4018/978-1-4666-4470-0.ch006

Titus, C. S. (2013). The use of developmental psychology in ethics: Beyond Kohlberg and Seligman? In F. Doridot, P. Duquenoy, P. Goujon, A. Kurt, S. Lavelle, N. Patrignani, & A. Santuccio et al. (Eds.), *Ethical governance of emerging technologies development* (pp. 266–286). Hershey, PA: IGI Global. doi:10.4018/978-1-4666-3670-5.ch018

Tiwary, U. S., & Siddiqui, T. J. (2014). Working together with computers: Towards a general framework for collaborative human computer interaction. In *Assistive technologies: Concepts, methodologies, tools, and applications* (pp. 141–162). Hershey, PA: IGI Global. doi:10.4018/978-1-4666-4422-9.ch008

Tomono, A. (2013). Display technology of images with scents and its psychological evaluation. In T. Nakamoto (Ed.), *Human olfactory displays and interfaces: Odor sensing and presentation* (pp. 429–445). Hershey, PA: IGI Global. doi:10.4018/978-1-4666-2521-1.ch022

Torres, G., Jaime, K., & Ramos, F. (2013). Brain architecture for visual object identification. *International Journal of Cognitive Informatics and Natural Intelligence, 7*(1), 75–97. doi:10.4018/jcini.2013010104

Trajkovski, G., Stojanov, G., Collins, S., Eidelman, V., Harman, C., & Vincenti, G. (2011). Cognitive robotics and multiagency in a fuzzy modeling framework. In G. Trajkovski (Ed.), *Developments in intelligent agent technologies and multi-agent systems: Concepts and applications* (pp. 132–152). Hershey, PA: IGI Global. doi:10.4018/978-1-60960-171-3.ch009

Tran, B. (2014). Rhetoric of play: Utilizing the gamer factor in selecting and training employees. In T. Connolly, T. Hainey, E. Boyle, G. Baxter, & P. Moreno-Ger (Eds.), *Psychology, pedagogy, and assessment in serious games* (pp. 175–203). Hershey, PA: IGI Global. doi:10.4018/978-1-4666-4773-2.ch009

Tran, B. (2014). The psychology of consumerism in business and marketing: The macro and micro behaviors of Hofstede's cultural consumers. In H. Kaufmann & M. Panni (Eds.), *Handbook of research on consumerism in business and marketing: Concepts and practices* (pp. 286–308). Hershey, PA: IGI Global. doi:10.4018/978-1-4666-5880-6.ch014

Travica, B. (2014). Homo informaticus. In *Examining the informing view of organization: Applying theoretical and managerial approaches* (pp. 34–66). Hershey, PA: IGI Global. doi:10.4018/978-1-4666-5986-5.ch002

Twomey, K. E., Horst, J. S., & Morse, A. F. (2013). An embodied model of young children's categorization and word learning. In L. Gogate & G. Hollich (Eds.), *Theoretical and computational models of word learning: Trends in psychology and artificial intelligence* (pp. 172–196). Hershey, PA: IGI Global. doi:10.4018/978-1-4666-2973-8.ch008

Ursyn, A. (2014). Cognitive processes involved in visual thought. In *Perceptions of knowledge visualization: Explaining concepts through meaningful images* (pp. 131–173). Hershey, PA: IGI Global. doi:10.4018/978-1-4666-4703-9.ch005

Ursyn, A. (2014). Communication through many senses. In *Perceptions of knowledge visualization: Explaining concepts through meaningful images* (pp. 25–60). Hershey, PA: IGI Global. doi:10.4018/978-1-4666-4703-9.ch002

Ursyn, A. (2014). Four trapped in an elevator. In *Computational solutions for knowledge, art, and entertainment: Information exchange beyond text* (pp. 322–329). Hershey, PA: IGI Global. doi:10.4018/978-1-4666-4627-8.ch016

Usart, M., & Romero, M. (2014). Time factor assessment in game-based learning: Time perspective and time-on-task as individual differences between players. In T. Connolly, T. Hainey, E. Boyle, G. Baxter, & P. Moreno-Ger (Eds.), *Psychology, pedagogy, and assessment in serious games* (pp. 62–81). Hershey, PA: IGI Global. doi:10.4018/978-1-4666-4773-2.ch004

Usoro, A., Majewski, G., & Bloom, L. (2012). Individual and collaborative approaches in e-learning design. In *Virtual learning environments: Concepts, methodologies, tools and applications* (pp. 1110–1130). Hershey, PA: IGI Global. doi:10.4018/978-1-4666-0011-9.ch514

van den Brink, J. C. (2014). How positive psychology can support sustainable project management. In *Sustainable practices: Concepts, methodologies, tools and applications* (pp. 958–973). Hershey, PA: IGI Global. doi:10.4018/978-1-4666-4852-4.ch053

van der Helden, J., & Bekkering, H. (2014). The role of implicit and explicit feedback in learning and the implications for distance education techniques. In T. Yuzer & G. Eby (Eds.), *Handbook of research on emerging priorities and trends in distance education: Communication, pedagogy, and technology* (pp. 367–384). Hershey, PA: IGI Global. doi:10.4018/978-1-4666-5162-3.ch025

van Mierlo, C. M., Jarodzka, H., Kirschner, F., & Kirschner, P. A. (2012). Cognitive load theory in e-learning. In Z. Yan (Ed.), *Encyclopedia of cyber behavior* (pp. 1178–1211). Hershey, PA: IGI Global. doi:10.4018/978-1-4666-0315-8.ch097

van Rosmalen, P., Wilson, A., & Hummel, H. G. (2014). Games for and by teachers and learners. In T. Connolly, T. Hainey, E. Boyle, G. Baxter, & P. Moreno-Ger (Eds.), *Psychology, pedagogy, and assessment in serious games* (pp. 243–269). Hershey, PA: IGI Global. doi:10.4018/978-1-4666-4773-2.ch012

Vega, J., Perdices, E., & Cañas, J. M. (2014). Attentive visual memory for robot localization. In *Robotics: Concepts, methodologies, tools, and applications* (pp. 785-811). Hershey, PA: IGI Global. doi:10.4018/978-1-4666-4607-0.ch038

Vinther, J. (2012). Cognitive skills through CALL-enhanced teacher training. In F. Zhang (Ed.), *Computer-enhanced and mobile-assisted language learning: Emerging issues and trends* (pp. 158–187). Hershey, PA: IGI Global. doi:10.4018/978-1-61350-065-1.ch008

Vogel, E. H., & Ponce, F. P. (2011). Empirical issues and theoretical mechanisms of Pavlovian conditioning. In E. Alonso & E. Mondragón (Eds.), *Computational neuroscience for advancing artificial intelligence: Models, methods and applications* (pp. 81–110). Hershey, PA: IGI Global. doi:10.4018/978-1-60960-021-1.ch005

Vragov, R. (2013). Detecting behavioral biases in mixed human-proxy online auction markets. *International Journal of Strategic Information Technology and Applications*, 4(4), 60–79. doi:10.4018/ijsita.2013100104

Wagner, C. L., & Delisi, J. (2010). Multi-sensory environments and augmentative communication tools. In S. Seok, E. Meyen, & B. DaCosta (Eds.), *Handbook of research on human cognition and assistive technology: Design, accessibility and transdisciplinary perspectives* (pp. 121–131). Hershey, PA: IGI Global. doi:10.4018/978-1-61520-817-3.ch008

Walk, A. M., & Conway, C. M. (2014). Two distinct sequence learning mechanisms for syntax acquisition and word learning. In *Computational linguistics: Concepts, methodologies, tools, and applications* (pp. 540–560). Hershey, PA: IGI Global. doi:10.4018/978-1-4666-6042-7.ch025

Wang, H. (2014). A guide to assistive technology for teachers in special education. In *Assistive technologies: Concepts, methodologies, tools, and applications* (pp. 12–25). Hershey, PA: IGI Global. doi:10.4018/978-1-4666-4422-9.ch002

Wang, J. (2012). Organizational learning and technology. In V. Wang (Ed.), *Encyclopedia of e-leadership, counseling and training* (pp. 154–170). Hershey, PA: IGI Global. doi:10.4018/978-1-61350-068-2.ch012

Wang, K. Y. (2014). Mixing metaphors: Sociological and psychological perspectives on virtual communities. In *Cross-cultural interaction: Concepts, methodologies, tools and applications* (pp. 116–132). Hershey, PA: IGI Global. doi:10.4018/978-1-4666-4979-8.ch008

Wang, Y. (2013). Neuroinformatics models of human memory: Mapping the cognitive functions of memory onto neurophysiological structures of the brain. *International Journal of Cognitive Informatics and Natural Intelligence*, 7(1), 98–122. doi:10.4018/jcini.2013010105

Wang, Y. (2013). The cognitive mechanisms and formal models of consciousness. *International Journal of Cognitive Informatics and Natural Intelligence*, 6(2), 23–40. doi:10.4018/jcini.2012040102

Wang, Y. (2013). Towards the synergy of cognitive informatics, neural informatics, brain informatics, and cognitive computing. In Y. Wang (Ed.), *Cognitive informatics for revealing human cognition: Knowledge manipulations in natural intelligence* (pp. 1–19). Hershey, PA: IGI Global. doi:10.4018/978-1-4666-2476-4.ch001

Wang, Y., Berwick, R. C., Haykin, S., Pedrycz, W., Kinsner, W., & Baciu, G. … Gavrilova, M. L. (2013). Cognitive informatics and cognitive computing in year 10 and beyond. In Y. Wang (Ed.), Cognitive informatics for revealing human cognition: Knowledge manipulations in natural intelligence (pp. 140-157). Hershey, PA: IGI Global. doi:10.4018/978-1-4666-2476-4.ch010

Wang, Y., Fariello, G., Gavrilova, M. L., Kinsner, W., Mizoguchi, F., Patel, S., & Tsumoto, S. et al. (2013). Perspectives on cognitive computers and knowledge processors. *International Journal of Cognitive Informatics and Natural Intelligence*, 7(3), 1–24. doi:10.4018/ijcini.2013070101

Wang, Y., Patel, S., & Patel, D. (2013). The cognitive process and formal models of human attentions. *International Journal of Software Science and Computational Intelligence*, 5(1), 32–50. doi:10.4018/ijssci.2013010103

Wang, Y., Pedrycz, W., Baciu, G., Chen, P., Wang, G., & Yao, Y. (2012). Perspectives on cognitive computing and applications. In Y. Wang (Ed.), *Breakthroughs in software science and computational intelligence* (pp. 1–12). Hershey, PA: IGI Global. doi:10.4018/978-1-4666-0264-9.ch001

Wang, Y., Widrow, B. C., Zhang, B., Kinsner, W., Sugawara, K., Sun, F., & Zhang, D. et al. (2013). Perspectives on the field of cognitive informatics and its future development. In Y. Wang (Ed.), *Cognitive informatics for revealing human cognition: Knowledge manipulations in natural intelligence* (pp. 20–34). Hershey, PA: IGI Global. doi:10.4018/978-1-4666-2476-4.ch002

Was, C. A., & Woltz, D. J. (2013). Implicit memory and aging: Adapting technology to utilize preserved memory functions. In R. Zheng, R. Hill, & M. Gardner (Eds.), *Engaging older adults with modern technology: Internet use and information access needs* (pp. 1–19). Hershey, PA: IGI Global. doi:10.4018/978-1-4666-1966-1.ch001

Wei, H. (2013). A neural dynamic model based on activation diffusion and a micro-explanation for cognitive operations. *International Journal of Cognitive Informatics and Natural Intelligence*, *6*(2), 1–22. doi:10.4018/jcini.2012040101

Wexler, R. H., & Roff-Wexler, S. (2013). The evolution and development of self in virtual worlds. *International Journal of Cyber Behavior, Psychology and Learning*, *3*(1), 1–6. doi:10.4018/ijcbpl.2013010101

Wickramasinghe, N. (2012). Knowledge economy for innovating organizations. In *Organizational learning and knowledge: Concepts, methodologies, tools and applications* (pp. 2298–2309). Hershey, PA: IGI Global. doi:10.4018/978-1-60960-783-8.ch616

Widrow, B. C., & Aragon, J. (2012). Cognitive memory: Human like memory. In Y. Wang (Ed.), *Breakthroughs in software science and computational intelligence* (pp. 84–99). Hershey, PA: IGI Global. doi:10.4018/978-1-4666-0264-9.ch006

Widyanto, L., & Griffiths, M. (2013). An empirical study of problematic internet use and self-esteem. In R. Zheng (Ed.), *Evolving psychological and educational perspectives on cyber behavior* (pp. 82–95). Hershey, PA: IGI Global. doi:10.4018/978-1-4666-1858-9.ch006

Wilson, M. S., & Pascoe, J. (2010). Using software to deliver language intervention in inclusionary settings. In S. Seok, E. Meyen, & B. DaCosta (Eds.), *Handbook of research on human cognition and assistive technology: Design, accessibility and transdisciplinary perspectives* (pp. 132–156). Hershey, PA: IGI Global. doi:10.4018/978-1-61520-817-3.ch009

Wilson, S., & Haslam, N. (2013). Reasoning about human enhancement: Towards a folk psychological model of human nature and human identity. In R. Luppicini (Ed.), *Handbook of research on technoself: Identity in a technological society* (pp. 175–188). Hershey, PA: IGI Global. doi:10.4018/978-1-4666-2211-1.ch010

Wilson, S. G. (2014). Enhancement and identity: A social psychological perspective. In S. Thompson (Ed.), *Global issues and ethical considerations in human enhancement technologies* (pp. 241–256). Hershey, PA: IGI Global. doi:10.4018/978-1-4666-6010-6.ch014

Winsor, D. L. (2012). The epistemology of young children. In S. Blake, D. Winsor, & L. Allen (Eds.), *Child development and the use of technology: Perspectives, applications and experiences* (pp. 21–44). Hershey, PA: IGI Global. doi:10.4018/978-1-61350-317-1.ch002

Winsor, D. L., & Blake, S. (2012). Socrates and Descartes meet the E*Trade baby: The impact of early technology on children's developing beliefs about knowledge and knowing. In S. Blake, D. Winsor, & L. Allen (Eds.), *Child development and the use of technology: Perspectives, applications and experiences* (pp. 1–20). Hershey, PA: IGI Global. doi:10.4018/978-1-61350-317-1.ch001

Yakavenka, H. (2012). Developing professional competencies through international peer learning communities. In V. Dennen & J. Myers (Eds.), *Virtual professional development and informal learning via social networks* (pp. 134–154). Hershey, PA: IGI Global. doi:10.4018/978-1-4666-1815-2.ch008

Yamaguchi, M., & Shetty, V. (2013). Evaluating the psychobiologic effects of fragrances through salivary biomarkers. In T. Nakamoto (Ed.), *Human olfactory displays and interfaces: Odor sensing and presentation* (pp. 359–369). Hershey, PA: IGI Global. doi:10.4018/978-1-4666-2521-1.ch017

Yan, Z., & Zheng, R. Z. (2013). Growing from childhood into adolescence: The science of cyber behavior. In R. Zheng (Ed.), *Evolving psychological and educational perspectives on cyber behavior* (pp. 1–14). Hershey, PA: IGI Global. doi:10.4018/978-1-4666-1858-9.ch001

Yildirim, G., & Gökçay, D. (2011). Problems associated with computer-mediated communication cognitive psychology and neuroscience perspectives. In D. Gökçay & G. Yildirim (Eds.), *Affective computing and interaction: Psychological, cognitive and neuroscientific perspectives* (pp. 244–261). Hershey, PA: IGI Global. doi:10.4018/978-1-61692-892-6.ch011

Younan, Y., Joosen, W., Piessens, F., & Van den Eynden, H. (2012). Improving memory management security for C and C. In K. Khan (Ed.), *Security-aware systems applications and software development methods* (pp. 190–216). Hershey, PA: IGI Global. doi:10.4018/978-1-4666-1580-9.ch011

Yu, C., & Smith, L. B. (2013). A sensory-motor solution to early word-referent learning. In L. Gogate & G. Hollich (Eds.), *Theoretical and computational models of word learning: Trends in psychology and artificial intelligence* (pp. 133–152). Hershey, PA: IGI Global. doi:10.4018/978-1-4666-2973-8.ch006

Yu, J., Chen, Z., Lu, J., Liu, T., Zhou, L., Liu, X., . . . Chui, D. (2013). The important role of lipids in cognitive impairment. In Bioinformatics: Concepts, methodologies, tools, and applications (pp. 268-272). Hershey, PA: IGI Global. doi:10.4018/978-1-4666-3604-0.ch014

Yu, Y., Yang, J., & Wu, J. (2013). Cognitive functions and neuronal mechanisms of tactile working memory. In J. Wu (Ed.), *Biomedical engineering and cognitive neuroscience for healthcare: Interdisciplinary applications* (pp. 89–98). Hershey, PA: IGI Global. doi:10.4018/978-1-4666-2113-8.ch010

Zelinski, E. M. (2013). How interventions might improve cognition in healthy older adults. *International Journal of Gaming and Computer-Mediated Simulations, 5*(3), 72–82. doi:10.4018/jgcms.2013070105

Zhang, J., Luo, X., Lu, L., & Liu, W. (2013). An acquisition model of deep textual semantics based on human reading cognitive process. *International Journal of Cognitive Informatics and Natural Intelligence, 6*(2), 82–103. doi:10.4018/jcini.2012040105

Zheng, R. Z. (2013). Effective online learning for older people: A heuristic design approach. In R. Zheng, R. Hill, & M. Gardner (Eds.), *Engaging older adults with modern technology: Internet use and information access needs* (pp. 142–159). Hershey, PA: IGI Global. doi:10.4018/978-1-4666-1966-1.ch008

Zhou, M., & Xu, Y. (2013). Challenges to use recommender systems to enhance meta-cognitive functioning in online learners. In *Data mining: Concepts, methodologies, tools, and applications* (pp. 1916–1935). Hershey, PA: IGI Global. doi:10.4018/978-1-4666-2455-9.ch099

Ziaeehezarjeribi, Y., & Graves, I. (2013). Behind the MASK: Motivation through avatar skills and knowledge. In R. Ferdig (Ed.), *Design, utilization, and analysis of simulations and game-based educational worlds* (pp. 225–239). Hershey, PA: IGI Global. doi:10.4018/978-1-4666-4018-4.ch014

Zoss, A. M. (2014). Cognitive processes and traits related to graphic comprehension. In M. Huang & W. Huang (Eds.), *Innovative approaches of data visualization and visual analytics* (pp. 94–110). Hershey, PA: IGI Global. doi:10.4018/978-1-4666-4309-3.ch005

Compilation of References

8. vo. (2005). *On the outside*. Lars Müller Publishers.

Abu-Dawas, R. B., Mallick, M. A., Hamadah, R. E., Kharraz, R. H., Chamseddin, R. A., Khan, T. A., & Rohra, D. K. et al. (2015). Comparative analysis of quantity and quality of biomedical publications in Gulf Cooperation Council countries from 2011-2013. *Saudi Medical Journal, 36*(9), 1103–1109. doi:10.15537/smj.2015.9.12369 PMID:26318469

Adams, P., & Ghose, R. (2003). India.Com: The Construction of a Space Between. *Progress in Human Geography, 27*(4), 414–437. doi:10.1191/0309132503ph437oa

Adams, S., Krolak, L., Kupidura, E., & Pahernik, Z. P. (2002). Libraries and resource centres: Celebrating adult learners every week of the year. *Convergence, 35*(2-3), 27–39.

Ahmed, A., Adam, M., Ghafar, N. A., Muhammad, M., & Ebrahim, N. A. (2016). Impact of article page count and number of authors on citations in disability related fields: A systematic review article. *Iranian Journal of Public Health, 45*(9), 1118–1125. PMID:27957456

Albert, R., & Barabási, A.-L. (2002). Statistical mechanics of complex networks. *Reviews of Modern Physics, 74*(1), 47–97. doi:10.1103/RevModPhys.74.47

Alexievich, S., & Gessen, K. (2006). *Voices from Chernobyl: The oral history of a nuclear disaster*. London: Macmillan.

Al-Mohammadi, N. (2017). Effectiveness of using infographics as an approach for teaching programming fundamentals on developing analytical thinking skills for high school students in the City of Makkah in Saudi Arabia. *Global Journal of Educational Studies, 3*(1), 22–42. doi:10.5296/gjes.v3i1.10854

Andersen, M., Wagner, J., & Warner, B. (2002). *Visual literacy, the Internet, and education*. Retrieved June 17, 2017, from http://www.cii.illinois.edu/InquiryPage/bin/docs/u12021_391finaldraft.doc

Anderson, C. (2008). *The End of Theory: The Data Deluge Makes the Scientific Method Obsolete*. Retrieved April 13, 2017, from https://www.wired.com/2008/06/pb-theory/

Anderson, E. (1957). A Semi-Graphical Method for the Analysis of Complex Problems. *Proceedings of the National Academy of Sciences, 13*(3), 923-927.

Anscombe, G. E. M. (1981). Memory, "Experience", and Causation. In G.E.M. Anscombe (Ed.), Collected Philosophical Papers (vol. 2, pp. 120-130). Oxford, UK: Blackwell.

Apanovich, Z. V., & Vinokurov, P. S. (2010b). *Ontology based portals and visual analysis of scientific communities*. Paper presented at the First Russia and Pacific Conference on Computer Technology and Applications (RussiaPacificComputer 2010), Vladivostok.

Apanovich, Z. V., & Vinokurov, P. S. (2010a). An extension of a visualization component of ontology based portals with visual analytics facilities. *Bulletin of the Novosibirsk Computing Center*, *31*, 17–28.

Arnaboldi, V., Dunbar, R. I. M., Passarella, A., & Conti, M. (2016). Analysis of Co-authorship Ego Networks. In A. Wierzbicki, U. Brandes, F. Schweitzer, & D. Pedreschi (Eds.), *Advances in Network Science* (pp. 82–96). Springer International Publishing. doi:10.1007/978-3-319-28361-6_7

Association of College & Research Libraries. (2011). *ACRL visual literacy competency standards for higher education*. Retrieved June 15, 2017, from http://www.ala.org/acrl/standards/visualliteracy

Avgerinou, M. D. (2001). *Visual literacy: Anatomy and diagnosis* (Unpublished doctoral dissertation). University of Bath, UK.

Axtell, R., Epstein, J. M., & Young, H. P. (2001). The Emergence of Economic Classes in an Agent-Based Bargaining Model. In S. In Durlauf & H. P. Young (Eds.), *Social Dynamics*. Cambridge, MA: MIT Press.

Azmi, H. (2014). *Media and visual competencies for information professionals in the Arab world challenges of the digital environment*. Retrieved September 28, 2017, from http://library.ifla.org/888/1/139-azmi-en.pdf

Balchin, J. A. (1970). The Song of Solomon. In The New Bible Commentary: Revised (3rd ed.; pp. 579-87). Grand Rapids, MI: Eerdmans.

Bamford, A. (2003). *The visual literacy white paper*. Retrieved June 17, 2017, from http://wwwimages.adobe.com/content/dam/Adobe/en/education/pdfs/visual-literacy-wp.pdf

Barabási, A. L. (2016). *Network Science*. Cambridge, UK: University Printing House.

Barajas, M. (2001). *Monitoring and evaluation of research in learning innovations (Merlin) - Final Report of project HPHA-CT2000-00042 funded under the Improving Human Research Potential & the Socio-economic Knowledge Base Directorate General Science, Research and Development European commission*. Retrieved December 15, 2016, from http://www.ub.edu/euelearning/merlin/docs/finalreprt.pdf

Barbiero, G. (2011). *Song of Songs: A Close Reading*. Danvers, MA: Brill. doi:10.1163/ej.9789004203259.i-542

Bardski, K. (2010). Oblubienica. In *Encyklopedia Katolicka. t.14*. Lublin, Poland: Towarzystwo Naukowe KUL.

Bardski, K. (2011). *Lektyka Salomona. Biblia – Symbol – Interpretacja, Rozprawy Naukowe 6*. Warszawa, Poland: Wydawnictwo Archidiecezji Warszawskiej.

Barrett, J. L. (1994). Process Visualization: Getting the Vision Right Is the Key. *Information Systems Management*, *11*(2), 14–23. doi:10.1080/10580539408964631

Bas, K., Dayangac, M., Yaprak, O., Yuzer, Y., & Tokat, Y. (2011). International collaboration of Turkey in liver transplantation research: A bibliometric analysis. *Transplantation Proceedings*, *43*(10), 3796–3801. doi:10.1016/j.transproceed.2011.09.081 PMID:22172849

Bassecoulard, E., & Zitt, M. (1999). Indicators in a research institute: A multi-level classification of scientific journals. *Scientometrics*, *44*(3), 323–345. doi:10.1007/BF02458483

Bassili, J. N. (1989). *On-line Cognition in Person Perception*. Psychology Press.

Bastian, M., Heymann, S., & Jacomy, M. (2009). Gephi: an open source software for exploring and manipulating networks. In *Proceedings of the Third International Conference on Weblogs and Social Media* (pp. 361–362). AAAI Press.

Beaudoin, J. E. (2016). Describing images: A case study of visual literacy among library and information science students. *College & Research Libraries*, *77*(3), 376–392. doi:10.5860/crl.77.3.376

Beaver, D. D., & Rosen, R. (1979). Studies in scientific collaboration: Part II: Scientific co-authorship, research productivity and visibility in the French elite. *Scientometrics*, *1*(2), 133–149. doi:10.1007/BF02016966

Behrman, A. L., Bowden, M. G., & Rose, D. K. (2013). Clinical trials in neurorehabilitation. *Handbook of Clinical Neurology*, *110*, 61–66. doi:10.1016/B978-0-444-52901-5.00005-8 PMID:23312630

Berner, A. (2015). AiryLight: Ambient Enviromental Data. In A. Ursyn (Ed.), *Maximazing Cognitive Learning through Knowledge Visualization*. IGI Global. doi:10.4018/978-1-4666-8142-2.ch017

Bertin, J. (1983). *Semiology of graphics: diagrams, networks, maps*. Madison, WI: The University of Wisconsin Press.

Bird, S., Klein, E., & Loper, E. (2009). *Natural language processing with Python. Analyzing text with the Natural Language Toolkit*. Pekin.

Bjelanović Dijanić, Ž. (2012). Some Methods for the Development of Students' Critical Thinking by ERR System. *Methodical Review. Journal of Philosophy of Education*, *19*(1), 163–179.

Boechat, M., & Venturini, T. (2016). From analysis to presentation: Information visualization for reifying issues and reenacting insights in visual data analysis. In *Les cahiers numériques: La visualization de données* (Vol. 12). Paris: Lavoisier.

Bogart, B. D. R., & Pasquier, P. (2013). Context Machines: A Series of Situated and Self-Organizing Artworks. *Leonardo*, *46*(2), 114–122. doi:10.1162/LEON_a_00525

Bonekamp, S., Halappa, V. G., Corona-Villalobos, C. P., Mensa, M., Eng, J., Lewin, J. S., & Kamel, I. R. (2012). Prevalence of honorary coauthorship in the American Journal of Roentgenology. *AJR. American Journal of Roentgenology*, *198*(6), 1247–1255. doi:10.2214/AJR.11.8253 PMID:22623536

Börner, K., Dall'Asta, L., Ke, W., & Vespignani, A. (2005). Studying the emerging global brain: Analyzing and visualizing the impact of co-authorship teams. *Complexity*, *10*(4), 57–67. doi:10.1002/cplx.20078

Börner, K., & Polley, D. E. (2014). *Visual Insights: a practical guide to making sense of data*. Cambridge, MA: Massachusetts Institute of Technology.

Borry, P., Schotsmans, P., & Dierickx, K. (2006). Author, contributor or just a signer? A quantitative analysis of authorship trends in the field of bioethics. *Bioethics*, *20*(4), 213–220. doi:10.1111/j.1467-8519.2006.00496.x PMID:17044155

Boullier, D. (2015). Les Sciences Sociales Face aux Traces du Big Data? Société, Opinion et Répliques. *Fondation Maison des Sciences de l'Homme*, *88*.

Brandt, T., & Bertram, M. (2016). Evidence-based neurorehabilitation. *Der Nervenarzt*, *87*(10), 1041–1042. doi:10.1007/s00115-016-0202-1 PMID:27613178

Brath, R., & MacMurchy, P. (2014). Information Visualization on Spheres. In E. Banissi, F. T. Marchese, & C. Forsell (Eds.), *Information Visualization: Techniques. Usability and Evaluation*. Cambridge Scholars Publishing.

Brewer, S., Jackson, S. T., & Williams, J. W. (2012). Paleoecoinformatics: applying geohistorical data to ecological questions. In *Trends in ecology and evolution* (vol. 27, Issue 2, pp. 104–112). Retrieved February 24, 2017 from http://www.cell.com/trends/ecology-evolution/fulltext/S0169-5347(11)00269-2

Bridges, P. H., Bierema, L. L., & Valentine, T. (2007). The propensity to adopt evidence-based practice among physical therapists. *BMC Health Services Research*, *7*(1), 103. doi:10.1186/1472-6963-7-103 PMID:17615076

British Columbia, Ministry of Education. (2016). *Inspiring libraries, connecting communities.* Retrieved June 20, 2017, from http://www2.gov.bc.ca/assets/gov/education/administration/community-partnerships/libraries/libraries-strategic-plan.pdf

Brown, D. (2003). *Angels and demons.* New York: Random House.

Brown, I. (2004). Global trends in art education: New technologies and the paradigm shift to visual literacy. *The International Journal of Arts Education, 2*(3), 50–61.

Brown, J. S. (2002). Learning in the Digital Age. In *Forum Futures 2002* (pp. 20–23). New York: Educause.

Brzegowy, T. (2007). *Pisma mądrościowe Starego Testamentu.* Tarnów, Poland: Biblos.

Buccino, G. (2014). Action observation treatment: A novel tool in neurorehabilitation. *Philosophical Transactions of the Royal Society of London. Series B, Biological Sciences, 369*(1644), 20130185. doi:10.1098/rstb.2013.0185 PMID:24778380

Budimir, I., Pasanec Preprotić, S., & Lukić, D. (2013). Cross-curricular linkage of mathematics and technology with applications in graphic technology. *The Holistic Approach to Environment, 3*(4), 223–230.

Budka, P., Brandi, B., & Fiser, A. (2009). MyKnet.org: How Northen Ontario's First Nations Communities Made Themeselves at Home on the World Wide Web. Community Informatics, 5(2).

Burkhard, R. A. (2005). Strategy Visualization: A New Research Focus in Knowledge Visualization and a Case Study. *Proceedings of I-KNOW.*

Buser, M., & Arthurs, J. (2013). *Connected Communities: Cultrual Activism in the Community.* Retrieved May 01, 2017, from http://www.culturalactivism.org.uk/wp-content/uploads/2013/03/CULTURAL-ACTIVISM-BUSER-Update.3.pdf

Buzing, P., Eiben, A., & Schut, M. (2005). Emerging communication and cooperation in evolving agent societies. *Journal of Artificial Societies and Social Simulation, 8*(1), 2. Retrieved from http://jasss.soc.surrey.ac.uk/8/1/2.html

Byrne, P et al. (Eds.). (2015). *Maximizing cognitive learning through knowledge visualization.* IGI Global.

Cairo, A. (2013). *The functional art: An introduction to information graphics and visualization.* Berkeley, CA: A New Riders. Retrieved June 17, 2017, from http://ptgmedia.pearsoncmg.com/images/9780321834737/samplepages/0321834739.pdf

Calvano, M. (2016). Models for Design: From Geometries to Generative Algorithms. In Handbook of Research on Visual Computing and Emerging Geometrical Design Tools (pp. 825-855). IGI Global.

Cambridge University Press. (2008). *Stemming and Lemmatization.* Retrieved from https://nlp.stanford.edu/IR-book/html/htmledition/stemming-and-lemmatization-1.html

Cañas, A. J., Carff, R., Hill, G., Carvalho, M., Arguedas, M., . . . Carvajal, R. (2005). Concept Maps: Integrating Knowledge and Information Visualization. In Lecture Notes in Computer Science: Vol. 3426. Knowledge and Information Visualization. Springer.

Card, S. K., Mackinlay, J. D., & Shneiderman, B. (1999). *Readings in information visualization: Using vision to think.* San Francisco, CA: Morgan Kaufmann Publishers Inc.

Carruthers, M. (1990). *The Book of Memory.* Cambridge, UK: Cambridge University Press.

Carswell, M., & Wickens, C. D. (1987). Information Integration and the Object Display: An Interaction of Task Demands and Display Superiority. *Ergonomics, 30*(3), 511–527. doi:10.1080/00140138708969741

Castells, M. (1997). *The Power of Identity, The Information Age: Economy, Society and Culture* (Vol. 2). Cambridge, MA: Blackwell.

CCL. (2013). Retrieved August 25, 2017, from http://nlp.pwr.wroc.pl/redmine/projects/corpus2/wiki/CCL_format

Chambers, J.M., Cleveland W.S., & Kleiner, B. (1983). *Graphical Methods for Data Analysis*. Wadsworth International Group.

Chen, Ch. (2006). *Information Visualization: Beyond the Horizon*. London: Springer-Verlag.

Chernoff, H. (1973). The Use of Faces to Represent Points in k-Dimensional Space Graphically. *Journal of the American Statistical Association*, *68*(342), 361–368. doi:10.1080/01621459.1973.10482434

Chinchilla-Rodríguez, Z., Vargas-Quesada, B., Hassan-Montero, Y., González-Molina, A., & Moya-Anegóna, F. (2010). New approach to the visualization of international scientific collaboration. *Information Visualization*, *9*(4), 277–287. doi:10.1057/ivs.2009.31

Chomsky, N. (1965). *Aspects of the Theory of Syntax*. MIT.

CLARIN-PL. (2015). Retrieved August 25, 2017, from http://clarin-pl.eu/pl/strona-glowna/

CLARIN-PL. (n.d.) Retrieved from http://ws.clarin-pl.eu/websty.shtml

Clegg, E., & DeVarco, B. (2010). *What is the Shape of Thought?* Retrieved July 20, 2017, from: http://shapeofthought.typepad.com/shape_of_thought/what-is-the-shape-of-thought/

Cleveland, W. S. (1994). *The elements of graphing data*. Hobart Press.

Cleveland, W. S., & McGill, R. (1984). Graphical Perception: Experimentation and Application to the Development of Graphical Methods. *Journal of the American Statistical Association*, *79*(387), 531–554. doi:10.1080/01621459.1984.10478080

Cohen, D. K., & Hill, H. C. (2001). *Learning Policy: When State Education Reform Works*. New Haven, CT: Yale University Press. doi:10.12987/yale/9780300089479.001.0001

Cohen, H. (1995). The further exploits of Aaron, painter. *Stanford Humanities Review*, *4*(2), 141–158.

Collado, A. S. (2012). Cyberactivisme et liens transnationaux au Rif. In Diaspora, Community and Communication: Internet Use in Transnational Haiti, Global Networks (Vol. 4). Academic Press.

Collado, A. S. (2013). Mouvement sociaux sur la Toile: les effets des TIC sur le militantisme Amazigh au Maroc. In *Le cyberactivisme au Maghreb et dans le monde arabe*. Paris: IRMC/Karthala.

Connell, K. (2015). Library exhibitions teach visual literacy. *Assessment*, *3*. Retrieved from https://www.ccsf.edu/dam/Organizational_Assets/Department/library/Assessment/Library%20Exhibition%20Assessment%203%20(1).pdf

Constant, J. (2015). Random Processes and Visual Perception. In A. Ursyn (Ed.), *Maximazing Cognitive Learning through Knowledge Visualization*. IGI Global. doi:10.4018/978-1-4666-8142-2.ch006

Cox, T. F., & Cox, M. A. A. (2001). *Multidimensional scaling* (2nd ed.). London: Chapman & Hall.

Cremante, S. (2014). *Leonardo da Vinci. The Complete Works*. A David and Charles Book.

Członkowska, A., & Sarzyńska-Długosz, I. (2002). Aims of neurorehabilitation. *Neurologia i Neurochirurgia Polska*, *36*(Suppl 1), 23–31. PMID:12189684

D3.js: Data-Driven Documents. (2017). Retrieved October 20, 2017 from https://d3js.org

Davenport, M. (2016, September). Nobel journeys in chemistry: Mapping the lives of laureates. *Chemical and Engineering News*, *94*(37), 24–25. Retrieved from https://cen.acs.org/articles/94/i37/Nobel-journeys-chemistry-Mapping-lives.html

Davidson, R. (2014). Using Infographics in the Science Classroom: Three Investigations in Which Students Present Their Results in Infographics. *Science Teacher (Normal, Ill.)*, *3*(81), 34–39.

Davis, M., & Quinn, D. (2014). Visualizing text: The new literacy of infographics. *Reading Today*, *31*(3), 16–18.

Dean-Baar, S., & Pakieser-Reed, K. (2004). Closing the gap between research and clinical practice. *Topics in Stroke Rehabilitation*, *11*(2), 60–68. doi:10.1310/GVP2-8CTV-QNGM-NG3U PMID:15118968

Debes, J. (1969). The loom of visual literacy: An overview. *Audiovisual Instruction*, *14*(8), 25–27.

DeFanti, T. A. (1976). The digital component of the circle graphics habitat. In *National Computer Conference* (pp. 195-203). Retrieved August 10, 2015 from http://excelsior.biosci.ohio-state.edu/~carlson/history/PDFs/cgh-defanti.pdf

Dennett, D. (2009). *Intentional Systems Theory*. Retrieved July 24, 2017 from https://ase.tufts.edu/cogstud/dennett/papers/intentionalsystems.pdf

Descartes, R. (1647). *Prinzipien der Philosophie. Aether vortex around suns and planets*. Retrieved July 20, 2017, from: ttps://commons.wikimedia.org/wiki/File:Descartes_Aetherwirbel.jpg

DH Awards: Digital Humanities Awards. (n.d.). Retrieved October 19, 2017 from http://dhawards.org

Diacu, F. (1996). The Solution of the n-body Problem. *The Mathematical Intelligencer*, *3*(3), 66–70. doi:10.1007/BF03024313

Digital Humanities Awards. (n.d.). Retrieved August 25, 2017, from http://dhawards.org

Diminescu, D. (2008). The Connected Migrant: An Epistemological Manifesto. *Social Sciences Information. Information Sur les Sciences Sociales*, *47*(4), 565–579. doi:10.1177/0539018408096447

Divjak, B. (2005). *First Steps in the Bologna Process), Tempus project, Croatia Bologna promoters team Cro4 Bologna*. Retrieved February 15, 2015, from http://www.kif.unizg.hr/_download/repository/Bologna.pdf

Divjak, B. (2008). *O ishodima učenja u visokom obrazovanju*. Retrieved July 19, 2017, from http://iu.foi.hr/upload_data/knjiga/Ishodi_ucenja_u_visokom_obrazovanju_12122008_F.pdf

Dohle, C., Tholen, R., Wittenberg, H., Quintern, J., Saal, S., & Stephan, K. M. (2016). Evidence-based rehabilitation of mobility after stroke. *Der Nervenarzt*, *87*(10), 1062–1067. doi:10.1007/s00115-016-0188-8 PMID:27531212

Dorling, D. (1991). *The Visualization of Spatial Structure* (PhD dissertation). Department of Geography, University of Newcastle upon Tyne, UK.

Dorogovtsev, S. N., & Mendes, J. F. F. (2003). *Evolution of Networks*. Oxford, UK: Oxford University Press. doi:10.1093/acprof:oso/9780198515906.001.0001

Doucet, B. M. (2013). Five years later: Achieving professional effectiveness to move neurorehabilitation forward. *The American Journal of Occupational Therapy*, *67*(5), e106–e119. doi:10.5014/ajot.2013.008417 PMID:23968801

Drucker, J. (2012). Humanistic Theory and Digital Scholarship. In M. K. Gold (Ed.), *Debates in Digital Humanities*. Minneapolis, MN: University of Minnesota Press. Retrieved March 15, 2017, from http://dhdebates.gc.cuny.edu/debates/text/34

Duron, R. (2006). Critical Thinking Framework for any discipline. *International Journal on Teaching and Learning in Higher Education*, *17*(2), 160–166.

Eco, U. (2010). *History of Beauty*. New York: Rizzoli.

EDUCAUSE. (2013). *7 things you should know about infographic creation tools*. Retrieved June 17, 2017, from https://net.educause.edu/ir/library/pdf/ELI7093.pdf

Einicke, G. A. (2012). *Smoothing, filtering and prediction: estimating the past, present and future*. Rijeka, Croatia: Intech.

Eisenberg, R. L., Ngo, L. H., & Bankier, A. A. (2014). Honorary authorship in radiologic research articles: Do geographic factors influence the frequency? *Radiology*, *271*(2), 472–478. doi:10.1148/radiol.13131710 PMID:24475845

Elmer, M. (2013). *The Trouble with Chernoff*. Retrieved October 29, 2017, from http://maphugger.com/post/44499755749/the-trouble-with-chernoff

Eppler, M. J. (2004). *Knowledge Communication Problems between Experts and Managers - an Analysis of Knowledge Transfer in Decision Processes*. University of Lugano. Retrieved October 29, 2017, from http://doc.rero.ch/record/5197

Epstein Ojalvo, H., & Doyne, S. (2010, August 24). Teaching with infographics. Social Studies, History, Economics. *The New York Times*.

Epstein, J. M. (2002). Modeling civil violence: An agent-based computational approach. In *PNAS* (vol. 99, suppl. 3, 7242). Retrieved February 25, 2017 from http://www.pnas.org/content/99/suppl_3/7243.full.pdf

Epstein, J.M., (1996). *Growing artificial societies: Social Science From the Bottom Up (Complex Adaptive Systems)*. Brookings Institution Press and MIT Press.

Epstein, J. M. (2007). *Generative Social Science: Studies in Agent-Based Computational Modeling*. Princeton University.

Epstein, J. M. (2014). *Agent_Zero: Toward Neurocognitive Foundations for Generative Social Science*. Princeton University.

Erickson, T. (1996). The World Wide Web as Social Hypertext. *Communications of the ACM*, *39*(1), 15–17. doi:10.1145/234173.234174

Fabrikant, S. I. (2000). *Cartographic Variations on the Presidential Election 2000 theme*. Retrieved October 29, 2017, from https://web.archive.org/web/20100818112308/

Falk, M. (1982). *Love Lyrics from the Bible: A Translation and Literary Study of the Song of Songs*. Sheffield, UK: The Almond Press.

Farmer, W. R. (Ed.). (2000). *Międzynarodowy komentarz do Pisma Świętego*. Warszawa, Poland: Vocatio.

Feramisco, J. D., Leitenberger, J. J., Redfern, S. I., Bian, A., Xie, X. J., & Resneck, J. S. Jr. (2009). A gender gap in the dermatology literature? Cross-sectional analysis of manuscript authorship trends in dermatology journals during 3 decades. *Journal of the American Academy of Dermatology*, *60*(1), 63–69. doi:10.1016/j.jaad.2008.06.044 PMID:19103359

Ferber, J. (1994). Simulating with Reactive Agents. In E. Hillebrand & J. Stender (Eds.), *Many Agent Simulation and Artificial Life* (pp. 8–28). Amsterdam: IOS Press.

Few, S. (2009). *Now You See It: Simple Visualization Techniques for Quantitative Analysis*. Oakland, CA: Analytics Press.

FextorEn. (2013). Retrieved August 25, 2017, from http://nlp.pwr.wroc.pl/redmine/projects/nlprest2/wiki/Fextor2_en

Flickr. (n.d.). *Networks of Abundance Lab*. Retrieved from https://www.flickr.com/photos/poptech/galleries/72157629723472161/

Flowingdata. (2017). Retrieved October 19, 2017 from http://flowingdata.com

Foam Tree. (2017). *Web service by Carrot Search*. Retrieved July 20, 2017, from: http://carrotsearch.com/foamtree

Fox, M. V. (1985). *The Song of Songs and the Ancient Egyptian Love Songs*. Madison, WI: University of Wisconsin Press.

Franchignoni, F., Muñoz Lasa, S., Ozçakar, L., & Ottonello, M. (2011). Bibliometric indicators: A snapshot of the scientific productivity of leading European PRM researchers. *European Journal of Physical and Rehabilitation Medicine*, *47*(3), 455–462. PMID:21946402

Francuz, P. (2007). *Obrazy w umyśle. Studia nad percepcją i wyobraźnią [Images in the mind. Studies of perception and imagination]*. Warszawa: Wyd. Naukowe Scholar.

Frank, E., Hall, M. A., & Witten, I. H. (2016). *The WEKA Workbench. Online Appendix for "Data Mining: Practical Machine Learning Tools and Techniques"*. Morgan Kaufmann. Retrieved October 19, 2017, from https://www.cs.waikato.ac.nz/ml/weka/Witten_et_al_2016_appendix.pdf

Friendly, M. (2010). *Re-Visions of Minard* Retrieved July 20, 2017, from: http://www.datavis.ca/gallery/re-minard.php

Friendly, M. (2008). The Golden Age of Statistical Graphics. *Statistical Science*, *23*(4), 502–535. doi:10.1214/08-STS268

Fry, B. (2007). *Visualizing Data*. Sebastopol, CA: O'Reilly Media.

Galanter, P. (2006). *Generative art and rules-based art*. Retrieved July 24, 2017 from http://vagueterrain.net/

Gallardo, D., Julià, C. F., & Jordà, S. (2008). *TurTan: a Tangible Programming Language for Creative Exploration*. Third annual IEEE international workshop on horizontal human-computer systems (TABLETOP). doi:10.1109/TABLETOP.2008.4660189

García, S., Luengo, J., & Herrera, F. (2015). *Data preprocessing in data mining*. New York: Springer. doi:10.1007/978-3-319-10247-4

Gardner, M. (1970). Mathematical Games. *Scientific American, 223*, 120-123.

Garet, M. S., Porter, A. C., Desimone, L., Birman, B. F., & Yoon, K. S. (2001). What makes Professional Development Effective? Results from a National Sample of Teachers. *American Educational Research Journal*, *38*(4), 915–945. doi:10.3102/00028312038004915

Garfield, E. (1984). Introducing The ISI Atlas of science: Biotechnology and molecular genetics, 1981/82 and bibliographic update for 1983/84. Essays of an Information Scientist, 7, 313-325.

Garfield, E. (1955). Citation index for science: A new dimension in documentation through association of ideas. *Science*, *122*(3159), 108–111. doi:10.1126/science.122.3159.108 PMID:14385826

Georgy Fedoseevich Voronoy. (2007). Retrieved July 20, 2017, from: http://www-history.mcs.st-andrews.ac.uk/Biographies/Voronoy.html

Gephi. The Open Graph Viz Platform. (2017). Retrieved October 21, 2017 from https://gephi.org

Ghitalla, F. (2008). La "Toile Européenne" Parcours Autour d'une Cartographie Thématique de Documents Web Consacrés au Thème de l'Europe et à ses Acteurs sur le Web Francophone. Communication & langages, 1(158).

Gillen, G. (2010). Rehabilitation research focused on neurorehabilitation. *The American Journal of Occupational Therapy*, *64*(2), 341–356. doi:10.5014/ajot.64.2.341 PMID:20437922

Ginsburg, F. (2002). *Mediating Culture: Indigenous Madia, Ethnographic film, and the Production of Identity. In The Anthropology of Media*. Oxford, UK: Backwell.

Glänzel, W. (2014). Analysis of co-authorship patterns at the individual level. *Transinformação, 26*(3), 229–238. doi:10.1590/0103-3786201400030001

Goh, K. I. (2007). The human disease network. *Proceedings of the National Academy of Sciences of the United States of America, 104*(2). Retrieved from http://im.ft-static.com/content/images/b678abae-e6fa-11e3-88be-00144feabdc0.gif PMID:17502601

Graham, S., Milligan, I., & Weingart, S. (2015). *Exploring Big Historical Data. The Historian's Macroscope.* London: Imperial College Press. Retrieved March 15, 2017, from http://www.themacroscope.org/2.0/

Grierson, M. (2008). Making music with images: Interactive audiovisual performance systems for the deaf. In *Proceedings of 7th ICDVRAT with ArtAbilitation.* Retrieved August 10, 2015 from http://doc.gold.ac.uk/~mus02mg/wp-content/uploads/m-grierson-icdvrat_artabilitation_2008_submissiondoc.pdf

Grimmer-Somers, K., Lekkas, P., Nyland, L., Young, A., & Kumar, S. (2007). Perspectives on research evidence and clinical practice: A survey of Australian physiotherapists. *Physiotherapy Research International, 12*(3), 147–161. doi:10.1002/pri.363 PMID:17624895

Gupta, M. R., & Chen, Y. (2010). Theory and Use of the EM Algorithm. *Foundations and Trends in Signal Processing, 4*(3), 223–296. doi:10.1561/2000000034

Hall. (2009). The WEKA Data Mining Software: An Update. *SIGKDD Explorations, 11*(1). Retrieved October 19, 2017, from http://www.kdd.org/exploration_files/p2V11n1.pdf

Harris S.R., Winstein C.J. (2017) The Past, Present, and Future of Neurorehabilitation: From NUSTEP Through IV STEP and Beyond. *Journal of Neurologic Physical Therapy, 41*(Suppl 3), S3-S9.

Harrison, L., Reinecke, K., & Chang, R. (2015). Infographic aesthetics: Designing for the first impression. In *Proceedings of the 33rd Annual ACM Conference on Human Factors in Computing Systems (CHI '15).* New York: ACM. doi:10.1145/2702123.2702545

Harzing, A. W. (2016). *Publish or Perish.* Retrieved on May 15, 2017, from https://harzing.com/resources/publish-or-perish

Hattwig, D., Bussert, K., Medaille, A., & Burgess, J. (2013). Visual literacy standards in higher education: New opportunities for libraries and student learning. *Libraries and the Academy, 13*(1), 61–89. doi:10.1353/pla.2013.0008

Haythornthwaite, C. (2010). Social Networks and Learning Networks: Using Social Network Perspectives to Understand Social Learning. *7th International Conference on Networked Learning.*

Healy, K., & Moody, J. (2016). Data Visualisation in Sociology. *Annual Review of Sociology, 40*(105).

Helland, C. (2007). Diaspora on the Electronic Frontier: Developing Virual Connections with Sacred Homeland. *Journal of Computer-Mediated Communication, 12.*

Henrich, K. J. (2014). *Visual literacy for librarians: Learning skills and promoting best practices.* Retrieved September 28, 2017, from https://theidaholibrarian.wordpress.com/2014/05/27/visual-literacy-for-librarians-learning-skills-and-promoting-best-practices/

Heymann, S. (2013). *Rebuilding Gephi's core for the 0.9 version.* Retrieved May 1, 2017, from https://gephi.wordpress.com/2013/03/05/rebuilding-gephis-core-for-the-0-9-version/

Heymann, S., Bastian, M., Jacomy, M., Maussang, C., Rohmer, A., Bilcke, J., & Jacomy, A. (2009). *GEXF File Format.* Retrieved March 13, 2017, from https://gephi.org/gexf/format/

Heymann, S. (2014). *Exploratory link stream analysis for event detection. Social and Information Networks.* Paris: Université Pierre et Curie.

Hey, T., Tansley, S., & Tolle, K. (2009). *The Fourth Paradigm: Data-Intensive Scientific Discovery.* Microsoft Research.

Hildegard of Bingen. (1990). *Scivias - Classics of Western Spirituality.* Mahwah, NJ: Paulist Press.

Hill, A. E. (1989). *The Song of Solomon. In The Evangelical Commentary on the Bible (pp. 452-66).* Grand Rapids, MI: Baker Book House.

Hiller, H., & Franz, T. (2004). New Ties, Old Ties and Lost Ties: The Use of the Internet in Diaspora. *New Media & Society, 6*(731).

Hollsanowa, J., Holmberg, N., & Holmqvist, K. (2009). Reading Information Graphics: The Role of Spatial Contiguity and Dual Attentional Guidance. *Applied Cognitive Psychology, 23*(9), 1215–1226. doi:10.1002/acp.1525

Holovatch, Yu., Kenna, R., & Thurner, S. (2017). Complex systems: Physics beyond physics. *European Journal of Physics, 38*(2), 023002. doi:10.1088/1361-6404/aa5a87

Hömberg, V. (2010). Neurological rehabilitation. *Internist, 51*(10), 1246–1253, 1248–1253. doi:10.1007/s00108-010-2624-3 PMID:20848072

Hopkins, D. (2006). *Multi Player SimCity for X11 TCL/Tk running on SGI Indigo workstation.* Retrieved from https://commons.wikimedia.org/w/index.php?search=simcity&title=Special:Search&go=Go&searchToken=69rsbzp0coqdrn 4b8qst7y6po#/media/File:SimCity-Indigo.gif

Howells, R., & Negreiros, J. (2013). *Visual Culture* (2nd ed.). Cambridge, UK: Polity Press.

Huang, T. H., & Huang, M. L. (2006). *Analysis and visualization of co-authorship networks for understanding academic collaboration and knowledge domain of individual researchers.* IEEE Xplore. doi:10.1109/CGIV.2006.20

Huang, W., & Tan, Ch. L. (2007). A system for understanding imaged infographics and its applications. In *Proceedings of the 2007 ACM symposium on Document engineering*, (pp. 9-18). New York: Association for Computing Machinery. doi:10.1145/1284420.1284427

Iles, R., & Davidson, M. (2006). Evidence based practice: A survey of physiotherapists' current practice. *Physiotherapy Research International, 11*(2), 93–103. doi:10.1002/pri.328 PMID:16808090

Ink.designhumanities. (n.d.). Retrieved from http://ink.designhumanities.org/voltaire/

Internet Mapping Project. (1998). *Map gallery.* Retrieved July 20, 2017, from: http://cheswick.com/ches/map/gallery/index.html

ISI Atlas of science: Biotechnology and molecular genetics, 1981/82 covering 127 Research Fronts Specialities. (1984). Philadelphia: Academic Press.

Jacomy, M., Venturini, T., Heymann, S., & Bastian, M. (2014). ForceAtlas2, a Continuous Graph Layout Algorithm for Handy Network Visualization Designed for the Gephi Software. *PLoS One, 9*(6), 2014. doi:10.1371/journal.pone.0098679 PMID:24914678

Jesus, T. S. (2016). Systematic Reviews and Clinical Trials in Rehabilitation: Comprehensive Analyses of Publication Trends. *Archives of Physical Medicine and Rehabilitation, 97*(11), 1853–1862.e2. doi:10.1016/j.apmr.2016.06.017 PMID:27424809

Jette, D. U., Bacon, K., & Batty, C. (2003). Evidence-based practice: Beliefs, attitudes, knowledge, and behaviors of physical therapists. *Physical Therapy*, *83*(9), 786–805. PMID:12940766

Junho, S. (in press). Roadmap for e-commerce standardization in Korea. *International Journal of IT Standards and Standardization Research*.

Kamada, T., & Kawai, S. (1989). An algorithm for drawing general undirected graphs. *Information Processing Letters*, *31*(1), 7–15. doi:10.1016/0020-0190(89)90102-6

Kamińska, A. M. (2017a). ProBIT – Prospektywna metoda tworzenia indeksów cytowań a problemy organizacji przestrzeni informacji w tradycyjnych bibliograficznych bazach danych [ProBIT - the prospective method of creating the traversable citation indices and the contemporary problems of the information space organization in traditional bibliographic databases]. *Zagadnienia Informacji Naukowej*, *1*(109).

Kamińska, A. M. (2017b). (in press). Wizualizacje wybranych wskaźników bibliometrycznych na przykładzie bibliograficznej bazy danych CYTBIN [Visualizations of selected bibliometric indicators on the example of the bibliographic database CYTBIN]. *Toruńskie Studia Bibliologiczne*, *2*(19).

Kaufman, R. R., & Chevan, J. (2011). The gender gap in peer-reviewed publications by physical therapy faculty members: A productivity puzzle. *Physical Therapy*, *91*(1), 122–131. doi:10.2522/ptj.20100106 PMID:21127164

Keel, O. (1997). *Pieśń nad Pieśniami. Biblijna pieśń o miłości*. Poznań, Poland: Zyski i Spółka.

Keller, T., & Tergan, S. (2005). *Knowledge and Information Visualization Searching for Synergies*. Berlin: Springer.

Kennedy, D. (2006). *Writing and Using Learning Outcomes*. Retrieved December 9, 2016, from https://www.cmepius.si/wp-content/uploads/2015/06/A-Learning-Outcomes-Book-D-Kennedy.pdf

Kessler, M. (1963). Bibliografic coupling between scientific papers. *American Documentation*, *14*(1), 10–25. doi:10.1002/asi.5090140103

Khosrow-Pour, M et al. (Ed.). (2016). *Big data: Concepts, methodologies, tools, and applications*. IGI Global.

Kierach, M., & Ogonowski, B. (2012). Wpływ ilości informacji i atrakcyjności wizualnej prezentacji na zapamiętywanie prezentowanych treści [The influence of the amount of information and visual attractiveness of the presentation on memorizing the presented content]. *e-Mentor*, 1. Retrieved March 15, 2017, from http://www.e-mentor.edu.pl/artykul/index/numer/43/id/905

Kim, J. H., Iyer, V., Joshi, S. B., Volkin, D. B., & Middaugh, C. R. (2012). Improved Data Visualization Techniques for Analyzing Macromolecule Structural Changes. *Protein Science*, *21*(10), 1540–1553. doi:10.1002/pro.2144 PMID:22898970

Kipphan, H. (Ed.). (2001). *Handbook of Print Media*. Berlin: Springer. doi:10.1007/978-3-540-29900-4

Knapiński, R. (2011). Biblia Pauperum – rzecz o dialogu słowa i obrazu [The Bible of Pauperum: the dialogue of words and images]. In M. Kluza (Ed.), *Materiały konferencji „Wizualizacja wiedzy. Od Biblii Pauperum do hipertekstu"* [Conference proceedings "Visualization of knowledge. From the Bible Pauperum to hypertext"] (pp. 10-36). Lublin: Wiedza i Edukacja.

Kondratov, A. (2016). Analyser les matérialités de l'espace public contemporain avec la méthode quantitative de visualisation. In *Les cahiers numériques: La visualization de données* (Vol. 12). Paris: Lavoisier. doi:10.3166/lcn.12.4.93-129

Kosara, R. (2007). *A Critique of Chernoff Faces*. Retrieved October 29, 2017, from https://eagereyes.org/criticism/chernoff-faces

Krauss, J. (2012). Infographics: More than words can say. *Learning and Leading with Technology, 39*(5), 10–14. Retrieved from http://files.eric.ed.gov/fulltext/EJ982831.pdf

Kręcidło, J. (2008). Miłość – płomień Jahwe (Pnp 8,5-7): Potęga miłości jako klucz interpretacyjny do Pieśni nad pieśniami. *Collectanea Theologica, 78*(4), 39–62.

Krolak, L. (2005). *The role of libraries in the creation of literate environments.* Retrieved June 18, 2017, from https://www.ifla.org/files/assets/literacy-and-reading/publications/role-of-libraries-in-creation-of-literate-environments.pdf

Kudelka, M., Horak, Z., Snasel, V., & Abraham, A. (2010). Social Network Reduction Based on Stability. *2010 International Conference on Computational Aspects of Social Networks.* Retrieved from IEEE Xplore Digital Library. doi:10.1109/CASoN.2010.120

Kuhlo, M. (2013). *Architectural Rendering with 3ds Max and V-Ray.* Taylor & Francis.

Kuhlo, M., & Eggert, E. (2010). *Architectural Rendering with 3ds Max and V-Ray: Photorealistic Visualization.* Focal Press.

Kühni, J. A. (2013). *Stemming and Lemmatizing for Natural Language Processing* (Unpublished master report). University of Neuchatel.

Kumar, S. (2015). Co-authorship networks: A review of the literature. *Aslib Journal of Information Management, 67*(1), 55–73. doi:10.1108/AJIM-09-2014-0116

Kwakkel, G. (2009). Towards integrative neurorehabilitation science. *Physiotherapy Research International, 14*(3), 137–146. doi:10.1002/pri.446 PMID:19634129

La Rooy, G. (2000). Charting Performance. *NZ Business,* 14.

Lamb, G. R., Polman, J. L., Newman, A., & Smith, C. G. (2014). Science News Infographics: Teaching Students to Gather, Interpret, and Present Information Graphically. *Science Teacher (Normal, Ill.), 3*(81), 25–30.

Lamb, W. E. Jr. (1964). Theory of an Optical Maser. *Physical Review, 134*(6A), A1429–A1450. doi:10.1103/PhysRev.134.A1429

Lamirel, J. C., Al Shehabi, S., & Francois, C. (2005). Evaluation of collaboration between European universities using dynamic interaction between multiple sources. In P. Ingwersen, & B. Larsen (Eds.), *Proceedings of ISSI 2005: 10th international conference of the International Society for Scientometrics and Informetrics, Stockholm, Sweden, July 24-28* (pp. 740-749). Stockholm: Karolinska University Press.

Landry, F. (1983). *Paradoxes of Paradise: Identity and Differences in the Song of Songs.* Sheffield, UK: The Almond Press.

Le Béchec, M. (2016). Le territoire comme un graphe: Pratiques, formes, éthique. In *Les cahiers numériques: La visualization de données* (Vol. 12). Paris: Lavoisier. doi:10.3166/lcn.12.4.131-156

Lee, L., & Amirfar, V. A. (2016). Infographics: Presenting data, telling a story through visuals. *Pharmacy Today, 22*(6), 46. doi:10.1016/j.ptdy.2016.05.021

Legrenzi, F. (2010). *VRay The Complete Guide* (2nd ed.). Industrie Grafiche Stilgraf.

Leskovec, J., Kleinberg, J., & Faloutsos, C. (2007). Graph evolution: Densification and shrinking diameters. *ACM Transactions on Knowledge Discovery from Data, 1*(1), 2, es. doi:10.1145/1217299.1217301

Leung, C. K. S., Carmichael, C. L., & Teh, E. W. (2011). Visual analytics of social networks: mining and visualizing co-authorship networks. In D. D. Schmorrow & C. M. Fidopiastis (Eds.), *Foundations of Augmented Cognition. Directing the Future of Adaptive Systems* (pp. 335–345). Berlin: Springer. doi:10.1007/978-3-642-21852-1_40

Levsky, M. E., Rosin, A., Coon, T. P., Enslow, W. L., & Miller, M. A. (2007). A descriptive analysis of authorship within medical journals, 1995-2005. *Southern Medical Journal*, *100*(4), 371–375. doi:10.1097/01.smj.0000257537.51929.4b PMID:17458396

Leydesdorff, L. (2007). On the normalization and visualization of author co-citation data: Salton's Cosine versus the Jaccard index. *Journal of the Association for Information Science and Technology*. doi:10.1002/asi.20732

Leydesdorff, L. (2010a). Eugene Garfield and algorithmic historiography: Co-words, co-authors, and journal names. *Annals of Library and Information Studies*, *57*(3), 248–260.

Leydesdorff, L. (2010b). What Can Heterogeneity Add to the Scientometric Map? Steps towards algorithmic historiography. In M. Akrich, Y. Barthe, F. Muniesa, & P. Mustar (Eds.), *Débordements: Mélanges offerts à Michel Callon* (pp. 283–289). Paris: Presses des Mines. doi:10.4000/books.pressesmines.756

Liepert, J. (2012). Evidence-based methods in motor rehabilitation after stroke. *Fortschritte der Neurologie-Psychiatrie*, *80*(7), 388–393. PMID:22760510

Lima, M. (2011). *Visual complexity: Mapping patterns of information*. New York: Princeton Architectural Press.

Lima, M. (2011). *Visual Complexity: Mapping Patterns of Information*. New York: Princeton Architectural Press.

Lima, M. (2014). *The Book of Trees. Visualizing Branches of Knowledge*. New York: Princeton Architectural Press.

Lima, M. (2014). *The Book of Trees: Visualizing Branches of Knowledge*. New York: Princeton Architectural Press.

Lima, M. (2017). *The Book of Circles: Visualizing Spheres of Knowledge*. New York: Princeton Architectural Press.

Linderman, M. G. (1997). *Art in elementary school*. Boston: Mc Gnow-Hill.

Literacy and School Libraries. (2013). *Examples of visual literacy lessons & programming for school libraries*. Retrieved September 28, 2017, from https://literacyandschoollibraries.wikispaces.com

Lloyd, M., & Bahr, N. (2010). Thinking Critically about Critical Thinking in Higher Education. *International Journal for the Scholarship of Teaching and Learning*, *4*(2), 1–16.

Lončar Vicković, S., & Dolaček Alduk, Z. (2009). *Ishodi učenja, priručnik za sveučilišne nastavnike*. Retrieved March 5, 2017, from http://www.azoo.hr/images/Natjecanja_2014./ishodi_ucenja.pdf

Long, B. (2014). *Complete Digital Photography* (8th ed.). Boston: Cengage Learning PTR.

Luft, A. R. (2012). How to gain evidence in neurorehabilitation: A personal view. *Biomedical Engineering*, *57*(6), 427–433. PMID:23023795

Lynch, E. A., Cumming, T., Janssen, H., & Bernhardt, J. (2017). Early mobilization after stroke: Changes in clinical opinion despite an unchanging evidence base. *Journal of Stroke & Cardiovascular Diseases*, *26*(1), 1–6. doi:10.1016/j.jstrokecerebrovasdis.2016.08.021 PMID:27612626

Mac Carron, P., & Kenna, R. (2012). Universal properties of mythological networks. *EPL*, *99*(2), 28002. doi:10.1209/0295-5075/99/28002

Malak, P. (2013) *The Polish Task within Cultural Heritage in CLEF (CHiC) 2013. In CLEF 2013 Evaluation Labs and Workshop Working Notes*. Retrieved August 25, 2017, from http://www.clef-initiative.eu/documents/71612/b00f7561-fadb-47a8-ab67-74f116ce062a

Maldenbrot, B. (1982). *Fractal Geometry of Nature*. New York: W. H. Freeman and Company.

Manning, C. D., Raghavan, P., & Schütze, H. (2008). *Introduction to information retrieval.* Cambridge University Press. Retrieved October 21, 2017 from: https://nlp.stanford.edu/IR-book/html/htmledition/irbook.html

Manovich, L. (2008). *Introduction to Info-Aesthetics.* Retrieved September 22, 2017 from http://manovich.net/content/04-projects/060-introduction-to-info-aesthetics/57-article-2008.pdf

Mapping Metaphor. (n.d.). Retrieved August 25, 2017, from http://mappingmetaphor.arts.gla.ac.uk

Mapping the Republic of Letters. (2013). Retrieved June 15, 2017, from http://republicofletters.stanford.edu/index.html

Marchese, F. T., & Banissi, E. (2013). *Knowledge visualization currents: from text to art to culture.* London: Springer. doi:10.1007/978-1-4471-4303-1

Marcinek, A. (2010). *Rethinking the library to improve information literacy.* Retrieved June 20, 2017, from https://www.edutopia.org/blog/rethinking-library-information-literacy

Markram, H. (2013). Seven challenges for neuroscience. *Functional Neurology, 28*(3), 145–151. PMID:24139651

Marshakova, I. (1973). System of document connections based on references [in Russian]. *Nauchno-Tekhnicheskaja Informacya. Ser. 2, N6,* 3–8.

Marshakova, I. (1981). Citation Networks in Information Science. *Scientometrics, 3*(1), 13–26. doi:10.1007/BF02021861

Marshakova, I. (1988). *The SCI system as a mean of monitoring of science development.* Moscow: Nauka. (in Russian)

Marshakova-Shaikevich, I. (2004a). Journal co-citation analysis in the field of Women's Studies. In H. Kretschmer, Y. Singh, & R. Kudra (Eds.), *WIS-2004, International Workshop on Webometrics, Informetrics and Scientometrics, 2-5 March 2004* (pp. 247-259). Roorkee: Central Library, Indian Institute of Technology.

Marshakova-Shaikevich, I. (2010a). Meeting Robert Merton: Discussion of co-citation maps of science and evaluation of scientific journals. *Sotsologija Nauki i Tekhnologij, 1*(4), 118-123.

Marshakova-Shaikevich, I. (2010b). Bibliometric maps of scientific Collaboration of UE countries in science and social science. *Sotsologija Nauki i Tekhnologij, 1*(2), 57-63.

Marshakova-Shaikevich, I. (2003). Journal Co-Citation Analysis in the Fields of Information Science and Library Science. In W. Krzemińska & P. Nowak (Eds.), *Language, Information and Communication Studies* (pp. 87–96). Poznań: Sorus.

Marshakova-Shaikevich, I. (2004b). Journal co-citaton analysis. *Journal of Information Management and Scientometrics, 1*(2), 27–36.

Marshakova-Shaikevich, I. (2005). Bibliometric maps of Field of Science. *Information Processing & Management, 41*(6), 1534–1547. doi:10.1016/j.ipm.2005.03.027

Marshakova-Shaikevich, I. (2006). Science collaboration of new 10 EU countries in the field of social sciences. *Information Processing & Management, 42*(6), 1592–1598. doi:10.1016/j.ipm.2006.03.023

Marshakova-Shaikevich, I. (2007a). The visualization of scientific collaboration of 15 'old ' and 10 'new' EU countries in the field of social sciences. *Collnet Journal of Scientometrics and Information Management, 1*(1), 9–16. doi:10.1080/09720502.2007.10700948

Marshakova-Shaikevich, I. (2007b). Memory and Memoriesa in lexical environment: Bibliometric analysis of SSCI DB. *Collnet Journal of Scientometrics and Information Management, 1*(2), 41–52. doi:10.1080/09737766.2007.10700830

Marshakova-Shaikevich, I. (2009). Information management as the part of Information and library science: bibliometric study. In B. F. Kubiak & A. Korowicki (Eds.), *Information Management* (pp. 498–506). Gdańsk: Gdansk University Press.

Martinez, E., Kwiatkowski, I., & Pasquier, P. (2011). *Towards a Model of Social Coherence in Multi-Agent Organizations*. Springer.

Mayer-Schnonberger, V., & Cukier, K. (2014). *Big Data: A Revolution That Will Transform How We Live, Work, and Think*. Boston: Houghton Mifflin Harcourt.

McCabe, J. (n.d.). *Nervous States*. Retrieved from https://www.flickr.com/photos/jonathanmccabe/albums/72157614673650974

McCabe, J. (n.d.). *Origami butterfly_0076*. Retrieved from https://www.flickr.com/photos/jonathanmccabe/albums/72157619224237107

McIntyre, A., Richardson, M., Janzen, S., Hussein, N., & Teasell, R. (2014). The evolution of stroke rehabilitation randomized controlled trials. *International Journal of Stroke*, *9*(6), 789–792. doi:10.1111/ijs.12272 PMID:24621406

McLean, A., & Wiggins, G. (2011). *Texture: Visual Notation for Live Coding of Pattern*. Centre for Cognition, Computation and Culture Department of Computing Goldsmiths, University of London.

Mendenhall, A. S., & Summers, S. (2015). Designing Research: Using Infographics to Teach Design Thinking in Composition. *Journal of Global Literacies, Technologies, and Emerging Pedagogies*, *1*(3), 359–371.

Meyer, R. (2009). *Knowledge Visualization*. Retrieved October 29, 2017, from http://citeseerx.ist.psu.edu/viewdoc/download?doi=10.1.1.164.3759&rep=rep1&type=pdf

Milgram, S. (1967). The small world problem. *Psychology Today*, *1*(May), 61–67.

Millington, J. D. A., O'Sullivan, D., & Perry, G. L. W. (2012). Model histories: Narrative explanation in generative simulation modelling. *Geoforum*, *43*(6), 1025–1034. doi:10.1016/j.geoforum.2012.06.017

Model Systems Knowledge Translation Center. (2015). *Presenting data using infographics*. Retrieved June 18, 2017, from http://www.msktc.org/lib/docs/KT_Toolkit/MSKTC_KT_Tool_Infographics_508.pdf

Moore, D. M., & Dwyer, F. M. (Eds.). (1994). *Visual literacy: A spectrum of visual learning*. Englewood Cliffs, NJ: Educational Technology Publications.

Moretti, F. (2005). *Graphs, Maps, Trees. Abstract Models for Literary History*. Brooklyn, NY: Verso.

Morgan, G. (1998). *Images of Organization*. Thousand Oaks, CA: Sage Publications.

Morris, S. A., & Yen, G. C. (2004). Crossmaps: Visualization of overlapping relationships in collections of journal papers. *Proceedings of the National Academy of Sciences of the United States of America*, *101*(Supplement 1), 5291–5296. doi:10.1073/pnas.0307604100 PMID:14762168

Moura, J. M. (2011). *Joao Martinho Moura*. Retrieved from http://jmartinho.net/

Mrvar, A., & Batagelj, V. (2016). Analysis and visualization of large networks with program package Pajek. *Complex Adaptive Systems Modeling*, *4*(1), 6. doi:10.1186/s40294-016-0017-8

Mryglod, O., Holovatch, Yu., Kenna, R., & Berche, B. (2016). Quantifying the evolution of a scientific topic: Reaction of the academic community to the Chornobyl disaster. *Scientometrics*, *106*(3), 1151–1166. doi:10.1007/s11192-015-1820-2

Murdock, K. L. (2013). *3ds Max 2012 Bible*. Indiana: Willey.

Murphy, R. E. (1986). History of Exegesis as a Hermeneutical Tool, The Song of Songs. *Biblical Theology Bulletin*, *16*(3), 87–91. doi:10.1177/014610798601600302

Murphy, R. E. (1990). *The Song of Songs. Hermeneia Commentary Series*. Philadelphia, PA: Fortress Press.

Murphy, R. E. (2001). Pieśń nad pieśniami. In R. E. Brown, J. A. Fitzmyer, & R. E. Murphy (Eds.), *Katolicki Komentarz Biblijny*. Warszawa, Poland: Vocatio.

Murtagh, F., & Legendre, P. (2011). *Ward's hierarchical clustering method: clustering criterion and agglomerative algorithm*. Retrieved October 21, 2017 from https://arxiv.org/pdf/1111.6285v2

Musso, P. (2010). Le Web: Nouveau Territoire et Vieux Concept. *Annales des Mines – Réalités Industrielles, 4*.

Najar, S. (Ed.). (2012). *Les nouvelles sociabilités du Net en Méditerranée*. Paris: IRMC/Karthala.

Nakata, M., Nakata, V., Gardiner, G., McKeough, J., Byrne, A., & Gisbon, J. (2008). Indigenous Digital Collections: An Early Look at the Organisation and Culture Interface. *Australian Academic and Research Libraries, 49*(4).

Nassery, F., Sikorski, P. (2015). New possibilities of using processing and modern methods of the "generative art" graphics in architecture. *Technical Transactions Architecture, 4-A/2015*.

National Qualifications Framework-Anniversary edition. (2015). *CROQF-Developments in Europe*. Retrieved March 12, 2016, from https://www.cedefop.europa.eu/files/4137_en.pdf

National Research Council. (2000). *Inquiry and the National Science Education standards: A guide for teaching and learning*. Washington, DC: The National Academies Press.

Nedelcu, M. (2009). Du Brain Drain à l'E-diaspora: Vers une Nouvelle Culture du Lien à l'ère du Numérique. TIC & Diaspora, 3(1-2).

Nelson, E., Dow, D., Lukinbeal, C., & Farley, R. (1997). Visual Search Processes and the Multivariate Point Symbol. *Cartographica, 34*(4), 19–33. doi:10.3138/15T3-3222-X25H-35JU

Nelson, N. (2004). Visual literacy and library instruction: A critical analysis. *Education Libraries, 27*(1), 5–10. doi:10.26443/el.v27i1.194

Newman, M. (2010). *Networks: An Introduction*. Oxford, UK: Oxford University Press. doi:10.1093/acprof:oso/9780199206650.001.0001

Newman, M. E. J. (2001). The structure of scientific collaboration networks. *Proceedings of the National Academy of Sciences of the United States of America, 98*(2), 404–409. doi:10.1073/pnas.98.2.404 PMID:11149952

Newman, M. E. J. (2004). Coauthorship networks and patterns of scientific collaboration networks. *Proceedings of the National Academy of Sciences of the United States of America, 101*(Suppl. 1), 5200–5205. doi:10.1073/pnas.0307545100 PMID:14745042

Newman, M., Barabási, A.-L., & Watts, D. J. (2006). *The Structure and Dynamics of Networks*. Princeton University Press.

Nordstrom, L. O. (1990). 'Bradford's Law' and the relationship between Ecology and Biogeography. *Scientometrics, 18*(3-4), 193–203. doi:10.1007/BF02017761

Nowosad, I. (2015). *Sound and Datasets graphical visualizations*. Fides, Ratio et Patria. In *Studia Toruńskie* (no. 3, pp. 82-98). Academic Press.

Nuñez, J. J. R., Rohonczi, A., Juliarena de Moretti, C. E., Garra, A. M., Rey, C. A., . . . Campos, M. A. (2011). Updating Research on Chernoff Faces for School Cartography. In A. Ruas (Eds.), Advances in Cartography and GI Science (vol. 2). Springer.

Nwana, H. S. (1996). Software Agents: An Overview. *The Knowledge Engineering Review*, *11*(3), 1–40. doi:10.1017/S026988890000789X

O'Connor, J. J., & Robertson, E. F. (1999). *John Wilder Tukey*. Retrieved July 20, 2017, from: http://www-history.mcs.st-and.ac.uk/Biographies/Tukey.html

Oiarzabal, P. (2012). Diaspora Basques and Online Social Networks: An Analysis of Users of Basque Institutional Diaspora Groups on Facebook. *Journal of Ethnic and Migration Studies*, *38*(9), 1469–1485. doi:10.1080/1369183X.2012.698216

Ollion, E., & Boelaert, J. (2015). Au Delà des Big Data: Les Sciences Sociales et la Multuplication des Données Numériques. Sociologie, 6(3).

Osińska V. (2011) Fractal Analysis of Knowledge Organization in Digital Library. *New Trends in Qualitative and Quantitative Methods in Libraries, 17–23.*

Osińska, W. (2017). *Wizualizacja informacji* [Visualization of information]. Retrieved March 15, 2017, from http://www.wizualizacjainformacji.pl/

Osińska, V. (2008). Wizualizacja i mapowanie przestrzeni danych w bibliotekach cyfrowych. *Toruńskie Studia Bibliologiczne*, *1*, 167–176.

Osinska, V. (2016). *Information Visualization. Information Science perspective*. Torun, Poland: Nicolaus Copernicus University Publishing. (in Polish)

Osińska, V. (2016). *Wizualizacja informacji. Studium informatologiczne*. Toruń, Poland: Wydawnictwo Naukowe Uniwersytetu Mikołaja Kopernika.

Osinska, V., & Bala, P. (2015). Study of dynamics of structured knowledge: Qualitative analysis of different mapping approaches. *Journal of Information Science*, *41*(2), 197–208. doi:10.1177/0165551514559897

Osinska, V., Jozwik, A., & Osinski, G. (2015). Mapping Evaluation for Semantic Browsing. In *Proceedings of the 2015 Federated Conference on Computer Science and Information Systems* (vol. 5, pp. 329-335). Los Alamitos, CA: IEEE. doi:10.15439/2015F50

Osinska, V., Osinski, G., & Kwiatkowska, A. B. (2015). Visualization in Learning: Perception, Aesthetics, and Pragmatics. In A. Ursyn (Ed.), *Maximazing Cognitive Learning through Knowledge Visualization*. Hershey, PA: IGI Global. doi:10.4018/978-1-4666-8142-2.ch013

Osinski, G. (2015). Information Visualization. The research of information structures in the search for truth. *Fides Ratio et Patria, 3*. (in Polish).

Osinski, G. *Retarius contra Sekutor*. WSKSiM, Torun 2018. (in Polish)

Oulhadj, L. (2005). *La ruée vers Internet*. Retrieved March 15, 2017, from http://tawiza.x10.mx/Tawiza92/oulhadj.htm

Paivio, A. (1990). *Mental Representations: A Dual Coding Approach.* Oxford University Press. doi:10.1093/acprof:oso/9780195066661.001.0001

Palfreyman, S., Tod, A., & Doyle, J. (2003). Comparing evidence-based practice of nurses and physiotherapists. *British Journal of Nursing (Mark Allen Publishing)*, *12*(4), 246–253. doi:10.12968/bjon.2003.12.4.11165 PMID:12671571

Palmer, D. D. (2010). Text Preprocessing. In N. Indurkhya & F. J. Damerau (Eds.), Handbook of Natural Language Processing (pp. 9-30). Chapman & Hall/CRC.

Pangburn, D. D. (2017). *Generative Algorithms and Acrylic Paint Create Profound Digital Paintings.* Retrieved from https://creators.vice.com/en_us/article/78e5qb/generative-paintings-acrylic-algorithms-helen-alexandra

Paradowski, M. (2011). Wizualizacja danych – dużo więcej niż prezentacja [Visualization of data - much more than presentation]. In M. Kluza (Ed.), *Materiały konferencji „Wizualizacja wiedzy. Od Biblii Pauperum do hipertekstu"* [Conference proceedings "Visualization of knowledge. From the Bible Pauperum to hypertext"] (pp. 37-60). Lublin: Wiedza i Edukacja.

Pareidolia. In (2017). In *Merriam-Webster's dictionary* (11th ed.). Springfield, MA: Merriam-Webster.

Partnership for 21st Century Learning. (2015). *P21's Framework for 21st Century Learning.* Retrieved July 05, 2017, from http://www.p21.org/about-us/p21-framework

Parts-of-speech.info. (n.d.). Retrieved from http://parts-of-speech.info/

Pasanec Preprotić, S. (2017). *Informacijski paket - Preddiplomski sveučilišni studij grafičke tehnologije.* Retrieved July 15, 2017, from http://www.grf.unizg.hr/informacijski-paket/

Pasanec, P. S. (2017, March). *From Visualization framework in teaching bookbinding at the Faculty of Graphic Arts.* Paper presented at the meeting International Conference Information Visualization in Humanities, Torun, Poland.

Pazienza, M. T., Pennacchiotti, M., & Zanzotto, F. M. (2005). Terminology extraction: An analysis of linguistic and statistical approaches. In S. Sirmakessis (Ed.), *Knowledge mining* (pp. 255–279). Berlin: Springer. doi:10.1007/3-540-32394-5_20

Pearson, M. (2011). *Generative Art: A practical guide using Processing.* Manning Publications.

Pereira, S., Graham, J. R., Shahabaz, A., Salter, K., Foley, N., Meyer, M., & Teasell, R. (2012). Rehabilitation of individuals with severe stroke: Synthesis of best evidence and challenges in implementation. *Topics in Stroke Rehabilitation, 19*(2), 122–131. doi:10.1310/tsr1902-122 PMID:22436360

Perianes-Rodríguez, A., Olmeda-Gómez, C., & Moya-Anegón, F. (2010). Detecting, identifying and visualizing research groups in co-authorship networks. *Scientometrics, 82*(2), 307–319. doi:10.1007/s11192-009-0040-z

Perriault, J. (2012). Réseaux Socionumériques et Frontières. Hermès, La revue, 2(63).

Perry, G. L. W., Wainwright, J., Etherington, T. R., & Wilmshurst, J. M. (2016, October). Experimental Simulation: Using Generative Modeling and Palaeoecological Data to Understand Human-Environment Interactions. *Frontiers in Ecology and Evolution, 13.* Retrieved from http://journal.frontiersin.org/article/10.3389/fevo.2016.00109/full

Petzold, A., Korner-Bitensky, N., & Menon, A. (2010). Using the knowledge to action process model to incite clinical change. *The Journal of Continuing Education in the Health Professions, 30*(3), 167–171. doi:10.1002/chp.20077 PMID:20872771

Phylogenetic Tree. (2008). Retrieved on November 30, 2015 from https://en.wikipedia.org/wiki/Phylogenetic_tree#/media/File:Tree_of_life_SVG.svg

Piasecki, M. (n.d.). *Fextor.* Retrieved August 25, 2017, from https://clarin-pl.eu/dspace/handle/11321/12

Piper, B., Ratti, C., & Ishii, H. (2002). Illuminating Clay: A Tangible Interface with potential GRASS applications. *Proceedings of the Open source GIS - GRASS users.* doi:10.1145/503376.503439

Pope, M. H. (1977). *Song of Songs. In The Anchor Bible (vol. 7c).* Garden City, NY: Doubleday & Sons, Inc.

Pope, M. H. (2008). *Song of Songs.* New Haven, CT: AYB.

Popova, M. (n.d.). *The Music Animation Machine*. Retrieved from https://www.brainpickings.org/2010/11/09/stephen-malinowski-music-animation-machine/

Potocki, S. (2007). *Rady mądrości*. Lublin, Poland: Wydawnictwo KUL.

Prokopowicz, P., Mikołajewski, D., Mikołajewska, E., & Kotlarz, P. (2017) Fuzzy system as an assessment tool for analysis of the health-related quality of life for the people after stroke. In *Artificial Intelligence and Soft Computing: 16th International Conference, ICAISC 2017, Proceedings, Part I*. Springer. doi:10.1007/978-3-319-59063-9_64

Przepiórkowski, A. (2011). *NKJP Tagset*. Retrieved October 23, 2017 from http://nkjp.pl/poliqarp/help/ense2.html

Pudovkin, A. I., & Fuseler, E. A. (1995). Indices of journal citation relatedness and citation relationships among aquatic biology journals. *Scientometrics, 32*(3), 227–236. doi:10.1007/BF02017642

Pudovkin, A. I., & Garfield, E. (2002). Algorithmic Procedure for finding semantically related journals. *Journal of the Association for Information Science and Technology, 53*(13), 1113–1110. doi:10.1002/asi.10153

Pulak, I., & Tomaszewska, M. (2011). Visual Literacy and Teaching with Infographics. In K. Denek (Ed.), Edukacja jutra. Edukacja w społeczeństwie wiedzy [Tomorrow's education. Education in the knowledge society]. Sosnowiec: Oficyna Wydawnicza "Humanitas".

Python Programming Language – Official Website. (2017). Retrieved August 25, 2017, from http://www.python.org/

Radomski, A. (2016). Wizualne analizy, wizualne narracje [Visual analyses, visual narrations]. In R. Bomba, A. Radomski, E. Solska (Ed.), Humanistyka cyfrowa. Badanie tekstów, obrazów i dźwięku [Digital humanities. Examination of texts, images and sound] (pp. 147-158). Lublin: Wyd. E-Naukowiec.

Radomski, A. (2013). Digital storytelling. Kilka słów o wizualizacji wiedzy w humanistyce [Digital storytelling. A few words about the visualization of knowledge in humanities]. In R. Bomba & A. Radomski (Eds.), *Zwrot cyfrowy w humanistyce [Digital turnaround in humanities]*. Lublin: Wyd. E-Naukowiec.

Radziszewski, A., & Warzocha, R. (2014). *WCRFT2, CLARIN-PL digital repository*. Retrieved August 25, 2017, from http://hdl.handle.net/11321/36

Ramachandran, V. S. (2012). *The Tell-Tale Brain. A Neuroscientists' Quest for What Makes Us Human*. New York: W. H. Freeman and Company.

Ramírez-Vélez, R., Correa-Bautista, J. E., & Muñoz-Rodríguez, D. I. (2015). Evidence-based practice: Beliefs, attitudes, knowledge, and skills among Colombian physical therapists. *Colombia Médica (Cali, Colombia), 46*(1), 33–40. PMID:26019383

Ravasi, G. (2005). *Pieśń nad pieśniami…jak pieczęć na twoim sercu*. Kraków, Poland: Salwator.

Reyes, J. J. (2009). Ideas for the Use of Chernoff Faces in School Cartography. The World's Geospatial Solutions. *CD Proceedings of ICA 24th ICC*.

Rock, D. (2009). *Your Brain at Work: Strategies for Overcoming Distraction, Regaining Focus, and Working Smarter All Day Long*. New York, NY: HarperBusiness.

Rogers, R. (2005). *Digital Methods*. Boston, MA: The MIT Press.

Rosenberg, W. M., & Donald, A. (1995). Evidence-based medicine: An approach to clinical problem solving. *BMJ (Clinical Research Ed.), 310*(6987), 1122–1126. doi:10.1136/bmj.310.6987.1122 PMID:7742682

Rosenstone, R. (2008). Historia w obrazach/historia w słowach: rozważania nad możliwością przedstawienia historii na taśmie filmowej [History in images/history in words: reflections on the possibility of presenting a story on a film tape]. In I. Kurz (Ed.), *Film i historia. Antologia [Film and history. Anthology]* (pp. 93–116). Warszawa: Wyd. Uniwersytetu Warszawskiego.

Rosiek, A., & Leksowski, K. (Eds.). (2016). *Organizational culture and ethics in modern medicine.* IGI Global. doi:10.4018/978-1-4666-9658-7

Rycroft-Malone, J., Seers, K., Titchen, A., Harvey, G., Kitson, A., & McCormack, B. (2004). What counts as evidence-based practice? *Journal of Advanced Nursing, 47*(1), 81–90. doi:10.1111/j.1365-2648.2004.03068.x PMID:15186471

Sackett, D. L., Rosenberg, W. M., Gray, J. A., Haynes, R. B., & Richardson, W. S. (1996). Evidence-based medicine: What it is and what it isn't. *BMJ (Clinical Research Ed.), 312*(7023), 71–72. doi:10.1136/bmj.312.7023.71 PMID:8555924

Salbach, N.M., Guilcher, S.J., Jaglal, S.B., & Davis, D.A. (2010). Determinants of research use in clinical decision making among physical therapists providing services post-stroke: A cross-sectional study. *Implementation Science, 14*(5), 77.

Salbach, N. M., Guilcher, S. J., Jaglal, S. B., & Davis, D. A. (2009). Factors influencing information seeking by physical therapists providing stroke management. *Physical Therapy, 89*(10), 1039–1050. doi:10.2522/ptj.20090081 PMID:19661160

Salbach, N. M., Jaglal, S. B., Korner-Bitensky, N., Rappolt, S., & Davis, D. (2007). Practitioner and organizational barriers to evidence-based practice of physical therapists for people with stroke. *Physical Therapy, 87*(10), 1284–1303. doi:10.2522/ptj.20070040 PMID:17684088

Sannino, C. (2012). *Photography and Rendering with V-Ray.* GC Edizioni.

Santos, J. A. C., & Santos, M. C. (2016). Co-authorship networks: Collaborative research structures at the journal level. *Tourism & Management Studies, 12*(1), 5–13. doi:10.18089/tms.2016.12101

Savoy, J. (2006). Light Stemming Approaches for the French, Portuguese, German and Hungarian Languages. *Proceedings ACM-SAC*, 1031-1035. doi:10.1145/1141277.1141523

Schellenberg, J. (2015). *Visual literacy practices in higher education* (Unpublished master dissertation). Oslo and Akershus University College of Applied Sciences, Norway. Retrieved June 20, 2017, from https://oda.hioa.no/en/visual-literacy-practices-in-higher-education

Schleser, J. (2013). Unprotected Memory: User-Generated and the Unintentional Archive. In *Proceedings of the Memory of the World in the Digital Age: Digitization and Preservation.* UNESCO.

Schnettler, B. (2008). W stronę socjologii wizualnej [Towards visual sociology]. *Przegląd Socjologii Jakościowej, 3,* 116–142.

Schroeder, R. (2004). Interactive info graphics in Europe--added value to online mass media: A preliminary survey. *Journalism Studies, 5*(4), 563–570. doi:10.1080/14616700412331296473

Sci2 Team. (2009). *Science of Science (Sci2) Tool.* Indiana University and SciTech Strategies. Retrieved on May 15, 2017 from http://sci2.cns.iu.edu

Severo, M., & Zuolo, E. (2012) Egyptian e-diaspora: migrant websites without a network? In Social Science information, (n° 51, pp. 521-533). Paris: SAGE Publications. doi:10.1177/0539018412456772

Shadgan, B., Roig, M., Hajghanbari, B., & Reid, W. D. (2010). Top-cited articles in rehabilitation. *Archives of Physical Medicine and Rehabilitation, 91*(5), 806–815. doi:10.1016/j.apmr.2010.01.011 PMID:20434622

Shaikevich, A. (2001). Contrastive and comparable corpora: Quantitative aspects. *International Journal of Corpus Linguistics, 6*(2), 229–255. doi:10.1075/ijcl.6.2.03sha

Shneiderman, B. (2009). *Treemaps for space-constrained visualization of hierarchies.* Retrieved July 20, 2017, from: http://www.cs.umd.edu/hcil/treemap-history/

Sidiakina, I. V., Dobrushina, O. R., Liadov, K. V., Shapovalenko, T. V., & Romashin, O. V. (2015). The role of evidence-based medicine in the neurorehabilitation: The innovative technologies (a review). *Voprosy Kurortologii, Fizioterapii, i Lechebnoi Fizicheskoi Kultury, 92*(3), 53–56. doi:10.17116/kurort2015353-56 PMID:26285335

Sigogneau, A. (1995). *The delimitation of the 'environment' research field by using reviews and journal citations.* In *Fourth International Conference on Science and Technology Indicators,* Antwerp, Belgium.

Sjöholm, A., Skarin, M., Linden, T., & Bernhardt, J. (2011). Does evidence really matter? Professionals' opinions on the practice of early mobilization after stroke. *Journal of Multidisciplinary Healthcare, 4,* 367–376. PMID:22096341

Slone, R. M. (1996). Coauthors' contributions to major papers published in the AJR: Frequency of undeserved coauthorship. *AJR. American Journal of Roentgenology, 167*(3), 571–579. doi:10.2214/ajr.167.3.8751654 PMID:8751654

Słownik, S. J. P. (n.d.). Retrieved October 21, 2017 from https://sjp.pl/

Smaldino, P. E., & McElreath, R. (2016). The natural selection of bad science. *Royal Society Open Science, 3*(9), 160384. doi:10.1098/rsos.160384 PMID:27703703

Small, H. (1973). Co-citation in the scientific literature: A new measure of the relationship between two documents. *Journal of the Association for Information Science and Technology, 24*(July/August), 256–269.

Smiciklas, M. (2012). *The power of infographics: Using pictures to communicate and connect with your audiences.* Indianapolis, IN: Que Publishing. Retrieved June 17, 2017, from http://ptgmedia.pearsoncmg.com/images/9780789749499/samplepages/0789749491.pdf

Sontag, S. (1998). *AIDS and Its Metaphors.* New York: Farrar, Straus and Giroux .

Sorensen, A., & Gardner, H. (2010). Programming With Time. Cyber-physical programming with Impromptu. *ACM SIGPLAN Notices, 45*(10), 822–834. doi:10.1145/1932682.1869526

Spitzer, K. L., Eisenberg, M. B., & Lowe, C. A. (1998). *Information literacy: Essential skills for the information age.* New York: ERIC Clearinghouse on Information & Technology.

Srinivasan, R. (2006). *Indigenous, Ethnic and Cultural Articulations of New Media, International Journal of Cultural Studies.* London: Sage Publications.

Stachowiak, L. (Ed.). (1990). *Wstęp do Starego Testamentu.* Poznań, Poland: Pallotinum.

Staley, D. J. (2003). *Computers, visualization, and history: how new technology will transform our understanding of the past.* Armonk, NY: M. E. Sharpe.

Stasko, J. (2001). *Sunburst.* Retrieved July 20, 2017, from: http://www.cc.gatech.edu/gvu/ii/sunburst/

Štěpánek, J., Syrový, V., Otčenášek, Z., Taesch, Ch., & Angster, J. (2005). Spectral features influencing perception of pipe organ sounds. *Proceeding of Forum Acusticum.*

Stevenson, K., Lewis, M., & Hay, E. (2004). Do physiotherapists' attitudes towards evidence-based practice change as a result of an evidence-based educational programme? *Journal of Evaluation in Clinical Practice, 10*(2), 207–217. doi:10.1111/j.1365-2753.2003.00479.x PMID:15189387

Stokes, S. (2002). Visual literacy in teaching and learning: A literature perspective. *Electronic Journal for the Integration of Technology in Education, 1*(1), 10-19. Retrieved June 13, 2017, from https://wcpss.pbworks.com/f/Visual+Literacy.pdf

Strotmann, A., Zhao, D., & Bubela, T. (2009) Author name disambiguation for collaboration network analysis and visualization. *Proceedings of the Association for Information Science and Technology.* doi:10.1002/meet.2009.1450460218

Strzemiński, W. (2016). Theory of Vison-the first edition with the critical commentary. Łódź Art Museum.

Strzeminski, W. (2015). Readability of Images. *Proceedings of the international conference devoted to the work of Władysław Strzemiński.*

Tager. (n.d.). Retrieved August 25, 2017, from http://ws.clarin-pl.eu/tager.shtml

TagerEn. (n.d.). Retrieved August 25, 2017, from http://ws.clarin-pl.eu/tagerEn.shtml

Taraszkiewicz, M. (1999). *Jak uczyć lepiej? Czyli refleksyjny praktyk w działaniu [How to teach better? Reflective practitioners in action].* Warszawa: Wyd. CODN.

Taylor, P. G. (2015). *Handbook of Research on Maximizing Cognitive Learning through Knowledge Visualization* (A. Ursyn, Ed.). Hershey, PA: IGI Global.

Teaching Tolerance. (2017). *Teaching Teachers: PD To Improve Student Achievement.* Retrieved August 8, 2017, from https://www.tolerance.org/professional-development/teaching-teachers-pd-to-improve-student-achievement

Teasell, R. (2012). Challenges in the implementation of evidence in stroke rehabilitation. *Topics in Stroke Rehabilitation, 19*(2), 93–95. doi:10.1310/tsr1902-93 PMID:22436356

Terzić, F. (2012). ERR Framework system and cooperative learning. *Metodički obzori, 7*(3), 47-50.

Thurner, S. (Ed.). (2017). *43 Visions for Complexity.* Singapore: World Scientific. doi:10.1142/10360

Tijssen, R. J. W. (2008). Are we moving towards an integrated European Research Area? Some macro-level bibliometric perspectives. In H. Kretschmer & F. Havemann (Eds.), *Proceedings of WIS 2008, Berlin. Fourth International Conference on Webometrics, Informetrics and Scientometrics & Ninth COLLNET Meeting* (pp. 19-25). Berlin: Humboldt-Universität zu Berlin.

Tillmann, A. (2012). What we see and why it matters: How competency in visual literacy can enhance student learning. *Honors Projects.* Paper 9. Retrieved June 13, 2017, from http://digitalcommons.iwu.edu/education_honproj/9

Tilson, J. K., Settle, S. M., & Sullivan, K. J. (2008). Application of evidence-based practice strategies: Current trends in walking recovery interventions poststroke. *Topics in Stroke Rehabilitation, 15*(3), 227–246. doi:10.1310/tsr1503-227 PMID:18647727

Timio, M., & Antiseri, D. (2000) Evidence-based medicine: reality and illusions. *Extension of epistemological reflexions, 1*(3), 411-414.

Treebenk. (2017). Retrieved October 20,2017 from https://en.wikipedia.org/wiki/Treebank

Treemaps of Race and Foreign-born by State. (n.d.). *Prints & posters of old maps, historic data viz and infographics from ages long past.* Retrieved July 20, 2017, from: http://vintagevisualizations.com/collections/charts-graphs/products/principal-constituent-elements-population-of-each-state

Tufte, E. (1990). *Envisioning Information.* Graphics Press LLC.

Tufte, E. R. (1997). *Visual Explanations: Images and Quantities, Evidence and Narrative.* Cheshire, CT: Graphics Press.

Tufte, E. R. (2001). *The Visual Display of Quantitative Information*. Cheshire, CT: Graphics Press.

Tulving, E. (1972). Episodic and semantic memory. In E. Tulving & W. Donaldson (Eds.), *Organization of memory* (pp. 381–403). New York: Academic Press.

Turner, P., & Whitfield, T. W. (1997). Physiotherapists' use of evidence based practice: A cross-national study. *Physiotherapy Research International*, *2*(1), 17–29. doi:10.1002/pri.76 PMID:9238748

Urbanc, K., & Kletečki Radović, M. (2007). Active learning and critical thinking in the context of supervisory, educational and helping relationship. *Annual of Social Work, 14*(2), 355-366.

Ursyn, A. (Ed.). (2015). Handbook of research on maximizing cognitive learning through knowledge visualization. Hershey, PA. Information Science Reference/an imprint of IGI Global. doi:10.4018/978-1-4666-8142-2

Ursyn, A. (Ed.). (2014). *Perceptions of knowledge visualization: explaining concepts through meaningful images*. Hershey, PA: Information Science Reference. doi:10.4018/978-1-4666-4703-9

Ursyn, A., & Mostowfi, M. (2015). Visualization by Coging: Drawing Simple Shapes and Forms in Various Programing Language. In A. Ursyn (Ed.), *Maximazing Cognitive Learning through Knowledge Visualization*. IGI Global. doi:10.4018/978-1-4666-8142-2.ch008

Vaisman, C. (2015). La visualisation, un langage sans parole. *NETCOM*, *29*(3/4), 2015.

Vakratsas, D., & Ambler, T. (1999). How Advertising Really Works: What Do We Really Know? *Journal of Marketing*, *63*(1), 26–43. doi:10.2307/1251999

Velden, T., Haque, A., & Lagoze, C. (2010). A new approach to analyzing patterns of collaboration in co-authorship networks: Mesoscopic analysis and interpretation. *Scientometrics*, *85*(1), 219–242. doi:10.1007/s11192-010-0224-6

Velders, T., de Vries, S., & Vaicaityte, L. (2007). Visual literacy and visual communication for global education: Innovations in teaching e-learning in art, design and communication. In *Designs on e-learning: the International Conference on Learning and Teaching in Art, Design and Communication, 12-14 September 2007, London, UK*. Retrieved June 13, 2017, from http://doc.utwente.nl/59769/1/Velders07visual.pdf

Venice Time Machine. (2016). Retrieved June 15, 2017, from https://vtm.epfl.ch/

Verson, J. (2007). Why We Need Cultural Activism? In *Do it Your Self: A Handbook for Changing our World*. London: Pluto Press. Retrieved April 05, 2017, from http://trapese.clearerchannel.org/chapters/HandbookForChangingOurWorld_chap11.pdf

Vintage visualization. Growth of the elements of the population: 1790 to 1890. (2017). Retrieved July 20, 2017, from: http://vintagevisualizations.com/collections/charts-graphs/products/growth-of-the-elements-of-the-population-1790-to-1890

Virtanen, P.K. (2015). Indigenous Social Media Pratices in Southwestern Amazonia. *AlterNative: An International Journal of Indigenous Peoples*, *11*(4).

Vis.js. (n.d.). Retrieved October 20, 2017 from https://visjs.org/

Visual Resources Association. (2009). *Advocating for visual resources management in educational and cultural institutions*. Retrieved June 16, 2017, from http://vraweb.org/wp-content/uploads/2016/09/vra_white_paper.pdf

Vizek Vidović, V. (Ed.). (2009). *Planiranje kurikuluma usmjerenoga na kompetencije u obrazovanju učitelja i nastavnika - Priručnik za visokoškolske nastavnike*. Zagreb, Croatia: University of Zagreb, Faculty of Humanities and Social Sciences & Faculty of Teacher Education.

Vlado, A. (2015). *Pajek: Program for large network analysis.* Retrieved April 1, 2015, from http://vlado.fmf.unilj.si/pub/networks/pajek/

Voltaire and the Enlightenment. (2013). Retrieved October 19, 2017, from http://republicofletters.stanford.edu/casestudies/voltaire.html

Von Ferber, C., Berche, B., Holovatch, T., & Holovatch, Yu. (2012). A tale of two cities. *Journal of Transportation Security, 5*(3), 199–216. doi:10.1007/s12198-012-0092-9

Voyant-tools. (2017). Retrieved October 21, 2017 from https://voyant-tools.org

Walker, M. F., Fisher, R. J., Korner-Bitensky, N., McCluskey, A., & Carey, L. M. (2013). From what we know to what we do: Translating stroke rehabilitation research into practice. *International Journal of Stroke, 8*(1), 11–17. doi:10.1111/j.1747-4949.2012.00974.x PMID:23280264

Walkowiak, T. (2016). Asynchronous System for Clustering and Classifications of Texts in Polish. In W. Zamojski, J. Mazurkiewicz, J. Sugier, T. Walkowiak, & J. Kacprzyk (Eds.), *Dependability Engineering and Complex Systems. Advances in Intelligent Systems and Computing* (Vol. 470). Cham: Springer. doi:10.1007/978-3-319-39639-2_46

Walrus — Graph Visualization Tool. (2005, March 30). Retrieved July 20, 2017, from: http://www.caida.org/tools/visualization/walrus/

Walton, J. H., Matthews, V. H., & Chavalas, M. W. (2005). *Komentarz historyczno-kulturowy do Biblii Hebrajskiej.* Warszawa, Poland: Vocatio.

Wardil, L., & Hauert, C. (2015). Cooperation and coauthorship in scientific publishing. *Physical Review E: Statistical, Nonlinear, and Soft Matter Physics, 91*(1), 012825. doi:10.1103/PhysRevE.91.012825 PMID:25679674

Ware, C. (2008). *Visual Thinking for Design.* San Francisco: Morgan Kaufman/Elsevier.

Ware, C. (2004). *Information Visualization: Perception for Design.* San Francisco: Morgan Kaufman.

Ware, C. (2012). *Information Visualization. Perception for Design.* Elsevier.

Watson, I. (2012). The Future Is Our Past: We once were sovereign and we still are. *Indigenous Law Bulletin, 8*(3).

Watts, A. (1958). *Nature, Man and Woman.* New York: Vintage Books.

WCRFT2. (2017). Retrieved August 25, 2017, from http://nlp.pwr.wroc.pl/redmine/projects/wcrft/wiki

Weick, K. E. (2009). *Sensemaking in Organizations.* Sage.

Weingart, S. (2013). *Diagrams of knowledge.* Retrieved July 20, 2017, from: http://www.scottbot.net/HIAL/

Weingart, S. (2013). From trees to webs: uprooting knowledge through visualization. In A. Slavic, A. Akdag Salah & S. Davies (Eds.), *Classification & visualization: Interfaces to knowledge. Proceedings of the International UDC Seminar,* (pp. 43-58). Würzburg: Ergon Verlag.

Weingart, S. (2013). From trees to webs: uprooting knowledge through visualization. In A. Slavic, A. Akdag Salah & S. Davies (Eds.). *Classification & visualization: Interfaces to knowledge. Proceedings of the International UDC Seminar,* (pp. 43-58). Würzburg: Ergon Verlag.

What is Circos? Circular visualization. (2009). Retrieved July 20, 2017, from: http://circos.ca/

Wheeldon, J., & Ahlberg, M. (2011). *Visualizing Social Sciences Research.* New York: SAGE Publications.

White, H. (2008). Historiografia i historiofotia (Historiography and historiophotics). In I. Kurz (Ed.), *Film i historia. Antologia [Film and history. Anthology]* (pp. 117–130). Warszawa: Wyd. Uniwersytetu Warszawskiego.

Wieviorka, M., & Diminescu, D. (Eds.). (2015). Le tournant numérique...et après ? *Socio, 4*.

Wilson, R. J. (2012). *Introduction to Graph Theory*. Cambridge, UK: Pearson Publishing.

Wishart, D. S., Yang, R., Arndt, D., Tang, P., & Cruz, J. (2004). Dynamic cellular automata: an alternative approach to cellular simulation. In Silico Biology 4, 0015. Bioinformation Systems e.V.

Witek, P. (2014). Metodologiczne problemy historii wizualnej [Methodological problems of visual history]. *Resena Historica (Mexico City, Mexico), 37*, 159–176.

World Statistics eXplorer. (2014). *Application developed by NComVA*. Retrieved July 20, 2017, from: https://mitweb.itn.liu.se/geovis/eXplorer

Wu, E., Carleton, R., & Davies, G. (2014). Discovering bin-Laden's Replacement in al-Qaeda, using Social Network Analysis: A Methodological Investigation. *Perspectives on Terrorism, 8*(1).

Wu, Y., & Duan, Z. (2015). Visualization analysis of author collaborations in schizophrenia research. *BMC Psychiatry, 15*(1), 27. doi:10.1186/s12888-015-0407-z PMID:25884451

Zanin-Yost, A. (2014). Visual literacy: Teaching and learning in the academic library of the 21st century and beyond. *AIB studi, 54*(2/3), 305-317. Retrieved June 20, 2017, from http://aibstudi.aib.it/article/download/9962/10179

Zeki, S. (2012). *Splendor and Miseries of the Brain. Love, Creativity, and the Quest for Human Happiness*. Willey-Blackwell.

Zhang, H., Hou, Y., Zhao, J., Wang, L., Xi, T., & Li, Y. (2016). Automatic Welding Quality Classification for the Spot Welding Based on the Hopfield Associative Memory Neural Network and Chernoff Face Description of the Electrode Displacement Signal Features. *Mechanical Systems and Signal Processing, 85*. doi:10.1016/j.ymssp.2016.06.036

Zhou, J. (2015). Connecting the Dots: Art, Culture, Science and Technology. In A. Ursyn (Ed.), *Maximazing Cognitive Learning through Knowledge Visualisation. IGI Global 2015*. doi:10.4018/978-1-4666-8142-2.ch011

Zinovyev, A. (2010) Data Visualization in Political and Social Sciences. International Encyclopedia of Political Science, 8.

Zoss, A. (2017). *Introduction to Data Visualization: About Data Visualization*. Retrieved March 15, 2017, from http://guides.library.duke.edu/datavis

Zuccala, A., & van Eck, N. J. (2011). Poverty research in a development policy context. *Development Policy Review, 29*(3), 311–330. doi:10.1111/j.1467-7679.2011.00535.x

About the Contributors

Veslava Osinska is an Assistant Professor at the Nicolaus Copernicus University in Torun. She has a physics background and holds a PhD in information sciences. She is specializing in the mapping of information, which is derived from both professional databases and Internet. She currently realizes the National Science Centrum Grant on visualisation the dynamics of digital knowledge (the website www. wizualziacjanauki.umk.pl) She is lecturing information visualization and graphic design, information architecture and database management. She has also a long experience in ICDL training. Veslava Osinska is collaborating with Places @ Spaces International Project and became its ambassadour in Poland. She is local coordinator of the Polish Chapter of ISKO and the member of Polish Information Processing Society. More at her blog: www.wizualizacjainformacji.pl

Grzegorz Osinski is computer scientist, cognitive scientist, quantum physicist. Head of the Institute of Computer Science at the College of Social and Media Culture in Toruń. He is involved in the analysis of nonlinear chaotic models in medical sciences and experimental psychology. In the years 2001-2002, a National Research Council grantee at the NASA / JPL laboratories in Pasadena, California. Author of numerous scientific publications on the use of numerical algorithms in experimental brain research. Currently he deals with cognitive issues of perception in the reception of visual messages. Author and co-author of popular interdisciplinary book titles, among others. "Clinical Neurology in Practice. Brain Inner "and" Chaos in the Head. Brain and life."

***

Bertrand Berche obtained his MSc in physics and applied physics in 1987 from Henri Poincaré University of Nancy, later completing his PhD studies here in 1991. Since then, he has remained at the same university, which in 2009 became a part of the University of Lorraine, as Maître de Conférences. He habilitated in 1997 and became a full professor in 1998. Between 2008-2011 he was president of the Condensed Matter Section of the National Council of Universities, France. In 2008-2013 he was Director of the Physics Department at the University of Lorraine, and since 2007, he is involved in the organization of a French-German doctoral college which then became the L4-collaboration between Leipzig, Lorraine, Lviv and Coventry. He was advisor and co-advisor of ten PhD students. He was awarded the degree of Doctor Honoris Causa of the Institute of Condensed Matter Physics of Lviv in 2016. His research concerns mainly Statistical Physics, Theoretical Condensed Matter Physics and History of Sciences.

Abdelaziz Blilid is a PhD student in the GERIICO laboratory at the University of Lille 3 - Charles de Gaulle. He prepares his thesis on "the role of digital media in the promotion of indigenous identities, in particular the Berbers, indigenous people of North Africa".

Jan Fazlagić is a professor in management at the Poznan University of Economics and Business in Poznan, Poland. He was responsible for the R&D at the Vistula University (2011-2014) – the fastest growing non-public HEI in Poland. His research interests include knowledge management, intellectual capital, service design, education and innovation management. He was a Senior Fulbright Scholar at Sam Houston University, TX, USA and Marie Curie Research Fellow at the Centre for Social Innovation (zsi.at) in Vienna, Austria. He is the author of the first Polish Intellectual Capital Report in a Higher Education Institution (2004). He is an author of 20 books and over 70 research papers. Prof. Fazlagic has participated in numerous research projects including Innovation Report on the Polish Pharma Sector (2012), Service Design (2013) and the national survey on the trust in Polish business sector (2015). He was one of the authors of the new law on Higher Education in Poland (Ustawa 2.0) in 2017. He is active as a business consultant and trainer. He also supports the development of European head teachers by organizing seminars and conferences aimed at improving leadership skills and marketing competences in schools.

Yurij Holovatch graduated from the Ivan Franko University of Lviv, 1979 and completed his Ph.D at the Bogolyubov Institute for Theoretical Physics in Kyiv (ITP), 1984 under the supervision of Prof. I. Yukhnovskii and Prof. I. Vakarchuk. He recieved his Doctor of physical and mathematical sciences in 1998. After completing his postgraduate studies he worked at the Lviv department of the ITP. Since 1990 he works at the Institute for Condensed Matter Physics, NAS of Ukraine. He was elected a full member of the Shevchenko Scientific Society in 2006 and the corresponding member of the National Acad. Sci. of Ukraine in 2015. He was invited professor at: Ivan Franko National University of Lviv, Johannes Kepler Universität Linz (Austria), Université Henri Poincaré (Nancy, France), Ukrainian Catholic University (Lviv). His scientific interests include the study of complex systems, physics of macromolecules, phase transitions and critical phenomena, complex networks, sociophysics, history of science.

Rigby Johnson is currently an undergraduate student of Public Health, Economics, and Astrophysics at the University of Colorado Denver. He serves as a multi-year intern for the University working to redesign the school's campus-wide wellness policies, is a member of the Auraria Student Wellness Center Advisory Board, and is the founding member of a University brain trust studying methods through which to improve college graduation rates.

Anna Małgorzata Kamińska is an employee of the Main Library of the Silesian University of Technology and, since 2017, assistant professor at University of Silesia in Katowice. She is a graduate of the University of Silesia in Katowice where, in 2016, she also defended PhD dissertation entitled "Scientific information on mining in the light of serials published by Polish technical universities (1945-1989)". Her research interests focus on several complementary areas: scientific information, bibliometrics, bibliographic databases, graphical languages of communication and information visualization. She is keen on books and Arduino platform.

Ralph Kenna is a statistical physicist who specialises in critical phenomena and sociophysics. He completed his PhD at the Karl-Franzens- Universitat Graz, Austria, in 1993. Kenna was a Marie Curie Research Fellow at the University of Liverpool (1994-1997) and Trinity College Dublin (1997-1999) where he lectured until 2002. He joined Coventry University in 2002 where he cofounded the Applied Mathematics Research Centre. He founded the Statistical Physics Group at Coventry and is Co-Director of the L4 Collaboration (Leipzig- Lorraine-Lviv-Coventry). His research concerns the statistical physics of phase transitions and complex systems. Kenna has generated over 100 published papers, has given a similar number of presentations internationally, and been awarded over 1M in grant income. He is an editor for Condensed Matter Physics and Advances in Complex Systems as well as the Springer book-series Simulating the Past.

Tomasz Komendziński, PhD, is senior lecturer at Department of Cognitive Science and Epistemology, Nicolaus Copernicus University in Toruń, and researcher at Neurocognitive Laboratory, Center for Modern Interdiscyplinary Technologies, Nicolaus Copernicus University in Torun. He is the initiator, co-creator and coordinator of InteRDoCTor research team, well known from many previous research projects and conferences. She has a Masters degree and a doctorate in philosophy. He is involved as researcher in several scientific projects concerning interdisciplinary studies and cognitive science and author in more than fifty articles and chapters. He also teaches courses on interdisciplinary studies and cognitive science at Nicolaus Copernicus University, Poland. His scientific interests focus on disorders of consciousness, human perception, sensory and cognitive processes.

Windham Loopesko has been assisting American and European businesses in setting up overseas operations since 1983. His firm, W.E. Loopesko and Associates, Inc., creates and implements international joint ventures, licenses and distribution agreements. Prior to beginning his international business development activity, Mr. Loopesko worked as head of mergers and acquisitions for the Bern-based division of a Swiss multinational. He has also practiced corporate law for six years both in private practice and with the Securities and Exchange Commission. Since January 2011, Mr. Loopesko has been teaching globalization and international business at the University of Colorado Denver, becoming an instructor in January 2017. He has also been a visiting professor and guest lecturer at universities in France, Peru and Poland. Mr. Loopesko has a law degree from Harvard University, an MBA from the University of Chicago and a Troisieme License from L'Universite Catholique de Louvain (Belgium), as well as an undergraduate degree from Dartmouth College (Phi Beta Kappa).

Piotr Malak works as an adjunct at Institute of Library and Information Science, University of Wrocław (UWr), Poland. Former he worked at Nicolaus Copernicus University, Toruń, Poland. He holds a PhD in humanities. His research interests concern: computational linguistics; Natural Language Processing; Information Visualization, Digital Humanities, time, information and tasks management. In years 2012-13 he was a fellow of SCIEX-NMS at University of Neuchatel, Switzerland, where he conducted research on texts classification for Polish. Currently he is involved in several national grants on information processing and texts classification and in creating of Digital Humanities Lab at UWr. He is also involved in CLARIN-PL works in the field of NLP web services designing and development. Author of two books and few peer-reviewed articles.

Leszek Matuszak, Ph.D., is an assistant professor in economics at the Poznan University of Economics and Business in Poznan, Poland. His research interests include data optimization strategies, commodity science, food safety, silver economy, information asymmetry, consumer research techniques. He has also experience as a secondary school teacher.

Emilia Mikołajewska, MSc, PhD, PT, is physiotherapist, assistant professor in Department of Physiotherapy, Ludwik Rydygier Collegium Medicum of the Nicolaus Copernicus University in Bydgoszcz, Poland and researcher in Neurocognitive Laboratory, Centre for Modern Interdisciplinary Technologies, Nicolaus Copernicus University in Toruń, Poland. She is also member of the InteRDoCTor research team. Author of 16 books, 50 book chapters, 260 articles in the area of neurorehabilitation and neurological physiotherapy. Member of 20 Editorial Boards. Reviewer in 110 scientific journals, book chapters, and grant applications. Emilia's research interests cover areas: neurorehabilitation of adult patients, including post-stroke, neurorehabilitation of children, increasing of patients' quality of life using: assistive devices, telemedicine, telerehabilitation, cybertherapy, rehabilitative robotics, applications of IT, AI and integrated systems in medicine, co-operation within therapeutic multidisciplinary team, evidence based medicine in clinical practice, biomedical engineering in rehabilitation. Emilia completed her PhD Thesis in 2007 at the Medical University in Poznań. She has also completed four-years postgraduate studies for governmental title 'specialist in physiotherapy', postgraduate studies in R&D projects management, and many additonal courses in neurorehabilitation of children and adults.

Dariusz Mikołajewski, PhD Eng, is engineer and scientist, specialist in IT, applications of IT in medical sciences, biocybernetics, and medical robotics. He works for two research centers: 1) Institute of Mechanics and Applied Computer Science, Kazimierz Wielki University in Bydgoszcz, 2) Neurocognitive Laboratory, Centre for Modern Interdisciplinary Technologies, Nicolaus Copernicus University in Toruń, Poland. He is also member of the InteRDoCTor research team. Author of more than 130 articles and chapters in the area of medical IT, biocybernetics, and biomedical engineering. His research interests cover areas medical IT, Assitive Technology and intelligent environments of disabled people, includin brain computer interfaces, biocybernetics and neurocybernetics, includig computational models of brain stem, generation of consciousness and its disorders, and simulation of cognitve aspects of various diseases, biomedical engineering. He graduated from Military University of Technology in Warsaw (MSc in telecommunication) and five postgraduate studies: in digital telecommunication, computer networks, project management (various methodologies), management of R&D projects, and MBA. His PhD Thesis covers topic of computational simulation of brain stem function (Thesis advisor: prof. Włodzisław Duch).

Olesya Mryglod received her MS in Computer and Information Technologies for Publishing from the Lviv Polytechnic National University in 2004. She completed her PhD in Information Technolodies here in 2009. Since then she works at the Institute for Condensed Matter Physics, NAS of Ukraine being a member of the Laboratory for Statistical Physics of Complex Systems. Her scientific interests include the study of complex systems, complex networks, scientometrics and sociophysics using different methods of data analysis.

Ilona Nowosad is a head of the Faculty of Social and Media Culture Sciences, employed at the Department of Informatics as a head of Multimedia Techniques Unit in College of Social and Media Culture in Toruń, Poland. She graduated from Nicolaus Copernicus University in Toruń (MSc in mathematics specialization in informatics). Her initial research has been focused on algebra and topology, algebraic and differential geometry, differential equations and their applications which resulted in obtaining a Phd in Mathematical Sciences at the Faculty of Mathematics and Computer Science of Nicolaus Copernicus University in Toruń. For many years now she is active in the field of computer science as a university and college lecturer and researcher, a member of Polish Information Processing Society and an author of computer science publications and coursebooks. Her recent research concerns computational creative processes, generative algorithms and programming, modern techniques of visualization and motion design, cognitive and perception processes, visual communication, hypermedia and hybridic space.

Nevzat Özel (PhD) is associate professor at Ankara University, Department of Information and Records Management. He graduated from Hacettepe University, Department of Library and Information Science in 2004 (BA), and got his master degree from Hacettepe University, Institute of Social Sciences in 2007 and PhD degree from Ankara University Institute of Social Sciences in 2014. He worked as a research assistant at Hacettepe University, Department of Information Management and specialist in Hacettepe University Libraries. He was also the president of University and Research Librarians' Association in Turkey between 2012-2015. His research interests are cataloging, classification, information and communication technologies, information literacy, library services and digital libraries.

Zbigniew Osiński graduated from higher education in 1984 at the Faculty of Humanities MCS University in Lublin: 1996-1999 employed as a teaching assistant, 1999 - 2008 as an assistant professor at the Institute of History; 2008 – 2012 as an assistant professor at the Institute of Library and Information Science, from 2012 as an associate professor at the same institute; from 2009 is a chief of Department of Information Science. Research interests: 1. Information science: educational and scientific Internet database; sources for humanities research available on the Internet; Internet as a space for humanists scientific communication; information architecture and usability of educational and scientific services; bibliometrics and webometrics; 2. Digital humanities: information visualization and data analysis of large collections of text and graphic objects, the efficiency of transfer of information and knowledge through infographics, humanities on the Internet.

Suzana Pasanec Preprotić graduated in 2001 and received her PhD in 2012 from the University of Zagreb. She is currently Assistant professor at the Department of Bookbinding and Packaging at the Faculty of Graphic Arts, University of Zagreb. Her basic areas of research are bookbinding finishing process including materials bindability - paper grades interactions with adhesives. Her list of publications is available at: http://bib.irb.hr/lista-radova?autor= 303526 Suzana teaches a number of graduate and postgraduate courses. She has participated in 4 scientific research projects financed by University of Zagreb. She is member of the Croatian Standard Institute -Division 130 -Graphic Technology. She is currently head of the Committee for Quality Assurance. She has exhibited students works in craft bookbinding exhibitions on several occasions.

Gorana Petković is a research assistant in the field of technical sciences, a scientific field of graphic technology at the University of Zagreb, Faculty of Graphic Arts (Department of Bookbinding and Packaging). After finishing the general high school, she graduated undergraduate and graduate studies at the Faculty of Graphic Arts, where he gained the title of MSc in Graphic Arts, field Graphic Technology. After graduation, she was working three years at the position of graphic designer in marketing agency and sign supply company. In 2015 she enrolls a postgraduate studies in graphic engineering and actively participates in domestic and international scientific conferences, scientific research projects and creative workshops for gifted children in elementary schools in Zagreb, Croatia. Scientific bibliography available on: https://bib.irb.hr/lista-radova?autor=347680.

Małgorzata Piotrkowska, Dańkowska, PhD, graduate of polish philology and philosophy on the John Paul II Catholic University of Lublin and biblical theology on Cardinal Stefan Wyszyński University in Warsaw. The author of the monograph "Winnice Engaddi. Biblijna droga do spotkania z Oblubieńcem" and other publications, focusing on the issues of biblical hermeneutics, synchronous methods of studying the Holy Bible and the aesthetics and symbolism of the Song of Songs.

Irina Marshakova-Shaikevich is a Professor Emeritus of Adam Mickiewicz University in Poznan, Poland. She also is a Leading Researcher in The Institute of Philosophy at Russian Academy of Science, Moscow, Russia (1988 – 2016). Her scientific research focus on bibliometrics and scientometrics, particularly widely used science mapping. Professor Marshakova-Shaikevich was invited as Visiting Professor at following institutions: Cambridge University, England in 2011 in the frame of TEMPUS Programme; Zulu Universiy, Shouth Africa in 2006 as Visiting Researcher - at the Institute for Scientific Information ISI, Philadelphia, USA in 1990.

Monika Szetela is a graduate of theology, social work, and political science at the University of Warmia and Mazury in Olsztyn and the Institute for Media Education and Journalism at the Cardinal Wyszyński University in Warsaw. Member of the Association of Fundamental Theologians and the Association of Polish Journalists. Chief editor in chief of magazine "Wzrastanie". An adjunct at College of Social and Media Culture in Torun. Author of the book "Pitfalls of political correctness."

Index

A

active teaching 243, 245
agent-based modeling 269
AIDA Model 198, 212
Architecture 11, 55, 216, 254, 257, 262
assessment of prior knowledge 250
Assessment of Prior Learning (APL) 250

B

bibliographic database 106, 151-152, 155, 168, 173
Bibliographic Record 154, 173
bibliography 154, 173
bibliometrics 121-122, 125, 129, 140, 146, 152, 154, 173
bio-interface 267
bookbinding engineering 239, 247, 250
Business Visions 199, 212

C

cellular automata 254, 264
Chernoff Faces 195-196, 200-204, 206-207, 209-210, 212-213
Chornobyl (Chernobyl) Disaster 106-108, 110-113, 118, 120
Circular Visualization 30
Citation Index 107, 126, 145, 148, 151, 174
co-authorship 106, 156
co-citation analysis 121-122, 127-128, 132, 146
Complex Network 108, 120, 239
complex networks 30, 107-108, 110, 120
Complex Systems 106-107, 119-120, 263
cooperative learning 241, 246, 248
Couple 70, 252, 266, 269
Critical Thinking 34, 39-40, 239-241, 243-245, 247-248
cultural activism 175, 182-184, 188, 191
Culture 11-12, 50, 52-53, 78, 106-107, 176, 181-187, 192, 238, 243, 257

D

Data Visualization 2, 30, 37-38, 88, 176-177, 191-192, 241-242, 270
Diagrams 2, 17, 19, 32-33, 37, 51, 55, 63, 200-201
Didactic Test With Test Materials 62
Digital Humanities 50-51, 55, 62, 86-89, 91, 261
digital media 50, 59
digital storytelling 52, 60, 62

E

educator 240, 245, 250
e-learning 242, 245, 247, 250
Emoticons 51, 206, 212
ERR framework system 241, 243, 245, 248
Evidence-Based Medicine (EBM) 274-279, 283, 287, 292
Evidence-Based Practice (EBP) 274-279, 283, 287, 292

F

fractal 1, 8-12, 15, 21, 24, 27

G

generative system 251-257, 263-264, 266-267
Gephi 91, 151, 153, 156, 158-159, 165, 168, 174, 177-178, 192, 261
Graph 4, 18, 22-23, 30, 84, 91, 109, 120, 152-153, 156, 158, 160-168, 174, 177-179, 200, 259, 261-262, 265, 281
Graphic Technology 237, 243, 250
Graphs 22-24, 38-39, 51, 55, 63, 120, 152-153, 156, 159, 162, 165, 168, 174, 177, 261, 281
GRUBA 151, 155, 168

H

Herman Chernoff 195, 212-213

I

Identity 175-177, 179, 181-188, 252
Indigenous People 175, 192
infographics 17, 19, 32-33, 37-39, 43, 48, 50, 53-55, 59, 62
information competencies 52, 55, 59, 62
information literacy 33, 40, 44, 48
information noise 50-52, 54, 59, 63
Information Technology 195, 213
Information Visualization 4, 13, 18, 27, 30-31, 37, 48, 51, 54, 63, 86-89, 91-93, 96, 102, 106, 119, 175, 197, 209, 213-214, 251, 261, 268

J

JCR 128, 130, 132, 145, 148
Journals 40, 108, 110, 121-122, 127-132, 145-147, 151, 155, 174, 238, 276, 279

K

Knowledge Base 197, 213

L

Learning Environment 33, 237, 242, 244-247
Learning Motivation 250
Learning Outcomes 43, 237, 239-243, 245, 247-248
lemmatization 95-96, 102
lexical analysis of keywords 121
library instruction 40, 43-44, 48
library instructions 32, 44
light algorithms 223
live coding 251, 259-261
love 68-73, 75-78, 80, 82

M

map of science 137
maps of science 121, 125-126, 145-147, 151
marriage 73-74, 185
Mind Space (MS) 1, 15
mining 23, 92, 151-152, 154-155
Multimodal Graph 174

N

National Science Indicators 148
Natural Language Processing 86-87, 92-93
Network 22-25, 30, 99, 108-117, 120-123, 152-154, 160, 164, 174, 177-178, 182, 184-187, 237, 239, 241, 247-248, 259, 261, 263-264, 266-267, 277, 281-285
network science 23, 30, 108-109
neurodynamics 13
Neuroesthetics 13, 15
Neurological Rehabilitation 292

O

Open-Ended Test Questions 63

P

Pareidolia 201, 213
Part-of-Speech Tagging 97
Perception 1-3, 8-13, 15, 19, 32, 39-40, 43, 52-54, 87, 169, 197, 215, 220, 256, 258, 261, 266-267
Periodicals 110, 151, 154, 174, 238
Playfair Charts 19, 30
Polish counties 195, 207, 209
Portfolio 250
Process Visualization 199, 213
Publications 39, 59, 107, 109-114, 118, 121-126, 132, 134, 136, 145-146, 151-152, 173, 179, 238, 269, 276, 278-286
Python 93-94, 259

R

ray tracing 225, 227
real-time city 270
Relation 17, 37, 71, 82, 122, 158, 162, 164, 174, 183, 270

S

sacral building 214, 233
Scale-Free Networks 120
Scientific Research 69, 121, 147, 151, 287
scientometrics 106-107, 110, 120, 129, 166
self-learning process 245
Simulation 158, 160, 214-215, 222-223, 225, 234, 255, 269
Small World Networks 120

Social Network Analysis (SNA) 23, 30, 152-154, 156, 158, 168-169, 174, 261
Socio-Economic 39, 201-203, 207, 209-210, 213
stemming 95-96, 101-102
Story 55, 68, 70, 72, 250-251
Sunburst 21, 31
synesthesia 11, 15

T

Teacher Motivation 250
Text Classification 92-93, 96
text preprocessing 86-87, 91-92, 100
timeline 71, 73, 75, 77, 79, 81-82
treemaps 19-21, 31

U

Unimodal Graph 174
Unintuitive Correspondence 204, 213

V

Visual Arts 37, 251, 268
visual literacy 32-37, 39-44, 48, 52-53
Visual Patterns 2, 254
Visualization Of Knowledge 84, 195-196, 199, 212

W

Web Mapping 175-177, 179
Web of Science 132, 145, 148, 152, 174
Web-Mapping 192

X

XML tags 94, 101

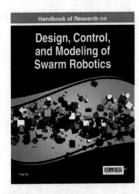

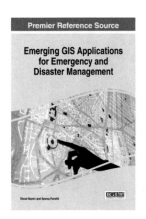
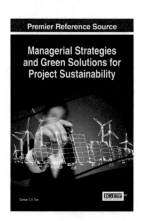

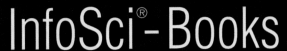
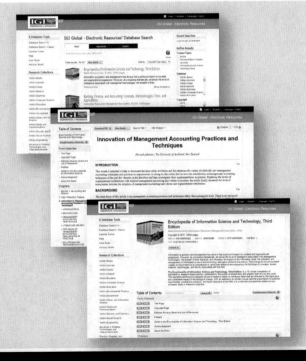

Information Resources Management Association

Advancing the Concepts & Practices of Information Resources
Management in Modern Organizations

Become an IRMA Member

Members of the **Information Resources Management Association (IRMA)** understand the importance of community within their field of study. The Information Resources Management Association is an ideal venue through which professionals, students, and academicians can convene and share the latest industry innovations and scholarly research that is changing the field of information science and technology. Become a member today and enjoy the benefits of membership as well as the opportunity to collaborate and network with fellow experts in the field.

IRMA Membership Benefits:

- **One FREE Journal Subscription**
- **30% Off Additional Journal Subscriptions**
- **20% Off Book Purchases**
- Updates on the latest events and research on Information Resources Management through the IRMA-L listserv.
- Updates on new open access and downloadable content added to Research IRM.
- A copy of the Information Technology Management Newsletter twice a year.
- A certificate of membership.

IRMA Membership $195

Scan code or visit **irma-international.org** and begin by selecting your free journal subscription.

Membership is good for one full year.